H4 L4   Room 354

CERTIFIED PUBLIC ACCOUNTANT
COBB FEDERAL BUILDING
MARIETTA, GEORGIA 30060

SAMUEL G. ANDERSON
CERTIFIED PUBLIC ACCOUNTANT
COBB FEDERAL BUILDING
MARIETTA, GEORGIA 30060

ACCOUNTING
PRINCIPLES AND
CONTROL

LAWRENCE L. VANCE, CPA
University of California, Berkeley

RUSSELL TAUSSIG, CPA
University of Hawaii

ACCOUNTING PRINCIPLES AND CONTROL

REVISED EDITION

HOLT, RINEHART and WINSTON
New York   Chicago
San Francisco   Toronto   London

Printed in the United States of America

Preface

This text is designed for a first course in accounting for college-level students, with emphasis on basic principles and concepts and the uses of accounting information. Special attention is given to the needs of management in terms of day-to-day control of the enterprise as well as in terms of those decisions involved in setting long-range goals, commitments, and policies.

This second edition includes the following changes:

1. Assignment material is substantially increased in quantity and variety. It appears at the end of each chapter under the headings of Questions, Exercises, and Problems.

2. A new chapter on responsibility accounting and departmental accounting has been introduced. This not only serves to acquaint the student with the important managerial tool of responsibility accounting, but also permits contrast and comparison of controllable costs with full costs, thus reinforcing each concept.

3. A new chapter on capital budgeting has been added. This extends the discussion on budgeting to one of its most prominent special applications and acquaints the student with another of the important managerial tools closely linked to accounting. The material is so presented that no algebra is required.

4. Funds and cash flow analysis has been set out in a chapter apart from other special statements, and the T account method has been used as a primary explanation of the derivation of a funds statement from account data. The work sheet method is also illustrated.

5. Branch accounts and consolidated statements have been presented in one chapter.

6. The introductory material presented in the first three chapters of the first edition is now presented in the first two, with some reduction in the extent of the illustration of hand account-keeping methods.

7. A brief illustration of a matrix formulation of accounting information is given in Part I, along with the traditional method, for three reasons: (a) It reinforces the idea that the double-entry system does not depend on traditional forms. (b) It serves as a good base for thinking about the organization of accounting data in computers. (c) It offers a starting point to instructors interested in a mathematical approach to accounting.

8. The voucher system is covered to the extent considered necessary in the chapters on cash and on purchases, so that a separate chapter on the system is no longer included.

9. The material on partnerships has been covered in one chapter instead of two.

In spite of the addition of new chapters, the consolidation of old ones has permitted an over-all reduction of two chapters in the length of the book. The new total of twenty-seven chapters is divided into six parts: the chapters may be conveniently divided between two semesters or three quarters of instruction. A great deal of flexibility continues to characterize the material, so that the instructor may omit chapters or change the order rather freely. For example, all of Part VI (Chapters 23–27) may be taken up as soon as Chapter 13 is completed, if the instructor so desires. Special cost analysis (Chapter 22) may be studied even if the preceding four chapters on cost accounting are omitted, to take a possibly extreme example.

The emphasis on managerial control and on managerial decisions generally has been maintained, and, as before, sufficient description of methods of handling data as well as presentations of basic concepts have been incorporated to give the student a solid base for understanding the nature of the information accumulated and hence its potential uses. At several points in this edition reference is made to differences in methods of obtaining accounting information in systems using computers, since the computer is increasingly important in accounting applications. No instructions for operating computers are offered, however.

We are indebted to many colleagues, to many teaching assistants, and to students who have used the first edition of the text and have made many helpful suggestions. Although their number is too large for individual mention here, we are grateful to each one. Professor Alan Cerf reviewed the chapter on payroll and income taxes and offered many helpful suggestions on it, as well as on other parts of the text. We are also indebted to The American Institute for Property and Liability Underwriters, Inc., The American Institute of Certified Public Accountants, and The Canadian Institute of Chartered Accountants for their kind permission to adapt for this text problems from their examinations.

We wish to express our thanks to Dun & Bradstreet, Inc., for permission to reproduce the Key to Ratings; to Buttes Gas & Oil Co. and to The Western Pacific Railroad Company, respectively, for permission to reproduce the stock certificate and the bond certificate.

We will always be most interested in hearing of the experiences of users of the book.

L. L. V.
R. T.

Berkeley, California
Honolulu, Hawaii
December 1965

Contents

PREFACE   *v*

PART I / BASIC PRINCIPLES

1   ACCOUNTING AND THE BALANCE SHEET   *3*

Nature of accounting control, *3*   Decision making and accounting, *4*
Specialization in accounting, *5*   The profession of accountancy, *6*   The
accounting entity, *7*   Users of accounting, *7*   Assets, *8*   Financial
interests, *8*   Identity of assets and financial interests, *9*   Accounting
equation, *9*   The balance sheet, *9*   Cost and value, *10*   Transactions,
10   Analysis of transactions, *10*   Types of transactions, *11*   Illustration of transaction analysis, *11*   Income statement, *16*   The account, *16*
Debit and credit, *17*   Equality of debits and credits, *17*   The ledger, *18*
Simple managerial uses of the ledger, *19*   Matrix formulation of accounting,
19   Form of the balance sheet, *21*   Proprietorship in the balance sheet,
22   Managerial use of the balance sheet, *23*

2   THE INCOME STATEMENT   *35*

Purposes of the income statement, *35*   Content of the income statement, *35*
Relation of the income statement to the balance sheet, *36*   Revenue and
revenue accounts, *38*   Expense and expense accounts, *38*   Expense account titles, *39*   The journal, *39*   Steps in journalizing, *41*   Usefulness of the journal, *41*   Posting the ledger, *42*   Illustration of journal and
ledger, *42*   The trial balance, *42*   Illustration of the trial balance, *44*
Closing the books, *45*   Illustration of the closing process, *46*   Alternative procedures, *56*   Ruling balance sheet accounts, *57*   Steps in the
accounting process, *58*   Disposition of income, *59*   Uses of the income
statement, *60*   Earnings that can be withdrawn, *60*   Basis for income
tax calculations, *60*   Basis for capital stock transactions, *60*   Managerial
and investor analysis for efficiency, *61*   Matrix formulation with income
statement data, *62*

3   MATCHING COSTS AND REVENUE   *76*

Matching costs and revenue, *76*   Means of matching costs and revenue, *76*
Recognition of revenue, *77*   Recognition of expense, *77*   Direct identification of expense with revenue, *78*   Identification with the accounting
period, *78*   Need for objectivity, *78*   Relation to the passage of time, *78*
Convenience, *79*   Adjusting entries, *79*   Nature of accruals, *79*   Accrued revenue, *80*   Accrued expense, *81*   Deferred revenue or income,
81   Deferred revenue adjustment, *82*   Deferred expense, *85*   Deferred or prepaid expense adjustment, *85*   Goods sold and supplies used,
88   Depreciation, *89*   Errors and omissions, *89*

4 MATCHING COSTS AND REVENUE AND THE WORK SHEET *104*

Merchandise accounts, *104*   Perpetual inventory method, *104*   Periodic inventory method, *105*   Entries illustrating periodic inventory method, *105* Inventory recorded with costs of goods sold account, *105*   Inventory recorded without costs of goods sold account, *106*   Merchandise inventory in the income statement, *106*   Accumulated depreciation, *109*   Bad debts and allowance for doubtful accounts, *109*   Property taxes, *111*   Income taxes, *112*   Illustration of accrual of federal income tax, *113*   Nature and function of the work sheet, *114*   Illustration of the work sheet, *114* Alternative work sheet procedures, *115*   Summary of preparation of the work sheet, *118*   Steps in formal closing, *118*

PART II / CONTROL AND ACCOUNTING
FOR BASIC FUNCTIONS

5 SALES ACCOUNTING AND CONTROL   *141*

Sales transactions, *141*   Sales and other excise taxes, *141*   Cash discounts, *142*   Recording cash discounts on sales, *143*   Trade discounts, *144*   Freight on sales, *145*   Sales returns and allowances, *145*   Sales accounts in the income statement, *146*   Sales records, *146*   Sales journal, *146*   Single-column credit sales journal, *147*   Multicolumn sales journal, *148*   Accounts receivable control account and subsidiary ledger, *148* Sales invoice or sales slips, *151*   Sundry original records, *152*   Sales records and computers, *156*   Internal control, *157*   Elements of good internal control, *157*   Specific control devices for sales activity, *159* Data for managerial decisions on sales, *160*   Distribution of sales revenue, *161*   Contribution theory and sales, *162*   Analysis of sales costs, *162* Other sales decisions and analyses, *163*

6 PURCHASES ACCOUNTING AND CONTROL   *173*

Purchase transactions, *173*   Freight in, *173*   Other acquisition costs, *174*   Purchase returns and allowances, *174*   Cash discounts on purchases, *175*   Purchase discounts lost, *176*   Purchases accounts in the income statement, *176*   Purchase records, *177*   Purchase requisition, *177*   Purchase order, *177*   Receiving report, *179*   Supplier's invoice, *180*   Purchases book, *180*   Multicolumn invoice register, *180*   Accounts payable control account and subsidiary ledger, *181*   Internal control for purchases, *181*   The voucher system, *184*   Records in the voucher system, *185*   Voucher document, *185*   Voucher register, *187* Variations in the voucher system, *187*   Cash disbursement system with vouchers, *189*   Voucher system and internal control, *189*   Other advantages of the voucher system, *190*   Managerial analysis of purchases, *190*   Important managerial purchase decisions requiring accounting data, *190*   Decision to make or buy an article, *191*

7 ACCOUNTING AND CONTROL OF CASH   *205*

Nature and composition of cash, *205*   Basic procedure for cash, *205* Cash receipts journal, *206*   Cash disbursements journal, *208*   Cash disbursements with the voucher system, *210*   Petty cash, *211*   Proof of petty cash, *212*   Cash over and short, *212*   Banking transactions, *212* Deposit slip, *213*   Bank check, *214*   Bank statement, *215*   Daily cash report, *216*   Bank reconciliation, *217*   Procedure in preparing the bank reconciliation, *218*   Adjustments from the reconciliation, *219*   Internal control of cash, *219*   Internal control procedures for cash receipts, *220*   Internal control procedures for cash disbursements, *220*   Data on cash for managerial decisions, *221*

8   CLOSING AND STATEMENTS   *241*

Steps in periodic closing of accounts and preparation of statements, *241* Illustration of end-of-period work, *241*   Comments on the work sheet, *243* Balance sheet, *246*   Classification of assets, *246*   Classification of liabilities, *248*   Classification of proprietorship, *248*   Income statement, *248*   Revenue section of the income statement, *248*   Cost of goods sold, *250*   Selling and general expenses, *250*   Other income and other deductions, *250*   Statement of retained earnings, *251*   Current-operating versus all-inclusive income statements, *251*   Combined income and retained earnings statement, *252*   Closing entries, *252*   Postclosing trial balance, *254*   Reversing entries, *255*   Application of reversing entries, *257*   Illustration of reversing entries, *257*   Statement problems of management, *257*   Popularized balance sheet, *258*   Single-step income statement, *258*   Use of less technical terminology, *260*

PART III / CONTROL AND ACCOUNTING FOR
PARTICULAR ASSETS AND LIABILITIES

9   ACCOUNTS RECEIVABLE   *279*

Transactions and procedures affecting accounts receivable, *279*   Sales discounts, *279*   Bad debts transactions, *281*   Bad debt recoveries, *282* Records and procedures for accounts receivable, *282*   Customer's statement, *284*   Direct posting, *284*   Machine posting, *286*   Estimation of collectible amount, *286*   Possible deductions from accounts receivable, *286* Estimating bad debts, *287*   Aging of accounts receivable, *288*   Internal control for accounts receivable, *289*   Management problems in extending and collecting credit, *290*   Identifying retail customers having acceptable credit, *290*   Identifying wholesale customers having acceptable credit, *290* Collection of accounts receivable, *292*   Credit policy, *292*

10   MERCHANDISE INVENTORY   *307*

Periodic inventory, *307*   Pricing periodic inventory, *308*   Identified-unit cost, *308*   First-in, first-out, *308*   Last-in, first-out, *309*   Average cost, *310*   Perpetual inventory method, *310*   Stores ledger account on a first-in, first-out basis, *311*   Stores ledger account on an average cost basis, *312*   Other methods for stores ledger accounts, *313*   Advantages of perpetual inventory, *313*   Inventory pricing in general, *314*   Summary of effects of different cost methods of inventory pricing, *314*   Inventory pricing that departs from the cost basis, *315*   Market price method, *315* Cost or market, whichever is lower, *316*   Modern application of the cost-or-market rule, *316*   Appraisal of the cost-or-market rule, *318*   Other inventory methods, *319*   Estimated inventories, *319*   Gross profits method, *319*   Retail inventory method, *320*   Internal control for inventory, *321*   Management problems with inventory, *322*   Traditional inventory quantity controls, *323*   Operations research approach to inventory management, *323*

11   FIXED AND INTANGIBLE ASSETS   *337*

Accounting for acquisition of fixed and intangible assets, *337*   Plant ledger accounts, *338*   Nature and recording of depreciation, *338*   Fallacies about depreciation, *339*   Calculation of depreciation, *339*   Straight line depreciation, *341*   Double declining balance depreciation, *341*   Sum-of-the-years'-digits depreciation, *342*   Selection of a depreciation method, *342*   Nature and calculation of depletion, *343*   Amortization of intangible assets, *343*   Patents, *344*   Copyrights, *344*   Franchises, *344*   Trademarks, *345*   Goodwill, *345*   Organization costs, *345*   Leaseholds and leasehold improvements, *345*   Balance sheet presentation of fixed and intangible assets, *346*   Revision of depreciation or depletion, *346*   Retirement of fixed and intangible assets, *347*   Abandonment, *347*   Sale of fixed assets, *347*   Trade-in of fixed assets, *348*   Tax rule on trade-ins, *348*   Internal control for fixed and intangible assets, *349*   Management decisions on fixed and intangible assets, *350*   Major new investments, *350*   Payout period, *350*   Replacement of a particular asset, *351*   The price level problem, *352*

12   NOTES, BONDS, AND INTEREST   *366*

Definitions, *366*   Calculation of interest, *367*   Notes payable, *370*   Notes receivable, *370*   Discounting notes payable, *371*   Discounting notes receivable, *372*   Contingent liability on notes receivable discounted, *373*   Dishonored notes receivable, *373*   Kinds of bonds, *374*   Issue of bonds, *374*   Recording discount on bonds payable, *375*   Recording premium on bonds payable, *375*   Investments in bonds, *376*   Bonds purchased between interest dates, *377*   Discount and premium in the balance sheet, *377*   Sinking funds, *378*   Mortgages paid on the installment plan, *378*   Internal control for notes and bonds, *379*   Management problems relating to notes receivable and bond investments, *379*   Management problems relating to notes payable, *380*   Management problems relating to bonds payable, *380*

13   PAYROLL AND INCOME TAXES   *392*

Nature and purposes of payroll taxes, *392*   Entries for payroll taxes, *393*   Calculation of withheld taxes, *394*   Payroll records, *396*   Records of work done, *396*   Payroll summary, *396*   Entries for the payroll in the illustration, *398*   Employee's individual earnings record, *400*   Other individual employee forms, *400*   Internal control for payroll, *400*   Federal income taxes, *402*   Cash versus accrual basis, *402*   Outline of computation of personal income tax, *403*   Content of gross income, *403*   Deductions from gross income, *403*   Deductions from adjusted gross income ("Itemized deductions"), *404*   Nondeductible expenditures, *405*   Exemptions, *405*   Capital gains and losses, *405*   Federal income tax rates, *405*   Illustration of the computation of the individual income tax, *406*   Estimated tax, *408*   Corporation income tax, *408*   Deferred income taxes payable, *408*   Internal control for taxes, *409*   Management problems relating to taxes, *410*

PART IV / PROBLEMS OF PARTICULAR ORGANIZATIONS

14   PARTNERSHIPS   *427*

Legal characteristics of partnerships, *427*   Formation by cash investment, *428*   Formation from prior proprietorship, *428*   Drawing accounts, *429*

Division of net income, *430*   Division of net income on fixed ratios, *430*
Division of net income on opening capital balances, *430*   Division of net
income on closing capital balances, *431*   Division of net income on average
capital balances, *432*   Division of net income on "salary," interest, and
fixed ratio, *432*   Division of net income when it is less than salary and interest, *433*   Statement of capital accounts, *433*   Partnership reorganization and dissolution, *434*   Admission of an additional partner, *434*   Purchase of an interest from another partner, *434*   Contribution of assets in
amount equal to the interest obtained, *435*   Contribution of assets in greater
or lesser amount than the interest obtained, *435*   Admission of new partner
—bonus method, *436*   Admission of new partner—goodwill method, *437*
Withdrawal of a partner, *438*   Withdrawing partner takes his recorded
capital balance, *439*   Withdrawing partner takes less than his recorded
capital, *439*   Withdrawing partner takes more than his recorded capital,
439   Liquidation of a partnership, *440*   Liquidation when a partner has
a deficit, *441*   Management considerations in forming and operating a
partnership, *441*   Personal qualifications of partners, *442*   Content of
the partnership agreement, *442*   Continuity of the partnership, *443*
Availability of capital, *443*   Income tax status, *444*

15   CORPORATIONS—FORMATION AND CAPITAL STOCK   *457*

Definition and nature of corporations, *457*   Organization of a corporation,
458   Proprietorship in a corporation, *458*   Kinds of capital stock, *459*
Preferred versus common stock, *460*   Classes of stock, *461*   Par versus
no-par stock, *461*   Paid-in surplus, *462*   Entries for issue of stock, *462*
Subscriptions to capital stock, *464*   Defaults on subscriptions to stock, *464*
Treasury stock, *465*   Treasury stock purchased, *466*   Resale of treasury
stock purchased, *467*   Special corporate records, *468*   Management
problems in deciding whether or not to use the corporate form of organization, *469*   Leverage through use of preferred stock, *469*   Possible loss
of control, *470*   Advantageous executive-compensation plans, *470*   Tax
on accumulated earnings, *471*   Minor problems, *471*

16   CORPORATIONS—RETAINED EARNINGS AND DIVIDENDS   *482*

Nature of retained earnings, *482*   Appropriations of retained earnings, *483*
Entries for appropriations of retained earnings, *483*   Statement of retained
earnings, *484*   Kinds of dividends, *484*   Ordinary dividends, *484*   Sig-
nificant dates for dividends, *486*   Entries for ordinary dividends, *486*
Nature of the liability for dividends, *487*   Financing of dividends, *487*
Dividends of wasting-asset companies, *488*   Liquidating dividends, *489*
Stock dividends, *489*   Stock split-up, *490*   Quasi reorganization, *490*
Appraisal capital, *492*   Managerial problems and dividends, *492*   Management of cash, *493*   Attracting or obtaining permanent investment funds,
493   Legal and contractual restrictions, *493*   Liability for illegal divi-
dends, *493*

PART V / COST CONTROLS AND ACCOUNTING

17   RESPONSIBILITY AND DEPARTMENTAL ACCOUNTING   *506*

Nature of responsibility accounting, *506*   Bases for effective use of responsibility accounting, *506*   Illustration of organizational and reporting
relationships, *507*   A case illustration of responsibility accounting, *510*
Departmental accounting, *511*   General objectives of departmental accounting systems, *511*   Departmental accounts, *512*   Forms of ledger

accounts, *512*   Journals for departmental accounts, *513*   Income statement with departmental gross margin figures, *515*   Distribution of expenses, *515*   Direct and indirect expenses, *515*   Selling and service
departments, *519*   Bases for distribution of indirect expenses, *519*   Sales
revenue as a basis for distribution of expenses, *520*   Departmental income
statement, *520*   Departmental expenses in the ledger, *523*   Departmental contribution, *523*   Internal control of departmental operations, *524*

18   MANUFACTURING ACCOUNTS   540

Nature of production cost accounts, *540*   Elements of productions costs,
541   Manufacturing accounts used, *541*   Manufacturing inventories,
542   Place of manufacturing accounts in the income statement, *542*
Statement of cost of goods manufactured, *543*   Manufacturing work sheet,
543   Adjusting and closing entries from the work sheet, *545*   Balance
sheet, *546*   Pricing of manufacturing inventories, *546*   Simple manufacturing accounts as a managerial device, *549*

19   JOB ORDER COST ACCOUNTING   560

The job order method, *560*   The job cost sheet, *561*   Materials, *561*
Labor cost, *563*   Factory overhead cost, *564*   Factory overhead variance, *565*   Finished goods, *566*   Illustration of job order cost accounting, *566*   Internal control for job order accounting, *575*   Managerial
decisions and cost accounting, *577*

20   PROCESS COST ACCOUNTING   588

General ledger accounts for process costs, *588*   Process costs under seasonal production, *591*   Process costs and service departments, *591*
Original records in process costs, *592*   Unit cost computations, *592*
Equivalent units with ending work in process, *592*   Equivalent units with
beginning work in process, *593*   Equivalent units with beginning and ending work in process, *593*   Materials complete when started, *593*   Unit
cost statement, *594*   Journal entries for process cost accounting, *596*
Internal control for process costs, *597*   Managerial problems with process
costs, *597*

21   STANDARD COST ACCOUNTING   605

Limitations of historical costs, *605*   Advantages of standard costs, *606*
General ledger accounts for standard costs, *606*   Original records for
standard costs, *607*   Illustrations of standard cost accounting, *609*   Analysis of materials and labor variances, *612*   Analysis of overhead variance,
615   Budget variance, *615*   Capacity variance, *615*   Overhead efficiency variance, *616*   Summary of factory overhead variance analysis, *616*

22   SPECIAL COST ANALYSIS   622

Break-even analysis, *622*   Data for the break-even chart, *623*   Uses of
the break-even chart, *624*   Limitations of the break-even chart, *625*   Applications of the contribution theory, *626*   Computation of the break-even
point, *626*   The contribution theory and planning, *626*   Contribution
theory and product selection, *627*   Contribution theory and appraisal of
sales effort, *628*   Differential cost and price discrimination, *628*   Variable and fixed cost and the decision to make or to buy, *630*   Opportunity
costs and the price level, *630*   Controllable versus uncontrollable costs in
reports, *631*

PART VI / SPECIAL CONTROLS AND ANALYSIS FOR MANAGEMENT AND INVESTORS

23 BUDGETING   *643*

Organization for budgetary control, *644*   Budget levels and employee motivation, *644*   Sales budget, *645*   Purchases budget, *645*   Operating expense budgets, *646*   Budgeted cash receipts from customers, *647* Budgeted payments on merchandise purchases, *648*   Budgeted income statement, *648*   Summary cash budget, *649*   Budgeted balance sheet, *651*   Journal entries expressing the budget, *655*

24 CAPITAL BUDGETING   *667*

Payout period, *668*   Rate of return on average investment, *669*   Discounted cash flow, *670*   Present value, *675*   Comparison of present value and discounted cash flow, *676*   Cost of capital, *677*   Economic life of equipment, *678*   Accounting for capital budgeting decisions, *679* Administration and control, *681*

25 BRANCH AND CONSOLIDATED ACCOUNTS AND STATEMENTS   *689*

Diversity of branches, *689*   Diversity of branch accounting systems, *690* Interbranch accounts, *691*   Illustration of branch accounting, *692*   Combined statements, *697*   Multiple branches, *697*   Internal control devices for branches, *697*   Branch cash controls, *699*   Other branch controls, *699*   Managerial decision to open or not to open a branch, *700*   Parent and subsidiary companies, *700*   Nature of consolidation, *701*   Illustration of a consolidated balance sheet—Case 1, *701*   Acquisition of a going concern, *704*   Intercompany profit in inventories, *705*   Changes in subsidiary's retained earnings after parent's acquisition, *705*   Illustration of a consolidated balance sheet—Case 2, *706*   Other possibilities in consolidated statements, *709*

26 FUNDS AND CASH FLOW ANALYSIS AND STATEMENTS   *720*

Nature and purpose of funds statements, *720*   Form and content of the funds statement, *720*   Preparation of the funds statement, *721*   Preparation of funds statement by T account method—Case 1, *723*   Preparation of funds statement by T account method—Case 2, *726*   Preparation of the funds statement—work sheet method, *731*   Preparation of the statement— Wilhoit Corporation—work sheet method, *732*   Popular form of "cash flow," *737*

27 ANALYSIS OF FINANCIAL STATEMENTS   *751*

Nature and purpose of statement analysis, *751*   Computation of ratios, *751* Summary analysis of the income statement, *751*   Summary analysis of the balance sheet, *752*   Other summary analyses, *754*   Other ratios, *755* Working-capital or current ratio, *755*   Acid-test ratio, *756*   Ratio of long-term debt to capital, *756*   Fixed-asset-to-long-term-debt ratio, *757* Times interest earned, *757*   Inventory turnover, *758*   Turnover and analysis of accounts receivable, *759*   Other turnovers, *759*   Book value per share of stock, *760*   Earnings per share of stock, *761*   Times dividends earned, *761*   Rate of return on total assets, *762*   Rate of return on proprietorship, *763*   Cautions for using financial statement ratios, *763*

INDEX   *777*

PART I

Basic Principles

1
Accounting and the Balance Sheet

NATURE OF ACCOUNTING CONTROL

Accounting provides information about the operations of an organization and its financial status at any date. This includes data on the properties owned and other investments made with which the organization carries on its activity; it includes information on the revenue earned over a given period and much data on the expenses associated with earning the revenue; it also includes information on the financial interests of various persons or other firms in the particular organization. The foregoing kinds of information are expressed in money, but other data associated with or necessary to the computation of the money data also make up a part of the accounting record. These include hours worked by employees, quantities of merchandise or raw materials used or sold, and number of tons of coal or gallons of oil burned or other supplies used in a period — to name just three examples of many. All these data are collected to facilitate *control* in one sense or another. They permit control of day-to-day operations, for example, by providing records of what is owed by customers (so the amounts can be collected); by giving information on the amount of time worked as compared with the product turned out (so the efficiency of the work may be measured and any needed action taken); by showing the revenue obtained from a particular product over a certain period (so its value as part of the line of merchandise carried can be decided) — and so on through an almost limitless list. From a broader viewpoint, *control* consists in part of making decisions about the major policies of an enterprise so its success can be assured. Thus, a decision may be made to produce new lines of products when older ones begin to lose favor in the market. To decide what new products to produce requires information about the costs of making them, about costs of soliciting orders for them, about warehousing them, and so on. Although much of this information must be estimated, the accounting record will aid in obtaining good estimates by supplying information on the cost of performing different functions and of purchasing various materials, supplies, and labor; and by disclosing the volume of work of various kinds that particular machines, individuals, or whole departments have been able to do in the past. Another type of control can be achieved through careful organization of the accounting system. This consists of dividing the work so that the results obtained by one person or department must fit in with the work done by another. Perhaps the simplest example of this kind of control is a record that shows the number of pieces of material delivered to a manufacturing department and the number of finished pieces returned to the storeroom. If the number of finished pieces that should be made from a piece of material is known, as it usually is, the record in the storeroom will serve as a check on the handling of material in the manufacturing department.

To summarize, accounting records make control effective by furnishing information required for day-to-day operation of an enterprise and for decisions of great or small import, and, when properly organized and maintained, by establishing an "accountability" between persons and departments.

DECISION MAKING AND ACCOUNTING

In speaking of decisions we are usually thinking of the more important decisions involving matters of general policy or unusually important transactions. Important decisions are illustrated by the following listing:

Sales decisions

Channels of distribution to be used (through wholesalers, direct to individual dealers, and others)
Methods of compensating salesmen
Kind of advertising media to be used
Location of warehouses
Form of delivery service to be offered

Purchasing and manufacturing decisions

Type of material to be used (for example, metal or plastic, copper or steel)
To make or to buy a part or a whole product
To rent or to own a machine or a building
To work two shifts in one plant or to acquire use of more space for a larger single shift
Whether or not to install labor-saving machinery

Financial decisions

Kind of financing to be used for expansion (sale of stock, sale of bonds, use of mortgage, or retention of earnings)
Amount to be paid in dividends
Use of short-term or long-term loans

Personnel decisions

Kind of pension plan to be offered
To fill open positions at distant branches by transferring employees (with the employer paying moving expense) or by recruitment at the location where the job is open
Whether or not to publish a company bulletin to give employees information about the company
Kinds of financial incentives to be offered employees

The reader will recognize that many factors will enter into all these decisions, including judgments on such intangibles as the effect of a particular decision on employee morale and productivity, the effect on the goodwill of customers, the possibility of giving competitors an advantage, and so on. However, a most important basic element in all these decisions will be the cost of doing a certain thing or the different costs of different alternatives. This is the information that accounting and accountants should supply. In many cases the specific information needed may not be accumulated in the routine established for the accounting system, but accounting techniques and skills will be the means of obtaining what is needed. Reference was made in the preceding section to the fact that some data needed for certain decisions may have to be estimated; this is especially noticeable where future cost trends are significant to the issue. This text will give information about the basic kinds of data collected by the accounting process; the records and procedures used and useful in getting them; the managerial controls that are helpful in assuring the accuracy and honesty of the data; the common accounting statements that present regular summaries of the data. Moreover, it will deal with managerial and external analysis and interpretation of the figures.

SPECIALIZATION IN ACCOUNTING

The decisions and operating controls for which accounting furnishes information may be further understood by observing the fields in which accountants specialize. These are discussed below.

General or financial accounting. This is the basic accounting required by all concerns. It is needed for the simplest kind of control over property and transactions, and is required for preparation of income tax returns, reports to owners, statements used in applying for credit, and reports required by government agencies.

Cost accounting. The cost accountant keeps records and renders reports that show the cost of producing a product or a service. His work usually involves a great deal of detail. Cost accounting is used chiefly by manufacturing concerns, but it may be applied to selling and administrative activity as well.

Auditing. Auditing is divided into *external* and *internal* auditing.

EXTERNAL auditing is the basic field of the public accountant. He comes in as an independent expert and examines the accounting records. He then renders an opinion on the fairness of the resulting statements and their conformity with generally accepted accounting principles. This opinion is important to creditors or stockholders who do not have the opportunity, ability, or time to examine the records themselves. The public accountant may call himself a "certified public accountant," or use the initials "CPA," if he has passed the required examination (given in each state for this purpose) and has met the experience and other requirements.

INTERNAL auditing is done by employees of the concern being audited. It is used in large enterprises to assure management that the accounting records are being properly kept. The internal auditor is in an excellent position to call management's attention to changed conditions that require action or to suggest improvements in the methods used.

Tax accounting. Income and other tax laws have become so complicated that many accountants specialize in this phase of accounting. These accountants render an important service to management by pointing out in advance the effect of different transactions on the tax to be paid. This prediction permits management to avoid paying more taxes than necessary. Public accountants often specialize in tax accounting, and many business firms have tax accounting specialists on their staffs. They prepare tax returns (reports to government) and may negotiate with representatives of government about disputed points in the returns.

Budgeting. A budget is a plan of operations presented in financial terms. The accountant is likely to have a leading role in the preparation of a budget, because the accounting records give most of the information used in it. He also prepares reports comparing the planned and the actual results at the end of the period. Budgeting is required by law in governmental units, and it is widely used in industry.

Controllership. An accountant in charge of the accounting of a business concern is often called a controller (also spelled "comptroller"). His work is especially concerned with the interpretation of the accounting record, and therefore represents a separate field. He can advise management on the financial condition of the firm, on the results of operations, and on the effect of possible new activities. His duties are the *control*, through the accounting records, of the property and transactions of the concern.

Governmental accounting. This is a separate specialty, because governments and business organizations use somewhat different types of accounting. The emphasis in governmental accounting is on compliance with the laws governing the collection of taxes and the disbursement of money. The emphasis in business concerns is on information for management, determination of financial position at any date, and calculation of profit or loss for a specified period. However, governments are using business accounting methods more and more.

Systems design. Systems which assure that all transactions are recorded, that no property is lost sight of, and that the records can be kept economically are necessary in all concerns. In large enterprises the design or the alteration of the system is placed in the hands of a specialist. He may be a member of the firm's own staff or a public accountant.

Management services. Accountants are frequently called upon by management to make recommendations that may not fit in the traditional areas of accounting service. This may involve advice on the kind of organization to set up to achieve effective managerial control, or advice on the suitability of a particular man or woman for a financial or accounting job. It may involve the use of one of the newer mathematical techniques such as statistical sampling or linear programming. It may be concerned with the kind of information that should be handled by an electronic computer. Large public accounting firms have separate departments to render this kind of service; accountants on the staffs of all kinds of organizations frequently participate in advising management on such problems. These services often overlap similar services offered by others, such as general management-consulting firms or industrial engineers, but accountants often have an advantage because of their knowledge of the sources of information and their familiarity with and over-all view of the organization, operations, and problems of the firm.

THE PROFESSION OF ACCOUNTANCY

Accounting is widely recognized as the newest of the major professions. In its most professional aspect it is practiced by individuals and firms that are available to the general public for accounting work. These are *independent* accountants; that is, they are independent of the special influence of any one client. This kind of practice is referred to as *public accounting*. In a majority of the states in the United States one must have a license to practice public accounting; this takes the form of a Certified Public Accountant certificate, or CPA. In some states another class of licenses exists in the form of a Public Accountant certificate, or PA. The latter have usually been created to provide for accountants who were in practice when the requirement of a license was first imposed; in almost all cases this group is not to be continued after the death of its current membership. One or two other special types of license exist. Acquisition of the CPA certificate requires specified education, experience, and the passing of a rigorous written examination. The issuance of CPA certificates developed before the requirement of a license to practice was established (beginning in the 1940s, for the most part), and in those states which have not required a license it still represents only a certification that the holder has met the required standards; this aids the public in seeking qualified accounting service. The bulk of the work of the public accountant consists of auditing and of preparation of tax returns and the related work, but branches out into all the specialities noted above.

The largest number of accountants is employed by individual organizations to maintain and improve their accounting systems and to analyze and interpret the resulting information. Those who work for the many governmental units — federal, state or local — are known as government accountants, and the others as private accountants. Government and private accountants have the opportunity to work in all the accounting specialties, and so can have wide experience, except that they rarely are in a position exactly comparable to the relationship of an independent professional practitioner and his client. In the higher positions in governmental and private accounting, managerial skills are required and proportionate opportunities exist; many corporation presidents have arrived at that position through the ranks of the accounting staff.

THE ACCOUNTING ENTITY

Each organization that keeps accounting records is said to have an *accounting system*, which consists of all the records used in recording and summarizing the transactions, properties, and related obligations of the concern. Each organization is said to constitute an accounting *unit* or *entity*. For example, a man who owns a dry goods store and a chain of filling stations will ordinarily have one accounting system for the store and another for the filling stations. A large manufacturing company with plants in several cities has one accounting system. Sometimes the records kept at the different locations are referred to as the "system" of that plant or branch. In any case, the accounting system serves one distinct organization under a single management.

USERS OF ACCOUNTING

Every organization that owns or manages property requires accounting records. Most property is owned by business concerns and by individuals for business purposes. As a result, most accounting is done for business units. The need for accounting in other types of organizations using or managing property is just as great. We have already mentioned governmental accounting; the large volume of government work could never be done successfully without very complete accounting records, whether for national, state, city, or county governments or for school districts and similar units. Nonprofit institutions such as schools, hospitals, libraries, and charities, whether privately or publicly owned, use accounting records. The need for records arises from the volume and complexity of the property and transactions involved. The discussion in this book is based on business organizations, but the principles apply to all types of enterprises.

ASSETS

Properties owned are called assets. There are many kinds of property, or assets. Some of those commonly used in business are:

Cash (currency, coin, and bank deposits)

Accounts receivable (amounts collectible from others, usually customers)

Merchandise (stock in trade)

Supplies (materials used in operating the business, such as wrapping paper, stationery, and dust cloths)

Prepaid expenses (payments made for services to be received in the future, such as insurance premiums paid in advance)

Land (a site or piece of ground)

Buildings (structures)

Machinery and equipment (movable and fixed machines and various kinds of tools and equipment, for example, lathes, ladders, and electric drills)

Office furniture and equipment (examples include desks, tables, and typewriters)

Store equipment (examples include counters, cash registers, and fans)

Trademarks (exclusive right to use a special design or a coined word)

Patents (exclusive right to produce a particular product, granted by the federal government)

Copyrights (exclusive right to reproduce a composition or a work of art, granted by the federal government)

Franchises (right granted by a public authority to operate a regulated service, such as sale of electric power or public transportation. Obtaining a franchise may require payment of attorney's fees and fees charged by the public authority.)

The essential feature of an asset is that it is useful in carrying on the activities of the concern. It may be acquired by donation or by purchase; in any event, it is an object or a right that has future usefulness.

FINANCIAL INTERESTS

A person who invests in a concern as an owner or who lends it money as a creditor is said to have a *financial interest* in it. The financial interests in a business concern take a variety of forms. The form depends on the kind of legal arrangement by which the person acquired or holds his interest. Some types of financial interests commonly found in the records of a business concern are given below.

Notes payable (debts owed by the business to a creditor, evidenced by a promissory note given to the creditor. A note payable is usually given in borrowing cash and may be used in buying merchandise.)

Accounts payable (debts owed by the business to a creditor for merchandise or services suppled by the creditor; no formal legal document is required.)

Taxes payable (amounts imposed by and owed to governmental units)

Mortgages payable (long-term promissory notes secured by pledging specific assets as security for their payment)

Bonds payable (long-term debts evidenced by a formal written contract or indenture. Usually, the liability extends to a number of creditors, each of whom holds one or more bond certificates.)

Proprietorship (the financial interest of the owners, arising from original investments and accumulated profits)

Financial interests in general are sometimes called *equities*. The *proprietorship*, or interest of the owners, is distinguished from the interests of creditors. The creditors' interests are called *liabilities*.

IDENTITY OF ASSETS AND FINANCIAL INTERESTS

The total amount of financial interests in any organization and the total amount of assets are identical, because they are two ways of describing the same thing. The assets describe the concern according to the *kinds of property owned*. The financial interests describe the concern according to the kinds of *interests* in it.

ACCOUNTING EQUATION

Because the assets and the interests in them are equal, the relationship may be stated in the form of an equation. Let

A stand for assets.
L stand for liabilities.
P stand for proprietorship.

Then
$$A = L + P$$

This fundamental expression of the identity of assets and interests is called the *accounting equation*. As in any equation, the symbols may be shifted from one side to the other if their sign is changed when they are shifted. Thus,

$$A - L = P$$
$$A - P = L$$

and
$$A - P - L = 0$$

THE BALANCE SHEET

The accounting equation is often called the *balance sheet equation*, because it expresses the fundamental relationship on which the balance sheet is based. The balance sheet is a statement of the assets, liabilities, and proprietorship (or properties and financial interests in them) on a given date. It is a statement of *financial condition*. An example is shown below.

VICTOR APPLIANCES
Balance Sheet
December 31, 1966

Assets		Liabilities and Proprietorship	
Cash	$ 4,570	Liabilities:	
Accounts Receivable	2,800	Accounts Payable	$ 4,000
Merchandise	20,300	Taxes Payable	50
Supplies	1,960	Total Liabilities	$ 4,050
		Proprietorship:	
		O. P. Victor, Capital	25,580
	$29,630		$29,630

COST AND VALUE

The assets are, by custom, initially listed in the balance sheet at cost, that is, at the actual number of dollars spent or promised for them. At the time of acquisition this is ordinarily the best evidence of their actual value. As time passes, however, conditions may change and the original or "historical" cost may no longer bear much resemblance to current value. This variance may occur because the general price level has changed, because conditions of supply and demand for this kind of asset have changed, or for other reasons. Normal declines in usefulness due to wear and tear, weathering, passage of time, and so on, are recorded and reflected in the balance sheet, but the other changes are not recorded in conventional accounting practice. The reason is that current values are not easy to determine for assets that are not actively traded and for those which are often more or less unique. Accountants are reluctant to introduce into the accounts figures which are not *objectively* determinable, that is, which cannot be arrived at (within close limits) independently by different accountants having the same general skills. They feel that the process of appraising an asset to obtain a current value for it may open the door to a wide range of possible values and to deliberate falsification as well. Historical cost, adjusted for expiration of useful life, on the other hand, *is* objectively determinable. Critics of the traditional use of historical cost point out that it does no good to have an objectively verifiable figure that is irrelevant to today's decisions, and suggest that some objectivity should be sacrificed for the greater relevance of current value information. Some accountants are convinced that satisfactorily objective methods for arriving at current values of assets may be devised. This is an area of warm debate in accounting at present, and although historical cost is still the accepted basis for asset "values," the future may see a change in the direction of more current values. However, basic accounting processes are the same whichever kind of "valuation" is used.

TRANSACTIONS

An event that changes the assets, liabilities, or proprietorship is a *transaction*. A large part of accounting work consists of recording the transactions of the concern in an orderly manner.

ANALYSIS OF TRANSACTIONS

To record a transaction properly it is necessary to determine how the transaction affects the assets, liabilities, or proprietorship. This determination is called an *analysis* of the transaction. This analysis must always conform to the basic principle that assets and the interests in them are equal, a test that is kept in mind each time a transaction is recorded. Because of this principle, any transaction may be expressed in terms of the accounting equation. No matter how many changes are made by transactions, the sum of the assets always equals the sum of the financial interests. The equality can be shown by drawing up a balance sheet after any transaction.

TYPES OF TRANSACTIONS

Transactions may affect only the assets, only the assets and the liabilities, or only the assets and proprietorship; they may affect only the liabilities, or the liabilities and proprietorship together. A transaction may affect all three elements of the accounting equation at the same time. The following examples illustrate some of the possibilities.

Increase in one asset, decrease in another

Merchandise increased, cash decreased by a cash purchase.
Cash increased, accounts receivable decreased when a customer pays for a charge sale.

Increase in assets, increase in liabilities

Cash increased, notes payable increased when money is borrowed on a note.
Supplies increased, accounts payable increased when supplies are bought on credit.

Increase in assets, increase in proprietorship

Land increased, proprietor's capital increased when proprietor brings his land into the business.
Cash increased, proprietorship increased when proprietor makes a sale for cash.

Decrease in assets, decrease in liabilities

Cash decreased, accounts payable decreased when bill for a charge (credit) purchase is paid.
Cash decreased, taxes payable decreased when taxes are paid.

ILLUSTRATION OF TRANSACTION ANALYSIS

The transactions that gave rise to the balance sheet of Victor Appliances (page 9) are analyzed in the following paragraphs.

When O. P. Victor started his appliance business on December 1, 1966, he invested $25,000 from his personal funds. This amount was deposited in a bank account for Victor Appliances. In terms of the balance sheet equation the transaction is analyzed as follows:

$$\text{Assets} = \text{Proprietorship}$$
$$\text{Cash} = \text{O. P. Victor, Capital}$$
$$\text{Transaction (1): } \$25,000 = \$25,000$$

Victor's firm buys merchandise costing $12,000, paying for it with cash:

	Assets		= Proprietorship
	Cash +	Merchan- dise	= O. P. Victor, Capital
Old balances:	$25,000		$25,000
Transaction (2):	−12,000	+ 12,000	= 0
New balances	$13,000 +	$12,000	= $25,000

The firm buys for cash supplies costing $2,000:

	Assets		= Proprietorship
	Cash + Merchandise + Supplies		= O. P. Victor, Capital
Old balances:	$13,000 + $12,000		= $25,000
Transaction (3):	−2,000	+ $2,000	= $ 0
	$11,000 + $12,000	+ $2,000	= $25,000

More merchandise is needed, and it is bought on credit; it costs $11,000. The new merchandise increases the assets, but the obligation to pay for it adds a liability:

	Assets		= Liabilities + Proprietorship
	Cash + Merchandise + Supplies		= Accounts Payable + O. P. Victor, Capital
Old balances:	$11,000 + $12,000	+ $2,000	= $25,000
Transaction (4):	+11,000		= +$11,000
	$11,000 + $23,000	+ $2,000	= $11,000 + $25,000

Merchandise is sold on credit for $5,200. This creates the asset *Accounts Receivable*, representing the right of the company to collect from the customers. Receipt of this asset, considered by itself, increases O. P. Victor's interest in the business:

	Assets				= Liabilities + Proprietorship
	Cash +	Accounts Receivable +	Mdse. +	Supplies	= Accounts Payable + O. P. Victor, Capital
Old balances:	$11,000		+ $23,000 +	$2,000	= $11,000 + $25,000
Transaction (5):		+ $5,200			= +5,200
	$11,000 +	$5,200	+ $23,000 +	$2,000	= $11,000 + $30,200

Of course, the sales require that merchandise be handed over to the customers. This merchandise cost $2,700, and the asset Merchandise is reduced by that amount. This delivery, considered by itself, reduces O. P. Victor's interest (comes out of his "pocket"):

	Assets				= Liabilities + Proprietorship
	Cash +	Accounts Receivable +	Mdse. +	Supplies	= Accounts Payable + O. P. Victor, Capital
Old balances:	$11,000 +	$5,200	+ $23,000 +	$2,000	= $11,000 + $30,200
Transaction (6):			−2,700		= −2,700
	$11,000 +	$5,200	+ $20,300 +	$2,000	= $11,000 + $27,500

Note that the net effect of the sale of $2,700 worth of merchandise (cost to O. P. Victor) for $5,200 (retail) is an increase in O. P. Victor's interest in the business by $2,500, the amount of the "margin."

One person was hired to help Mr. Victor in the store; his semimonthly salary of $225 is paid in cash; this outlay reduces what O. P. Victor otherwise would have:

	Assets				= Liabilities + Proprietorship
	Cash +	Accounts Receivable	+ Mdse.	+ Supplies =	Accounts Payable + O. P. Victor, Capital
Old balances:	$11,000 +	$5,200	+ $20,300	+ $2,000 =	$11,000 + $27,500
Transaction (7):	− 225			=	− 225
	$10,775 +	$5,200	+ $20,300	+ $2,000 =	$11,000 + $27,275

The customers pay $2,400 on their accounts, with these results:

	Assets				= Liabilities + Proprietorship
	Cash +	Accounts Receivable	+ Mdse.	+ Supplies =	Accounts Payable + O. P. Victor, Capital
Old balances:	$10,775 +	$5,200	+ $20,300	+ $2,000 =	$11,000 + $27,275
Transaction (8):	+2,400	−2,400		=	
	$13,175 +	$2,800	+ $20,300	+ $2,000 =	$11,000 + $27,275

During the period supplies costing $40 are used up. This amount comes out of O. P. Victor's interest:

	Assets				= Liabilities + Proprietorship
	Cash +	Accounts Receivable	+ Mdse.	+ Supplies =	Accounts Payable + O. P. Victor, Capital
Old balances:	$13,175 +	$2,800	+ $20,300	+ $2,000 =	$11,000 + $27,275
Transaction (9):				− 40 =	− 40
	$13,175 +	$2,800	+ $20,300	+ $1,960 =	$11,000 + $27,235

Various taxes assessed against the business are calculated at $50. Although these taxes have not yet been paid, the sum is a liability and must be recorded. Its incurrence reduces the interest that O. P. Victor would otherwise have in the business:

	Assets				=	Liabilities		+ Proprietor-ship
Cash +	Accounts Receiv-able	+ Mdse.	+ Sup-plies		= Accounts Payable	+ Taxes Pay-able	+ O. P. Victor, Capital
Old balances: $13,175 +	$2,800	+ $20,300	+ $1,960	= $11,000			+ $27,235
Transaction (10):						+ $50	− 50
$13,175 +	$2,800	+ $20,300	+ $1,960	= $11,000	+ $50	+ $27,185

The rent for the month is paid, $300. This payment reduces cash and Victor's interest:

	Assets				=	Liabilities		+ Proprietor-ship
Cash +	Accounts Receiv-able	+ Mdse.	+ Sup-plies		= Accounts Payable	+ Taxes Pay-able	+ O. P. Victor, Capital
Old balances: $13,175 +	$2,800	+ $20,300	+ $1,960	= $11,000	+ $50	+ $27,185
Transaction (11): −300						−300
$12,875 +	$2,800	+ $20,300	+ $1,960	= $11,000	+ $50	+ $26,885

The second half month's salary is paid to the employee. This outlay reduces cash and Victor's interest:

	Assets				=	Liabilities		+ Proprietor-ship
Cash +	Accounts Receiv-able	+ Mdse.	+ Sup-plies		= Accounts Payable	+ Taxes Pay-able	+ O .P. Victor, Capital
Old balances: $12,875 +	$2,800	+ $20,300	+ $1,960	= $11,000	+ $50	+ $26,885
Transaction (12): −225						−225
$12,650 +	$2,800	+ $20,300	+ $1,960	= $11,000	+ $50	+ $26,660

The firm pays $7,000 on its liability for the merchandise bought on credit (transaction 4); since this liability has already been recorded, the payment reduces cash and the liability but does not affect proprietorship:

	Assets				=	Liabilities		+ Proprietor-ship
Cash +	Accounts Receiv-able	+ Mdse.	+ Sup-plies		= Accounts Payable	+ Taxes Pay-able	+ O. P. Victor, Capital
Old balances: $12,650 +	$2,800	+ $20,300	+ $1,960	= $11,000	+ $50	+ $26,660
Transaction (13): −7,000					−7,000		
$ 5,650 +	$2,800	+ $20,300	+ $1,960	= $ 4,000	+ $50	+ $26,660

During the month the firm pays $80 for light and heat and other bills. These items reduce what Victor would otherwise have had; they are recorded together in transaction 14:

	Assets			=	Liabilities		+ Proprietorship
Cash +	Accounts Receivable +	Mdse. +	Supplies	= Accounts Payable +	Taxes Payable +	O. P. Victor, Capital
Old balances:	$ 5,650 +	$2,800 +	$20,300 +	$1,960 =	$ 4,000 +	$50 +	$26,660
Transaction (14):	−80						−80
	$ 5,570 +	$2,800 +	$20,300 +	$1,960 =	$ 4,000 +	$50 +	$26,580

Victor withdraws $1,000 cash from the business to use for his personal expenses:

	Assets			=	Liabilities		+ Proprietorship
Cash +	Accounts Receivable +	Mdse. +	Supplies	= Accounts Payable +	Taxes Payable +	O. P. Victor, Capital
Old balances:	$ 5,570 +	$2,800 +	$20,300 +	$1,960 =	$ 4,000 +	$50 +	$26,580
Transaction (15):	−1,000						−1,000
	$ 4,570 +	$2,800 +	$20,300 +	$1,960 =	$ 4,000 +	$50 +	$25,580

Summary of illustration. The transactions of Victor Appliances are summarized in a single table on this page. The balances shown in the summary are the ones in the balance sheet on page 9.

SUMMARY OF TRANSACTIONS OF VICTOR APPLIANCES

	Assets				= Liabilities		+ Proprietorship
	Cash +	Accounts Receivable +	Mdse. +	Supplies	= Accounts Payable +	Taxes Payable +	O. P. Victor, Capital
Transaction:							
(1)	+ $25,000						+ $25,000
(2)	− 12,000		+ $12,000				
(3)	− 2,000			+ $2,000			
(4)			+ 11,000		+ $11,000		
(5)		+ $5,200					+ 5,200
(6)			− 2,700				− 2,700
(7)	− 225						− 225
(8)	+ 2,400	− 2,400					
(9)				− 40			− 40
(10)						+ $50	− 50
(11)	− 300						− 300
(12)	− 225						− 225
(13)	− 7,000				− 7,000		
(14)	− 80						− 80
(15)	− 1,000						− 1,000
Balances	$ 4,570 +	$2,800 +	$20,300 +	$1,960 =	$ 4,000 +	$50 +	$25,580

INCOME STATEMENT

The summary of all transactions provides the statement called a *balance sheet*, as the summary tabulation above indicates. Another important statement is provided by summarizing only the transactions that determine the amount of income earned by the business. This is called an *income statement*, a *statement of profit and loss*, or an *operating statement*. It is drawn up to reflect a specific period – a month or a year. It shows the changes that have occurred in the proprietorship during the period in consequence of the income-earning activities. The income statement of Victor Appliances for December 1966 is shown below. The figures in it can be observed in the O. P. Victor, Capital, column of the summary of transactions, along with other figures there.

VICTOR APPLIANCES

Income Statement

Month of December, 1966

Sales......................................		$5,200
Cost of Goods Sold.......................		2,700
Gross Margin on Sales...................		$2,500
Expenses:		
Salaries............................	$450	
Rent...............................	300	
Taxes..............................	50	
Supplies Used......................	40	
Other Expenses....................	80	920
Net Income.............................		$1,580

THE ACCOUNT

An account is a record of transactions affecting one balance sheet figure or one income statement figure. There is an account for each asset, liability, or proprietorship item. Sometimes the information about one element of the statement will be subdivided into two or more accounts. For example, if a concern has money in three banks, it will have an account for each one, but the three will be combined in the one figure on the balance sheet under Cash. In the pages above we recorded each transaction by changing the balance sheet. This operation is obviously not practical as a regular business procedure, so a record is accumulated separately in accounts for each element of the statement. A typical account has the following appearance:

Account Title No.

DATE	EXPLANATION	REF.	DEBIT	DATE	EXPLANATION	REF.	CREDIT
1966				1966			
Jan 1	Balance		800 00	Jan 18			400 00
14			30 00				
27			60 00				

Periodically the additions to and deductions from the item described by the account are summarized, and a net amount or balance is carried forward in the account. Such a net total appears in the illustration under date of January 1, 1966. Since this represents the beginning figure in the account illustrated, it is referred to as the *opening* balance.

Note that provision for four kinds of information is made in the body of the account:

1. The date on which the transaction affecting the account was entered
2. Any explanation desired
3. A column in which reference (Ref.) may be made to the source of information about the transaction
4. The amount entered as a debit or credit.

DEBIT AND CREDIT

The terms *debit* and *credit* refer to amounts entered on the left (debit) or the right (credit) sides of the typical account. They are abbreviated *dr.* and *cr.* These terms come down to us from early Renaissance times when Latin was used in account books, the Latin being *debitur* and *creditur*. Their only modern significance is to designate the left and the right sides of the common form of account. We also speak of *debiting* or *crediting* an account. One side of an account is used to record increases in the asset, liability, or proprietorship item it represents, and the other side is used to record decreases. Which side represents increases and which one decreases depends on the type of account. One can remember which side to use for a particular account if he keeps in mind the common arrangement of the balance sheet with assets on the left and liabilities and proprietorship on the right. The asset accounts (appearing on the left side of the balance sheet) are increased by debits and decreased by credits; the reverse is true of liabilities and proprietorship items (appearing on the right side). The increases go on the same side of the account as the item does on the balance sheet; the decreases go on the opposite side from the increases. This explanation may be summarized as follows:

	Debits	*Credits*
Assets	Increase	Decrease
Liabilities	Decrease	Increase
Proprietorship	Decrease	Increase

The relationship is also indicated in the diagram on page 18, where the accounts of Victor Appliances (in skeleton or T form) are shown below the balance sheet with their balances on the proper side. Note the correspondence between the position of the balance of each account and the position of the same figure on the balance sheet.

EQUALITY OF DEBITS AND CREDITS

Throughout the whole system of accounts, debits must always equal the credits. This equality follows from the balancing feature of the balance sheet. Assets are equal to the financial interests because these things are two ways of describing the concern. Since they describe the same thing, they add to the same total. Transactions that change one element of the balance sheet have a corresponding effect on some other element. When each transaction is ana-lyzed, its effect is expressed in debits and credits. For each transaction, and of course for any series of transactions, the debit amounts always equal the credit amounts.

BALANCE SHEET ACCOUNTS

VICTOR APPLIANCES
Balance Sheet

December 31, 1966

Assets		Liabilities and Proprietorship	
Cash	$ 4,570	Liabilities:	
Accounts Receivable	2,800	Accounts Payable	$ 4,000
Merchandise	20,300	Taxes Payable	50
Supplies	1,960	Total Liabilities	$ 4,050
		Proprietorship:	
		O. P. Victor, Capital	25,580
	$29,630		$29,630

Cash		**Accounts Payable**	
4,570			4,000

Accounts Receivable		**Taxes Payable**	
2,800			50

Merchandise		**O. P. Victor, Capital**	
20,300			25,580

Supplies	
1,960	

THE LEDGER

A ledger is a set of accounts. Originally, ledgers were bound books, and some still are. However, loose-leaf ledgers are now typical of the larger con-cerns and are common in small ones. They may consist of cards in trays, punched sheets kept in a binder, or similar devices. Traditional use of bound books for ledgers and other accounting records explains the term "books of account" or simply the "books."

The ledger contains the account balances from which the statements are prepared. For convenience in drawing up the statements and as a method of indexing, accounts are frequently arranged in the ledger in the order in which they appear on the statements. In this case, assets come first, liabilities next, and proprietorship last.

SIMPLE MANAGERIAL USES OF THE LEDGER

The ledger is a constant source of information for managerial action. For example, the balance shown in the Cash account, plus or minus any receipts or disbursements not yet entered in the ledger, shows what is available to be spent at any time. From this the manager can decide that a particular bill can be paid today, or that it must wait until some more cash receipts come in. By looking at the Accounts Receivable account he can see how long ago a customer was debited ("charged") for some merchandise, and whether or not the customer should be sent another notice or be asked to pay up. If he is considering trading off a certain machine and wants to know how long the machine has been used and what it cost, the manager may look up the debit that recorded its purchase in the Machinery and Equipment account, which will give him the date of acquisition and cost. If a creditor sends a statement showing $5,825 due, it may be compared with the record kept in the company's own Accounts Payable account. If that account shows only $4,225 due, the difference may be investigated and the proper amount determined. More elaborate uses are made of the data in the ledger, but it serves important uses in providing a continuous record of the transactions affecting each account. This record (1) provides information for day-to-day decisions, and (2) helps protect the concern against loss of assets.

On the latter point, note that a properly kept ledger will show what assets should be on hand. For example, it will show the amount of cash in the bank; if embezzlement occurs, the loss will be disclosed when the bank's statement is compared with the company's ledger. The ledger also controls other assets, such as equipment and merchandise. It facilitates collection of debts and prevents overpayment to creditors.

MATRIX FORMULATION OF ACCOUNTING

The relationship of assets and the interests in them — an equality — was expressed above in the form of the accounting equation, $A = L + P$, or assets = liabilities + proprietorship. The effect of transactions on the equation and the accounts can also be displayed in the form of a matrix, as shown on page 20 for the transactions of Victor Appliances.

Note that a debit to an account is indicated by a figure in a column, while the same figure indicates a credit to the account for the row it is in. For example, the entry of $2,400 in the column for Cash on the row for Accounts Receivable represents a debit to Cash and a credit to Accounts Receivable. By this method one figure serves to indicate both a debit and a credit, and the "double-entry" feature of accounting appears in the double set of captions for the accounts, rather than in the use of two figures for each transaction. The matrix formulation may be thought of as a more realistic picture of accounting data kept in an electronic computer, with each cell of the matrix representing a memory location. It also serves the purpose here of emphasizing the fact that the

MATRIX FORMULATION OF ACCOUNTING
VICTOR APPLIANCES

| | Debits | | | | | | | | |
	Cash	Accounts Receivable	Merchandise	Supplies	Accounts Payable	Taxes Payable	O. P. Victor, Capital	Totals	Balances
Cash			12,000	2,000	7,000		225 300 225 80 1,000	22,830	
Accounts Receivable	2,400							2,400	
Merchandise							2,700	2,700	
Supplies							40	40	
Accounts Payable			11,000					11,000	4,000
Taxes Payable							50	50	50
O. P. Victor, Capital	25,000	5,200						30,200	25,580
Totals	27,400	5,200	23,000	2,000	7,000		4,620	69,220	
Balances	4,570	2,800	20,300	1,960					29,630

Credits

traditional two-sided account customarily used in hand-kept records is only a mechanical device and not the essence of the information system that accounting represents.

FORM OF THE BALANCE SHEET

Asset, liability, and proprietorship items may be arranged on the balance sheet in various ways. The form most commonly used has two major features:

1. The assets are listed on the left, and the liabilities and proprietorship on the right.

2. Assets and liabilities are grouped into certain classes. The asset groups commonly used are:

Current assets. This term includes assets that are turned over rapidly in the operation of the business, usually within a year. For example, cash is used to buy merchandise, merchandise is sold on credit and becomes accounts receivable, and the accounts receivable are collected in cash — all within a matter of weeks. Supplies and prepaid insurance are other examples of current assets. Most current assets are liquid; that is, they may readily be turned into cash. Current assets include cash, accounts receivable, merchandise, supplies, and prepaid items such as insurance.

Fixed assets. This term denotes land, buildings, and equipment. The term is sometimes used to refer to all assets of long duration in the business.

Intangible assets. Intangibles are long-lived assets whose value does not depend on any physical quality of the asset. In this respect they are in contrast to the fixed asset as defined above. Copyrights, trademarks, franchises, and patents are prominent intangible assets.

Deferred charges. The terms *prepaid expenses* and *deferred charges* are used interchangeably, but sometimes the latter refers only to the longer lived items. Many accountants now show the short-lived prepayments as current assets, but the traditional practice of placing them in a separate group is still widely followed.

Assets that do not fit into any of these categories are shown separately on the balance sheet. "Investment in Affiliated Companies" is an example.

The liability groups commonly used are:

Current liabilities. These debts are payable in a short time, usually within a year. Notes payable, accounts payable, wages and salaries payable, and taxes payable are examples.

Long-term liabilities. These liabilities fall due later than one year from the balance sheet date; they are also called "noncurrent liabilities" or "fixed liabilities." Examples include long-term notes, bonds, mortgages, and installment contracts payable.

The balance sheet of Pomeroy Building Materials (below) illustrates the form and classification just described. The form in which it appears is called the *account* form. The *report* form, in which liabilities and proprietorship are listed below the assets, is useful when a balance sheet is published on a single narrow page.

POMEROY BUILDING MATERIALS
Balance Sheet
June 30, 1966

Assets			*Liabilities and Proprietorship*		
Current Assets:			**Current Liabilities:**		
Cash	$12,000.00		Notes Payable	$15,000.00	
Accounts Receivable	18,421.00		Accounts Payable	28,515.00	
Merchandise	62,500.00		Wages Payable	785.00	
Trucking Supplies	827.00		Taxes Payable	1,200.00	
Office Supplies	200.00		Total Current Liabilities		$ 45,500.00
Prepaid Insurance	350.00		**Long-term Liabilities:**		
Total Current Assets		$ 94,298.00	Contracts Payable	$ 4,000.00	
Fixed Assets:			Mortgage Payable	6,000.00	
Trucks	$ 8,000.00		Total Long-term Liabilities		10,000.00
Buildings	12,000.00		Total Liabilities		$ 55,500.00
Land	5,000.00		**Proprietorship**		
Office Equipment	1,850.00		John J. Pomeroy, Capital		75,648.00
Total Fixed Assets		26,850.00			
Intangible Asset—Patent		10,000.00			
Total Assets		$131,148.00	Total Liabilities and Proprietorship		$131,148.00

PROPRIETORSHIP IN THE BALANCE SHEET

When the business is owned by one person, his interest appears on the balance sheet as shown above. If the business is owned by two or more partners (a partnership), it is shown by separate figures for the capital, or interest, or each partner. For example, a partnership with two owners might have the following proprietorship section in its balance sheet:

Albert M. Franks, Capital	$ 16,438	
Jonathan B. Senn, Capital	28,915	
Total Capital		$ 45,353

If the business is a corporation, separate figures are shown for capital stock and for any additional elements of proprietorship. The most common additional item results from leaving earnings in the business. Such a figure is called "retained earnings" or "earned surplus." A corporation balance sheet may therefore include:

Capital Stock	$115,000	
Retained Earnings	78,226	
Total Capital		$193,226

The form used by corporations results from legal requirements applicable only to corporations.

MANAGERIAL USE OF THE BALANCE SHEET

The balance sheet shows what kinds of assets the business has and, in terms of money, the amount of each. It shows what amounts are owed, and whether or not the amounts are due soon or over a longer period. If the assets are large relative to the liabilities, the business is presumably in good financial condition, because the assets then can provide enough to pay all the debts, even though their values shrink considerably. Ordinarily it is expected that the business will keep on operating indefinitely. Assets that are large relative to liabilities indicate that large temporary losses could be incurred without causing liquidation of the business.

More detailed analysis is helpful to management. Four items in particular are commonly used in this connection and are computed from the balance sheet:

Working capital, calculated by subtracting current liabilities from current assets. Taking figures from page 22, we get

$$\begin{aligned} W.C. &= C.A. - C.L. \\ &= \$94,298 - \$45,500 \\ &= \$48,798 \end{aligned}$$

This shows how much investment the proprietors (and possibly long-term creditors) have in current assets. The rest of the current assets are presumably derived from the short-term creditors (current liabilities). It shows how well the firm can stand temporary losses, which reduce current assets, and still pay its current debts.

Current ratio, calculated by dividing current assets by current liabilities. The formula is

$$C.R. = \frac{C.A.}{C.L.}$$

Using the figures of page 22, we get

$$C.R. = \frac{C.A.}{C.L.} = \frac{\$94,298}{\$45,500} = 2.07 \text{ to } 1$$

Since current assets are more than twice the amount of current liabilities, the firm could pay its current liabilities even if the assets had to be sold at a loss of one half.

Fixed assets—fixed liabilities ratio, calculated by dividing fixed assets by fixed (long-term) liabilities, as follows (figures from page 22):

$$\frac{F.A.}{F.L.} = \frac{\$26,850}{\$10,000} = 2.685 \text{ to } 1$$

From a managerial viewpoint, a high ratio of fixed assets to fixed liabilities indicates that funds received from use of the fixed assets should be more than adequate to permit payment of the debts. From the viewpoint of the creditors it has the same significance and means that the debts could be collected even though the assets had to be sold at a loss to meet the debt.

Percent of proprietory investment, calculated by dividing the proprietorship by the total of liabilities and proprietorship (financial interests). To illustrate (figures from page 22):

$$\%P = \frac{P}{L + P} = \frac{\$\ 75,648}{\$131,148} = 57.68\%$$

This indicates that approximately 58 percent of the assets used in the business have been supplied by the proprietor and that 42 percent of them have been acquired from creditors. A large percentage of proprietory interest indicates safety. Debts have to be paid regardless of losses, and losses can be absorbed without affecting the creditors' interests if proprietorship is relatively high.

Creditors are also interested in these calculations, because they indicate something about the collectibility of the debts. Owners and prospective owners are interested in them because of the information they give on the financial health of the organization. Managers especially will watch the changes in the ratios from one period to another to see if any unfavorable trends are developing that require corrective action, or to keep favorable trends going.

SUMMARY

Accounting provides control of property by means of records. Organizations with reasonably complete accounting have records that show what properties are owned (assets) and also the financial interests in the assets (liabilities and proprietorship). The assets of a concern and the financial interests in it describe the one concern from two viewpoints and therefore add to the same total. This is the basis for the balance sheet—the statement of financial condition—and is the key to analysis of transactions. It is the basis for double-entry accounting. The income statement shows the results of the income-earning activities. Management and other interested persons use the balance sheet as an index to the financial health of the concern. In this connection, ratios that disclose significant relationships of different asset, liability, and proprietorship items are calculated.

QUESTIONS

1.1 Accounting control may be classified as:

control for day-to-day operations
control for making decisions
control for establishing accountability

Give two concrete examples of each of the three kinds of control and discuss each briefly.

1.2 Describe briefly how a theater uses control to prevent embezzlement of cash receipts.

1.3 Management of the Stalker Chemical Co. is confronted with the alternative of working three shifts in the present plant or acquiring more space for a larger shift.

What accounting information is relevant to making a decision between these alternatives? What other factors should be considered?

1.4 Accounting provides information as to amounts and kinds of properties owned, debts owed, owners' equities, revenues earned, and expenses incurred; but accounting is not restricted to providing this information. List some of the other functions of accounting.

1.5 Suggest things that an accountant specializing in each of the following fields might do: financial accounting, cost accounting, auditing—external, auditing—internal, tax accounting, budgeting, controllership, governmental accounting, systems design, and management services.

1.6 It has been alleged that electronic computers will diminish the need for accountants. Comment.

1.7 H. Higgins borrows $50,000 on his life insurance and puts the proceeds into an appliance business. During the year he pays $3,000 interest on the loan. Is the interest a business expense? Comment on the facts in relation to the concept of an accounting entity.

1.8 The H National Bank is not audited by certified public accountants. What reasons might be advanced by the directors of the bank for this situation? Suggest reasons why the bank should be audited by certified public accountants.

1.9 How will accounting education change as a result of an expansion in the field of management services?

1.10 What is meant by "objectivity" in accounting? How does it apply to the basis for reporting assets?

1.11 On December 31, 1966, the M Company constructed a warehouse for a contract price of $50,000. The directors were advised by the contractor that costs had been underestimated and that he had lost money on the contract. The contractor states that a fair charge for the construction would have been $70,000. As a result of this information, the directors wish to report the warehouse at $70,000 in the December 31, 1966, balance sheet, because in their opinion that is the fair market value of the property. Comment.

1.12 Why must the accounting equation always balance?

1.13 The sum of Nagel Miner's assets is $20,000, and the sum of his liabilities is $25,000. What is his proprietorship? What are the factors that might account for such a financial condition?

1.14 In what ways are the interests of bondholders and stockholders similar? In what ways are they different?

1.15 (1) Define assets. (2) Name five assets that might appear on the balance sheet of a firm of certified public accountants. (3) Name two additional assets that might appear on the balance sheet of a department store. (4) Name two additional assets that might appear on the balance sheet of a railroad. (5) Name two additional assets that might appear on the balance sheet of a typewriter manufacturer.

1.16 (1) Define liabilities. (2) List five liabilities that might be found on the balance sheet of a manufacturer of synthetic detergents.

1.17 Suggest transactions that would do each of the following things:

(1) Increase one asset and decrease another.
(2) Increase an asset and increase a liability.
(3) Increase an asset and increase proprietorship.
(4) Decrease an asset and decrease a liability.
(5) Decrease an asset and decrease proprietorship.
(6) Increase a liability and decrease proprietorship.

1.18 In what way will the balance sheets of corporations, partnerships, and sole proprietorships in the same line of business differ even if they do the same kind and amount of business?

1.19 What groupings are usually made in presenting figures in a balance sheet?

1.20 Suggest some uses that management of a concern may make of the balance sheet.

1.21 It is impractical to record business transactions by changing figures on the balance sheet for each transaction. What device is actually used to accumulate information about each item on the balance sheet?

1.22 What information is recorded in an account?

1.23 What does the instruction "debit Cash $5,000, credit Accounts Receivable $5,000," mean?

1.24 Translate each of the following into either debit or credit:

(1) Increase in an asset
(2) Decrease in proprietorship
(3) Increase in a liability
(4) Increase in proprietorship
(5) Decrease in an asset
(6) Decrease in a liability

1.25 For each of the following transactions, state what kind of account (asset, liability, or proprietorship) is affected by the *debit*, and whether the account is increased or decreased:

(1) The proprietor delivers some counters to a new store as part of his investment.
(2) A loan is obtained from a bank; the proceeds are left on deposit at the bank.
(3) A loan from a private party, evidenced by a promissory note, is paid off.
(4) The concern buys a patent for $10,000.
(5) The proprietor withdraws $500 cash for personal use.
(6) The proprietor takes home a toaster as a gift for his wife.
(7) A freezer is sold to a customer on credit.
(8) The lot next door is purchased for use as a parking lot for customers.
(9) A "premium" (price) of $400 is paid for an insurance policy that furnishes protection for three years ahead.
(10) A truck is purchased for $1,200 down and a promise to pay $3,800 more in future installments.

1.26 For each of the following transactions, state what kind of account (asset, liability, or proprietorship) is affected by the *credit*, and whether the account is increased or decreased:

(1) A corporation receives $12,000 as an investment and issues shares of capital stock.
(2) A customer pays a 20-day-old bill for merchandise that he bought on credit.
(3) Taxes are assessed against the company.
(4) Supplies are used in operating a retail store.
(5) Merchandise is bought on credit.
(6) A partner is admitted to a firm; he contributes a patent to obtain an interest in the firm.
(7) Wages earned by employees but not yet paid are recorded on the books.
(8) A customer who finds that he cannot pay his bill on time offers a 30-day promissory note, which the firm accepts.
(9) A firm wishes to have a longer time to pay off its bank loan, so it gives the bank a mortgage on its real estate and extends the loan.
(10) A firm invests some of its idle cash in the bonds of another company.

1.27 Why is it said that debits and credits must always balance?

1.28 What is a ledger? Suggest a method of arranging the contents of a ledger.

1.29 How does a ledger help protect a concern against loss of assets?

1.30 Does the matrix formulation result in single-entry accounting? Explain.

EXERCISES

1.1 The following accounts appear in the ledger of Doveco, Inc.:

Accounts Payable	Equipment
Accounts Receivable	Retained Earnings
Capital Stock	Unearned Rent Income
Cash	Unexpired Insurance

Arrange the accounts in the order in which they would probably appear in the ledger.

1.2 Laguna Shores, a 101-unit motel, was constructed July 1, 1960, on leased land at a cost of $400,000. The lease runs for forty years, at the end of which time Laguna Shores will have no economic interest in the properties. The general price level increased 10 percent from July 1, 1960, to July 1, 1965, and values of motel properties in the neighborhood of Laguna Shores increased 50 percent. What is the accepted basis for reporting the motel building on July 1, 1965? Why?

1.3 Indicate (by ± A, ± L, or ± P) the increase or decrease in assets, liabilities, and proprietorship resulting from each of the following transactions:

(1) Invested cash and equipment.
(2) Purchased supplies for cash.
(3) Bought additional equipment on credit.
(4) Borrowed cash on a promissory note.
(5) Paid trade creditors on account.

1.4 Record the transactions below in tabular form, using the following headings: Cash + Supplies + Plant = Liabilities + Proprietorship. Compute balances after each transaction.

(1) Issued for cash 1,000 shares of $10 par stock at face value.
(2) Issued to the First Bank a 5-year $5,000 note, bearing interest at 8 percent per year.
(3) Purchased furniture and fixtures for $3,000; paid $500 and signed an installment contract for the balance.
(4) Purchased office supplies for cash, $300.
(5) Acquired a building for $30,000; issued a check for $1,000 and signed a mortgage for the balance.

How would repayment of the 5-year note affect proprietorship, if at all?

1.5 The accounts of H. B. Smith showed the following balances on December 24, 1966: Cash, $2,000; Accounts Receivable, $3,000; Equipment, $5,000; Notes Payable, $1,000; Accounts Payable, $4,000; H. B. Smith, Capital, $5,000. Transactions for the period from December 24 to December 31 were:

(1) Smith contributed a $1,000 calculating machine from another business.
(2) Collected from customers on account, $1,000.
(3) Bought filing cabinets and a copy machine on credits, $4,000.
(4) Paid promissory note in full.
(5) Issued a check for $200 to Mrs. H. B. Smith as a gift.

Required:

1. Open skeleton accounts and record the transactions. Cross-number the entries.
2. Prepare a balance sheet dated December 31, 1966. Omit asset classifications.

1.6   Entries for a series of transactions are shown in the skeleton accounts below. Indicate the probable nature of each transaction.

Cash		Equipment		Accounts Payable	
(a) 10,000	(c) 5,000	(d) 6,000		(f) 2,000	(b) 1,200
	(d) 1,000				(d) 5,000
	(e) 1,000				
	(f) 2,000				

Marketable Securities		Land		Mortgage Payable	
(c) 5,000		(e) 5,000			(e) 24,000

Supplies		Buildings		Capital Stock	
(b) 1,200		(e) 20,000			(a) 10,000

1.7   El Monte Properties (a cooperative apartment) completed six transactions in January. These transactions resulted in accounts with debit and credit totals as follows:

Cash		Accounts Payable		Notes Payable to Stockholders	
24,000	7,300	300	800		10,000

Prepaid Rent		Contracts Payable		Capital Stock	
6,000			4,000		10,000

Equipment		Deposits Refundable		Premium on Capital Stock	
5,800			2,000		2,000

State the probable nature of each of the six transactions. Notes were issued as part of the initial capitalization, additional funds were then received from tenants, and a small piece of equipment was purchased on open account.

1.8   Classify the following balance sheet items as (CA) current assets, (FA) fixed assets, (CL) current liabilities, (LL) long-term liabilities, or (P) proprietorship.
   (1) Refining and gas processing facilities
   (2) Marketable securities
   (3) Prepaid insurance
   (4) Unsecured short-term notes payable
   (5) Deferred income from sale of oil production payments (realizable after one year)

(6) Accrued income taxes
(7) Capital in excess of par value
(8) Investments in unconsolidated subsidiaries
(9) Retained earnings
(10) Mortgage payable (portion due in one year)

1.9 The JD Co. has assets of $1,200,000 and liabilities of $300,000. Draft the proprietorship section of the balance sheet for the following cases:

(1) JD Co. is a corporation with 10,000 shares of $100 par common stock authorized and outstanding. The stock was issued at par.
(2) JD Co. is a partnership. J. Johnson owns 90 percent, D. Dillon owns 10 percent.

1.10 The following assets and liabilities appear on the balance sheet of a bank: assets—Cash in Banks, Loans and Discounts, Prepaid Rent; liabilities—Demand Deposits, Unearned Discount. What are the corresponding titles of the liability and asset accounts for the other party to the transaction?

1.11 Below are condensed balance sheets for two companies in the truck transportation industry at the end of five years of operations. Neither company has paid dividends since incorporation.

	M	N
Cash	$15,000	$ 8,000
Freight Accounts Receivable	20,000	10,000
Operating Supplies	2,000	1,000
Tires and Tubes in Service	3,000	1,000
Property, Plant, and Equipment	90,000	50,000
	$130,000	$70,000
Notes Payable to Banks	$ 8,000	$ 2,000
Accounts Payable and Accrued Expenses	18,000	7,000
Federal and Other Taxes on Income	4,000	1,000
Mortgage and Equipment Notes due after 1 year	55,000	10,000
Common Stock	10,000	45,000
Retained Earnings	35,000	5,000
	$130,000	$70,000

1. Compute working capital, current ratio, fixed-asset–fixed-liabilities ratio, and percent of proprietary investment for each company.
2. Which company has the better working capital position? Why?
3. What is the apparent relationship between profitability and risk in the two companies?

1.12 Elizabeth Bailey opened a dress shop on December 1, 1966, and completed the following transactions during December:

(1) Invested cash, $25,000.
(2) Purchased merchandise for cash, $15,000.
(3) Purchased merchandise on credit, $10,000.
(4) Paid expenses, $2,000.
(5) Paid $5,000 on account.
(6) Sold for $12,000 cash merchandise costing $8,000.
(7) Sold on credit for $6,000 merchandise costing $4,000.

Record the transactions in a matrix, using the following accounts: Cash, Accounts Receivable, Merchandise, Accounts Payable, E. Bailey, Capital. (Amounts may be entered in thousands of dollars.)

1.1   The accounting records of the Travel Lodge Motel contain the following information at December 31, 1966:

Accounts Payable	$ 2,000
Accounts Receivable	1,000
Buildings	80,000
Cash on Hand and in Banks	2,000
Contracts Payable	
Due within one year	1,000
Due after one year	5,000
Franchise	3,000
Furniture and Fixtures	15,000
Land	20,000
Mortgage Payable	
Due within one year	10,000
Due after one year	40,000
Note Payable to First National Bank	1,000
Prepaid Insurance	1,000
Supplies	3,000
Taxes Payable	2,000
Wages Payable	1,000
Walter A. Young, Capital	?

Prepare a classified balance sheet.

1.2   The following information as of December 31, 1966, is available concerning Charles W. Jones and Peter B. Smith, doing business as C. W. Jones and Co. (a copartnership): The partnership has $5,000 due from customers, owes $3,000 on open account, has a truck with a depreciated cost of $1,000, and has $1,000 in the bank. Smith's personal automobile cost $4,000; his residence, on which there is a mortgage of $10,000, is valued at $30,000. For all practical purposes, Jones has no assets other than his investment in the partnership. Each partner has an equal interest in the capital of the partnership.

Required:

1. Prepare the balance sheet of C. W. Jones and Co. (omit captions classifying assets and liabilities).
2. An equipment vendor is considering the sale of special-purpose machinery to the partnership for $5,000, on terms requiring no payment until one year after the date of sale. Evaluate the credit of C. W. Jones and Co. on the basis of the limited information appearing above.

1.3   A clerk for Bay, Inc., submitted the following balance sheet as of June 30, 1966:

BAY, INC.

BALANCE SHEET, JUNE 30, 1966

Assets		*Liabilities*	
Retained Earnings	$ 4,000	Capital Stock	$10,000
Equipment	11,000	Merchandise	5,000
Trade Creditors	4,000	Cash	2,000
	$19,000	Prepaid Insurance	1,000
		Taxes Payable	1,000
			$19,000

1. Prepare a corrected balance sheet.

2. How do you explain the fact that the cash is less than the retained earnings?

1.4 The following table shows the financial condition of the Varsity Theater as of January 1, 1966, and the effect of transactions for the month of January:

	Cash	+	Supplies	+	Equipment	=	Liabilities	+	Proprietorship
(a)	2,000 − 500	+ +	3,000 500	+	5,000	=	4,000	+	6,000
(b)	1,500	+	3,500	+ +	5,000 700	=	4,000 + 700	+	6,000
(c)	1,500 −1,000	+	3,500	+	5,700	=	4,700 −1,000	+	6,000
(d)	500 +3,000	+	3,500	+	5,700	=	3,700	+ +	6,000 3,000
(e)	3,500 −1,200	+	3,500	+	5,700	=	3,700	+ −	9,000 1,200
(f)	2,300 −	+	3,500 400	+	5,700	=	3,700	+ −	7,800 400
	2,300	+	3,100	+	5,700	=	3,700	+	7,400

All changes in proprietorship are the result of operations. There have been no drawings in January.

1. Describe each of the transactions.
2. What is the net income for the month?

1.5 John Walsh has opened an appliance service business. His transactions for the first month were as follows:

(1) Deposited $15,000 in a commercial account at First National Bank for use in the business.
(2) Contributed hand tools, welding apparatus, and other equipment for use in the business, $6,000.
(3) Purchased a used lathe and other equipment for $10,000; terms $2,000 down and the balance due in five equal annual installments. A note secured by the equipment was given in evidence of the balance due.
(4) Bought supplies on credit, $3,000.
(5) Invested idle cash in marketable securities, $2,000.
(6) Paid trade creditors, $500.
(7) Issued a check to Mrs. Walsh for household expenses, $200.

Required:

1. Record the transactions in tabular form, using the following headings: Cash + Marketable Securities + Supplies + Equipment = Accounts Payable + Contracts Payable + J. Walsh, Capital.
2. How would you obtain the $6,000 figure for the equipment in transaction 2? Why should John Walsh be concerned whether this amount is proper or not?

1.6 On January 1 the business assets and liabilities of Don Carlson, doing business as Don's Candies, were as follows:

$$
\begin{array}{lr}
\text{Cash} \dots\dots\dots\dots\dots\dots & \$20,000 \\
\text{Accounts Receivable} \dots\dots & 35,000 \\
\text{Merchandise} \dots\dots\dots\dots & 52,000 \\
\text{Store Supplies} \dots\dots\dots\dots & 2,000 \\
\text{Notes Payable} \dots\dots\dots\dots & 10,000 \\
\text{Accounts Payable} \dots\dots\dots & 20,000 \\
\end{array}
$$

Transactions for January were:

(1) Purchased on credit $30,000 of merchandise and $2,000 of supplies.
(2) Paid $5,000 on notes and $10,000 on account.
(3) Sold on credit for $18,000 merchandise that cost $10,000.
(4) Collected cash from customers on account, $20,000.
(5) Cash sales, $5,000; the goods cost $3,000.
(6) Paid expenses, $6,000.
(7) Supplies used, $1,000.
(8) Withdrew cash for personal expenses, $1,000.

Required:

1. Record in tabular form the January 1 balances and the transactions for January, using the following headings: Cash + Accounts Receivable + Merchandise + Store Supplies = Notes Payable + Accounts Payable + D. Carlson, Capital.
2. What was the net income (or loss) for January?
3. Explain the difference between the net income (or loss) and the change in proprietorship for January.

1.7   T. Vanda opened the Aloha Launderette, a self-service laundry, on April 1, 1966. Record in T accounts the preoperating transactions given below, and prepare a balance sheet at April 1, 1966, in good form. The following account titles are suggested:

Accounts Payable	Prepaid Insurance
Cash	Prepaid Rent
Contracts Payable	Supplies
Laundry Equipment	Unearned Income
Leasehold Improvements	Utility Deposits
Notes Payable	T. Vanda, Capital

A summary of the April 1 transactions follows:

(1) T. Vanda deposited $20,000 at the Statewide Bank in the name of the business.
(2) Twenty automatic washers were purchased for $6,000; one-half the price was paid by check, and the balance is payable in ten equal monthly installments.
(3) Various supplies were purchased for cash from Multiproducts Co., $700.
(4) The laundry premises were leased for five years at a monthly rental of $200. A check for $400 was drawn to Brevet and Holbrook, Realtors, for the first two months' rent.
(5) A check for $2,000 was drawn for improvements completed to make the premises usable as a self-service laundry.
(6) Insurance was placed with Pacific Mutual Insurance Co. The premium of $720 is payable thirty days from April 1.
(7) A deposit of $100 was paid the South Bay Muncipal Utility District for water service. (The deposit will be returned at the end of a year.)
(8) Drying machines were purchased on credit from Hopaco, Inc., $800.
(9) A check for $500 was received from the Tradewinds Hotel to apply on laundry services to be performed during the month.

(10) A loan of $5,000 was received from N. Morley on a 3-year note.

1.8 W. S. Beeson and J. A. Smith form a partnership to practice law. The transactions for the first month are:

(1) Beeson contributes a law library, which is to be recorded in the partnership accounts at $3,000.

(2) Smith contributes 400 shares of Sperry Rand Corp., quoted at $20 per share. The partners expect to sell these shares within the year.

(3) Beeson, the senior partner, has been in practice many years. The partners agree that Beeson should be credited with $5,000 in recognition of his clients and reputation.

(4) Three hundred shares of Sperry Rand Corp. are sold at $24. Profits and losses are divided equally between the partners.

(5) Office equipment is bought for $10,000; terms, $2,000 down and the balance on a contract. The first installment on the contract is due one year after the purchase of the equipment.

(6) Five thousand dollars is borrowed from the bank on a 6 percent 60-day note.

(7) Office supplies are purchased for cash, $1,000.

Enter the transactions in skeleton accounts and prepare a balance sheet dated January 31, 1966. Cross-number the transactions.

1.9 The first month's transactions of The Crossroads Bookstore, Inc., which was incorporated on January 1, 1966, were:

(1) Issued for cash 1,000 shares of capital stock at $20 par.

(2) Paid incorporating and legal fees, $1,000. (Debit the asset Organization Costs.)

(3) Issued 250 shares of stock to an investor for merchandise which cost him $5,000.

(4) Purchased shelving, cash registers, and other equipment for cash, $6,000.

(5) Purchased merchandise on credit, $30,000.

(6) Received $10,000 from the Transamerica Corp. for bonds issued. The indenture specifies, among other things, that payments on principal begin five years after date of the loan.

(7) Purchased office supplies for cash, $2,000.

(8) Purchased a truck for $8,000; terms, $2,000 down and a contract payable in twelve monthly installments.

(9) Paid perchandise creditors on account, $10,000.

(10) Repurchased from a dissident shareholder 100 shares of capital stock at par.

Enter the transactions in skeleton accounts and prepare a balance sheet dated January 31, 1966. Cross-number the transactions.

1.10 On December 1, 1966, Rip Matson established Royal Gardens to develop lands in Lehua, Hawaii. Transactions for December are summarized below:

(1) Deposited $100,000 in the Bishop National Bank for Royal Gardens.

(2) Acquired land for $150,000; assumed a mortgage of $120,000 and paid the balance by check.

(3) Received invoices for road improvements chargeable to the land inventory, $50,000.

(4) Purchased equipment, $5,000, paying $3,000 cash and agreeing to pay the balance in thirty days.

(5) Sold for $20,000 cash land costing $10,000.

(6) Sold on credit for $30,000 land costing $15,000.

(7) Paid expenses, $40,000.

(8) Paid trade creditors on account, $5,000.

(9) Withdrew $2,000 for personal use.

(10) Interest accrued during December amounts to $1,000. (This is the interest incurred on the mortgage to December 31.)

Record the transactions in a matrix; include rows and columns for totals and balances. Use the following accounts: Cash, Accounts Receivable, Inventory, Equipment, Accounts Payable, Interest Payable, Mortgages Payable, Rip Matson, Capital. (Amounts may be entered in thousands of dollars.)

1.11 L. C. Ness plans to open Tradeways, Inc., a retail furniture store, on January 1, 1966. He estimates his capital requirements as follows:

Annual income required from the enterprise	$12,000
Percent of net income to sales common to the industry	5%
Estimated sales volume	$240,000
Common rate of merchandise turnover in this business	4
Estimated inventory at retail prices	$60,000
Average percent of cost to retail	70%
Opening stock of merchandise	$42,000
Store fixtures and equipment	10,000
Cash funds for organization costs of $1,000, plus peak merchandise needs, expenses for one turnover period, and personal and business emergencies	5,000
Total capital required	$57,000

He estimates the sources of his capital as follows:

(1) Trade creditors will allow a 30-day line of credit to the limit of the cost of merchandise that will be sold in an average month. Sales at retail per month will be $20,000, which is $14,000 at cost.

(2) Store fixtures and equipment can be purchased on terms of 20 percent down and the balance on a 12-month installment contract.

(3) The First National Bank will lend the company $5,000 on a 6 percent 6-month promissory note.

(4) The Bank of Commerce will finance $10,000 of the business on an 8 percent long-term note, the first payment on principal due five years after January 1, 1966.

(5) Ness plans to borrow $20,000 from relatives, which will be invested in the business for 2,000 shares of $10 par stock.

Draft a *pro forma* balance sheet as of January 1, 1966, reflecting the expected financial condition after incorporation and acquisition of merchandise and equipment.

2

The Income Statement

PURPOSES OF THE INCOME STATEMENT

The income statement presents the results of operations for a period. It describes in summary form the transactions that make a profit or a loss for the owners. It is the means of analyzing, from an over-all point of view, the effectiveness of the organization. The latter refers not only to the net result but also to the analysis that may be made by comparing one element of the statement with another. For example, the amount of selling expense incurred to produce the volume of sales revenue may be observed in a reasonably complete income statement; this will give an indication of efficiency in selling activity that can be compared with the concern's past experience (disclosing trends) and with other firms similarly engaged (disclosing relative efficiency). The income statement is sometimes called an operations statement, statement of profit and loss, profit and loss statement, or income account. The latter term is confusing, because "account" is used to describe the device for collecting data about one element of either the balance sheet or income statement. Authoritative accounting organizations in the United States prefer "income statement," the term used in this book.

CONTENT OF THE INCOME STATEMENT

The income statement of Pomeroy Building Materials for July 1966 appears on page 36. Six sections of the statement may be distinguished in the case of a merchandising business, as follows:

Revenue section. The revenue in a concern selling merchandise is called "sales"; it represents the amounts charged to customers as the sale price of the goods.

Cost of goods sold section. This shows the cost to the business of the merchandise delivered to customers. Usually it also includes the cost of any merchandise damaged or lost while being held for sale, since such merchandise costs are normally incurred to some degree in merchandising. Cost of goods sold is an expense, that is, something that must be deducted from revenue to calculate net income.

Selling expenses. These are the expenses of carrying on the selling activity for the period. They include the expenses of soliciting sales and waiting on customers, of storing merchandise awaiting sale, and of delivering the merchandise.

General and administrative expenses. These are the expenses of carrying on the main activity of the business other than cost of merchandise and the expenses directly identifiable with selling activity. They include the cost of the accounting work, salaries of general officers, legal expenses, and so on.

Other income. Income not derived from the main object of the business is shown here. Pomeroy Building Materials owns a vacant lot, not used in the building materials business, that it rents for parking.

Other deductions. Expenses not incurred in connection with the main object of the business are shown here. Interest paid on borrowed money is not essential to the merchandising business; a firm operating without borrowed funds would not have this expense. It is accordingly shown separately from the operating expenses.

Concerns that do not sell merchandise will not have the cost of goods sold section. They commonly will not have operating expenses separated into selling expenses and general and administrative expenses, since this segregation is applicable chiefly to companies selling merchandise of some kind.

POMEROY BUILDING MATERIALS
Income Statement

Month of July, 1966

Sales			$14,000
Cost of Goods Sold			8,000
Gross Margin on Sales			$ 6,000
Operating Expenses:			
Selling Expenses:			
Salesmen's Salaries	$1,270		
Advertising	80		
Delivery Wages	400		
Truck Repairs	150		
Other Delivery Expense	200		
Rent of Yard	150	$2,250	
General and Administrative Expenses:			
General Salaries	$1,310		
Rent of Office	50		
Supplies Used	25		
Payroll Taxes	75		
Insurance	120		
Postage, Telephone, and Telegraph	80		
Other General Expenses	140	1,800	4,050
Net Operating Income			$ 1,950
Other Income: Rent			100
			$ 2,050
Other Deductions: Interest			50
Net Income			$ 2,000

RELATION OF THE INCOME STATEMENT TO THE BALANCE SHEET

The transactions summarized in the income statement all affect one balance sheet element: proprietorship. In a sole proprietorship their net effect appears in the proprietor's capital account. In a partnership the net income is divided among the partners according to their profit-sharing agreement, and the results appear in each partner's capital account. In a corporation, where separate accounts are kept for Capital Stock and Retained Earnings, the income figure goes into the Retained Earnings account. The income statement accounts are used to accumulate data for a specific period. The period may be as short as a month or as long as a year. This is called the *fiscal* period or *accounting* period. The accounts are then summarized and the figures transferred to the appropriate proprietorship account or accounts. This process is called *closing the books*. After the closing, the accounts immediately begin to accumulate the same kind of data for the next period, and the process is repeated. The income statement accounts have been called temporary or nominal accounts, because they do not accumulate a figure continuously and indefinitely, but only periodically. By contrast, the balance sheet accounts run on indefinitely as long as the asset, liability, or proprietorship item exists. Balance sheet accounts have been called permanent or real accounts. The debit and credit rules for income statement accounts follow the rules for proprietorship, of which these accounts are a part. These normal account relationships are shown in diagram form below. The accounts appear in the illustration in skeleton account or

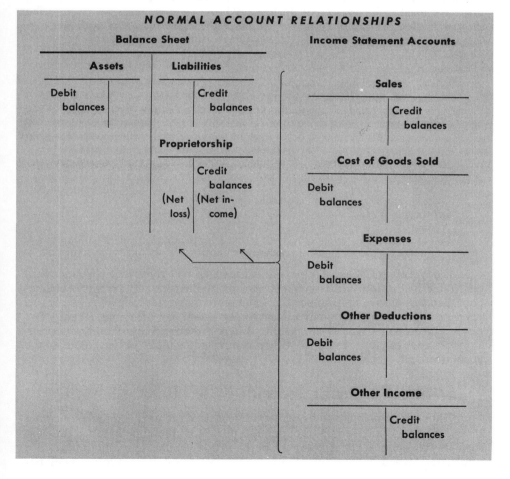

T account form. This is a simple form with a horizontal and vertical line arranged like a letter T. It is useful in informal work, such as solving accounting problems in school or for work on scratch paper elsewhere. The revenue and other income accounts that increase proprietorship are increased by credits, as is proprietorship. The expenses and other deductions that decrease proprietorship are increased by debits, which, like debits made directly to a permanent proprietorship account, decrease proprietorship.

REVENUE AND REVENUE ACCOUNTS

Revenue is what a concern gets from customers for the merchandise or services sold. Earnings from investments, such as interest on bonds, may also be called revenue. In the case of a government with tax revenue, the services rendered may not be directly related to the collection of revenue. Revenue has the aspect of both asset and financial interest. For example, we commonly speak of revenue being received in cash, referring to the asset obtained. In accounting, the revenue *accounts* record the effect of acquiring the asset on the financial interests — in this case, proprietorship. A variety of revenue account titles are used in business and professional and other enterprises to describe the particular revenue of each one. Some of these revenue accounts are:

Sales. This records revenue from sales of merchandise.
Fees. This commonly refers to the charges made by professional people. Thus we find medical fees, legal fees, accounting fees, and dental fees.
Service charges, repair charges, or *service fees.* These account titles are used by concerns doing repair work and other types of service work. For example, a garage might keep accounts for Towing Service and for Repair Charges.
Commissions. This describes the service charges of persons or concerns that charge on the basis of a percentage of the value of the thing handled. Agents handling such produce as vegetables use it; so do real estate agents.
Interest, or *interest income.* These are revenues of concerns lending money, such as banks and mortgage investment companies.
Rent or *rent income.* These accounts record the revenue of landlords and of concerns renting equipment, costumes and other property.
Subscriptions. This is the revenue of publishers of periodicals, including newspapers.
Ticket sales. This revenue account is used by theaters, carnivals, promoters of auto races, and all kinds of concerns promoting performances or selling tickets.

In a government, Taxes, Fines, and Licenses will represent revenue. In a charitable institution, Gifts or Subscriptions or Pledges may be a revenue account. In the service enterprises the same word may refer to an expense or to a revenue. For example, we have Rent Expense and Rent Income, Repairs Expense and Repair Charges or Income. Where there is any possibility of confusion, "Expense" or "Income" or an equivalent should be included in the account title.

EXPENSE AND EXPENSE ACCOUNTS

Expense is what has to be deducted from revenue to calculate net income. It represents assets used up or expenditures or commitments made in order to earn the revenue. *Expenses* are to be contrasted with *assets*. The latter are properties owned or investments made that are useful in the future. They become expenses as they are used up in earning revenue. The expenses connected directly with the major purpose of the concern—to sell merchandise, for example—are called operating expenses. The others are nonoperating expenses. In a concern that manufactures and sells merchandise, or buys and sells it, a major element of operating expense is the cost of goods sold. Because of its importance, this expense is deducted from sales revenue as a separate item in the traditional income statement. This subtraction gives the gross margin on sales, commonly called gross profit. The latter figure is of special interest, particularly in a purely merchandising or trading concern. The reason is that obtaining adequate sales at a figure sufficiently higher than the cost of the merchandise is the essential basis for merchandising success. To obtain them the concern must select merchandise for which there will be a demand, price it properly, handle it so as to avoid deterioration and physical loss, and avoid acquiring excess stocks that can be sold only at a loss. If these things are accomplished, a gross margin large enough to cover the other expenses and to provide a net income or profit will be provided. The gross margin figure is therefore an indication of merchandising effectiveness, especially when compared with the sales revenue.

Selling expenses and general and administrative expenses are deducted from gross margin to get the net operating income. This figure shows what the concern got from its main activity as distinct from any expenses or incomes not directly connected with the major activity. The figure is also of special interest to managers and investors. It indicates what the concern has done and something of what it can continue to do in the line of activity that it presumably is best qualified to pursue.

Nonoperating, or "other," income arises from sources not connected directly with the main activity. Examples include interest or dividends earned on investments in securities held by a concern whose business is not of an investment type, rents from real estate not used in the regular line of work, and profits on the sale of assets other than merchandise.

Nonoperating expenses, or "other deductions," often include interest paid on borrowed funds, expenses connected with property not used in the regular activity, and losses on sales of assets other than merchandise.

EXPENSE ACCOUNT TITLES

Expense accounts may be kept by *object of expenditure* or by *functions*. "Object of expenditure" refers to the kind of thing bought or used, such as salaries, supplies, or advertising. "Function" refers to a particular activity or performance, for example, maintenance of building, delivery expense, or entertainment expense. Different kinds of supplies and wages as well as other expenses may be charged to each functional account. Each concern uses such expense accounts as are needed to describe its transactions and to provide information desired by management.

THE JOURNAL

Figures are usually entered in the ledger accounts from information in a journal. A journal is a chronological record of transactions in which each transaction is set down in its entirety. A journal is called a *book of original entry*, because it traditionally is the first record in which the accounting analysis of a transaction is recorded. The traditional form of the journal has the appearance shown below.

This form is called a general journal because it can readily accommodate any transaction. When the volume of transactions increases beyond a few dozen a month, special journals are needed. These are designed to record certain kinds of transactions with less effort than in a general journal, and will be considered in later chapters. In a very small concern the general journal is sufficient.

VICTOR APPLIANCES
General Journal

Page 1

DATE	EXPLANATION	REF.	DEBIT	CREDIT
1966				
Dec 1	Cash	1	25000 00	
	O. P. Victor, Capital	7		25000 00
	(to record O. P. Victor's investment)			
3	Merchandise	3	12000 00	
	Cash	1		12000 00
	(Purchased merchandise for cash from Appliance Distributors)			
4	Supplies	4	2000 00	
	Cash	1		2000 00
	(Purchased supplies for cash from Store Supplies, Inc.)			

Note that the journal gives:

1. Date of the entry
2. Names of the accounts debited and credited
3. Amounts
4. Explanation of the transaction
5. Reference

The reference may be the page of the ledger on which the account affected is located, or, as in the illustration above, the number of the account. This reference permits figures to be traced to the ledger; the references in the ledger accounts are to journal pages, so the tracing can go both ways. Names of the accounts debited are listed at the left side of the space, and the names of the accounts credited are indented to the right. Indention helps the reader to recognize easily the accounts being debited and credited. It is also customary to list first the accounts debited, and then the accounts credited, in case more than two accounts are involved in a single transaction. When more than two accounts appear in one entry, it is called a *compound* journal entry.

The journal provides a complete analysis of each transaction. It is thus in contrast with the ledger account, which shows in each account only the transactions that affect it. To find out what other account was affected by a transaction in a particular account, it is usually necessary to refer back to the journal to see the transaction in its entirety. Sometimes explanations are written in ledger accounts that disclose what other account is involved, but ordinarily they are not. In extremely simple organizations (such as a small estate, for example) a ledger may be used without a journal or journals; when transactions become fairly numerous, a journal is needed.

STEPS IN JOURNALIZING

Recording a transaction in a journal is called *journalizing*. The steps in journalizing are:

1. Write the year at the top of the date column.
2. Write the month and day in the date column on the first line to be used for the particular transaction.
3. Write the name of the account to be debited in the explanation space.
4. Write the amount to be debited in the debit amount column on the same line with the account name.
5. Write the name of the account to be credited on the next line, indenting to the right.
6. Write the amount to be credited in the credit amount column on the same line with the account name.
7. Write an explanation of the transaction. This may give additional information, such as the name of a concern paid or from whom something was purchased.

Note that no entry in the reference column was specified above. The reference to a ledger page ("folio") or account number is best inserted after the debits and credits called for in the journal entry have been entered in their ledger accounts. It then serves not only as a means of looking up the item in the account, but also as an indication that the entry required by the journal has been made in the ledger. It is customary to leave a blank line between journal entries. Sometimes journal entries are numbered.

USEFULNESS OF THE JOURNAL

The journal provides:

1. A chronological record of transactions
2. A full view of each transaction in one place
3. An explanation and supplementary information about each transaction

The basic function of the journal is to provide an orderly record from which entries may be made in the accounts. However, the characteristics listed above give the journal further usefulness. For example, suppose that a customer comes in and says, "I paid my bill on the twentieth of last month and you sent me a statement showing that I still owe it." A clerk can then go through the transactions entered on or near the twentieth of last month and may discover that the customer's remittance was credited to the wrong account. Recording the transactions in chronological order makes this review possible. Putting the whole transaction down in one place gives anyone interested a chance to notice any error, and particularly to notice if the debits and the credits are equal, as they always must be. If a figure is entered in the wrong account in the ledger, a person may notice that something is wrong with that account, then look up the transaction in the journal, and determine the proper treatment. Use of the journal also permits a division of labor; one bookkeeper may analyze the transactions and enter them in the journal, and another may make the entries in the ledger from the journal.

POSTING THE LEDGER

Posting is the process of entering in the ledger the information given in the journal. The steps in posting are:

1. Find the ledger account named on the first line of the journal entry (a debit).
2. Enter in the proper columns in this account the date, journal page number, and amount of debit as given in the journal.
3. Enter the number of the ledger account in the reference column of the journal.
4. Take the same steps for the other accounts named in the journal entry, being careful to enter the data for accounts credited on the *right* side of the account.

ILLUSTRATION OF JOURNAL AND LEDGER

Use of the journal and ledger is illustrated with the transactions of Victor Appliances. The transactions given in the journal are the first seven of those presented in Chapter 1. The general journal of Victor Appliances is shown on page 43. The first four accounts of the ledger of Victor Appliances are shown on page 44. The other accounts follow the same form.

THE TRIAL BALANCE

The trial balance is a list of account balances taken from the figures appearing in the ledger. Its purpose is to determine whether or not debit and credit amounts in the accounts are evidently equal. Debits and credits are expected to be equal because every transaction has a twofold aspect — debit and credit. This dual aspect is derived from the fact that the ultimate summary of transactions for any enterprise becomes a balance sheet, which shows the condition of the enterprise from two viewpoints: nature and amount of assets held and nature and amount of financial interests in the assets. If the trial balance, or listing of account balances, shows debit balances equal in total to credit balances, it is assumed that no error in arithmetic is involved. But this may not be true, because the wrong amount may have been used in both the debit and the credit entries for a transaction; yet the fact that the equality of debits and credits must be maintained is a good check on accuracy. The name of the trial balance indicates its role as a "trial" of the equality of debits and credits.

The trial balance is also useful in drawing up the financial statements, since it presents the account balances in a convenient form.

VICTOR APPLIANCES
General Journal

Page

DATE	EXPLANATION	REF.	DEBIT	CREDIT
1966				
Dec 3	Cash	1	2500000	
	O P Victor, Capital	7		2500000
	(to record O P Victor's investment)			
3	Merchandise	3	1200000	
	Cash	1		1200000
	(Purchased merchandise for cash			
	from Appliance Distributors)			
4	Supplies	4	200000	
	Cash	1		200000
	(Purchased supplies for cash from			
	Store Supplies, Inc.)			
5	Merchandise	3	1100000	
	Accounts Payable	5		1100000
	(Purchased merchandise on account			
	from Household Products Co)			
15	Salaries	10	22500	
	Cash	1		22500
	(Paid salary to Thomas Marks for			
	first half of Dec.			
31	Accounts Receivable	2	520000	
	Sales	8		520000
	(charge sales for the month)			
31	Cost of Goods Sold	9	270000	
	Merchandise	3		270000
	(cost of goods sold for the month)			

VICTOR APPLIANCES
Ledger

Cash   Acct. No. 1

DATE	EXPLANATION	REF.	DEBIT	DATE	EXPLANATION	REF.	CREDIT
1966				1966			
Dec 3		1	25000 00	Dec 3		1	1200 00
31	4,570.00	2	2400 00	4		1	2000 00
			27400 00	15		1	225 00
				31		2	300 00
				31		2	225 00
				31		2	1000 00
				31		2	800 00
				31		2	1000 00
							22830 00

Accounts Receivable   Acct. No. 2

DATE	EXPLANATION	REF.	DEBIT	DATE	EXPLANATION	REF.	CREDIT
1966				1966			
Dec 31	2,800.00	1	5200 00	Dec 31		2	2400 00

Merchandise   Acct. No. 3

DATE	EXPLANATION	REF.	DEBIT	DATE	EXPLANATION	REF.	CREDIT
1966				1966			
Dec 3		1	12000 00	Dec 31		1	2700 00
5	20,300.00	1	11000 00				
			23000 00				

Supplies   Acct. No. 4

DATE	EXPLANATION	REF.	DEBIT	DATE	EXPLANATION	REF.	CREDIT
1966				1966			
Dec 4	1,960.00	1	2000 00	Dec 31		2	40 00

ILLUSTRATION OF THE TRIAL BALANCE

The trial balance of Victor Appliances is given in the accompanying illustration. The first four account balances may be compared with the ledger accounts shown above, from which they came.

The financial statements are drawn up after the trial balance is completed. The income statement accounts must be combined with the regular capital account to get the final capital balance for the balance sheet.

VICTOR APPLIANCES
Trial Balance

December 31, 1966

Cash	$ 4,570.00	
Accounts Receivable	2,800.00	
Merchandise	20,300.00	
Supplies	1,960.00	
Accounts Payable		$ 4,000.00
Taxes Payable		50.00
O. P. Victor, Capital		24,000.00
Sales		5,200.00
Cost of Goods Sold	2,700.00	
Salaries	450.00	
Rent	300.00	
Taxes	50.00	
Supplies Used	40.00	
Other Expenses	80.00	
	$33,250.00	$33,250.00

CLOSING THE BOOKS

The balances accumulated in the revenue and the expense accounts for a period are transferred into a summary account at the end of the period. This account is usually called *Profit and Loss* account; it may be called *Profit and Loss Summary* or *Revenue and Expense Summary*. The balance of Profit and Loss is then transferred to the proper proprietorship account. In a sole proprietorship or a partnership this is the capital account of the proprietor or of each partner. In a corporation it is the Retained Earnings account. Retained Earnings account was formerly called Earned Surplus, and some concerns still use this term. The transfers are made in formal style by journal entry. For example, the entry to transfer a sales balance of $14,000 into Profit and Loss is:

Sales	$14,000	
Profit and Loss		$14,000

The entry to transfer a balance of $1,270 from Salesmen's Salaries to Profit and Loss is:

Profit and Loss	$ 1,270	
Salesmen's Salaries		$ 1,270

When all the transfers have been made, the revenue and the expense accounts and the Profit and Loss account will have zero balances. They will be "closed" for the period. The purpose of "closing the books" is to summarize the results of operations for the period and to clear the accounts in preparation for the accumulation of similar data for the next period. The only accounts "open" at this time will be balance sheet accounts.

ILLUSTRATION OF THE CLOSING PROCESS

The revenue and the expense accounts of Pomeroy Building Materials and Pomeroy's Capital account are shown on pages 46–49 as they appeared at the end of July 1966, but before closing. At this point all the regular transactions for the month have been entered and subtotals have been taken. Pages 50 and 51 present the general journal of the company with the closing entries for the month. Pages 52–55 show the revenue and expense accounts, the Profit and Loss account, and the Capital account after the closing entries were posted. Note that the revenue and the expense accounts are "ruled up" after their balances have been transferred. In this procedure a total is taken on each side (note that it is written on the same line on each side), and a double rule under each total indicates that computations stop at that point. If there is only one figure on each side of a balanced account, no total is required and the double rule alone is used.

Note that the names of accounts closed to Profit and Loss are written in the explanation columns of that account. This practice is not universal but is often employed to permit easy reference to past profit and loss figures in the ledger account.

POMEROY BUILDING MATERIALS
Revenue and Expense Accounts and Capital Account
before Closing
July, 1966

Sales   Acct No. 18

DATE	EXPLANATION	REF.	DEBIT	DATE	EXPLANATION	REF.	CREDIT
				1966			
				July 9		27	3200 00
				16		29	3600 00
				23		31	3800 00
				30		33	3400 00
							14000 00

Cost of Goods Sold   Acct No. 19

DATE	EXPLANATION	REF.	DEBIT	DATE	EXPLANATION	REF.	CREDIT
1966							
July 9		27	1720 00				
16		29	1860 00				
23		31	2580 00				
30		33	1840 00				
			8000 00				

Salesmen's Salaries   Acct No 20

DATE	EXPLANATION	REF.	DEBIT	DATE	EXPLANATION	REF.	CREDIT
1966							
July 16		29	635 00				
30		33	635 00				
			1270 00				

Advertising   Acct No 21

DATE	EXPLANATION	REF.	DEBIT	DATE	EXPLANATION	REF.	CREDIT
1966							
July 28		32	80 00				

Delivery Wages   Acct No 22

DATE	EXPLANATION	REF.	DEBIT	DATE	EXPLANATION	REF.	CREDIT
1966							
July 16		29	200 00				
30		33	200 00				
			400 00				

Truck Repairs   Acct No 23

DATE	EXPLANATION	REF.	DEBIT	DATE	EXPLANATION	REF.	CREDIT
1966				1966			
July 13		28	100 00				
28		33	50 00				
			150 00				

Other Delivery Expense   Acct No 24

DATE	EXPLANATION	REF.	DEBIT	DATE	EXPLANATION	REF.	CREDIT
1966				1966			
July 23		31	180 00				
30		33	20 00				
			200 00				

Rent of Yard   Acct. no. 25

DATE	EXPLANATION	REF	DEBIT	DATE	EXPLANATION	REF.	CREDIT
1966				1966			
July 1		26	150 00				

General Salaries   Acct. no. 30

DATE	EXPLANATION	REF	DEBIT	DATE	EXPLANATION	REF.	CREDIT
1966				1966			
July 16		29	655 00				
30		33	655 00				
			1310 00				

Rent of Office   Acct. no. 31

DATE	EXPLANATION	REF	DEBIT	DATE	EXPLANATION	REF.	CREDIT
1966							
July 1		26	50 00				

Supplies Used   Acct. no. 32

DATE	EXPLANATION	REF	DEBIT	DATE	EXPLANATION	REF.	CREDIT
1966							
July 30		33	25 00				

Payroll Taxes   Acct. no. 33

DATE	EXPLANATION	REF	DEBIT	DATE	EXPLANATION	REF.	CREDIT
1966							
July 16		29	37 50				
30		33	37 50				
			75 00				

Insurance   Acct. no. 34

DATE	EXPLANATION	REF.	DEBIT	DATE	EXPLANATION	REF.	CREDIT
1966							
July 30		33	120 00				

Salesmen's Salaries   Acct. No. 20

DATE	EXPLANATION	REF.	DEBIT	DATE	EXPLANATION	REF.	CREDIT
1966							
July 16		29	635 00				
30		33	635 00				
			1270 00				

Advertising   Acct. No. 21

DATE	EXPLANATION	REF.	DEBIT	DATE	EXPLANATION	REF.	CREDIT
1966							
July 28		32	80 00				

Delivery Wages   Acct. No. 22

DATE	EXPLANATION	REF.	DEBIT	DATE	EXPLANATION	REF.	CREDIT
1966							
July 16		29	200 00				
30		33	200 00				
			400 00				

Truck Repairs   Acct. No. 23

DATE	EXPLANATION	REF.	DEBIT	DATE	EXPLANATION	REF.	CREDIT
1966				1966			
July 13		28	100 00				
28		33	50 00				
			150 00				

Other Delivery Expense   Acct. No. 24

DATE	EXPLANATION	REF.	DEBIT	DATE	EXPLANATION	REF.	CREDIT
1966				1966			
July 23		31	180 00				
30		33	20 00				
			200 00				

Rent of Yard   Acct. no. 25

DATE	EXPLANATION	REF.	DEBIT	DATE	EXPLANATION	REF.	CREDIT
1966				1966			
July 1		26	150 00				

General Salaries   Acct. no. 30

DATE	EXPLANATION	REF.	DEBIT	DATE	EXPLANATION	REF.	CREDIT
1966				1966			
July 16		29	655 00				
30		33	655 00				
			1310 00				

Rent of Office   Acct. no. 31

DATE	EXPLANATION	REF.	DEBIT	DATE	EXPLANATION	REF.	CREDIT
1966				1966			
July 1		26	50 00				

Supplies Used   Acct. no. 32

DATE	EXPLANATION	REF.	DEBIT	DATE	EXPLANATION	REF.	CREDIT
1966							
July 30		33	25 00				

Payroll Taxes   Acct. no. 33

DATE	EXPLANATION	REF.	DEBIT	DATE	EXPLANATION	REF.	CREDIT
1966							
July 16		29	37 50				
30		33	37 50				
			75 00				

Insurance   Acct. no. 34

DATE	EXPLANATION	REF.	DEBIT	DATE	EXPLANATION	REF.	CREDIT
1966							
July 30		33	120 00				

Postage, Telephone, and Telegraph — Acct. No. 35

DATE		EXPLANATION	REF.	DEBIT	DATE	EXPLANATION	REF.	CREDIT
1966								
July	9		27	30 00				
	30		33	50 00				
				80 00				

Other General Expense — Acct. No. 36

DATE		EXPLANATION	REF	DEBIT	DATE	EXPLANATION	REF.	CREDIT
1966								
July	13		28	20 00				
	19		30	80 00				
	30		33	40 00				
				140 00				

Rent Income — Acct. No. 40

DATE	EXPLANATION	REF.	DEBIT	DATE		EXPLANATION	REF.	CREDIT
				1966				
				July	1		26	100 00

Interest — Acct. No. 41

DATE		EXPLANATION	REF	DEBIT	DATE	EXPLANATION	REF.	CREDIT
1966								
July	30		33	50 00				

W. R. Pomeroy, Capital — Acct. No. 17

DATE	EXPLANATION	REF.	DEBIT	DATE		EXPLANATION	REF.	CREDIT
				1966				
				July	1	Balance brought forward		75648 00

POMEROY BUILDING MATERIALS
General Journal with Closing Entries
July, 1966

Page 34

DATE	EXPLANATION	REF.	DEBIT	CREDIT
1966				
July 31	Sales	18	14000 00	
	Profit and Loss	50		14000 00
	(to close Sales)			
31	Profit and Loss	50	8000 00	
	Cost of Goods Sold	19		8000 00
	(to close Cost of Goods Sold)			
31	Profit and Loss	50	1270 00	
	Salesmen's Salaries	20		1270 00
	(to close Salesmen's Salaries)			
31	Profit and Loss	50	80 00	
	Advertising	21		80 00
	(to close Advertising)			
31	Profit and Loss	50	400 00	
	Delivery Wages	22		400 00
	(to close Delivery Wages)			
31	Profit and Loss	50	150 00	
	Truck Repairs	23		150 00
	(to close Truck Repairs)			
31	Profit and Loss	50	200 00	
	Other Delivery Expense	24		200 00
	(to close Other Delivery Expense)			
31	Profit and Loss	50	150 00	
	Rent of Yard	25		150 00
	(to close Rent of Yard)			
31	Profit and Loss	50	1310 00	
	General Salaries	30		1310 00
	(to close General Salaries)			

DATE		EXPLANATION	REF.	DEBIT	CREDIT
1965					
July	31	Profit and Loss	50	50 00	
		Rent of Office	31		50 00
		(to close Rent of Office)			
	31	Profit and Loss	50	25 00	
		Supplies Used	32		25 00
		(to close Supplies Used)			
	31	Profit and Loss	50	75 00	
		Payroll Taxes	33		75 00
		(to close Payroll Taxes)			
	31	Profit and Loss	50	120 00	
		Insurance	34		120 00
		(to close Insurance)			
	31	Profit and Loss	50	80 00	
		Postage, Telephone, and Telegraph	35		80 00
		(to close Postage, Telephone, and Telegraph)			
	31	Profit and Loss	50	140 00	
		Other General Expense	36		140 00
		(to close Other General Expense)			
	31	Rent Income	40	100 00	
		Profit and Loss	50		100 00
		(to close Rent Income)			
	31	Profit and Loss	50	50 00	
		Interest	41		50 00
		(to close Interest)			
	31	Profit and Loss	50	2000 00	
		W. R. Pomeroy, Capital	17		2000 00
		(to close net income for July)			

POMEROY BUILDING MATERIALS
Revenue and Expense Accounts and Capital Account
After Closing
July, 1966

Sales
Acct. No. 18

DATE	EXPLANATION	REF.	DEBIT	DATE	EXPLANATION	REF.	CREDIT
1966				1966			
July 31		34	14000 00	July 9		27	3200 00
				16		29	3600 00
				23		31	3800 00
				30		33	3400 00
							14000 00
			14000 00				14000 00

Cost of Goods Sold
Acct. No. 19

DATE	EXPLANATION	REF.	DEBIT	DATE	EXPLANATION	REF.	CREDIT
1966				1966			
July 9		27	1720 00	July 31		34	8000 00
16		29	1860 00				
23		31	2580 00				
30		33	1840 00				
			8000 00				
			8000 00				8000 00

Salesmen's Salaries
Acct. No. 20

DATE	EXPLANATION	REF.	DEBIT	DATE	EXPLANATION	REF.	CREDIT
1966				1966			
July 16		29	635 00	July 31		34	1270 00
30		33	635 00				
			1270 00				
			1270 00				1270 00

Advertising　　　　　　　Acct. No. 21

DATE	EXPLANATION	REF.	DEBIT	DATE	EXPLANATION	REF.	CREDIT
1966				1966			
July 28		32	80 00	July 31		34	80 00

Delivery Wages　　　　　　　Acct. No. 22

DATE	EXPLANATION	REF.	DEBIT	DATE	EXPLANATION	REF.	CREDIT
1966				1966			
July 16		29	200 00	July 31		34	400 00
30		33	200 00				
			400 00				
			400 00				400 00

Truck Repairs　　　　　　　Acct. No. 23

DATE	EXPLANATION	REF.	DEBIT	DATE	EXPLANATION	REF.	CREDIT
1966				1966			
July 13		28	100 00	July 31		34	150 00
28		33	50 00				
			150 00				
			150 00				150 00

Other Delivery Expense　　　　　　　Acct. No. 24

DATE	EXPLANATION	REF.	DEBIT	DATE	EXPLANATION	REF.	CREDIT
1966				1966			
July 23		31	180 00	July 31		34	200 00
30		33	20 00				
			200 00				
			200 00				200 00

Rent of Yard   Acct no. 25

DATE	EXPLANATION	REF.	DEBIT	DATE	EXPLANATION	REF.	CREDIT
1966				1966			
July 1		26	150 00	July 31		34	150 00

General Salaries   Acct no. 30

DATE	EXPLANATION	REF.	DEBIT	DATE	EXPLANATION	REF.	CREDIT
1966				1966			
July 16		29	655 00	July 31		34	1310 00
30		35	655 00				
			1310 00				
			1310 00				1310 00

Rent of Office   Acct. no. 31

DATE	EXPLANATION	REF.	DEBIT	DATE	EXPLANATION	REF.	CREDIT
1966				1966			
July 1		26	50 00	July 31		35	50 00

Supplies Used   Acct. no. 32

DATE	EXPLANATION	REF.	DEBIT	DATE	EXPLANATION	REF.	CREDIT
1966				1966			
July 30		33	25 00	July 31		35	25 00

Payroll Taxes   Acct. no. 33

DATE	EXPLANATION	REF.	DEBIT	DATE	EXPLANATION	REF.	CREDIT
1966				1966			
July 16		29	37 50	July 31		35	75 00
30		33	37 50				
			75 00				75 00

Insurance   Acct. No. 34

DATE	EXPLANATION	REF.	DEBIT	DATE	EXPLANATION	REF.	CREDIT
1966				1966			
July 30		33	120 00	July 31		35	120 00

Postage, Telephone, and Telegraph   Acct. No. 35

DATE	EXPLANATION	REF.	DEBIT	DATE	EXPLANATION	REF.	CREDIT
1966				1966			
July 9		27	30 00	July 31		35	80 00
30		33	50 00				
			80 00				
			80 00				80 00

Other General Expense   Acct. No. 36

DATE	EXPLANATION	REF.	DEBIT	DATE	EXPLANATION	REF.	CREDIT
1966				1966			
July 13		28	20 00	July 31		35	140 00
19		30	80 00				
30		33	40 00				
			140 00				
			140 00				140 00

Rent Income   Acct. No. 40

DATE	EXPLANATION	REF.	DEBIT	DATE	EXPLANATION	REF.	CREDIT
1966				1966			
July 31		35	100 00	July 1		26	100 00

Interest   Acct. No. 41

DATE	EXPLANATION	REF.	DEBIT	DATE	EXPLANATION	REF.	CREDIT
1966				1966			
July 30		33	50 00	July 31		35	50 00

Profit and Loss   Acct. no. 50

54

DATE	EXPLANATION	REF.	DEBIT	DATE	EXPLANATION	REF.	CREDIT
1966				1966			
July 31	Cost of Goods Sold	34	8000 00	July 31	Sales	34	14000 00
31	Salesmen's Salaries	34	1270 00	31	Rent Income	35	100 00
31	Advertising	34	80 00				
31	Delivery Wages	34	400 00				
31	Truck Repairs	34	150 00				
31	Other Delivery Exp.	34	200 00				
31	Rent of Yard	34	150 00				
31	General Salaries	34	1310 00				
31	Rent of Office	35	50 00				
31	Supplies Used	35	25 00				
31	Payroll Taxes	35	75 00				
31	Insurance	35	120 00				
31	Postage, Tele. and Teleg.	35	80 00				
31	Other General Exp.	35	140 00				
31	Interest	35	50 00				
31	To Capital	35	2000 00				
			14100 00				14100 00

W. R. Pomeroy, Capital   Acct. no. 17

DATE	EXPLANATION	REF.	DEBIT	DATE	EXPLANATION	REF.	CREDIT
				1966			
				July 1	Balance brought forward		75648 00
				31	Profit and Loss	35	2000 00

ALTERNATIVE PROCEDURES

Entries are made individually in the general journal (pages 50–51) to close each revenue and each expense account. An alternative procedure is to make one or more compound journal entries. For example, three journal entries may be used, one to close the revenue and other income accounts, one to close the expense accounts, and one to close the Profit and Loss summary account. These entries would have the following appearance:

```
Sales..............................................$14,000
Rent Income.......................................     100
        Profit and Loss............................              $14,100
(to close revenue and income accounts)

Profit and Loss...................................$12,100
        Cost of Goods Sold........................              $ 8,000
        Salesmens' Salaries.......................                1,270
        Advertising...............................                   80
        Delivery Wages............................                  400
        Truck Repairs.............................                  150
        Other Delivery Expense....................                  200
        Rent of Yard..............................                  150
        General Salaries..........................                1,310
        Rent of Office............................                   50
        Supplies Used.............................                   25
        Payroll Taxes.............................                   75
        Insurance.................................                  120
        Postage, Telephone, and Telegraph.........                   80
        Other General Expense.....................                  140
        Interest..................................                   50
(to close expense accounts)

Profit and Loss...................................$ 2,000
        W. R. Pomeroy, capital....................              $ 2,000
(to close Profit and Loss)
```

Another possibility is to use a single compound journal entry and to omit use of the Profit and Loss account altogether. Most people prefer to use the Profit and Loss account so as to have a ledger record summarizing revenues and expenses.

RULING BALANCE SHEET ACCOUNTS

It is customary to rule the balance sheet accounts at the end of an accounting period, to bring the balance forward. Without this ruling, the sub-totals of the debits and the credits would be carried on indefinitely. These sub-totals would soon become cumbersome. When the balance sheet accounts are ruled, the balance is first entered on the side with the smaller total and dated as of the last day of the period. The two sides are then added to the same total, since the smaller side plus the balance equals the larger side. The ruling is made and the balance is then entered on the side that previously was the larger. Here it is dated as of the first day of the new period. This is the side that the balance represents. The balance figures do not record any new transactions in the account; they are simply a means of summarizing the figures in the account for a period and starting off with the net amount in the new period. This process is illustrated by the accounts shown below. It is frequently referred to as "ruling and balancing the accounts." When the balance figure is inserted on the smaller side and that side is added to the same figure as on the larger side, a check on the arithmetic is obtained.

ILLUSTRATION OF RULING AND BALANCING
THE ACCOUNTS

Asset Account:

Supplies

DATE	EXPLANATION	REF	DEBIT	DATE	EXPLANATION	REF.	CREDIT
1966				1966			
Jan 1	Balance		408 00	Jan 31		J 26	628 00
4		J 16	200 00	31	Balance		505 00
16		J 20	350 00				
22	505.00	J 22	175 00				
			1133 00				
			1133 00				1133 00
Feb 1	Balance		505 00				

Liability Account:

Accounts Payable

DATE	EXPLANATION	REF	DEBIT	DATE	EXPLANATION	REF	CREDIT
1966				1966			
Jan 3		J 15	1428 00	Jan 1	Balance		1428 00
15		J 19	400 00	10		J 17	400 00
31	Balance		1870 00	14		J 18	370 00
				22	1,870.00	J 22	1500 00
							3698 00
			3698 00				3698 00
				Feb 1	Balance		1870 00

STEPS IN THE ACCOUNTING PROCESS

The steps in the accounting process studied to this point are the following:

1. Recording of transactions in the journal.
2. Posting of transactions from the journal to the ledger.
3. Preparation of a preclosing trial balance of the ledger accounts and financial statements.
4. Closing of revenue and expense accounts and ruling and balancing balance sheet accounts.

To this list may now be added,

5. Preparation of a postclosing trial balance.

"Postclosing" of course means "after closing." This trial balance gives assurance that the closing work has been done accurately. The other trial balance, called a "preclosing" trial balance, performs the same function for the work done in recording and posting the transactions and calculating balances before the closing process. The postclosing trial balance contains only balance sheet accounts and is otherwise like the preclosing trial balance.

DISPOSITION OF INCOME

The immediate effect of earning a net income is to increase the assets and the proprietorship by the same amount. The particular assets affected cannot usually be identified for long, because many other transactions occur to change them. Cash received from cash sales will be used to buy new merchandise or new fixed assets, to pay off liabilities, or for some other purpose. Accounts receivable created by sales will be collected and the cash used in many ways.

The effect on proprietorship may be changed by subsequent losses or by withdrawals of assets by the owners. In a sole proprietorship or a partnership withdrawals may be made at the will of the owners, subject to any agreement between partners governing withdrawals. The entry to record a withdrawal of $400 cash by J. F. Hicks, a sole proprietor, is:

```
J. F. Hicks, Capital . . . . . . . . . . . . . . . . . . . . . . . . . . . $400
    Cash . . . . . . . . . . . . . . . . . . . . . . . . . . . . . . .        $400
```

The entry would be the same if Hicks were a partner. Usually no effort is made to distinguish withdrawals of current net income from withdrawals of original investment or of net income accumulated in prior periods in the case of a sole proprietorship or a partnership. Withdrawals are eventually debited to the individual's capital account, even though they are first accumulated in a separate account.

Disbursement of income by a corporation requires the formal declaration of a dividend by the board of directors. A legal declaration of a dividend creates a liability of the corporation. Usually the payment date follows the declaration date by one or more weeks. A complete recording of a dividend requires the following entries:

```
Dividends . . . . . . . . . . . . . . . . . . . . . . . . . . . . . . . . . xxx
    Dividends Payable . . . . . . . . . . . . . . . . . . . . . . .        xxx
(to record declaration of dividend)

Dividends Payable . . . . . . . . . . . . . . . . . . . . . . . . . . . xxx
    Cash . . . . . . . . . . . . . . . . . . . . . . . . . . . . . . . . .        xxx
(to record payment of dividend)

Retained Earnings . . . . . . . . . . . . . . . . . . . . . . . . . . . xxx
    Dividends . . . . . . . . . . . . . . . . . . . . . . . . . . . . .        xxx
(to close Dividends account)
```

If no closing date occurs between the declaration and the payment, the Dividends Payable account may be omitted and the Dividends account charged when the cash is paid. Furthermore, if the separate ledger record provided by the Dividends account is not wanted, it also may be omitted. The only entry then required would be:

```
Retained Earnings . . . . . . . . . . . . . . . . . . . . . . . . . . . $xxx
    Cash . . . . . . . . . . . . . . . . . . . . . . . . . . . . . . . . .        $xxx
(to record declaration and payment of dividend)
```

USES OF THE INCOME STATEMENT

Uses of the income statement are discussed under the following headings:

1. Earnings that can be withdrawn
2. Basis for income tax calculations
3. Basis for capital stock transactions_
4. Managerial and investor analysis for efficiency

EARNINGS THAT CAN BE WITHDRAWN

A useful definition of business net income in a general sense is "that which one can spend and still be as well off as before." The income statement presents a figure that may be interpreted in this sense. However, most successful business concerns never disburse all their income—for three principal reasons:

1. Prudence requires that some income be retained in case of unusual losses. The losses can then be absorbed in the Retained Earnings account (in the case of a corporation) and will not reduce the original capital.

2. Retained earnings permit growth of the business without the need for going into the capital market to sell more stock or to borrow additional money.

3. Owing to rising price levels, it often costs more in dollars to replace worn-out equipment than the old equipment cost. If all income were paid out, it might be impossible to replace worn-out equipment. Another way of saying the same thing is that the dollar income arrived at by conventional accounting methods is not necessarily "real" income. Some of the accounting income is accordingly retained to make up for this discrepancy.

BASIS FOR INCOME TAX CALCULATIONS

Both individuals and corporations are subject to income tax in the United States. The data in the income statement provide the basic data for the income tax return. The return is a report of income and the tax thereon required to be filed by each taxpayer. The figure on which the tax is calculated is often not exactly the same as the net income figure in the income statement of a business concern. This difference is due chiefly to special rules in the tax law for the calculation of income subject to tax. For example, the tax law does not recognize gain or loss when a piece of equipment is traded in on another piece of substantially the same character. Regular accounting does recognize this gain or loss. In many cases the differences are insignificant; in others they are very important. In any case the income statement is the starting point for income tax calculations and provides most of the data for them.

BASIS FOR CAPITAL STOCK TRANSACTIONS

When an ownership interest in a business concern is to be sold, the major question is usually the earning power of the company. For this reason the income statements, showing earnings for a period of past years, are of special importance. The earnings per share of stock are often published as an aid to investors considering purchase or sale of the stock. The real basis for the price of a share, however, is ordinarily the expectations of the persons involved as to the *future* earnings. These expectations take into consideration general business conditions and all prospects of a company. Nevertheless, one of the best indications of what a company may be able to do in the future is the record of what it actually has earned in the past. The latter is supplied by the income statements of the prior years.

MANAGERIAL AND INVESTOR ANALYSIS FOR EFFICIENCY

Reference has already been made to the importance of the gross margin on sales shown in the income statement. A margin of 40 percent is obviously better than one of 30 percent, other things being equal. Managers and others also calculate the relationship of various expenses to revenue and to each other where significant relationships can be observed. For example, income statements may disclose that one concern is able to operate with general and administrative expenses of 10 percent of revenue, whereas another in the same type of business requires 15 percent. Management of the second one is then alerted to the possible need to improve its efficiency in the area of general and administrative expenses. A similar advantage is gained by observing any changes in amounts of revenue and expense and their relationships from one period to the next. Management may take steps to counteract unfavorable trends or to create favorable ones. Investors or creditors may invest or lend money freely to a company that shows a good and improving record; they will usually avoid those which show declining records. The details of the analysis of the income statement are the subject of a later chapter, but one type of analysis is given below as an illustration. This percentage analysis is applied to a comparative, condensed income statement. The percentages are obtained by dividing each figure by the sales figure, except where they can be obtained by adding or subtracting other percentages. This analysis is often done for a single income statement as well as for more detailed income statements.

PERCENTAGE ANALYSIS OF THE INCOME STATEMENT

POMEROY BUILDING MATERIALS
Condensed Income Statements

Months of July, 1966 and 1965

	1966	1965	1966	1965
Sales	$14,000	$13,500	100.0%	100.0%
Cost of Goods Sold	8,000	8,600	57.1	63.7
Gross Margin on Sales	$ 6,000	$ 4,900	42.9	36.3
Operating Expenses:				
Selling Expense	$ 2,250	$ 2,000	16.1	14.8
General and Administrative Expense	1,800	1,700	12.9	12.6
	$ 4,050	$ 3,700	29.0	27.4
Net Operating Income	$ 1,950	$ 1,200	13.9	8.9
Other Income	100	100	0.7	0.7
	$ 2,050	$ 1,300	14.6	9.6
Other Deductions	50	80	0.4	0.6
Net Income	$ 2,000	$ 1,220	14.2	9.0

MATRIX FORMULATION WITH INCOME STATEMENT DATA

The reader will recall that Chapter 1 included a formulation of accounting in matrix form. At that point only balance sheet accounts were given, all entries affecting proprietorship going directly to the proprietor's capital account. This scheme is easily expanded by adding columns and rows for each revenue and expense account that is to be maintained. The scheme must provide for addition of balances brought forward from the prior period in the permanent, or balance sheet, accounts, so a column (for old balance sheet credit balances) and a row (for old balance sheet debit balances) are added for these figures. To provide for the new totals, a column for total credits and a row for total debits are added, giving space to record the addition of the current transactions to the old balances. Before the final additions are made, however, the net balance of the revenue and the expense accounts will be obtained and an entry made to cancel out the several revenue and expense amounts that make up this net total and to enter it in the proprietorship account or accounts. Then when the old balances are added to the totals of the transactions for the year, the

MATRIX PROVIDING FOR INCOME STATEMENT DATA

	Balance Sheet Accounts	Income Statement Accounts	Old Balance Sheet Credit Balances	Totals	New Balance Sheet Credit Balances
Balance Sheet Accounts					
Income Statement Accounts					
Old Balance Sheet Debit Balances					
Totals					
New Balance Sheet Debit Balances					

operator (or the machine) will be in a position to take the last step, which is to compare the credits with the debits for the various balance sheet accounts and so to calculate the new balances. The new credit balances may then be entered in the column added to the matrix for this purpose, and the new debit balances may be entered on the row added for it. The matrix then will have the form shown in the accompanying illustration.

Once again, note that this matrix may be thought of as a kind of model for the way accounting data are accumulated in an electronic computer. One may provide for the future reproduction of figures that exist in the memory locations indicated by our matrix cells (but which are sometimes removed when added to other figures) when actually using a computer, by having the machine record them on magnetic tape, on punched tape, or on punched cards, or by assigning different locations for their preservation. They may also be printed out at whatever stage one wishes to record. Note again also that the debit and credit mechanism may take forms which have no physical resemblance to the traditional ledger account, but which nevertheless reflect the same basic principle expressed in the accounting equation.

SUMMARY

The income statement presents the results of operations for a period. The accounts that provide the data for the statement describe what is happening to proprietorship as a result of the income-earning activities. They accordingly follow the rules of debit and credit that apply to the permanent, or balance sheet, proprietorship accounts. The traditional income statement for a concern selling merchandise has sections for sales and cost of goods sold, the difference being gross margin on sales. It has sections for selling expenses and general and administrative expenses. These constitute the operating expenses and, when deducted from gross margin, give net operating income. The remaining sections show the nonoperating incomes and deductions or expenses.

Entries are usually posted to the ledger from a journal, which is a chronological record of the transactions. It provides for complete explanations when necessary, and it facilitates review and control of entries in the accounting records. After the ledger is posted, a trial balance is generally prepared to test the equality of debits and credits and to serve as a basis for drawing up the financial statements.

The revenue and expense accounts are designed to accumulate data for one accounting period (not more than a year) and are closed out to proprietorship through the Profit and Loss account at the end of the year. The many uses of the income statement are summarized under these topics: Earnings That Can Be Withdrawn, Basis for Income Tax Calculations, Basis for Capital Stock Transactions, and Managerial and Investor Analysis for Efficiency.

The basic accounting principles reflected traditionally in the journal and ledger procedures of this chapter may also be formulated in the form of a matrix. The matrix formulation of accounting may be thought of as a kind of model for the way accounting data are accumulated in an electronic computer.

QUESTIONS

2.1 Robert Fuller is the owner-manager of Chicago Custom Electronics, a firm specializing in the sale and maintenance of hi-fidelity systems and components. Fuller tells you that his sales volume has increased for each of the five years since he organized his business, and that his markup is higher now than five years ago. Nevertheless, he is concerned because his "profit" has been decreasing.

On questioning, Fuller reveals that he draws from the business bank account all cash in excess of $5,000. The amount of his annual drawing he considers his "profit."

Discuss briefly the adequacy of Fuller's profit determination, indicating the major elements of revenue and expense he has failed to consider.

2.2 (1) Describe how the information in a conventional income statement is arranged and what each section contains.
(2) What figures are computed on the face of the income statement?

2.3 (1) What is the relationship between the income statement and the balance sheet?
(2) How is the change in proprietorship during a fiscal period related to net income?
(3) State the net income in each of the following cases:

	Case A	Case B	Case C	Case D
Capital, January 1	$18,000	$15,000	$20,000	$28,000
Capital, December 31	33,000	30,000	18,000	10,000
Invested during year	10,000	—	—	—
Drawing during year	—	5,000	6,000	6,000

2.4 "The rules for debit and credit of asset and expense accounts are the same, but for different reasons." Explain.

2.5 (1) State what revenue is, and name five revenue accounts that may be used by different kinds of concerns.
(2) Indicate whether revenue has been realized in each of the following instances:
  (a) A theater sells tickets for a performance during its next fiscal period.
  (b) Cash is collected from a customer for merchandise sold during the last fiscal period.
  (c) An architect sends out bills for work performed; cash is expected during the next fiscal period.
  (d) Cash was collected by a landlord during a previous fiscal period for rents applicable to the current period.
  (e) A metal fabricator manufactures machinery for its own use at a profit.

2.6 (1) Define expense and distinguish expense accounts representing functions from those representing object of expenditure.
(2) As a company grows, the expenses tend to be classified more by function and less by object. Why?

2.7 By using the appropriate letter, indicate whether the debit for each of the following is made to (a) an asset account, (e) an expense account, or (s) some other kind of account:

(1) Merchandise is purchased for credit.
(2) Cost of goods sold is recorded by a deduction from inventory.
(3) Salaries for the month are paid.
(4) An insurance premium is paid on a 3-year policy.
(5) A bill is paid for last week's newspaper advertising.
(6) Salesmen's commissions for the month are calculated and recorded; they will be paid next month.

(7) A new partner is admitted; his contribution to capital consists of office equipment.

(8) Supplies on hand are counted and the usage for the month is calculated. (Supplies purchased were charged to the Supplies on Hand account.)

(9) One of the partners withdrew $800 in cash because he expected that his share of profit would equal at least that much.

(10) A corporation declared a dividend of $50,000.

2.8 "Every expenditure is not an expense." Give an example of (1) an expenditure that is an expense, (2) an expenditure that is not an expense, and (3) an expense that is not an expenditure.

2.9 (1) All the information contained in the journal is repeated in the ledger. What are the advantages, then, of maintaining both records?

(2) How may the reference column in the journal be best used?

2.10 Under what situations in actual accounting practice would general journal entries require complete explanations? What are the essentials of information that should be contained by such explanations?

2.11 (1) What is the function of a trial balance?

(2) How does the trial balance differ from the balance sheet?

(3) Name three errors that will be revealed by a trial balance, and three that will not.

2.12 Explain what might cause each of the following differences between total debits and total credits of a trial balance:

(1) Debits were $540 larger than credits.

(2) Credits were $432 larger than debits.

2.13 (1) Following are selected accounts taken from the ledger of Talbot's Bookmart. Arrange them in the order in which they would usually be found in the ledger.

Accounts Payable	Interest Expense
Accounts Receivable	Merchandise Inventory
Advertising Expense	Mortgage Payable
Cash Discounts Taken	Store Equipment
Cost of Periodical Sales	Sales of Periodicals
Geo. Talbot, Proprietor	Wages Payable

(2) Put an X next to the accounts that normally have a credit balance.

2.14 In a certain insurance agency the accounting books are kept according to the double-entry system. It is the custom of the agency to have the books closed twice each year, as of the close of business on June 30 and on December 31. Before the books are closed, a trial balance of the ledger accounts is prepared. Among the accounts appearing in the trial balance are the following:

Accounts Payable	Office Salaries
Cash	Office Supplies Used
Commissions Earned	

1. For each account listed above explain whether it would have a debit or a credit balance at the time of closing the books and whether it is a balance sheet or income statement account.

2. Why must a trial balance actually balance if the books are correctly kept? Explain.

3. Explain the meaning of "closing the books" and illustrate by showing its effect on each of the accounts referred to in this problem.

(CPCU — adapted)

2.15 (1) Give the steps in the accounting process as you know it thus far.

(2) Can you explain why, in actual practice, the closing entries are often prepared after the balance sheet has been drafted?

2.16 (1) Distinguish between expenses and dividends.

(2) What is the advantage of debiting a Dividends account rather than Retained Earnings for the declaration of a dividend?

2.17 (1) Explain how matrix accounting may be thought of as a model of the way accounting data is processed in an electronic computer.

(2) Write in ordinary English directions which might be translated into computer language, instructing a computer to accumulate revenue and expense data on a year-to-date basis and to print out monthly income statements.

2.18 (1) "A trial balance need never be taken to prove the equality of debits and credits in the matrix form of accounting." Explain.

(2) Although matrix accounting eliminates the need for a trial balance, it does not eliminate the possibility of arithmetical errors. Name four kinds of errors that may still occur.

2.19 The transaction matrix of Chapter 2 is partitioned into four sections. Give an example and explain the effect on net income of an understated entry in the upper left-hand part, the lower right-hand part, the lower left-hand part, and the upper right-hand part.

2.20 The office manager of a moderate-sized insurance agency is not too well versed in accounting procedures. The young woman who is doing the bookkeeping has had several years of accounts receivable ledger experience and is good on detail; however, she has had no formal training in accounting and is not too well versed in the handling of the general ledger.

The office manager knows the books should be "closed," but he is not too sure about just what should be done. Explain the purpose of closing, and submit model closing entries in journal form using "xxx" in place of dollars for debit and credit amounts.

EXERCISES

2.1 Compute net income for the year in each case below.

	Case A	Case B	Case C	Case D
Capital, January 1	$25,000	$20,000	$50,000	$50,000
Capital, December 31	75,000	30,000	70,000	40,000
Invested during year	40,000	—	5,000	—
Withdrew during year	—	15,000	12,000	12,000

2.2 (1) From the following alphabetical list of revenue and expense accounts prepare an income statement for A and W Wholesalers for the month of January 1966. Include a column on the income statement for percent of sales and show percentages for cost of goods sold, gross profit, operating expenses, net operating income, other deductions, and net income.

Advertising	$ 1,000
Cost of Goods Sold	12,000
General Salaries	2,400
Interest Paid	200
Office Rent	600
Sales	20,000
Sales Salaries	2,000
Sundry General Expense	200

(2) The percentage of gross profit to sales last month was 42 percent. What two price changes might explain the difference between the percentage last month and this month?

2.3　The ledger of the World Wide Travel Agency contained the following accounts on December 31, 1966. Prepare the annual income statement.

Land	$125,000	Insurance	$ 6,210
Accounts Receivable	43,610	Capital Stock	100,000
Building	173,000	Advertising Expense	38,893
Cash	20,250	Repairs to Building	10,330
Prepaid Rent	1,107	Interest Earned	4,213
Notes Payable	60,000	Taxes	5,800
Taxes Payable	6,300	Postage	2,980
Accounts Payable	54,330	Dividends	5,000
Commissions Earned	250,000	Depreciation Expense	10,000
Retained Earnings	165,457	Travel Expense	45,000
Salaries	150,000	Prepaid Insurance	3,120

2.4　The Aloha Pool Service was organized January 1, 1966, to maintain commercial and residential swimming pools. Enter the following transactions for January directly into T accounts, identifying each debit and credit by the number of the transaction, and prepare a trial balance. Use the following accounts: Cash, Accounts Receivable, Supplies, Truck, Contracts Payable, L. Ash, Capital, L. Ash, Drawings, Service Charges, Salaries, Supplies Used, Interest.

(1) L. Ash invested $5,000 cash.
(2) Purchased a truck for $2,000 cash plus a contract of $6,000.
(3) Purchased supplies for $500 cash.
(4) Received $1,000 cash for services rendered.
(5) Billed customers $2,000 for services rendered.
(6) Paid assistant's salary, $500.
(7) Paid $500 principal and $60 interest on the contract.
(8) Collected from customers $700 on account.
(9) Supplies used, $100.
(10) L. Ash drew a "salary" of $500 for personal use. (Charge Drawings.)

2.5　The October transactions of King Co. are shown below. Explain each transaction.

Cash		Accounts Payable		Profit and Loss	
(1) 10,000	(2) 1,000	(3) 2,000	(2) 2,500	(11) 6,000	(10) 10,000
(4) 4,000	(3) 2,000			(12) 4,000	
(7) 3,000	(6) 5,000				

Accounts Receivable		Taxes Payable		Revenues	
(5) 6,000	(7) 3,000		(9) 200	(10) 10,000	(4) 4,000
					(5) 6,000

Supplies on Hand		John King, Capital		Expenses	
(2) 3,500	(8) 800		(1) 10,000	(6) 5,000	(11) 6,000
			(12) 4,000	(8) 800	
				(9) 200	

2.6　Prepare a chart analyzing the transactions below, showing the names of the accounts affected, the kind of account (asset, liability, or proprietorship), whether the accounts are increased or decreased, and the resulting debits and credits. Transaction O illustrates the form.

Transaction	Accounts Affected	Kind of Account	Increase or Decrease	Debit or Credit
O	Cash	A	+	Dr
	Accounts Receivable	A	−	Cr

(0) Collected cash on account.
(1) Purchased a desk on credit.
(2) Paid note payable by check.
(3) Received promissory note from customer on account.
(4) Paid salaries.
(5) Purchased supplies on credit.
(6) Charged supplies used to expense.
(7) Purchased merchandise for cash.
(8) Purchased merchandise on credit.
(9) Sold merchandise for cash.
(10) Determined cost of merchandise sold.

2.7 The trial balance of International Data Corporation at December 31, 1966, follows:

Cash	$ 26,000	
Accounts Receivable	21,000	
Furniture and Fixtures	20,000	
Accounts Payable		$ 12,000
Capital Stock		20,000
Retained Earnings		2,000
Data Processing Charges		142,000
Set-up Charges		6,000
Salaries and Wages	70,000	
Equipment Rental	32,000	
Office Expense	13,000	
	$182,000	$182,000

Draft T accounts for Profit and Loss and Retained Earnings and demonstrate closing the books by entering the closing entries directly in those accounts. What is the purpose of closing the books at the end of each accounting period?

2.8 The DR Land Co. was formed December 1, 1966. Journal entries for December were:

Dec. 1	Cash	$25,000	
	J. Doe, Capital		$25,000
2	Land Inventory	25,000	
	R. Roe, Capital		25,000
3	Rent Expense	300	
	Cash		300
4	Office Equipment	5,000	
	Cash		1,000
	Contracts Payable		4,000
5	Supplies Inventory	500	
	Accounts Payable		500
15	Land Inventory	10,000	
	Cash		2,000
	Mortgage Payable		8,000
30	Cash	8,000	
	Cost of Land Sold	5,000	
	Sales		8,000
	Land Inventory		5,000
31	Supplies Used	100	
	Supplies Inventory		100

Required:

1. Write an explanation for each entry.
2. Draft closing journal entries. The partners share profits and losses equally.
3. Prepare a schedule of cash receipts and disbursements for December 1966. Comment on the difference between the excess of receipts over disbursements for the month and net income for the month.

2.9   The trial balance of M. Wray Sales at January 31, 1966, follows:

Cash	$ 3,530	
Accounts Receivable	28,920	
Supplies	420	
Furniture and Fixtures	5,300	
Accounts Payable		$14,460
M. Wray, Capital		8,400
Sales		20,100
Salaries	340	
Rent	1,700	
	$40,210	$42,960

The trial balance contains the following errors:

(1) The sum of the credit postings to Sales was computed as $8,400; the correct total is $8,300.
(2) A cash payment of $630 was posted to Cash as $360; the debit was recorded properly.
(3) A $460 payment to a supplier was not posted to Accounts Payable; the rest of the entry was recorded properly.
(4) A $200 purchase of supplies was posted as a credit to Supplies; the rest of the entry was posted properly.
(5) The balance of $3,400 in the Salaries account was copied as $340 into the trial balance.
(6) The offset to cash on a $500 collection from a customer was *debited* to Rent; the rest of the entry was posted properly.
(7) No entry was made to record partitions installed by a contractor. The work was done in exchange for a $1,200 piano taken from the residence of M. Wray.

Prepare a corrected trial balance.

2.10   Following are statements of cash receipts and disbursements and comparative financial condition of B Co. for 1966. Compute revenues and expenses, and reconcile net income with the change in capital for the year.

B CO.

STATEMENT OF CASH RECEIPTS AND DISBURSEMENTS

Year Ended December 31, 1966

Receipts:	
Collections from Customers	$27,000
Investments by Owner	5,000
Total Receipts	$32,000
Disbursements:	
Expenses	24,000
Increase in cash during year	$ 8,000

B CO.

STATEMENT OF COMPARATIVE FINANCIAL CONDITION

As of December 31, 1966 and 1965

	December 31	
	1966	1965
Cash	$13,000	$ 5,000
Accounts Receivable	28,000	25,000
	$41,000	$30,000
Accounts Payable	$12,000	$10,000
Capital	29,000	20,000
	$41,000	$30,000

2.11 Explain the lettered entries in the matrix below.

Dr. Cr.	Cash	Accounts Receivable	Merchandise	Accounts Payable	R. Albert, Capital	Sales	Cost of Sales	Expenses	Old Balance Sheet Credit Balances	Totals	New Balance Sheet Credit Balances
Cash								(e) 1		1	
Accounts Receivable	(g) 2									2	
Merchandise							(d) 3			3	
Accounts Payable				(a) 4					(f) 1	1	6	6
R. Albert, Capital						(h) 7				8	15	10
Sales	(c) 1	(b) 6								7	
Cost of Sales				(h) 3						3	
Expenses				(h) 2						2	
Old Balance Sheet Debit Balances	2	4	3						9		
Totals	5	10	7		5	7	3	2		39	
New Balance Sheet Debit Balances	4	8	4								16

2.12 The December 1, 1966, trial balance of Island Pest Control follows:

Cash	$ 500	
Supplies	400	
Equipment	3,000	
Accounts Payable		$2,000
Kimo McVay, Capital		1,900
	$3,900	$3,900

The December transactions were:

(1) Received $500 cash for services rendered.
(2) Purchased $200 of supplies and $1,000 of equipment; paid $500 cash and charged the balance.
(3) Paid operating expenses, $200.
(4) Used supplies, $100.
(5) Depreciation of equipment, $50.

    1. Record the transactions and closing entries in a matrix. In addition to the trial balance accounts above, use accounts for Service Charges and Expenses. Columns and rows should also be provided for old balances, totals, and new balances.

    2. Instead of letting columns and rows show debits and credits respectively, would it be just as convenient to denote column and row entries respectively as simply increases and decreases? Explain.

PROBLEMS

2.1   Prepare the income statement of Wilson Wholesale Sporting Goods for June 1966 from the revenue and the expense accounts below.

Advertising	$ 1,000
Cost of Goods Sold	10,000
Delivery Expense	800
General Salaries	5,000
Interest Paid	100
Office Rent	500
Office Supplies Used	300
Patent Royalties Earned	500
Sales	27,000
Sales Returns and Allowances	2,000
Sales Salaries	3,000
Sales Supplies Used	300
Sundry General Expense	200
Taxes — Property and Payroll	1,000
Travel and Entertainment	500
Warehouse Rent	400

Compute percentages of gross margin and net operating income to net sales. Last month the percent of gross margin to net sales was 65 percent. What are some of the reasons which would account for a difference between this month and last month?

2.2   The ledger of International Products Co. contains a Cash account in balance form, as shown below.

		CASH			ACCT. NO. 101	

Date	Explanation	Ref.	Debit	Credit	Dr. or Cr.	Balance
1966						
Jan. 1		J1	8,000			
15		J1		2,000		
31		J1	4,000		Dr.	10,000

Required:

1. Draft a similar form, starting with the February 1 balance. Enter the following transactions from page 2 of the journal and balance the account at February 28.

Feb. 1 Issued additional capital stock for cash, $10,000.
       5 Paid February rent on the store, $1,000.
      10 Purchased merchandise for cash, $8,000.
      15 Sold merchandise for cash, $4,000.
      18 Paid $6,000 to suppliers on account.
      27 Collected $10,000 from customers on account.
      28 Paid salaries, $2,000.

2. Discuss the advantages of the balance form of ledger account over the traditional divided form of ledger account.

2.3   The balance sheet accounts of the Eastman Residence Club at January 1, 1966, are as follows:

Cash in Bank	$ 2,000	
Accounts Receivable	500	
Furniture and Fixtures	8,000	
Land	5,000	
Buildings	12,000	
Accounts Payable		$ 400
J. Eastman, Capital		27,100
	$27,500	$27,500

A summary of transactions for January follows:

(1) Additional cash invested by owner, $500.
(2) Collections on rents billed in December 1965, $300.
(3) Receipts for rent earned during the current month, $600.
(4) Check written for a 1-year insurance policy, $120.
(5) Two apartments previously rented as unfurnished were converted to furnished apartments; total cost of kitchen equipment, beds, and other furnishings, paid in cash, $300.
(6) Checks written for invoices recorded during previous accounting periods, $350.
(7) Check written for January electric bill, $55.
(8) Check written for utility man's January salary, $200.
(9) Check written to Robinson Service Company for regular tune-up and cleaning of air-conditioning motor, $20.
(10) An invoice was received during January, but was not paid, for plumbing work required by negligence of a tenant and chargeable to his account, $30.
(11) Insurance expired for the month is written off (see entry 4).
(12) Check for $300 was written against the company bank account to buy a gold locket for Mrs. Eastman, wife of the owner.

Open T accounts and record the opening balances and transactions for the month. Prepare the January 31 trial balance, marking with an X the name of each account that would be closed at the end of the fiscal period. Accounts to be used in addition to those in the opening trial balance are Rent Revenue, Prepaid Insurance, Utilities Expense, Salaries Expense, Repairs, Insurance Expense, J. Eastman, Drawing.

2.4   The KL Trading Co. completed the transactions below (among others) in December 1966. Draft general journal entries. Explanations may be omitted.

(1) Purchased a delivery truck for $6,000 cash.
(2) Paid $300 wages of delivery-truck driver for first half of December.

(3) Purchased $400 gasoline on credit.
(4) Recorded consumption of gasoline: on hand December 1, $100; on hand December 31, $200.
(5) Purchased garage site for $1,000 cash plus a 6 percent 6-month note for $4,000.
(6) Received $100 rent for December from a tenant, who will occupy the garage site until construction begins.
(7) Paid $400 principal and $100 interest on the long-term mortgage on land and buildings.
(8) Paid trade creditors $5,000 on account.
(9) Received a $500 invoice for December radio advertising.
(10) Cash sales amounted to $20,000.
(11) Charge sales amounted to $40,000.
(12) Recorded cost of goods sold for December. Merchandise on hand at December 1 cost $36,000. Purchases of $12,000 during December were charged to the Merchandise account. Merchandise on hand at December 31 cost $18,000.
(13) Closed the Sales account for December, $63,000.
(14) Closed Delivery Wages for December, $600.
(15) Closed net income of $6,000 for the month to the partners' Capital accounts: R. S. Kay, $2,000; B. S. Lee, $4,000.

2.5   The balance sheet of Casper Caterers at August 1, 1966, was as follows:

CASPER CATERERS
BALANCE SHEET
August 1, 1966

Cash	$ 4,000	Notes Payable	$ 5,000
Accounts Receivable	6,000	Accounts Payable	11,000
Merchandise	10,000	Total Liabilities	$16,000
Supplies	1,000	O. H. Casper, Capital	5,000
	$21,000		$21,000

During August 1966 the company used the following revenue and expense accounts: Sales, Cost of Goods Sold, and Expenses. Transactions for August 1966 are given below.

(1) H. O. Casper deposited $5,000 to the credit of Casper Caterers as an additional investment.
(2) Borrowed $10,000 on a promissory note.
(3) Paid $9,000 on accounts payable.
(4) Purchased merchandise on credit, $16,000.
(5) Charge sales, $24,000.
(6) Received cash: sales, $25,000; accounts receivable, $15,000.
(7) Paid wages, $14,000.
(8) Received bills: supplies, $1,000; expenses, $11,000.
(9) Paid $5,000 noninterest-bearing note.
(10) Returned to suppliers defective merchandise, $1,000.
(11) Determined by inventory cost of goods sold for August, $15,000.
(12) Supplies used, $1,000.
(13) Closed the Sales account.
(14) Closed the Cost of Goods Sold and Expenses accounts.

Prepare a matrix with rows and columns for the balance sheet and income statement accounts. Include rows and columns for opening balances, totals, and closing balances. Enter the transactions and balance the accounts.

2.6   The Town House is an apartment hotel with 100 apartments rented at $200 to $500 per month and a number of hotel rooms rented on a weekly basis. The December 1, 1966, trial balance was as follows:

105	Cash	$ 5,000	
122	Accounts Receivable	3,000	
131	Prepaid Insurance	2,000	
161	Furniture and Fixtures	320,000	
206	Accounts Payable		$ 10,000
231	Rents Received in Advance		20,000
291	J. Smith, Capital		160,000
301	Rent Revenues		430,000
505	Rent Expense	215,000	
508	Repairs	40,000	
511	Salaries	20,000	
514	Utilities	10,000	
519	Unclassified	5,000	
		$620,000	$620,000

Transactions for December were:

Dec.   2 Smith invested an additional $5,000.

3 Issued a check for insurance premiums, $1,200.

4 Paid $100 on c.o.d. parcels, cleaning service, and laundry for tenants.

5 Received $2,500 on account from tenants.

6 Collected from tenants for December rent, $18,000.

7 Paid creditors on account, $9,500.

8 Paid repair bill for December services, $1,800.

15 Paid semimonthly salaries, $1,000.

16 Received invoice for repainting an apartment, $200.

20 Purchased air conditioner on 30-day credit, $20,000.

30 Paid semimonthly salaries, $1,000.

30 Paid December charges: rent of building, $20,000; gas and electricity, $600; telephone, $400.

30 Collected rents from tenants for January 1967, $22,000.

31 Charged other tenants for December 1966 rent, $2,000.

31 During December certain rents received prior to December 1 were earned. The entire $20,000 balance in the Rents Received in Advance account at December 1 was for occupancy during the period from December 1 to December 31. (Debit Account 231 and credit Account 301.)

31 Insurance expired in December, $200.

31 Depreciation for December was $300. (Credit Account 161.)

31 Smith withdrew $500 for personal use.

Required:

1. Enter the trial balance amounts directly into ledger accounts. A Profit and Loss account (Account 601) may be used in addition to the trial balance accounts.
2. Draft dated journal entries for the December transactions, omitting explanations.
3. Post the transactions, using the account numbers as ledger references.
4. Take a trial balance.
5. Prepare a balance sheet and an income statement. Use the following form for the income statement:

THE TOWN HOUSE
INCOME STATEMENT
For Month and Year Ended December 31, 1966

	This Month		Year to Date	
	Amount	Percent	Amount	Percent
Rent Revenues	$xxx	xxx%	$xxx	xxx%
Expenses: (detail)	$xxx	xxx%	$xxx	xxx%

6. Journalize and post the closing entries.

Matching Costs and Revenue

MATCHING COSTS AND REVENUE

Calculation of the net income for a specified period requires that the revenue earned during that period and the costs of earning it be properly identified. The whole process of earning revenue and of incurring costs in most enterprises is a continuous one, but measures of results are needed period by period. The result is that some basis is needed for deciding at what point in the series of steps required to earn revenue it is reasonable to conclude that the revenue is "earned." Accountants in the past have often taken a legal view toward the earning of revenue, recording it when enough has been done to justify a legal claim on the customer. Recent thought on the subject tends to support an economic view of the process and to encourage recognition of revenue earlier in the process of earning it.

Recognition of costs as expenses incurred in earning revenue presents problems for three basic reasons. Some of the costs represent expenditures made in past periods but used in later periods; some expenses may be contracted for in one period and used for its benefit but paid in later periods. Some costs benefit many periods or products, so the amount to be "matched" with revenue of a particular period is not definite or certain.

This chapter presents the fundamental concepts that accountants have developed for determining when revenue should be recognized and recorded and which expenses should be matched with it in determining net income for a period.

MEANS OF MATCHING COSTS AND REVENUE

To assure a proper matching of costs and revenue, attention must be given to the following matters, which are discussed in this chapter:

1. Recognition of revenue
2. Recognition of expense
3. Adjusting entries:
   (a) Accrued revenue
   (b) Accrued expense
   (c) Deferred revenue
   (d) Deferred expense
   (e) Goods sold and supplies used
   (f) Depreciation
   (g) Errors and omissions

RECOGNITION OF REVENUE

Revenue from services is normally recognized and recorded when the services are performed. Performance of a service under a valid contract creates a right to collect for the work. For convenience the entry is usually made when a particular job is finished. If the job extends over more than one accounting period, the portion of the revenue earned to the end of the accounting period should be recorded for strict accuracy. This is the practice of contractors, especially those working on large projects. It may not be followed as a practical matter if the amount involved is not important.

Revenue from the sale of goods is usually recorded when the goods are shipped to a customer. The essential event is the "passage of title" to the buyer. In retail trade, title ordinarily passes when the goods are handed to the customer. In wholesale trade, goods are often shipped by common carrier, for example, a railroad or trucking line. The commonest arrangement is for the shipper to send the goods "f.o.b. shipping point" ("free on board" the common carrier's vehicle at the shipping point, which is usually the shipper's place of business). This expression means that the costs beyond that point are paid by the buyer; in other words, he pays the freight bill. In this case the law regards the common carrier as the agent of the buyer, and title passes to the buyer when the seller delivers the goods to the carrier. When this delivery is made, the seller is entitled to record the sale.

Other arrangements may be made as the buyer and the seller wish. Some other common arrangements automatically imply an intention to have title pass at a particular time. For example, if you say to a used-car dealer, "I'll take the third car from the left end in the first row" and you sign an order for it, the car becomes yours at that moment even though you take delivery later. You may also accomplish passage of title if you sign nothing but pay down a certain amount—in some states, $50. This is a sale of "specific" goods. If goods are shipped "f.o.b. destination," the seller pays the freight and is responsible for safe delivery. The carrier in this case is agent for the seller, and title does not pass until the goods are delivered to the customer by the carrier. Other special rules apply to certain special situations.

Strictly speaking, a sale of goods should be recorded when the title passes to the buyer. This also applies to the recording of the purchase by the buyer. Some types of contracts, such as "conditional sales" contracts, declare that the seller retains title to the goods until the buyer pays for them. In spite of the legal formalities, the essential part of the title *does* pass to the buyer in a case of this kind. The real test is, who loses if the goods are accidentally destroyed? Not the seller, who kept title to the goods, but the buyer. The retention of title in a case of this kind is really retention of a security interest in the goods; that is, the right to take them back if the buyer does not pay for them. This is only a small part of the whole title, which is a divisible thing.

RECOGNITION OF EXPENSE

Many expenses are readily identified with related revenue, but in some cases the relationship is not perfectly clear. For these cases businessmen have developed some generally recognized practices. The methods of associating expense with revenue are described under the following headings:

1. Direct identification with revenue
2. Identification with the accounting period, because of
   (a) Need for objectivity
   (b) Relation to the passage of time
   (c) Convenience

DIRECT IDENTIFICATION OF EXPENSE WITH REVENUE

The Cost of Goods Sold account records the cost of merchandise sold and is therefore directly identifiable with the related revenue. Commissions paid to salesmen are computed on the sales made and easily follow the revenue into the record. Delivery expenses, especially where delivery charges are paid to an outside concern, also follow directly from sales made. The income tax for a period is calculated on net income, and hence follows directly from the revenue earned. The recording of such items in the expenses of the proper period involves no difficult accounting principle; it is easy to "match" revenue and related expenses in these cases.

IDENTIFICATION WITH THE ACCOUNTING PERIOD

Expenses that cannot easily and clearly be identified with particular revenue are identified with accounting periods.

NEED FOR OBJECTIVITY

In general, any expenditure that has future usefulness is an asset, and should be charged to an asset account. However, in some cases where future usefulness is possible or even expected it is not possible to *prove* the existence of it or to *measure* it accurately. For example, a newspaper advertising campaign carried out in December *may* increase sales in the following January and February. In so far as it does, the expenditure is theoretically an asset. But there is no way, at December 31, to prove or measure this asset.

Accounting must be objective; that is, different accountants with the same facts must be able to get substantially the same results. They cannot be influenced by something so much a matter of personal opinion (subjective) as the future value of an advertising campaign. Such expenditures are therefore charged to expense in the period in which the service paid or contracted for is given. In the case of the newspaper advertising, this is the period in which the advertising is published.

This category includes all promotional expenditures, such as salesmen's salaries, catalogues issued, favors given prospective customers, and so on. It includes charitable contributions and other expenses that have a theoretical but immeasurable future benefit.

RELATION TO THE PASSAGE OF TIME

Some expenses are directly related to the passage of time. Salaries are customarily paid by the month. Taxes on real estate and personal property are assessed each year and collected to finance the governmental unit for a particular twelve-month period. Payroll taxes are assessed on payrolls and are therefore partly a function of time. Supplies are used up partly as a function of time; each day a little more sweeping compound is used, and each day the delivery truck burns some more gasoline. Repairs may also be thought of as arising with the passage of time. These items and others like them are recorded in the accounting period in which the material is used or the service is performed. For salaries, it is the period in which they are earned; for supplies or repairs, the period in which they are issued and used or the work done.

CONVENIENCE

Some items in practice are not handled as they theoretically should be, because it is inconvenient to do so and the difference is not very important. For example, supplies purchased are sometimes charged immediately to Supplies Expense instead of being charged to the Supplies (on hand) account even though they are not used at once. Again, the costs incurred to purchase goods, such as the buyer's salary, ideally should be identified with the goods and go into expense when the cost of the goods goes into Cost of Goods Sold. This would be complicated and also involves some uncertainties, so the buyer's salary is recognized as an expense of the period in which it is earned. In a fairly large concern the difference in the income statement caused by this treatment is not likely to be significant, since purchases and usage of supplies, for example, will be about equal over a year. The asset will not appear on the balance sheet, however, and this involves some error. In most companies it is insignificant.

In conclusion, it should be noted that costs incurred by a manufacturing concern to produce product give rise to an asset. These costs often have the same appearance as expenses in a merchandising concern—salaries, for example—but the services paid for are *used* differently. The accounting involved is discussed in the chapters on manufacturing.

ADJUSTING ENTRIES

Most of the revenues and expenses of a period are recorded during the period. This recording occurs as the revenue is earned, and the expenses identifiable with it or with the period are paid or recorded on receipt of bills or preparation of payrolls. Some transactions that must be recognized do not arise automatically and are recorded at the end of the period by *adjusting entries*. Adjusting entries are entries made at the end of the period to bring the accounts up to date so that accurate statements may be prepared. The adjustments involved at this point concern accrued revenue and expense, deferred revenue and expense, goods sold and supplies used, depreciation, and correction of errors and omissions.

NATURE OF ACCRUALS

The word *accrue* means to grow or increase. In a broad sense, it is used to distinguish accrual-basis accounting from cash-basis accounting. Under the *accrual basis*, revenues and expenses are recognized whether or not they are received or expended in cash at the time of recording. This is accrual accounting, the kind used by most business concerns and the kind discussed here.

Under the *cash basis*, revenues and expenses are recorded only when received or paid. In its narrowest sense, *accrue* refers only to those transactions that "grow" as time passes. A good example is interest on a debt; each day the amount of interest one must pay on an outstanding debt grows a little larger. The same is true of rent, salaries, income taxes, and similar items. The term is used in this narrow sense in connection with adjusting entries.

ACCRUED REVENUE

To record accrued revenue at the end of a period, an asset is debited and an income or revenue account is credited. For example, the Heald Investment Co. owns $10,000 of Clay Corporation bonds that pay 4 percent interest per year, half on March 31 and half on September 30. It closes its books annually on December 31. To record the interest Heald has earned since the last payment was received on September 30, it makes the following entry at December 31, 1966:

```
Accrued Interest Receivable...........................$ 100
     Interest Income.................................         $ 100
(to record interest for fourth quarter of 1960 on $10,000 of
Clay Corporation 4% bonds)
```

The *Accrued Interest Receivable* account is an asset representing the right to collect the interest accrued but not yet paid. It is similar to an account receivable growing out of the sale of goods, but differs in that the amount grows, or accrues, with time. The Interest Income account is a revenue account. In practice, the asset may be called simply "Accrued Interest," and a debit balance in the account will disclose that it is an asset, not a payable.

When the next interest is paid on March 31, 1967, Heald may make this entry:

```
Cash...........................  .......................$ 200
     Accrued Interest Receivable...................         $ 100
     Interest Income...............................           100
(to record collection of interest on $10,000 of Clay Corporation
4% bonds)
```

Another example of accrued income is the rental of trucks and other equipment of the Parkman Equipment Co., which closes its books on September 30. At September 30, 1966, the company had in the hands of renters various pieces of equipment on which the rental charges to September 30 totaled $6,248. The entry to record this accrual is:

```
Accrued Rent Receivable...........................$6,248
     Rental Income................................         $6,248
(to record rents accrued on equipment)
```

Rent on real estate is usually paid in advance, but if it is payable at the end of a period an accrual entry may be necessary. City Properties Co. has a warehouse on which the rent is $800 per month, payable on the fifteenth of each month for the period from the fifteenth of the last month to the fifteenth of the present one. When this company closes its books on December 31, the entry for accrued rent is:

Accrued Rent Receivable............................$ 400
      Rent Income................................. $ 400
(to record accrued rent on warehouse for the half month ended
Dec. 31, 1966)

ACCRUED EXPENSE

Accrued expense is recorded by a debit to an expense account and a credit to a liability account. The transaction is an "accrued liability" as well as an "accrued expense." Expenses that accrue include interest, rent, salaries or wages, and various taxes. For example, the interest receivable by Heald Investment Co., referred to in the preceding section, is an accrued expense to Clay Corporation. Clay Corporation also closes its books on December 31; its accrual of this item at December 31, 1966, is entered as follows:

Interest Expense...................................$ 100
      Accrued Interest Payable..................... $ 100
(to record accrued interest on $10,000 of 4% bonds out-
standing)

When the interest is paid on March 31, 1967, the payment may be recorded thus:

Accrued Interest Payable...........................$ 100
Interest Expense................................... 100
      Cash....................................... $ 200
(to record semiannual payment of interest on $10,000 4%
bonds outstanding)

Other examples of adjusting entries for accrued expenses follow.

Wages...$1,842
      Accrued Wages Payable...................... $1,842
(to record wages for last 3 days of December, 1966)

Real Estate Taxes.................................$ 90
      Accrued Real Estate Taxes.................. $ 90
(to record real estate taxes accruing during Oct., 1966)

Federal Income Tax................................$2,800
      Federal Income Tax Payable................. $2,800
(to record federal income tax payable on net income of July,
1966)

Such titles as "Wages Payable" or "Real Estate Taxes Payable" may be used instead of "Accrued Wages Payable" and so on.

DEFERRED REVENUE OR INCOME

Revenue collected in advance of the period in which it is earned must be *deferred*. In other words, it must be shown as a liability in the balance sheet until the period in which it is earned arrives. It is then taken into a revenue account. Examples of income commonly collected in advance are rent, subscriptions to magazines, sales of coupons or tokens redeemable in merchandise or services, insurance premiums, and theater admissions.

The nature of the adjustment made for deferred revenue at the end of a period depends upon the kind of entry made when the revenue was collected. The collection may be credited (1) to a deferred revenue (liability) account or (2) to a regular revenue account. In the first case an adjustment is needed at the end of the accounting period to remove the part earned, if any, from the deferred account. In the other case the adjustment takes out of the regular revenue account the part not yet earned.

DEFERRED REVENUE ADJUSTMENT — COLLECTIONS DEFERRED FROM THE START

The first case is illustrated by the transactions of Theatrical Productions, Inc. This company owns a theater and the adjoining lot and presents plays. The lot is rented to a parking-lot operator who pays six months' rent in advance every March 1 and September 1. The rent is $12,000 per year. The company records each collection like the following one for September 1, 1966:

Cash. $6,000	
Deferred Rent Income.	$6,000
(to record rent received on lot for the six months to February 28, 1967)	

When the books are closed for the month on September 30, 1966, this adjusting entry is made:

Deferred Rent Income. $1,000	
Rent Income.	$1,000
(to record rent earned for September, 1966)	

The same entry is made at the end of each succeeding month. Assuming that the lot was first rented on September 1, 1966, the Deferred Rent Income and Rent Income accounts will appear on December 31, 1966, as shown below.

MONTHLY CLOSING

THEATRICAL PRODUCTIONS, INC.

Deferred Rent Income[a]

Date		Explanation	Ref.	Debit		Date		Explanation	Ref.	Credit	
1966						1966					
Sept.	30		23	1 000	00	Sept.	1	6,000.00	20	6 000	00
Oct.	31		30	1 000	00			4,000.00			
Nov.	30		37	1 000	00			3,000.00			
Dec.	31		44	1 000	00			2,000.00			
	31	Balance		2 000	00						
				6 000	00					6 000	00
						1967					
						Jan.	1	Balance		2 000	00

[a]The Deferred Rent Income account may be ruled and balanced each month if desired; but when there are no more entries than here, it is not necessary.

Rent Income

Date	Explanation	Ref.	Debit	Date	Explanation	Ref.	Credit
1966				1966			
Sept. 30	To P & L	24	1 000 00	Sept. 30		23	1 000 00
Oct. 31	To P & L	31	1 000 00	Oct. 31		30	1 000 00
Nov. 30	To P & L	38	1 000 00	Nov. 30		37	1 000 00
Dec. 31	To P & L	45	1 000 00	Dec. 31		44	1 000 00

DEFERRED REVENUE ADJUSTMENT — COLLECTIONS CREDITED TO INCOME

The second case is also illustrated by transactions of Theatrical Productions, Inc. The company credits all ticket sales to the revenue account, in this manner:

```
Cash. . . . . . . . . . . . . . . . . . . . . . . . . . . . . . . . . . . . . . . . . . . .$160,000
        Admissions Income. . . . . . . . . . . . . . . . . . . . . . .        $160,000
        (to record ticket sales for September, 1966)
```

At the end of each month the value of tickets sold for performances in the next month or later is calculated by reference to the unsold ticket files (tickets not in the files for future performances have been sold). At September 30, 1966, the advance sales amounted to $4,200. The entry to adjust the revenue at this date is:

```
Admissions Income. . . . . . . . . . . . . . . . . . . . . . . . . . . . .$   4,200
        Deferred Admissions. . . . . . . . . . . . . . . . . . . . .        $   4,200
        (to record deferred income from ticket sales)
```

Most of this deferred income will be earned in October, so the whole amount is taken into income in October. If any belongs in November or later months, it will be taken out again by the November adjusting entry. The entry to transfer the income deferred at September 30 into the October revenue account is:

```
Deferred Admissions. . . . . . . . . . . . . . . . . . . . . . . . . . . .$   4,200
        Admissions Income. . . . . . . . . . . . . . . . . . . . . .        $   4,200
        (to transfer income deferred at Sept. 30 to October in-
        come account)
```

The Admissions Income and Deferred Admissions accounts for the period September 1 (season opening) to December 31, 1966, are shown below. The sales and deferred income during this period were as follows:

	Tickets Sold during the Month	Deferred Income at End of Month
September	$160,000	$4,200
October	185,000	4,800
November	190,000	5,200
December	200,000	5,500

Note that in making an adjustment for a deferred revenue item, one must first notice whether collections have been credited to an income or a deferred income account. The amount to be deferred can then be taken out of income or left in the deferred account as the case requires.

MONTHLY CLOSING

THEATRICAL PRODUCTIONS, INC.

Deferred Admissions

Date		Explanation	Ref.	Debit		Date		Explanation	Ref.	Credit	
1966						1966					
Oct.	1		24	4 200	00	Sept.	30		23	4 200	00
Nov.	1		31	4 800	00	Oct.	31		31	4 800	00
Dec.	1		37	5 200	00	Nov.	30		37	5 200	00
						Dec.	31		44	5 500	00

Admissions Income

Date		Explanation	Ref.	Debit		Date		Explanation	Ref.	Credit	
1966						1966					
Sept.	30		23	4 200	00	Sept.	30		22	160 000	00
	30	To P & L	24	155 800	00						
				160 000	00					160 000	00
Oct.	31		31	4 800	00	Oct.	1		24	4 200	00
	31	To P & L	31	184 400	00		31		29	185 000	00
				189 200	00					189 200	00
Nov.	30		37	5 200	00	Nov.	1		31	4 800	00
	30	To P & L	38	189 600	00		30		36	190 000	00
				194 800	00					194 800	00
Dec.	31		44	5 500	00	Dec.	1		37	5 200	00
	31	To P & L	45	199 700	00		31		43	200 000	00
				205 200	00					205 200	00

DEFERRED EXPENSE

Expenses paid in advance of the period to which they apply must be deferred. The deferred expense — often called prepaid expense — is an asset. It is a kind of investment in future services. Expenses frequently paid in advance include rent, insurance premiums, subscriptions to magazines, licenses, some taxes, and dues to organizations. Postage stamps and supplies on hand are commonly classified with prepaid expenses or "deferred charges." Tokens, coupons, and theater tickets are held chiefly by individuals who do not keep formal accounts, but may appear as assets in the accounts of business organizations that buy them.

Here again the adjusting entry needed at a closing date depends on the account used to record the payment. Two possibilities exist here, as in the case of deferred revenue: The payment may be charged (debited) (1) to a prepaid expense (asset) account or (2) to a regular expense account. A prepaid expense account is adjusted at the end of the period by removing the part "expired" — the amount of expense assignable to that period. This adjustment consists of a credit to the prepaid account and a debit to the proper expense account. If the payment was debited to a regular expense account, the adjustment removes from that account any prepaid portion. This adjustment consists of a credit to the expense account and a debit to the prepaid expense account.

DEFERRED OR PREPAID EXPENSE ADJUSTMENT — PAYMENT DEBITED TO PREPAID EXPENSE AT THE START

The first possibility is illustrated from the accounts of Harman Co. It purchased a 3-year fire insurance policy on July 1, 1966, paying a premium of $900. It recorded the purchase thus:

```
Prepaid Insurance...................................$900
     Cash..........................................          $900
(to record purchase of 3-year fire insurance policy)
```

On July 31, 1966 the following adjusting entry was made (the company closes its books monthly):

```
Insurance Expense...................................$ 25
     Prepaid Insurance..............................          $ 25
(to record insurance premium expired from July 1 to July 31, 1966)
```

The Prepaid Insurance and Insurance Expense accounts for this case are shown below; they cover the period from the purchase of the policy to the end of 1966.

MONTHLY CLOSING
HARMAN CO.
Prepaid Insurance[a]

Date		Explanation	Ref.	Debit	Date		Explanation	Ref.	Credit
1966					1966				
July	1	*875.00*	14	900	July	31		18	25 00
		850.00			Aug.	31		22	25 00
									50 00
		825.00			Sept.	30		26	25 00
									75 00
		800.00			Oct.	31		30	25 00
									100 00
		775.00			Nov.	30		34	25 00
									125 00
		750.00			Dec.	31		39	25 00
									150 00
						31	Balance		750 00
				900 00					900 00
1967									
Jan.	1	Balance		750 00					

Insurance Expense

Date		Explanation	Ref.	Debit	Date		Explanation	Ref.	Credit
1966					1966				
July	31		18	25 00	July	31	To P & L	19	25 00
Aug.	31		22	25 00	Aug.	31	To P & L	23	25 00
Sept.	30		26	25 00	Sept.	30	To P & L	27	25 00
Oct.	31		30	25 00	Oct.	31	To P & L	31	25 00
Nov.	30		34	25 00	Nov.	30	To P & L	35	25 00
Dec.	31		39	25 00	Dec.	31	To P & L	40	25 00

[a]The Prepaid Insurance account may be ruled and balanced monthly if desired; but where there are no more entries than here, it is not necessary.

DEFERRED OR PREPAID EXPENSE ADJUSTMENT — PAYMENT DEBITED TO EXPENSE ACCOUNT

Bridgeford, Inc., subscribes to several magazines and pays dues to some associations of which it is a member. These expenditures are recorded in an account for Dues and Subscriptions, an expense account. Most of the dues and subscriptions are for a calendar year, which is also the fiscal period of Bridgeford, Inc. However, a very few items are paid for a fiscal year different from the calendar year. These items result in some prepaid expense at December 31 of each year. These amounted to $230 at December 31, 1966, and the adjusting entry required on that date is:

```
Prepaid Dues and Subscriptions.........................$230
    Dues and Subscriptions..........................         $230
    (to record dues and subscriptions prepaid at December 31, 1966)
```

These items all become expense during the following year, so they are put back into the expense account on January 1, 1967, by this entry:

```
Dues and Subscriptions................................$230
    Prepaid Dues and Subscriptions....................         $230
    (to transfer prepaid dues and subscriptions to the expense account)
```

The Prepaid Dues and Subscriptions account and the Dues and Subscriptions account are shown here for the three years 1966 (inception of the company) through 1968. The accounts reflect the following data:

	Dues and Subscriptions	
	Prepaid at Dec. 31	Total expenditures (charged to expense)
1966	$230	$2,780
1967	245	2,610
1968	210	2,460

Note that in making an adjustment for deferred expense one must first determine whether expenditures have been debited to a prepaid (asset) account or to an expense account. The amount to be deferred can then be left in the prepaid account or taken out of the expense account as the case may be.

ANNUAL CLOSING
BRIDGEFORD, INC.
Prepaid Dues and Subscriptions

Date	Explanation	Ref.	Debit	Date	Explanation	Ref.	Credit
1966				1967			
Dec. 31		62	230 00	Jan. 1		64	230 00
1967				1968			
Dec. 31		108	245 00	Jan. 1		110	245 00
1968							
Dec. 31		152	210 00				

Dues and Subscriptions

Date	Explanation	Ref.	Debit	Date	Explanation	Ref.	Credit
1966	(Total of various debits)		2 780 00	1966 Dec. 31		62	230 00
				31	To P & L	63	2 550 00
			2 780 00				2 780 00
1967 Jan. 1		64	230 00	1967 Dec. 31		108	245 00
	(Total of various debits)		2 610 00	31	To P & L	109	2 595 00
			2 840 00				2 840 00
1968 Jan. 1		110	245 00	1968 Dec. 31		152	210 00
	(Total of various debits)		2 460 00	31	To P & L	153	2 495 00
			2 705 00				2 705 00

SUMMARY TABLE OF ACCRUALS AND DEFERMENTS

The nature of accruals and deferments is summarized briefly in a table that may help in keeping them in mind.

SUMMARY TABLE OF ACCRUALS AND DEFERMENTS		
	Not Yet Paid or Received (Accruals)	Paid or Received in Advance (Deferments)
Revenue	Accrued revenue (earned, not collected)	Deferred revenue (collected, not yet earned)
Expense	Accrued expense (incurred, not paid)	Deferred (prepaid) expense (paid for a future period)

GOODS SOLD AND SUPPLIES USED

An adjusting entry is ordinarily necessary to record cost of goods sold and the expense of supplies used, because it is usually inconvenient or expensive to record these items day by day. The amount of these expenses is commonly obtained by taking a "physical inventory," which means counting the items left on hand at any date. The price for each item is then looked up and multiplied by the quantity to get the amount. The amounts are added to get the total inventory. The inventory on hand is then deducted from the total of the goods acquired to compute the amount used up. If the total amount of goods acquired has been recorded in a single asset account for merchandise or supplies, the adjusting entry simply transfers the amount sold or used up to an expense account. The entries, already familiar from prior chapters, for goods sold costing $52,600 and supplies used costing $640 are:

```
Cost of Goods Sold.............................$52,600
      Merchandise..............................              $52,600
(to record cost of merchandise sold for the period)

Supplies Used..................................$    640
      Supplies.................................              $    640
(to record supplies used for the period)
```

If Supplies is an expense account in a particular ledger, the amount left on hand is removed by the adjusting entry and charged to Supplies on Hand or Supplies Inventory. The procedure in this case is the same as that given under the section on adjustment for deferred expense, where the payment is debited to the expense account (see p. 87). A more elaborate accounting for merchandise is used in practice and is taken up in later chapters.

DEPRECIATION

Depreciation is the cost involved in using up the investment in fixed assets other than land. These fixed assets are such items as machinery, furniture and fixtures, office equipment, automobiles, buildings, and so on. Some of these assets often seem permanent, but experience shows that they never prove to be so. A judge once recognized this principle in a case in which it was an issue by saying that "every asset is on an irresistible march to the grave." Depreciation occurs as a result of wear and tear, weathering, and the progress of invention. An asset that is no longer useful because it is outmoded is just as thoroughly used up for ordinary business purposes as one that has rusted away. It is therefore necessary to make an adjusting entry each period to record as expense a portion of the amount invested in the depreciable fixed assets. To make this entry it is necessary to estimate the useful life of each asset. The cost of an asset is commonly spread evenly over its expected life. Consider an automobile costing $4,000 that is expected to be traded in on a new car in five years with a trade-in value of $800. The depreciable amount is $3,200, or $640 per year. Assuming that the car was bought at the beginning of the calendar year 1966, the depreciation entry at December 31, 1966, may be made as follows:

```
Depreciation of Automobile............................$    640
      Automobile.....................................           $    640
(to record depreciation of auto for 1966)
```

In practice, a separate account is kept to accumulate the credits for depreciation which have been made in the asset account above. This account will be discussed in the next chapter.

ERRORS AND OMISSIONS

It is wise to look over the accounts and related records at the end of a fiscal period to see if anything needs correction and whether or not anything has been omitted. For example, a bill for goods or services may have been received that is not yet entered. Omissions present no special problem; the entry that should have been made in the regular course of business is made when the oversight is discovered. The correction of errors takes whatever form is necessary in light of the particular error. For example, check number 1420 was made out (properly) for $810 but entered as $180. It represented a payment for repairs that had not been previously recorded as a payable. The correcting entry in this case is:

Repairs. $630
       Cash. $630
(to correct entry of check No. 1420, entered as $180, should have been $810)

Corrections may be made at any time, but special care should be taken to make them all at a closing date, since the major object of the closing is to produce accurate statements.

SUMMARY

The proper calculation of net income requires a matching of revenues and expenses. Some expenses, such as cost of goods sold and salesmen's commissions, can easily be matched with revenue because they are directly related to it. Other expenses must be matched with revenue by relating the expenses to the accounting period in which they are incurred. The proper accounting period for expenses may be decided because of the need for objectivity (asset accounts cannot be created on the basis of personal opinion alone). It may be determined by the fact that some expenses are closely related to the passage of time, or, in insignificant cases, by convenience alone. Adjusting entries are needed at the end of a fiscal period to bring the accounts up to date for preparation of accurate statements. These include entries for revenues and expenses that have accrued, for deferring revenues and expenses that have been received or paid but which belong in a future period, for recognizing the cost of merchandise and supplies used, for recording depreciation of fixed assets, and for correction of errors and omissions.

QUESTIONS

3.1   Income has been characterized as a flow of wealth into an organization, that might be measured at various points: production, shipment, collection.

(1) Indicate an industry in which each basis of income recognition would be appropriate and explain the reason for your answer.

(2) Consolidated Electric Co. owns many corporations. These subsidiaries sell products and services to one another. Should revenue be recognized on such transfers? How would your answer differ if the subsidiaries were merely unincorporated divisions of Consolidated Electric Co.? Discuss.

3.2   (1) What is the difference between the cash and the accrual basis of income recognition?

(2) When is it appropriate to recognize income on a cash basis?

(3) List four types of adjustments required to convert income from a cash to an accrual basis. Give a numerical example of each.

3.3 State in each case when revenue may be recognized as earned, and your reason.

(1) An appliance repairman overhauls a motor.

(2) A bridge-building company comes to the end of its fiscal year with a large bridge half erected.

(3) Goods are shipped f.o.b. seller's factory.

(4) Goods are shipped f.o.b. destination.

(5) A financially responsible customer signs an order for a certain 1912 automobile for his antique collection, but asks that it be held three months for him while he is in Europe.

(6) Cash in the amount of $10,000 is borrowed from the First National Bank.

3.4 Revenue was recognized (and not subsequently adjusted) when the event or events described in each of the following cases occurred. State whether or not the recognition was proper for accrual accounting at that time, and your reason.

(1) A customer's order is received for ten boxes of twelve-penny nails. It is approved by the credit department.

(2) A repairman did some work a year ago, but waited until now to record the revenue because it took that long to collect the bill.

(3) A retail merchant sold some silverware to a customer, who took it with him. The merchant charged the customer's account.

(4) An order is received by a wholesale merchant. It is approved by the credit department, and a shipping order is sent to the shipping department. It specifies shipment f.o.b. destination.

(5) Goods are shipped f.o.b. shipping point by a merchant in response to a customer's order.

3.5 Why is revenue recognized when an article is sold under a conditional sales contract that specifies the vendor retains title to the goods?

3.6 In what two ways may expenses be associated with revenue? Give examples.

3.7 State in each case whether an expense was incurred in 1966, and your reason.

(1) Insurance is paid December 31, 1966, on a 3-year policy.

(2) Borrowed money on an interest-bearing note dated December 26, 1966. Interest is not due until maturity, six months after date of the note.

(3) Paid in 1966 a bonus based on 1965 sales.

(4) During 1966 paid freight on machinery and equipment purchased f.o.b. factory.

(5) Paid in December of 1966 for an advertising campaign. Management expects the advertising to benefit future accounting periods.

3.8 (1) What is meant by "matching costs and revenue"?

(2) International Airlines defers the costs of new routes and certain preoperating costs, then amortizes these charges against future revenues. Comment briefly on this accounting procedure relative to the general objective of matching costs and revenues. In a particular decision by management to defer or not to defer costs, can you see a conflict between the attempt to match costs and revenues on the one hand and the attempt to measure income objectively on the other hand?

(3) Do you think all airlines should follow the same accounting methods for preoperating costs?

(4) Comment briefly on the problem of securing uniformity in accounting practice within the industry.

3.9 Name five kinds of adjusting entries and state briefly what each kind does.

3.10 Identify each of the items below as one of the following: accrued revenue, accrued expense, deferred revenue, deferred expense.

(1) Rent for 1966 received on January 1, 1966, by the owner of a warehouse.

(2) Interest on a note due to a bank in four months. Interest is payable at maturity.

    (3) Cash received by a magazine publisher for subscriptions running through the next year.

    (4) Dues to a professional association for 1966 paid on January 2, 1966. Answer from the viewpoint of the paying member.

    (5) Interest at December 31, 1966, on an investment owned since July 1, 1966, that pays $200 per year each June 30.

3.11 (1) Would it be possible to keep accounts in such a manner that adjusting entries would not be required at the end of the fiscal period?

    (2) What is the relationship, if any, between the length of the accounting period and the number of adjusting entries?

    (3) Is the net income on a carefully prepared income statement an exact figure or an approximate figure?

    (4) What is the relationship between the length of the accounting period and the precision of income measurement?

3.12 "Entries which convert income from a cash basis to an accrual basis always affect both a real account and a nominal account. They never affect Cash." Discuss.

3.13 (1) Define "accrue" and "accrued receivable." Give three examples of accrued receivables.

    (2) Is Cash ever debited or credited to record an accrual? Why?

    (3) Which title do you prefer: Accrued Interest Payable, Accrued Interest, or Interest Payable? Why?

    (4) Under what circumstances, if any, would Accrued Interest Receivable appear in the income statement?

    (5) What is the difference between an accrued liability and any other liability?

3.14 (1) Define "deferred expense" and "deferred income." Give three examples of each.

    (2) What is the difference between accrued expense and prepaid expense? Describe transactions resulting in each.

    (3) Insurance paid may be charged either to an asset account or to an expense account. Describe the adjustment for each alternative and give illustrative journal entries for each.

    (4) The receipt of rent in advance may be credited either to a liability account or to an income account. Describe the adjustment for each alternative and give illustrative journal entries for each.

    (5) "Deferred income" has been called a misnomer. Why is it a misnomer? Suggest an alternative title.

3.15 (1) "The asset Plant and Equipment is logically similar to deferred expenses such as the payments in advance for rent, interest and taxes."—Henry Rand Hatfield. Compare depreciation of plant with the amortization of deferred expenses. Is the computation of expired services equally objective for both types of assets?

    (2) The owners of Concord Arms Hotel object to the recording of depreciation, contending that the building has not declined in value over recent years, but rather that it has appreciated with increased demand for hotel space. Discuss.

3.16 Marshall Stores charges both beginning inventory and purchases to a Merchandise Stock account. It takes a physical inventory at the end of each period. (1) Explain how the cost of goods sold is computed and recorded. (2) Prepare the entry to record the cost of goods sold if the balance of Merchandise Stock is $82,000 and the ending inventory is $12,000.

3.17 It was held in the case of New Capitol Hotel, Inc., that advance receipt of rental by an accrual-basis hotel was taxable income in the year received rather than in a subsequent year when earned. (1) Under what circumstances would this method of accounting result in a fair presentation of income? (2) How will it affect the presentation of financial condition?

3.18 Indicate for each of the following errors whether 1966 income is overstated or understated: (1) omitted accrued receivables at December 31, (2) omitted accrued payables at December 31, (3) understated merchandise inventory at December 31, (4) understated deferred expenses at December 31, (5) overstated deferred income at December 31.

EXERCISES

3.1 The following income statement was prepared from the check records of S. D. Hamilton at the end of his first year of operations.

HAMILTON AND CO.
INCOME STATEMENT
Year Ended December 31, 1966

Sales..............................		$55,000
Cost of Goods Sold		40,000
Gross Margin on Sales		$15,000
Expenses:............................		
Equipment	$10,000	
Other	20,000	30,000
Net (loss)		$(15,000)

Hamilton is vexed by the apparent loss. He finds the results of operations inconsistent with the net income he has obtained in managing a similar business for others during the past ten years. Your investigation reveals the statement was prepared on a cash basis:

(1) Sales represent only cash collected from customers; in addition to these collections, $5,000 of uncollected receivables were outstanding on December 31, 1966.

(2) Cost of goods sold represents the total merchandise purchased in 1966, of which $4,000 was on hand at December 31.

(3) The equipment purchased January 1 is expected to have a life of ten years.

Revise the income statement from a cash to an accrual basis.

3.2 The average payroll for a 5-day week at Dwan & Co. amounts to $4,000. (1) If December 31 falls on a Tuesday, what adjusting entry is required? (2) What entry would be made to pay the payroll of $4,000 in January of the following year? (3) State the effect on the income statement and on the balance sheet of failure to make the adjusting entry for accrued wages.

3.3 On January 1, 1966, Island Holidays paid $6,000 insurance for a 3-year period. What adjustment is required on December 31 if the payment was charged to an asset account? to an expense account?

3.4 Compute depreciation for 1966 on the following assets:

Asset	Date Acquired	Cost	Scrap Value	Life (years)
Store fixtures	1/1/64	$ 5,000	$ —	10
Office equipment	1/1/64	12,000	2,000	5
Electric sign	7/1/66	12,000	—	8
Motor vehicles	7/1/66	6,000	2,000	4

3.5   A comparative balance sheet for the S Co. as of December 31, 1966 and 1965, is as follows:

	December 31	
	1966	1965
Cash.	$ 6,000	$ 5,000
Receivables	15,000	4,000
Equipment	14,000	11,000
	$35,000	$20,000
Liabilities	9,000	8,000
B. T. Smith, Capital	$26,000	$12,000

Smith's drawings for 1966 were $6,000.

Required:

1. Compute the net income for 1966 from the above data.
2. Adjust the 1966 net income to reflect the following facts:
    (a) Omission of $2,000 of accrued payables at December 31, 1966
    (b) Omission of $1,000 of prepaid expenses at December 31, 1966
    (c) Omission of $500 of accrued receivables at December 31, 1965

3.6   On January 1, 1966, Doyle-McDuffie & Co. received $18,000 rent for a 3-year lease of properties owned by the company. What adjustment is required at December 31 if the receipt was credited to a liability account? to an income account?

3.7   The trial balance of Murphy Capital Corporation at December 31, 1966, was as follows:

MURPHY CAPITAL CORPORATION

TRIAL BALANCE

December 31, 1966

Cash.	$101,000	
Investments in Bonds	200,000	
Prepaid Insurance	2,500	
Deferred Commission Income		$ 4,000
Capital Stock		300,000
Interest Income.		21,000
Rent Expense	7,000	
Salaries Expense	11,500	
Office Expense	3,000	
	$325,000	$325,000

The data for adjustments at December 31, 1966, was:

(1) Accrued interest on bonds, $1,000
(2) Accrued salaries, $500
(3) Prepaid insurance, $1,500
(4) Prepaid rent, $1,000
(5) Commissions earned, $3,000

Prepare the income statement.

3.8   Submit the adjusting entries at December 31, 1966, for Universal Marine from the income statement and the unadjusted trial balance given below:

UNIVERSAL MARINE
INCOME STATEMENT
Year Ended December 31, 1966

Commissions Earned.................		$108,000
Expenses:..........................		
Salaries	$84,000	
Supplies..........................	1,000	
Rent	6,000	
Depreciation	1,000	92,000
Net income........................		$ 16,000

UNIVERSAL MARINE
TRIAL BALANCE
December 31, 1966

Cash..............................	$ 50,000	
Supplies	3,000	
Equipment	10,000	
Unearned Commissions................		$110,000
Capital Stock		30,000
Retained Earnings...................		10,000
Salaries...........................	80,000	
Rent..............................	7,000	
	$150,000	$150,000

3.9 The Hotel Continental completed the following transactions during 1966:

Oct. 1   Paid 6 months' rent at $10,000 per month, on leasing the property.

1   Paid 20,000 cash for leasehold improvements with an estimated useful life of five years.

1   Collected 6 months' rent at $1,000 per month from Michel Cartier, who will operate a restaurant on the first floor.

Dec. 1   Rented a shop to P. Patou for a beauty parlor. A monthly rent of 5 percent of gross income is due ten days after the end of the month.

31   Patou reported gross income of $4,000 for December (See December 1).

31   Property taxes from October 1 to December 31 are estimated at $600.

Required:

1. Draft journal entries to record the transactions in 1966.
2. Draft entries to record the year-end adjustments at December 31.

3.10 The X-L Corp. borrowed $10,000 on a 6 percent 90-day note on November 1, 1966. The company closes its books annually on December 31. Submit journal entries to record the accrual of interest on December 31, 1966, and the payment of the note and interest on January 30, 1967.

3.11 The Hillavator Co. holds the exclusive patent rights on a hillside elevator, which it licenses to manufacturers for a royalty. A schedule of royalty receipts, accrued royalties, and unearned royalties for the first three years of the company's operations is as follows:

	1965	1966	1967
Royalty receipts	$50,000	$100,000	$200,000
Accrued royalties	10,000	20,000	–
Unearned royalties	–	–	50,000

Compute the royalties earned by years.

3.12 The trial balance of C. Dana and Co. as of December 31, 1966, is shown below.

Cash	$37,700	
Supplies on Hand	500	
Accounts Payable......................		$ 3,500
Unearned Rent........................		1,500
C. Dana, Capital......................		20,000
Commissions Income		48,000
Salaries	25,500	
Rent.................................	6,000	
Insurance............................	1,800	
Taxes...............................	1,500	
	$73,000	$73,000

The books are adjusted and closed annually. Additional information follows:

(1) Commissions accrued December 31, $3,000.
(2) Salaries totaling $500 for a 5-day week are paid every Friday. December 31 of the current year falls on a Thursday.
(3) Supplies on hand December 31, $200.
(4) Insurance of $1,800 was paid January 1 for a 3-year policy.
(5) $1,500 was collected for office space rented for three months beginning December 1, 1966.

Required:

1. Adjusting entries.
2. Closing entries at December 31, 1966.

3.13 State the amount of revenue to be recognized in 1966 for each of the following items and give the reasons for your answers.

(1) A steamship company collected $50,000 in December 1966 for a cruise scheduled for January 1967.
(2) On December 1 an appliance service company collected $12,000 cash on service warranty policies. The company agreed to repair, without further charge for a period of one year from the date of warranty, appliances covered by the contracts.
(3) A construction company completes 40 percent of a bridge in 1966; the contract price is $5,000,000.
(4) Merchandise is sold for $1,000 f.o.b. shipping point. The goods were put in the hands of the carrier on December 28, 1966, and were received by the customer on January 5, 1967. No explicit agreement was made regarding the passage of title, and the goods were not identified by the buyer and the seller.
(5) Merchandise is sold for $1,000 f.o.b. destination. The goods were put in the hands of the carrier on December 28, 1966, and were received by the customer on January 5, 1967. No explicit agreement was made regarding the passage of title, and the goods were not identified by the buyer and the seller.
(6) Fabrication was completed December 30 on a special-order machine for $10,000. Delivery was postponed until after December 31, pending completion of construction work on the customer's factory.

(7) Merchandise is sold on December 15 for $5,000 with a 20 percent down payment on a conditional sales contract, legal title to the merchandise being retained by the vendor until the full contract price is collected in twenty equal monthly payments.

(8) The owner of a herd of cattle finds that the value of his livestock held for sale has increased $20,000 during 1966 because of births, reclassifications from calves to heifers, and reclassifications from heifers to cows.

(9) Machinery to be used on a company's production line was constructed in its own shop at a cost of $20,000, after the company had refused a bid of $25,000 for the job from an outside fabricator.

(10) Land acquired in 1956 at $50,000 is conservatively appraised in December 1966 at $120,000.

3.14 State the amount of expense to be recorded in 1966 for each of the following items:

(1) Paid $2,400 property taxes July 1 for the period July 1, 1966, to July 1, 1967.

(2) Paid $5,000 on January 1, 1966, for partitions and painting on leased premises. The term of the lease is five years from January 1, 1966.

(3) Paid $2,000 on January 2, 1966, for interest accrued during 1965.

(4) Paid $1,000 on January 14, 1967, for payroll taxes applicable to 1966 wages.

(5) Paid $5,000 on December 28, 1966, for an advertising campaign completed in 1966. The vice president of marketing estimates the campaign will contribute $10,000 to profits in early 1967.

PROBLEMS

3.1 C. D. Roe, a wheat farmer from Alberta, Canada, tells you he is in trouble with the U. S. Internal Revenue Service. He has been wintering in southern California the past few years, expecting to retire there eventually. On January 1, 1966, he purchased a cooperative apartment, which he rented for most of 1966. A "tax expert," who set up his office in the local supermarket during tax season, prepared his 1966 income tax return, including the following schedule of rents:

Total rents received		$4,800
Less:		
Repayment of mortgage debt	$4,080	
Maintenance payments	1,200	5,280
Net (loss) from rents		($ 480)

You find the rents received to be correct. You also find the maintenance payments, which comprise repairs, taxes, and other expenses, to be correct and proper deductions. Of course, the mortgage payments are not.

You also learn that the apartment was purchased on January 1, 1966, for $40,000, subject to a mortgage of $30,000. Of the mortgage payments during the year, $1,500 applies to interest and $2,580 to principal. Depreciation on the building is allowable for tax purposes at the rate of 10 percent.

Required:

1. Prepare a revised schedule of rent income.
2. Draft a brief note to Roe explaining the difference between net income and cash flow.

3.2 Prepare adjusting and closing entries for the year ended December 31, 1966, from the following trial balance and data for adjustments:

ACME PAINT SHOP
Trial Balance
December 31, 1966

Cash	$ 800	
Notes Receivable	5,000	
Supplies on Hand	1,200	
Land	10,000	
Capital Stock		$10,000
Retained Earnings—January 1, 1966		4,600
Dividends	2,000	
Service Revenue		12,000
Rent Revenue		2,600
Salaries and Wages	7,000	
Advertising Expense	2,100	
Office Expense	1,200	
Miscellaneous Expense	200	
Interest Income		300
	$29,500	$29,500

Data for adjustments at December 31, 1966:

(1) Accrued interest receivable, $100
(2) Accrued wages payable, $500
(3) Supplies on hand, $400
(4) Prepaid advertising, $300
(5) Rents received but not earned, $200

3.3 During 1966, the first year of operations, the Fairchild Co. completed the following transactions, among others:

(1) Paid fire insurance premiums for the period April 1, 1966, to April 1, 1967, $8,000.
(2) Received $9,000 representing advance rental for a portion of the company's properties for the period September 1, 1966, to March 1, 1967.

Prepare adjusting entries, assuming:

  1. The transactions were recorded initially in asset and liability accounts.
  2. The transactions were recorded initially in income and expense accounts.

3.4 St. Helena Vintners completed the following transactions during 1966, its first year of operations.

(1) Paid $9,000 rent for the period August 1, 1966, to August 1, 1967.
(2) Received $2,700 royalties on a patented process for the period October 1, 1966, to June 30, 1967.

Prepare adjusting entries at December 31, 1966, assuming:

  1. The original transactions were recorded in real accounts.
  2. The original transactions were recorded in nominal accounts.

3.5 Prepare adjusting entries from the following information regarding Lake, Inc., for the year ended June 30, 1966:

(1) Wages of $2,000 for the last three days of June were paid with the rest of the wages earned in the week ended July 2.
(2) Insurance premiums, charged to Prepaid Insurance when paid, expired in the amount of $600 during the fiscal year.
(3) The Merchandise account, which contains the beginning inventory and purchases, has a balance of $36,000. At June 30, 1966, $4,000 of the merchandise was still on hand.
(4) Dues and subscriptions, charged to expense when paid, apply to the period subsequent to June 30, 1966, in the amount of $400.

(5) Rent was received April 1, 1966, in the amount of $4,000 to cover the four months from April 1 to August 1, 1966, and was credited to Rents Received in Advance.

3.6 Consolidated Van and Storage Company closes its books annually on September 30. Prepare adjusting entries as required by the data below for September 30, 1966.

(1) All purchases of supplies were charged to Supplies Expense. At September 30, $200 of supplies was still on hand.

(2) On July 1, 1966, $12,000 rent on a new warehouse was paid for a year in advance. Prepaid Rent was debited for the payment.

(3) The company borrowed $50,000 on a note payable dated April 1, 1966, due April 1, 1967 with interest at 6 percent.

(4) Storage charges paid in advance by customers were credited to Storage Income. At September 30, 1966, $4,000 of these credits was unearned.

(5) Storage charges accumulated on goods stored for others during the year amounted to $8,000 at September 30, 1966. No customer will be billed until his goods are withdrawn and the specific charge to him is ascertained.

3.7 Prepare dated journal entries for the following transactions of the Regent Company. The company closes its books annually on June 30.

Feb. 1   Borrowed $5,000 at the bank on a 2-month 6 percent note.
Apr. 1   Paid the note and interest.
May 1   Borrowed $10,000 on a 3-month 6 percent promissory note.
June 30   Recorded the adjusting and the closing entries.
July 1   Paid the note and interest.

3.8 Following are some transactions of the Saxton Company.

Jan. 1   Received $50,000 proceeds from a promissory note issued to Equity Capital Corporation. Interest at 6 percent per year is payable on June 30 and December 31.
June 30   Paid interest on the note.
Sept. 30   Recorded the adjusting and the closing entries.
Dec. 31   Paid interest on the note.

Required:

1. Prepare dated journal entries. The company closes its books annually on September 30.
2. Prepare the entries for March 31 and June 30, assuming the company closes quarterly instead of annually.

3.9 The Kona Press completed its first year of operations on December 31, 1966. The trial balance at that date contained, among other items, the balances listed below:

Notes Receivable......................	$10,000
Prepaid Insurance	1,200
Tools	5,000
Deferred Subscription Revenues	64,000
Debentures Payable....................	60,000
Rent Income	6,000
Supplies Expense.....................	3,200

Additional information obtained from the company records is as follows:

(1) The note receivable, dated August 1, pays 6 percent interest per year, half on February 1 and half on August 1.

(2) Interest on the debentures, dated March 1, is payable annually at the rate of 8 percent per year.

(3) Cash collections during the year on annual subscriptions to a quarterly publication printed by the company are as follows:

Quarter	Amount
First	$12,000
Second	8,000
Third	24,000
Fourth	20,000
Total	$64,000

The subscriptions begin in the quarter following receipt of the cash. For example, the subscriptions received during the first quarter are earned in the year beginning April 1.

(4) Land owned by the company was rented on June 1 at an annual rent of $6,000, payable in advance.

(5) The insurance premiums are for a 3-year policy beginning January 1, 1966.

(6) The inventory of supplies on hand December 31 amounted to $800.

(7) Tools are estimated to have a useful life of ten years. (Credit the Tools account directly.)

Draft the year-end adjusting entries with explanations.

3.10 The trial balance of the XYZ Company appears below. The books are closed semiannually June 30 and December 31.

XYZ COMPANY
TRIAL BALANCE
December 31, 1966

Cash.	$ 3,700	
Accounts Receivable.	5,100	
Notes Receivable	5,000	
Merchandise	30,200	
Store Supplies Inventory	360	
Prepaid Insurance	300	
Leasehold Improvements.	22,000	
Accounts Payable		$10,590
Property Taxes Payable		200
6% Bonds Payable		10,000
Capital Stock		20,595
Sales		35,000
Rent Income.		2,400
Office Supplies Expense	410	
Selling Expenses.	2,500	
Wages and Salaries Expense	9,215	
	$78,785	$78,785

Give adjusting entries, when necessary, for the following data:

(1) Wages accrued at December 31, $130.

(2) The only note receivable is a 4-month 8 percent note dated October 1.

(3) Store supplies on hand December 31, $120.

(4) Office supplies on hand December 31, $150.

(5) Merchandise inventory December 31, $7,800.

(6) Unexpired insurance at December 31, $120.

(7) Leasehold improvements represents the cost of a building constructed on leased land. The lease expires twenty years from June 30, 1966.

(8) Unpaid property taxes at December 31, $800.

(9) Interest on the bond issue is payable July 1 and January 1.

(10) Cash of $3,600 was received April 1 for 9 months' rent of the second floor of the building.

3.11 The following account balances were taken from the ledger of the Anchor Co. on
March 31, 1966:

Notes Receivable....................	$ 1,000
Notes Payable......................	2,500
Sales.............................	30,000
Store Supplies on Hand................	75
Employer Payroll Deductions...........	312
Bank.............................	1,140
Prepaid Insurance..................	230
Salaries Expense...................	3,200
Tax Expense.......................	490
Cost of Sales......................	14,000
Furniture and Fixtures................	3,300
Rent Expense......................	1,200
Insurance........................	335
Capital Stock......................	7,800
Employer Payroll Taxes Payable.........	128
Supplies Used.....................	960
Retained Earnings..................	3,250
Cash Register Fund..................	350
Merchandise Stock..................	12,470
Miscellaneous Expense...............	2,450
Accounts Receivable.................	1,360
Accounts Payable...................	790
Sales Tax Payable...................	900
Delivery Equipment..................	3,120

Journalize the closing entries.

3.12 The accountant for Elizabeth Foods Co. left the country shortly after he prepared the income statement for the year ended February 28, 1966. The adjustments had not yet been posted to the ledger.

From the trial balance and income statement below, draft the entries required
to adjust and close the books for the year.

ELIZABETH FOODS CO.
TRIAL BALANCE
February 28, 1966

Cash.............................	$ 23,900	
Accounts Receivable..................	42,000	
Merchandise and Products..............	471,200	
Prepaid Insurance....................	6,100	
Plant and Equipment (net).............	73,000	
Accounts Payable....................		$ 13,300
Common Stock......................		50,000
Retained Earnings...................		93,000
Sales.............................		606,000
Rent Income.......................		3,000
Salaries and Wages..................	74,100	
Supplies..........................	43,000	
Utilities...........................	19,000	
Taxes............................	6,200	
Repairs and Maintenance...............	6,800	
	$765,300	$765,300

ELIZABETH FOODS CO.
INCOME STATEMENT
Year Ended February 28, 1966

Sales.............................		$606,000
Cost of Goods Sold....................		456,000
Gross Margin on Sales................		$150,000
Expenses:............................		
Salaries and Wages	$76,000	
Supplies............................	38,000	
Utilities............................	19,000	
Taxes	9,000	
Repairs and Maintenance	6,800	
Depreciation	6,000	
Insurance	4,800	159,600
Net loss from operations		($ 9,600)
Rent Income.........................		2,400
Net loss for the year		($ 7,200)

3.13 The trial balance of The Ritz French Restaurant at December 31, 1966, and the data needed for year-end adjustments are presented below.

THE RITZ FRENCH RESTAURANT
TRIAL BALANCE
December 31, 1966

Cash.............................	$ 5,000	
Inventory	10,000	
Prepaid Insurance	4,000	
Land.............................	100,000	
Building and Equipment (net)............	100,000	
Taxes Payable.......................		$ 1,000
R. Descartes, Capital.................		200,000
R. Descartes, Drawing	5,000	
Sales.............................		227,000
Cost of Sales........................	118,000	
Labor	60,000	
Payroll Taxes	10,000	
Laundry and Linen	8,000	
Heat, Light, and Power	7,000	
Repairs and Maintenance..............	6,000	
Advertising and Promotion	5,000	
Licenses and Sundry Taxes	2,000	
Miscellaneous Expense	1,000	
Rent Income........................		13,000
	$441,000	$441,000

Data for adjustments:

(1) Accrued payroll taxes at December 31 are $2,000.

(2) Depreciation for the year amounts to 10 percent of the December 31 unadjusted balance of net buildings and equipment.

(3) Insurance expired for the year is $3,000.

(4) Advertising and promotion includes payments of $1,000 for TV shows to be aired in January and February of 1967.

(5) The inventory taken on December 31, 1966, amounts to $15,000.

(6) The parking lot is sublet to a concessionnaire for $1,000 per month.

Required:

1. Prepare adjusting entries with explanations.
2. Prepare closing entries. (The Drawings account is closed to Capital at the end of each year.)
3. Descartes is undecided as to whether he should continue in business. He has been offered $120,000 for that half of the land now used as a parking lot. Draft a brief comment, including computations of the ratio of net operating income to sales and net income to capital invested at the beginning of the year.

4

Matching Costs and Revenue

and the Work Sheet

This chapter continues the discussion of expenses that must be recognized to obtain a proper matching of costs and revenue. It also describes some special accounts and the technique of using a work sheet. The following topics are taken up:

1. Merchandise accounts
2. Accumulated depreciation
3. Bad debts and allowance for doubtful accounts
4. Tax accruals
5. The work sheet

MERCHANDISE ACCOUNTS

The use of a single asset account for merchandise is already familiar from prior chapters. Such an account may be used in practice in precisely the way it has been described, but a slightly more elaborate procedure is usually used. Two different methods of accounting for merchandise are common. These are (1) perpetual inventory method, (2) periodic inventory method.

PERPETUAL INVENTORY METHOD

In this method an asset account is kept for merchandise, with purchases being debited and the cost of goods sold being credited to that account. The account therefore gives a running record of the merchandise on hand. The method also customarily includes a separate, or subsidiary, record of each kind of merchandise carried. This "stores" record, or ledger, has a sheet or account for each article. Each sheet shows the units, price, and dollar amount of that article on hand. Units purchased are shown with their price and amount; units issued are similarly entered. A running balance of units and amount is ordinarily calculated. By means of this subsidiary stores record and related documents, entries for cost of goods sold can be made frequently. This method is used by manufacturing concerns that need to know what materials are on hand at all times. It is also used in merchandising activities where its higher cost is not prohibitive and where it is necessary to keep close check on the merchandise. For example, it is used by stores carrying expensive jewelry, by fur shops, and by furniture stores. When the perpetual inventory method is used, it is still necessary to count the stock now and then. Otherwise, errors in the record or in handling merchandise, deterioration, or theft of stock may go unnoticed.

PERIODIC INVENTORY METHOD

Most merchandising concerns use the periodic inventory method. This means that they get the inventory figures for the balance sheet and the cost of goods sold figure only at the end of the accounting period. The figures are obtained after a physical inventory is taken, which involves counting, listing, pricing, extending (multiplying prices by quantities), and footing (adding) to get the final inventory figure. Beginning inventory plus purchases minus the ending inventory gives cost of goods sold. This procedure is usually employed just once a year. Some firms that close their books more often take a physical inventory more often, but frequent physical inventorying is too expensive for most of them. The latter firms often get monthly or quarterly statements by using estimated inventory figures.

Merchandising companies customarily use the asset account for inventory only to record the amount obtained periodically from the physical count. The record of purchases made during the period is accumulated in a separate account called *Purchases*. The calculation of cost of goods sold is made by bringing together the information about beginning and ending inventory and purchases in the adjusting and closing process at the end of a period. A separate account may be used for cost of goods sold, or the figure may be calculated on the income statement without the use of an account.

ENTRIES ILLUSTRATING PERIODIC INVENTORY METHOD

Journal entries in the following sections show how the inventory figures are recorded under the periodic inventory method. The entries are posted to the accounts shown on pages 107–108. Two procedures are shown: with and without a Cost of Goods Sold account. The beginning inventory, recorded last period, is $14,000, and the ending inventory is $13,000. Purchases were made on March 31 and August 31.

INVENTORY RECORDED WITH COST OF GOODS SOLD ACCOUNT

In this illustration, two purchases of merchandise were made, but in practice there would be many more in a period:

Purchases..$16,000		
Accounts Payable or Cash....................		$16,000
(to record merchandise purchased)		

Purchases..$12,000		
Accounts Payable or Cash....................		$12,000
(to record merchandise purchased)		

Adjusting and closing entries:

Cost of Goods Sold.............................	$14,000	
Merchandise..............................		$14,000
(to close opening inventory to Cost of Goods Sold)		
Cost of Goods Sold.............................	$28,000	
Purchases.................................		$28,000
(to close Purchases to Cost of Goods Sold)		
Merchandise....................................	$13,000	
Cost of Goods Sold........................		$13,000
(to record ending inventory of merchandise)		
Profit and Loss..................................	$29,000	
Cost of Goods Sold........................		$29,000
(to close Cost of Goods Sold)		

INVENTORY RECORDED WITHOUT COST OF GOODS SOLD ACCOUNT

This illustration uses the same figures as above. When the Cost of Goods Sold account is omitted, the entries that would otherwise be posted to it are posted directly to the Profit and Loss account. The accounts both for this and for the procedure described above are shown on pages 107–108.

Purchases.......................................	$16,000	
Accounts Payable or Cash...................		$16,000
(to record merchandise purchased)		
Purchases.......................................	$12,000	
Accounts Payable or Cash...................		$12,000
(to record merchandise purchased)		

Adjusting and closing entries:

Profit and Loss..................................	$14,000	
Merchandise..............................		$14,000
(to close opening inventory to Profit and Loss)		
Profit and Loss..................................	$28,000	
Purchases................................		$28,000
(to close purchases to Profit and Loss)		
Merchandise....................................	$13,000	
Profit and Loss...........................		$13,000
(to set up ending merchandise inventory)		

MERCHANDISE INVENTORY IN THE INCOME STATEMENT

Figures on inventories and purchases are often shown in the income statement whether or not a Cost of Goods Sold account is used. These figures develop the cost of goods sold amount, and are taken from the Cost of Goods Sold account or the Profit and Loss account, as the case may be. The following section of an income statement shows the presentation of the data used in the illustrations above.

Sales.		$48,000
Cost of Goods Sold:		
Inventory January 1, 1966	$14,000	
Purchases.	28,000	
	$42,000	
Deduct: Ending Inventory.	13,000	
Cost of Goods Sold		29,000
Gross Margin on Sales.		$19,000

Purchases is an asset account in so far as it represents merchandise on hand. It is an expense account in so far as it represents merchandise that has been sold. The same is true of the Merchandise account at any time after the close of business on the ending day of a period, because units of the merchandise are continually being sold. Such accounts are called *mixed accounts*, because they contain elements of both asset and expense at most times. Some mixed accounts contain elements of liability and income. For example, Deferred subscriptions is a liability on the closing date, but some of it is earned in the next month when the publication is delivered. One of the purposes of the

MERCHANDISE INVENTORY ACCOUNTS

I. With Cost of Goods Sold Account

Merchandise

Date		Explanation	Ref.	Debit	Date		Explanation	Ref.	Credit
1966					1966				
Jan.	1	Balance		14 000 00	Dec.	31		47	14 000 00
Dec.	31		49	13 000 00		31	Balance		13 000 00
				27 000 00					27 000 00
1967									
Jan.	1	Balance		13 000 00					

Purchases

Date		Explanation	Ref.	Debit	Date		Explanation	Ref.	Credit
1966					1966				
Mar.	31		18	16 000 00	Dec.	31		48	28 000 00
Aug.	31		32	12 000 00					
				28 000 00					28 000 00

Cost of Goods Sold

Date	Explanation	Ref.	Debit	Date	Explanation	Ref.	Credit
1966				1966			
Dec. 31		47	14 000 00	Dec. 31		49	13 000 00
31		48	28 000 00	31		50	29 000 00
			42 000 00				42 000 00

Profit and Loss

Date	Explanation	Ref.	Debit	Date	Explanation	Ref.	Credit
1966							
Dec. 31		50	29 000 00				

MERCHANDISE INVENTORY ACCOUNTS

II. Without Cost of Goods Sold Account

Merchandise

Date	Explanation	Ref.	Debit	Date	Explanation	Ref.	Credit
1966				1966			
Jan. 1	Balance		14 000 00	Dec. 31		47	14 000 00
Dec. 31		49	13 000 00	31	Balance		13 000 00
			27 000 00				27 000 00
1967							
Jan. 1	Balance		13 000 00				

Purchases

Date	Explanation	Ref.	Debit	Date	Explanation	Ref.	Credit
1966				1966			
Mar. 31		18	16 000 00	Dec. 31		48	28 000 00
Aug. 31		32	12 000 00				
			28 000 00				28 000 00

Profit and Loss

Date	Explanation	Ref.	Debit	Date	Explanation	Ref.	Credit
1966				1966			
Dec. 31		47	14 000 00	Dec. 31		49	13 000 00
31		48	28 000 00				

end-of-period adjusting entries is to separate the assets from expenses and the liabilities from revenues in accounts where both are present. This separation is accomplished in the periodic inventory method, when the ending inventory (asset) is recorded and thereby deducted from beginning inventory plus purchases to get cost of goods sold (expense).

ACCUMULATED DEPRECIATION

In the preceding chapter depreciation was recorded by debiting an expense account and crediting the asset account. In practice the credit is almost always carried in a separate account that shows the amount of depreciation accumulated against the asset. This account may be called *Accumulated Depreciation, Allowance for Depreciation*, or *Reserve for Depreciation*. "Reserve," the older term, is in disfavor with authorities because it has been used in too many ways. The term Accumulated Depreciation, which is growing in popularity and is particularly apt, is used in this text.

Each ledger account for a depreciable asset is accompanied by an Accumulated Depreciation account. Thus we have an account for Buildings and one for Accumulated Depreciation on Buildings. We have an account for Office Equipment and one for Accumulated Depreciation on Office Equipment. The amount of accumulated depreciation is deducted from the cost figure as shown in the regular asset account when a balance sheet is prepared. A reasonably detailed balance sheet shows both the original cost figure and the accumulated depreciation figure. The fixed asset section of a balance sheet may therefore have this appearance:

Fixed Assets:			
Land		$16,000	
Building	82,000		
Less: Accumulated Depreciation	22,000	60,000	
Machinery and Equipment	$124,000		
Less: Accumulated Depreciation	42,000	82,000	
Total Fixed Assets			$158,000

Accounts that are deducted from asset accounts are called contra-asset, deduction, or valuation accounts. They are part of the information about the asset account but are carried separately for convenience. It is easier to get the amount of accumulated depreciation if it is not mixed up in the regular asset account with other entries, which include additions to and other deductions from the amount originally invested in the fixed asset, such as sales or retirements.

BAD DEBTS AND ALLOWANCE FOR DOUBTFUL ACCOUNTS

Concerns that sell goods or render service on credit take precautions against extending credit to persons or organizations that may not be able to pay. Nevertheless, experience has shown that some accounts receivable prove to be uncollectible. Sales revenue that is never collected cannot give rise to net income, so some provision for deducting the amount not collected must be made. Making this provision is complicated by the fact that the particular customer who cannot or does not pay cannot be identified, as a rule, until long after the sale is made. Hence a deduction made only when the uncollectibility is finally discovered comes too late. The income statement of the period in which the uncollectible sale was made is past history by that time. The solution is to *estimate* the amount that may prove uncollectible. This estimate can be made on the basis of past experience. The entry to record estimated bad debts of $1,800 for a period is:

```
Bad Debts...........................................$1,800
    Allowance for Doubtful Accounts.................            $1,800
(to record estimate of bad debts for the period)
```

Allowance for Doubtful Accounts was formerly called Reserve for Bad Debts, a term still widely used in practice. It is in disfavor with accounting authorities for the same reason that Reserve for Depreciation is frowned upon. Allowance for Bad Debts is also used, but many accountants prefer to refer to the accounts as in part "doubtful" until actual uncollectibility is established.

The Allowance account is used instead of crediting Accounts Receivable for two reasons: (1) the particular customer cannot yet be identified, so one cannot tell which account to remove from the list; (2) the separate account permits showing in the statements the amount billed and the part not claimed as collectible, and this separation improves the information given. When a particular account is discovered to be uncollectible, it is "written off" as follows:

```
Allowance for Doubtful Accounts........................$  400
    Accounts Receivable............................            $  400
(to write off uncollectible account of A. B. Estor Company)
```

This entry may be thought of as bringing together the debit and the credit that removes it, this having been impossible before because the particular item that was uncollectible could not be identified.

BAD DEBTS AND ALLOWANCE FOR DOUBTFUL ACCOUNTS IN THE STATEMENTS

The Allowance for Doubtful Accounts is a contra-asset, deduction, or valuation account. It is deducted from Accounts Receivable in the balance sheet. Its function in the balance sheet is to eliminate from the accounts receivable the amount that may not be collected. When there is an Allowance for Doubtful Accounts, the accounts receivable section of the balance sheet has the following appearance:

```
Accounts Receivable...................................$29,468
    Less: Allowance for Doubtful Accounts.................   1,628
                                                                  $27,840
```

Opinion differs among accountants as to the place of the Bad Debts account in the income statement. The most widespread practice, which is to show it as a general and administrative expense, is advocated on the theory that the officers who approve credits and those responsible for collections are responsible for the bad debts figure. This practice excludes the item from the selling expenses, but gives no consideration to the question of whether or not the deduction should be made directly from sales revenue. Many accountants wish to show in revenue only the amount of cash that can be expected to come in from customers (if it has not already been collected in cash). They say that showing amounts *charged* to customers but not expected to be *collected* from them presents a misleading figure for revenue. From this viewpoint the estimated bad debts should be deducted from sales revenue to get a net sales figure, the method followed in this text. The sales section of an income statement with deduction for bad debts has the following appearance:

```
Sales .................................... $228,967
    Less: Bad Debts ......................     5,100
        Net Sales Revenue ................               $223,867
```

PROPERTY TAXES

Local governments assess taxes each year on the value of personal and real property (real estate). Several months may elapse between the assessment date and the payment dates. Often the payment may be made in two installments. This variety of significant dates raises a question as to the period in which the tax should be shown as an expense. The date favored by the American Institute of Certified Public Accountants for beginning the accrual of property taxes is the beginning of the fiscal year of the governmental unit levying them.[1] In this way the tax expense is spread over the year in which the government uses the money. For example, Bestor Co. acquired property on June 30, 1966, in a county with a fiscal year beginning July 1. The tax for the year beginning July 1, 1966, is $6,000. If the accrual is to be made monthly, the entry for July is:

```
Property Taxes............................... $ 500
    Property Taxes Payable ................            $ 500
    (to record property-tax accrual for July)
```

Property Taxes is an expense account. Payments are debited to the liability account, Property Taxes Payable. If payments are required so that the tax is fully paid up before the end of the government's fiscal year, prepaid property tax will be recorded. At the time of such a payment, the debit may be divided between the amount needed to eliminate the credit balance in Property Taxes Payable, any portion assignable to the current month as expense, and the charge to Prepaid Property Taxes. The prepaid tax is then written off month by month with debits going to Property Taxes. For example, Bestor Co. pays the first half of the annual tax on December 10 and the last half on April 5. Accrual entries are made monthly except in months when payments are made. The payment entries then are:

```
Dec. 10  Property Taxes Payable ..................... $2,500
         Property Taxes .............................      500
             Cash...................................              $3,000
         (to record payment of first half of 1966–1967 property
         taxes)

Apr. 5   Property Taxes Payable ..................... $1,500
         Property Taxes .............................      500
         Prepaid Property Taxes .....................    1,000
             Cash...................................              $3,000
         (to record payment of second half of 1966–1967 property
         taxes)
```

[1] *Restatement and Revision of Accounting Research and Terminology Bulletins*, Chapter 10 (AICPA, 666 Fifth Avenue, New York, N. Y. 10019.)

Bestor Co. closes its books annually on December 31. Its property tax accounts, including the monthly accruals, the prepaid tax, and the monthly writeoff of the prepayment, are shown on this page and page 113.

INCOME TAXES

Income taxes are levied by the federal and state governments on the net income of individuals and corporations. In the eyes of the law, a corporation is an artificial person separate from its owners. No income taxes are levied on sole proprietorships or partnerships as such, because these organizations are only the owners acting in their natural capacities. Individual proprietors and partners must include in their personal tax returns any income earned by operating the proprietorship or the partnership. No income taxes appear in the statements of the latter organizations, because they are not subject to the tax. Income taxes do appear in the statements of corporations. The "net income" shown in the conventional corporate income statement is the net income earned by the stockholders. To get this figure, any amount paid or pay-

PROPERTY TAX ACCOUNTS
(with Monthly Entries but Annual Closing at December 31)

BESTOR CO.

Property Taxes

Date		Explanation	Ref.	Debit		Date		Explanation	Ref.	Credit	
1966						1966					
July	31		77	500	00	Dec.	31	To P & L	103	3 000	00
Aug.	31		82	500	00						
				1 000 00							
Sept.	30		87	500	00						
				1 500 00							
Oct.	31		92	500	00						
				2 000 00							
Nov.	30		97	500	00						
				2 500 00							
Dec.	10		98	500	00						
				3 000	00					3 000	00
1967											
Jan.	31		107	500	00						
Feb.	28		112	500	00						
				1 000 00							
Mar.	31		117	500	00						
				1 500 00							
Apr.	5		118	500	00						
				2 000 00							
May	31		127	500	00						
				2 500 00							
June	30		132	500	00						
				3 000 00							

able as income tax must be deducted from revenue. From the viewpoint of the stockholders it is an expense. It is shown last in the income statement because it is calculated on income left after other expenses are deducted from revenue.

Tax rates and rules change from time to time. Recently the federal government established a corporate tax rate of 22 percent on the first $25,000 of net income and 48 percent on all income above $25,000. State income taxes vary, from zero to 8 percent (at present).

ILLUSTRATION OF ACCRUAL OF FEDERAL INCOME TAX

Photomat Corp. closes its books annually on December 31. During 1966 its net income, before income taxes, was $68,000. Its federal income tax for 1966 is computed as follows:

$$
\begin{array}{rll}
\text{First } \$25,000 \times 22\% = & \$\ 5,500 \\
\text{Remaining } \underline{\ 43,000} \times 48\% = & \underline{\ 20,640} \\
\text{Total } \underline{\underline{\$68,000}} & \underline{\underline{\$26,140}}
\end{array}
$$

Property Taxes Payable

Date	Explanation	Ref.	Debit	Date	Explanation	Ref.	Credit
1966				1966			
Dec. 10		98	2 500 00	July 31		77	500 00
				Aug. 31		83	500 00
							1 000 00
				Sept. 30		87	500 00
							1 500 00
				Oct. 31		92	500 00
							2 000 00
				Nov. 30		97	500 00
							2 500 00
			2 500 00				2 500 00
1967				1967			
Apr. 5		118	1 500 00	Jan. 31		107	500 00
				Feb. 28		112	500 00
				Mar. 31		117	500 00
			1 500 00				1 500 00

Prepaid Property Taxes

Date	Explanation	Ref.	Debit	Date	Explanation	Ref.	Credit
1967				1967			
Apr. 5		118	1 000 00	May 31		127	500 00
				June 30		132	500 00
			1 000 00				1 000 00

This obligation is recorded at December 31, 1966, by this entry:

Federal Income Tax	$26,140	
Federal Income Tax Payable		$26,140
(to record federal income tax for 1966)		

The Federal Income Tax account is an expense (for the purpose of calculating net income of the owners) and the payable account is a liability. It may be accrued throughout the year whenever net income is calculated, if so desired.

NATURE AND FUNCTION OF THE WORK SHEET

A work sheet is a columnar analysis that summarizes the adjusting and closing process. An illustration appears on pages 116–117. The work sheet has three purposes:

In regular account keeping:

1. It permits a preview of the adjusting and closing entries before they are entered in the journal and the ledger. In this preview, errors and omissions can be noticed and corrected before they affect the formal records.

2. It permits adjustments to be applied and proper statements to be prepared conveniently at dates on which a formal closing is not desired. For example, a firm may not wish to record a formal closing more than once a year, but may wish proper statements monthly. The data for the monthly statements may be assembled on the work sheet alone and the ledger left undisturbed.

In solving accounting problems:

3. The work sheet is convenient for handling accounting data that must be adjusted and summarized to solve an accounting problem. It is therefore used in schoolwork and in examinations elsewhere.

A complete work sheet shows in adjacent pairs of columns the preclosing trial balance, the adjusting entries, an adjusted trial balance, the income statement figures, and finally the balance sheet figures. The adjusted trial balance may be omitted to save effort.

ILLUSTRATION OF THE WORK SHEET

The preclosing trial balance of McCarty Wholesale Grocery, Inc., can be seen in the first two amount columns of the work sheet shown on pages 116–117. Those balances represent the transactions recorded during the year 1966 to December 31, with the exception of adjusting and closing entries for the year. The company records bad debt estimates, certain expense accruals, and depreciation monthly, but closes the books annually. It accrues income tax only at the year end. The company uses the periodic inventory method. Data on adjustments needed at December 31 are as follows:

1. Ending inventory of merchandise is $42,000.
2. Bad debts estimated on the basis of December sales are $500.
3. Delivery truck is depreciated at $100 per month.
4. The building is expected to last 33⅓ years and to have no salvage value.
5. Office furniture and fixtures are depreciated for December at $40.

6. The December accrual for property tax, not yet recorded, is $60.
7. Prepaid insurance has expired during December in the amount of $75.
8. Interest on the note payable is 6 percent per year. The December accrual has not been recorded.
9. The company is subject to the regular federal income tax on corporations.

COMMENTS ON THE ILLUSTRATED WORK SHEET

The adjustments are numbered in the McCarty work sheet to correspond with the numbers given to the adjustment data above. The company sets up a Cost of Goods Sold account as part of its adjusting and closing procedure. The entries for it are numbered 1a, 1b, and 1c in the work sheet. Note that any account needed but not in the preclosing trial balance is added at the bottom of the sheet. As an accountant you are expected to determine what accounts are needed and to open them.

After the adjusting entries (except the income tax entry) are entered, they are subtotaled to make sure that they are in balance. The adjustments are then added or deducted from the figures in the preclosing trial balance on the corresponding lines. This procedure gives the adjusted trial balance (except for the income tax figures), which is also subtotaled to check the arithmetic. The adjusted balance sheet figures may then be carried over into the Balance Sheet columns and the adjusted revenue and expense may be taken into the columns for that statement. When the income statement figures are subtotaled, a scratch-paper calculation of the net income before income tax may be made. The income tax is then calculated and entered as the last adjusting entry. For the McCarty work sheet the income tax is calculated as follows:

$$\begin{array}{r} \$25,\!000 \times 22\% = \$\ \ 5,\!500 \\ \underline{14,\!600} \times 48\% = \underline{\ \ \ 7,\!008} \\ \$39,\!600 \qquad\qquad \$12,\!508 \end{array}$$

The final net income is entered to transfer the balance of the income statement section to the balance sheet. This last entry may be thought of as the equivalent of a closing entry transferring the balance of the Profit and Loss account to Retained Earnings. The preclosing balance of retained earnings and the net income figure are separated in the balance sheet section as a result of this procedure, but they are easily brought together when the statements are prepared. Computation of final totals in the Adjustments, Adjusted Trial Balance, and statements columns completes the work sheet and proves the arithmetic of the final steps taken in it.

ALTERNATIVE WORK SHEET PROCEDURES

Reference has already been made to the fact that the adjusted trial balance may be omitted in preparing a work sheet. The resulting eight-column work sheet involves less work. However, it gives no opportunity to check the arithmetic involved in adding the adjustments to the first trial balance figures until the Balance Sheet columns are footed.

Alternative means of handling merchandise inventory are also common but are not described here, as they are likely to be confusing at this stage.

McCARTY WHOLESALE GROCERY, INC.
Work Sheet
Year ended December 31, 1966

	Trial Balance		Adjustments		Adjusted Trial Balance		Income Statement		Balance Sheet	
	Debit	Credit	Debit	Credit	Debit	Credit	Debit	Credit	Debit	Credit
Cash	27 176 00				27 176 00				27 176 00	
Accounts Receivable	47 600 00				47 600 00				47 600 00	
Allowance for Doubtful Accounts		3 600 00		(2) 500 00		4 100 00				4 100 00
Merchandise	39 000 00		(1c) 42 000 00	(1a) 39 000 00	42 000 00				42 000 00	
Prepaid Insurance	1 875 00			(7) 75 00	1 800 00				1 800 00	
Land	50 000 00				50 000 00				50 000 00	
Building	100 000 00				100 000 00				100 000 00	
Accumulated Depreciation—Building		5 750 00		(4) 250 00		6 000 00				6 000 00
Delivery Equipment	5 200 00				5 200 00				5 200 00	
Accumulated Depreciation—Delivery Equipment		2 300 00		(3) 100 00		2 400 00				2 400 00
Office Furniture and Fixtures	10 000 00				10 000 00				10 000 00	
Accumulated Depreciation—Office Furniture and Fixtures		1 040 00		(5) 40 00		1 080 00				1 080 00
Notes Payable		20 000 00				20 000 00				20 000 00
Accounts Payable		24 800 00				24 800 00				24 800 00
Property Taxes Payable		180 00		(6) 60 00		240 00				240 00
Accrued Interest Payable		1 100 00		(8) 100 00		1 200 00				1 200 00
Capital Stock		150 000 00				150 000 00				150 000 00
Retained Earnings		34 356 00				34 356 00				34 356 00
Sales		208 000 00				208 000 00		208 000 00		
Bad Debts	5 500 00		(2) 500 00		6 000 00		6 000 00			
Purchases	124 000 00			(1b) 124 000 00						
Sales Salaries	10 500 00				10 500 00		10 500 00			
Delivery Expense	4 200 00				4 200 00		4 200 00			

Account	Trial Balance Dr	Trial Balance Cr	Adjustments Dr	Adjustments Cr	Adjusted Trial Balance Dr	Adjusted Trial Balance Cr	Income Statement Dr	Income Statement Cr	Balance Sheet Dr	Balance Sheet Cr
Advertising	1 600 00				1 600 00		1 600 00			
Depreciation of Delivery Equipment	1 100 00		(3) 100 00		1 200 00		1 200 00			
Sundry Selling Expense	500 00				500 00		500 00			
Office Salaries	15 600 00				15 600 00		15 600 00			
Depreciation of Building	2 750 00		(4) 250 00		3 000 00		3 000 00			
Depreciation of Office Furniture and Fixtures	320 00		(5) 40 00		360 00		360 00			
Property Taxes	780 00		(6) 60 00		840 00		840 00			
Insurance	825 00		(7) 75 00		900 00		900 00			
Sundry General Expenses	1 500 00				1 500 00		1 500 00			
Interest	1 100 00		(8) 100 00		1 200 00		1 200 00			
	451 126 00	451 126 00								
Cost of Goods Sold			(1a) 39 000 00 (1b) 124 000 00	(1c) 42 000 00	121 000 00		121 000 00			
Subtotals			206 125 00	206 125 00	452 176 00	452 176 00	168 400 00	208 000 00	283 776 00	
Income-tax expense			(9) 12 508 00		12 508 00		12 508 00			
Income tax payable			218 633 00	(9) 12 508 00 218 633 00	464 684 00	12 508 00 464 684 00				12 508 00
Net income							27 092 00			27 092 00
							208 000 00	208 000 00	283 776 00	283 776 00

SUMMARY OF PREPARATION OF THE WORK SHEET

Preparation of a work sheet involves the following steps:

1. Copy the preclosing trial balance on the work sheet and foot it.
2. Make the needed adjusting entries directly on the face of the work sheet and foot them.
3. Add the preclosing trial balance and adjusting-entry figures across, line by line. Note that in this process debits and credits have their usual offsetting character.
4. Enter the adjusted figures in the statement columns in which they belong.
5. Add the income statement figures. Calculate and enter any required income tax figure, then transfer the net income to the balance sheet section.
6. Foot the balance sheet section to prove the results.

STEPS IN FORMAL CLOSING

The formal closing of the books may proceed as soon as the work sheet has been scrutinized and has been found complete. The closing involves all the steps that would have been taken without the work sheet, but the adjusting and closing entries may be made more easily from the work sheet. The steps in the adjusting and closing process are:

1. Enter adjusting journal entries and post to the accounts.
2. Enter closing entries and post to the accounts.
3. Take postclosing trial balance.
4. Rule the income statement accounts, and rule and balance the balance sheet accounts.

The adjusting entries are copied from the work sheet if a work sheet has been used. The closing entries can be entered by going down the income statement figures in the work sheet and noting the entry to close each one to Profit and Loss and to close the balance of Profit and Loss to a proprietorship account.

Statements may be prepared as soon as the work sheet is complete. If the work sheet is used to obtain proper statements at a date on which there is no formal closing, it is made up in exactly the same way. In this case no adjusting entries are made unless the company wants to bring certain accounts up to date without a closing, and of course, no closing entries are made.

The process that has been described here applies to hand-kept records or to those kept on bookkeeping machines operated like typewriters. Where computers are used, the information for the adjusting and closing entries will be fed into the computer, which automatically adds it to the proper account balances. If the operator wishes, he can instruct the computer to print out information, such as a trial balance, at any stage, but many such intermediate steps can be skipped on the computer, statements being printed out immediately after all the data are in.

SUMMARY

Merchandise transactions may be recorded by a perpetual inventory or a periodic inventory procedure. In the former the Merchandise account gives a running record of the merchandise on hand, purchases being debited to it and cost of goods sold being credited. It is accompanied by a subsidiary record giving units, prices, and amounts of the various articles on hand. In the periodic inventory method the Merchandise account records only the amount of inventory established by a physical count at the end of a period. Between closing dates the purchases are recorded in a Purchases account. At the end of the period, cost of goods sold is calculated by bringing together the opening balance from the Merchandise account and the purchases, and crediting against this total the new merchandise inventory figure, which is debited to the Merchandise account. These figures are brought together in a Cost of Goods Sold account or in the Profit and Loss account, as the accountant prefers.

The credits for depreciation on fixed assets are usually accumulated in separate accounts for Accumulated Depreciation. This isolation avoids confusion in the regular asset account and facilitates presentation of both original cost and total depreciation recorded against it. Provision must also be made for the reduction of revenue resulting from inability to collect for all sales. This is done by estimating, from experience, the amount that may be lost. It is recorded by a debit to Bad Debts and a credit to Allowance for Doubtful Accounts.

The work sheet is a convenient device for getting a preview of the adjusting and closing process. It is useful also in assembling the data for statements when a formal closing is not desired, and helpful in solving accounting problems in or out of school.

QUESTIONS

4.1 (1) Give the steps in the accounting process as explained thus far.

(2) In view of the fact that a work sheet produces the same figures as the formal adjusting and closing process in the journal and ledger, why use a work sheet?

4.2 (1) Differentiate between perpetual and periodic inventories.

(2) Explain the reason for the Purchases account.

(3) You are asked by a company employee whether Purchases is an asset or an expense account. What is your answer?

(4) If a perpetual inventory is maintained, is a physical inventory needed regularly? Explain.

4.3 The following amounts apply to Deken Co. for the month of July 1966: beginning inventory, $6,000; purchases, $22,000; ending inventory, $4,000. The company uses the periodic inventory method.

(1) Give the adjusting and closing entries when a Cost of Goods Sold account is used.

(2) Give the adjusting and closing entries when a Cost of Goods Sold account is not used.

(3) Construct the income statement down to gross margin on sales. The percent of gross margin to sales was 60 percent.

4.4 During 1966 the Samarang Boat Works had a beginning inventory of $120,000. Purchases for the year were $250,000; sales were $600,000. The ending inventory amounted to $100,000.

On January 5, 1966, catamaran No. 57, which cost $2,500, was sold for $3,000 cash.

(1) Give the entries to record the January 5 sale under the perpetual inventory method.

(2) Give the entry to record the January 5 sale under the periodic inventory method.

(3) Give the adjusting entry at December 31 under the periodic inventory method, using a Purchases and a Cost of Goods Sold account.

(4) Prepare the gross margin section of the income statement, showing details of cost of goods sold.

4.5 The "days purchases in accounts payable" is sometimes defined as $\frac{\text{accounts payable}}{\text{purchases}} \times 365$. It is an index of the age of creditors' accounts.

(1) Compute the days purchases in accounts payable from the following data:

> Beginning inventory $50,000
> Ending inventory   75,000
> Cost of goods sold   225,000
> Accounts payable   25,000

(2) Discuss the debt-paying practice of the company if the terms of credit in the industry require payment within forty days.

4.6 (1) What is a valuation account?

(2) What are the advantages in carrying the credit for depreciation in an account separate from the regular asset account?

(3) Why is an Allowance for Doubtful Accounts necessary?

(4) Suggest two different places for Bad Debts in the income statement, and give a reason for each.

4.7 The balances of trucks less accumulated depreciation for two companies at a given date were as follows:

	M Co.	N Co.
Trucks	$10,000	$50,000
Accumulated Depreciation	5,000	45,000
Net	$ 5,000	$ 5,000

Discuss the implications in terms of cash required for replacement of trucks.

4.8 The adjusted trial balance of Norsco contains the following balances: Accounts Receivable, $24,000; Allowance for Doubtful Accounts, $2,600; Bad Debts, $1,200.

(1) Why does the balance in Allowance for Doubtful Accounts exceed that of Bad Debts?

(2) How will these balances be extended on the work sheet?

(3) What entry is made to record an uncollectible account?

4.9 The December 31, 1966, balance sheet of Burgess Metals of Canada, Ltd., shows under liabilities a Reserve for Depreciation of $412,634.87.

(1) Is the Reserve for Depreciation a liability?

(2) What are the purposes of the Depreciation and Accumulated Depreciation Accounts? Where should they be shown on the financial statements?

4.10 In practice, real and personal property taxes have been charged against the income of the following periods: calendar year in which paid, fiscal year of taxpayer in which paid, year ending on assessment date, year beginning on assessment date, and fiscal year of governing body levying the tax.

Discuss the acceptability of these alternative bases of accounting for property taxes.

4.11 Calco pays property taxes in two installments, November 1 and February 1.

The taxes become a lien on the property the first Monday in March, when the tax is assessed by the county, whose fiscal year begins July 1. The company adjusts its accounts monthly and closes annually on December 31. What are the amounts in the balance sheet accounts relating to taxes on each of these dates: July 31, November 30, December 31, January 31, March 31?

4.12 (1) Would you expect to find a figure for income taxes in the income statements of sole proprietorships, partnerships, and corporations? Why?

(2) M, Inc., issues semiannual financial statements. The company is subject to income taxes at 22 percent on the first $25,000 of income and 48 percent on the remainder. During the first half-year, operations result in a loss of $10,000. During the last half-year, operations result in a net income before income taxes of $45,000. What amounts should appear in the balance sheet and the income statement for income taxes in the second half of the year?

4.13 (1) Explain how a work sheet facilitates the preparation of interim statements.

(2) Prepare the cost of goods sold section of the income statement for September from the following data:

	Year to Date	
Cost of Goods Sold:	August 31	September 30
Opening Inventory	$ 20,000	$ 20,000
Purchases	180,000	190,000
Total.	$200,000	$210,000
Closing Inventory	25,000	30,000
Cost of Goods Sold	$175,000	$180,000

4.14 The following errors were made in extensions in a work sheet:

(a) The balance of Accrued Utilities was entered in the Income Statement Credit column.

(b) The balance in the Allowance for Doubtful Accounts was entered in the Balance Sheet Debit column.

(c) The balance of Interest Receivable was entered in the Income Statement Debit column.

(1) How will each error affect the balancing of the work sheet?

(2) How will each error affect the computation of net income?

4.15 (1) Can the work sheet be prepared without the Adjusted Trial Balance columns? Would you recommend the omission?

(2) Some accountants adjust inventories on a work sheet in the following manner: (a) They enter the new Inventory in the Balance Sheet Debit column and Income Statement Credit column, (b) they enter the old Inventory in the Income Statement Debit column, and (c) they extend Purchases to the Income Statement Debit column. What do you think of this plan? Give a numerical example of the method by constructing the relevant portions of a work sheet.

(3) Some accountants charge purchases directly to a Cost of Goods Sold account, then at the end of the year they adjust the inventory to the periodic count with a compensating debit or credit to Cost of Goods Sold. Comment.

4.16 Tay Lind has been doing business as Tay's Jewelers for the past three years, selling custom-made jewelry bought from various small craftsmen. Miss Lind has always thought of herself more as an artist than as a businesswoman, and has kept virtually no accounting records.

The state government is investigating Tay's Jewelers, as Miss Lind has never filed a state sales tax return. She has consulted a lawyer, who has advised her that she is liable for taxes, interest, and penalties. Furthermore, the lawyer learned that Miss Lind has never filed an individual income tax return. Miss Lind cannot understand why she should have filed income tax returns, as she has been living with her uncle, who has paid all her personal living expenses and has contributed sizable sums to pay for inventories and equipment.

The lawyer asks you to get such bank records, sales slips, purchase invoices, and merchandise inventories as are available for Tay's Jewelers. From these you are requested to reconstruct the records for the past three years.

(1) Comment briefly on the type of work sheet you might use to prepare the annual statements, stating the column headings of the work sheet and the sources of information for the entries.

(2) Explain the probable cause of confusion in Tay Lind's mind regarding net income and cash flow, as evidenced by her failure to file an income tax return. What has she disregarded?

4.17 The trial balance of W Co. before adjustments appears below:

Accounts Payable		$xxx
Accounts Receivable	$xxx	
Accrued Salaries		xxx
Accumulated Depreciation		xxx
Allowance for Bad Debts		xxx
Bad Debts	—	
Cash	xxx	
Capital Stock		xxx
Cost of Goods Sold	—	
Depreciation	—	
Equipment	xxx	
Income Tax	—	
Income Tax Payable		—
Insurance	—	
Interest	xxx	
Interest Payable		—
Inventory of Supplies	—	
Merchandise	xxx	
Notes Payable		xxx
Prepaid Insurance	xxx	
Purchases	xxx	
Retained Earnings		xxx
Salaries	xxx	
Sales		xxx
Supplies	xxx	

(1) Indicate whether each account would be debited or credited to record typical adjustments in the Adjustments column of a work sheet.

(2) Indicate the final column to which each balance would be extended.

4.18 The following accounts are selected from the ledger of the M Co.

No.	Name	No.	Name
111	Allowance for Doubtful Accounts	320	Commissions Earned
120	Prepaid Insurance	410	Bad Debts
151	Accumulated Depreciation	420	Depreciation
220	Unearned Commissions	430	Insurance
230	Interest Payable	440	Interest
240	Income Tax Payable	450	Income Taxes

Prepare a matrix designating rows and columns by account numbers. Place a mark in each cell affected by the annual adjustments. The company records all deferred items initially in real accounts.

EXERCISES

4.1 The following three accounts contain the property tax transactions of Dillco, Inc., for the four months ended October 31, 1966. The property is located in a county whose fiscal year begins July 1. The 1966-1967 tax is $9,000. The company records the tax expense monthly and closes its books annually. The tax is paid in two installments on September 10 and February 10. Name each account and explain each entry.

Account A			Account B			Account C		
9/10	1,500	7/31 750	7/31	750		9/10	3,000	9/30 750
		8/31 750	8/31	750				10/31 750
			9/30	750				
			10/31	750				

4.2 Sections of two unrelated work sheets appear below. Explain for each work sheet what the adjustment represents and why it is made.

(1)

Account	Trial Balance		Adjustments		Income Statement		Balance Sheet	
	Debit	Credit	Debit	Credit	Debit	Credit	Debit	Credit
Merchandise	18,000		22,000	18,000			22,000	

(2)

Account	Trial Balance		Adjustments		Income Statement		Balance Sheet	
	Debit	Credit	Debit	Credit	Debit	Credit	Debit	Credit
					84,000	116,000		
Income tax					11,140		11,140	
Net income					20,860			20,860
					116,000	116,000	227,450	227,450

4.3 The merchandise purchases and inventories of Barker Co. for 1966 were as follows:

Inventory brought forward January 1, 1966 . . . . $12,500
Purchases for 1966 (all on credit).   30,000
Inventory on hand December 31, 1966   10,000

Required:

1. Journalize the purchases for the year. The company uses a Purchases account.
2. Prepare the adjusting and closing entries at December 31, 1966. The company uses a Cost of Goods Sold account.
3. Post the entries to all accounts except Accounts Payable.

4. Prepare the adjusting and closing entries, without using a Cost of Goods Sold account.

4.4 Following is a schedule of fixed assets of the Dedman Co.:

Asset	Acquired	Cost	Scrap	Life (years)	Depreciation Prior to 1/1/66
Building	1/1/60	$48,000	$ —	20	$14,400
Office equipment	1/1/66	7,500	300	10	—
Machinery	6/30/65	72,800	800	12	3,000
Truck	9/30/66	5,500	700	4	—

Required:

1. Compute the depreciation for 1966.
2. Journalize the depreciation on buildings.
3. Prepare the fixed assets section of the balance sheet on December 31, 1966.

4.5 The trial balance of Trion, Inc., at December 31, 1966, is as follows:

Cash..............................	$12,000	
Merchandise	9,000	
Furniture and Fixtures	20,000	
Allowance for Depreciation..............		$ 8,000
Capital Stock		22,000
Sales		50,000
Purchases............................	30,000	
Salaries..............................	8,000	
Miscellaneous Expense	1,000	
	$80,000	$80,000

From the following information prepare a work sheet for the year ended December 31, 1966:

(1) Merchandise inventory at December 31, 1966, is $10,000. The company uses a Cost of Goods Sold account.
(2) The furniture and fixtures is being depreciated over ten years with no scrap value.
(3) The company is subject to income taxes of 22 percent on the first $25,000 of net income and 48 percent on the rest.

4.6 The accounts of the XYZ Co. relating to customers and bad debts have the following balances at December 31, 1966:

Accounts receivable	$20,000 dr.
Allowance for doubtful accounts	500 dr.
Bad debts.........................	—

Required:

1. Explain why the Allowance for Doubtful Accounts has a debit balance.
2. Give the entry to record estimated bad debts of $2,000 for 1966.
3. Why credit estimated bad debts to Allowance for Doubtful Accounts rather than to Accounts Receivable?
4. Give the entry to record sending to an attorney customer John Barkhorn's account for $500 for collection.
5. How does entry 4 affect total assets? proprietorship?

4.7 A work sheet, minus the Adjustments columns, of the Lanai Co. for the year ended December 31, 1966, appears below. State six adjustments contained in the work sheet and present them in journal form.

	Trial Balance		Income Statement		Balance Sheet	
	Debit	Credit	Debit	Credit	Debit	Credit
Cash	$ 7,800				$ 7,800	
Accounts Receivable	40,000				40,000	
Allow. for Doubtful Accts.		$ 100				$ 1,000
Merchandise	15,100				16,200	
Prepaid Taxes	–				4,000	
Equipment	20,000				20,000	
Allow. for Depreciation		10,000				12,000
Advances from Customers		–				5,000
Capital Stock		30,000				30,000
Sales		185,000		$180,000		
Bad Debts	–		$ 900			
Cost of Goods Sold	–		90,100			
Purchases	91,200		–			
Salaries	40,000		40,000			
Property Taxes	8,000		4,000			
Depreciation	–		2,000			
Other Expense	3,000		3,000			
Income Taxes	–		12,700			
Income Taxes Payable		–				12,700
Net Income			27,300			27,300
	$225,100	$225,100	$180,000	$180,000	$88,000	$88,000

4.8 The unadjusted trial balance of Custom Appliance Company at December 31, 1966, is as follows:

Cash.	$ 2,000	
Accounts Receivable.	12,000	
Allowance for Doubtful Accounts		$ 200
Merchandise.	6,000	
Equipment	15,000	
Accumulated Depreciation		3,000
Notes Payable		5,000
Advances on Service Work		6,000
Capital Stock		10,000
Retained Earnings.		2,400
Sales		70,000
Purchases.	46,000	
Supplies	10,000	
Utilities*	4,400	
Unclassified	1,200	
	$96,600	$96,600

* Meters are read on the 20th of each month.

Analyze the trial balance to determine eight possible adjusting entries. ("Unclassified" requires no adjustment.) Draft adjusting entries in journal form, using "xxx" in place of amounts.

4.9 Because of the length of the trial balance, the cost and expense accounts of Morgan's Mart are listed on a supporting work sheet, while only the total is listed on the master work sheet. Cost and expense balances at December 31, 1966, follow:

Cost of Sales	$ —
Advertising	10,000
Depreciation	—
Heat, Light, and Water	4,000
Insurance	—
Rent	14,000
Salaries	10,600
Supplies	2,000
Taxes	1,900
Telephone and Telegraph	2,400
Miscellaneous Expense	600
Total	$45,500

Additional data:

(1) Inventory January 1, 1966, $60,000; purchases for year, $480,000; inventory, December 31, 1966, $65,000.
(2) The unrecorded balance due on 1966 TV programs at December 31, 1966, amounts to $500.
(3) Depreciation of furniture and fixtures, 10 percent on $35,000.
(4) Company records show that telephone and telegraph usage from the last billing date to December 31, 1966, amounts to $200.
(5) Insurance policies (all for twelve months):

Date of Policy	Total Premium	Date of Policy	Total Premium
4/2/65	$1,200	4/2/66	$1,800
7/31/65	600	7/31/66	720

(6) Rent is $1,000 per month.
(7) Supplies on hand at December 31, 1966, amount to $900. Supplies purchased during the year have been charged to expense.
(8) Taxes include a $600 payment on October 5, 1966, of half of the annual taxes for the government's fiscal year beginning August 1.

Prepare a work sheet containing details of costs and expenses and including the following four columns: Trial Balance Dr., Adjustments Dr. and Cr., and Income Statement Dr.

4.10 After the financial statements of Classic Furniture Co. have been prepared, it is discovered that a page of the inventory amounting to $1,000 was omitted from the total. What is the effect of the error on working capital, current ratio, percent of net income to sales, percent of margin to sales, income taxes payable?

4.11 Compute the useful lives remaining from December 31, 1966, for the fixed assets of the Norton Co. listed below.

Asset	Acquired	Cost	Scrap	Acc. Depr. 12/31/66
Building	1/1/62	$23,800	$ —	$5,950
Office equipment	1/1/63	9,400	400	3,000
Truck	7/1/65	6,200	700	1,650

4.12 Compute 1966 bad debts of the M Co. from the information below. The company reports sales net of bad debts.

Inventory—January 1, 1966	$ 21,300
Purchases	86,300
Inventory—December 31, 1966	22,400
Sales	120,500
Gross margin on sales	34,700

4.13 Robert F. Palmer has been offered the Waikiki Hale Apartments for $600,000 cash plus a $300,000 8 percent mortgage. The vendors project a "cash income" of $60,000 for 1966, as shown below.

WAIKIKI HALE APARTMENTS
PROJECTED CASH INCOME
Year Ended December 31, 1966

Gross Rents		$130,000
Expenditures Other Than Loan Repayments:		
Interest	$24,000	
Taxes and Insurance	13,000	
Land Rents	12,000	
Utilities............................	5,000	
Repairs and Maintenance	3,000	
Salaries and Wages	3,000	60,000
Net before Loan Repayments		$ 70,000
Loan Repayments		10,000
Cash Income.........................		$ 60,000

The property is located on Waikiki Beach on land leased from the Steiner Trust Co. The lease has thirty years to run, with no option to renew. At the termination of the lease all improvements revert to the lessor. The principal of the $300,000 mortgage is payable in equal annual installments over a 30-year period.

Required:

1. Compute the projected net income for 1966 on an accrual basis.
2. Palmer asks your advice regarding purchase of the property. He tells you that, on investments of like risk, he customarily earns 10 percent on acquisition price before income taxes. State your opinion, showing appropriate computations.

4.14 As surety bond manager of a large insurance corporation, you are presented with an urgent request for a performance bond for the B Construction Corporation. Statements are not available, but you are supplied with the following trial balance taken from the records of the company as of the close of the year's business December 31, 1966. All accounting processes for 1966 have been completed except the preparation of year-end statements.

Wages Payable		$ 3,000
Prepaid Insurance	$ 1,300	
Allowance for Depreciation		6,500
Insurance Expense	2,650	
Allowance for Bad Debts..............		700
Sales...............................		95,200
Dividends	1,000	
Common Stock		28,000
Depreciation of Equipment	1,000	
Cash...............................	11,800	
Patents (net)	10,000	
Accounts Payable		5,000
Retained Earnings		6,300
Rent Expense	6,000	
Equipment	12,000	
Notes Payable—Noncurrent		2,500
Accounts Receivable	13,500	
Construction Labor Expense	50,450	
Cost of Materials Used	18,000	
Inventory of Materials (12/31/66).........	5,500	
Administrative and Office Expense........	14,000	
	$147,200	$147,200

Required:

1. Answer the following questions. Show all calculations necessary to secure your answers.
    (a) What was the net income or net loss for 1966?
    (b) What are the retained earnings as of December 31, 1966?
    (c) What is the working capital as of December 31, 1966?
    (d) What is the book value of tangible fixed assets on December 31, 1966?
2. Briefly explain the nature of the following items appearing above: Dividends, Patents (net), Allowance for Depreciation, and Notes Payable, Noncurrent.
3. Is the company maintaining its records on the cash or the accrual basis of accounting? Point out several reasons why you believe your answer is correct.

(CPCU — adapted)

PROBLEMS

4.1 On July 1, 1966, the York Company bought real estate subject to property tax of $7,200 for the governmental unit's fiscal year beginning July 1, 1966. Half the tax is paid October 2, 1966; the other half will be paid by February 5, 1967. The company adjusts monthly but closes annually on December 31.

Required:

1. Give dated journal entries required in connection with this tax for 1966, including the entry to close the tax expense.
2. Post the entries to the accounts affected, except Cash and Profit and Loss.

4.2 On July 1, 1966, the Calway Development Co. bought an apartment house subject to property tax of $9,600 for the government's fiscal year beginning July 1, 1966. Half the tax is paid October 5, 1966, and the other half February 5, 1967. The company records adjusting journal entries quarterly but closes annually on March 31.

Required:

1. Give dated journal entries required in connection with this tax for the fiscal year ended March 31, 1967, including the entry to close the tax expense.
2. Post the entries to the accounts affected, except Cash and Profit and Loss.

4.3 The merchandise transactions of B Trading Co. for 1966 are summarized below.

Inventory brought forward January 1, 1966 . . . . $25,000
Purchases on account 45,000
Inventory on hand December 31, 1966 15,000
Sales on account 75,000

Required:

1. Draft journal entries to record purchases and sales for the year. The company uses a Purchases account.
2. Draft the adjusting and closing entries at December 31, 1966, using a Cost of Goods Sold account.
3. Post the entries and opening inventory balance to the appropriate accounts (omit Accounts Payable and Accounts Receivable).

4. Draft the adjusting and closing entries, without using a Cost of Goods Sold account.
5. Prepare the income statement to gross margin on sales.
6. The merchandise turnover is defined as the ratio of the cost of goods sold to the average inventory. Statistics for the industry show a median turnover of 2.4 per year. How does the company compare with the median?

4.4 (1) Prepare journal entries to record the depreciation for 1966 on the fixed assets listed below.

	Cost	Salvage Value	Useful Life (years)	Age as of 12/31/66 (years)
Building	$200,000	$ —	50	9
Delivery truck	6,200	700	5	4
Office equipment	32,000	2,000	15	2

(2) Prepare the fixed assets section of the balance sheet as of December 31, 1966.

4.5 The account balances of F. B. McNulty at December 31, 1966, are as follows:

Cash	$15,000
Accounts Receivable	3,000
Prepaid Insurance	1,500
Supplies	1,000
Furniture and Fixtures	5,000
Accounts Payable	12,000
Inspection Revenue Received in Advance	18,000
F. B. McNulty, Capital	2,000
Delivery Service Revenue	14,000
Salaries	18,000
Taxes	1,000
Advertising	1,000
Miscellaneous Expense	500

Data for adjustments for the year ended December 31, 1966, are:

(1) Accrued advertising, $300.
(2) Supplies on hand, $400.
(3) Taxes paid in advance, $200.
(4) Inspection services earned, $16,000.
(5) All furniture and fixtures are expected to have a useful life of ten years and no salvage value. Additions costing $2,000 were made to furniture and fixtures on July 1; the rest of the furniture and fixtures was acquired January 1.
(6) Prepaid insurance consists of two policies:

Acquired	Term (years)	Premium
January 1, 1966	3	$900
July 1, 1966	1	600

(7) Ten percent of the accounts receivable are expected to be uncollectible.

Prepare a work sheet.

4.6 The trial balance and data for adjustments of the Coast Land Co. at December 31, 1966, are as follows:

Accounts Receivable..................	$ 5,000	
Advertising Expense	2,000	
Capital Stock		$ 50,000
Cash..............................	15,000	
Fees..............................		30,000
Insurance Expense	–	
Interest Earned......................		1,500
Interest Receivable	–	
Land..............................	35,000	
Mortgages Receivable	25,000	
Prepaid Advertising..................	–	
Prepaid Insurance	3,000	
Rents Earned	–	
Retained Earnings, January 1, 1966		11,500
Salaries Expense	18,000	
Salaries Payable	–	
Travel Expense......................	4,000	
Unearned Rent		14,000
	$107,000	$107,000

Data for adjustments:
(1) Accrued salaries, $2,000
(2) Accrued interest on the mortgages, $500
(3) Rents earned for year, $12,000
(4) Insurance expired, $1,000
(5) Prepaid advertising expense, $200
The company elects to be treated as an unincorporated business under Subchapter S of the Internal Revenue Code, and as such is not subject to income taxes.
Prepare a work sheet. (Leave accounts in alphabetical order.)

4.7 Auto Supplies, Inc., conducts a wholesale business in certain lines of auto supplies. Its trial balance on June 30, 1966, was as follows:

Cash	$ 1,400	
Accounts Receivable...........................	4,500	
Allowance for Doubtful Accounts		700
Merchandise.................................	16,600	
Store Supplies...............................	840	
Store Fixtures................................	18,000	
Accumulated Depreciation—Store Fixtures		$ 600
Office Furniture and Fixtures	10,500	
Accumulated Depreciation—Office Furn. and Fixt.		350
Notes Payable		2,000
Accounts Payable.............................		3,200
Capital Stock		20,000
Retained Earnings.............................		13,675
Sales		97,315
Purchases...................................	54,000	
Sales Salaries	15,000	
Advertising..................................	1,200	
Sundry Selling Expense........................	2,400	
Office Salaries...............................	8,000	
Rent.......................................	2,400	
Sundry General Expense........................	1,600	
	$137,140	$137,140

The company's fiscal year ends on June 30. Data needed for year-end adjustments on June 30, 1966, are as follows:

(1) Merchandise inventory at June 30, 1966, is $18,100. The company uses a Cost of Goods Sold account.

(2) Bad debts for the year are estimated at $1,000.

(3) Store fixtures are being depreciated over ten years with no salvage value. No acquisitions or retirements have been made during the year.

(4) Office furniture and fixtures are being depreciated over 15 years with no salvage value. No acquisitions or retirements have been made during the year.

(5) Interest in the amount of $75 is accrued on the note payable.

(6) Property taxes are accrued in the amount of $240.

(7) Store supplies used amount to $400.

(8) The company is subject to income tax at the rate of 22 percent on the first $25,000 and 48 percent on the remainder.

Prepare a work sheet.

4.8   Ace Patio Materials Co. sells garden-construction materials. It closes its books annually on September 30. Its trial balance for September 30, 1966, is given below. Prepare a work sheet from the following information:

(1) Merchandise inventory is $14,800. The company uses a Cost of Goods Sold account.

(2) Supplies are debited to Supplies Expense when bought. At September 30, 1966, $150 of supplies was still on hand.

(3) The insurance policies were renewed October 1, 1965, at a premium of $360 for a term of three years.

(4) The building is being depreciated over twenty years; no salvage is expected.

(5) The truck is expected to last four years and to have a trade-in value of $500.

(6) Wages of the delivery-truck driver amounting to $105 are unpaid for the last five days of the year; they will be paid along with the pay for Saturday, October 1, as usual.

(7) Bad debts for the year are estimated at $480.

(8) Property taxes have accrued in the amount of $300.

(9) The company is subject to income taxes of 22 percent on the first $25,000 of net income and 48 percent on the remainder.

The trial balance at September 30, 1966, is:

Cash	$ 1,600	
Accounts Receivable	5,000	
Allowance for Doubtful Accounts		$ 100
Merchandise	15,000	
Prepaid Insurance	360	
Land	4,000	
Building	8,000	
Accumulated Depreciation – Building		1,600
Delivery Truck	3,500	
Accumulated Depreciation – Delivery Truck		550
Accounts Payable		2,100
Capital Stock		15,000
Retained Earnings		5,905
Sales		95,120
Purchases	60,000	
Delivery Wages	5,095	
Advertising	400	
Sundry Selling Expense	1,300	
Supplies Expense	310	
General Salaries	14,000	
Sundry General Expense	1,810	
	$120,375	$120,375

4.9 The account balances listed below were taken from the ledger of Tab Co. at December 31, 1966.

Accumulated Depreciation—Office Equipment	$10,000
Accumulated Depreciation—Store Fixtures	5,000
Accrued Advertising	1,200
Advertising	10,200
Allowance for Doubtful Accounts	800
Bad Debts	1,000
County Property Taxes Payable	500
Depreciation—Office Equipment	1,000
Depreciation—Store Equipment	4,000
Dividends	4,000
General Salaries	15,400
Office Equipment	10,000
Insurance	2,600
Interest Expense	1,200
Interest Payable	500
Inventory, January 1, 1966	25,000
Payroll Taxes	4,800
Prepaid City Property Taxes	400
Property Taxes	2,400
Purchases	88,000
Rent of Office	3,600
Rent of Showroom	6,000
Sales	200,000
Sales Salaries	48,000
Store Fixtures	20,000
Supplies Used	800
Telephone and Telegraph	1,000

Adjustments are required for the following data:

(1) Inventory, December 31, 1966, $35,000

(2) Income taxes of 22 percent on the first $25,000 of net income and 48 percent on the remainder

Prepare the annual income statement.

4.10 Transactions of E. S. Neal and Co. for the year ended December 31, 1966, are summarized below.

(1) Invested cash, $50,000.

(2) Purchased merchandise on credit, $140,000.

(3) Sold merchandise on credit, $150,000.

(4) Cash disbursements:

Merchandise	$120,000
Salaries	25,000
Furniture and Fixtures	6,000
Rent	6,000
Motor Vehicle	4,000
Taxes	3,000
Unclassified Expense	1,000
Total disbursements	$165,000

(5) Collected from customers on account, $120,000.

Additional data for adjustments at December 31 are as follows:

(1) The merchandise inventory at December 31, 1966, is $40,000.

(2) The fixed assets were purchased on January 1. The furniture and fixtures are expected to be useful for ten years and are expected to have no salvage value. The motor vehicle is expected to be useful for three years and is expected to have a salvage value of $1,000.

(3) Bad debts are estimated at 0.5 percent of sales for the year.

(4) The taxes were levied on March 1 for the city and county fiscal year July 1, 1966, to June 30, 1967.

Required:

1. Enter the transactions in T accounts.
2. Enter the adjustments in the T accounts.
3. Prepare a balance sheet and an income statement.
4. Enter the closing entries in the T accounts.
5. In the early evening of December 31, 1966, Neal telephones to inform you that an automobile salesman has been trying to persuade him to buy a new truck so that he can "take it off his 1966 income tax." Neal asks your opinion. Draft a brief reply.

The following accounts are suggested: Cash, Accounts Receivable, Allowance for Doubtful Accounts, Merchandise, Prepaid Taxes, Furniture and Fixtures, Accumulated Depreciation—Furniture and Fixtures, Motor Vehicle, Accumulated Depreciation—Motor Vehicle, Accounts Payable, E. S. Neal, Capital, Profit and Loss, Sales, Bad Debts, Cost of Goods Sold, Purchases, Rent, Salaries, Taxes, Depreciation, Unclassified Expense.

4.11 Following is a comparative balance sheet of Zack's TV Service as of December 31, 1967 and 1966:

	December 31	
Assets	*1967*	*1966*
Cash	$ 5,000	$ 4,000
Accounts Receivable	11,500	10,000
Supplies	700	500
	$17,200	$14,500

Liabilities and Proprietorship		
Liabilities:		
Accounts Payable (supplies)	$ 5,800	$ 5,000
Wages Payable	700	1,000
Proprietorship:		
Zack Smith, Capital	10,700	8,500
	$17,200	$14,500

Disbursements for the year ended December 31, 1967, consisted of wages, $4,000; supplies, $1,000; unclassified expenses, $2,000; and drawings, $3,000. Prepare the 1967 income statement.

4.12 A. S. Francis, doing business as Francis Cameras, sells and services a complete line of photographic equipment. He is located in a rapidly expanding population area, and his sales volume has increased with the growth of the area. Francis has five employees; three years ago, when he started business, he had none. Francis acts as manager and bookkeeper and still does some selling.

Francis tells you that he has received a letter from the Internal Revenue Service asking him to bring in his accounting records and supporting documents. He is worried, because he has never filed a tax return. He tells you he wants no trouble from the government, and explains that he has not filed a return because he has "yet to see a year in which the business breaks even." He explains that he has borrowed from a wealthy aunt for the past three years to meet his personal and business debts.

On investigation, you find that the accounting records consist only of his bank statements, canceled checks, duplicate deposit slips, unpaid bills, and uncollected sales tickets. Francis has prepared from these the following statement for 1966:

FRANCIS CAMERAS
INCOME STATEMENT
Year Ended December 31, 1966

Sales		$230,000
Cost of Goods Sold		155,000
Gross Margin on Sales		$ 75,000
Expenses:		
Operations and Supervision	$65,000	
Equipment	15,000	80,000
Net Loss		$(5,000)

(1) Sales of $230,000 consist of cash receipts from customers during 1966. Balances due from customers on December 31 amount to $21,000. The balances due from customers on January 1, 1966 amounted to $15,000.

(2) The cost of goods sold of $155,000 is the total of checks issued to merchandise suppliers during 1966. Unpaid bills show that amounts due to creditors were $10,000 on January 1 and $15,000 on December 31.

(3) Francis has taken an inventory at the end of each year for stock control and reordering, but has never included the value of the inventory in his income statement. The inventory at the end of 1966 was $50,000; the inventory at the end of the prior year was $40,000.

(4) Operations and supervision represents 1966 disbursements for operating expenses. Because of a cash shortage, Francis was in arrears $2,000 in paying his employees on January 1, but these obligations were liquidated during the current year.

(5) Equipment costing $15,000 was bought in the middle of the year. It is expected to have a 10-year life. Other equipment owned by the business had a remaining depreciable basis of $17,500 at the beginning of the year and a remaining useful life of seven years.

Required:

1. Prepare an income statement for 1966 on the accrual basis, with notes explaining the computation of the principal items.
2. Explain why Francis found it necessary to borrow from his aunt although his business was profitable.

4.13 Consolidated Marine, Inc., was incorporated March 1, 1966, to engage in the ship charter and brokerage business. Simple records of receipts and disbursements were maintained. At the end of the first year of operations the records showed:

(1) Receipts:

Charter parties	$251,150
Brokerage	48,000
Common stock	5,000
Notes payable to officers (due after 3/1/68)	5,000
	$309,150

(2) Disbursements:

Time charter hire	$230,000
Office equipment	3,000
Automobile	5,000
Loans to Down International (due after 3/1/68)	2,000
Officers salaries	20,000
Office salaries	1,500
Telephone and telegraph	9,000
Office expense	2,000
Travel and entertainment	5,000
Taxes	2,500
Rent	2,000
Costs of incorporation	1,000
	$283,000

Additional data, derived from an examination of invoices and other documents:

(3) Unpaid invoices—February 28, 1967:
   American President Lines:
      Time charter of President Taylor $10,000
   Pacific Telephone & Telegraph Co.:
      Cable service for February, 1967 700
(4) Accrued expenses:
      Auditing 500
      Payroll taxes 450
(5) Depreciation and amortization:
      Office equipment 10%
      Automobile 20%
      Organization costs 20%
(6) Revenue on charter parties is not recognized until a ship completes the voyage. The S/S Milne (voyage 6601) is at sea on February 28, 1967. Receipts of $40,000, included under charter parties, pertain to this vessel; also disbursements of $30,000, included under time charter hire, pertain to this vessel.
(7) Income taxes:
   The company is subject only to federal income taxes. These taxes are 22 percent on the first $25,000 of taxable income and 48 percent on all income over $25,000.
   1. Prepare a balance sheet as of February 28, 1967, and an income statement for the year then ended. (A work sheet may be helpful in developing the information for the statements. Columns may be included for Cash Transactions, Adjustments, Income Statement, and Balance Sheet.)
   2. Can you suggest why the company selected a fiscal year ending in February?

4.14 The net income after income taxes per general ledger of H Co. for the year ended December 31, 1966, is $43,000. An inspection of the accounting records and supporting documents reveals:

(1) Prepaid insurance was charged for premiums paid during the year. The balance of that account at December 31, 1966, was $1,200; the unexpired premium amounted to $300.
(2) The December 31, 1965, balance of accrued salaries, $1,400, was left unchanged during 1966. Accrued salaries at December 31, 1966, were $1,000.
(3) An unused warehouse was sublet by the company for six months on Decem-

ber 1, 1966. Rental income was credited with the $2,400 received; no adjustment was made to this account at the end of the year.

(4) The company bought a truck on July 1, 1966, signing a 1-year contract including interest of $520, charged to expense. Only $420 of the interest is applicable to 1966. No adjustment was made for this item at December 31, 1966.

(5) Federal and state income taxes of 50 percent of taxable income are provided for in the financial statements.

Enter the net income after income taxes per general ledger in a skeleton account titled Profit and Loss. Enter the adjustments for above items directly in the skeleton account, and balance the account with the adjusted net income after income taxes. Submit calculations for adjustment 5.

4.15 Robert A. Martin, doing business as The Audio Center, has been in the business of installing and servicing high-fidelity sound systems for one year on December 31, 1966. Martin retains you to help him determine the financial position of his business on December 31, 1966, and the results of operations for the year then ended. He tells you he "has a horrible feeling that he is going faster and faster, but has no idea where he is going." He cannot understand why his checks are dishonored and his creditors are dunning him.

Your investigation shows that the accounting records, such as they are, have been kept by Mrs. Martin, who has no formal training in bookkeeping. She produces for your examination the following statement of cash receipts and disbursements.

THE AUDIO CENTER
STATEMENT OF CASH RECEIPTS AND DISBURSEMENTS
Year Ended December 31, 1966

Receipts:

Investment	$ 5,000	
Customers	31,000	
Total Receipts		$36,000

Disbursements:

Tubes and Parts	$14,000	
Labor	9,000	
Furniture and Equipment	5,000	
Rent	3,500	
Auto Expense	3,000	
Office Expense	1,000	
Utilities	500	
Repair and Maintenance	400	
Taxes	400	
Miscellaneous Expense	200	
Total Disbursements		37,000
Overdraft, December 31, 1966		($ 1,000)

You find the statement to be correct. From various business papers you ascertain the following additional facts:

(1) A list of balances due from customers totals $9,000.

(2) An inventory of tubes and parts on hand amounts to $6,000.

(3) A list of outstanding balances due to trade creditors for purchase of tubes and parts amounts to $2,000.

(4) The business operates on leased premises, on which rent of $250 per month is payable at the beginning of each month. During 1966 the last two months'

rent under the 5-year lease was paid in addition to the twelve regular monthly payments.

(5) Furniture and equipment, acquired January 1, 1966, is expected to have a life of five years.

(6) In addition to the balance due trade creditors it is estimated that expenses accrued but unpaid comprise taxes of $200 and utilities of $100.

Prepare a balance sheet as of December 31, 1966, and an income statement on the accrual basis for the year ended December 31, 1966. Draft a brief note explaining the principal factors accounting for the difference between the excess of disbursements over receipts and the excess of revenues over expenses.

PART II

Control and Accounting
for Basic Functions

Sales Accounting and Control

This chapter deals with three general topics involving sales. First are the sales transactions, with the documents and records required to record them on a day-to-day basis. These records provide data for the conventional statements, for collecting the amounts owed by customers, and for analyses needed for managerial decisions. Second, the devices of internal control that are closely related to sales accounting and management are discussed. These give assurance that customers are sent the goods they order, that they are charged for goods they are sent, and so on. Last, some of the managerial decisions required in forming sales policy are described and the contribution of the sales accounting records to them is pointed out. This same pattern is followed in succeeding chapters wherever it is appropriate.

SALES TRANSACTIONS

The time for recognizing a sale was discussed in Chapter 3 under the heading of Recognition of Revenue. Passage of title to the goods, in the sense that risk of loss passes to the buyer, was the essential condition. Other transactions involving the sale of goods are as follows:

1. Sales and other excise taxes
2. Cash discounts
3. Freight out and freight paid for customers
4. Sales returns and allowances

SALES AND OTHER EXCISE TAXES

Many states levy a tax on sales transactions, usually 2, 3, or 4 percent. The federal government levies special excise taxes on many sales or service transactions. For example, there has been an excise tax of 10 percent on jewelry, furs, watches and clocks, toilet preparations, and luggage, and a 10 percent tax on the charges for telephone and similar messages and on transportation of persons, and so on. Such taxes are collected by the seller from the buyer of the goods or the user of the service. They must be reported and paid to the government at specified intervals—usually quarterly. They are not revenue of the business. The entry for a charge sale of $800 subject to a 3 percent sales tax is:

Accounts Receivable..............................$ 824		
Sales..	$ 800	
Sales Tax Payable.........................	24	

The entry for a $500 charge sale subject to a 3 percent sales tax and to a 10 percent federal excise tax is:

Accounts Receivable................................$	565	
Sales.....................................		$ 500
Sales Tax Payable........................		15
Federal Excise Tax Payable................		50

To make the above entries, one must keep separate records of the price of the merchandise (sales revenue) and the tax on each sale. Some concerns record the sales revenue and sales tax in one figure. On sales of $18,000 subject to a 3 percent tax, the record would show:

Accounts Receivable................................$18,540	
Sales.....................................	$18,540

If this practice is followed, it is necessary to separate the sales tax liability from the sales revenue at each closing date. In doing so, one has to remember that the sales figure is 100 percent, the tax 3 percent (in this case), and the two together are 103 percent. Thus 1 percent is calculated by dividing the combined figure by 103, and the tax is three times 1 percent. Thus:

$$\$18,540 \div 103 = \$180$$
$$3 \times \$180 = \$540 = \text{the sales tax}$$

This entry is then made:

Sales...$	540	
Sales Tax Payable........................		$ 540
(to segregate sales tax from sales)		

This method is not satisfactory unless all sales are subject to the sales tax or unless separate sales accounts for taxable and nontaxable sales are kept. It is not satisfactory if some of the sales subject to sales tax are also subject to certain federal excise taxes—unless, again, a separate sales revenue account is kept for each class. As a rule, sales made for resale, that is, to dealers, are not taxable, because the intent is to levy the tax only on the ultimate consumer.

CASH DISCOUNTS

It is a common practice in wholesale trade to offer a small discount for prompt payment of a charge sale, practically all the sales being charge sales. These discounts are called cash discounts or sales discounts. The discount, if any, is indicated on the sales invoice under "terms." It is expressed in abbreviations, as follows:

1/10 n/30. Read: "one ten net thirty." (A 1 percent discount is allowed if paid within ten days from the invoice date, otherwise the whole amount ["net"] is payable in thirty days.)

2/10 n/30. Read: "Two ten net thirty." (Same as above except that the discount is 2 percent. This is a very popular arrangement.)

2/10 e.o.m. Read: "two ten end of month." (A 2 percent discount is allowed if paid within ten days after the end of the month in which the bill is rendered.

Final time for payment is not expressed here, but it is ordinarily expected in 30 days.)

2/10 n/60. Read: "two ten net sixty." (A variation of the first two given above.)

net 10 prox. Read: "net tenth proximo." (Must be paid without discount by the tenth of the month following the invoice date.)

Net. This means that no discount is allowed.

Bills may be marked "payable when rendered," or other special terms may be given.

RECORDING CASH DISCOUNTS ON SALES

The seller records a sale subject to discount in the usual way. He has to do something about the discount only when it is taken. The following entries illustrate a sale of $500 subject to a 2 percent discount where the bill was paid within the discount period:

Accounts Receivable	$500	
Sales		$500
Cash	$490	
Sales Discount	10	
Accounts Receivable		$500

If sales tax is involved it should be noted that discounts do not apply to the tax. But this fact need not affect the computation of the amount to be paid, because a reduction in the amount paid for the goods permits a proportional reduction in the tax. For example, assume a sale of $600 with sales tax of 3 percent on terms of 2/10 n/30, and payment made within the discount period. The sale is recorded as follows:

Accounts Receivable	$618	
Sales		$600
Sales Tax Payable		18

The payment may be calculated by either of the following methods:

First method		Second method	
Total charged	$618.00	Charged for goods	$600.00
Less 2% discount	12.36	Less 2% discount	12.00
Cash paid	$605.64		$588.00
		Add 3% tax	17.64
		Cash paid	$605.64

The amount of sales tax ($18) as originally recorded before the discount was taken is therefore slightly overstated. A proper entry of the receipt of cash by the seller is as follows:

Cash	$605.64	
Sales Discount	12.00	
Sales Tax Payable	0.36	
Accounts Receivable		$618.00

Sales discounts were formerly shown in the income statement in the section for other deductions—a nonoperating item. However, if the desire is to show sales revenue at the net amount of cash collected or collectible, sales discounts must be deducted from the gross sales figure. This is the basis for the statement of revenue adopted in Chapter 4, and in the case of sales discounts it is evidently now the most widespread practice. Sales discount is therefore shown in this text, along with bad debts, as a deduction from the gross sales figure. For accurate results, the sales discount figure should be based on the discounts estimated to be taken on the sales made in a period but not yet paid for, as well as on the discounts already taken in that period. This estimate may be made and recorded in precisely the same way that bad debts are provided for. For example, if the concern's terms are 2/10, n/30 and half the sales are discounted, discounts will average 1 percent of sales. Then, on sales of $60,000 for a period, sales discounts would be provided for by this entry:

Sales Discount	$600.00	
Allowance for Sales Discount		$600.00

When a payment is received for a sale of $800 on which the discount is taken, the entry is:

Cash	$784.00	
Allowance for Sales Discount	16.00	
Accounts Receivable		$800.00

The Allowance for Sales Discount account has the same kind of function as Allowance for Bad Debts account; it is deducted from Accounts Receivable to show the net amount expected to be collected in cash.

TRADE DISCOUNTS

Cash discounts must be distinguished from trade discounts. A cash discount is a price concession given for prompt payment of the bill. A trade discount is a device for calculating from a list price the sales price to be billed a particular customer. Different trade discounts are applied to the same list price to determine what a wholesaler will pay as compared with a retailer. The wholesaler gets a larger discount (lower price) so that he can sell to the retailer and earn a profit. Trade discounts are also used where catalogues are large and expensive, as in the wholesale hardware trade, and prices must be changed more frequently than catalogues can be economically issued. When prices change, the seller simply sends out a new set of discounts. Trade discounts are often "chain discounts," that is, a string of percents, each of which is applied to the figure obtained by taking the prior percent off the price to which it applies. For example, the discount 20–8–3 (read "twenty, eight, three"), when applied to an article listed at $400, would give the following price calculation:

List price	$400.00
Less 20% of $400	80.00
	$320.00
Less 8% of $320	25.60
	$294.40
Less 3% of $294.40	8.83
Invoice price	$285.57

Chain discounts may be converted to a single discount figure by substituting 100 percent for the list price in the above computation, and proceeding as before, thus:

Base.	100.000%
Less 20% of 100	20.000
	80.000
Less 8% of 80	6.400
	73.600
Less 3% of 73.60	2.208
Basis for invoice price	71.392%

list price ($400) × discount rate (71.392) = invoice price ($285.57)

If it were desired to cut prices 2 percent, the above discount of 20–8–3 might be changed to 20–8–3–2; to raise prices, the 3 could be dropped or changed to a smaller figure.

FREIGHT ON SALES

Many sales are made f.o.b. shipping point, so there is no freight cost to the seller. When the seller ships by common carrier and does stand the freight expense (f.o.b. destination) the cost of freight is charged to an expense account commonly called Freight Out, which is a selling expense. Sometimes the seller does not stand the cost but pays it for the convenience of the customer, who is charged for it. In this case a Freight Paid for Customers account is used. It is a clearing account, because every debit will promptly be balanced by a corresponding credit, or vice versa. To illustrate, assume that goods are sold for $250 and that $27 freight is paid for the customer. The entries are:

Accounts Receivable.	$277	
Sales.		$250
Freight Paid for Customers		27
(to record sale with freight paid for account of the customer)		
Freight Paid for Customers.	$ 27	
Cash.		$ 27
(to record payment of freight for customer)		

If the account Freight Paid for Customers has a debit balance, it represents a receivable that soon will be shifted to a customer's account. If it has a credit balance, it represents a liability to pay the freight, assuming that all entries to date are correctly made.

SALES RETURNS AND ALLOWANCES

Merchandise is sometimes returned for credit with the consent of the seller, and occasionally the seller allows a reduction in price when it is discovered that the goods are not of the quality intended, or for other special reasons. It is desirable to have a record of the amount of returns and allowances as a check on the effectiveness with which customers' orders are being filled. An account for Sales Returns and Allowances is kept for this purpose, or a separate account for each customer may be kept. If a charge customer returns merchandise that sold for $85, the entry is:

```
Sales Returns and Allowances.............................$ 85
       Accounts Receivable............................          $ 85
```

If the bill has been paid and a cash refund is made, Cash instead of Accounts Receivable would be credited. The Sales Returns and Allowances account in effect partly cancels sales entries previously made. It is therefore deducted from sales in the income statements to arrive at net sales. It would be possible to estimate returns and allowances that probably will be made on charge sales not yet paid for, in which case an Allowance for Sales Returns and Rebates could be used. However, returns and allowances (or refunds or rebates) are very irregular and even uncommon in most businesses, so this account is rarely used.

SALES ACCOUNTS IN THE INCOME STATEMENT

The revenue section of the income statement of a concern selling merchandise in which the net cash collectible is the basis for the presentation of revenue has the following appearance:

```
Sales..........................................            $182,465
Deduct: Returns and Allowances.........................$4,875
        Bad Debts.....................................  6,400
        Sales Discounts...............................  2,700       13,975
    Net Sales.......................................            $168,490
```

The net sales figure represents the net amount of cash collectible from this period's sales.

SALES RECORDS

Records required for sales transactions are:

1. Sales journal
2. Accounts Receivable control account and subsidiary ledger
3. Sales invoices or sales slips
4. Sundry original records:
   (a) Customers' order
   (b) Shipping order
   (c) Bill of lading
   (d) Debit memorandum and credit memorandum

SALES JOURNAL

The sales journal serves the same purpose for sales transactions that the general journal would serve if there were no sales journal. The sales journal is one of the *special* journals, that is, a journal designed exclusively for one kind of transaction. Special journals have the following advantages:

1. Some postings may be made in total instead of individually.
2. Explanations may be abbreviated or omitted; the nature of the journal tells the nature of the transaction.
3. Work involving the journals may be divided among several persons, as is necessary when transactions are voluminous.
4. Specialization on the part of both employees and equipment permits economy in recording transactions.

SINGLE-COLUMN CREDIT SALES JOURNAL

The simplest form of special journal is a one-column journal. A single-column credit sales journal is shown below. In this journal each charge sale is recorded on one line. Note that the total is posted as a credit to the Sales account, thus saving many postings as compared with the general journal method. This sales journal, or sales book, also shows the total charges posted as one figure to a general ledger Accounts Receivable account. The numbers in the reference column indicate that this posting and the posting to Sales have been made. The check marks (✔) in the Reference column indicate that the individual debits have been posted to individual accounts for the various customers in the separate, or subsidiary, record for them. (The subsidiary record of customers accounts is discussed below in the section on Accounts Receivable Control Account and Subsidiary Ledger.) It would be possible to have a separate general ledger account for each customer, or to write their names opposite the entries for each one in a single general ledger account, but these methods suffice if there are only a few charge customers. Ordinarily a separate record of the amounts owed by each customer is kept, with the total owing by all customers carried in the general ledger account for Accounts Receivable.

SINGLE-COLUMN CREDIT SALES JOURNAL

	Sales Journal		Page ___	
Date	**Sold to**	**Ref.**	**Amount**	
1966				
June 1	Aberson Bros..................................	✔	682	10
2	Bateman, Inc.................................	✔	100	00
3	Capewell Stores..............................	✔	500	20
6	Dunlee Co....................................	✔	80	50
9	Epperson & Spear............................	✔	108	40
14	Fenware Stores...............................	✔	540	00
16	Gearheart Co.................................	✔	94	20
21	Hurlburd & Son..............................	✔	517	80
23	Ingwell Associates...........................	✔	44	60
25	Jackman, Inc.................................	✔	102	10
28	Kohlman Company............................	✔	435	00
29	Lormer Bros..................................	✔	321	20
	Dr. Accounts Receivable, Cr. Sales	6,22	3 526	10

Entries are made in the sales journal from invoices, a copy of each one being kept by the seller. Entries for cash sales are usually made in the journal for cash receipts, which is discussed in a later chapter.

The single-column sales journal is inconvenient if sales taxes must be collected, and especially if both taxable and tax-exempt sales are made.

MULTICOLUMN SALES JOURNAL

A multicolumn journal for credit sales is shown on page 149. This provides for sales tax and, in the Sundry columns, for unusual transactions. It has a separate column for debits to Accounts Receivable. In this journal the column totals for Accounts Receivable, Sales, and Sales Tax Payable are posted to the accounts indicated by those columns. The entries in the Sundry columns must be posted individually, as they would be if they were entered in a general journal. Also, the individual amounts in the Accounts Receivable column must be posted to the separate record of accounts with individual customers. Posting for the individual Accounts Receivable accounts and the general ledger sundry accounts is indicated by check marks or account numbers in the Reference column; when a column total is posted, the reference is placed below the figure.

Some of the sales in the illustrated journal are subject to a 3 percent state sales tax, which is recorded in the column for Sales Tax Payable. Now and then a note is taken in connection with a sale, and such a transaction is recorded on June 3 in the illustration. Sometimes a sale is subject to both a state sales tax and a federal excise tax of 10 percent; one of these occurred on June 30. Although the Sundry column totals are not posted, they are added to check the equality of debits and credits for the whole period in the journal. This proof is made for the multicolumn journal shown as follows:

Debit totals		Credit totals	
Accounts Receivable	$2,884.68	Sales	$3,413.50
Sundry	618.00	Sales Tax Payable	69.18
		Sundry	20.00
Total	$3,502.68	Total	$3,502.68

Every invoice may be recorded in the sales journal and posted from journal to ledger when only a few sales are made each day. When the number of sales is large and each amount is small, it is generally convenient to post the customers accounts directly from the sales invoices and enter only the daily total of the charge sales in the sales journal. This plan is called *direct posting*.

ACCOUNTS RECEIVABLE CONTROL ACCOUNT AND SUBSIDIARY LEDGER

When the number of charge customers is more than about twenty, it is not convenient to keep a separate account for each customer in the regular ledger or to make entries for all of them in one regular ledger account. Instead, an account for the total accounts receivable is kept in the regular ledger, called the *general ledger*, and accounts for each customer are kept in a separate ledger called a *subsidiary ledger*. If the work is complete and has been accurately done, the total of the accounts in the subsidiary ledger at any time will equal the

MULTICOLUMN JOURNAL FOR CREDIT SALES

Sales Journal

Page 18

Date	Sold to	Invoice Number		Accounts Receivable Debit	Credit Sales	Sales Tax Payable	Sundry Debit	Sundry Credit	Sundry Ref.	Sundry Account
1966 June 1	Madewell Factors........	101	✓	432 60	420 00	12 60				
2	Newman Co..........	102	✓	515 00	500 00	15 00				
3	Opel Distributors, Inc....	103	✓		600 00	18 00	618 00		3	Notes Receivable
6	Parker Commission Co...	104	✓	308 00	308 00					
9	Quill Bros..........	105	✓	211 15	205 00	6 15				
14	Roberts & Frank.......	106	✓	400 00	400 00					
16	Stillmere Co.........	107	✓	82 40	80 00	2 40				
21	Tubman & Son........	108	✓	104 03	101 00	3 03				
23	Upman Associates......	109	✓	99 50	99 50					
25	Van Dyke, Inc........	110	✓	170 00	170 00					
28	Webster Shops........	111	✓	206 00	200 00	6 00				
29	The Young Co........	116	✓	130 00	130 00					
30	A. X. Zeitman........	113	✓	226 00	200 00	6 00	618 00	20 00	16	Fed. Excise Tax Payable
				2 884 68	3 413 50	69 18	618 00	20 00		
				4	27	15				

balance in the *control account* in the general ledger. At the end of each month the balances in the subsidiary accounts are listed. This listing is called a *schedule* or a *trial balance* of the subsidiary ledger. It is then checked with the control account. If there is a discrepancy, the work is retraced to locate the error. A control account with a subsidiary ledger is used whenever too much detail would otherwise accumulate in the general ledger. In addition to the accounts receivable ledger there are accounts payable ledgers, plant ledgers (to record detail of plant and equipment), and stores ledgers (to record individual items of inventory). A concern that has accounts in many banks may have a bank or cash in banks ledger. The sales journal and accounts below show the relationship of the sales journal, the general ledger control account, and the subsidiary ledger. Note that the individual charges have been posted to the subsidiary ledger accounts, while the column total has been posted both as a debit to the Accounts Receivable control account and as a credit to the Sales account in the general ledger. Thus the general ledger is in balance and the subsidiary ledger has a net balance that agrees with its control account.

SALES JOURNAL AND ACCOUNTS RECEIVABLE ACCOUNTS

Sales Journal		page 2	
Date	**Sold to**	**Ref.**	**Amount**
1966			
Aug. 1	Ace Company		40 00
11	Bee, Incorporated		100 00
19	Cid Brothers		32 00
26	Dar, Limited		18 00
31	Eel Association		25 00
	Dr. Accounts Rec., Cr. Sales	2,4	215 00

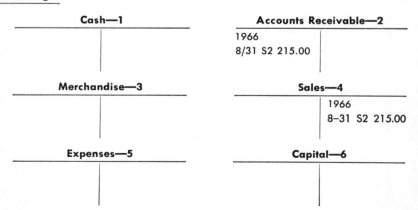

General Ledger

Cash—1

Accounts Receivable—2
1966
8/31 S2 215.00

Merchandise—3

Sales—4
1966
8–31 S2 215.00

Expenses—5

Capital—6

Accounts Receivable (Subsidiary) Ledger

Ace Company		Bee, Incorporated	
1966		1966	
8–1 S2 40.00		8–11 S2 100.00	

Cid Brothers		Dar, Limited	
1966		1966	
8–19 S2 32.00		8–26 S2 18.00	

Eel Association	
1966	
8–31 S2 25.00	

SALES INVOICE OR SALES SLIPS

The ledger classifies transactions by accounts and summarizes them. The journals give a chronological record of transactions in terms of debits and credits. One more type of record completes the basic list. This is the *original record* or *business paper.* It is the document that first records the transaction. Original records take many forms; the common ones for credit sales are the *sales invoice* or the *sales slip.* The bill we get at the end of a month from the

CUSTOMER'S ORIGINAL INVOICE

THE GREAT WESTERN SUGAR COMPANY   NO. 4427
P. O. BOX 5308—TERMINAL ANNEX

ORDER NO 410
CAR INITIAL AND NO GN 18–642–228
JOBBER'S ORDER NO 1217   DENVER, COLO., April 18,   1966
ROUTING   DRG
FACTORY
DESTINATION

SOLD TO A. S. Wise Stores, Inc.

1418 Pueblo Ave.
                                          TERMS: 2/10 n/30
Phoenix, Arizona

400	100 lb. sacks white granulated sugar at $60	$24,000.00

BROKER   ALF

gas company or the telephone company is an invoice, though sometimes labeled "statement." Most of us are familiar with the sales slip that records our purchase in a department store. Cash sales are often recorded only by a cash register, the tape from the register serving as the original record of the cash sales for a day. As was noted earlier, cash sales are usually recorded through the cash records rather than the sales records. Whatever the form of the original record, it contains the information required for the journal entries. Frequently the original records are numbered when printed or made out and the number is recorded along with the other information about the transaction when the journal entry is made. This facilitates subsequent reference to the original document. The illustrations given here show an invoice of the type common in wholesale trade and in much retail trade, and a sales slip of the sort often used in retail stores.

No.856-38   Date 6-17 1966

Name R. M. Salter

Address 410 W. 27th St. City

SOLD BY	CASH	C. O. D.	CHARGE	ON ACCT.	MDSE. RETD.	PAID OUT
ML	✓					

QUAN.		DESCRIPTION	PRICE	AMOUNT	
2	1	36 exp. K135	2 20	4	40
	2				
	3	Tax			18
	4			4	58
	5				
	6				
	7				
	8				
	9				
	10				
	11				
	12				

Customer's Order No.	Rec'd By

KEEP THIS SLIP FOR REFERENCE

5H 528 Rediform

SUNDRY ORIGINAL RECORDS

Various records that are not directly the basis for a journal entry are needed to facilitate the handling of merchandise or the rendering of service. Five documents of this sort are important in connection with sales; namely:

1. Customer's order
2. Shipping order
3. Bill of lading
4. Debit memorandum
5. Credit memorandum

PURCHASE ORDER

No. **1940**   REQ. NO. __976__   DATE __7-14__ 19 __66__

TO __H. K. Lehrman Co.__

ADDRESS __1710 West Olive St., St. Louis, Mo.__

SHIP TO __S. O. Bateman, Inc.__

ADDRESS __110 9th St., Elgin, Ill.__

FOR	DATE REQUIRED	HOW SHIP	TERMS
	at once	truck	

	QUANTITY	PLEASE SUPPLY ITEMS LISTED BELOW	PRICE	UNIT
1	10	3/4" gal. unions	80	ea
2	40	3/4" gal. 90° ells	15	"
3	20	1" gal. 45° ells	23	"
4				
5				
6				
7				
8				
9				
10				
11				

IMPORTANT
OUR ORDER NUMBER MUST APPEAR ON
ALL INVOICES - PACKAGES, ETC.
   PLEASE NOTIFY US IMMEDIATELY IF YOU
ARE UNABLE TO SHIP COMPLETE ORDER BY DATE
SPECIFIED.

PLEASE SEND 2 COPIES OF YOUR INVOICE

B. M. Ladd
PURCHASING AGENT

Rediform
1S142

ORIGINAL

Customer's Order. The customer's order may be sent in on a form supplied by the seller or his salesman. It may be on a special form supplied by the customer, in which case it is usually called a *purchase order*. It may be very informal. In any case it is preserved for some time after the goods are shipped or the service rendered, since it is evidence of the contract between the buyer and seller. A customer's order form is shown on page 153.

SHIPPING ORDER

MARJORIE-ANN CREATIONS
430 Santa Clara Ave.   TEmplebar 6-4299   Oakland 10, California

CUSTOMER ORDER NO.	1829	DATE	Nov. 10	1966

SOLD TO Vardon, Inc.   SHIP TO Same

43 Maiden Lane

Westwood, South Carolina

| DATE SHIPPED | 11-10-66 | SHIPPED VIA | Parcel Post | ORDER FILLED BY | a a Heald | ORDER WRAPPED BY | Boyce | ORDER PACKED BY | AC. |

QUANTITY ORDERED	QUANTITY SHIPPED	DESCRIPTION	UNIT PRICE
12	12	#14 ASSORTED JEWELRY	
2	2	#27-98 Pins	
6	6	#27-101 Earrings	
4	4	#41-70 Rings	

SPECIAL INSTRUCTIONS: *Insured for $200.00*

Shipping Order. The shipping order instructs the shipping clerk or department to send the specified goods to the specified person. It has space in which the shipping clerk enters the date of shipment and perhaps the name of the carrier. The signature of the shipping clerk indicates that the shipment has been properly sent out. This document is also kept as evidence of performance of the seller's contract and for reference in case of difficulty. A shipping order is shown here.

Bill of Lading. The written contract and receipt between the shipper and the carrier of the goods is called a bill of lading. Two forms are used: the *straight* bill of lading and the *order* bill of lading. The straight bill of lading authorizes the carrier to deliver the goods only to the customer named in the bill. The order bill of lading provides for endorsing the bill over to someone else by the shipper or his agent. It is used to make c.o.d. (cash-on-delivery) shipments and for shipments that are to be sold, perhaps while in transit, and for which the final customer is not known at the time the shipment is made. In wholesale

Form 43—ORIGINAL

(Uniform Domestic Order Bill of Lading Adopted by Carriers in Official, Southern, Western and Illinois Classification Territories, March 15, 1922, as Amended August 1, 1930, and June 15, 1941.)

UNIFORM ORDER BILL OF LADING

ORIGINAL

Shipper's No._____

Agent's No._____

THE_____RAILWAY CO.   Loaded on_____

RECEIVED, subject to the classifications and tariffs in effect on the date of the issue of this Bill of Lading.

At_____   19____

From NATIONAL ALFALFA DEHYDRATING AND MILLING COMPANY

the property described below, in apparent good order, except as noted (contents and condition of contents of packages unknown), marked, consigned, and destined as indicated below, which said company (the word company being understood throughout this contract as meaning any person or corporation in possession of the property under the contract), agrees to carry to its usual place of delivery at said destination, if on its own road or its own water line, otherwise to deliver to another carrier on the route to said destination. It is mutually agreed, as to each carrier of all or any of said property over all or any portion of said route to said destination, and as to each party at any time interested in all or any of said property, that every service to be performed hereunder shall be subject to all the conditions not prohibited by law, whether printed or written, herein contained, including the conditions on back hereof, which are hereby agreed to by the shipper and accepted for himself and his assigns.
    The surrender of this Original ORDER BILL of Lading properly endorsed shall be required before the delivery of the property. Inspection of property covered by this Bill of Lading will not be permitted unless provided by law or unless permission is endorsed on this Original Bill of Lading or given in writing by the shipper.

Consigned to ORDER of NATIONAL ALFALFA DEHYDRATING AND MILLING COMPANY

Destination_____State of_____County of_____

Notify_____

At_____State of_____County of_____

Route_____

Delivering Carrier_____Car Initial_____Car No._____

NO. PACKAGES	Description of Articles. Special Marks, and Exceptions	*Weight (Subject to Correction)	RATE THRU	PAID IN	BAL.	EXTEN-SION	Subject to Section 7 of conditions, if this shipment is to be delivered to the consignee without recourse on the consignor, the consignor shall sign the following statement:
							The carrier shall not make delivery of this shipment without payment of freight and all other lawful charges. National Alfalfa Dehydrating and Milling Company By_____ (Signature of Consignor.) If charges are to be prepaid, write or stamp here, "To be Prepaid." Received $_____ to apply in prepayment of the charges on the property described hereon. Agent or Cashier. Per_____ (The signature here acknowledges only the amount prepaid.) Charges advanced: $_____

This shipment is correctly described.

Correct weight is_____lbs.

Subject to verification by the Western Weighing and Inspection Bureau in accordance with Agreement No.

NATIONAL ALFALFA DEHYDRATING AND MILLING COMPANY

_____per_____

*If the shipment moves between two ports by a carrier by water, the law requires that the Bill of Lading shall state whether it is "carrier's or shipper's weight."

Note—Where the rate is dependent on value, shippers are required to state specifically in writing the agreed or declared value of the property.

The agreed or declared value of the property is hereby specifically stated by the shipper to be not exceeding

INBOUND REFERENCE

Tender is hereby made of the following recorded Freight Bills or Transit Tonnage Credit Slips, to be applied on the above outbound shipment:

Bureau Number	PRO. No.	PRO. Date	From	WAY-BILL No.	WAY-BILL Date	Rate	Com-m'd'y	Actual Transit Weight	Actual Transit Weight used	Balance Due Transit House	Transit Operation

NATIONAL ALFALFA DEHYDRATING AND MILLING COMPANY

_____Agent

Per_____

Permanent postoffice address of shipper, LAMAR, COLORADO   Per_____

trade, c.o.d. shipments are often made by sending an order bill of lading to a bank, which collects for the goods or obtains a signature as specified on the required document before it gives the bill of lading to the customer. The bill of lading must be presented to the carrier's freight agent by the customer before he may obtain the merchandise. An order bill of lading is shown on this page.

Debit Memorandum. A debit memorandum notifies the person to whom it is addressed that the sender is debiting the account of the addressee on the sender's books. It is used for unusual transactions. For example, a seller noticed that the invoice sent to a customer a few days before had been made out for

● DEBIT MEMO ●

PISTON SERVICE Inc.

EAst 2-4242   905 EAST UNION   SEATTLE 22, WASHINGTON

DATE 4-20-66   YOUR INVOICE NO. 1848   YOUR INVOICE DATE 4-5-66

TO   Acme Tool Co.

     2710 Washburn Ave.

     Portland, Ore.

WE DEBIT YOUR ACCOUNT AS FOLLOWS:

For underextension on our invoice

     No. 4423 $18.00

DM 2570

PLEASE REFER TO THIS DR NUMBER ON ALL CORRESPONDENCE.
PLEASE FORWARD CREDIT MEMO IN DUPLICATE IMMEDIATELY TO BALANCE ACCOUNT.

100 units at $3 and that the amount extended was $30 instead of $300. The seller made out a debit memorandum for $270 and sent it to the customer with the explanation "to correct error in extension on our invoice No. 8283." A debit memorandum is shown on this page. Transactions involving debit memorandums are entered in the general journal, because they do not occur frequently enough to justify a special journal.

Credit Memorandum. The credit memorandum notifies the addressee that the sender is crediting the account of the addressee on the sender's books. It may be issued to acknowledge acceptance of returned merchandise, for example. In this case it is the basis for a debit to Sales Returns and Allowances and a credit to Accounts Receivable in the general journal. Note that when an unusual entry of this sort is made to Accounts Receivable in the general journal, the Accounts Receivable entry must be made in the subsidiary ledger account as well as in the general ledger control account. A credit memorandum usually has the same form as a debit memorandum.

SALES RECORDS AND COMPUTERS

Some form of original document for each of the transactions described in the preceding paragraphs will be needed even though a computerized accounting system is being used, at least during the present stage of development. Savings may be made, however, by using documents designed in the form of a card in which holes may be punched that the computer can read, or by using magnetic ink that some computer equipment can read. The sales registers described and other journals may be eliminated in a computer system, since the computer may total the transactions and automatically record them in "accounts" (memory locations) once the original transaction is read in. Computer specialists and others interested in systems developments predict that eventually almost all business concerns will have computers, that they will be interconnected, and that much business will be done automatically. In such a system, the computer of a merchant will notice when stock of an item is low, then order more stock by sending the necessary information to the computer of the supplier, which in turn will produce the shipping instructions. After the goods are received, the computer of the merchant will authorize the computer at the bank to transfer enough of the cash balance of the merchant to the account of the supplier, and it will notify the supplier's computer that it has done so and the bank's computer will confirm that fact. The supplier's computer, which had debited the merchant's account for the shipment, will then debit Cash and credit the merchant's account, and the transaction will be closed — all without intervention of the human mind, except perhaps at the points where the shipment went out and where it was received. This situation seems to be still a considerable distance in the future, and in the meantime many of the simpler devices described above will still be used. Knowledge of them will not only enable the student to be oriented to actual situations that he will later meet, but will also enable him to visualize the kinds of summaries and account relationships that are involved, regardless of the mechanical process by which the data are assembled.

INTERNAL CONTROL

Internal control "comprises the plan of organization and all of the coordinate methods and measures adopted within a business to safeguard its assets, check the accuracy and reliability of its accounting data, promote operational efficiency, and encourage adherence to prescribed managerial policies."[1] This definition includes more than accounting. However, the accountant is concerned with records covering all phases of the business. He is therefore in an especially favorable position to see that adequate control devices are used in all departments. The term "controller," used as a title for the accounting executive, recognizes this fact.

It is important that the student who wishes to use accounting as a tool of management (which includes accountants and many others) realize the usefulness of internal control devices. This text accordingly takes up the control measures that are especially important in connection with the discussion of each function of the enterprise, such as sales activity, and also in connection with the discussion of individual assets, such as accounts receivable or merchandise. Internal control protects a concern against fraud and embezzlement as well as against errors and inefficiency.

ELEMENTS OF GOOD INTERNAL CONTROL

The American Institute of Certified Public Accountants has suggested that four elements determine a good internal control system:

[1] American Institute of Certified Public Accountants, *Internal Control*, p. 6.

1. Organization
2. System of authorization and records
3. Sound practices
4. Adequacy of personnel

Organization. From the standpoint of control, good organization requires that operating, custodian, and accounting departments be separate. For example, the manufacturing department (which uses materials), the storeroom (in which materials are kept before use), and the accounting department (which records the flow of materials in stores accounts) are separate but cooperating units in the larger well-managed concerns. A similar example is the division of duties between the sales department (taking orders and requesting that shipments be made), the warehouse, and the accounting department. Under these circumstances neither the operating department (manufacturing or sales) nor the custodian department (storeroom or warehouse) can cover up its errors or misuse the materials without the likelihood that the accounts will show that some materials are not properly accounted for. This shortage would lead to an investigation that could uncover the error or misuse.

It is also important that responsibilities be clearly defined, preferably in an organization chart and an organization manual. Such a chart shows the positions and indicates who reports to and is responsible to what executive, and a manual describes the duties of the various positions in more detail.

System of Authorization and Records. The documents and other records required to carry on operations smoothly and to accumulate adequate accounting information about them constitute the system of authorization and records.

Of first importance here is a chart of accounts, which is a list of the accounts to be used in recording the assets, the liabilities, and proprietorship items and transactions, including revenues and expenses. Second, an accounting manual is helpful — and in complicated enterprises, essential; it describes the transactions to be recorded in each account. The third requirement is appropriate original records and forms. Three characteristics are desirable in an original record:

SIMPLICITY. The record should be as simple as possible, for ease of understanding and efficiency in recording data.

MULTIPLE USE. It should be designed for all its possible uses. For example, a sales invoice form, made up with several carbon copies, may be used for making the entry in the sales journal, for authorization for the shipment (shipping order), for summarizing sales by products, customers, territories and so on, and for calculating salesmen's commissions — to mention only a few possibilities.

AUTOMATIC CONTROL DEVICES. Forms should provide space for the initials or signature of persons using them; requiring initials or signature tends to assure that the individuals who sign them have done the required work. The use of forms prenumbered by the printer helps assure that no forms are destroyed. Even forms that are accidently spoiled should be marked "void" and filed in proper sequence. Other devices of this sort include alignment of space for figures to facilitate computations and inclusion of routing instructions on the form.

The original records discussed in prior sections of this chapter provide the needed forms for the common sales transactions.

Beyond the foregoing three requirements, certain collateral control devices are very useful. These include budgets (which permit checking results against plans), cost accounting systems (which require detailed accounting for materials and labor and also disclose errors or bad performance when costs show up out of line), and production control systems (that provide for checking on the progress of materials through the manufacturing process), and so on.

Sound Practices. Practice is sound or weak according to the way in which the forms are handled and the duties performed. The purposes of good organization and good forms and procedures can be defeated if sound practices do not accompany them.

The basic principle here is that duties should be divided among persons so that no one person has control over a transaction from start to finish. In other words, it is desirable to divide the work so that the work of one must tie in with, and therefore be checked by, that of another. For example, a general ledger bookkeeper may post the totals from the columns of a special journal to the general ledger accounts. Another bookkeeper may post the individual debits to the customer's accounts in the subsidiary ledger (either from the detail in the journal or directly from the invoices listed in the journal). If one makes an error, the chances are that the other will not make the same error. When the schedule of subsidiary account balances is compared with the control account balance, a difference will ordinarily appear if any errors are present; hence, the work of one bookkeeper checks that of the other. A great deal of internal control is based on this principle. It is used on the assumption that collusion or conspiracy to defraud a concern is unlikely; no system is secure against a sufficiently widespread conspiracy.

Another example of sound practices related to sales activity is the practice of keeping merchandise in a locked warehouse, with access given only authorized persons who can then be held responsible for it.

Adequacy of Personnel. A system that is good on paper can be defeated by incompetent or improperly trained personnel. Adequate internal control from the viewpoint of the personnel employed requires these steps:

1. Job analysis that discloses the personal qualifications needed on the job
2. Hiring of employees according to the qualifications needed
3. Adequate employee training for the job
4. Means of measuring the quality of performance on the job, such as:
   (a) Arranging duties so that the work of one employee is a check on that of another (see preceding section)
   (b) Regular review of work of subordinates by supervisors
   (c) Special control devices such as budgets, standard costs, internal audit staff, and, for some jobs, time and motion studies

SPECIFIC CONTROL DEVICES FOR SALES ACTIVITY

The principles of internal control outlined above are applicable to all phases of business. The following specific devices are especially useful for sales functions and are closely connected with the accounting process.

Separation of handling of merchandise and cash. This separation is easy in most wholesale trade; the shipping department is separate from the cashier and is not allowed to take cash for occasional cash sales. Department stores often separate the two functions by setting up cashier cages at various points and requiring the salesperson to give the merchandise to the cashier for wrapping, checking the sales slip, and making change for the customer. The salesperson has no good way to get and keep cash, as he has no supply of change and the customer is usually aware of the cashier system. Hence the salesperson has no incentive to understate the amounts on sales slips. The cashier can be checked on, because the salesperson sends sales slips to the accounting office that show what the cashier should have taken in.

Use of mechanical sales (or cash) registers. The "visible" register shows the amounts being rung up; modern registers produce a printed list for the customer; old ones ring a bell. Modern ones make a noise in recording the sale that attracts the customer's (or supervisor's) attention and causes him to notice if the sale is not being recorded. Thus the customer or the supervisor can check the salesperson or the cashier. Usually the register produces a tape that remains locked in the machine until taken out by an authorized person, thus giving a record not easily manipulated by the operator. Most modern machines also produce a receipt for the customer, which he has come to expect and can check.

Use of inventory control. This consists of keeping a record that shows how much stock should be on hand. Specific methods for it are discussed in the chapter on merchandise. When available it gives a check on the use of the stock because the stock is occasionally counted. If the count is less than the amount shown by the record, the shortage can be investigated.

Requirement of credit approval before making charge sales. In wholesale trade the credit department places a signature on the customer's order or on some other document to signify that the credit is approved. If this is lacking the shipping department will not ship the goods. In department stores the sales clerk calls the credit "board" on a special telephone if the sale is over a certain figure. If the credit is all right, the person at the board presses a button after finding the card for the customer. This signal causes a mark to be put on the sales slip, which was previously inserted in the telephone device. In smaller stores someone in charge may initial a sales slip to indicate approval of credit.

Preparing at one writing by means of carbon paper the customer's copy of the invoice, the office copy, and the shipping order. The use of carbons assures that the shipping department is authorized to send only what the customer is billed for, and that the company's record will show the same amount due that the customer is instructed to pay. If some information is not wanted on some copies, such as prices on the shipping order, that part of that copy may be printed over with dark crosshatching. This will make the prices or other data virtually unreadable.

DATA FOR MANAGERIAL DECISIONS ON SALES

The basic managerial decisions about sales are these:

1. Products to sell
2. Channels of distribution to use
3. Territories in which to sell

These basic decisions are not made permanently. As the firm operates, decisions are constantly reviewed and changed if need be. For example, some products may become obsolete and be dropped, while new products may appear and become profitable. New channels of distribution may develop.

("Channels of distribution" refers to the organizations sold to or through, such as wholesalers, dealers, or retailers.) For example, chain grocery stores have grown so much that the selling methods of food processors have changed in recent years. Similarly, a territory once profitable may decline, and another, once of no importance, may become profitable as population shifts or new industries develop.

Two steps of analysis that are useful in making basic sales decisions are (1) distribution of sales revenue, and (2) analysis of costs of earning the revenue.

DISTRIBUTION OF SALES REVENUE

"Distribution of sales revenue" refers to the process of sorting the sales figures into classes. If decisions about products to be sold are involved, the sales revenue is divided into different categories of products. For example, a farm-machinery dealer who also sells some industrial equipment might distribute sales into classes of products as follows:

Farm machines
Industrial machines
Replacement parts
Fertilizer
Other farm supplies

A concern may distribute sales figures by wholesalers, retailers, and local dealers, or by territories, such as states. The information is often obtained continuously. To assemble it an *analysis sheet* may be used. Each invoice is listed and the amounts of sales of the different products are entered in the columns for those products. Totals taken at the end of the month then show the revenue obtained for each class of product (or channel of distribution or territory in other cases). Analysis sheets are used for many similar purposes in accounting. This illustration shows an analysis sheet for the farm- and industrial-equipment dealer mentioned above.

SALES ANALYSIS SHEET BY PRODUCTS

		Sales Analysis			Month of May 1966
Invoice Number	Farm Machines	Industrial Machines	Replace- ment Parts	Fertilizer	Other Farm Supplies
804	1,800.00				
805		400.00			
806	2,000.00			1,600.00	180.00
807			427.00		232.00
808	3,600.00		140.00		80.00
809		2,400.00			
810		1,500.00	200.00		
811	2,700.00			3,200.00	300.00
812				800.00	200.00
813		840.00	40.00		
814	2,200.00				60.00
	12,300.00	5,140.00	807.00	5,600.00	1,052.00

The sales analysis may be made in the sales journal by including columns for the different sales classes. The analysis may also be recorded in a ledger; in this case the sales analysis totals are posted to sales accounts. If a control account for sales is used, it will appear in the general ledger and the sales distribution accounts will be in a subsidiary ledger. Otherwise, separate accounts may be kept in the general ledger for the several classes of sales.

From the figures in the sales distribution a manager can see what kinds of sales are lagging. He can decide whether to take steps to improve them or perhaps to drop them from the list. However, better decisions can be made if costs as well as revenue are considered. The consideration of costs involves the *contribution* theory.

CONTRIBUTION THEORY AND SALES

The contribution theory provides a way of analyzing sales costs (or expenses) in relation to the revenue. From the viewpoint of this theory, each dollar of sales consists of two things: the amount necessary to cover the variable cost of earning that dollar, and the remainder. The remainder is the *contribution* made by the sales dollar to cover fixed costs and possibly to make a profit. *Variable* costs are those that vary directly with production and sales. For example, the material used in a product and the salesman's commission on its sale are variable costs. Another sale means the incurring of some more of these costs. *Fixed* costs are those that do not vary with production or sales. Examples are depreciation, salaries of permanent officers and employees, insurance premiums, and rent. Another sale in a particular period does not require incurring more of these fixed costs. Managers evidently find it helpful to think in terms of the sales contribution, and accountants therefore may calculate the contribution made by sales of different classes of product, of sales to different classes of customers (channels of distribution), or of sales made in different territories. Any contribution improves the profit.

ANALYSIS OF SALES COSTS

Analysis of sales costs includes the analysis of variable costs into the same classes used for the analysis of sales revenue. Making this analysis requires that the sales expenses which vary with sales be identified and listed for the different sales classes, just as sales revenue is. The process requires examining each expense account and then identifying any variable part of it with the sales class affected. Sometimes the expense can be calculated without reference to the account for it. For example, the cost of goods sold in a merchandising concern can be obtained by multiplying the units sold by the purchase price per unit, and the sales commissions can be computed by multiplying the sales revenue by the percent of commission. Sales returns and allowances must be similarly analyzed. For completeness, bad debts and sales (or cash) discounts must also be included. Each of the costs or expenses may be accumulated on a separate analysis such as the one illustrated in the product sales analysis. The totals may then be brought together as in the contribution analysis illustrated here, which shows the contribution made toward covering the fixed costs and possible profit by the sales revenues already analyzed. From such an analysis a manager can see which types of sales are making a

CONTRIBUTION ANALYSIS

		Contribution Analysis		Month of May 1966	
Account	Farm Machines	Industrial Machines	Replacement Parts	Fertilizer	Other Farm Supplies
Sales..................	12,300.00	5,140.00	807.00	5,600.00	1,052.00
Less: Sales Returns, Discounts and Bad Debts......	1,100.00	400.00	50.00	400.00	40.00
Net Sales Revenue......	11,200.00	4,740.00	757.00	5,200.00	1,012.00
Cost of Goods Sold.........	6,400.00	2,600.00	400.00	2,500.00	520.00
Advertising...............	200.00	300.00	40.00	1,400.00	40.00
Sales Commissions..........	1,230.00	514.00	—	560.00	—
Freight Out...............	200.00	150.00	160.00	600.00	200.00
Other Variable Costs........	900.00	100.00	30.00	100.00	50.00
Total Variable Costs.....	8,930.00	3,664.00	630.00	5,160.00	810.00
Contribution..............	2,270.00	1,076.00	127.00	40.00	202.00

helpful contribution to cover fixed costs and which are not. If a contribution is not satisfactory, steps may be taken to make it so; for example, costs may be cut by giving less service, or commissions on that item may have to be reduced. If the contribution is negative, the item may be dropped.

A word of caution is needed at this point. Many factors must be considered in any basic sales policy decision. The decision will not usually be made solely on the information about the current sales contribution of the item. For example, the figures in the contribution analysis shown here indicate that fertilizer sales are making almost no contribution to fixed costs and profit. However, the company has been putting special effort into promoting this item because it is new. It is expected that the variable costs associated with it will decline relative to the revenue as soon as it is established in the business. The item will therefore be continued at least until it has had a chance to become known and accepted by the firm's customers. However, the amount of contribution will be an important factor in any fundamental sales decision.

OTHER SALES DECISIONS AND ANALYSES

Decisions must be made about many sales activities other than the fundamental ones noted above. These include:

1. Whether or not to accept very small orders
2. What methods of solicitation to use (salesmen, telephone solicitation, mail solicitation, for example)
3. Methods of delivery (railroad, trucker, ship or barge, own trucks, mail, express, air)
4. What kinds of customers to cater to (industries, dealers, individuals)
5. Where to locate warehouses
6. Whether or not to use branch offices

The distinction between fixed and variable costs is often helpful in making decisions on these and similar problems. For example, a management thinking of opening a branch office can calculate the amount that would be added to fixed costs for depreciation, insurance, permanent salaries, taxes, and so on. Then it will know the amount of sales contribution necessary to cover these fixed costs. From this, assuming that the percent (ratio) of variable costs to sales is known, the amount of sales necessary to break even is computed. For example, a new branch office will involve fixed costs of $12,000 per year. Variable costs are 60 percent of sales. On each sales dollar, 40 cents is the contribution to cover fixed costs and to make a profit. The number of sales dollars needed to break even at this branch is then:

$$\frac{\text{fixed costs}}{\text{contribution per sales dollar}} = \frac{\$12,000}{0.40} = \$30,000$$

It is also possible to analyze total costs (including the fixed costs) by sales classes. The methods used are described in Chapter 17 on departmental accounting.

SUMMARY

Sales transactions explained in this chapter are:

1. Sales and other excise taxes
2. Cash discounts and trade discounts
3. Freight out and freight paid for customers
4. Sales returns and allowances

The documents and records used in the day-to-day recording of sales are:

1. Sales journal
2. Accounts Receivable control account and subsidiary ledger
3. Sales invoices or sales slips
4. Sundry original records:
   (a) Customer's order
   (b) Shipping order
   (c) Bill of lading
   (d) Debit memorandum and credit memorandum

The principles of internal control were presented as follows:

1. Organization
2. System of authorization and records
3. Sound practices
4. Adequacy of personnel

Devices of internal control especially useful in assuring an accurate and honest record of sales were also suggested.

The analysis of sales revenue by classes such as type of product, channels of distribution, and territories was described for its use in making managerial decisions. An analysis sheet was illustrated. The analysis of variable costs or expenses by the same sales classes to obtain the contribution of sales toward fixed costs and profit was also described. The viewpoint of the contribution theory, that each sales dollar consists of the amount necessary to cover the variable costs of earning it and the remainder, which is the contribution it makes to fixed costs and profit, was stated. Other possible cost analyses related to sales are possible but are beyond the scope of this chapter.

QUESTIONS

5.1 All of Othman Company's sales are subject to a 3 percent sales tax. The company records the total amount of its invoices, including sales tax, as a credit in the Sales account. How can the amount of tax be determined and separated from sales revenue at the end of the month?

5.2 (1) What are the purposes of trade discounts?
(2) Explain the difference between a trade discount and a cash discount.
(3) Explain the basic difference in the accounting treatment of the two types of discounts.
(4) What is the reason for this difference in treatment?

5.3 The Masterco Press sells f.o.b. its warehouse, but it pays the postage, which is added to the amount of the sales invoice. Give the entries required to record the sale and the payment of postage on a $500 order for which $25 of postage was paid.

5.4 (1) Manufacturing and trading companies generally use a Sales account, while real estate developers and construction companies generally do not. Why?
(2) The owner of a medium-sized retail store objects to the Sales Returns account as being unnecessary. He suggests that returned sales should be charged directly to the Sales account. Explain the reason for the Sales Returns account.

5.5 (1) Sales made near the end of the month that are subject to a cash discount result in an accounts receivable balance larger than the amount likely to be collected. What can the accountant do about this situation?
(2) During the month the Tilden Sales Co. sells $5,000 of merchandise on terms 5/10 n/30. It collects on account $4,000 less discounts of $200. Customers are expected to take all cash discounts. Give the entries to record the sale, collection, and adjustment at the end of the month if the company uses an Allowance for Sales Discounts account.
(3) Give the entries for the Tilden Sales Co. if the company does not use an Allowance for Sales Discounts account.
(4) Differentiate between the Allowance for Sales Discounts account and the Sales Allowances and Discounts account.

5.6 (1) What are the specific laborsaving advantages obtained through the use of special journals? What are other reasons for the use of special journals?
(2) What is the basic factor in determining the columns that should be provided in a special journal?
(3) A multicolumn sales journal has the following column headings:

Date	Credit Sales
Sold to	Credit Sales Tax Payable
Invoice Number	Sundry Debit
Ref.	Sundry Credit
Debit Accounts Receivable	Ref.
	Account

Describe the posting of this journal.

5.7 (1) What are the principal advantages of control accounts?

(2) List five common control accounts in the ledger of a retail corporation.

(3) Describe the posting of a one-column sales journal in each of the following cases:

(a) The general ledger contains a single Accounts Receivable account and there is no subsidiary ledger.

(b) The general ledger contains an account for each customer.

(c) The general ledger contains an Accounts Receivable account and there is an account for each customer in a subsidiary ledger.

5.8 State the function of each of the following documents: sales invoice, shipping order, bill of lading, debit memorandum, credit memorandum.

5.9 Data processing by computers may be classified as "off line" or "real time." Under the former, sales invoices are sorted into batches and processed by groups; under the latter, each transaction is processed as it occurs. Can you explain why most accounting installations are of the off-line variety at the present time?

5.10 Answer the following questions about the principles of good internal control:

(1) What does good organization for internal control imply about the creation of different departments?

(2) What four things make up a good system of authorization and records?

(3) What kind of arrangement of the duties of different employees is the basis for many sound practices in internal control?

5.11 (1) "The handling of ticket sales in a motion picture theater vividly illustrates two necessary conditions for internal control; namely, division of labor and prenumbered forms." Discuss.

(2) Eaton's uses a central cashier system. Sales tickets are prepared in triplicate. The original is given to the customer, the duplicate is sent to the sales audit department, and the triplicate is retained by the salesman. When a sale is made, the customer is taken to a cashier, who wraps the merchandise and either collects cash or charges the customer's account. Explain how this system prevents fraud.

5.12 Suggest a specific internal control device or sales activity that would tend to prevent each of the following frauds:

(1) A salesclerk wrote "$8.40" on the sales slip for a sale totaling $18.40, and kept the extra $10 when the customer paid the $18.40.

(2) A salesclerk did not ring up part of the customer's purchase on the cash register and kept the difference when the customer paid the full amount of the sale.

(3) The manager of a branch feed mill sold grain and pocketed the proceeds without recording the sales.

(4) The shipping department received a shipping order for a certain sale calling for shipment of 100 units, and it shipped that quantity. The sales invoice was made out for the quantity the customer ordered, but the dollar amount was for the price of 10, not 100, units. The customer was dishonest and did not mention the discrepancy.

5.13 University Housing operates seven student dormitories on the campus of a Western university. Daily cash receipts from about one hundred persons, mostly for room and board, range from $500 to $1,000. All cash is received in one central office, which consists of the manager and two clerks. The accounting functions are to be divided among these three.

Outline the duties of each person with respect to receipt of cash, preparation of daily deposits, posting of receivables, and related functions so as to secure optimum internal control.

5.14 (1) Suggest three bases of classification for analyzing sales revenue incident to the making of basic sales decisions.

(2) Describe a working paper form for making the analysis.

(3) What is the "contribution theory"?

(4) How is it used in making sales decisions?

5.15 (1) Distinguish between fixed costs and variable costs and give examples of each.

(2) During the past year the JR Company earned $4,000 on a sales volume of $300,000. Fixed expenses amounted to $116,000; variable expenses amounted to $180,000. The manager is contemplating hiring another man at an annual cost of $12,000. He expects the new man to increase sales by 15 percent. Compute the break-even point under present and proposed conditions.

EXERCISES

5.1 The Furniture Mart is located in a state which taxes all retail sales made within the state at 4 percent. Charge sales in January amount to $20,000 plus tax.

Required:

1. Submit journal entries to record the sales if (a) the tax liability is recorded at the time of sale and (b) the tax liability is recorded only at the end of the month.
2. Submit the journal entry required to adjust the sales for the tax liability when sales and tax are not segregated in the records at the date of sale.
3. What is the disadvantage of not recording the tax liability on the date of sale?

5.2 Allied Paper records discounts only when payment is received.

Required:

1. Draft journal entries for the following transactions:
   Mar. 5   Sold merchandise for $1,000, terms 2/10 e.o.m.
   Apr. 8   Received payment for the above sale.
2. Draft journal entries to record the transactions and the March 31 adjustment if the company uses an Allowance for Sales Discounts account. (Record the allowance at March 31 based on the discount available for the March 5 sale.)
3. What is the advantage of using the Allowance for Sales Discounts account?

5.3 Malibu Sales Co. sold merchandise for $2,000 f.o.b. shipping point and paid freight charges of $300, which is added to the invoice.

Draft journal entries to record the sale and the payment of the freight for the customer.

5.4 Sales and sales returns of Florence and Mary's for the years 1966 to 1968 are as follows:

	1966	1967	1968
Sales	$200,000	$300,000	$500,000
Sales returns	10,000	21,000	50,000

Discuss the significance of these figures, and comment on the control provided by maintaining separate accounts for gross sales and returned sales.

5.5 Classic Furniture Company is located in a state in which a 4 percent sales tax applies to the gross receipts of retailers from the sale of tangible personal property. A sale for resale is exempt from tax. If the tax collected is less than 4 percent of taxable sales, the deficiency is paid by the retailer.

The balances of the Sales and the Sales Tax Payable accounts at March 31 and June 30 appear below. The March 31 balances are after the adjustment for the sales tax liability and the balances on June 30 are before the adjustment for the sales tax liability.

	Year to Date	
	March 31	June 30
Sales	$40,100	$120,400
Sales Tax Payable	1,532	3,101

Sales during the quarter ended June 30 include merchandise sold for resale in the amount of $2,400.

1. What was the amount of tax-exempt sales in the quarter ended March 31?
2. Give the entry to adjust the sales tax liability account at June 30 for the uncollected sales tax, supported by a schedule in good form.

5.6   Bruxbo, Inc., sells to both the wholesale and the retail trade. Wholesale prices are list less 40 percent. Terms of sale are 2/10 n/30 wholesale, n/30 retail. Some small items are sold for cash. Retail sales are subject to a 4 percent sales tax unless delivery is made out of state. A number of sales are made f.o.b. shipping point; delivery charges are paid by the company and added to the invoice.

Design a multicolumn sales journal suitable for this company.

5.7   Rollo Company recorded sales and cash receipts for July 1966 in a multicolumn journal as shown below.

Cash Dr.	Accts. Rec. Dr.	Date	Explanation	Accts. Rec. Cr.	Sales Cr.
	400	July 6	Customer A		400
	500	7	Customer B		500
200		15	Cash sale		200
100		22	Customer A	100	
300		28	Customer B	300	
200		30	Cash sale		200
800	900			400	1,300

Balances due from customers at July 1, 1966, were as follows:

Customer A $100
Customer B   200
Total $300

Post to T accounts for the general and the subsidiary ledgers, ignoring the opening balances in the general ledger accounts except Accounts Receivable. Prepare a schedule of customers accounts at July 31, 1966, and compare the total to the general ledger control.

5.8   Following is a schedule of various invoices:

Date of Invoice	List Price	Trade Discounts	Credit Terms	Date Paid
Jan. 5	$1,000	40%	2/10 n/30	Jan. 15
12	2,000	30-20-10%	2/10 e.o.m.	Feb. 9
15	5,000	30-20%	5/10 1/30 n/60	Feb. 15

Compute the net cash proceeds received in settlement of each invoice.

5.9 Operations of the H Co. for 1966 are summarized below.

Sales		$200,000
Fixed costs	$ 60,000	
Variable costs	120,000	180,000
Net income before income taxes		$ 20,000

Management believes that sales can be increased 20 percent by the addition of an outside salesman at an annual cost of $14,000.

Required:

1. Calculate sales at the break-even point under the present conditions and under proposed conditions.
2. Calculate the pretax net income under the proposed conditions if management's estimates of sales increase are realized.
3. Calculate the sales necessary under the proposed conditions if the current pretax net income is to be maintained.

5.10 The Decorating Center sells furniture, appliances, and rugs. Using the following data for August 1966, prepare an analysis sheet that shows the contribution to fixed costs and profits made by each line of merchandise. Identify any line that appears to be making an inadequate contribution.

In the groups of three figures given below, the first represents furniture, the second appliances, and the third rugs. Sales for August were $360,000, $170,000, and $70,000. Returns, discounts, and bad debts were $3,000, $2,000, and $1,000. Cost of goods sold amounted to $285,000, $160,000, and $56,000. Delivery and installation charges absorbed by the company were $13,400, $4,600, and $4,800. Depreciation totaled $10,000, allocated respectively to the three items 50%, 30%, and 20%. Miscellaneous variable costs were $6,100, $3,200, and $900.

5.11 Prepare journal entries for the following transactions completed by the Emperor Sales Co.

Jan. 11 Sold $2,500 of merchandise, f.o.b. shipping point, terms 2/10 e.o.m. Freight charges of $100 were prepaid and added to the invoice.
　　 12 Paid the freight charges.
　　 20 Issued a credit memorandum for merchandise returned with an invoice price of $1,000.
Feb. 10 Received a check in full of the invoice less discount. No discount is allowed on the prepaid freight.

PROBLEMS

5.1 The following data are taken from the records of the N Co. The company recognizes sales discounts only when an account is collected. Prepare the entries required in general journal form.

(1) A check is received from a customer for a cash sale. The sales slip shows merchandise amounting to $100 and sales tax of 3 percent.
(2) An invoice is issued for merchandise $500, sales tax 3 percent, and excise tax 10 percent.
(3) A check is received from a customer in full of account less discount. His account has a balance of $2,200 for an invoice of $2,000 plus 10 percent excise tax; terms, 2/10 n/60.
(4) An invoice is issued for merchandise $300, sales tax $9, and freight $25.
(5) A check is issued in payment of freight on the above shipment.
(6) An invoice is issued for merchandise $700, f.o.b. destination, terms 2/10 e.o.m.

(7) A check is received in full of the foregoing invoice less discount and $40 freight paid by the customer.

(8) An invoice is issued for 1,000 units of merchandise at a list price of $8 less trade discount of 20-10-5.

(9) A credit memorandum is issued for the net cash price of goods billed at $50, terms 2/10 n/60.

(10) The sales tax return for the prior quarter is filed with a check in the amount of $650.

5.2 Accounts receivable of Norsco at December 31, 1966, were as follows:

Customer	Date	Terms	Amounts
Layton's	12/1/66	2/10 e.o.m.	$2,000
Mikesell, Inc.	12/10/66	2/10 e.o.m.	6,000
Nan & Co.	12/10/66	2/10, n/30	3,000
O'Day's Fashions			(1,000)
			$10,000

The credit balance in O'Day's Fashions represents the invoice price of merchandise returned. The company records discounts when cash is received. The following selected transactions occurred during January 1967:

(1) Received a check from Layton's for $1,960 in full of account.

(2) Received a check from Nan & Co. for $3,500 in settlement of account plus a $500 advance payment.

(3) Received a check from Mikesell, Inc., for $4,900 in partial payment of the account. The partial payment was received within the discount period, and the 2 percent cash discount was allowed on the pro rata portion of the invoice price.

(4) Sold Layton's 50 tables at a list price of $200 per table less trade discounts 50-25-20; terms 2/10 e.o.m.

(5) Sold land acquired as an investment at cost for $5,000 cash.

(6) Sold merchandise to O'Day's Fashions at list $5,000 less 50-20; terms 2/10 n/30.

(7) Received a check from O'Day's Fashions in full of account. The check was received within the discount period.

(8) Issued a credit memorandum to Mikesell, Inc., for merchandise returned at the invoice price of $600.

Required:

1. Prepare general journal entries. Explanations may be omitted.
2. How would entry 7 differ if the accounting procedures of the company were such that the January 1 credit in O'Day's Fashions represented the net cash price of goods returned?
3. Post Accounts Receivable control and the subsidiary ledger. Prepare a schedule of accounts receivable and compare it with the control.
4. Where should the credit balance in the Nan & Co. account be shown in the balance sheet?

5.3 Delro Co. carries three lines of products: wholesale hardware, retail hardware, and builders' specialties. Using the following data for July 1966, prepare an analysis sheet and compute the contribution to fixed costs and profit made by each class of products. Identify any class that appears to be making an inadequate contribution. In each group of three figures given below, the first represents wholesale hardware, the second retail hardware, and the third builders' specialties.

Sales for the month were $18,420, $9,680, and $4,125. Returns, allowances, discounts, and bad debts were $1,100, $480, and $80. Cost of goods sold totaled $8,400, $5,050, and $2,200. Advertising was $2,100, $970, and $570. Sales commissions were $910 for wholesale hardware and $260 for builders' specialties. Freight out was $1,005 for wholesale hardware and $810 for builders specialties. Miscellaneous variable costs were $175, $580, and $85. Depreciation on the equipment used for each class of product was $2,200, $3,200, and $1,800.

5.4   The trial balance of the ATC Co. at June 30, 1967, is as follows:

Cash	$ 4,100	
Accounts Receivable	10,100	
Inventories	20,000	
Accounts Payable		$ 8,000
Sales Tax Payable		1,900
Advances from Customers		—
A. Taylor, Capital		9,000
Merchandise Sales		200,100
Labor Sales		60,100
Cost of Merchandise Sales	—	
Purchases	160,000	
Purchase Returns and Allowances		5,000
Expenses	89,900	
	$284,100	$284,100

The bookkeeper neglected to post the sales and cash receipts journal for June. Totals of that journal for June appear below. (The company charges trade-ins to Purchases and credits damage claims to Purchase Returns and Allowances.)

Left page

Other, Dr.		Cash	Accts.		
Name	Amount	Received	Rec., Dr.	Date	Description
Trade-ins	1,000	16,000	36,000		

Right page

Accts.	Sales		Sales	Other, Cr.	
Rec., Cr.	Merchandise	Labor	Tax	Name	Amount
15,000	30,000	5,000	1,000	Damage claims	2,000

Examination of the accounting records discloses the following additional errors:

(1) The $8,000 balance of Accounts Payable in the trial balance is the amount that was due trade creditors January 1, 1967. Payments from January to June were charged to Purchases. The total due trade creditors on June 30 is $10,000.

(2) The list of customers' balances at June 30 totals $30,536. A review of the sales and cash records discloses that the balance in the W. C. Adams account was overstated because an invoice of $904 was posted as $940 to the subsidiary ledger, but was posted correctly to the general ledger; that a $500 invoice was posted twice in error to the account of C. W. Jones; and that a March invoice for a nontaxable sale of labor was overstated $100 when recorded in the sales and cash receipts journal but was posted in the correct amount to the subsidiary ledger.

(3) All merchandise sales are taxable at 4 percent; labor sales are exempt. Sales tax returns are filed quarterly. Merchandise sales for April and May amounted to $45,000. The company neglected to include the proper sales tax on some invoices and is liable for the uncollected tax.

(4) Some customers pay in advance for certain merchandise. At June 30 a total of $5,200 (merchandise $5,000, tax $200) is included in the Merchandise Sales and Sales Tax Payable accounts for goods to be purchased by the company and delivered to customers in the next month.

(5) The Purchases, Purchase Returns and Allowances, and Inventories accounts are to be adjusted to reflect a cost of merchandise sold amounting to 60 percent of merchandise sales.

Required:

1. Open T accounts for the June 1 balances, and post the sales and cash receipts journal for June. Adjust the accounts to correct the additional errors.

2. Prepare an income statement for the six months ended June 30, 1967.

5.5 The Muller Manufacturing Company began business on January 1, 1966. All sales are made on terms of 2/10 n/30. Sales, cash receipts, discounts taken, and accounts written off for the three years ended December 31, 1968, are as follows:

	1966	1967	1968
Sales at gross prices	$80,000	$120,000	$240,000
Collections from customers:			
Cash received	60,000	100,000	180,000
Discounts taken	900	1,500	3,000
Accounts written off as uncollectible	—	1,000	4,000

Required:

1. Present the revenues section of the income statement under each of the following assumptions:

(a) Sales discounts are recognized only when they are taken; bad debts are recorded only when customers' accounts are removed from the accounts receivable ledger.

(b) Sales discounts are recognized only when they are taken; bad debts are estimated at 1½ percent of sales.

(c) Bad debts are estimated at 1½ percent of sales; sales discounts are estimated to be taken on 80 percent of the sales for the year.

2. Present the accounts receivable section of the balance sheet at the end of each year for the three assumptions.

5.6 A company is considering the addition of a new line of products. Different product lines that could be added have different ratios (percents) of variable costs to sales. They also involve different kinds of facilities with different fixed costs. The five sets of figures given below represent five different possible new product lines that the company is considering. The first figure in each case represents the percent of variable costs to sales of the line. The second one is the annual fixed cost figure involved in the facilities required. You are to determine which new line will be adopted, using the figures below and the following two assumptions: (1) sales will be $100,000 regardless of the line selected; (2) the line to be selected is the one that will make the largest contribution to general fixed costs and profit over and above its own fixed costs.

The figures referred to are: 60%, $24,000; 80%, $36,000; 50%, $40,000; 40%, $36,000; 35%, $44,000.

Purchases Accounting and Control

The term *purchases* refers to commodities and to various services as well, but in business usage it is often restricted to the purchase of merchandise. For example, the Purchases account records purchases of merchandise. This chapter gives special attention to merchandise purchases, but also covers other purchases. It is concerned with three things: the transactions and the records made of them; the internal control measures for purchases; the managerial decisions about purchases that accounting or accounting methods can help with. Thus it is parallel to Chapter 5, which dealt with sales.

PURCHASE TRANSACTIONS

The student is already acquainted (Chapter 4) with the Purchases account, to which acquisitions of merchandise are debited. Purchases of other assets, such as machinery and equipment or supplies, are charged to accounts for those assets. Services, such as advertising, are ordinarily debited to expense accounts, because they are usually used up by the time the entry is made. When they are going to be useful over a period of time, as is the premium on an insurance policy that will run for three years, they are frequently charged to an asset account such as Prepaid Insurance. This chapter will deal with purchases made on credit, but of course purchases may be also made for cash. In the latter case the credit is made to Cash instead of Accounts Payable or Vouchers Payable. Other transactions involving purchases are the following:

1. Freight in and other acquisition costs
2. Purchase returns and allowances
3. Cash discounts on purchases

FREIGHT IN

The cost of any asset is not merely the amount paid to the supplier. It includes any amounts spent to get the asset in a position to be used by the buyer. The cost of merchandise, for example, frequently includes freight, because most shipments in wholesale trade are made f.o.b. shipping point. When merchandise is bought, this cost is customarily debited to a separate account called Freight In, as follows:

Freight In $800
    Accounts Payable $800
(to record freight bill payable to S.P.R.R. Co. for purchase from Zee Co. received 6/16/66)

In some cases there is an additional cost for cartage, which is transportation within the local area from the railroad's delivery point to the plant of the buyer. In these cases an account for Freight and Cartage In is ordinarily used for the two items. Such accounts are added to Purchases when an income statement is drawn up. Other costs involved in getting merchandise into a position to be used occur in special cases and may be recorded in accounts similar to the two mentioned. For example, sometimes goods must be tested chemically or inspected by expensive procedures.

OTHER ACQUISITION COSTS

In all cases there are costs that are theoretically part of the cost of the asset but are not large enough to justify the trouble of accounting for them as acquisition costs. These include the costs of operating a purchasing department, a receiving department, and a storeroom, where merchandise and supplies are kept before use or sale. These latter costs are troublesome when treated as freight in was in the preceding section, because unit costs must be calculated for inventory purposes. At the end of the period the inventory of merchandise is recorded, when the periodic inventory method is used, as follows:

Merchandise $10,000
  Cost of Goods Sold (or Profit and Loss) $10,000
(to record ending inventory of merchandise)

To get the figure for this entry, the number of units of each item on hand is multiplied by the cost per unit. This unit cost must include freight in and any other acquisition costs added to purchases in the income statement. However, costs such as purchasing department, receiving department, and storeroom costs are difficult to identify with individual units of material. There is little identification difficulty with freight in, since freight is calculated as so much per 100 pounds. As a result, the other acquisition costs are usually recorded as expenses in the period in which they are incurred, and nothing is added to purchases or included in inventory figures for them.

Freight and any other acquisition costs (such as cost of a special permit) that are identified with assets other than merchandise are charged directly to the particular asset account. Freight on a piece of machinery is charged to the Machinery account; a permit to erect an advertising sign is charged to the Sign or the Equipment account.

PURCHASE RETURNS AND ALLOWANCES

A sales return on the seller's books is a purchase return on the buyer's books. Accounts for Purchase Returns and Allowances are accordingly used by the buyer to record these transactions. The entry to record a purchase return or allowance is:

Accounts Payable $1,400
  Purchase Returns and Allowances $1,400

The Purchase Returns and Allowances account has a credit balance, as it reduces the Purchases account. It is deducted from Purchases in the income statement. Notice of entry is given to the seller by means of a *debit* memorandum, which was described in Chapter 5.

If the bill has been paid and the Accounts Payable account shows a debit balance because of the return or allowance, this balance is shown as a receivable in the balance sheet.

CASH DISCOUNTS ON PURCHASES

The discount allowed for prompt payment of cash is a sales discount to the seller and a purchase discount to the buyer. The cash discount on purchases is ordinarily recorded only when it is actually taken. The entry is:

```
Accounts Payable.......................................$400
       Cash.........................................         $392
       Purchase Discount.............................           8
(to record payment of A. J. Co. bill with 2% discount)
```

The Purchase Discount account is often called Discount Taken or Discount Earned. It is frequently shown as a nonoperating income on the income statement. However, many thoughtful accountants have concluded that one cannot "earn" money by paying only the minimum one has to pay for a purchase. This conclusion also agrees with the view that purchases should be stated on the income statement at the net cash amount. The authors concur in this view, and Purchase Discount is deducted from purchases in the illustrations in this text.

It is interesting to note that purchases are probably most often shown at their net cash amount in actual business, in spite of the practice of showing Purchase Discount (or Discount Taken or Earned) as a nonoperating income. The reason is that the most popular method of recording purchases is to record them when the payment is made and not before. Under this procedure the net amount to be paid is calculated and no discount is recorded. For the transaction used above, the entry would be:

```
Purchases.........................................$392
       Cash.........................................         $392
```

The Purchase Discount account arises only because the purchase was previously recorded at the invoice or gross amount. When less is paid, the difference must be accounted for. But if the gross amount is never recorded, there is no problem. Many concerns need a record of purchases more promptly than they would have if they waited until payment to make the entry. Furthermore, many prefer to have the running record of accounts payable (without it the open accounts payable must be recorded by an adjusting entry at the end of a period). These concerns will have Purchase Discount accounts, but they are a minority. In this chapter it is assumed that purchases on credit will be recorded as accounts payable before payment; cash transactions will be considered in the next chapter.

Purchase discounts on items other than merchandise are preferably credited directly to the accounts for those items; this procedure requires no separate account.

PURCHASE DISCOUNTS LOST

Management is usually alert to the need to take all available cash discounts. Some lines of business have a net profit of only 2 percent of sales or less, and if the companies did not take their available cash discounts they would have little or no net profit. It is therefore important that management know of any failure to take a discount. In this respect, however, the conventional accounting that records a cash discount only when one is taken is not very helpful. Not all purchases are subject to discount, so there is no fixed percentage of discounts to purchases and therefore little chance to notice that discounts are too low when only the discounts taken are recorded. Management would have a better tool if all purchases were recorded at the net cash amount, whether made on credit or not. Payments would be made for the recorded amount when discounts were taken on credit purchases, and no discount account would then appear. However, if the discount were not taken, a larger payment would be required than the amount originally recorded. This excess — the difference between gross and net price — should then be charged to a Discounts Lost account. Similarly, Discounts Lost should be charged with the same amount if the purchase were recorded only when paid, assuming the payment was made too late to get the discount. For a $400 purchase subject to 2 percent discount but paid for too late to get the discount, the entries are:

Credit purchase recorded before payment:

Purchases	$392	
Accounts Payable		$392
Accounts Payable	$392	
Purchase Discount Lost	8	
Cash		$400

Purchase recorded only when paid for:

Purchases	$392	
Purchase Discount Lost	8	
Cash		$400

Purchase discount lost in these cases should be considered an administrative expense, as it is not a necessary part of the cost of the goods or the service received. Although this method seems useful, it is rarely if ever seen in practice.

PURCHASES ACCOUNTS IN THE INCOME STATEMENT

The accounts describing purchases appear in the income statement in the cost of goods sold section as follows:

Cost of Goods Sold:			
Inventory Jan. 1, 1966			$ 42,000
Purchases		$112,000	
Add: Freight In		2,600	
		$114,600	
Deduct:			
Returns and Allowances	$3,800		
Purchase Discount	1,400	5,200	109,400
			$151,400
Inventory Dec. 31, 1966			34,000
Cost of Goods Sold			$117,400

The figure of $109,400 in this illustration is net purchases. Some bills may not have been paid but will be paid in the next period and the discount taken. Aside from these few items, the net purchases represent net cash prices.

PURCHASE RECORDS

The accounting and closely related records used for purchases are:

1. Purchase requisition
2. Purchase order
3. Receiving report
4. Supplier's invoice
5. Purchases book or invoice register
6. Accounts Payable control account and subsidiary ledger

PURCHASE REQUISITION

This form is used in larger firms to notify the purchasing department that certain materials are wanted. It may be issued by an operating department, by a storekeeper, or by a planning department. It provides for the signature of the person issuing it; this tends to prevent unauthorized requests. A purchase requisition form is shown below. At least two copies should be prepared: one for the purchasing department and one for the files of the issuer.

			SCOTTSDALE PUBLIC SCHOOLS **REQUISITION ON PURCHASING DEPT.** (NOT A PURCHASE ORDER)			
8817 __P. O. NUMBER			☒ HIGH ☐ ELEMENTARY		A	5001
SCHOOL OR DEPARTMENT Oak Valley Consolidated				DATE__July 11, 1966		
SUGGESTED VENDOR AND ADDRESS Westport Janitorial Supply Co.				DATE REQUIRED__		
CODE	QUANTITY	ARTICLE AND DESCRIPTION			ESTIMATED UNIT PRICE	TOTAL
	10	boxes sweeping compound #38			1.50	15.00
BUDGET $__		BALANCE AVAILABLE $ 1,400.00	BUSINESS OFFICE			
ORIGINAL - BUSINESS OFFICE		AMOUNT THIS PURCHASE $ 15.00	ORDERED BY			
		REMAINING BALANCE $ 1,385.00	APPROVED BY			

PURCHASE ORDER

A purchase order is a written offer to purchase something from the supplier to whom it is sent. When he accepts it a binding contract is ordinarily formed, although most American businessmen permit cancellation of orders before shipment. In large organizations the purchase order is issued by a separate purchasing department. In smaller ones a certain individual may be designated as purchasing agent. The order often specifies the requirements for the product, the price, the shipping directions, and any special conditions, as well as the description of the product and the quantity desired. At least three copies are often prepared: one for the supplier, one for the receiving department as notice of what should be received, and one for the purchasing department files. Another may be used to notify the requisitioning department that the goods have been ordered. A purchase order is illustrated below.

GENERAL ATOMIC

DIVISION OF GENERAL DYNAMICS CORPORATION
P O. BOX 608.   SAN DIEGO 12.   CALIFORNIA

PURCHASE ORDER

No. 10302

THE ABOVE NUMBER MUST SHOW ON ALL PACKING LISTS, INVOICES, AND COMMUNICATIONS

| ACCOUNT NO | REQUISITION NO | TERMS | BUYER | W O NUMBER | DATE |
| | | | | | Sept. 6, 1966 |

| SHIP VIA | | DESTINATION | | WHEN SHIP |
| Truck | | OUR PLANT [X]   F.O B | | at once |

TO . Delmar Engine Works   SHIP TO . above
   . 840 Division St.   .
   . Pasadena, Calif.   .

ITEM	QUANTITY	UNIT	DESCRIPTION	UNIT PRICE	TOTAL
—	22	boxes	#44 welding rods	6.40	140.80
—					

INSPECTION: ALL MATERIAL SUBJECT TO   U.S.   INSP AT   San Diego   TOTAL AMOUNT OF ORDER   140.80

ACCEPTANCE: THIS PURCHASE ORDER CONSTITUTES BUYER'S OFFER TO SELLER, AND BECOMES A BINDING CONTRACT ON THE TERMS AND CONDITIONS SET FORTH HEREIN, INCLUDING THOSE ON THE REVERSE SIDE HEREOF, WHEN IT IS ACCEPTED BY THE SELLER EITHER BY ACKNOWLEDGMENT OR THE COMMENCE-MENT OF PERFORMANCE HEREOF NO REVISIONS OF THIS ORDER OR ANY OF THE TERMS AND CONDITIONS THEREOF SHALL BE VALID UNLESS IN WRITING AND SIGNED BY AN AUTHORIZED REPRESENTATIVE OF BUYER; AND NO CONDI-TION STATED BY SELLER IN ACCEPTING OR ACKNOWLEDGING THIS ORDER SHALL BE BINDING ON BUYER IF IN CONFLICT WITH, INCONSISTENT WITH, OR IN AD-DITION TO THE TERMS AND CONDITIONS CONTAINED HEREIN UNLESS EXPRESSLY ACCEPTED IN WRITING BY BUYER

SHIPPING NOTICES, PACKING LISTS, INVOICES, MONTHLY STATEMENTS, AND CERTIFICATES SHALL BE HANDLED IN ACCORDANCE WITH PARAGRAPHS 1, 3, AND 5, ON REVERSE SIDE.

GENERAL ATOMIC - DIVISION OF GENERAL DYNAMICS CORPORATION

BY_____ O. L. Freeman _____

VENDOR'S COPY

RECEIVING REPORT

A report from the receiving department shows what was received, from whom, and in what condition. One report is made for each shipment. It is signed by the person responsible for the report. At least two copies are needed: one goes to the purchasing or the accounting department and the other is kept in the receiving department. The purchasing or the accounting department compares its copy with a copy of the purchase order and the supplier's invoice to see that the goods ordered were received in good condition and that what was ordered and received is billed. A receiving report is shown here.

RECEIVING RECORD		
3420	DATE *Oct. 4 1966*	PURCHASE ORDER NO. OR RETURNED GOODS *2185*
RECEIVED FROM *Wilson Mfg. Co.*		PREPAID
ADDRESS *1610 Allen Ave. Pittsburgh, Pa*		COLLECT
VIA *Penn - St. RR.*	FREIGHT BILL NO. *77- 9864*	

	QUANTITY	ITEM NUMBER	DESCRIPTION
1	*10 gross*		*40 x40 fused glass sheets*
2			
3			
4			
5			
6			
7			
8			
9			
10			
11			
12			
13			

REMARKS: CONDITIONS, ETC. *OK*

NO. PACKAGES	WEIGHT	RECEIVED BY	CHECKED BY	DELIVERED TO
10		*W. A. S.*	*same*	*stock*

Rediform
2S260

BE SURE TO MAKE THIS RECORD ACCURATE AND COMPLETE

SUPPLIER'S INVOICE

The buyer's copy of the seller's sales invoice is the supplier's invoice, and is illustrated on page 151. It is the record used to make the entry in the purchases book (journal) or the invoice register. The entry is customarily made as soon as the goods and invoice are received, the goods inspected, and the receiving report, purchase order, and invoice compared. A notation is usually made on the invoice, which gives the date of entry, the initials of the person who enters it, and perhaps other information.

PURCHASES BOOK

A special journal is kept for purchases. When the title "purchases book" is used, it commonly refers to a journal that records only purchases of merchandise. The simplest purchases book is a one-column journal, which is illustrated below. The total is posted as a debit to Purchases and as a credit to Accounts Payable control in the general ledger. The detail figures are posted as credits to the individual accounts in the subsidiary accounts payable ledger. The postings to the general ledger are indicated by account numbers in the reference column (for example, 32 for Purchases, 14 for Accounts Payable). The postings to the subsidiary accounts payable ledger are indicated by check (✔) marks in the reference column.

SINGLE-COLUMN MERCHANDISE PURCHASES BOOK

Purchases Book			Page 86	
Date	**Purchased from:**	**Ref.**	**Amount**	
1966				
July 1	Woodward Co.	✔	1 428	00
5	Manchester Supply	✔	720	00
8	Donovan Bros., Inc.	✔	42	00
12	Markwell Mfg. Co.	✔	860	00
14	Exeter Supplies	✔	510	00
19	Willowby Shops	✔	77	00
25	Manfred, Ltd.	✔	224	00
27	Ascay Co.	✔	16	00
29	Wunderline Products Co.	✔	8	00
	Dr. Purchases, Cr. Accounts Payable	32,14	3 885	00

MULTICOLUMN INVOICE REGISTER

Purchases on credit include things other than merchandise. If these obligations are to be recorded currently, provision must be made for them as well as for merchandise purchases. This record can best be kept in a multicolumn purchases book or invoice register. Such a journal is illustrated on page 182. The entries are made from the invoices received from suppliers. Occasionally an entry may be made for a purchase where a note payable or an installment contract is given. See, for example, the transaction on July 14 in the illustration. Even in these cases an invoice is usually provided, but it does not result in an entry to Accounts Payable; Notes Payable or Contracts Payable is used instead. Posting references are handled in the same way as in the single-column purchases book. Proof that the journal is balanced as to debits and credits is shown by the following tabulation:

Debit totals		Credit totals	
Purchases	$ 7,530	Accounts Payable	$ 9,428
Office Supplies	208	Sundry	1,800
Sales Supplies	540		
Sundry	2,950		
Total	$11,228	Total	$11,228

The columns used for only one account are called "special columns." They permit charges or credits for a period to be added and posted as one figure. Whenever a number of transactions affecting one account are likely to occur in a period, a special column for that account is advisable. Each concern uses the columns required by its transactions.

ACCOUNTS PAYABLE CONTROL ACCOUNT AND SUBSIDIARY LEDGER

Unless accounts are kept with very few creditors, the control account and subsidiary ledger arrangement is needed for accounts payable. As before, the posting from the invoice register to the general ledger control account is from the column total, and the postings to the individual accounts in the subsidiary ledger are from the individual figures in the same column. Sometimes the individual accounts are posted directly from the invoices; this procedure is called *direct posting*. Direct posting has important advantages: the possible division of work and control of accuracy. Work may be divided so that one employee makes entries in the journal while another posts subsidiary ledger accounts from invoices. Thus both jobs can go on at once, or all the time if necessary. Accuracy is increased because the control account is posted with figures entered by one person, while the subsidiary accounts contain figures handled by another. It is not likely that each of the bookkeepers will copy the same figure in the same wrong way from the invoice. As a result, an error by one will cause the subsidiary ledger schedule of balances to differ from the control account balance, and the error can then be located. The illustration on page 183 shows the relationship of a purchases journal (or invoice register) to the general ledger and subsidiary ledger accounts.

Posting references in ledger accounts indicate the purchases book with a "P" or the invoice register with an "I" or "IR."

INTERNAL CONTROL FOR PURCHASES

The principles previously listed for internal control in general were:

1. Organization
2. System of authorization and records
3. Sound practices
4. Adequacy of personnel

MULTICOLUMN INVOICE REGISTER

Invoice Register

Page 28

Date	Due to	✓	Accounts Payable Credit	Debit — Purchases	Debit — Office Supplies	Debit — Sales Supplies	Sundry Debit	Sundry Credit	Sundry Ref.	Sundry Account
1966 July 1	Hanover Co.	✓	1410 00	1410 00						
5	Base Metals Co.	✓	800 00				800 00			Machinery
7	Forman Industries	✓	220 00			220 00				
8	Mak-Pak Co., Inc.	✓	1050 00	1050 00						
11	Denver Motors Co.	✓	2000 00	2000 00						
14	Devise Process Company	✓		1800 00				1800 00	17	Notes payable
19	Opter, Inc.	✓	128 00		128 00					
21	Affeld Industrial Co.	✓	950 00				950 00		11	Office Equip.
22	Parker Shops, Inc.	✓	320 00			320 00				
25	Harmer & Co.	✓	870 00	870 00						
27	Fritz Bros., Inc.	✓	80 00		80 00					
28	Harmony Products Co.	✓	400 00	400 00						
29	Epworth, Inc.	✓	1200 00				1200 00		36	Advertising
			9428 00	7530 00	208 00	540 00	2950 00	1800 00		
			16	32	8	9				

PURCHASES JOURNAL AND ACCOUNTS PAYABLE ACCOUNTS

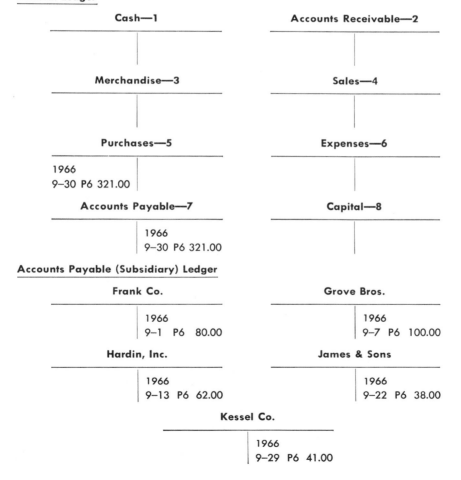

Purchases Journal				Page 6
Date	**Purchased from:**	**Ref.**	**Amount**	
1966				
Sept. 1	Frank Co..........................	✓	80	00
7	Grove Bros........................	✓	100	00
13	Hardin, Inc.......................	✓	62	00
22	James & Sons.....................	✓	38	00
29	Kessel Co.........................	✓	41	00
	Dr. Purchases, Cr. Accounts Payable......	5, 7	321	00

General Ledger

Cash—1

Accounts Receivable—2

Merchandise—3

Sales—4

Purchases—5

1966
9–30 P6 321.00

Expenses—6

Accounts Payable—7

1966
9–30 P6 321.00

Capital—8

Accounts Payable (Subsidiary) Ledger

Frank Co.

1966
9–1 P6   80.00

Grove Bros.

1966
9–7 P6 100.00

Hardin, Inc.

1966
9–13 P6 62.00

James & Sons

1966
9–22 P6 38.00

Kessel Co.

1966
9–29 P6 41.00

Organization for Purchases. Good organization requires that the purchasing function be separated from operating activities and from accounting. If operating departments do their own purchasing they may tend to order goods that are easiest to use or which can be obtained with the least purchasing effort, and these may not be the most economical. If purchasing and accounting are combined, there is greater danger that some employee's personal purchases will be included with the company's, to the company's loss. Having a separate purchasing department or at least a specially designated purchasing agent is the best practice.

System of Authorization and Records for Purchases. The documents discussed earlier in this chapter constitute the important ones for purchase activities. The purchase requisition restricts purchase requests to authorized persons. The purchase order, controlled by the purchasing department, restricts the actual placement of orders. The receiving report assures an opportunity to check what is sent by the supplier against what was ordered and what was billed by the supplier. All these records provide a written history of the transaction and tend to prevent error and misunderstanding

Sound Practices for Purchasing. The division of duties among persons is sufficiently provided for by the departmental division of duties between requesting an order, placing it, and recording receipt of the goods. It is important, however, that someone be specially designated to compare the purchase order, receiving report, and supplier's invoice to see that the right goods were shipped and billed for. This check is sometimes made in the purchasing department but more frequently, in the authors' experience, in the accounting department. As was noted earlier, the person who does this comparing is normally required to initial the invoice to show that he has done the work. It is also necessary to check the arithmetic on the supplier's invoice; this is ordinarily done by a calculating-machine operator, using a type of machine that permits rapid work. Some progressive concerns now check only a sample of incoming invoices for arithmetical accuracy and proper prices. The sampling procedure should be designed scientifically by use of statistical-sampling principles.

Adequacy of Personnel in Purchasing. This requirement of good internal control is easily, but not automatically, satisfied if a separate purchasing department is used. If a concern is too small for a purchasing department or even a full-time purchasing agent, it should give special training in purchasing to the person doing this work. Purchasing of special equipment is handled outside the purchasing department, or by the purchasing department in consultation with the executive who has special knowledge of the thing needed. For example, a new and expensive knitting machine would be decided upon by the plant superintendent, the plant engineer, and perhaps other high executives in consultation with the purchasing department.

THE VOUCHER SYSTEM

The voucher system consists of records and procedures designed to control the recording and the payment of current purchases and to economize by eliminating the separate purchase journal and the subsidiary accounts payable ledger. It features excellent internal control devices often employed even when the complete voucher system is not used. There are, in general, three methods of accounting for current purchases of goods and services that are to be paid for within a short period (a few days to three or four months):

Cash disbursement system. The purchase is recorded only when payment is made, at which time Cash is credited and the account chargeable with the product or the service acquired is debited. This system is popular because it involves a minimum of work. It is usually operated with a multicolumn cash disbursement journal in which checks are entered.

Invoice register and accounts payable system. In this system each invoice received is entered in a journal and credited to Accounts Payable unless it is paid at once. An Accounts Payable control account and a subsidiary ledger are kept. This is a traditional method, and is the basis for the preceding discussion in this chapter. It involves a great deal of work in keeping a ledger account for each creditor and is less used than the other two methods.

Voucher system. This system is described in detail in the following sections.

RECORDS IN THE VOUCHER SYSTEM

The voucher system requires use of the following records: vouchers and voucher register.

As each invoice is received and checked against the purchasing order and receiving report (if goods are involved), a voucher for it is prepared. In general, the term *voucher* refers to any document supporting a transaction. In the voucher system, the voucher consists of the several documents used in carrying out the transaction, such as supplier's invoice, purchase order, receiving report, and perhaps others. They may be stapled together with a cover, or placed in an envelope that is printed to serve as a cover. The cover gives the journal entry to be made.

The voucher is entered in a voucher register, which is a multicolumn journal. It provides a credit to Vouchers Payable and debits to any other accounts required. The listing of vouchers in the Vouchers Payable column of the register and the file of vouchers are the only detail provided for the general ledger account for Vouchers Payable. There is no subsidiary ledger for accounts payable. The general ledger account does give a continuous record of current accounts payable, however, so statements can be made up without adjustments to record these payables.

The vouchers are filed in a *tickler* file. This file is partitioned according to days of the month. Each voucher is dropped into the slot for the day on which it is to be paid. Each day the vouchers for that day are removed and checks are made out in payment. This practice facilitates taking all purchase discounts.

The check issued in payment of the bill represented by the voucher is entered in a check register, which is the only journal for cash disbursements when a voucher system is used. One of the features of the voucher system is the requirement that no check be issued without the prior preparation of a voucher. Each check therefore results in a debit to Vouchers Payable. One of the controls provided by the system is the requirement that a voucher with related documents be submitted to the person who signs the check.

VOUCHER DOCUMENT

The voucher brings together the major documents that describe the transaction. It permits the transaction to be reviewed in terms of the purchase order, the receiving report, the supplier's invoice, and often other documents. These include purchase requisition, copy of the bill of lading, copy of the freight bill, advices of various sorts, and any other document desired. Accountants speak of this documentation as "support" for the transaction; it proves the validity of the transaction and justifies the expenditure. The voucher cover typically provides space for the name of the creditor, the journal entry required, and the signature of an executive, who reviews the voucher when it is presented

WAYS DRAYAGE, INC.

In favor of: *Hanover Oil Co.*   No. **218**

1816 10th St.
Tulsa, Okla.   Date **7-8** 19**66**

Accounts	Debit	Credit
Gasoline and Oil	130 —	
Vo. Payable		130 —

Explanation: *Invoice of 7-6-66*

Prepared by:	Approved:	Date Paid:	Check No:
O. Sexton	*E F G*	7-15	872

for payment. The accompanying illustration shows a voucher cover. Before payment, the voucher is held in the tickler file; after payment, it is typically filed in numerical order, though some accountants prefer to file paid vouchers in alphabetical order by the creditor's name. Alphabetical filing makes it more difficult to locate a voucher by proceeding from an entry in the register, and so is not popular with auditors. The summary of the transactions with each supplier, for which the alphabetical voucher file serves, is usually provided by other means. It can be done with duplicate copies of the voucher covers or with alphabetical files of copies of the purchase orders or the supplier's invoices. The voucher is a useful document in proving expenditures to management, to income tax authorities, to general auditors, and to others. For example, if one must prove costs to government auditors in connection with a contract to supply goods to the government, the voucher document with its rather complete description and evidence of the nature of the transaction is very helpful.

The voucher is prepared by an accounting employee who matches the documents relating to the transaction with the supplier's invoice. Sometimes the matching process is carried on in the purchasing department, in which case the accounting department receives the matched documents for completion of the voucher.

VOUCHER REGISTER

The journal of the voucher system is called a voucher register. An example is given on page 188. The voucher register is similar to the invoice register, but the former name implies use of the voucher system in which there is no subsidiary accounts payable ledger, while the latter implies use of such a ledger. As in other multicolumn journals, special columns are provided for whatever accounts are frequently used. Each concern sets up such columns as its transactions require. Note that provision is made for entering the voucher number and date paid as well as date of entry, creditor's name, and debit and credit amounts. The details of the balance of Vouchers Payable can be made up and compared with the ledger account balance at any time that the Vouchers Payable account is posted up to date, by listing the vouchers for which no payment date is shown in the voucher register. This comparison should be made periodically to catch errors. For example, if a voucher were mislaid and were not paid, such a listing would disclose that an old voucher had not been paid and it could be investigated.

The payroll entries in the Holdmere voucher register (on April 15 and April 30) indicate that one check was issued in each case. This is the check on the general bank account deposited in a special payroll bank account. It simply transfers the amount necessary to pay the workers from the general bank account to the special one. The individual payroll checks are drawn on the special account and are listed in the payroll sheet or book for each pay period. These checks, or course, amount to the total deposited.

Postings of special-column totals and individual items from the sundry-account columns are made, as in the case of other special journals.

VARIATIONS IN THE VOUCHER SYSTEM

Persons using the voucher system make such changes as their needs indicate. One important variation consists of preparing the check and the voucher cover at the same time, the cover being a carbon copy of the check. When this is done in a regular voucher system, the check is kept in a tickler file until payment date. It is then taken out, given a check number, entered in the check register, countersigned, and mailed. This procedure has the advantage of

VOUCHER REGISTER

THE HOLDMERE COMPANY
Voucher Register

Page 22

Date	In favor of	Vou. No.	Payment Date	Check No.	Vouchers Payable Credit	Purchases (Debit)	Supplies (Debit)	Sundry Debit	Sundry Credit	Sundry Ref.	Sundry Account
1966 Apr. 4	Hanover Co.	1810	4/13	370	1400 00	1400 00					
7	Appleton Machine Works	1811			2800 00			2800 00		8	Machinery & Equip.
11	Dunmar Co.	1812	4/20	372	68 00		68 00				
12	Simon Bros. Co.	1813	4/21	373	722 00	722 00					
14	The Office Supply Co.	1814			125 00		125 00				
15	Payroll	1815	4/15	371	3530 00			4000 00		24	Salaries
	—								370 00	14	Fed. Inc. Tax With.
	—								100 00	15	Payroll Tax With.
18	Famous Products Co.	1816	4/28	374	1200 00	1200 00					
20	Hammer, Inc.	1817			420 00	420 00					
21	The Paper House	1818			170 00		170 00				
25	Dahl Bros.	1819			220 00			220 00		37	Truck Repairs
26	A. B. Keller Co.	1820			940 00	940 00					
28	The Deakin Co.	1821			98 00	98 00					
30	Payroll	1822	4/30	375	3530 00			4000 00		24	Salaries
	—								370 00	14	Fed. Inc. Tax With.
	—								100 00	15	Payroll Tax With.
					15 223 00	4780 00	363 00	11 020 00	940 00		
					(12)	(20)	(4)				

making one writing do for both the check and the voucher, but it makes checks prenumbered by the printer impractical—a serious disadvantage.

CASH DISBURSEMENT SYSTEM WITH VOUCHERS

As was noted earlier, many concerns record their acquisitions of goods and services only when they pay for them, except that open obligations at the end of an accounting period will be recorded by an adjusting entry. They therefore use a cash disbursements book where others would use a voucher register or an invoice register. In this case they often use the voucher document as a basis for the entries in the cash disbursements book. This method is desirable, because the document and the procedures it involves provide useful internal control regardless of the fact that a running ledger record of current payables is not kept. This method also makes practical the procedure of preparing the voucher cover as a carbon copy of a prenumbered check, since voucher and check are entered as one item. Sometimes the cash disbursement book is referred to as a voucher register in these cases; one must notice whether Vouchers Payable or Cash is credited to know whether or not that term indicates that the regular voucher system is being followed.

VOUCHER SYSTEM AND INTERNAL CONTROL

The voucher system is an excellent device for facilitating internal control. The following five points indicate how the system, through use of the voucher document, aids in applying the principles of internal control.

1. It provides evidence of performance of duties by the separate departments and individuals. This evidence makes it much easier for an executive to review a transaction to see if it has been properly carried out. This reviewing is often done when the voucher is completed but before it is entered. It may also be done by the executive who signs the check when the voucher is paid.

2. The ease of executive review provided by the voucher stimulates good performance by the various departments and individuals who perform the separate tasks of ordering, receiving, checking, and paying for the acquisition of goods and services.

3. Ease of executive review makes it convenient for executives who are not closely concerned with the accounting but who have to countersign the check, to see that the check is justified. In this connection, recall that it is desirable to deface the voucher once it has been paid so the documents in it cannot be used again. Defacing may be done with a machine that punches holes in the voucher, or with a rubber stamp that prints "paid" on it. If the stamp is used, it should be applied to all the documents in the voucher.

4. Paying bills on the basis of vouchers facilitates the scheduling of payments and helps in taking cash discounts. The tickler file provides nearly automatic control of payment dates. This is to be contrasted with the older method of making payments by reference to accounts in the accounts payable ledger, often in round amounts, not identifiable with particular invoices. The tickler file can be used with invoices and an invoice register as well as in the voucher system.

5. Paying specific invoices prevents confusion about what is being paid. Being specific is especially important if some invoice is being challenged and is not to be paid until the dispute is settled. The rule of law on the point is that the creditor has the right to apply the payment to the oldest part of the obligation if no indication is made by the debtor of what part of the debt he is paying. Specific invoices can also be paid under other systems, but this method is easier under the voucher system.

OTHER ADVANTAGES OF THE VOUCHER SYSTEM

The voucher system has the following advantages in addition to those enumerated above:

Prompt entry. The accounting record is much more up to date than it can be under the popular cash disbursements method.

Economy. The record of liabilities it provides is more economically maintained than an accounts payable ledger system.

MANAGERIAL ANALYSIS OF PURCHASES

Management information about sales needed to determine whether or not a line of products is producing a satisfactory contribution to profit was outlined in Chapter 5. It was noted that such analyses could also be made for territories, classes of customers, or other classifications. To compute the contribution, the costs or expenses that had to be incurred immediately to produce the sales had to be gathered and deducted from the sales. Prominent in the expenses is the cost of the goods sold. These data may be accumulated by analyzing the Purchases account and any related accounts such as Freight In, Purchase Returns and Allowances, and Purchase Discount. A similar analysis of beginning and ending inventories is also needed. These analyses can be made on sheets similar to the sales analysis illustrated on page 161. For purchases the information would come from supplier's invoices or vouchers. When all the analyses are made, they may be arranged as in the contribution analysis on page 163. Concerns that wish to make such analyses continually may provide extra columns in the invoice register in which the amount of each purchase entry is broken down by products or otherwise. Other devices for accumulating the data are also used, including electronic computers that receive information about the different kinds of purchases and then summarize it and print the results when instructed to do so. The various means of accumulating such data are the subject matter of books on accounting systems.

IMPORTANT MANAGERIAL PURCHASE DECISIONS REQUIRING ACCOUNTING DATA

Certain important purchasing decisions can be properly made only after analysis of information recorded in the accounts. These are:

1. Determination of quantities of inventory to carry and the frequency and size of orders
2. When to replace major items of equipment
3. Choice between making or buying an article

The first of these topics is considered in Chapter 10 and the second in Chapter 11. The third is the subject of the next section.

DECISION TO MAKE OR TO BUY AN ARTICLE

Whether to make or to buy something depends upon costs. In considering the costs, however, it is important once again to distinguish between fixed and variable costs. Suppose a concern has some building space and equipment that it could use in producing an article of merchandise it regularly sells. The costs of producing a unit are calculated to be the following:

```
Fixed costs:
    Depreciation . . . . . . . . . . . . . . . . . . . . . . . . . . . . $3.08
    Taxes . . . . . . . . . . . . . . . . . . . . . . . . . . . . . . .  .04
    Insurance . . . . . . . . . . . . . . . . . . . . . . . . . . . . .  .03
    Miscellaneous . . . . . . . . . . . . . . . . . . . . . . . . . . .  .06    $3.21

Variable costs:
    Wages . . . . . . . . . . . . . . . . . . . . . . . . . . . . . . . $1.85
    Power . . . . . . . . . . . . . . . . . . . . . . . . . . . . . . .  .02
    Materials . . . . . . . . . . . . . . . . . . . . . . . . . . . . . 1.10
    Miscellaneous . . . . . . . . . . . . . . . . . . . . . . . . . . .  .12     3.09
            Total cost per unit . . . . . . . . . . . . . . . . . . . . .      $6.30
```

Assuming that the concern can buy the article from outsiders for $5.65, should it make the article or buy it? The answer depends on the facilities represented by the fixed costs. If there is no other use for them and they could not even be rented to someone else, the answer is that the article should be made, not bought. The fixed costs in this case are "sunk"; the concern has no choice but to incur them. The important comparison is between what must be spent under the two alternatives to get additional units of product. Since the firm has to spend only an additional $3.09 (the variable cost per unit) to get a unit of product if it makes it, but has to spend $5.65 to buy it, the answer is clear.

If it is assumed that the facilities represented by the fixed costs could be used equally well for another profitable purpose, the answer is different. In this case the fixed costs must be counted with the variable costs. The reason lies in the fact that the concern is making a current sacrifice by giving up the alternative profitable use of the facilities. The total sacrifice required to get a unit of the product amounts to $6.30, and it should be bought for the smaller amount of $5.65 rather than made.

The regular purchase records show how much the cost of material for this product was; they would also contain information on the power, taxes, and insurance. These items, as well as depreciation, would have to be converted into cost per unit of product by cost accounting methods.

SUMMARY

Purchase transactions involve freight in, returns and allowances, and cash discounts on purchases in addition to the invoice price of materials and services bought. Theoretically, other acquisition costs such as purchasing department, receiving department, and stores department costs should be accounted for as part of the cost of merchandise or materials and therefore as an asset – an investment that has future usefulness – until the goods are sold. This practice is rare, because of the difficulties of determining the cost per unit of merchandise for these items.

It would be of more use to management to record purchase discounts lost rather than purchase discounts taken, but custom has developed the other way so far.

The records required by or closely associated with a prompt accounting for purchases are the purchase requisition, purchase order, receiving report, supplier's invoice, purchases book or invoice register, and Accounts Payable control account and subsidiary ledger.

Good internal control for purchases requires that the functions of requisitioning, ordering, and receiving goods be performed by separate departments or persons. It also requires that someone compare the purchase order, receiving report, and supplier's invoice to see that the goods are received, that the ones ordered were sent, and that the charges are in conformity with the goods and the order. Supplier's invoices must be checked for arithmetic and prices; this may be advantageously done on a sampling basis if scientific sampling methods are used.

The voucher system provides superior control, prompt entry, and economical recording of the acquisition of goods and services. It uses the voucher document, including the supplier's invoice and related papers, and the voucher register – a multicolumn journal. It provides a running record of accounts payable in the general ledger account for Vouchers Payable and in the voucher register without use of an accounts payable ledger. It facilitates internal control by providing a documented history of each transaction that aids managerial review of the transaction and stimulates the persons who must contribute to the record to perform the work properly. It makes the scheduling of payments easy and reliable, facilitates the paying of specific invoices, and discourages arbitrary "payments on account."

Management needs accounting data in order to make defensible decisions on important purchases and purchase policies. These include the quantity of inventory to carry and the frequency and size of orders for it; when to replace major equipment; and whether to make or to buy an article. In analyzing costs for the last decision it is important to distinguish between fixed and variable costs.

QUESTIONS

6.1   Saxton's Emporium, a retailer of quality home furnishings, has enjoyed a slow but steady increase in sales and net income over the ten years that the company has been in business. Lloyd Saxton, owner of the store, has been proud of what he calls his conservative approach toward all aspects of his business. During the past decade he has never borrowed one cent from a bank and has never been delinquent in paying his bills. However, he frequently has had to wait until the last day to pay trade creditors and has never taken a cash discount.

Charles Hitch, manager of the local bank, has suggested that Saxton could increase his net income by borrowing at 6 percent to take advantage of cash discounts. The normal credit terms on purchases, which are made uniformly through-out the year, are 2/10 n/40. The income statement for last year follows:

Sales		$540,000
Cost of Goods Sold:		
Beginning Inventory	$ 19,000	
Purchases	240,000	
	$259,000	
Ending Inventory	21,000	238,000
Gross Margin		$302,000
Operating Expenses		215,000
Net Income		$ 87,000

What do you think of Hitch's suggestion? What would have been the effect on net income if the suggestion had been followed last year?

6.2 (1) What rate of interest is implicit in the loss of discounts of 2/10 n/30?
(2) Explain a method of accounting for purchase discounts that records discounts lost rather than discounts taken.
(3) For both the conventional and the discounts-lost methods, make up an example and give journal entries for purchase and payment in time, and too late, to get the discount.
(4) Can discounts lost be recorded if invoices are journalized only when paid?
(5) Where should discounts lost be reported in the income statement? Why?
(6) Explain how discounts lost may be recorded yet accounts payable recorded at the invoice price through the use of an Allowance for Purchase Discounts account. Comment on the relative merits of this system.
(7) Under the discounts-lost method should an entry be made at the end of the fiscal period to record the expiration of discounts on unpaid invoices?

6.3 Federated Stores purchased floor coverings from Eaton Carpets on terms 2/10 e.o.m., paying the invoice within the discount period. Federated Stores subsequently returned some of the goods that were not up to specification and received a credit memo for the list price.
(1) What entries should be made by Federated Stores to record the return, a subsequent purchase, and payment of the second invoice within the discount period under the conventional method?
(2) What entries should be made if the company records discounts lost?

6.4 (1) Why is freight on f.o.b. shipping point purchases considered to be part of the cost of the merchandise?
(2) What account is debited when freight is paid on f.o.b. destination purchases? Why?
(3) What charges other than freight are part of the cost of merchandise purchased? What are the difficulties of including such charges in the cost of merchandise for inventory purposes?
(4) During World War II, price control made it necessary to maintain a Freight In account separate from Purchases in order to justify prices based on landed cost. From a managerial point of view can you suggest any other reason for use of a Freight In account?

6.5 (1) Describe the purpose of each of the following: purchase requisition, purchase order, receiving report, supplier's invoice.
(2) The purchase order of S. O. Bateman, Inc., is prepared in triplicate. Describe the function of each copy.
(3) Some companies provide the receiving department with a carbon copy of the purchase order on which prices and quantities do not appear. Comment on the advantages and the disadvantages of this procedure.

6.6   The following errors were made in recording and posting a single-column purchases book. How might each error have been discovered, and what action should be taken to rectify each?

(1) The purchases book was incorrectly footed as $67,246 instead of $68,246.

(2) A $1,200 purchase of merchandise was made by signing a 90-day trade acceptance. The transaction was recorded in the purchases book as a credit to Accounts Payable, and was posted to the Accounts Payable account in the general ledger.

(3) A $2,500 invoice for merchandise from American Products Co. was recorded as received from American Producers Ltd.

(4) Among the invoices entered in the purchases book was one for $200 from Charles Hadley and Company for office supplies.

6.7   (1) Willmot, Inc., uses a one-column purchases book. It buys all merchandise on credit and maintains an accounts payable ledger. It does not use direct posting. Describe the posting of this firm's purchases book.

(2) What would your answer be if the company used direct posting?

(3) The Madison Advertising Agency records in its invoice register bills for art work, advertising space, and other charges to customers. What special column would it use in its invoice register that would not be used by a trading company?

6.8   The Yankee Company purchased a large truck for $18,000. It agreed to pay $3,600 in thirty days and signed a contract to pay the rest in installments over three years. This transaction is recorded in the invoice register. Describe the entry, giving the column and the account used for each figure.

6.9   (1) Describe three general methods of accounting for the purchase of goods and services that have to be paid within a short time.

(2) What records make up the voucher system?

(3) Suggest documents that you think would desirably be included in a voucher.

(4) Describe two methods of filing paid vouchers, and cite one advantage of each.

(5) Bothwell Company uses a voucher system. All invoices received have been vouchered. The manager wishes to know how much is owed to a supplier. Suggest means of getting the data for an answer to the manager's question.

6.10 (1) Some users of the regular voucher system prefer to make up the check in preliminary form at the same time the voucher is made up. Later the check is completed, entered, and mailed. What form of control becomes impractical when this procedure is used?

(2) Voucher 1818 of the Forest Skills Company was made out for $1,284 and entered in the voucher register on April 15, 1966. Later it was discovered that some of the goods were defective and were returned. Suggest methods for changing the record, assuming (a) that the voucher register has been footed for the month and (b) that it has not.

6.11 (1) What division of responsibility between departments is required for good internal control over purchases?

(2) Aside from segregation of duties among departments, what purchasing procedures would you recommend as a matter of sound internal control?

(3) It has been discovered that the manager of the kitchen department at York General Hospital has been receiving more than $20,000 a year in kickbacks from the suppliers of meats. He has been ordering and approving receiving reports for meat of a higher grade than actually received. Discuss methods for avoiding this fraud.

6.12 (1) A company ran short of a certain material although the manager remembered paying a bill recently for enough material to serve all current needs. Investigation showed that the shipment was short, although the bill did not indicate this.

What procedure regularly used in the voucher system would have prevented the overpayment?

(2) Goods were received from a supplier in the proper quantity, but grade B was delivered instead of grade A, which had been ordered. The supplier's invoice billed for grade A, higher in price than B. What regular voucher system procedure would prevent acceptance of this substitution?

6.13 Indicate in each of the following cases what procedure in handling of vouchers was neglected:

(1) The H Company covers all its telephone bills in one voucher each month. The person who made up the vouchers included his personal telephone bills with the company's bills, and the vouchers were paid for several months before the fraud was discovered.

(2) The voucher clerk took invoices from old vouchers, changed the dates on them, and made up new vouchers for them. After obtaining the signature of an executive on the checks for these vouchers, the clerk cashed the checks through a bank account he opened in the name of the payee.

6.14 The East Side Dairy uses a variation of the voucher system which it calls the voucher-check system. A check with remittance advice attached is prepared in duplicate from invoices. The remittance advice, or voucher portion of the check, is written with a ball-point pen over a special journal form called a "check register," and carbon paper carries the impression onto the journal. One copy of the check is mailed to the supplier; the other is filed in numerical order. Under this plan the voucher register is eliminated and the distribution of charges is made in the check register. Checks are mailed to suppliers as funds are available. A journal entry is made at the end of the month debiting Cash in Bank and crediting Vouchers Payable for the amount of unmailed checks. Comment on this system.

6.15 Indicate by letter where each of the numbered items below would be classified in the financial statements. Place a "—" next to the letter if the item is to be deducted on the statements.

(A) Asset   (S) Sales
(L) Liability   (C) Cost of Goods Sold
(P) Proprietorship (E) Expenses

(1) Allowance for bad debts   (6) Advances from customers
(2) Purchase discounts   (7) Sales allowances
(3) Freight in   (8) Freight paid for customers
(4) Purchase discounts lost   (credit balance)
(5) Debit balances in accounts payable   (9) Allowance for sales discounts
                                    (10) Allowance for purchase discounts

6.16 Burton's Wholesale makes no cash sales. Almost all cash receipts come through the mail. Outline the system of internal control on collections. Personnel available for processing receipts include a trusted personal secretary to Gordon Burton, who opens all the mail; an accounts receivable bookkeeper, who posts customers accounts; and an office manager, who prepares the daily bank deposit.

If the secretary is absent from the office for a day or two, who should take over her work—the office manager or the accounts payable bookkeeper? Why?

6.17 Auberts/Berkeley, a retailer of contemporary design furnishings, uses two copies of a purchase requisition, three copies of a purchase order, and files one copy of the incoming invoice. The purchase of merchandise for stock involves four different people in the store: the head of the particular selling department making the order, the purchasing agent, the receiving clerk, and the accounts payable bookkeeper.

For each business paper, indicate who receives the form and how it should be filed. Support your discussion with a diagram showing the flow of the forms. Why does this system prevent unauthorized purchases by the head of a particular department? by the purchasing agent?

6.18 (1) Suggest some important managerial decisions regarding purchases that can be reached properly only after analysis of accounting data. Describe briefly the nature of the accounting data required for these decisions.

(2) The Warren Co. has some unused facilities that could be used to manufacture one of the articles it sells. In assembling data relative to this decision the company has classified its costs between fixed and variable. Give three examples of each, and explain briefly how you might determine empirically whether a particular cost is fixed or variable.

(3) Before a company can decide if it is more economical to make an article than it is to buy it, must the price from an outside vendor be greater than the fixed plus variable cost or just greater than the variable cost? Comment on the relevance of fixed costs to the make-or-buy decision.

EXERCISES

6.1 XYZ Co. purchased $1,000 of merchandise on terms 2/10 n/60. Record the purchase of the merchandise and payment for it under (1) the conventional method and (2) the discounts-lost method, assuming (a) the invoice is paid in time to get the discount and (b) the invoice is paid too late to get the discount.

6.2 Western Retailers purchased $10,000 of merchandise from Eastern Wholesalers, f.o.b. shipping point, n/30. Freight charges amount to $100. Use the conventional method for cash discounts.

Give general journal entries:

1. To record the purchase of merchandise, payment of freight, and payment of the invoice.
2. To record the purchase of merchandise, payment of freight, and payment of the invoice, assuming the terms were f.o.b. shipping point but Eastern Wholesalers prepaid the freight and added it to the invoice.
3. To record the purchase of merchandise, payment of freight, and payment of the invoice, assuming the price quoted was $10,100 f.o.b. destination but Western Retailers paid the freight and deducted it from its remittance.

6.3 Lysenko & Co. purchased a truck on January 1, 1966, at $6,000 list less 20 percent trade discount plus 4 percent sales tax; terms 2/10 n/60, f.o.b. factory. The invoice was paid on time to get the cash discount; and, in addition, $200 of transportation charges were paid on delivery of the vehicle, plus a $100 vehicle license for one year. The truck has an expected life of five years with a residual value of 10 percent. What is the depreciation for 1966?

6.4 Regional Bolt Works purchased $2,640 of merchandise, 5/10 n/60, and paid the invoice within the discount period. Discovering that some of the shipment did not conform to metallurgical standards, the company returned items with an invoice price of $860. Purchase discounts are recorded under the conventional method.

Required:

1. What entry should be made to record the return if a cash refund is received?
2. What entry should be made to record the return if a credit adjustment is received?
3. What entry should be made to record a subsequent purchase of $1,200 on the same terms and a payment within the discount period?
4. How would your answers change if the company used the discounts-lost method?

6.5 An examination of the records of the May Sales Company disclosed the following errors at December 31, 1966:

(1) A $2,000 purchase of office equipment was recorded as a purchase of merchandise for resale.

(2) A refund from a supplier for freight damage was credited to Sales.

(3) A payment of $60 freight charges on merchandise bought f.o.b. destination was charged to Freight In.

(4) Payment of $196 on an invoice of $200 less 2 percent was recorded as a debit to Accounts Payable and a credit to Cash in the amount of $196. (The company uses the conventional method of recording purchase discounts.)

(5) The purchase of a $500 color television set for the owner, R. S. May, was charged to Purchases.

Give the journal entries to correct the records, assuming the accounts have not yet been closed for the year.

6.6 Compute the January 1 inventory of Dwan & Company, Inc., from the following information:

Discounts allowed	$ 815
Discounts taken	824
Inventory, December 31	17,420
Freight in	2,106
Gross margin on sales	16,115
Purchases	42,170
Returned purchases	1,245
Returned sales	321
Sales	61,205

6.7 Desnor Company has some unused facilities that could be used in the manufacture of one of the articles it sells. Cost investigations show that the per unit cost to manufacture the product would be:

Fixed costs:		
Depreciation	$1.50	
Taxes and insurance	.09	
Sundry	.10	$1.69
Variable costs:		
Wages	$2.08	
Material	1.75	
Sundry	0.26	4.09
Total unit cost		$5.78

Should the company make or buy the article, assuming that:

(1) It can buy the article from an outside concern for $4.75 per unit?

(2) It can buy the article for $4.02 per unit?

(3) It can rent the facilities profitably and can buy the article from outsiders for $5.10 per unit?

PROBLEMS

6.1 The following transactions were completed by Frasers/Wholesale of Chicago during November 1966:

Nov. 1 Purchased merchandise from WMF Co., list $10,000 less 50-20; terms 2/10 n/60, f.o.b. New York.

2 Paid Brevet & Holbrook in full of invoice of October 15 for $3,600; terms 2/10 e.o.m.

    3 Purchased a duplicating machine from Fisher Supply Co. $1,400 plus 4 percent sales tax; terms 2/10 n/30.

  10 Paid Acme Fast Freight $300 transportation charges on the WMF Co. invoice of November 1.

  10 Paid WMF Co. invoice of November 1.

  12 Paid Fisher Supply Co. invoice of November 3. (Do not credit Purchase Discounts.)

  15 Purchased merchandise from Arsburg & Co. of Seattle, $2,000 less 30-20-10; terms 2/10 n/30, f.o.b. Chicago.

  20 Paid National Freightways $200 transportation charges from Seattle to Chicago on Arsburg & Co. shipment of November 15.

  25 Paid Arsburg & Co. invoice less discount and freight.

  30 Received a cash refund from Arsburg & Co. for return of merchandise with a list price of $500. (Record a cancellation of part of the discount.)

Required:

1. Give general journal entries; explanations may be omitted. The company uses the conventional method of recording purchase discounts.
2. Prepare the cost of goods sold section of the income statement for November based on the foregoing transactions and inventories of $2,400 at November 1 and $1,800 on November 30.

6.2 Kramer's records accounts payable at the net cash price. If a discount is not taken, it is charged to purchase discounts lost when the payment is made. The following transactions occurred during November:

(1) An invoice dated November 1 of $2,000 for merchandise from Altman and Co., Inc., terms 2/10 n/60, is approved for entry in the records.
(2) Freight of $200 is paid November 2 on the Altman invoice.
(3) A checking of the goods received from Altman and Co., Inc., reveals some defective items. These are returned on November 3 with a debit memo for $100, the invoice price of the items.
(4) The Altman invoice is paid on November 10.
(5) An invoice is approved for a truck brought from Mac's Motors for $6,000 on November 5; terms 5/10 n/30.
(6) The Mac's Motors invoice is paid on November 14.
(7) An invoice dated November 5 for $5,000 of merchandise from Fuzzy Lamb of California is approved for entry; terms 2/10 m.o.m.
(8) Through an oversight, the Fuzzy Lamb invoice is not paid until November 30, by which date the discount period had expired.

Required:

1. Record the transactions in general journal form without explanations.
2. Prepare the cost of goods sold section of the income statement for November based on the foregoing transactions. The inventories were $10,000 at November 1 and $9,962 at November 30.
3. Compute the approximate rate of interest implied in the terms 5/10 n/30 offered by Mac's Motors.
4. Should the company take all cash discounts on 5/10 n/30 datings?
5. What would you consider the cost of the truck if the Mac's Motors invoice had been paid after expiration of the discount period?

6.3 Exeter Appliances, Inc., sells and repairs household appliances. It uses an invoice register like the one shown on page 182 except that it has columns for Repair Parts and Shop Supplies instead of Office Supplies and Sales Supplies. During May 1966 it received and recorded the following invoices:

(1) Engel Co. for repair parts, $400.
(2) Wagner Products Co. for merchandise, $1,100.

(3) Silva Industries, for shop supplies, $320.
(4) Quill, Inc., for merchandise, $650.
(5) McDowell Corp., for merchandise, $1,200. A note is given for this so Accounts Payable account is not used.
(6) Van Dyke Process Co., for repair parts, $150.
(7) Engel Co., for shop supplies, $80.
(8) Milton Corp., for an adding machine for the office, $400.
(9) Lehman Co., for merchandise, $1,400.
(10) King Works Inc., for merchandise, $300, and for repair parts, $300.
(11) E. O. Hart Co., for merchandise, $550, and for shop supplies, $200.

The general ledger accounts affected by these transactions and their numbers are:

Repair Parts	6	Accounts Payable	18
Shop Supplies	7	Notes Payable	19
Office Equipment	10	Purchases	32

Opening balances in accounts payable are as follows:

	Credit
E. O. Hart Co.	$100.00
Lehman Co.	350.00
Wagner Products Co.	75.00
Balance per control	$525.00

Required:

1. Prepare an invoice register and enter the transactions for May 1966. The register page is no. 6.
2. Post the register for the month to general and subsidiary ledger accounts. Enter the opening balances of accounts payable; ignore other possible opening balances.
3. Prepare a schedule of the subsidiary ledger to check the accuracy of the posting.

6.4   The record of invoices for Johnson Brothers has the following form:

Gen. Led., Cr.		Accounts Payable	Invoice					Gen. Led., Dr.	
Acct.	Amount	Credit	Date	No.	Description	Purch.	Supp.	Acct.	Amount

During October 1966 the following invoices and other documents were recorded in the record of invoices:

Oct. 3   Brown Co., inv. 1001 for merchandise, $2,000.
  6   Dart Products, inv. 1002 for supplies, $500.
 10   Royce Bros., inv. 1003 for office equipment, $1,000.
 12   Brown Co., inv. 1004 for merchandise, $800.
 15   Bart Co., inv. 1005 for merchandise, $2,000. A 6 percent 60-day promissory note is issued to Bart Co. for this purchase. (Credit Notes Payable.)
 20   Debit memo D1001 was issued to Brown Co. for $200 of merchandise returned. (Enter this transaction in the usual columns for a purchase, but indicate it is a return by enclosing the amounts in parentheses.)

A schedule of accounts payable at October 1 follows:

Brown Co.	$400
Dart Products	200
Royce Bros.	300
Balance per control	$900

Required:

1. Prepare a record of invoices and enter the October transactions.
2. Post the general ledger and accounts payable ledger. Make a check mark in the invoice record to indicate an amount is posted. Ignore opening balances in all general ledger accounts other than Accounts Payable.
3. Prepare a schedule of accounts payable at October 31 and reconcile the schedule with the control.
4. Should the date of invoice or the date on which the invoice is received be recorded in the invoice register? Why?
5. Under what circumstances will it be desirable to use a record of invoices such as this one, rather than simply recording the total of unpaid invoices at the end of the month by a general journal entry?

6.5 Cranwell Corporation merchandises canvas goods and sometimes cuts and sews material to a customer's specifications. As many of its products are sold chiefly to farmers, it advertises widely in rural newspapers. It accordingly has a voucher register with a special column for advertising. Set up the voucher register for Cranwell Corporation for October 1966, using the form of the example on page ■ except that the column for Supplies in the example will be Advertising in this case. Enter the vouchers noted below. The voucher register page number is 41. The data on the vouchers follow:

228	Oct. 1	Concord Cloth Mills, $1,800 for merchandise.
229	Oct. 3	Bessemer Weekly News, $60 for advertising.
230	Oct. 6	Ace Machine Shop, $120 for repairs.
231	Oct. 10	Williston Bee, $75 for advertising.
232	Oct. 11	Huntington Co., $400 for merchandise.
233	Oct. 13	Wills Machine Tool Co., $1,200 for a sewing machine.
234	Oct. 15	Payroll, $7,400 gross, with deductions of $700 for federal income tax withheld and $185 for payroll taxes withheld.
235	Oct. 18	Havenford News, $200 for advertising.
236	Oct. 22	The Eames Co., $800 for merchandise.
237	Oct. 26	Weekly Sentinel, $90 for advertising.
238	Oct. 28	Greene Stationery, $60 for supplies.
239	Oct. 31	Payroll: figures are the same as those for October 15.

The following payments were made on the foregoing vouchers during the month:

Voucher No.	Date	Check No.
228	10/10	128
229	10/3	126
230	10/8	127
231	10/10	129
232	10/18	132
234	10/15	130
235	10/18	131
237	10/27	133
238	10/31	134
239	10/31	135

6.6 Delta Retail, Inc., keeps a voucher register like the one on page 188 except that it has the following debit columns in addition to the one in the Sundry accounts section:

> Purchases
> Freight In
> Supplies
> Miscellaneous Selling Expense
> Miscellaneous General Expense

During July 1966, the following vouchers were made up and entered on the dates shown:

July 1   The William O. Bell Co., $125 for supplies; voucher No. 81.

2   Concord Trading Corp., merchandise invoiced at $1,400; terms 2/10 n/30.

5   A. P. Sharpe Co., $80 for note-paper holders for salesmen.

6   Walter Bros. Trucking, $110 for freight on the Concord Trading shipment.

8   Ghent Works, $840 for merchandise; 1/10 n/30.

12   O. F. Johnson, Inc., $170 for bookkeeping service.

14   The Moore Company, $320 for merchandise; 2/10 n/30.

15   Payroll. The salaries total $8,200, from which $790 is withheld for federal income tax and $205 for payroll taxes.

18   Verdi Shops, $285 for gifts for customers.

20   Sharman, Inc., $1,600 for merchandise; 2/10 n/30.

21   T. F. Casey Co., $160 freight on the Sharman, Inc., shipment.

25   Verlin Bros., $220 for appraisal of property for insurance purposes (a miscellaneous general expense).

26   A. B. Getz & Son, $170 for supplies.

28   Palmer and Palmer, legal fee, $820.

29   Williams & Norden, $40 for interest on a debt.

30   Payroll. Figures are the same as those for July 15.

Payments were made in July on vouchers entered in June, as follows:

Date	Check No.	Vou. No.	In Favor of	Amount of Voucher
7/1	42	79	Comstock & Co.	$ 400.00
7/2	43	77	Holberg Company	116.00
7/5	44	78	Sanborn Trading Co.	1,300.00
7/7	46	80	The Zilke Co.	226.00

Payments were made for vouchers entered in July, as follows:

Date	Check No.	Vou. No.	Date	Check No.	Vou. No.
7/6	45	84	7/19	53	89
7/8	47	82	7/21	54	87
7/11	48	83	7/21	55	91
7/12	49	81	7/27	56	90
7/13	50	86	7/29	57	95
7/15	51	88	7/30	58	96
7/16	52	85			

Prepare the voucher register of Delta Retail, Inc., for July, entering the data on payments as well as vouchers.

6.7   Carlson Factors purchases a single product on terms of 2/10 n/30. Activity in accounts payable at invoice prices for the first three years of operations was as follows:

	1966	1967	1968
Accounts payable, Jan. 1	$ 0	$ 20,000	$ 36,000
Purchases	100,000	160,000	200,000
Totals	$100,000	$180,000	$236,000
Less: accounts payable repaid			
With discounts taken	$ 72,000	$124,000	$160,000
With discounts lost	8,000	20,000	36,000
Totals	$ 80,000	$144,000	$196,000
Accounts payable, Dec. 31	$ 20,000	$ 36,000	$ 40,000

Inventories and sales:	1966	1967	1968
December 31 inventories at invoice prices	$ 40,000	$ 70,000	$ 85,000
Sales	$200,000	$300,000	$420,000

Prepare a schedule of gross margin on sales under each of the following accounting procedures:

1. The conventional method is used for cash discounts, which are reported as deductions from purchases. Inventories are valued at invoice prices.
2. The discounts-lost method is used for cash discounts, which are reported as an operating expense. Inventories are valued at invoice prices less cash discounts.

6.8   As a member of the investment department of a large insurance company you are asked to evaluate the operations of the Y Manufacturing Co. An income statement for the year 1966 (shown below) shows a substantial profit from operations; however, the market demand for the product manufactured by this company has decreased in 1967. You are convinced that this slump is temporary but it is doubtful that the trend will be reversed in 1967. Through examination of company records you have determined that the expenses marked (v) are variable and those marked (f) are fixed.

Y MANUFACTURING COMPANY
STATEMENT OF INCOME
Year Ended December 31, 1966

Sales (net)		$1,200,000
Expenses		
Manufacturing labor (v)	$220,000	
Raw materials (v)	130,000	
Manufacturing overhead (v)	230,000	
(other than depreciation)		
Depreciation (f)	130,000	
Executive salaries (f)	110,000	
Other administrative expense (f)	30,000	
Selling commissions (v)	100,000	
Other sales expenses (v)	120,000	1,070,000
Net income		$ 130,000

Required:

1. Using the above expenses as examples, what are the characteristics of variable expenses as distinguished from fixed expenses? Explain.
2. The Y Company executives estimate that their net sales for 1967 will total $960,000. Your company decides that it will invest in Y Company stock if this sales volume will not cause the Y Company to show a loss for the year 1967. Would such net sales exceed the break-even point for the Y Company? Show all calculations.

(CPCU — adapted)

6.9 National Batteries, Inc., has some unused facilities and is considering using them to manufacture a product that it now purchases from others. The accountant has calculated the cost of the new product as follows:

Cost	Cost per Product Unit
Depreciation on building	$0.15
Labor	2.00
Insurance on building and equipment	0.05
Power...	0.03
Water	0.02
Depreciation of equipment..................................	0.06
Materials...	1.25
Property taxes..	0.04
Payroll taxes, insurance, and welfare contributions	0.30
Ground rent	0.10
Total...	$4.00

Analyze the costs and indicate whether the company should make or buy the new product under each of the following alternatives:

1. The product can be bought from outsiders at $3.50 per unit.
2. The product can be bought from outsiders at $3.65 per unit.
3. The idle facilities could be rented for 20 cents per unit and the product could be bought for $3.75 per unit.
4. The idle facilities could be rented for 45 cents per unit and the product could be bought for $4.25 per unit.

6.10 Farnhurst Electronics has some unused facilities and is considering using them to manufacture a product that they now purchase from others. The accountant has prepared calculations of the cost of the new product, as follows:

Cost	Cost per Product Unit
Depreciation of building	$0.10
Labor	1.85
Insurance on building and equipment	.03
Power...	.04
Water	.01
Depreciation of equipment..................................	.06
Materials...	1.18
Property taxes..	.02
Payroll taxes..	.05
Employee welfare contributions (made at about 1% of payrolls)	.02
Ground rent	.03
Total...	$3.39

Analyze the costs by whatever method you consider appropriate and give your recommendation, under the following assumptions:

1. The product can be bought from outsiders at $3 per unit.
2. It can be bought for not less than $3.20 per unit.
3. The idle facilities could be rented for the equivalent of 10 cents per unit and the product could be bought for no less than $3.20.
4. The product can be bought only for $3.25 and the facilities can be rented out for the equivalent of 20 cents per unit.
5. The product can be bought for no less than $3.50 and the facilities could be rented out for the equivalent of 25 cents per unit.

7

Accounting and Control of Cash

The importance of careful control and accounting for cash can hardly be overemphasized. Cash is readily spendable and is therefore a prime temptation to dishonest persons. It is frequently a part of business transactions and accordingly is often a key to the adequate recording of transactions affecting many other accounts. This chapter takes up the fundamental cash records and transactions, the internal control of cash, and the most important data for managerial decisions about cash.

NATURE AND COMPOSITION OF CASH

Cash consists of coin, currency (paper money), checks, money orders, and bank deposits. Its essential quality is that it is a *medium of exchange*; it is freely accepted in payment of debts. To be classified on the balance sheet as "Cash" with no qualifying words, it must be available for any purpose of the business. Cash that is set aside for some special purpose is given another description and carried in a separate account. For example, cash advanced to an executive or a salesman for travel expenses but not yet spent is called "Travel Advances"; cash that is set aside to pay off a long-term debt will be in an account for "Sinking Fund." This chapter is concerned with the freely spendable cash, listed as such in the balance sheet.

BASIC PROCEDURE FOR CASH

The best practice in accounting for cash is to deposit all receipts in a bank account. Under this practice all disbursements must be made by check, except that special provision may be made for minor disbursements as described later in this chapter under Petty Cash. The advantages of this system are:

1. Only small amounts of currency and coin will be on hand at any time, thus minimizing opportunities for theft.

2. All important disbursements, being made by check, can be kept under the control of the persons authorized to sign checks.

3. The use of the check assures a record of each disbursement, since the canceled check is returned to the maker by his bank. The bank also has a record of it. The alternative is to make payments from currency and coin on hand, and this gives opportunities for errors in counting money and failure to make a record or get a receipt.

4. The bank check automatically provides a receipt for the payment.

5. When all cash received is deposited intact, the bank's record of deposits automatically provides a means of verifying the accuracy of the depositor's record of receipts.

CASH RECEIPTS JOURNAL

The *cash receipts journal,* or *cash receipts book,* is a special journal for cash receipts. On page 207 is an illustration of a cash receipts journal. The column headed Cash in this book represents deposits in the bank, as all receipts are deposited intact by this concern. The proof that the book is in balance follows:

Debits		Credits	
Cash	$8,404.80	Accounts Receivable	$6,895.00
Sales Discount	108.20	Sales	1,070.00
		Sundry	548.00
Total	$8,513.00	Total	$8,513.00

The entries in the cash receipts journal are made from these sources:

Remittance advices. When a customer sends a check by mail he usually indicates on a special form called a "remittance advice" what he is paying. (Many business checks are printed with a remittance advice, attached by perforations.) He may send a letter instead. The document he sends is kept as a source of information for the entry.

Cash register tapes. Cash received over the counter and rung up on a cash register is recorded on the tape, which then serves as the original record.

Cash receipts forms. Cash received over the counter and not rung up on a conventional cash register is often recorded on a form that provides an original and one or more carbon copies. One copy is given to the customer as a receipt and one or more are kept by the business for its records. The forms may come in pads or in continuous rolls. In the latter case they are handled in a small machine that exposes one at a time for writing. Remittances sent in by mail without a remittance advice may be recorded on the receiver's cash receipts form or on a cash register. A cash receipt form is shown here.

Postings of the cash receipts journal are handled in the same way as postings in other special journals. The numbers below the column totals and in the Sundry reference column indicate that those figures have been posted to

Cash Receipts Journal

Date	Received from:	Cash Debit	✓	Accounts Receivable Credit	Sales Credit	Sales Discount Debit	Sundry Credits Amount	Ref.	Account
1966 April									
2	Jones & Scully	400 00	✓	400 00					
4	A. B. Hickman Co.	666 40	✓	680 00		13 60			
9	Cash Sales	320 00			320 00				
11	Everett & Co.	500 00					500 00	5	Notes Receivable
12	Crump Bros.	1 568 00	✓	1 600 00		32 00			
13	Darnell, Inc.	185 00	✓	185 00					
16	Cash Sales	210 00			210 00				
18	Konrad Sales Co.	1 176 00	✓	1 200 00		24 00			
19	The Rogers Company	48 00					48 00	26	Rent Income
23	Cash Sales	260 00			260 00				
25	Phillips Industries	760 00	✓	760 00					
26	Boland, Calvin & Co.	803 60	✓	820 00		16 40			
27	Young and Wilson	1 087 80	✓	1 110 00		22 20			
28	Harper & Co.	140 00	✓	140 00					
30	Cash Sales	280 00			280 00				
		8 404 80		6 895 00	1 070 00	108 20	548 00		
		1		3	22	24			

general ledger accounts. The check marks in the Accounts Receivable column show that the individual accounts receivable subsidiary ledger accounts have been posted.

CASH DISBURSEMENTS JOURNAL

As was noted above, the best practice is to make all cash disbursements by check except those made from the special petty cash funds. The cash disbursements journal then becomes a listing and distribution of the checks issued. The check numbers, as well as the name of the payee and the debit and credit amounts, are entered in the journal. A page from a cash disbursements journal is illustrated here.

The proof of balance in this example follows:

Debits		Credits	
Accounts Payable	$10,128.00	Cash	$ 9,292.40
Sundry	1,060.00	Purchase Discount	95.60
		Sundry	1,800.00
Total	$11,188.00		$11,188.00

As before, the figures below the column totals and in the Sundry Reference column indicate postings of the related amounts to general ledger accounts. The check marks in the column along the accounts payable figures show that they have been posted to the accounts payable subsidiary ledger accounts.

Entries in the cash disbursements journal are commonly made from the checks themselves before they are mailed out. Many firms prepare their checks on a typewriter and use a form that provides a carbon copy of the check which may be used for entries in the journal. Very small firms may use checks with stubs like those used for personal accounts. In this case the date, amount, and name of payee are entered on the stub, as well as the previous balance and the new balance of cash in the bank account. Entry in the journal can then be made from the data on the stubs. This form is shown here. Note that the stylized figures in the lower left-hand corner are used in sorting the checks by computerized equipment (the letters are in ink that can be magnetized by the computer and then read).

Cash Disbursements Journal

Date	Paid to:	Check No.	Cash Credit	✓	Accounts Payable Debit	Purchase Discount Credit	Sundry Debit	Sundry Credit	Ref.	Account
1966 April										
4	Helm Hardware	321	392 00	✓	400 00	8 00				
6	LaPlant Works	322	800 00	✓	1 600 00			800 00	22	Notes Payable
7	Edison Co.	323	931 00	✓	950 00	19 00				
9	Patten Corporation	324	1 800 00	✓	1 800 00					
11	McGuire Bros. Co.	325	60 00	✓	60 00					
13	Overstreet and Lamb	326	350 00				350 00		48	Legal Expenses
14	Perly Agency	327	128 00	✓	128 00					
19	Keller Mfg. Co.	328	1 176 00	✓	1 200 00	24 00				
21	Bush Industries	329	607 60	✓	620 00	12 40				
22	Wolfe and Marker Co.	330	686 00	✓	700 00	14 00				
25	Fosket, Hart & Co.	331	400 00	✓	1 400 00			1 000 00	25	Capital Stock
27	Groves Advertising Agency	332	710 00				710 00		36	Advertising
29	Moore & McLain	333	891 80	✓	910 00	18 20				
30	H. A. Stratton Co.	334	360 00	✓	360 00					
			9 292 40		10 128 00	95 60	1 060 00	1 800 00		
			1		23	29				

Note that checks 326 and 332 in the illustration of the cash disbursements journal represent transactions that do not involve accounts payable. In these cases the bill was paid at once and was not recorded in Accounts Payable before payment. Check 322 represents a transaction in which some special merchandise was bought and recorded in the invoice register with a credit to Accounts Payable. Arrangements were then made to pay half the bill in cash on April 6 and to give a promissory note for the rest. This settlement is recorded in the cash disbursements journal on April 6. Check 331 was issued in settlement of a bill for which the creditors agreed to take $1,000 worth of the capital stock of the buyer.

CASH DISBURSEMENTS WITH THE VOUCHER SYSTEM

The voucher system, described in the preceding chapter, is a method of recording purchases in which a voucher document is used to bring together the invoice, the receiving report, and related papers supporting the purchase or similar transaction. It requires no accounts payable ledger, as the file of unpaid vouchers serves the same purpose. In the voucher system the voucher register serves as the book of original entry. In this system the cash disbursements book is simplified, because all payments are first recorded on vouchers; the checks issued are then all debited to the Vouchers Payable account. The cash disbursements book in this case is customarily called a check register and has the appearance shown in the accompanying illustration.

CHECK REGISTER

THE HOLDMERE COMPANY
Check Register   page 17

Date	Vou. No.	In favor of	Check No.	Cash Credit	Purchases Discount Credit	Vouchers Payable Debit
1966						
Apr. 1	1802	Blaisdell, Inc.	364	1 100 00		1 100 00
4	1803	Pacific Electric Co.	365	180 00		180 00
6	1805	The Donover Co.	366	431 20	8 80	440 00
7	1806	Markers Machine Shops	367	170 00		170 00
8	1808	Altman Supply Co.	368	72 00		72 00
11	1809	Herbert Bros. Co.	369	128 00		128 00
13	1810	Hanover Co.	370	1 372 00	28 00	1 400 00
15	1815	The Holdmere Company—Payroll	371	3 530 00		3 530 00
20	1812	Dunmar Co.	372	68 00		68 00
21	1813	Simon Bros. Co.	373	714 78	7 22	722 00
28	1816	Famous Products Co.	374	1 176 00	24 00	1 200 00
30	1822	The Holdmere Company—Payroll	375	3 530 00		3 530 00
				12 471 98	68 02	12 540 00

PETTY CASH

Some small expenditures would be a nuisance if they had to be made by check. Control of these small items is maintained by use of an *imprest fund*, or a *petty cash fund*. A petty cash fund is established by drawing a check for the required amount payable to the petty cashier. The entry for the check establishing a $100.00 fund is:

```
Petty Cash . . . . . . . . . . . . . . . . . . . . . . . . . . . . . . . . . . . . . . $100.00
        Cash (or Cash in Bank) . . . . . . . . . . . . . . . . . . . .           $100.00
    (to establish petty cash fund)
```

The check is cashed and the currency and coin are placed in a box or drawer. When a small expenditure is made, currency and coin are used and a slip or petty cash voucher for the amount spent is placed in the cash box with

CASH VOUCHER		No. 226	
		DATE *July 21* 19 66	
PAY TO *Railway Express Agency*			
	DESCRIPTION	AMOUNT	ACCOUNT NUMBER
1 pkg	*express on grain sample from Minot*	1 85	
APPROVED	ENTERED	RECEIPT OF ABOVE IS HEREBY ACKNOWLEDGED	
BY *A. H. P.*	BY	BY *A. Smiley*	

the remaining currency and coin. This voucher may be something obtained from the payee or a form supplied by the payer, or both. An example of such a form is illustrated.

No entry is made in the regular double-entry system until the fund is reimbursed. Reimbursement is made when the supply of the currency and coin get low. It should also be done at the end of each accounting period so the expenditures can be recorded in the proper period. When the fund is to be reimbursed, the vouchers are summarized according to the accounts to be charged. This summary may be made on an analysis sheet in which voucher numbers are listed at the left and columns are headed with account names, thus:

Voucher No.	Total	Delivery Expense	Office Expense	Sales Expense	Sundry Amount	Account

The totals of the columns and any individual items in the Sundry column give the charges to be recorded. A check is drawn on the regular bank account for the total amount expended, and it is recorded by debits and credits similar to the following:

Delivery Expense..$xx.xx	
Office Expense.. x.xx	
Sales Expense .... x.xx	
etc.	
Cash..	$xx.xx

The check that establishes the fund and those that reimburse it are of course entered in the cash disbursements book. The illustrative entries above are given in general journal form, but the general journal would not be used to record checks issued unless the enterprise is so small that it has very few transactions.

PROOF OF PETTY CASH

When an imprest fund is used, it can be proved at any time by counting the currency and coin and adding in the amounts of any vouchers. The total should be the amount shown in the ledger account. If the fund is used often, the custom is to count it once each day.

Note that no entries need be made in the general ledger account for an imprest fund once it is established, unless it is done away with. Reimbursing checks are the basis for entry of all its expenditures, and these do not have to be run through the Petty Cash account.

CASH OVER AND SHORT

Imprest funds are often used for change funds. In this case the fund is put each morning in a cash drawer, perhaps the drawer of a cash register. At the end of the day it is taken out and set aside from the rest of the currency, coin, and checks that have been received during the day. At the same time all the contents of the drawer are counted. The total obtained should equal the original fund plus the receipts taken in and recorded on the cash register tape or otherwise.

If the count of an ordinary petty cash fund or a change fund is more or less than the record indicates it should be, it is either *over* or *short* (of the record). A slip is made for this difference and the actual receipts are deposited. When the receipts are recorded, or, in the case of an ordinary petty cash fund, when the fund is reimbursed, the overage or shortage is entered in a general ledger account for Cash Over and Short. A cash shortage creates a debit; a cash overage, a credit. If the cause of the overage or shortage is not found and corrected within a reasonable time, the balance of Cash Over and Short is closed into Profit and Loss as a general expense or a miscellaneous income.

BANKING TRANSACTIONS

The maintenance of a checking account at a bank involves the following records:

1. Deposit slip
2. Bank check
3. Bank statement

4. Daily cash report
5. Bank reconciliation

These records are the subjects of the sections that follow.

DEPOSIT SLIP

A deposit slip accompanies the cash deposited when it is sent or taken to the bank; a specimen is shown below. The totals for the currency and the coin deposited are entered respectively on the lines marked Currency and Coin. The checks deposited are listed individually. They are identified with the number of the bank on which they are drawn. Most checks include this number; it appears in this form:

$$\frac{90\text{-}1281}{1211}$$

The upper numbers designate the bank and are the ones written on the deposit slip; the lower ones are used by the banks in their system for transferring checks between banks — the "clearing" system.

The deposit slip is usually made in duplicate, the original being kept by the bank and the carbon by the depositor. The carbon copy may also serve as a

```
              DEPOSITED WITH
      METROPOLITAN BANK
        FOR CHECKING ACCOUNT OF

      Wm. S. Childs Co
      40 Victor St.

   DATE            Aug 31      19 66
                          DOLLARS    CENTS

   CURRENCY                  75    00
   COIN                      17    15
   CHECKS
   LIST BY BANK NUMBER
          1-10      1       128    30
          18-40     2        74    22
          19-1280   3       176    00
          16-123    4        22    75
          14-91     5        14    90
          2-16      6        12    16
                    7
                    8
                    9
                    10
                            520    48
```

receipt form, in which case it is initialed by the teller who takes the deposit, or stamped by him. The older method of recording the receipt of the deposit is also still in use. This is the use of a "passbook," which is a small blank book ruled so that the date, the teller's initials, and the amount of a deposit can be written on each line. The passbook is kept by the depositor and is ordinarily presented to the teller only long enough to permit him to record the deposit. In large modern systems the deposit slip, like the check, includes the depositor's number and the bank's number, both printed in ink that a computer can magnetize and read. The amount of the deposit (or check) is also put on the document by bank personnel in similar ink so that amounts can be entered by the computer.

BANK CHECK

The check is an order addressed by the maker instructing the bank to pay a sum of money to the payee. The check is signed by the maker. In making it out he dates it and writes in the name of the payee and the amount to be paid. The amount is commonly written twice: once in figures and once in words. In large organizations checks are written by machines. The check is given or sent to the payee, to whom it is a cash receipt. As a rule he deposits it in his bank account, endorsing it on the back. The endorsement may be in blank— that is, it may consist only of the payee's name—but it is preferable to use a restrictive endorsement, such as "For deposit only, John Jones." The endorsement is usually necessary to transfer ownership of the check from one person

---

CROWN ZELLERBACH CORPORATION

PORT ANGELES, WASHINGTON_____June 16, 1966_____

19-28
1250

No. 03409

REVOLVING
FUND

TO THE
ORDER OF

Everhard Mfg. Co.
Seattle, Wash.

PAY FIVE HUNDRED TWENTY-FOUR AND 18/100. . . . . .DOLLARS $ 524.18

TO
·THE PACIFIC NATIONAL BANK OF SEATTLE
SEATTLE, WASHINGTON

SPECIMEN

CROWN ZELLERBACH CORPORATION
PORT ANGELES, WASH.
PAID BY CHECK OF LIKE DATE, AMOUNT AND NUMBER
ENDORSEMENT AND COLLECTION OF CHECK ACKNOWLEDGES PAYMENT IN FULL FOR ACCOUNT AS NOTED BELOW
DETACH BEFORE DEPOSITING—IF INCORRECT PLEASE DEPOSIT AND ADVISE US OF DIFFERENCE

No. 03409

	ACCOUNT DISTRIBUTION	AMOUNT
Your invoice of May 11, 1966	8821	524.18

to another. When the check arrives at the bank of the maker, that bank charges it to the maker's account and cancels the check by running it through a machine that punches holes in it. It is then kept with other checks drawn by that depositor until the end of the monthly accounting period, at which time the canceled checks are sent, along with any debit and credit memorandums, to the depositor with a statement. The illustration given here shows a bank check that has a remittance advice attached at the bottom. This advice is removed by the payee, and may be used in his accounting procedure.

BANK STATEMENT

The bank statement lists the beginning balance, the deposits, the charges (mostly for checks drawn), and the ending balance of the depositor. A bank statement is illustrated below. Balances and other data appear at the bot-

STATEMENT OF ACCOUNT WITH

CENTRAL OFFICE

METROPOLITAN BANK

SINCE 1950

PLEASE CALL ►
IF YOU HAVE ANY QUESTIONS ABOUT THIS STATEMENT

0129 229720
ACCOUNT NUMBER

A. F. Zeeman Company
468 Braman St.
Chicago, Illinois

10 19 ⁿ/ₒ 11 20 66   1
STATEMENT PERIOD   PAGE NO.

CHECKS AND OTHER ITEMS PAID (READ ACROSS)						DEPOSITS	
DATE	AMOUNT	DATE	AMOUNT	DATE	AMOUNT	DATE	AMOUNT
10 21	5 00	10 21	5 46	10 22	8 99	10 27	13 00
10 22	50 00	10 22	233 10	10 23	9 21	11 2	1 115 37
10 23	14 44	10 23	16 12	10 26	3 43	11 4	237 10
10 26	25 00	10 27	15 00	10 29	10 00	11 9	230 68
10 29	30 45	11 2	20 50	11 2	50 00	11 19	480 90
11 2	142 00	11 3	41 60	11 4	23 53		
11 4	100 00	11 4	170 00	11 6	7 34		
11 6	8 27	11 6	12 46	11 6	16 00		
11 9	70 00	11 10	13 78	11 11	24 00		
11 13	50 00	11 17	16 55	11 17	17 11		
11 17	139 03	11 18	2 00	11 18	19 00		
11 18	20 00	11 19	2 00	11 19	7 90		
11 19	9 38	11 19	12 27	11 19	29 91		
11 19	1 24S						

A - AUTOMATIC TRANSFER   B - BANK ORIGINATED ENTRY   L - SUMMARY ENTRY TOTAL   S - SERVICE CHARGE   OD - OVERDRAFT

BALANCE PREVIOUS STATEMENT	CHECKS AND OTHER ITEMS PAID NUMBER	TOTAL AMOUNT	DEPOSITS AND OTHER CREDITS NUMBER	TOTAL AMOUNT	NEW BALANCE (AS OF STATEMENT DATE)
1 524 25	39	1 452 07	5	2 077 05	2 149 23

AVERAGE LEDGER BALANCE	MIN. BALANCE LESS THAN	ITEMS SUBJECT TO SERVICE CHARGE	AMOUNT OF SERVICE CHARGE	REPORT ANY ERRORS OR OMISSIONS WITHIN 10 DAYS OTHERWISE STATEMENT WILL BE CONSIDERED CORRECT	ACCOUNT NUMBER
1 635	1200	39	1 24		

tom; charges are detailed by days in the large center portion of the statement; and deposits are listed on the right. The material at the bottom includes minimum and average balances for the period on which the service charge is based. This statement is an example of the type prepared by an electronic computer, which also calculates the totals, balances, and service charge.

Banks are often requested to collect "bills of exchange" used in some lines of trade. When such a collection is made, the depositor's account is credited and he is sent a notice. The amount collected will appear in the deposit column of the statement; any charge made for this service appears among the other charges. Banks will charge the depositor a bank service charge if his average balance is too small to justify the handling cost. It also charges him for any check he has deposited that turns out to be "bad," that is, uncollectible. A notice is sent for this, too, along with the uncollected check, and a copy of the notice is enclosed with the checks drawn and paid by the bank when the statement is sent; the charge also appears on the statement. The depositor charges the bad check back to the account receivable of the customer who gave it; the bad check ceases to be any concern of the depositor's bank.

DAILY CASH REPORT

Control of cash requires a knowledge of the amount of cash on deposit each day and its location, as well as the amounts that must be paid. In a large concern the amount of cash available each day is shown on a *daily cash report* such as that illustrated. The day's receipts and disbursements are given as well as the opening and closing balances and the distribution by banks. From this the treasurer or other disbursing officer can see what is available and on what banks he can make withdrawals of various amounts.

DAILY CASH REPORT

	Daily Cash Report April 14, 1966			
Bank	Bal- ance A.M.	Re- ceipts De- posited	Dis- burse- ments	Bal- ance P.M.
A	8 421 00	2 810 00	2 460 00	8 771 00
B	9 680 00	4 110 00	5 200 00	8 590 00
C	6 750 00	1 488 00	1 292 00	6 946 00
D	5 700 00	2 020 00	2 390 00	5 330 00
	30 551 00	10 428 00	11 342 00	29 637 00

In small concerns with only one bank account, a running record of the bank balance may be kept on the check stub. A check and stub designed for this use is shown on page 208. This method is inconvenient if transactions are numerous, because it requires copying the balance and calculating a new balance after each check is written. It is easier to add up the checks for a day and make one calculation of the balance.

BANK RECONCILIATION

The bank statement shows what the bank has recorded in the depositor's account. This may be, and in most cases is, somewhat different from the record on the books of the depositor. Checks issued by the depositor are deducted from the cash account on his books, but not all of them will be presented at the bank in time to be deducted from his balance on the bank's books in the same month. A deposit made up and recorded on the last day of the period by the depositor may not reach the bank until the next day's business, and so it may appear on the bank's statement for the month after the depositor recorded it on his books. Other kinds of transactions may be recognized by one party in one month and the other in another. Furthermore, errors may be made by the depositor or the bank. If the depositor is going to know whether or not an error exists, all the differences between the two records must be identified. The statement or calculation in which this is done is called a *bank reconciliation*. A bank reconciliation is illustrated here. This form is convenient in mak-

ARBOR APPLIANCE CO.
Bank Reconciliation

April 30, 1966

Balance per bank $1,842.00		Balance per our ledger $1,240.18	
Add: Deposit of April 30 in transit . . . 650.82		Add: Collection by bank from A B	
Error by bank; deposit of April		Co. not recorded	
14 entered as $300.00,		by us 375.00	
should be $400.00 . . . . 100.00		$1,615.18	
$2,592.82			
Deduct: Checks outstanding:		Deduct:	
No. Amount		Bad check returned	
310 $187.00		April 30, 1966; X	
340 314.00		Z Co., including	
341 98.40		bank handling	
342 227.10		charge $15.00	
344 208.54 1,035.04		Bank service charge. 12.40	
		Error by us; check no.	
		290 entered as	
		$60.00, actually is	
		$90.00 . . . . 30.00 57.40	
Adjusted balance $1,557.78		Adjusted balance $1,557.78	

ing adjusting entries that originate from the bank reconciliation. Note that any item requiring an adjustment on the books of the depositor is added to or deducted from the unadjusted balance on the depositor's books. Any items not requiring adjustment of the depositor's books — items that presumably will soon be recognized by the bank in the regular course of business — are added to or deducted from the balance given by the bank statement. Each of these calculations gives the adjusted figure for the depositor's books, that is, the figure that the depositor's books will show after the adjustments are made and that the bank's books would show if it had received a record of everything the depositor did. When the two sides of the calculation arrive at an identical figure it may be presumed that all differences, including any errors, have been identified.

PROCEDURE IN PREPARING THE BANK RECONCILIATION

Differences between the depositor's record and the bank's statement may be identified by following these steps:

1. Compare the returned checks and other vouchers with the debits on the bank statement to see that vouchers have been supplied for all charges. The bank presents the vouchers arranged in the order of their entry on the statement, and they should be kept in this order in this step; checking them against the statement is inconvenient once they are out of order. If they should get out of order, however, the comparison can be made by looking at the cancellation on the check and thus finding the date of entry on the bank statement.

2. Sort the returned checks into numerical order. This places the checks in the order of their entry in the depositor's cash disbursements journal.

3. Compare the returned checks, one by one, first with the list of outstanding checks on the prior month's reconciliation, and second with the entries for checks in the cash disbursements book for the month being reconciled. In this operation a check mark (✔) is ordinarily placed beside the figure in the book to indicate that the canceled check is in hand.

4. List on the reconciliation as outstanding checks the amounts of checks that were outstanding on the prior reconciliation and have still not come in and those not checked off in the cash disbursements book for the month being reconciled.

5. Trace any deposits in transit in accordance with the prior month's reconciliation to the current month's bank statement, and compare with this statement deposits made during the current month as shown by the depositor's duplicate deposit slips. A memorandum column showing the total of each deposit is often added to the cash receipts journal, and this column simplifies the checking of deposits. On the reconciliation, list any deposit not shown on the bank statement as a deposit in transit. Record on the reconciliation as an item for adjustment any deposit recorded by the bank but not yet recorded by the depositor.

6. Trace to the depositor's records any vouchers returned by the bank. For example, the bank may not be able to collect a check that has been deposited. It will charge the check to the depositor's account and send it back to him. The depositor then debits the account receivable of the customer who gave the check and credits Cash for the amount of the check plus the charge made by the bank for handling such items. If the transaction occurs late in the month and has not been recorded by the depositor by the time the reconciliation is being made, it must be listed with the other items to be adjusted on the depositor's books.

At this point the reconciliation should be in balance. If it is not, one must look for errors. The following steps may be necessary:

1. Add the items and check the calculation of the balance on the bank statement.

2. Check footings in the depositor's cash receipts and cash disbursements journals and in the ledger account for Cash, and check the calculation of the Cash balance.

3. Compare bank vouchers and deposits with the depositor's records again to see if a discrepancy escaped the prior checking.

Errors by the bank are listed on the left of the reconciliation form illustrated and the bank is notified to make the correction. Errors by the depositor are listed on the right side and are included in his adjusting entries or corrected without entry. An error in footing a journal, for example, would be corrected without any entry.

ADJUSTMENTS FROM THE RECONCILIATION

Adjustments required on the depositor's books by the illustrated reconciliation are:

Cash	$375.00	
Accounts Receivable—A B Co.		$375.00
Accounts Receivable—X Y Co.	$ 15.00	
Collection and Exchange Expense	12.40	
Cash		$ 27.40
Office Salaries	$ 30.00	
Cash		$ 30.00

Check 290 was an office-salary check that was entered as $60, when it was actually $90, hence the additional charge of $30 to Office Salaries. The error by the bank requires no adjustment on the depositor's books; the bank will adjust its books.

For maximum accuracy these adjustments must be recorded in the month being reconciled, but in practice they are often recorded in the next one. Note that the process of closing the books at the end of a period requires collection of data over a period after the closing date. Accordingly, such operations as reconciling the bank statement may be done before the record is closed.

INTERNAL CONTROL OF CASH

It has already been noted that the spendability of cash makes it a prime target for fraud; consequently, cash requires the most careful control. The general principles of internal control apply to the handling and recording of cash but they must be applied with special vigor. These principles have been mentioned as good organization (separation of departmental functions), a good system of authorization and records, sound practices, and adequate personnel. Wherever possible the firm should be organized so that cash is handled by a separate department, and beyond that, the accounting for the cash is desirably separate from the handling of it. The record system described in the previous sections of this chapter provides the essential records, but note that the pre-numbering of documents by the printer, such as checks, is especially important in cash work. Prenumbering helps to prevent misuse of documents because their disappearance can be noted by the missing numbers. Adequate personnel is of course important in cash work as elsewhere. Two practices apply to all cash work: (1) the bonding of employees and (2) the taking of vacations or the occasional rotating of jobs so that no one has control over a substantial part of the work indefinitely. A person who has sole control of a cash journal over a long period, for example, has a better opportunity to embezzle. A fidelity bond, which is an insurance policy that will reimburse the employer if an employee embezzles funds, is a desirable protection.

The following two sections give internal control practices separately for cash receipts and cash disbursements that fall chiefly under the heading of sound practices, but are in part matters of organization.

INTERNAL CONTROL PROCEDURES FOR CASH RECEIPTS

The following practices are recommended.

1. Have cash receipts listed by someone not involved with the other cash records, who then turns the cash over to a cashier for deposit and the list to a third person. This person will later check to see that the proper amount was deposited. In the smaller organizations, where this much division of labor may not be practicable, the mail may be opened by an executive who later turns over the cash to a cashier-bookkeeper, who records and deposits it. The fact that the executive knows the customers and what they owe, and notices when they pay makes it difficult for the cashier to withhold any of the cash.

2. Deposit all receipts intact. The general advantages of this rule were outlined in an earlier section of this chapter. For cash receipts these were that only small amounts of currency and coin remain on hand, and the bank's record of deposits is a check on the accuracy of the depositor's books. In addition to having these advantages, the rule is helpful because the banks and others come to expect the firm's checks to be deposited with the endorsement "for deposit only," and any other handling arouses suspicion.

3. Never allow cashiers to do the accounts receivable work, particularly the cashier who keeps the cash receipts journal. If an employee records cash receipts and also makes the accounts receivable postings, he can withhold cash and conceal the shortage by making a false entry in the customer's account, or he can keep it from notice by sending the customer a statement showing that his bill is paid when the ledger account does not show this.

4. Separate the job of accounting for cash receipts from that of making cash payments. If one person has control of both the cash receipts and the cash disbursements journals, a shortage in receipts can be covered up by entering a false disbursement.

5. Keep inventory records that show how much merchandise and materials should be on hand. In other words, use inventory control. This discourages the fraudulent employee from selling the company's merchandise and pocketing the proceeds with no record being made.

6. Have the bank reconciliation made by someone who does not do other cash work. A shortage in cash may be concealed by falsifying the reconciliation.

INTERNAL CONTROL PROCEDURES FOR CASH DISBURSEMENTS

The following practices are recommended.

1. Make all disbursements by check except small ones from the petty cash fund. One of the previously noted advantages for this rule is that a record and receipt are automatic, and since only the signatures of authorized persons are

acceptable on the checks, disbursements are thus controlled. It is still possible for an embezzler to forge a signature, but if a forgery is discovered the money can be recovered from the bank, which is permitted to accept only genuine signatures.

2. Make all checks to specific payees; for example, to "John P. Derward, Petty Cashier," instead of to "Cash" or "Bearer." Checks payable to "Cash" or "Bearer" can be cashed by anyone.

3. Require two signatures of responsible persons on each check. One signature is often that of the person who keeps the cash disbursements journal; the other that of an executive who is in a position to see that the expenditure is in order.

4. Use protective devices such as check-writing machines and special paper for checks. Checks are normally printed on paper that has an overlay pattern of color which rubs off if the check is erased, but mechanical check protectors are commonly used in addition. These are small machines that print the amount of the check in ink which is difficult to remove. On some special papers the word "void" appears if ink remover is placed on the paper.

5. Guard the supply of unused checks and prenumber and account for them. Fraud is discouraged if persons who might commit forgery cannot obtain any of the blank forms of the concern or if the loss of forms or stationery cannot be concealed.

6. Separate the work of making and recording checks from the work of keeping the accounts payable records. Control of both records facilitates the issue of extra checks that may be converted to the embezzler's use.

7. Have supporting documents presented with the check to the executive who places the second signature on it. These include the supplier's invoice and the receiving report. The documents should then be defaced so that they cannot be submitted another time.

8. Have the signer pass the check on to a mailing department so that persons who handled it previously cannot get it back and thus have an opportunity to use it for themselves.

The foregoing discussion may appear to reflect an unduly cynical view of people. However, fraud and embezzlement occur frequently enough to require careful preventive attention. Furthermore, good internal control that makes fraud difficult may benefit the employee who might otherwise find the temptation overpowering and get into trouble.

DATA ON CASH FOR MANAGERIAL DECISIONS

Management's day-to-day concern with the amount and location of cash funds available has been mentioned above in the discussion of the daily cash report. Good management also requires that the *need* for funds be anticipated so the firm will not be caught short of cash. This foresight may involve short-term borrowings at the banks to provide cash for seasonal needs; for example, buildup of a stock of goods for the Christmas trade or purchase of a crop of wheat as it is harvested. It may involve issuance of bonds or long-term notes or the sale of capital stock to provide cash for new buildings or equipment. The best approach to the problem is the preparation of a *cash budget*. This shows what receipts are anticipated from customers and any other sources and what

Cash Budget **3d and 4th Quarters, 1966** (cents omitted)				

Item	July 1966	August 1966	September 1966	4th Quarter 1966
1. Cash balance, beginning.............	38 000	41 970	19 832	47 923
Receipts:				
2. Accounts receivable, beginning.........	100 000	112 000	120 000	132 000
3. Sales.............................	1 000 000	900 000	800 000	2 400 000
4. Bank loans.........................	—	—	250 000	500 000
5. Subtotal.........................	1 100 000	1 012 000	1 170 000	3 032 000
Deduct:				
6. Bad accounts......................	5 000	6 200	7 100	24 000
7. Sales discounts.....................	9 830	8 858	7 809	17 520
8. Accounts receivable, ending...........	112 000	120 000	132 000	160 000
9. Total deductions...................	126 830	135 058	146 909	201 520
10. Cash receipts (5 minus 9).............	973 170	876 942	1 023 091	2 830 480
11. Total cash available (1 plus 10)........	1 011 170	918 912	1 042 923	2 878 403
Disbursements:				
12. Merchandise purchases...............	403 200	508 080	617 000	1 500 000
13. Selling expenses....................	220 000	210 000	201 000	615 000
14. General expenses...................	180 000	169 000	165 000	510 000
15. Property tax.......................	14 000	—	—	—
16. Interest...........................	12 000	12 000	12 000	36 000
17. Dividends.........................	40 000	—	—	80 000
18. Payments on notes..................	100 000	—	—	100 000
19. Total disbursements................	969 200	899 080	995 000	2 841 000
20. Cash balance, ending (11 minus 19)......	41 970	19 832	47 923	37 403

expenditures are to be made. The cash budget will indicate when borrowing is necessary. A cash budget is shown on this page. It may be drawn up for various periods; the company whose budget is shown makes up monthly budgets for one quarter of a year ahead and quarterly budgets for one to three quarters beyond that. The considerations one must have in mind in drawing up a budget and some of the calculations one must make are presented in Chapter 23. Note that in the illustrated cash budget the disbursements listed do not include all the selling and general expenses. Such expenses as depreciation and prepaid insurance expired do not require a current disbursement. Note also that the merchandise purchases figure refers only to cash disbursed to creditors for purchases, not to the amount of purchases made in the period.

A difficult management decision is the determination of the amount of cash to carry, since some balance over absolute needs must be maintained as a safety factor. Theoretically this should be solved by comparing the interest one gives up by carrying "idle" cash (instead of investing the funds) with the losses one could incur by being caught short. Purchase discounts obviously could be lost if cash is short. The firm could suffer the effects of poor labor relations if a cash shortage causes paychecks to be late. This kind of problem is studied in the field of *operations research*, and the techniques cannot be described in this text. However, many of the data used in operations research constitute costs that are recorded in or calculated from the accounting records.

SUMMARY

Because cash is readily spendable it requires especially careful control. The records used in accounting and control of cash are the cash receipts and cash disbursements journals, daily cash report, deposit slip, bank check, bank statement, and bank reconciliation.

Good control requires that all receipts be deposited intact. All disbursements are then made by check, except that small payments may be handled in an imprest petty cash fund.

Internal control procedures for cash include a separation of duties between the cashier and the people keeping accounts receivable and accounts payable records. Several other important internal control devices are also important.

Management data needed for decisions regarding cash consist first of the daily cash report and secondly of a cash budget showing planned receipts and disbursements over a period. The decision of how large a continuing cash balance is to be maintained can be approached through the methods of operations research that use accounting and other data.

QUESTIONS

7.1 State whether or not each of the following would appear in the amount under the caption "Cash in Banks and on Hand" on the balance sheet:

(1) Cash held by the president of the company for travel funds.

(2) Cash deposited.with a trust company to buy outstanding bonds of the firm.

(3) Cash deposited with the state highway department as a guarantee that the company will perform its road-building contract properly. It will get the cash back when the job is done.

(4) Cash on deposit in a bank that went bankrupt. The trustee in bankruptcy anticipates that after the bank's assets are sold, the creditors will probably be paid 75 cents on each dollar of their claims.

(5) Cash on deposit in the firm's regular checking account.

7.2 (1) It is often recommended that all cash receipts be deposited intact. What are the general advantages of this practice?

(2) Lapping is the unauthorized borrowing of cash receipts covered by crediting customer A with receipts from customer B, then crediting B with the receipts from C, and so on. At each step the borrower generally removes additional

currency to make the bank deposit agree exactly with the credit to Accounts Receivable. Discuss briefly how the requirement of depositing all receipts intact facilitates the review of cash transactions to detect lapping.

(3) What sources of information may be used in making entries in a cash receipts journal?

(4) If cash receipts are deposited intact, what will be the source of information for entry in the cash disbursements journal?

7.3 (1) What is an imprest petty cash fund? How are the disbursements from an imprest petty cash fund recorded in the double-entry system?

(2) What device does an imprest fund have for determining whether or not an error has occurred?

(3) What journal entry is made to increase the size of a petty cash fund maintained on an imprest basis?

(4) Should the petty cash fund be reimbursed at the end of every accounting period? Why? If it is not reimbursed, what entry is required? What entry should then be made when the fund is reimbursed in the following period?

7.4 (1) In examining the petty cash fund, you find it contains a small amount of cash, several IOU's from members of the office staff, an employee's postdated check, and another employee's check marked "N.S.F." What can be done to discourage employees from borrowing from the fund?

(2) At Design and Color, the petty cash fund is kept in a locked cash register used exclusively for petty cash disbursements. Every payment is rung up on the register. At noon the cashier goes to lunch, leaving the key in the register so that payments can be made by any of three persons who remain in the office. Comment.

(3) At Antioch Motors, Inc., the petty cash fund is in the custody of the regular cashier. Every day the cashier attaches to the daily cash received report petty cash vouchers evidencing payments. The payments are recorded in a Petty Cash column of the cash receipts journal. The total of this column is posted as a credit to Petty Cash and a debit to Miscellaneous Expense. At irregular intervals the fund is replenished by an arbitrary amount debited to Petty Cash. What do you think of this plan?

7.5 (1) At the end of the day the cashier of the Apparel Arts Store has counted her cash and found that she has $5 less than the amount rung up on the cash register. The error cannot be located, at least not for a day or two. What should be done about this $5 difference when the cash sales for the day are recorded?

(2) The Bookmart records cash sales in both the sales journal and the cash receipts journal, using a Cash Sales Clearing column in each journal. Present in general journal form the entry to be made in the sales journal and in the cash receipts journal to record the following facts:

May 1	Opening register reading	$1,260.20
	Closing register reading.	1,821.50
	"Over" rings	1.00
	Refunds ($25 plus $1 sales tax)	26.00
	Cash count	531.05
	Cash sales ($538.75 plus tax)	560.30

The company records the sales tax when the sale is journalized.

(3) In what ways can the use of cash registers contribute to the effectiveness of internal control over receipts from cash sales? Explain.

7.6 (1) What records other than journals and ledgers are used in maintaining an ordinary bank account, and what is the function of each?

(2) What is the advantage of a daily cash report such as that illustrated on page 216 if the company keeps all cash in a single bank?

    (3) Why does a bank debit memo evidence a reduction in the depositor's account when a debit to the Cash account represents an increase?

    (4) Suggest a method for recording dishonored checks received from charge customers by a wholesaler? How would the procedure differ for cash customers of a supermarket?

7.7 (1) Give the steps you would take in reconciling a bank statement to the depositor's balance.

    (2) In reconciling the bank account of the ABC Co. at December 31, 1966, you have added the checks returned by the bank and find they amounted to $29,219. Comparing these checks to those outstanding on November 30, 1966, and those issued in December, you find that $4,800 of those listed as outstanding on November 30 were not returned by the bank with the December 31 statement, and of those issued per books in December $3,600 were not returned. The cash disbursements journal for December shows a total credit to Cash of $11,241. The list of checks outstanding on the November 30, 1966, reconciliation, which was prepared by another person, amounted to $21,378. What is the amount of the discrepancy between disbursements per books and disbursements per bank? Suggest four possible explanations for the condition existing here, and state what your action would be in each case, including any necessary journal entry.

7.8 In preparing the December 31, 1966, bank reconciliation in a form which will reconcile both the general ledger balance and the bank statement balance with the correct cash in bank for financial statement purposes, indicate for items 1 to 10 below whether:

(a) To add it to the bank statement balance.

(b) To deduct it from the bank statement balance.

(c) To add it to the general ledger balance.

(d) To deduct it from the general ledger balance.

(e) To exclude it from the reconciliation.

The bank debit and credit memos have not been recorded by the company.

    (1) Bank service charges of $30 for December.

    (2) A credit memo dated December 31, 1966, for $150 of interest on bonds held by the bank as collateral for a loan.

    (3) A charge of $90 dated December 30, 1966, for a customer's check returned marked "N.S.F."

    (4) A comparison of checks returned by the bank with those outstanding at November 30, 1966, and those issued during December discloses checks amounting to $1,416 outstanding at December 31, 1966.

    (5) Receipts of $827 were recorded by the company on December 31, 1966, and were placed in the bank's after-hours depository.

    (6) The bank statement includes a $5,000 credit memo representing the proceeds of a loan made to the company on December 30, 1966.

    (7) The company was credited on December 28, 1966, with the receipts of another depositor in the amount of $1,627.

    (8) Among the canceled checks returned is one dated December 28, 1966, in the amount of $2,415 drawn on the Payroll account of the company.

    (9) Among the canceled checks is one for $200 written by the president in November 1966 while on a buying trip. The check was not listed as outstanding on the November 30, 1966, reconciliation and was not recorded in the December record of checks drawn.

   (10) The December bank statement contains a credit memo for $10 adjusting for November service charges. This memo corrects an error reported by the company as a result of the November reconciliation.

(If any of the items are ambiguous, make assumptions and state them as notes to your answer.)

7.9 (1) Outline a division of duties among several employees to secure good internal control over incoming mail receipts on accounts receivable. Point out the controls over error or fraud on the part of each employee.

(2) The owner of a small business mistakenly believes that internal control is impossible for him. "After all," he says, "you just can't divide a one-girl office." What internal control procedures are possible with respect to mail receipts in a small business?

7.10 State whether or not each of the following bank reconciliation items would give rise to an adjusting entry on the depositor's books.

(1) Checks totaling $1,850 were issued by the depositor but were not received by the bank.

(2) A bill of exchange was collected by the bank for the depositor, but notice of it did not get to the depositor until after the end of the month.

(3) The last day's receipts were not entered as a deposit by the bank until after the end of the month.

(4) The depositor issued a check for $180 but entered it in his records as $810.

(5) The bank paid a check for $150 but entered it as $510.

(6) The bank charged back an $85 bad check that it had received in a deposit. The depositor got notice of this just after the close of the period.

(7) The bank made an error in footing its record; the balance shown was $2,800, but should have been $2,600.

7.11 (1) List specific procedures for handling and recording cash receipts that will give good internal control of them.

(2) A 300-room hotel has three people working in the office between 8 A.M. and 5 P.M. — all of whom perform jointly the duties of writing out cash receipts, making up a list of the cash to be deposited each day, and posting to the guests subsidiary ledger. Posting to the general ledger is done by an independent public accountant. The manager suspects that all cash collected from guests is not being deposited in the hotel's bank account. Suggest a plan for the improvement of internal control and point out how the plan would operate.

7.12 D. A. Carter Co. owns 100 machines vending candy in various office buildings throughout the city. Outline a system of inventory control to prevent the misappropriation of cash receipts.

7.13 (1) List specific procedures for handling and recording cash disbursements that will give good internal control.

(2) Clarence Wheelwright, office manager for Ridge Properties, Inc., is authorized to sign checks for the company. Among Wheelwright's duties are those of preparing the daily deposit and reconciling the bank account. On the evening of June 15, 1966, Wheelwright suddenly left town without a forwarding address. An audit discloses that he had embezzled over $40,000, primarily by two devices:

(a) Checks were made payable to tenants for refunds which were not actually due them and which were never recorded in the books. Then, under the pretext of cashing the checks as a convenience for the tenants, Wheelwright had included these checks with the bank deposit for Ridge Properties in lieu of a like amount of currency and coin. The bank accepted the checks for deposit without endorsement.

(b) Checks from tenants properly journalized in the receipts records were cashed and the funds were converted by Wheelwright. He purported to reconcile the bank account by omitting long-outstanding checks from the reconciliation.

Discuss the principles of internal control which have been violated and the changes in procedure which would prevent the frauds.

7.14 (1) A. S. Bauer suspects that there is something drastically wrong with the accounting for his business. According to the monthly income statements prepared by the accountant, net income has been increasing regularly at a brisk rate, yet Bauer finds that he is unable to pay company bills on time. Suggest an explanation other than fraud.

(2) Bauer is perplexed further by the fact that the current ratio on the last balance sheet stands at 2.5 to 1, yet he is unable to pay bills on time. Explain.

7.15 The Local Sales Co. was incorporated on January 1, 1966, to sell motor scooters. Monthly sales of 125 units are expected at $300 each. Eighty percent of these sales will be on an installment basis: 20 percent down, the balance in six monthly payments with no carrying charge. Management is considering holding the installment paper rather than selling it to a finance company, and wishes to know the maximum amount that will be invested in this paper. Assume sales are dated the first of the month and monthly payments begin one month later.

(1) Prepare the required calculation.

(2) What will be the annual cost of the cash invested in this paper at 10 percent a year?

EXERCISES

7.1 Smith & Co. are manufacturers' representatives for a line of home elevators. The company has prospered over its thirty-year history despite the somewhat informal procedures of the founders, Joe and John Smith. The Smith brothers have always felt that a primary reason for their success has been the spirit of trust they managed to convey to their customers and employees. Much of this confidence, they explained, was due to the fact that theirs was a family business. For example, they were pleased to note that John Smith, Jr., had been the shop foreman for fifteen years and that his wife, Mary, the treasurer of the company, had been in charge of the office for that same period.

Mary Smith maintained the accounting records and prepared the financial statements with the help of two assistants, made bank deposits, signed checks, and prepared bank reconciliations. She also signed most checks, along with any of three other officers of the company. Because these officers were frequently out of town, they generally signed a few checks in blank so that Mary could make emergency payments.

On the evening of Friday, April 13, Mary cashed a company check for $2,000 made out to Payroll and suddenly disappeared. Auditors, retained to examine the accounting records, discovered the following irregularities:

(1) Cash had been abstracted from nonoperating receipts. Checks received from freight companies in settlement of damage claims and from insurance companies as dividends on mutual policies had not been recorded; an equivalent amount of currency was taken, and the checks were substituted for the currency, thereby making the bank deposit agree with the recorded receipts.

(2) Cash discounts had been overstated. Checks received from customers after the expiration of the discount period were recorded as though the discount had been actually taken by the customer, and currency was abstracted from the cash sale of parts.

(3) Accounts receivable from some charge sales were written off to Allowance for Bad Debts, though the accounts were good. Cash receipts from these accounts were deposited but were not recorded in the record of cash received. Subsequently, Mrs. Smith drew checks payable to Payroll, cashed the checks, kept the money, and destroyed the checks when they were returned by the bank.

(4) Mrs. Smith abstracted other amounts by cashing checks payable to Petty Cash or Payroll. She omitted these checks from the check register and falsified the bank reconciliations, thus concealing the fact that the balance per bank was less than the amount shown in the ledger.

    1. Comment briefly on the general principles of internal control which had been violated.

    2. For each of the numbered types of embezzlement, describe specific internal practices that would have prevented the occurrence of such a loss.

7.2   The Timberline Co. uses a *voucher system* and makes small disbursements from a petty cash fund maintained on an imprest basis. Show in general journal form the entries required *in each journal* to record the following transactions:

Jan. 2   The fund was established in the amount of $20.

      31   A count on January 31 disclosed:

Currency and coins	$ 2
Freight bills for merchandise received	15
Cash shortage	3
Total...............................	$20

The fund was replenished and increased to $50.

7.3   The journals of Jackson's Supermarket for January 1966 are presented below. (Debits and credits have been omitted from the column headings in this exercise).

SALES JOURNAL		PURCHASES JOURNAL	
A Co.	100	X Co.	2,000
B Co.	300	Y Co.	500
C Co.	600		2,500
	1,000		

CASH RECEIPTS JOURNAL

	Sundry Accounts	Accounts Receivable	Sales Discounts	Cash
C Co.		600	12	588
Notes payable	2,000			2,000
B Co.		200	4	196
Capital stock	1,000			1,000
	3,000	800	16	3,784

CASH DISBURSEMENTS JOURNAL

	Sundry Accounts	Accounts Payable	Purchase Discounts	Cash
X Co.		2,000	40	1,960
Equipment	500			500
Y Co.		200	4	196
Salaries	500			500
	1,000	2,200	44	3,156

Required:

    1. Open general ledger and subsidiary ledger accounts and post the journals. Ignore opening balances (see following list of accounts).

General Ledger Accounts	*Accounts Receivable*
Cash	A Co.
Accounts Receivable	B Co.
Equipment	C Co.
Notes Payable	
Accounts Payable	*Accounts Payable*
Capital Stock	X Co.
Sales	Y Co.
Sales Discounts	
Purchases	
Purchase Discounts	
Salaries	

2. Prepare schedules of receivables and payables as of January 31.

7.4 Prepare a bank reconciliation and make any entries required for the Vanda Company at June 30, 1966, from the following data:

BANK RECONCILIATION
May 31, 1966

Bank balance $5,397.50
Less outstanding checks:
   69 . . . . $100.00
   72 . . . . 416.10
   78 . . . . 56.20
   81 . . . . 14.70   587.00
Ledger balance $4,810.50

The bank statement at June 30 from the First National Bank reveals:

Date	Debits		Deposits		Balance
June 1					5,397.50
4	416.10	65.40		115.10	
11	76.70	56.20	69.25	315.60	
16	10.15	25.40			
18	115.60			195.90	
22	101.20				
24	74.25	64.80		211.60	
30	3.85	(service charge)			5,156.80

The deposits in the cash receipts book were:

June 4	$115.10	June 18	$195.90	June 30	$215.60
11	315.60	24	211.60		

The cash disbursements book contained the following checks:

#82	$65.40	#85	$69.25	#88	$ 42.90	#91	$74.25
83	99.80	86	10.15	89	115.60	92	64.80
84	76.70	87	25.40	90	101.20		

The ledger balance of Cash on June 30 was $5,118.85.

7.5 From the following information prepare a bank reconciliation as of January 31, 1966 for the H Co.

The general ledger account shows:

Balance 1/1/66		$ 494
Add: Deposits in January	$15,000	
Less: Checks in January	14,265	735
Balance 1/31/66		$ 1,229
Balance per bank statement 1/30/66		$ 1,479

Deposits per bank statement, including a $300 deposit on 12/31/65 .. 15,225

Canceled checks returned by bank with January statement, including checks of $400 outstanding on 12/31/65 14,340

Deposit of another depositor credited by bank to the company 59

Proceeds of January sight draft on foreign sale (not recorded by company):

Gross amount	$310	
Collection fee	5	305

Bank charges for January (not recorded by the company) 20

Check #112 for $75 to a trade creditor entered in the check register on 1/15/66 as $57 cleared the bank at the correct amount 18

7.6 Give the journal entries which would be made on the bank's books and the depositor's books after preparation of the following reconcilation. The depositor's books have not been closed for May.

EXACTO, INC.
BANK RECONCILIATION
May 31, 1966

Balance per bank statement, June 1, 1966		$3,723
Checks written on June 1, 1966		25
		$3,748
Less: Outstanding checks	$1,567	
Deposit of XYZ Company entered in error	523	
June 1, 1966, deposit	258	
		2,348
Adjusted bank balance as of May 31, 1966		$1,400
Balance per books, May 31, 1966		$1,403
Error in May 16, 1966, deposit. A check for $51 received in a cash sale was journalized as $50. The bank corrected the deposit slip		1
Check #256, written three years ago, has never been returned. It is now canceled and payment is stopped at the bank		5
		$1,409
Collection and service charges		9
Adjusted book balance, May 31, 1966		$1,400

7.7 Sales for F Co. for January are expected to be $10,000 and to increase $5,000 a month. Sales for a given month are collected two months later (for example, $10 of January sales result in $10 of March receipts.) Fixed expenses are $3,000 a month. Variable expenses are 60 percent of sales. Expenses are paid in the month incurred.

1. Prepare a forecast of income and expense by months for the period January 1 to June 30, 1966.
2. Prepare a forecast of cash receipts and disbursements for the same period. Include a line showing the cumulative cash deficit.
3. What is the maximum cumulative cash deficit? When does it occur?

7.8 As the accountant for the K Corporation you are requested to prepare a cash budget for July, August, and September 1966. In a conference with the owner and the sales force, the accounting records for the past three years are reviewed and the following estimates prepared for the four months—June through September 1966.

	June	July	August	September
Commissions earned	$20,000	$25,000	$18,000	$10,000
Investment revenue	1,200	1,800	1,000	800
Payroll (including owner's salary).................	10,000	12,000	10,000	9,000
Travel expense............	4,000	5,000	4,000	5,000
Office rent	800	800	800	800
Misc. office expense	2,000	3,000	3,000	2,000

Fifty percent of the commissions are received in the month of the billing and 50 percent in the following month. Investment revenue is received in cash in the month shown. Payroll and office rent are paid by check in the month shown. Travel expense and miscellaneous office expense are paid by check, 90 percent in the month shown and 10 percent in the following month. A mortgage payment of $8,000 must be made in July 1966.

The cash balance is not to be permitted to fall below $6,000. When the expected balance is below this figure, a 30-day loan is to be secured from the bank in amounts of even thousands of dollars. Such loans must be repaid in the following month. When the expected cash balance is above $10,000, U. S. bonds are to be purchased in amounts of even thousands of dollars to reduce the balance to just above $6,000. It is anticipated that the cash balance on July 1, 1966, will be $6,800. Clearly label each item you use in presenting the cash budget to the owner.

(CPCU—adapted)

PROBLEMS

7.1 National Factors does not have a satisfactory system of internal control over cash receipts and disbursements. John Smith, the bookkeeper, received cash, made some disbursements from cash receipts for freight and postage, maintained the accounting records, and prepared the bank reconciliations. Smith terminated his employment without notice on December 31, 1966, after taking all cash on hand in excess of $3,700. In an attempt to conceal his theft he prepared the following "reconciliation":

Balance per ledger		$40,000
Add outstanding checks:		
# 1281..............................	$380	
# 1282..............................	416	
# 1283..............................	290	1,086
Total..		$41,086
Deduct cash on hand		3,700
Balance per bank...............................		$37,386
Deduct unrecorded credit........................		1,000
Balance per bank, as adjusted		$36,386

The company's books showed a $40,000 balance of cash as of December 31, including cash on hand. The bank statement balance was $37,386, and the actual checks outstanding were:

# 62	$220	# 1281	$380
64	300	1282	416
66	500	1283	290

A credit memorandum of $1,000 on the bank statement, representing the collection of a sight draft, does not appear on the company's records.

Required:

1. Prepare a corrected reconciliation, showing the adjusted cash balance that will appear in the balance sheet.
2. What was the amount of Smith's defalcation? How did he attempt to conceal his theft?
3. Suggest improvements in the internal control of cash.

7.2 A bank statement of Communications Engineering, Inc., at December 31, 1966, shows a balance of $1,821, while the Cash account on this date shows a balance of $407.

The bookkeeper (a brother-in-law of the chairman of the board) is in complete charge of the office. He supervises the collection of cash, at times personally handles cash receipts, prepares bank deposits with the help of several assistants, signs checks, and reconciles the bank account.

Because of an unexpected business opportunity and the consequent requirements of additional financing, the company needs certified statements. Auditors, retained to perform an examination of financial condition as of December 31, 1966, discover that:

(1) The December 31, 1966, cash balance included a $200 change fund, which contained $185 in currency and coin. The difference of $15 arose from shortages in making change.
(2) The cash balance also included a $300 petty cash fund. Inspection of the fund revealed $120 cash on hand and a replenishing check for $180.
(3) The bookkeeper had misappropriated $700 of the collections from charge customers, which amount he attempted to conceal by crediting the original customers with subsequent collections from other customers, then crediting these customers with collections from still other customers, and so on in turn — always crediting prior customers for current receipts, so that a customer would not be dunned for a paid account.
(4) The bookkeeper had written off $1,800 of good accounts to the Allowance for Bad Debts and abstracted the receipts. Confronted with these facts, the bookkeeper confessed to the embezzlements and admitted to a further embezzlement of $2,500 during the past year. This fraud he had effected by having one of the officers sign blank checks, which he made out to himself and cashed. He destroyed the canceled checks when they were returned from the bank, and raised other checks in payment of Travel and Entertainment in an attempt to hide the defalcation. Because of a desire to avoid criminal action against his brother-in-law, the chairman of the board insists on making restitution personally for the entire loss.

The following additional items were discovered when reconciling the bank statement:

(1) The company was charged with a $165 N.S.F. check from a customer.
(2) Bank charges for December were $24.
(3) A check for $172 drawn by Comac, Inc., had incorrectly been charged to the company.

(4) December 31 receipts of $1,925 were omitted from the bank statement.
(5) Outstanding checks amounted to $4,200, including the $180 check in petty cash.

Required:

1. Prepare a bank reconciliation, using a form which results in the adjusted cash balance.
2. Prepare the journal entries required by the foregoing data.
3. Describe some internal control procedures that would prevent the recurrence of such frauds.

7.3 Following are the voucher register, check register (record of disbursements by check), and general journal of Holcomb Co. for January 1966:

VOUCHER REGISTER

Vo. Pay.	Vo. No.	Date	Ck. No.	Payee	Purchases	Freight In	Sundry Account	Amount
1,500	1-1	Jan 2	2	A Co.	1,500			
40	1-2	2	1	SP		40		
400	1-3	5	3	B Co.	400			
600	1-4	20	J	C Co.	600			
50	1-5	21	4	CF		50		
200	1-6	23		D Co.	200			
400	1-7	24	5	E Co.			Advertising	400
200	1-8	26	6	F Co.			Rent	200
1,000	1-9	31	7	X			Note Payable	1,000

CHECK REGISTER

Purch. Disc.	Net Check	Ck. No.	Payee	Vo. Pay.
	40	1	SP	40
30	1,470	2	A Co........................	1,500
8	392	3	B Co........................	400
	50	4	CF.........................	50
	400	5	E Co........................	400
	200	6	F Co........................	200
	1,000	7	X..........................	1,000

JOURNAL

Jan. 2

Cash	10,000	
Capital stock		10,000

Jan. 2

Cash	1,000	
Notes payable		1,000

Jan. 30

Vouchers payable	600	
Notes payable		600

1. Post the general ledger.
2. Take a trial balance.

7.4   Prepare the following forms for the Food Pantry on a sheet of 14-column paper, allowing approximately ten lines for each form. (On all forms the blank columns will be used for explanation.)

Record of Sales:
  Cash Sales — column 1
  Accounts Receivable, Retail — column 2
  Accounts Receivable, Wholesale — column 3
  Sales Tax — column 11
  3½% Sales — column 12
  3% Sales — column 13
  Exempt Sales — column 14
Record of Cash Received:
  Net Amount Received — column 1
  Discount Allowed — column 2
  Cash Over or (Short) — column 11
  Wholesale Accounts Receivable — column 12
  Retail Accounts Receivable — column 13
  Cash Sales — column 14
Record of Invoices:
  Accounts Payable Credit — column 1
  Merchandise Stock — column 10
  Expenses — columns 11 and 12 (11, Name; 12, Amount)
  General Ledger — columns 13 and 14 (13, Name; 14, Amount)
Record of Checks Drawn:
  Employee Payroll Deductions — column 1
  Cash Discounts Taken — column 2
  Net Amount of Check — column 3
  Accounts Payable — column 10
  Expenses — columns 11 and 12 (Name, Amount)
  General Ledger Dr. — columns 13 and 14

Record the following transactions in the special journals. Key each transaction into the record of original entry by means of the transaction number.

(1) A summary of the sales slips shows the following charge sales. (Record the entry on a single line.)

$$
\begin{aligned}
&\text{Wholesale sales (tax exempt)} \dots\dots\dots\dots\$1,700\\
&\text{Retail sales:}\\
&\quad\text{City sales (taxable at 3½\%)} \dots\dots\dots\dots\ 1,000\\
&\quad\text{Out-of-city sales (taxable at 3\%)} \dots\dots\dots\ 500\\
&\quad\text{Out-of-state sales (tax exempt)} \dots\dots\dots\ 300\\
&\text{Sales tax} \dots\dots\dots\dots\dots\dots\dots\dots\dots\ \underline{50}\\
&\text{Total charge sales and tax} \dots\dots\dots\dots\ \underline{\underline{\$3,550}}
\end{aligned}
$$

(2) The reconciliation of cash sales shows:

$$
\begin{aligned}
&\text{Total cash sales (city retail)} \dots\dots\dots\dots\ \$2,000\\
&\text{Sales tax} \dots\dots\dots\dots\dots\dots\dots\dots\dots\ \underline{70}\\
&\text{Total} \dots\dots\dots\dots\dots\dots\dots\dots\dots\dots\ \$2,070\\
&\text{Less: Shortages due to making change} \dots\dots\ \underline{10}\\
&\text{Cash deposited in bank} \dots\dots\dots\dots\dots\ \underline{\underline{\$2,060}}
\end{aligned}
$$

(Enter cash sales in both the record of cash received and record of sales; use a Cash Sales account in each case.)

(3) Collections on account:

```
                Retail . . . . . . . . . . . . . . . . . . . . . . . . . $4,500
                Wholesale . . . . . . . . . . . . . . . . . . . . . . .   2,000
                    Total accounts credited . . . . . . . . . . . . . $6,500
                Less: Discounts allowed . . . . . . . . . . . . . .     300
                    Cash deposited in bank . . . . . . . . . . . . . $6,200
```

(4) Paid creditor:
```
                Total accounts payable paid . . . . . . . . . . . . $5,000
                Discounts taken . . . . . . . . . . . . . . . . . . . .    100
                    Net amount of check . . . . . . . . . . . . . . . $4,900
```

(5) Check for freight charges on various invoices of merchandise:
```
                Shipping terms f.o.b. destination . . . . . . . . . $   25
                Shipping terms f.o.b. shipping point . . . . . . .    475
                    Total of check . . . . . . . . . . . . . . . . . . . . $  500
```

(Freight and purchases are combined in the Merchandise Stock account.)
  (6) Check drawn to Alameda Boat Sales for $7,500 for 30-foot Tahiti ketch to
      be used for the owner's pleasure.
  (7) Purchased goods for resale, from H. Miller Company; terms 2/10 e.o.m.,
      f.o.b. shipping point.
```
                List price . . . . . . . . . . . . . . . . . . . . . . . . $1,550
                Less 50% trade discount . . . . . . . . . . . . . .     775
                    Difference . . . . . . . . . . . . . . . . . . . . . . . $  775
                Freight paid by shipper . . . . . . . . . . . . . . .     25
                Balance due . . . . . . . . . . . . . . . . . . . . . . . $  800
```

  (8) Issued a check to Parcel Post for $300 delivery charges on sales. (Expense
      to be borne by the store.)
  (9) Issued a check for payroll:
```
                Total salaries expense . . . . . . . . . . . . . . . . $1,250
                Less: Employees payroll deductions . . . . . . .     250
                    Net amount of check . . . . . . . . . . . . . . . $1,000
```

(10) Issued a check for one year's insurance premium, $120.
(11) Purchase from the Bookmart a used calculator for the office, $400.
(12) Received an invoice from Ross and Stevens for public accounting services,
     $100. The bill is recorded but is not paid at this time.
(13) A retail customer's check for $13, which had been returned by the bank
     marked N.S.F. and had been recorded in the check register and charged
     back to Accounts Receivable, is now redeposited.
(14) At the time the bank account is reconciled, a previously unrecorded debit
     memo for $90 is received:
```
                Bank activity charge . . . . . . . . . . . . . . . . . $   10
                Interest on loan #C-12-47 . . . . . . . . . . . . . .     80
                    Total . . . . . . . . . . . . . . . . . . . . . . . . . . . . $   90
```

     (Record the interest, a nonoperating expense, in the General Ledger column.)
(15) Returned merchandise purchased from H. Miller Company, $200 (see trans-
     action 7).

7.5 The unaudited balance sheet of Contract Sales Company at December 31, 1966,
     contains cash in the amount of $42,300. This amount has been reconciled to the
     bank balance as follows:

Balance per bank statement		$16,500
Add: Cash placed in escrow with Title Guarantee Co. as a deposit on land for new plant site	$ 3,200	
Sight drafts on Canadian customers drawn in late December, collections of which were not reported by December 31, 1966.................................	24,500	
Cash receipts of December 31, 1966, not deposited in bank until January 2, 1967......................	12,200	
Advances to president for travel expense	2,500	
Interest for the quarter ended December 31, 1966, on a note payable to the bank; debit memo for interest recorded by company January 2, 1967	1,000	
Imprest cash funds of $1,000, composed of $500 cash, $200 employee IOU's, and $300 vouchers for miscellaneous expense	1,000	
Cash in a Dealer's Reserve account held by the bank until contracts assigned to the bank were collected	6,400	50,800
		$67,300
Less: Checks issued through December 31, 1966, but not presented to the bank at December 31, 1966	$ 8,000	
Checks recorded in the cash disbursements journal during December but not mailed to creditors until January 1967	15,000	
Deposit of December 27, 1966, by Comstock Sales Co. posted in error	2,000	25,000
Cash per balance sheet		$42,300

Required:

Preface a schedule showing the corrected balance of cash and the disposition of each of the foregoing items not included in that balance.

7.6   The bank reconciliation of Mademoiselle's Candy Co. on June 30, 1966, was as follows:

Bank balance, June 30		$6,210.15
Checks outstanding:		
No. 1156	$118.20	
1185	256.40	
1188	98.60	
1192	110.15	
1203	25.50	
1206	165.30	
1211	215.25	
1212	648.20	
1225	96.80	1,734.40
		$4,475.75
Deposit, June 30, not credited by bank		726.10
		$5,201.85
N.S.F. check		20.00
		$5,221.85
Bank charges		6.15
Ledger balance, June 30		$5,228.00

The cash receipts journal showed the following deposits for July:

$$\begin{array}{llll} \$317.80 & \$543.10 & \$177.40 & \$415.90 \\ 786.20 & 540.25 & 116.80 & 795.40 \end{array}$$

The following amounts were entered in the cash disbursements journal during July:

Check No.	Amount	Check No.	Amount	Check No.	Amount
	$ 20.00	1236	$ 77.20	1244	$110.40
	6.15	1237	166.80	1245	79.60
1230	185.90	1238	595.10	1246	42.30
1231	116.10	1239	28.70	1247	215.20
1232	172.40	1240	90.50	1248	194.40
1233	78.60	1241	87.40	1249	60.50
1234	15.70	1242	177.20		
1235	98.10	1243	93.80		

The bank statement for July showed the following debits and credits:

Debits						Credits
No. 1156	$118.20	No. 1233	$ 78.60	No. 1243	$ 93.80	$726.10
1188	98.60	1234	15.70	1244	110.40	317.80
1192	110.15	1236	77.20	1247	215.20	543.10
1203	25.50	1237	166.80	Bank charges	5.85	177.40
1206	165.30	1238	595.10			415.90
1211	215.25	1239	28.70			786.20
1225	96.80	1240	90.50			540.25
1230	185.90	1241	87.40			116.80
1231	116.10	1242	177.20			

These transactions resulted in a bank statement balance of $7,009.45 at July 31 compared with a ledger balance of $6,258.80.

Required:

1. Prepare the bank reconciliation at July 31, 1966, in a form which shows the adjusted cash balance.
2. Prepare journal entries for the company resulting from the reconciliation.

7.7 The cash records of the Y Company for August 1966 are as follows:

CASH RECEIPTS JOURNAL

			Debits		Credits			
			Cash	Sales Disc.	Accts. Rec.	Sales	General Acct.	Amt.
Date	Name	Explanation						
8/1	Cash balance	1,389						
8/4	T. Yate	Inv. 8/1 less 2%	329	8	400			
8/11	Sales	Cash sales	263			263		
8/18	P. White	On account	575		575			
8/31	Tunick, Cap.	Investment	158				Invest.	158
			1,325	8	975	263		158
9/1	Cash balance	1,474						

CASH DISBURSEMENTS JOURNAL

| | | | | | Credits | Debits |
| | | | | | Purchase | Accounts |
Date	Ck. No.	Payee	Explanation	Cash	Discounts	Payable
8/4	2188	Wm. Smith	On account	400		400
8/6	2189	F. Jones	Inv. 8/2 less 2%	343	7	350
8/7	2190	J. Merrill	On account	200		200
8/21	2191	P. Hallet	On account	147		147
8/22	2192	P. Harmon	Inv. 8/9 less 2%	98	2	100
8/30	2193	M. Ross	On account	52		52
				1240	9	1,249

The reconciliation at July 31, 1966, was as follows:

```
Bank balance, July 31 . . . . . . . . . . . . . . . . . . . . . $1,528
Less outstanding checks:
      No. 2186 . . . . . . . . . . . . . . . . . . . . . $ 10
           2187 . . . . . . . . . . . . . . . . . . . . .   294      304
                                                                   $1,224
      Add deposit in transit . . . . . . . . . . . . . . . . . . .    165
      Balance per books, July 31 . . . . . . . . . . . . . . . . $1,389
```

The bank statement for August 1966 showed the following:

CITY BANK
ACCOUNT WITH: Y COMPANY

Date	Checks		Deposits	
Aug. 2	294		CM	1,000
2	982			165
7				392
8	392DM	2DM		
10	400	200		
10	343			
13				263
15			CM	303
19				575
22	98			
30	145	3SC		

CM – Credit Memo   Opening balance   1,528
DM – Debit Memo   Closing balance   1,367
SC – Service Charges

Canceled checks returned with the above bank statement were as follows:

Check No.	Payee	Amount	Paid
2187	P. Roe	$294	Aug. 2
2188	Wm. Smith	400	Aug. 10
2189	F. Jones	343	Aug. 10
2190	J. Merrill	200	Aug. 10
2191	P. Hallet	145	Aug. 30
2192	P. Harmon	98	Aug. 22
7081	L. Mart (drawn by W Company)	982	Aug. 2

The following debit memorandums accompanied the bank statement:

> Aug. 8 Yate's check returned for insufficient funds $392
> 　　　8 Protest fee on Yate's check　　　　　　　　　2

The following credit memorandums accompanied the bank statement:

> Aug. 2 Proceeds of demand note issued to the bank $1000
> 　　　15 Collection of Morse note $300
> 　　　　　Interest for 60 days . . . .　3　　303

Required:

1. Prepare a reconciliation of the company's bank account as of August 31, 1966.
2. Prepare one or more journal entries to adjust the company's bank balance at August 31, 1966. (If further data are required, make reasonable assumptions and state them.)

7.8　In reconciling the bank balance of the Ametel Co. at December 31, 1966, with that shown in the company's ledger, you observe the following facts:

Balance per bank statement, December 31, 1966 . . . . $88,489
Balance per ledger, December 31, 1966 . . . .　58,806
Outstanding checks, December 31, 1966 . . . .　32,108
Receipts of December 31, 1966, deposited January 2, 1967 . . . .　5,317
Service charge for November 1966, per bank memo of December 15, 1966 . . . . 　38
Proceeds of bank loan, December 31, 1966, evidenced by demand note executed to bank with interest at 6% per year, omitted from company books . . . . 　10,000
Deposit of December 23, 1966, omitted from bank statement . . . .　2,892
Check of Pogo Products, Inc., charged back on December 22, 1966, for absence of countersignature and redeposited with complete signature on January 5, 1967, no entry on books having been made for chargeback or redeposit . . . . $　417
Error on bank statement in entering deposit of December 16, 1966:
　Correct amount $3,182
　Entered in statement . . . . 3,172　　　10
Check No. 3917 of Ametek Manufacturing Co., charged by bank in error to Ametel Co. account . . . . 　2,690
Proceeds of note of H. Hatfield & Co. collected by bank, December 10, 1966, not entered in cash book:
　Principal $2,000
　Interest . . . .　20　　2,020
Erroneous debit memo of December 23, 1966, to charge company's account with settlement of bank loan, which was paid by check No. 8714 on the same date . . . .　5,000
Error on bank statement in entering deposit of December 4, 1966:
　Entered as $4,817
　Correct amount . . . . 4,717　　100
Deposit of Ametek Manufacturing Co. of December 6, 1966, credited in error to Ametel Co. . . . .　1,819

Required:

1. Prepare a bank reconciliation at December 31, 1966.
2. Prepare one or more journal entries to adjust the ledger to reflect the correct bank balance at December 31, 1966.

7.9 The Pots and Pans Co. has secured the exclusive franchise to distribute a patented appliance in twelve Western states as of January 1, 1966. Management wants to know the amount of cash required to finance the project, and has retained you to assist in this matter. Each appliance will be sold for $40 on an installment contract, 10 percent down and six monthly payments of $6 each.

The appliances cost $10 each. Their purchase will be financed by payment of 20 percent down with a noninterest-bearing floor-plan note for the balance. (This balance must be paid at the end of the month in which the appliance is sold.) An inventory of 2,000 units at the beginning of each month will be maintained, and the same purchase terms apply to all replacements. Salesmen are paid a commission of $2 per unit; other variable expenses are $3 per unit. Fixed expenses are estimated at $2,000 per month. These payments will be made on the last day of each month. Estimated sales in units by months are as follows:

January	1,000
February	1,600
March	1,800
April	2,200
May	3,800
June	4,000

The company agrees to maintain a minimum bank balance of $15,000. Experience with similar enterprises has shown that credit losses are negligible and may be ignored in forecast computations.

Required:

1. Prepare a forecast summarizing cash receipts, cash disbursements, receipts less disbursements, and cash deficits by months. It may be convenient to support the forecast with a schedule by months showing units bought and sold and resulting payments.
2. What is the minimum cash requirement of the company?

Closing and Statements

This chapter summarizes the closing process, incorporating the transactions discussed since the closing was first described. It presents more complete financial statements, including the statement of retained earnings, and considers some of the debatable points about them. Finally, it considers management's statement problems and gives the forms developed in an effort to make financial statements understandable to persons untrained in accounting.

STEPS IN PERIODIC CLOSING OF ACCOUNTS AND PREPARATION OF STATEMENTS

The steps in adjusting and closing the accounts and preparing statements and the related work are listed below. They involve proving the record (trial balances and schedules of subsidiary ledgers), adjusting and closing the accounts, preparing financial statements, and using reversing entries. The steps may be taken in various orders, but the following order is common:

1. Take a trial balance of the general ledger and prepare schedules of the subsidiary ledgers (to check against control accounts).
2. Prepare data for adjusting entries after scrutinizing the accounts to note those probably requiring adjustment.
3. Prepare a work sheet.
4. Prepare financial statements from the work sheet.
5. Enter the adjusting entries in the general journal and post them.
6. Enter closing entries in the general journal and post them.
7. Rule and balance the general ledger accounts.
8. Prepare a postclosing trial balance.
9. Prepare, enter in the general journal, and post any desired reversing entries under date of the new period. The reversing entries are discussed in a later section of this chapter.

ILLUSTRATION OF END-OF-PERIOD WORK

The preclosing trial balance of Wholesale Auto Parts, Inc., as of December 31, 1966, is given on page 242. This company closes its books annually on December 31. It records supplies and insurance premiums in asset accounts and adjusts them for supplies used and insurance expired at the year end. No accruals are recorded until adjusting entries are made at the close. The periodic inventory method is used. The trademark was purchased from a predecessor company and does not expire as long as it is used.

241

WHOLESALE AUTO PARTS, INC.
Trial Balance

December 31, 1966

	Debit	Credit
Cash	$ 11,800.00	
Petty Cash	200.00	
Notes Receivable	13,500.00	
Accounts Receivable	14,600.00	
Allowance for Doubtful Accounts		$ 1,800.00
Merchandise	46,000.00	
Warehouse Supplies	1,610.00	
Office Supplies	840.00	
Prepaid Insurance	3,470.00	
Land	5,000.00	
Building	58,000.00	
Accumulated Depreciation—Building		2,900.00
Delivery Equipment	3,000.00	
Accumulated Depreciation—Delivery Equipment		500.00
Office Furniture and Fixtures	8,200.00	
Accumulated Depreciation—Office Furniture and Fixtures		1,640.00
Warehouse Equipment	4,800.00	
Accumulated Depreciation—Warehouse Equipment		900.00
Trademark	2,000.00	
Notes Payable		12,600.00
Accounts Payable		13,900.00
Income Tax Withheld		400.00
Payroll Taxes Withheld		120.00
Mortgage Payable		7,200.00
Capital Stock		100,000.00
Retained Earnings		9,880.00
Dividends	2,000.00	
Sales		195,400.00
Sales Returns and Allowances	4,100.00	
Bad Debts	2,200.00	
Sales Discounts	1,770.00	
Purchases	91,000.00	
Purchase Returns and Allowances		3,800.00
Purchase Discounts		1,200.00
Freight In	1,640.00	
Salesmen's Salaries	22,000.00	
Advertising	3,900.00	
Delivery Expense	8,100.00	
Freight Out	9,200.00	
Sundry Selling Expense	3,750.00	
Office Salaries	20,000.00	
Payroll Taxes	2,700.00	
Property Taxes	2,460.00	
Postage and Express	1,600.00	
Sundry General Expense	2,800.00	
	352,240.00	352,240.00

Adjusting entries required by Wholesale Auto Parts, Inc., at December 31, 1966 are described in the following listing. The data are numbered to correspond with the entries in the company's work sheet, which is given on pages 244-245.

1. Interest of $210 is accrued on the notes receivable.
2. Merchandise on hand cost $50,000. The company uses a Cost of Goods Sold account in its adjusting and closing process.
3. An addition of $150 to Allowance for Doubtful Accounts is needed to record estimated bad debts on December sales.
4. Warehouse supplies on hand cost $120.
5. Office supplies on hand cost $65.
6. Insurance prepaid amounted to $680.
7. The building is to be depreciated over twenty years; no salvage value is expected.
8. Delivery equipment is expected to last five years and to have a trade-in value of $500.
9. Office furniture and fixtures will be used twenty years and will have no salvage value.
10. Warehouse equipment is expected to last ten years and to have no salvage value.
11. Interest accrued on the notes payable amounts to $378.
12. Property taxes accrued are $1,250.
13. Payroll taxes accrued amount to $675.
14. Interest accrued on the mortgage payable amounts to $150.
15. Dividends of $3,000 were declared on December 15, 1966, payable on January 31, 1967, to stockholders of record on January 15. They have not been recorded.
16. The corporation is subject to federal income tax of 22 percent of the first $25,000 of taxable net income and 48 percent of any amount over $25,000. Assume that it operates in a state that does not levy an income tax. Taxable net income and ordinary net income are the same in this case.

COMMENTS ON THE WORK SHEET

The work sheet of Wholesale Auto Parts, Inc., given on pages 244-245, is an eight-column work sheet, without columns for an adjusted trial balance. If the work is done accurately, this omission causes no trouble; if not, one simply has to look over a little more work to find the error, since there is no chance to catch it at a halfway point. Note that the accounts not open in the preclosing trial balance but needed when adjustments are made, are listed at the bottom as their need appears. Interest Expense and Accrued Interest Payable require two lines each, and Cost of Goods Sold three lines. In these cases it is helpful to anticipate the need if possible and to allow the extra space, but two figures may often be written on one line legibly. Since net income must be calculated before the income tax can be computed, it is more convenient to enter the income tax after the Income columns are totaled. Income tax may be entered in the Adjustment columns if desired, but it is usually entered only in the Income Statement and Balance Sheet columns.

WHOLESALE AUTO PARTS, INC.
Work Sheet
For Year Ended December 31, 1966

	Trial Balance		Adjustments		Income Statement		Balance Sheet	
	Debit	Credit	Debit	Credit	Debit	Credit	Debit	Credit
Cash	11 800 00						11 800 00	
Petty Cash	200 00						200 00	
Notes Receivable	13 500 00						13 500 00	
Accounts Receivable	14 600 00						14 600 00	
Allowance for Doubtful Accounts		1 800 00		(3) 150 00				1 950 00
Merchandise	46 000 00		(2a) 50 000 00	(2b) 46 000 00			50 000 00	
Warehouse Supplies	1 610 00			(4) 1 490 00			120 00	
Office Supplies	840 00			(5) 775 00			65 00	
Prepaid Insurance	3 470 00			(6) 2 790 00			680 00	
Land	5 000 00						5 000 00	
Building	58 000 00						58 000 00	
Accumulated Depreciation—Building		2 900 00		(7) 2 900 00				5 800 00
Delivery Equipment	3 000 00						3 000 00	
Accumulated Depreciation—Delivery Equipment		500 00		(8) 500 00				1 000 00
Office Furniture and Fixtures	8 200 00						8 200 00	
Accumulated Depreciation—Office Furniture and Fixtures		1 640 00		(9) 410 00				2 050 00
Warehouse Equipment	4 800 00						4 800 00	
Accumulated Depreciation—Warehouse Equipment		900 00		(10) 480 00				1 380 00
Trademark	2 000 00						2 000 00	
Notes Payable		12 600 00						12 600 00
Accounts Payable		13 900 00						13 900 00
Income Tax Withheld		400 00						400 00
Payroll Taxes Withheld		120 00						120 00
Mortgage Payable		7 200 00						7 200 00
Capital Stock		100 000 00						100 000 00
Retained Earnings		9 880 00						9 880 00
Dividends	2 000 00		(15) 3 000 00				5 000 00	
Sales		195 400 00				195 400 00		
Sales Returns and Allowances	4 100 00				4 100 00			
Bad Debts	2 200 00		(3) 150 00		2 350 00			
Sales Discounts	1 770 00				1 770 00			

Account	Trial Balance Dr	Trial Balance Cr	Adj. Ref (Dr)	Adjustments Dr	Adj. Ref (Cr)	Adjustments Cr	Income Statement Dr	Income Statement Cr	Balance Sheet Dr	Balance Sheet Cr
Purchase Returns and Allowances		3 800 00	(2d)	3 800 00						
Purchase Discounts		1 200 00	(2e)	1 200 00						
Freight In	1 640 00				(2f)	1 640 00				
Salesmen's Salaries	22 000 00						22 000 00			
Advertising	3 900 00						3 900 00			
Delivery Expense	8 100 00						8 100 00			
Freight Out	9 200 00						9 200 00			
Sundry Selling Expense	3 750 00						3 750 00			
Office Salaries	20 000 00						20 000 00			
Payroll Taxes	2 700 00		(13)	675 00			3 375 00			
Property Taxes	2 460 00		(12)	1 250 00			3 710 00			
Postage and Express	1 600 00						1 600 00			
Sundry General Expense	2 800 00						2 800 00			
	352 240 00	352 240 00								
Accrued Interest Receivable			(1)	210 00					210 00	
Interest Income					(1)	210 00		210 00		
Cost of Goods Sold			(2b) 46 000 00; (2c) 91 000 00; (2f) 1 640 00		(2a) 50 000 00; (2d) 3 800 00; (2e) 1 200 00		83 640 00			
Warehouse Supplies Used			(4)	1 490 00			1 490 00			
Office Supplies Used			(5)	775 00			775 00			
Insurance Expense			(6)	2 790 00			2 790 00			
Depreciation of Building			(7)	2 900 00			2 900 00			
Depreciation of Delivery Equipment			(8)	500 00			500 00			
Depreciation of Office Furniture and Fixtures			(9)	410 00			410 00			
Depreciation of Warehouse Equipment			(10)	480 00			480 00			
Interest Expense			(11) 378 00; (14) 150 00				528 00			
Accrued Interest Payable					(11) 378 00; (14) 150 00					528 00
Property Taxes Accrued					(12)	1 250 00				1 250 00
Payroll Taxes Accrued					(13)	675 00				675 00
Dividends Payable					(15)	3 000 00				3 000 00
				208 798 00		208 798 00	180 168 00	195 610 00		
Federal Income Tax							3 397 00			3 397 00
Net Income							12 045 00			12 045 00
							195 610 00	195 610 00	177 175 00	177 175 00

BALANCE SHEET

The balance sheet of Wholesale Auto Parts, Inc., for December 31, 1966, is given on page 247. The statement is made up from the Balance Sheet columns of the work sheet on pages 244-245. Note that Allowance for Doubtful Accounts is deducted from the combined total of Notes Receivable and Accounts Receivable. Since notes as well as accounts may prove uncollectible, the allowance is designed to cover both assets. Note also that certain amounts that appear individually in the columns of the work sheet are combined for the balance sheet. These are the two cash figures and the dividends, net income, and retained earnings figures. The latter three are all part of the Retained Earnings account after the books are closed. The balance sheet of Wholesale Auto Parts, Inc. is in *account* form. Where the space available requires it, the balance sheet is presented in *report* form, that is, with the liabilities and capital listed below the assets instead of being placed to the right of them.

CLASSIFICATION OF ASSETS

The balance sheet of Wholesale Auto Parts, Inc., is classified in the conventional way. Current assets include assets of short life (usually one year or less) in the enterprise, including any prepayments. However, in cases where the normal operating cycle is longer, as in the aging of tobacco or wines and liquors, that period is used instead. Formerly, prepaid expenses were not grouped with the current assets but were shown in a "deferred charges" section at the bottom of the asset side, as is still the practice of some companies. The reason was the preference for restricting current assets to items that were closer to being turned into cash. Analysts for credit grantors still often prefer this classification, but the trend seems to be the other way.

The term "fixed assets" has been used in practice to mean land, buildings, and machinery, or, as it is often expressed in practice, "property, plant, and equipment" or "property and plant." This usage is followed here, although some authors prefer to use the term to designate all noncurrent assets. Frequently there is another group of assets between the current and the fixed assets, namely, permanent or long-term investments. These usually consist of investments in companies controlled by or closely affiliated with the investing company for some business purpose. They are expected to be retained over a long period and so cannot be classified as current assets even though the securities are readily salable. Investments are classified as current assets when held as temporary repositories of funds with the expectation that they may be sold at any time.

The trademark is one of the group usually termed "intangible" assets. This group consists of goodwill, trademarks, patents, copyrights, and some others. Leaseholds, for example, are sometimes classified as intangibles and sometimes as fixed assets. Goodwill is the excess over the amount paid for other assets less any applicable liabilities. It may appear legitimately on a balance sheet as a result of the purchase of one business by another that pays something more than the values of the regular assets because of the reputation and superior earning power of the old business. It cannot be recorded on the books of the concern that developed it, since this practice would open the way to arbitrary estimates of the amount and it would also confuse the record of the

Balance Sheet

December 31, 1966

Assets

Current Assets

Cash in Bank and on Hand		$12,000.00	
Notes Receivable	$13,500.00		
Accounts Receivable	14,600.00		
	$28,100.00		
Less: Allowance for Doubtful Accounts	1,950.00	26,150.00	
Accrued Interest Receivable		210.00	
Merchandise		50,000.00	
Warehouse Supplies		120.00	
Office Supplies		65.00	
Prepaid Insurance		680.00	$ 89,225.00

Fixed Assets

Land		$ 5,000.00	
Building	$58,000.00		
Less: Accumulated Depreciation	5,800.00	52,200.00	
Delivery Equipment	$ 3,000.00		
Less: Accumulated Depreciation	1,000.00	2,000.00	
Office Furniture and Fixtures	$ 8,200.00		
Less: Accumulated Depreciation	2,050.00	6,150.00	
Warehouse Equipment	$ 4,800.00		
Less: Accumulated Depreciation	1,380.00	3,420.00	$ 68,770.00

Intangible Asset—Trademark	2,000.00
Total Assets	$159,995.00

Liabilities and Proprietorship

Current Liabilities

Notes Payable	$ 12,600.00	
Accounts Payable	13,900.00	
Income Tax Withheld	400.00	
Payroll Taxes Withheld	120.00	
Accrued Interest Payable	528.00	
Property Taxes Accrued	1,250.00	
Payroll Taxes Accrued	675.00	
Dividends Payable	3,000.00	
Federal Income Tax Payable	3,397.00	$ 35,870.00

Long-term Liability—Mortgage Payable	7,200.00
Total Liabilities	$ 43,070.00

Proprietorship

Capital Stock	$100,000.00	
Retained Earnings	16,925.00	116,925.00

Total Liabilities and Proprietorship	$159,995.00

amount of investment in the business. When goodwill is purchased, it represents an actual investment by the buyer and it is recorded as part of the costs of his assets.

Trademarks represent the right to use a unique design or coined word to identify the user's product or service.

Copyrights are exclusive rights to publish material such as pictures, books, or music, representing artistic or literary creations. In the United States, they are good for twenty-eight years and renewable for another twenty-eight, but expire after that. Patents are exclusive rights to manufacture and sell a mechanical invention, and run for seventeen years in the United States; they are not renewable. None of these assets are likely to appear on a balance sheet except as the result of a purchase. It is sometimes possible to trace accurately the costs of developing an invention, and any legal costs of establishing the validity of any of these assets may properly be charged to an asset account. As a rule, however, the developer cannot identify specific costs with them sufficiently well to justify an asset charge.

CLASSIFICATION OF LIABILITIES

Current liabilities, like current assets, are those expected to be "turned over" or liquidated in a year or in one operating cycle. This cycle is a year in most concerns but may be longer in some. Liabilities that are due in a longer period are called "long-term," "noncurrent," or "fixed." They consist chiefly of long-term notes, bonds, or mortgages and are sometimes referred to as "funded debt." As liabilities ordinarily have very specific due dates, they are easy to classify.

CLASSIFICATION OF PROPRIETORSHIP

In a sole proprietorship or a partnership a single Capital account for the owner or one for each of the owners suffices. In a corporation the declared value of the capital stock, which is established under legal requirements for a declared value, is separately reported. Two other kinds of proprietorship accounts may be present in a corporation. There may be "Paid-In Surplus," sometimes called "Capital Surplus." Almost always there will be "Retained Earnings," sometimes called "Earned Surplus." Further divisions of corporation proprietorship are discussed in Chapters 15 and 16. Proprietorship is often referred to as "capital" or "net worth"; it is frequently titled "stockholders' equity" in annual reports to stockholders.

INCOME STATEMENT

The income statement of Wholesale Auto Parts, Inc., for the year ended December 31, 1966, is shown on page 249. The sections of the statement are identified as follows: revenue, cost of goods sold (or cost of sales), selling and general expenses, and nonoperating income and deductions.

REVENUE SECTION OF THE INCOME STATEMENT

The revenue section develops the net sales figure by deducting any returns and allowances, bad debts, and discounts from the gross sales figure. In a

WHOLESALE AUTO PARTS, INC.
Income Statement
Year Ended December 31, 1966

Sales...			$195,400.00
Less: Sales Returns and Allowances...............		$ 4,100.00	
Bad Debts................................		2,350.00	
Sales Discounts...........................		1,770.00	8,220.00
Net Sales....................................			$187,180.00
Cost of Goods Sold:			
Merchandise Inventory, January 1, 1966...........		$ 46,000.00	
Purchases....................................	$91,000.00		
Add: Freight In...........................	1,640.00		
	$92,640.00		
Less: Purchase Returns and			
Allowances...............	$3,800.00		
Purchase Discounts............	1,200.00	5,000.00	87,640.00
		$133,640.00	
Less: Merchandise Inventory, December 31, 1960		50,000.00	83,640.00
Gross Margin on Sales............................			$103,540.00
Selling Expenses:			
Salesmen's Salaries	$22,000.00		
Advertising.................................	3,900.00		
Delivery Expense............................	8,100.00		
Freight Out.................................	9,200.00		
Warehouse Supplies Used.....................	1,490.00		
Depreciation of Delivery Equipment.............	500.00		
Depreciation of Warehouse Equipment...........	480.00		
Sundry Selling Expense	3,750.00	$ 49,420.00	
General and Administrative Expenses:			
Office Salaries..............................	$20,000.00		
Payroll Taxes...............................	3,375.00		
Property Taxes..............................	3,710.00		
Postage and Express.........................	1,600.00		
Office Supplies Used.........................	775.00		
Insurance Expense	2,790.00		
Depreciation of Building......................	2,900.00		
Depreciation of Office Furniture and Fixtures.......	410.00		
Sundry General Expense......................	2,800.00	38,360.00	87,780.00
Net Income from Operations.....................			$ 15,760.00
Other Income: Interest			210.00
			$ 15,970.00
Other Deductions: Interest			528.00
			$ 15,442.00
Federal Income Tax............................			3,397.00
Net Income...................................			$ 12,045.00

service enterprise the returns and allowances and discounts would not usually be involved, and, of course, the term "sales" would not be used. The service revenue account titles are peculiar to the field, such as "Freight Revenue" or "Professional Fees." When bad debts and discount are deducted in the revenue section, the effect is to state revenue at the amount of cash collected or expected to be collected. If sales discounts are not set up on an "allowance" basis, this objective will not be achieved precisely, because in that case some discounts may be taken in the next period on recent sales of this period that are charged to sales discount in the new period. These are certain to be small and are usually insignificant in relation to the income statement figures for a year.

COST OF GOODS SOLD

The cost of goods sold section of the income statement calculates cost of goods sold by adding up all the costs representing goods available for sale and then deducting what is left unsold in inventory. The deduction of discounts puts the purchases figure on the basis of cash paid or expected to be paid for the goods bought. The inventory figures are usually obtained by a physical count. When the various items are priced to compute the cost of each lot, the price should be consistent with the price basis of purchases in the income statement. In other words, if there is freight in and if discounts are deducted from purchases in the income statement, freight per unit should be added and an average percent of discount should be deducted from the supplier's invoice price to get the inventory price.

SELLING AND GENERAL EXPENSES

The selling expenses and the general and administrative expenses, together with the cost of goods sold, constitute the operating expenses of the concern. Operating expenses are the expenses necessary to carry on the main purpose or purposes of the enterprise. The selling expenses are those definitely identifiable with selling activity alone. This activity includes the storage of merchandise before sale and the delivery of it as well as solicitation of sales. In merchandising businesses those expenses which contribute to both selling and general or administrative activities are usually shown as general expenses. In other words, no attempt is normally made to divide them. This separation can be made, however, and is done when cost accounting techniques are used. In the case of Wholesale Auto Parts, Inc., the building depreciation could be so divided, since the building is used both for the warehousing and for the general office activity.

OTHER INCOME AND OTHER DEDUCTIONS

Other income and other deductions make up the nonoperating section of the income statement. It contains incomes that do not result from the main object of the business, such as interest earned in a merchandising concern. Similarly, any expenses or losses not a necessary or regular part of the main activity are deducted here. Interest again is a nonoperating deduction, since it is not essential to borrow money to operate; it is possible to operate with proprietary capital alone. Unusual losses, such as fire and windstorm damage, if not covered by insurance, are deducted here. Collateral activities, such as holding an unused piece of land for sale in a manufacturing business, give rise to nonoperating deductions. Taxes on income are set aside in a special class in the nonoperating group because of their importance.

STATEMENT OF RETAINED EARNINGS

The statement of retained earnings, sometimes known as a statement of earned surplus, shows in summary form the changes in the Retained Earnings account for the period. The retained earnings statement of Wholesale Auto

---

WHOLESALE AUTO PARTS, INC.
Statement of Retained Earnings

Year Ended December 31, 1966

Balance January 1, 1966	$ 9,880.00
Add: net income for the year	12,045,00
	$21,925,00
Less: dividends paid or declared	5,000.00
Balance December 31, 1966	$16,925,00

Parts, Inc. is given here. In the case of this company there were no charges or credits in the Retained Earnings account other than the net income and dividends. As is indicated in the following section, sometimes unusual transactions are entered in Retained Earnings rather than in ordinary expense or income accounts. In sole proprietorships and partnerships a "statement of capital" takes the place of a retained earnings statement. These statements show the changes in capital during the period and include net income credited to the accounts and any additional contributions of capital and any withdrawals from it.

CURRENT-OPERATING VERSUS ALL-INCLUSIVE INCOME STATEMENTS

There is a difference of opinion among accountants with regard to the treatment of unusual or nonrecurring transactions. If a company sells its plant and has a large gain or a large loss, it has such a transaction; it also has one if it suffers a large casualty loss or if it makes a large gain by buying in its own bonds. Adjustments of revenue and expense transactions of prior periods also fall in this class. If such transactions are shown in the income statement, there is no question that they are nonoperating items. But many accountants do not wish to show them in the income statement; they wish to carry them directly to the Retained Earnings account. This viewpoint is known as the current-operating concept of the income statement. It excludes any significant nonrecurring transaction in order to present a net income figure considered more representative of the continuing activity of the concern. The opposite viewpoint, known as the all-inclusive viewpoint of the income statement, would show all incomes and expenses and all unusual gains and losses in the income statement. This is also known as the "clean-surplus" viewpoint, since it results in a surplus account without entries except for net income and dividends. Its advocates point out that the result of excluding unusual transactions from the income statement is to misrepresent the total amount gained or lost over a period. The issue centers on the question of how best to report net income in view of the presumption that many people form their ideas about a company simply by looking at a newspaper release of the "net income per share." This is computed by dividing the net income shown in the income statement by the number of shares. The object, of course, is to give in this one statistic the most accurate possible indication of how the fortunes of the company have fared during the period. The American Institute of Certified Public Accountants has advocated the current-operating viewpoint for some time, and other authorities have recently tended to go along with this position.

Nonrecurring gains and losses are generally reported net of the income taxes resulting from such transactions, thus identifying the tax with the income on which it is based. In the case of an extraordinary gain, the extra tax is deducted from the gain instead of being shown as part of the regular income tax deduction. In the case of an extraordinary loss, the regular income tax figure is shown at what it would be without regard to the loss (and hence at an appropriate figure for the regular income), and a corresponding deduction is made from the loss to show it net of its tax effect. One may think of this last treatment as resulting from a debit to the regular income tax figure (as determined on the income tax return), and a credit to the loss account, for the amount of tax reduction caused by the loss.

COMBINED INCOME AND RETAINED EARNINGS STATEMENT

The retained earnings statement is often combined with the income statement. This combination gives one statement that shows first, what revenues and expenses produced the income and, second, what was done with the income. The combination is made by adding to the net income figure at the bottom of a regular income statement the beginning balance of retained earnings, and then adding or deducting any transactions carried directly into the Retained Earnings account for the period, to arrive at the closing balance of retained earnings. For Wholesale Auto Parts, Inc., this addition appears as follows (all of the income statement except the last line is omitted here because it can be seen in the statement on page 249):

Net Income	$12,045.00
Add: Balance of Retained Earnings, January 1, 1966 . . .	9,880.00
	$21,925.00
Less: Dividends Paid or Declared	5,000.00
Balance of Retained Earnings, December 31, 1966	$16,925.00

The combined statement is desirable because it puts before the reader in one place all transactions affecting earnings even though some unusual ones may have been carried directly to retained earnings. It does not prevent the careless observer from looking at the figure labeled "net income" and ignoring all else. A common title for this statement is "statement of income and retained earnings."

CLOSING ENTRIES

The closing entries for Wholesale Auto Parts, Inc., are shown on page 253 as they appear in the general journal. The Purchases and its related accounts were "closed" by the adjusting entries that opened the Cost of Goods Sold account, and hence do not appear in the regular closing entries. If the Cost of Goods Sold account had not been used, Purchases and its related accounts would have been closed to Profit and Loss along with the others. The closing entries are indicated by that heading in the journal and so do not require individual explanations. The closing entries required may be found by observing the figures on the income statement or noting the open balances in the Income Statement columns of the work sheet, and by remembering that Dividends and Profit and Loss must be closed into Retained Earnings. The adjusting entries have not been presented in journal form because they can be easily identified in the work sheet (page 245), but in practice they would of course be written in

WHOLESALE AUTO PARTS, INC.
General Journal   Page 27

Date			
1966	*Closing entries*		
Dec. 31	Sales	195,400.00	
	Sales Returns and Allowances		4,100.00
	Bad Debts		2,350.00
	Sales Discounts		1,770.00
	Profit and Loss		187,180.00
31	Profit and Loss	171,420.00	
	Cost of Goods Sold		83,640.00
	Salesmen's Salaries		22,000.00
	Advertising		3,900.00
	Delivery Expense		8,100.00
	Freight Out		9,200.00
	Warehouse Supplies Used		1,490.00
	Depreciation of Delivery Equipment		500.00
	Depreciation of Warehouse Equipment		480.00
	Sundry Selling Expense		3,750.00
	Office Salaries		20,000.00
	Payroll Taxes		3,375.00
	Property Taxes		3,710.00
	Postage and Express		1,600.00
	Office Supplies Used		775.00
	Insurance Expense		2,790.00
	Depreciation of Building		2,900.00
	Depreciation of Office Furniture and Fixtures		410.00
	Sundry General Expense		2,800.00
31	Profit and Loss	3,715.00	
	Interest Income	210.00	
	Interest Expense		528.00
	Federal Income Tax		3,397.00
31	Profit and Loss	12,045.00	
	Retained Earnings		12,045.00
31	Retained Earnings	5,000.00	
	Dividends		5,000.00

the journal and posted, or run into the computer, if one is used. The reader will recall that the accounts may be closed one by one instead of by groups, if the accountant prefers. They may also be closed in one all-embracing entry if desired, in which case the Profit and Loss account may be skipped.

POSTCLOSING TRIAL BALANCE

Proof that the closing entries are in balance and that the postings and footings have been properly done is obtained by taking a postclosing trial balance. It is not absolute proof; compensating errors can be made. However, when the

WHOLESALE AUTO PARTS, INC.
Post-Closing Trial Balance
December 31, 1966

	Debit	Credit
Cash	$ 11,800.00	
Petty Cash	200.00	
Notes Receivable	13,500.00	
Accounts Receivable	14,600.00	
Allowance for Doubtful Accounts		$ 1,950.00
Accrued Interest Receivable	210.00	
Merchandise	50,000.00	
Warehouse Supplies	120.00	
Office Supplies	65.00	
Prepaid Insurance	680.00	
Land	5,000.00	
Building	58,000.00	
Accumulated Depreciation—Building		5,800.00
Delivery Equipment	3,000.00	
Accumulated Depreciation—Delivery Equipment		1,000.00
Office Furniture and Fixtures	8,200.00	
Accumulated Depreciation—Office Furniture and Fixtures		2,050.00
Warehouse Equipment	4,800.00	
Accumulated Depreciation—Warehouse Equipment		1,380.00
Trademark	2,000.00	
Notes Payable		12,600.00
Accounts Payable		13,900.00
Income Tax Withheld		400.00
Payroll Taxes Withheld		120.00
Accrued Interest Payable		528.00
Property Taxes Accrued		1,250.00
Payroll Taxes Accrued		675.00
Dividends Payable		3,000.00
Federal Income Tax Payable		3,397.00
Mortgage Payable		7,200.00
Capital Stock		100,000.00
Retained Earnings		16,925.00
	$172,175.00	$172,175.00

postclosing trial balance proves to be in balance, the probability that there are no mechanical errors is very high. The postclosing trial balance of Wholesale Auto Parts, Inc., at December 31, 1966, is shown here. Since the postclosing trial balance is taken immediately after the closing of the income statement accounts, it contains only balance sheet accounts.

REVERSING ENTRIES

Reversing entries are useful in those cases where an adjustment would have to be referred to in the new period to find what entry to make for a new transaction. They eliminate the need for this reference. For example, suppose a concern has a large number of notes receivable on which interest accrues. A list of the makers is prepared at the end of the period and the interest accrued on each note is calculated and written opposite the name of that debtor. The total is recorded as follows:

Dec. 31	Accrued Interest Receivable	$8,210	
	Interest Income		$8,210

If the adjusting entry is not reversed at the beginning of the new period, the various collections will be recorded as in the following example. D. B. Blake's $3,000 note had accrued interest of $80 at the recent closing, and had a total of $120 interest due when he paid it. The entry for the payment is:

Cash	$3,120	
Notes Receivable		$3,000
Accrued Interest Receivable		80
Interest Income		40

In order to make this entry it is necessary to refer to the list of notes with the amounts of interest accrued on each one used for the adjustments at the prior closing date. This list shows the amount of accrued interest now being collected from Blake. As a payment on a note is received, it is necessary to refer to this list for every note that had accrued interest on it at the closing date. Obviously, this involves much work, which can be avoided by reversing the adjusting entry at the beginning of the new period, as follows:

Jan. 1	Interest Income	$8,210	
	Accrued Interest Receivable		$8,210

After this reversal the collections are recorded as in the following entry (using Blake's case again):

Cash	$3,120	
Notes Receivable		$3,000
Interest Income		120

The accrued income previously recorded for Blake's note is already in the Interest Income account as a debit, and automatically affects that portion of the income collected and credited there. This leaves a net of $40 as income for the current period. The reversing entry in this case permits all collections of income to be credited to the income account, regardless of whether or not part of the income has been accrued. The ledger examples given here show accounts for the accrued interest and interest income containing only the D. B. Blake data and showing first, the entries with no reversing entry and, second, the use of the reversing entry. In the case of an accrued expense the debit and credit arrangement is, of course, the reverse of the one shown for an accrued income.

ACCOUNTS WITH AND WITHOUT A REVERSING ENTRY

Without a Reversing Entry

Accrued Interest Receivable (D. B. Blake)

Date	Explanation	Ref.	Debit	Date	Explanation	Ref.	Credit
1966 Dec. 31	Accrual	J6	80 00	1967 Mr. 20		CR18	80 00

Interest Income

Date	Explanation	Ref.	Debit	Date	Explanation	Ref.	Credit
1966 Dec. 31	To P & L	J7	80 00	1966 Dec. 31	Accrual	J6	80 00
				1967 Mr. 30		CR18	40 00

With a Reversing Entry

Accrued Interest Receivable (D. B. Blake)

Date	Explanation	Ref.	Debit	Date	Explanation	Ref.	Credit
1966 Dec. 31	Accrual	J6	80 00	1967 Jan. 1	Reversal	J8	80 00

Interest Income

Date	Explanation	Ref.	Debit	Date	Explanation	Ref.	Credit
1966 Dec. 31	To P & L	J7	80 00	1966 Dec. 31	Accrual	J6	80 00
1967 Jan. 1	Reversal	J8	80 00	1967 Mr. 20		CR18	120 00

APPLICATION OF REVERSING ENTRIES

Reversing entries, as explained above, are most useful in cases where reference would otherwise have to be made to the adjusting entry data when subsequent transactions are recorded. This is the case with accruals, whether receivable or payable, and is most important where the accrual consists of many independent items. Deferred items, such as prepaid insurance or deferred subscription income, do not require reversing entries if the balance sheet account is used for all payments or collections. Then the amount to be transferred to expense or income is calculated at the end of the period and entered by an adjusting entry. The balance sheet account remains to show the asset or the liability for the balance sheet and to carry on the process in the next period. If, however, payments are charged to expense and if collections are credited to income regardless of whether or not they are prepayments, the adjusting entry sets up the balance sheet account at the end of the period. In order to carry on in the same manner in the next period (using only an expense or an income account), it is necessary to transfer the prepaid expense or the deferred income balance back into the expense or the income account. This back transfer is done by a reversing entry. The reader will recall that the transfer back to the Profit and Loss statement account was used in Chapter 3, but the term "reversing entry" was not applied to it there. It is common practice to set up accounts for deferments and accruals only by adjustment at the end of the period, and as a result to reverse the adjustments for deferments as well as accruals at the beginning of the new period.

ILLUSTRATION OF REVERSING ENTRIES

Wholesale Auto Parts, Inc., reverses only those adjusting entries that would have to be referred to as receipts or payments arise in the new period. The only accounts involved in this case are those for interest and its accruals. The reversing entries appear below in a section of the general journal of Wholesale Auto Parts, Inc. After posting of the reversing entries the transactions for the new period are entered in the ordinary way without reference to the old period.

WHOLESALE AUTO PARTS, INC.
General Journal   Page 28

Date		Debit	Credit
1967			
Jan. 1	Interest Income..	$210.00	
	Accrued Interest Receivable........................		$210.00
	(to reverse Dec. 31, 1966 accrual)		
1	Accrued Interest Payable.............................	528.00	
	Interest Expense.......................................		528.00
	(to reverse Dec. 31, 1966 accrual)		

STATEMENT PROBLEMS OF MANAGEMENT

Management is responsible for presenting proper statements for the company. Most corporations are required to prepare statements also for state authorities so that they may be made a matter of public record. If the stock is listed on a stock exchange the statements must be filed with the exchange for the information of traders. If the stock is traded in interstate commerce in sufficiently large amounts it must be registered with the United States Securities and Exchange Commission; this requirement entails the filing of statements with the SEC. Creditors often require statements as a basis for loans.

Note that management may improve the salability of the company's stock and bonds by giving complete financial information. Frequently the statements must be accompanied by the opinion of a certified public accountant who has examined the company's records. For these purposes the forms of statements described previously in this chapter are used.

However, in recent years a large segment of management has become concerned with the public-relations aspect of its financial statements. This concern was crystallized a few years ago when a study revealed that the general public was ignorant of business affairs and had some very wrong impressions of financial statements. Many people thought that there was something suspicious in the fact that the balance sheet balanced; many thought that earned "surplus" was something over and above what was really needed. In an attempt to make financial statements less technical and more understandable to the uninitiated, some managements have done three things to the statements in their annual reports; they have:

1. Rearranged the balance sheet.
2. Simplified the income statement.
3. Adopted less technical terminology.

These popularizing devices are not helpful to trained analysts; in the income statement especially, they obscure information the analyst desires. However, they are not intended for the trained analyst, and he can usually get the more conventional forms and details from sources other than the concern's annual reports. Because they represent a vigorous effort to solve an especially difficult managerial problem, brief descriptions of these statement forms are given in the following paragraphs.

POPULARIZED BALANCE SHEET

The popularized balance sheet shown below presents the figures in more condensed form than does the balance sheet on page 247, and it uses some of the less technical terminology previously referred to. Both these qualities are characteristic of statements in annual reports designed for stockholders, employees, and the public generally. Features of the statement are: working capital is computed on the face of the statement; net assets are computed on the statement; net assets and "ownership" are shown as equivalent items (which they are). This form of statement avoids somewhat the technicalities of an account-form balance sheet with its more obvious "balancing" feature. The basic principle on which the balancing depends is, of course, still present in the popularized form.

SINGLE-STEP INCOME STATEMENT

The simplification of the income statement for popular reports results in the "one-step" or "single-step" income statement. This statement avoids the

POPULARIZED BALANCE SHEET

WHOLESALE AUTO PARTS, INC.
Statement of Financial Position
December 31, 1966

Current Assets
Cash. . . . .$ 12,000.00
Notes, Interest, and Accounts Receivable 26,360.00
Merchandise and Supplies. 50,185.00
Prepaid Expenses. 680.00

  Total Current Assets. . . . .$ 89,225.00
Less: Current Liabilities
Notes and Accounts Payable and Accrued Liabilities. . . . .$ 32,473.00
Federal Income Tax Payable 3,397.00

  Total Current Liabilities . . . .$ 35,870.00

    Working Capital. . . . .$ 53,355.00
Property, Plant and Equipment 68,770.00
Other Assets. 2,000.00

  Total Assets Less Current Liabilities. $124,125.00
Deductions
Long-Term Debt. 7,200.00

Excess of Assets over Liabilities—Ownership $116,925.00

Ownership evidenced by:
Capital Stock. $100,000.00
Earnings Reinvested in the Business. 16,925.00

                                                                          $116,925.00

computation of gross margin on sales, net operating income, and other figures shown in the conventional form. It does so by showing all revenue in one computation or listing at the top and all deductions in one listing in the middle. The total revenue less total deductions or expenses gives net income. The reason for the use of this kind of statement is the desire to eliminate technical terms and computations that are puzzling to persons unfamiliar with accounting. Here again the purposes of the analyst or competent observer are not well served; such people wish information about the ratio of gross margin to sales, of net operating profit to sales, and so on, and often they can get it, at more effort, through other sources than the company's annual report.

The tendency to condense and the tendency to use more popular terminology are present in the simplified or popularized income statement as well as in the related balance sheet. One other practice is also often used in this statement: the classification of expenses by object of expenditure exclusively. As was explained in Chapter 2, expenses may also be classified by function. Salaries is an object of expenditure; cost of merchandise sold is an object of expenditure; but delivery expense is a functional class, and may contain salaries, depreciation, gasoline, oil and grease, and so on. Object-of-expenditure accounts are thought to be more understandable to the uninitiated, hence the preference for them in some popular-form income statements. The income statement of Wholesale Auto Parts, Inc., in single-step form is on page 260;

SINGLE-STEP INCOME STATEMENT

WHOLESALE AUTO PARTS, INC.
Statement of Income
For the year 1966

Revenue	
Sales of merchandise....................................	$187,180.00
Interest income..	210.00
	$187,390.00
Deductions	
Operating charges:	
Cost of merchandise sold.............................	$ 83,640.00
Taxes, other than income taxes.......................	7,085.00
Depreciation..	4,290.00
Other selling and administrative expense..............	76,405.00
Interest..	528.00
Provision for federal income tax......................	3,347.00
	$165,345.00
Net Income...	$ 12,045.00

the same account classifications are used as in the form on page 249, but some of them are combined and some of the popularized terminology is used.

USE OF LESS TECHNICAL TERMINOLOGY

Much may no doubt be gained by making accounting terminology less technical. As a result of efforts in this direction in recent years by accountants in public practice, in corporations, and in academic life, changes have been made that have gained wide use. Some of these have been noted previously. They are:

1. Accumulated depreciation *for* reserve *or* allowance for depreciation
2. Retained earnings *for* earned surplus
3. Allowance for doubtful accounts *for* reserve for doubtful accounts *or* reserve for bad debts.
4. Gross margin on sales *for* gross profit
5. Income statement *for* profit and loss statement

These changes are examples of improvement in technical terms, which may make the terms less misleading but still leave them technical and obscure to the uninformed. Some companies in presenting their popular-form statements give descriptions in nontechnical language devised to make sense to those unfamiliar with accounting terms. Substitutions such as the following may be made:

For "sales": "Amounts charged to customers for our goods and services"
For "depreciation": "Wear and exhaustion of facilities"

Anyone can develop his own descriptions; the student may find it useful to do so as a method of testing his knowledge of the meaning of technical terms. In doing the exercises in this book the student will be expected to use conventional accounting terminology, unless advised to the contrary by his instructor.

SUMMARY

The steps in adjusting and closing the accounts and the related work are (1) take a trial balance of the general ledger and prepare schedules of subsidiary ledgers; (2) prepare adjusting entry data; (3) prepare work sheet; (4) prepare financial statements; (5) enter and post adjusting entries; (6) enter and post closing entries; (7) rule and balance general ledger accounts; (8) prepare a postclosing trial balance; (9) enter and post any reversing entries desired at the start of the new period.

Major classifications on the balance sheet are: current assets (used up or turned over in one operating cycle, usually a year or less); permanent or long-term investments; fixed assets (property, plant, and equipment); intangible assets; current liabilities; long-term liabilities; and proprietorship. Proprietorship is shown in Capital accounts for the owner or owners in sole proprietorships and partnerships, but in accounts for Capital Stock and Retained Earnings in corporations.

The income statement has sections for revenue, cost of goods sold, selling and general expenses, and nonoperating income and deductions. The retained earnings statement shows the changes in the Retained Earnings account during the period. It may be combined with the income statement in a statement of income and retained earnings.

Accountants differ on the question of whether to show all gains and losses in the income statement ("all-inclusive" or "clean-surplus" viewpoint), or to put the unusual ones directly in the Retained Earnings account ("current-operating" viewpoint).

Reversing entries are useful where reference would otherwise have to be made to details of an adjusting entry when receipts or payments involving previously recorded accruals are made.

Management has, in many cases, reacted to the need to make financial statements more understandable to the general public by rearranging the balance sheet, simplifying the income statement, and using popular or less technical terminology.

QUESTIONS

8.1 The president of a small factory has come to you for advice. His bookkeeper tells him each year that the business has been just about breaking even. The president says that the inventories, receivables, and payables have not varied much since the corporation was organized ten years ago but that cash has been constantly increasing. He thinks that the business has been making money and that there is an error. He states there has been no sale of assets, refinancing of indebtedness, or change in corporate structure such as sale of stock.

(1) Present briefly the explanation that you would give the president for the contined increase in cash.

(2) Give examples of transactions that would illustrate your explanation.

8.2 (1) List sequentially the steps in the typical accounting cycle of a company that prepares financial statements only once a year.

(2) Explain why the preparation of a work sheet is commonly included as a step in the periodic closing of accounts and preparation of statements.

(3) Why are closing entries generally prepared after preparation of the balance sheet, although this statement reflects proprietorship balances after the accounts are closed?

(4) Why do some companies prepare monthly work sheets even when they close their accounts annually?

(5) Explain how interim statements can be prepared from work sheets without recording adjusting entries in the ledger. Comment particularly on the handling of merchandise inventories in the preparation of monthly income statements from successive year-to-date work sheets.

8.3 In each of the following statements an error on a work sheet is described. For each one, state whether or not the error would cause the work sheet to be out of balance and whether or not the balance sheet or the income statement would be in error (aside from the fact that any error in the income statement finally affects the balance sheet).

(1) Accrued real estate tax is computed as $480 when it should be $460.

(2) An inventory of office supplies costing $125 is overlooked. The company records supplies purchased in the Supplies Expense account.

(3) The preclosing trial balance was copied onto the work sheet with Notes Payable as $2,000 instead of $2,500, the figure that actually was on the original trial balance. The footings were also copied from the original trial balance, where they were correct and in balance.

(4) The adjusting entry for depreciation of building was recorded as follows:

Depreciation of Building $1,800
    Accumulated Depreciation — Building $1,600

The Adjustments columns were not footed because footing was considered unnecessary.

(5) When the figure for advertising expense was written in the Income Statement columns, it was put on the credit side.

(6) When the figure for sales salaries was written in the Income Statement columns, it was copied as $14,800 when it actually was $18,400 per the Trial Balance columns, which were correct.

(7) Depreciation on office equipment was carried to the Income Statement columns as $800 when it should have been $600 (and was $600 in the Adjustments column), and at the same time the figure for sundry selling expense was transferred to the Income Statement columns as $1,600 although the prior columns showed that it was $1,800.

(8) The Dividends account was extended to the Balance Sheet columns as $4,200 when it actually was $4,500; at the same time, an error in addition was made in which the trial balance figure of $2,500 for Accumulated Depreciation — Truck was added to the adjustment of $900 and extended as $3,100. An eight-column work sheet is used.

8.4 State in what section of the balance sheet each of the following accounts would appear (use the classification illustrated in the text).

(1) Sales Supplies on Hand

(2) Bonds Payable

(3) Investment in Subsidiary Company

(4) Petty Cash

(5) Delivery Trucks

(6) Investment in U. S. Government Bonds

(7) Notes Payable (payable in five years; the company is a department store)

(8) Federal Income Tax Payable

(9) Land (used as a factory site)

(10) Copyrights on Books (purchased from another company)

(11) Allowance for Doubtful Accounts
(12) Retained Earnings
(13) Notes Receivable (due in 90 days)
(14) Accumulated Depreciation — Machinery and Equipment
(15) Capital Stock

8.5   State the section of the income statement in which each of the following accounts would appear (assume the same arrangement as that in the conventional income statements given in the text):

(1) Bad Debts
(2) Sales Supplies Expense
(3) Insurance Expense
(4) Freight In
(5) Rent Income (from parking lot in another city owned by a bank)
(6) Sales Discounts
(7) Purchase Discounts
(8) Office Salaries
(9) Sales Returns
(10) Merchandise Inventory
(11) Federal Income Tax
(12) Purchases

8.6   (1) Explain what is meant by the current-operating viewpoint and the all-inclusive viewpoint regarding the income statement.
    (2) The income statement prepared by the bookkeeper of the M Co. for the year ended December 31, 1966, showed a net income of $5 per share. Independent accountants audited the company for 1966 and proposed no material adjusting entries; however, the income statement certified by the auditors showed a net income of only $3 per share. Suggest two specific items which could explain the difference.
    (3) Discuss briefly the arguments for and against the current-operating and all-inclusive viewpoints of income.

8.7   (1) What information does the statement of retained earnings contain?
    (2) What controversy is at least partially solved by a statement of income and retained earnings?
    (3) Prepare a statement of retained earnings for the N Co. according to the current-operating concept of income based on the following data for 1966:

Gross margin on sales	$500,000
Retained earnings, January 1, 1966	150,000
Operating expenses	520,000
Dividends paid	20,000
Loss on disposal of foreign plant	50,000

8.8   The ledger of the California Copper Co. contained the following nominal accounts at the end of 1966:

Sales of product	$460,754,000
Costs and expenses	437,554,000
Loss on sale of Pinole properties	10,800,000

The company is subject to a federal income tax of 22 percent on the first $25,000 of taxable net income and 48 percent on any amount over $25,000. The company prepares its income statement in accordance with the current-operating viewpoint.

(1) Prepare the income statement, showing the provision for income taxes on the basis that the extraordinary loss is reported in the statement of retained earnings net of tax.
(2) Prepare the income statement, showing the provision for income taxes on the

basis that the extraordinary loss is reported without allocation of income taxes.

(3) Discuss the comparative advantages of (1) and (2) above.

(4) Some people consider income taxes an "expense" of doing business, others as a "distribution" of net income — like dividends to stockholders. How are these alternative viewpoints relevant to whether a loss should or should not be reported net of tax?

8.9 (1) What is a reversing entry? Under what conditions are reversing entries most useful?

(2) Select from the following cases one that you think is the most likely to require reversing entries:

(a) The company has prepayments but no accruals.

(b) The only adjustments are for merchandise and supplies.

(c) The only adjustments are for omitted invoices.

(d) The company has many small accrual transactions, but few other adjustments.

(3) The ledger of a company contains accounts for Interest Payable and Dividends Payable. Which account is most likely to be reversed? Why?

8.10 (1) Name some of the persons or organizations that expect or require financial statements.

(2) In what manner are the information requirements of investors, creditors, and tax authorities at variance? Can a set of general-purpose financial statements be prepared which satisfies all these requirements? Discuss.

8.11 (1) What problems have led management to change the traditional forms of financial statements presented in annual reports? (2) What kind of changes, in general, have been made?

8.12 (1) The traditional balance sheet contains a figure for total assets and an equal figure for total liabilities and proprietorship. What two figures are equated in the rearranged balance sheet presented in some annual reports? (2) In what way is simplification attempted in the simplified income statement used in some annual reports? (3) Give the traditional term for each of the following: retained earnings, gross margin on sales, allowance for doubtful accounts, accumulated depreciation.

8.13 In the preparation of the financial statements of Baber Sales Co. for the year ended December 31, 1966, the following errors were committed:

(1) The employer's share of accrued payroll taxes for the last quarter of 1966 was not recorded.

(2) One page of the December 31, 1966, inventory was omitted from the recapitulation.

(3) The 1966 depreciation of buildings was overstated.

(4) The nominal account for advertising allowances received in 1966 but applicable to 1967 promotions was not adjusted at December 31, 1966.

(5) Merchandise bought f.o.b. shipping point, which was in transit at December 31, 1966, was omitted from inventory and invoice record at the end of 1966.

Indicate the effect of each error on the items below by a "+" for overstated and "−" for understated.

(a) Net income, year ended December 31, 1966

(b) Retained earnings, as of December 31, 1966

(c) Net income, year ended December 31, 1967

8.14 (1) A stockholder who owns some stock in a listed corporation is concerned because she receives such small dividends. She has reviewed the last stockholders' report and has concluded there is ample cash available for much larger dividends. In addition to cash in banks, the corporation's balance sheet shows the following items which she believes represent cash funds: a large reserve for depreciation, plenty of Earned Surplus, and a substantial reserve for bad debts. In simple, nontechnical language, explain the nature of the items the stockholder has confused with cash.

(2) "Problems of accounting are partly communication and partly measurement." Discuss. Suggest alternative titles which might be used in published annual reports to stockholders for Allowance for Doubtful Accounts, Prepaid Insurance, Sales, Depreciation.

8.15 Listed below are beginning and ending balances of various accounts and additional information. One item has been omitted from the explanation of the change in each account. Submit the journal entry to record the missing item.

| | Balances | | Partial Explanation |
	Beginning	Ending	of Charges
(1) Prepaid Insurance	$ 3,600	$ 2,400	Paid premiums, $1,400
(2) Advertising Expense	–0–	22,000	Paid invoices, $24,000
(3) Interest Payable	600	1,000	Interest expense, $8,400
(4) Unearned Rent	2,000	4,000	Rent revenue, $24,000
(5) Allowance for Doubtful Accounts	3,000	5,000	Bad debts, $12,000
(6) Accounts Payable	12,000	15,000	Net checks issued to creditors, $92,500; discounts taken, $200.

8.16 After preparation of the financial statements of Dana Stores for 1966, the following errors were discovered:

(1) The accrual of interest on customer's notes had been omitted.
(2) Depreciation had been overstated.
(3) An order of merchandise had been omitted from the inventory and invoice record.
(4) The adjustment to defer royalties received in 1966 for the use of franchises in 1967 had been omitted.
(5) The journalization of accounts receivable sent to the attorneys for collection had been omitted. (The company uses the allowance method on bad debts.)

Indicate the effect of these errors on:

(a) current assets	(d) retained earnings
(b) current liabilities	(e) net income
(c) fixed assets	(f) working capital

8.17 After the statements of Great Eastern, Inc., for the year 1966 had been submitted to the stockholders and the accounts had been closed, the following errors were discovered:

(a) The inventories at December 31, 1966, were understated $2,000.
(b) The Repairs account for 1966 was debited $12,000 for an air-conditioning unit that should have been charged to Leasehold Improvements.
(c) Depreciation and amortization for 1966 was understated because of the error in recording the leasehold improvement. The air-conditioning unit is expected to have a useful life of five years from July 1, 1966.
(d) Prepaid rent at December 31, 1966, was understated $1,000.
(e) Accrued payroll taxes at December 31, 1966, were understated $500.

The company reverses all accruals and deferred items.

(1) Present the correcting entries to be recorded in 1967, using the Retained Earnings account for corrections of prior years' profits.

(2) Prepare a statement of retained earnings for 1967, assuming net income before taxes of $10,000, dividends paid of $6,000, a January 1 balance in Retained Earnings of $50,000, and an income tax rate of 30 percent. The company follows the current-operating concept of income and shows the correction of prior years' profit net of tax.

8.18 (1) The auditors of Island Airlines discovered that various imprest cash funds had not been replenished at the close of the fiscal year. They proposed adjusting entries to reduce the funds for expense vouchers, and suggested these entries be reversed after closing. Explain why these reversing entries were recommended by the auditors.

(2) The controller of Electrosonics, Inc., tells you he is considering a change in the accounting procedures to include reversing entries, and asks your advice. You find the company has expanded rapidly, but the accounting system has not kept pace. Management has been asking for monthly statements. At present the company adjusts and closes annually. Under what conditions would it be convenient to reverse Interest Payable if the company closes annually?

(3) Show the monthly adjusting entries for November and December on a $100,000 6 percent 6-month note payable dated November 1, assuming Electrosonics, Inc., uses reversing entries. How would these entries differ if the company did not use reversing entries? Comment on the desirability of reversing entries under a manual system of accounting.

(4) How would your answer change if the company put its general ledger on a computer?

EXERCISES

8.1 Consolidated Investments, Inc., and National Refining Co. have entered into an agreement whereby Consolidated will purchase all the common stock of National for a price of fifteen times annual net income, based on the average for the past five years. A summary of net income for that period is as follows:

Year	Net Income before Taxes	Income Taxes	Other Credits	Increase in Retained Earnings
1962	$46,761	$18,100	$10,680[a]	$39,341
1963	69,055	33,100	11,441[b]	47,396
1964	63,188	30,600	12,100[c]	44,688
1965	76,708	33,300	–	43,408
1966	81,530	35,600	13,300[d]	59,230

[a] Gain from sale of sections of Garfield Plantation, net after taxes.
[b] Gain from sale of sections of Southern Plantation, net after taxes.
[c] Correction for overdepreciation in prior years, net after taxes.
[d] Gain from sale of sections of Garfield Plantation, net after taxes.

Required:

1. What is the purchase price if earnings are defined to exclude other credits arising from sales of land and revisions of depreciation?
2. What is the purchase price if earnings are defined to include the other credits?
3. Discuss the relative merits of the foregoing definitions of net income in connection with the purchase price for National.

8.2 Indicate by letter, from the statement sections below, where each of the following numbered items should be shown. The company follows the current-operating concept of the income statement.

(1) Accrued interest receivable
(2) Allowance for doubtful accounts
(3) Depreciation of office equipment
(4) Sales discounts
(5) Mortgage payable-due in 5 years
(6) Accrued interest on mortgage
(7) Freight in
(8) Freight out
(9) Patents
(10) Premium on common stock
(11) Purchase discounts
(12) Interest paid on mortgage
(13) Loss on sale of obsolete plant
(14) Allowance for depreciation
(15) Leasehold improvements
(16) Organization costs
(17) Rents received in advance
(18) Prepaid insurance
(19) Rents on unused land
(20) Corrections of prior years' income-
        overstated depreciation

Balance sheet:
(A) Current assets
(B) Investments
(C) Fixed assets
(D) Intangibles
(E) Current liabilities
(F) Long-term liabilities
(G) Stockholders' equity

Income statement:
(H) Sales
(I) Cost of goods sold
(J) Selling expenses
(K) General and administrative
        expenses
(L) Other income
(M) Other deductions
(N) *Statement of retained earnings*

8.3 The balance sheet accounts of B Co. at December 31, 1966, were as follows:

Accounts Payable	$ 40,000
Accounts Receivable	20,000
Accrued Interest Receivable	1,000
Accrued Rent Payable	3,600
Advances from Customers	4,000
Allowance for Depreciation	20,000
Allowance for Doubtful Accounts	3,000
Bank of B — General Account	34,000
Bank of B — Payroll Account	18,000
Bank of B — Pension Fund Account	12,000
Buildings	80,000
Cash-Surrender Value of Life Insurance	3,800
Common Stock	250,000
Income Taxes Payable	28,000
Interest Received in Advance	2,400
Investment in Stock of Subsidiary	40,000
F.I.C.A. Taxes Payable	2,000
Land	20,000
Marketable Securities	16,500
Merchandise Inventory	120,000
Mortgage Payable (in installments of $20,000 on July 1 of each year)	80,000
Notes Receivable from Customers	20,000
Petty Cash	2,000
Prepaid Taxes	3,200
Retained Earnings (debit balance)	40,000
Unexpired Insurance	2,500

Prepare a balance sheet in popularized form, setting out the working capital as a subtotal on the statement.

8.4 From the data below for the fiscal year ended December 31, 1966, prepare a combined income and retained earnings statement for the C Co., following the current-operating concept of income.

Net sales		$48,000
Retained earnings, January 1, 1966		41,000
Selling and administrative expenses		5,600
Royalties earned		2,600
Cost of goods sold		20,000
Loss on sale of obsolete equipment:		
Book value	$35,000	
Proceeds	25,000	10,000
Error in prior years' net income — understatement of depreciation		5,000
Dividends paid		8,000

Prepare the income statement in single-step form, and show extraordinary losses net of tax. Provide for income taxes on all items at the rate of 22 percent.

8.5 The D Cooperative, whose fiscal year ends on December 31, 1966, has secured some of its funds from the issuance of approximately two hundred notes in denominations of from $100 to $10,000. Interest is payable annually at various dates throughout the year at rates from 4 to 6 percent.

The manager of the cooperative has heard of reversing entries, but is not sure he understands how they are used or why they should be used. Explain the use of reversing entries by showing the entries on December 31, 1966, January 1, 1967, and March 1, 1967, for a $10,000 1-year note dated March 1, 1966, with interest payable at 6 percent per year at maturity.

Prepare the entries both with and without the use of reversing entries.

8.6 T Co.'s transactions for 1966, the first year of business, included the following:

(1) Paid $4,000 for supplies, of which $1,000 are on hand December 31.

(2) Received $12,000 rent for the twelve months ended June 30, 1967.

Submit adjusting entries for the year ended December 31, 1966, and reversing entries when they might be useful, assuming:

1. The original transactions were recorded in real accounts.
2. The original transactions were recorded in nominal accounts.

8.7 The trial balance of International Products contains the following balances on December 31, 1966, the end of the fiscal year:

Notes Receivable	$ 5,000	
Merchandise Stock	45,000	
Prepaid Insurance	440	
Supplies on Hand	500	
Prepaid Property Taxes	360	
Building	95,800	
Accumulated Depreciation — Building		$16,000
Equipment	12,500	
Accumulated Depreciation — Equipment		6,000
Sales Tax Payable		1,040
Notes Payable		10,000
Sales		51,000
Sales Returns	1,000	
Bad Debts	—0—	

The following facts are ascertained on this date on examination of the company's records.

(1) The net sales for the final quarter amount to $30,000. All sales are taxable at 4 percent. Sales taxes are remitted to the state quarterly within thirty days after the calendar quarter.

(2) The bad debts experience indicates a loss of 1 percent of net sales for the year.

(3) Notes receivable consists of a single 90-day 6 percent note dated December 1.

(4) The inventory of stock in trade at December 31 totals $15,000.

(5) The inventory of supplies on hand at December 31, 1966, amounts to $300.

(6) Property taxes are assessed in advance for the taxing body's fiscal year, which begins July 1. These taxes, paid on June 20, 1966, for the 1966-1967 year in the amount of $360, were charged to Prepaid Property Taxes.

(7) Payments for insurance coverage in force at December 31, 1966, were as follows:

Policy Dates	Coverage (years)	Premium
May 1, 1965	3	$180
Sept. 30, 1966	1	120
Nov. 30, 1966	1	180

(8) There were no additions to or retirement of equipment during the year. Depreciation is based on an expected life of five years and an estimated scrap value for all equipment of $2,500.

(9) The building is being depreciated over a 50-year life with no scrap value. The balance of the Building account at the beginning of the year was $80,000. A new addition was completed on June 1, 1966, at a cost of $15,800.

(10) The balance of the Notes Payable account represents a single 6 percent note dated March 1 on which interest is paid semiannually on September 1 and March 1.

Required:

1. Submit adjusting entries for the year ended December 31, 1966, as necessary.
2. Submit reversing entries at January 1, 1967, which might be appropriate for this company.

8.8 The errors described below, applicable to the year ended December 31, 1966, the past fiscal year of Q Co., were discovered in January 1967. The company reverses all accruals and it reverses deferrals originally recorded in expense accounts.

(1) Depreciation of buildings was understated $2,000.

(2) The entire payment of $5,000 to Fidelity Assurance Co. was debited erroneously to Mortgages Payable; $4,000 applies to interest, $1,000 to principal.

(3) The December 31, 1966, merchandise inventory was overstated by $3,000.

(4) No adjustment was made for supplies used. The Supplies on Hand account at December 31 had a balance of $3,000; the inventory of supplies was $1,000.

(5) No adjustment was made for prepaid rent of $2,400 at December 31. (Rent Expense was closed with the other nominal accounts at the end of the year.)

Required:

1. Present journal entries dated January 25, 1967, to correct the errors. The company adjusts and closes annually. Record corrections to prior years' profits by debits or credits to Retained Earnings.

    2. Submit the last section of the income statement for 1967 beginning with net income from operations, which amounts to $10,000. Use the all-inclusive concept of net income. Provide for income taxes on all items at 22 percent.

    3. Submit the statement of retained earnings for the year ended December 31, 1967. Dividends paid in 1967 were $4,000.

8.9 Prepare the 1966 income statement for the R Co., whose cash receipts and disbursements for the year ended December 31, 1966, were as follows:

```
Receipts:
    Customers . . . . . . . . . . . . . . . . . . . . . . . . . . . . .$152,000
    Long-term notes . . . . . . . . . . . . . . . . . . . . . . . .    50,000
                                                                     $202,000

Disbursements:
    Merchandise creditors  . . . . . . . . . . . . . $85,000
    Operating expenses . . . . . . . . . . . . . . . .  52,000
    Equipment . . . . . . . . . . . . . . . . . . . . . .  20,000      157,000
Excess of receipts over disbursements  . . . . . . . . . . . $ 45,000
```

Balance sheet items, other than the liability for federal and state taxes on income at January 1 and December 31, 1966, were as follows:

	January 1	December 31
Cash	$10,000	$55,000
Accounts Receivable	20,000	25,000
Merchandise Inventory	30,000	40,000
Prepaid Expenses	3,000	5,000
Equipment(net)	50,000	68,000
Accounts Payable	16,000	22,000
Accrued Expenses	2,000	6,000
Long Term Notes Payable	−0−	50,000

The company provides for federal and state taxes on income during 1966 at 30 percent of net income before taxes.

8.10 The trial balance of M Co. at January 1, 1966, after reversing entries is as follows:

```
Cash . . . . . . . . . . . . . . . . . . . . . . . . . $6,000
Capital  . . . . . . . . . . . . . . . . . . . . . . .           $7,500
Commissions . . . . . . . . . . . . . . . . . .  2,000
Expenses . . . . . . . . . . . . . . . . . . . . .               500
                                                $8,000  $8,000
```

During 1966 the company collected $25,000 of commissions and paid $15,000 of expenses. Data for adjustments at December 31 were:

(1) Prepaid taxes $400.
(2) Wages payable $600.
(3) Unearned commissions $3,000.

Set up a matrix with the following columns (debits), and rows (credits):

(1) Cash	(6) Commissions
(2) Prepaid Taxes	(7) Expenses
(3) Wages Payable	(8) Old Balances
(4) Unearned Commissions	(9) Totals
(5) Capital	(10) New Balances

Suggestion: Use the numbers from the above list instead of titles as descriptions of the rows and the columns.

Required:

1. Enter the January 1 balances; record the cash transactions and adjustments for the year; record the closing entries for the year; and compute the new balances.
2. Prepare another matrix with the same rows and columns. Enter the December 31 postclosing balances, record reversing entries for the accrual and deferred items, and compute the new balances.

PROBLEMS

8.1 The account balances required for the February 28, 1966, balance sheet for Pacifica, Limited, are included in the following list:

Rents Received in Advance.................... $	85,792
Payroll Taxes Payable........................	409,929
Unexpired Insurance.........................	105,306
Accounts Receivable.........................	2,701,475
First National Bank..........................	600,900
Bank of the Pacific	1,050,006
Imprest Funds	5,000
Sales Commissions Expense	28,415
Prepaid Taxes...............................	90,090
Supplies Inventories	733,625
Supplies Used...............................	46,126
Common Stock, par $5 – authorized 500,000 shares, issued 400,000 shares.......................	2,000,000
Accumulated Depreciation – Buildings	6,613,797
Notes Receivable	473,548
Buildings	9,762,655
Mortgage Payable (due after Feb. 28, 1967)	2,000,000
Merchandise Inventories	2,525,530
Purchases	12,121,180
Rents Earned	2,465,121
Taxes Expense	685,000
Income Taxes Payable........................	840,108
Investment in 50 percent-Owned Company........	473,548
Land......................................	583,042
Accounts Payable	764,171
Sales......................................	14,616,156
Retained Earnings, Feb. 28, 1966	3,324,516
Equipment.................................	602,471
Additional Paid-in Capital	4,000,000
Advances to 50 percent-Owned Company – due after Feb. 28, 1967	537,623
Accumulated Depreciation – Equipment	103,060
Freight In..................................	2,161
Rent of Land...............................	22,416
Allowance for Doubtful Accounts	103,446

Required:

1. Prepare a classified balance sheet.
2. Prepare a popularized balance sheet, or statement of financial condition, which shows the working capital on the face of the statement.
3. Compare the working capital position of the company with that of the prior year. At that time the current ratio was 5 to 1, and working capital was $6,812,521.
4. The president of the company states that while the balance sheet conforms to generally accepted accounting practices, it does not show the practical financial condition of the company. He asserts that a substantial part of the "true retained earnings" is represented by the reduction in mortgage debt over the years. To the extent these repayments are made, he points out, it is usually possible after a period of time to refinance the mortgages and thereby provide the company with new funds. He further points out that the balance sheet shows the real estate at cost less depreciation. The property located in Bellingham, Washington, was acquired before World War II, and since that date similar real estate has sold at prices per square foot ranging from three to five times that paid for the real estate owned by the company. Comment on the remarks concerning "true retained earnings."

8.2 Among the items listed below for the Valley Coal Company are the operating and retained earnings data for the year ended December 31, 1966.

Net sales		$285,100
Provision for depreciation		14,700
Gain on disposal of reserve coal lands:		
Proceeds	$30,000	
Book value	20,000	10,000
Advances from customers		2,600
Retained earnings, Jan. 1, 1966		50,000
Dividends paid		6,000
Allowance for doubtful accounts		1,500
Cost of goods sold		216,000
Purchases		246,000
Selling and administrative expenses		50,400
Accrued interest receivable		1,600
Interest income		6,000
Mining royalties applicable to operations after Dec. 31, 1966		122,400

Required:

1. Prepare a combined income and retained earnings statement for the year ended December 31, 1966. Use the current-operating concept and single-step form for the income statement section. Show the gain on disposal of reserve coal lands net of tax. The income tax rate is 25 percent on the gain from sale of land and 22 percent on all other income.
2. Prepare the 1966 income statement under the all-inclusive concept, using a form that shows gross margin on sales. Do not allocate income taxes between the gain on sale of land and ordinary income.
3. Discuss the comparative advantages of the alternative concepts of net income implied by operating reports prepared in (1) and (2) above.
4. Why is depreciation itemized separately?

8.3 Prepare a work sheet for January 1966 for the Red Hill Market. The ledger balances at January 31 are as follows:

Bishop Bank .... $ 1,674
Accounts Receivable 3,500
Allowance for Doubtful Accounts 50
Notes Receivable 1,000
Accrued Interest Receivable .... —
Merchandise Inventory 4,000
Furniture and Fixtures 12,000
Accumulated Depreciation 1,800
Prepaid Rent .... —
Prepaid Insurance 270
Store Supplies 345
Bonus and Salaries Payable .... —
Accounts Payable 1,500
Taxes Payable 1,000
Accrued Interest Payable .... —
Income Taxes Payable .... —
Mortgage Payable 3,000
Capital Stock 7,150
Retained Earnings 5,815
Sales 51,000
Sales Returns and Allowances 1,000
Bad Debts .... —
Cost of Sales .... —
Purchases 38,000
Taxes 500
Advertising 215
Depreciation .... —
Insurance .... —
Rent 1,400
Salaries 5,750
Supplies .... —
Unclassified 1,661
Interest Earned .... —
Interest Expense .... —
Income Taxes .... —

Data for Adjustments:
(1) The ending inventory of merchandise is $6,000.
(2) The Notes Receivable account represents a single note for $1,000, dated January 1, 1966. It is a 6 percent 90-day note, interest payable at maturity.
(3) Bad debts are estimated at 1 percent of gross sales.
(4) Furniture and fixtures have an estimated life of ten years, with no salvage value.
(5) Insurance premiums were paid July 1, 1965. All policies run for three years.
(6) The inventory of store supplies on January 31 is $300.
(7) The $3,000 mortgage payable bears interest at 6 percent per year, payable semiannually on July 31 and December 31.
(8) The sales manager earns a bonus of $\frac{1}{2}$ percent of net sales as part of his salary. This bonus is paid on the 15th of the month following that in which it was earned. Other salaries accrued on January 31, 1966, amount to $250.
(9) Two months' rent, at $700 per month, was paid on January 15, 1966.
(10) Provide for taxes on income at 50 percent.

8.4 Following is a trial balance at March 31, 1966, of John Powers and Company, distributors of Dodge and Plymouth motor cars. The last closing of the accounts was December 31, 1965.

Bank of America	$ 19,500	
Customer Notes	800,000	
Customer Notes Discounted		$ 765,000
Customer Accounts	40,000	
Allowance for Doubtful Accounts		300
Vehicles and Parts in Stock	150,000	
Building Equipment	45,000	
Allowance for Depreciation—Bldg. Equip.		22,500
Machinery, Tools, and Shop Equipment	90,000	
Allowance for Depreciation—Mach., Tools, and Shop Equipment		40,000
Office Furniture and Fixtures	20,000	
Allowance for Depreciation—Office Furniture and Fixtures		10,000
Company Cars and Service Vehicles	28,000	
Allowance for Depreciation — Company Cars and Service Vehicles		14,000
Prepaid Insurance	3,600	
Prepaid Taxes	4,800	
Prepaid Advertising	—	
Notes Payable to Bank of America		—
Accounts Payable to Factory		70,000
Customer Deposits		1,000
Accrued Payroll		—
Accrued Interest		—
Accrued Taxes and Withholding		600
Mortgage Payable		40,000
Capital Stock		100,000
Retained Earnings		54,700
Sales		640,000
Bad Debts		—
Cost of Sales	450,500	
Operating Expenses (allow 5 lines)	106,900	
Interest Earned		200
Interest Expense	—	
	$1,758,300	$1,758,300

Additional data available at the end of the quarter:

(1) March 31, 1966, falls on a Thursday. Shop employees are paid every Saturday. Salaries in the amount of $150 are unpaid on March 31.

(2) Payroll taxes accrued and not recorded amount to $200.

(3) Bad debts average $\frac{1}{4}$ percent of sales.

(4) Depreciation is based on the life of the asset, as follows:

	Years
Buildings equipment	10
Machinery, tools, and shop equipment	$4\frac{1}{2}$
Office furniture and fixtures	8
Company cars and service vehicles	$3\frac{1}{2}$

(5) All insurance policies are for a 3-year term. They were renewed at January 1, 1966, and the premiums were paid in the amount shown in the trial balance.
(6) Property taxes for one year were paid on July 1, 1965, in the amount of $9,600.
(7) Interest on the mortgage is payable semiannually on December 31 and June 30 at the rate of 4 percent per year.
(8) A "packaged" radio show was bought from the Coast Broadcasting Company for three months beginning February 1, 1966. The full cost of the series, $3,000, was charged to expense in February; however, it is expected that the advertising will benefit sales in equal proportions each month the program is on the air.
(9) The bank reconciliation at March 31, 1966, is summarized below.

Balance per books $19,500
Add: Outstanding checks 10,000
   Proceeds of short-term loan negotiated
   at bank, March 31, 1966, on the company's 4% note   5,000

Balance per bank $34,500

(10) Provide for federal and state income taxes at 50 percent.

Required:

Prepare an eight-column work sheet for the three months ended March 31, 1966. Charge Operating Expenses for adjustments to expense accounts; do not open new expense accounts.

8.5 On January 1, 1966, the Bishop Land Co. owned real estate known as Colony Surf Properties, which had been leased by Capital Realty at $2,000 a month. Capital had subleased part of Colony Surf to Dilco, Ltd., for $1,500 a month. All leases were renegotiated March 1, 1966, from which date Capital agreed to a rent of $2,500 a month and Dilco agreed to a rent of $2,000 a month. The following transactions occurred during 1966:

Feb. 1 Capital paid Bishop $12,000.
Mar. 15 Dilco paid Capital $6,000.
June 5 Capital paid Bishop $12,000.
July 20 Dilco paid Capital $7,500.
Oct. 12 Dilco paid Capital $4,000.
Dec. 15 Capital paid Bishop $8,000.

The ledger of Bishop showed Rent Receivable of $2,000 at December 31, 1965, while Dilco showed $1,500 Prepaid Rent at the same date.

Required:

1. Journal entries and T accounts for 1966 rent transactions of Bishop, including adjusting entries, closing entries, and reversing entries. Bishop closes annually and uses reversing entries.
2. Journal entries and T accounts for 1966 rent transactions of Dilco, including adjusting entries, closing entries, and reversing entries. Dilco closes at the end of each calendar quarter and uses reversing entries.
3. Journal entries and T accounts for rent transactions and adjustments in 1966 of Capital. Capital closes monthly but does not make reversing entries. (Omit journal entries for the monthly closings.)

8.6 The owner of Maclean's Co., an unincorporated manufacturing business, has been approached by a syndicate interested in purchasing the business. It has been agreed that goodwill will be calculated on the following basis:

(a) Adjustments will be made to the recorded net income of each year for any errors or omissions.

(b) The lowest annual net income selected from the three years 1965, 1966, and 1967 will be multiplied by a factor of 10. (Losses on abandonment of equipment are not to be deducted in the computation of net income for this purpose.)

(c) The resulting product less the net worth at December 31, 1967, (adjusted for any errors or omissions) is the price to be paid for goodwill.

Data follow:

(1) Net profits as reported by the bookkeeper: 1965 — $37,000; 1966 — $41,000; 1967 — $42,000.

(2) Items charged to maintenance and repairs, which are fixed assets: 1965 — $4,000; 1966 — $1,000. The company depreciates such assets at the straight line rate of 10 percent per year calculated from January 1 of the year acquired.

(3) Amounts not set up at year end:

	Accrued Liabilities	Prepaid Expenses
1965	$ 950	$1,800
1966	1,100	1,395
1967	1,225	650

Accrued liabilities at December 31 were paid in the following year; prepaid expenses at December 31 expired during the following year.

(4) Inventories at December 31 per books and as revised:

	Per Books	As Revised
1965	$12,000	$11,000
1966	14,000	10,000
1967	15,000	12,000

(5) No provisions have been made for doubtful accounts, which at December 31, 1967, were estimated at $800. Accounts written off, which in all cases were incurred in the year prior to the write-off: 1966 — $900; 1967 — $1,050. It has been agreed that for the purposes of computing goodwill, bad debts are to be matched with revenue by years.

(6) Included in the fixed assets accounts is an amount of $10,000 less accumulated depreciation of $6,800, which represents assets that were abandoned as useless in January 1966. The company has continued to charge depreciation on these assets at the rate of 20 percent on the straight line basis for the years 1966 and 1967.

(7) Net worth, as reported by the bookkeeper at December 31, 1967, was $370,275.

Required:

Prepare schedules showing the determination of the goodwill.

Suggestion: Prepare a work sheet to correct net income by years, with column headings as follows: Explanation, Net Income 1965 Dr. and Cr., Net Income 1966 Dr. and Cr., Net Income 1967 Dr. and Cr., Balance Sheet Accounts December 31, 1967 Dr. and Cr., Name.

(ICAC — adapted)

PART III

Control and Accounting
for Particular Assets
and Liabilities

Accounts Receivable

This chapter is concerned with accounts receivable from five points of view:

1. Transactions affecting accounts receivable
2. Records and procedures involved
3. Estimation of the amount that is collectible
4. Internal control that is desirable
5. Management problems in extending and collecting credit

TRANSACTIONS AND PROCEDURES AFFECTING ACCOUNTS RECEIVABLE

Transactions previously discussed are summarized in the following journal entries.

Accounts Receivable............................$	8,000	
Sales.....................................		$ 8,000
Sales Returns and Allowances....................$	400	
Accounts Receivable......................		$ 400
Cash...$	2,940	
Sales Discounts...............................	60	
Accounts Receivable......................		$ 3,000
Bad Debts.....................................$	1,100	
Allowance for Doubtful Accounts............		$ 1,100
Allowance for Doubtful Accounts..................$	280	
Accounts Receivable......................		$ 280

Additional attention is given to sales discounts and to bad debts in the next two sections.

SALES DISCOUNTS

Questions about discounts may arise when goods are returned, when partial payments are made, when the customer makes deductions for freight that he pays for the account of the seller, and when sales taxes are charged.

If goods are returned after the invoice has been paid at a discount, should the credit be recorded at gross or net price? For example, a sale was made for $5,000 subject to a 1 percent cash discount. The invoice was paid within the discount period with $4,950 cash. Subsequently, $800 worth (original invoice price) of the goods was returned. This $800 worth of goods represents only

$792 of cash. The common practice is to record the return at the invoice price, $800 in this case. The entry is:

Sales Returns and Allowances................... $	800	
Accounts Receivable...................		$ 800

This entry is proper if, as is commonly the case, the credit will be used up by future purchases by the customer. He will then have the benefit of his prompt payment in obtaining the new merchandise. If, however, the customer asks for a cash refund, it must be noted that he is not entitled to the invoice amount in cash. If a cash refund is made, the discount is canceled and the entry is:

Accounts Receivable.......................... $	800	
Sales Discounts........................		$ 8
Cash		792

Ordinary discount terms require full payment by the purchaser in order to qualify for the discount. However, the seller may allow a discount on a partial payment made within the discount period if he chooses to do so. This discount is recorded in the same way as a full-payment discount, except that it is calculated on the partial payment.

Sometimes freight is allowed by the seller when it is paid by the buyer. For example, $1,800 is charged for merchandise on a 2/10 n/30 basis. Freight paid by the buyer chargeable against the seller is $120. The discount in this case is taken on the cost of the merchandise, or $1,800. The fact that part of the payment is made to the railroad or trucker does not change the fact that the whole obligation is being discharged by prompt payment. The buyer instead of the seller makes the payment for freight as a matter of convenience. The entry on the books of the seller is:

Cash	$1,644.00	
Freight Out.............................	120.00	
Sales Discounts	36.00	
Accounts Receivable.................		$1,800.00

On the books of the buyer it is:

Freight Paid for Suppliers................... $	120.00	
Cash.............................		$ 120.00

Purchases	$1,800.00	
Cash.............................		$1,644.00
Freight Paid for Suppliers		120.00
Purchase Discounts		36.00

Freight Paid for Suppliers is a clearing account that has no balance after all elements of the purchase and payment have been recorded.

Sales taxes are not subject to discount. They are added to the invoice on the basis of the gross price, because the discount sometimes is not taken. If the discount is taken, the tax recorded on the seller's books should be revised. Consider a sale invoiced at $1,400 plus sales tax at 4 percent, or $56. It is paid less a discount of 2 percent. The presence of sales tax and discount creates no problem for the buyer; his cost includes the tax, and the tax is not distinguished from the rest of the cost on his books. He simply records a payable of $1,456 and a purchase discount of $29.12 when he pays the net cash of $1,426.88. However, from the seller's viewpoint the tax liability is reduced when the discount is taken. His computation is:

Invoice price of goods	$1,400.00
Less 2% discount	28.00
Net price of goods	$1,372.00
Sales tax at 4%	54.88
Cash received	$1,426.88

The seller's entry to record the receipt is:

Cash	$1,426.88	
Sales Discounts	28.00	
Sales Tax Payable ($56.00 – $54.88)	1.12	
Accounts Receivable		$1,456.00

The reduction in sales tax of $1.12 is 2 percent of the $56 originally computed on the gross invoice price.

BAD DEBTS TRANSACTIONS

Bad debts transactions include two methods of recording bad debts and two methods of recording recoveries on bad debts.

The charge to Bad Debts may be made on the basis of an estimate as previously explained. This method results in the following entry:

Bad Debts	$xxx	
Allowance for Doubtful Accounts		$xxx

This is known as the *allowance* or *reserve* method of recording bad debts. It has the advantage of matching the bad debts with the sales giving rise to them, provided that the estimate is reasonably accurate. The alternative method sets up no allowance. It consists of writing off the bad account directly to Bad Debts, thus:

Bad Debts	$xxx	
Accounts Receivable		$xxx

This method, called the *direct writeoff* method, has the advantage of simplicity and is fairly popular in practice. It has the disadvantage of presenting on the balance sheet inadequate information about the amount to be collected, since no provision is made for future writeoffs of the existing balances. Once the firm is established, this method may not distort results on the income statement significantly, since the amount of bad debts estimated on current sales and the amount written off from prior periods' sales may be about equal. However, if the level of sales and the ability of customers to pay vary, as they do between periods of recession and prosperity, the direct writeoff may be significantly in error. The allowance method is accordingly preferred.

BAD DEBT RECOVERIES

Accounts written off are sometimes collected later in whole or in part. Two methods of recording recoveries may be used; one treats the recovery as a reversal of the original writeoff, the other as a reduction of the bad debts charge. The former is appropriate where the allowance method of recording bad debts is used; the latter is appropriate when the direct writeoff method is used. Suppose a management decides that an account for $500 is uncollectible, and the allowance method is in use. The writeoff is made by this entry:

```
Allowance for Doubtful Accounts.....................$500.00
    Accounts Receivable.........................            $500.00
```

Subsequently the debtor pays off his old debt. The seller's entry, following the method of reversing the writeoff, is:

```
Accounts Receivable...............................$500.00
    Allowance for Doubtful Accounts...............            $500.00

Cash.............................................$500.00
    Accounts Receivable..........................            $500.00
```

This method has the advantage of leaving a record of the collection in the debtor's account. Since the entry to Bad Debts each period is presumably made on the basis of a percent of *net* writeoffs over a period, no correction is required by the fact that a particular recovery occurs.

The alternative method is rather commonly practiced. It records the recovery in a separate account used as an offset to or a reduction of the Bad Debts account in the income statement. For the case given above, the entry is:

```
Cash.............................................$500.00
    Recoveries of Bad Debts......................            $500.00
```

This method has one advantage—simplicity. But unless common practice is ignored and the extra entry is made to run the transaction through the debtor's account, this method gives no record in that account of the payment of the debt. It is appropriate to credit Bad Debts with recoveries when bad debts are determined by a direct writeoff method, as the amounts written off exceed the final loss experienced. However, these transactions are spread over a long time in many cases, so they are not well matched with each other and with revenue. The allowance method is therefore preferred.

RECORDS AND PROCEDURES FOR ACCOUNTS RECEIVABLE

The records and procedures with which we are concerned here are the customer's ledger account, the customer's statement, and the procedures of direct and machine posting. The reader is already familiar with the use of a general ledger control account and a subsidiary ledger for accounts receivable.

Special needs have resulted in the widespread use of the balance-column form of account for Accounts Receivable. The example below illustrates the form.

BALANCE-COLUMN ACCOUNT
John H. More Company

Date			Ref.	Debit		Credit		Balance	
1966									
June	1	Balance forward						800	20
	3		1841	600	00			1 400	20
	7		1866	55	00			1 455	20
	10		CR10			800	20	655	00
	14		1898	427	00			1 082	00
	17		1914	67	00			1 149	00
	22		CR13			600	00	549	00
	28		1944	125	00			674	00
	30		CR15			55	00	619	00

Note that the three-column arrangement of this account provides for calculating the balance after each entry or group of entries is made. This running balance enables management to know how much credit has been extended to the customer at any time. This form is economical when the account is kept by use of a bookkeeping machine. A common form of bookkeeping machine is operated by inserting the account in the machine, punching into the machine the last balance in the account, then punching in the debits and the credits. Debits and credits are printed on the account as they are punched in, and the machine automatically adds the debits to the old balance and deducts the credits. Depression of the balance key causes the automatically computed new balance to be printed.

The great volume of work involved in keeping customer's accounts has encouraged many schemes designed to cut cost. Two are especially prominent; these may be called the "unit-slip" method and the "microfilm" method.

In the unit-slip method a file of invoice copies under the name of each customer takes the place of the regular account. When the bill is paid, the invoice is marked "paid" and removed. If a partial payment is made, it is recorded on the bottom of an invoice retained in the active file. The balance of an account consists of the combined totals of the several invoices in the active file for that account. This method gives a less reliable permanent record than an ordinary account, but is alleged to save clerical time.

The microfilm method has been used chiefly by department stores. In it, sales slips, remittance slips, and any debit or credit memos are collected under the customer's name until his billing date (the same date each month). Then they are listed on a statement, together with any opening balance (from the last statement) and a new balance is calculated and also listed. Then the whole group of documents is photographed on microfilm. The documents are sent to the customer and the microfilm is filed. This method provides a permanent record for any future reference, avoids repeated handling of a ledger account and saves much filing space.

CUSTOMER'S STATEMENT

The customer's statement is a notice to the customer, usually sent monthly, showing what he owes. Most commonly it is a transcription (listing of all transactions) of his account, but sometimes it is a list of only the unpaid bills, and sometimes it shows the transactions in summary form. It typically includes opening and closing balances. When an ordinary ledger account is kept for the customer, the statement and the account are often made together by means of carbon paper. They stay together throughout the month, and at the end of the month the statement is removed and mailed to the customer. This procedure is especially convenient when the accounts are posted on book-keeping machines. In other cases the statement is written specially at the end of the month. Not all firms send statements; after all, the customer has received an invoice for each purchase. However, they are usually used and are especially important in retail trade. A statement form designed for general use is shown below, as is a statement of the type used by department stores that send the sales slips and other documents to the customer with the statement.

DATE **Sept. 30** 19 **66**

TO **The Benson Supply Co.**

ADDRESS **1641 Tenth Street**

CITY **Wilmington, Del.**

9	1	Balance	48	80		
	6		67	10		
	10				48	80
	13		27	90		
	16		14	72		
	20				67	10
	26		30	08		
	29		5	40		
		Balance owing			78	10

Redifprm 8S882

STATEMENT

DIRECT POSTING

Accounts receivable offer an outstanding opportunity for direct posting, that is, for posting from the original record directly to the ledger account. The transaction is entered in a journal, but only the general ledger control account is posted from the journal; as a rule only a monthly posting of the total of a journal column is required. Direct posting is done from invoice or sales-slip copies for charges and from remittance advices or similar slips made by the sellers' cashiers for credits. It permits work to be done on the journal by one person and on the subsidiary ledger by another at the same time. It offers a valuable control on accuracy, because the entries in the journals that determine the control account balance and those made in the subsidiary ledger must give the same result when the schedule of subsidiary balances is compared with the control account balance. Thus the work of one person checks that of another. Invoice numbers are commonly used as the posting reference in customer's accounts.

LOUISVILLE 2, KY.
501 S. FOURTH STREET

Stewart's

LEXINGTON 6, KY.
130 E. MAIN STREET

Mr. and Mrs. C. S. Harper
2966 Overlook Court
Lexington, Ky.

PLEASE DETACH AND RETURN THIS PART OF BILL WITH YOUR REMITTANCE

FROM YOUR PREVIOUS BALANCE OF:	WE HAVE DEDUCTED PAYMENTS OF:	AND ADDED CHARGES OF:	DEDUCTED RETURNS OF:	AND ON THIS DATE:	THERE IS A BALANCE DUE OF:
48.80	20.00	16.10			
		4.32			
		5.70			
			5.70		
PAYMENTS, CREDITS OR CHARGES WHICH REACHED OUR OFFICE AFTER DATE SHOWN WILL APPEAR ON YOUR NEXT STATEMENT.		8.40		Jul 20 '66	57.62

Original sales checks, credit slips and payment vouchers for this billing period are enclosed. Please retain them until your bill is paid in full. Inquiry concerning any item on this statement should be accompanied by the sales check or credit slip and directed to our adjustment department.

Stewart's

Louisville JUniper 4-3261
Lexington phone 2-2210

MACHINE POSTING

Reference has been made above to the use of bookkeeping machines in handling accounts receivable. It is worthy of note that this practice permits the writing at one time of the customers' statement, his account, and the sales or cash receipts journal. This combined writing is accomplished by placing the statement, ledger card or sheet, and journal all in the machine at once with carbon paper between them. As each invoice is posted, the same information—date, invoice number, and amount—are thus written on the statement, the subsidiary ledger account, and the sales journal. When cash receipts are posted, the cash receipts journal goes in the machine with the statement and the account. A journal remains in the machine while the transactions of a variety of customers are recorded, the journal sheet being moved up one line as each transaction is entered. The machines have "registers" that accumulate the totals needed for the footings of the journal columns, in addition to making calculations of the account balances automatically. More elaborate systems using punched cards or electronic computers are also used. When accounts are kept on a computer, the original record is used to put the data into a form that the computer can read (cards or tape), and all subsequent processing is done in the machine. Accounts and a journal (if desired) are printed out on order.

ESTIMATION OF COLLECTIBLE AMOUNT

The process of determining what amount should be shown for an asset is called "valuation" of the asset, but the term is misleading to the uninitiated. It does not usually refer to a value that could be obtained by sale of the asset. Cost is the basis for most asset "valuation" in accounting, because it is objective and can be verified and because it produces a record of what was invested with which the income from the investment can be usefully compared. In the case of accounts receivable the "valuation" goes a little beyond cost, because it includes the element of profit or income that compensates the organization for its effort and the use of its facilities. This addition is justified by the fact that responsible customers have made legally binding promises to pay the amounts recorded. However, two questions arise in determining the amount to be shown for accounts receivable: What items are the customers entitled to deduct in paying? To what extent will the customers take advantage of the deductions they can take and to what extent will they fail to pay altogether?

POSSIBLE DEDUCTIONS FROM ACCOUNTS RECEIVABLE

The gross amount of a charge may be reduced by cash discount, returns and allowances, and freight allowances. Very strict accuracy would require that allowance accounts similar to the Allowance for Doubtful Accounts be set up for these other items. The entries would be based on estimates of the percentage of sales that discounts and returns and allowances would be and on actual freight allowances applicable to the particular shipments. Assume that experience shows that 1 percent of sales are allowed as cash discounts; that $\frac{1}{2}$ percent of sales are returned and reduced by allowance for defects, errors in grading, or otherwise; and that $480 of freight is allowable against the $18,000 of sales made in July 1966. The entries to set up allowance accounts for these items are:

```
Sales Discount......................................$180.00
        Allowance for Sales Discount..................        $180.00

Sales Returns and Allowances.......................$ 90.00
        Allowance for Returns and Adjustments..........        $ 90.00

Freight Out.......................................$480.00
        Allowance for Freight......................        $480.00
```

If discounts of $75, a return for $40, and freight deductions of $310 are taken on bills paid during July 1966, on which the gross billing was $12,000, the entry, in summary form, would be:

```
Cash.......................................$11,575.00
Allowance for Sales Discount....................    75.00
Allowance for Returns and Adjustments............    40.00
Allowance for Freight..........................   310.00
        Accounts Receivable....................        $12,000.00
```

Cash discounts still to be taken at the end of a month are usually a very small part of the gross balances of accounts receivable. In most lines of business returns and allowances are also very small, and most concerns do not handle freight on a customer-allowance basis. As a result one does not see allowances for these items except in unusual cases where the trade practice involves large returns or where freight allowances are regularly extended to customers.

ESTIMATING BAD DEBTS

There are two ways of estimating the amount to be debited to Bad Debts and credited to Allowance for Doubtful Accounts. One is to compute the percent of sales that actual writeoffs have constituted in the past, and to use this figure. The other is to examine the accounts closely and, using such information as is available about them, arrive at a judgment as to the amount of allowance required. The second method sounds less scientific than the first, but it is needed when economic conditions are changing. In times of recession collections often slow up and business failures increase. A constant percent of sales is likely to be inadequate as an allowance at such times. The judgment method must be used by auditors who examine a set of accounts and render an opinion on their fairness at a certain date. They cannot wait for an average percent to work out. In an examination of accounts receivable for this purpose, all available information may be used: the paying habits of certain customers (some are always slow, but good); the financial condition of particular customers (financial statements may be available; credit-rating agencies furnish information on customers); and the customer's replies to collection efforts. As a starting point and a means of getting a summary of the condition of the accounts, an *aging* is often prepared.

AGING OF ACCOUNTS RECEIVABLE

An aging is an analysis of the balances according to the age of the charges in the accounts. The accompanying illustration shows The Keld Co. account and the columnar working form for aging of that account. Note that the analysis provides for identifying the current amount (not yet due) and the amounts that are past due for certain numbers of days. Terms given by the seller in the illustrated case are 1/10 n/30, so the last month's charges are current and any prior months' charges are past due. The analysis is easier to make if the names of the months appropriate to the particular case are written over the columns headed "Current," "1–30," and so on. Note also that offsetting debits and credits in the account must be watched for. Customers normally pay specific charges or invoices, so the charge and its payment can be matched. For example, in the case of The Keld Co., the charges of April 21 and May 4 were evidently paid by the remittance of May 13. If the customer does not indicate what invoice he

ACCOUNT AND AGING

The Keld Co.

Date	Explanation	Ref.	Debit	Date	Explanation	Ref.	Credit
1966				1966			
Jan. 1	Balance	S1	400 00	Feb. 10		CR4	400 00
8		S1	38 00	Mr. 8		CR5	133 00
Feb. 26		S3	133 00	Apr. 12		CR6	200 00
Mr. 17		S4	200 00	May 13		CR7	186 00
Apr. 5		S5	50 00	June 30	Balance		588 00
21		S5	111 00				
May 4		S6	75 00				
17		S6	22 00				
June 2		S7	390 00				
16		S7	88 00				
			1 507 00				1 507 00
June 30	Balance		588 00				

Accounts Receivable Aging

As at June 30, 1966

Account	Balance	Current	Past Due—Days				Remarks
			1–30	30–60	60–90	Over 90	
The Keld Co.	588 00	478 00	22 00	50 00		38 00	Jan. 8—in dispute

is paying, the creditor has the legal right to apply the payment against the oldest charge. If the customer pays round amounts not identical with any charge, he is not indicating specific invoices. Such an account may be aged by taking the latest charges as constituting the balance. Bookkeepers often make check marks in the account to indicate debits and credits that have been matched so the unpaid charges are more easily noted.

When all the accounts are aged and listed on the working paper, the columns are totaled. A summary of the aging of the accounts receivable is thus obtained. From this it may be decided that the allowance for doubtful accounts should be large enough to cover, say, 75 percent of the accounts over ninety days past due, and lesser percents, if any, of the others. These percents must be based on experience and judgment, as well as on consideration of the special circumstances surrounding the particular accounts present.

The aging may also be done on a sample basis; if the sample is chosen on a random or equivalent basis it may be assumed to be representative of all the accounts.

If the decision is that the allowance should be larger, Bad Debts is debited and Allowance for Doubtful Accounts is credited with the added amount; if the contrary is true, the debit and the credit are reversed.

INTERNAL CONTROL FOR ACCOUNTS RECEIVABLE

The four principles of internal control cited previously are:

1. Organization
2. System of authorization and records
3. Sound practices
4. Adequacy of personnel

Good organization for control of accounts receivable in large concerns requires separate departments for soliciting orders, approving credit of customers, preparing the bills, shipping the goods, receiving the cash payments, and keeping the accounts. The credit department approves credit and also carries on collection effort where it is needed.

The system of authorization and records should include the requirement of credit department approval on any order before goods can be shipped on credit. The use of a shipping order, customer's invoice, and office copy of the invoice that are made at one writing by means of carbon paper, previously mentioned in connection with sales, is also a good safeguard against loss through errors in shipments or in billing or bookkeeping.

Sound practices for accounts receivable include the prelisting of documents transferred from one department to another. For example, when a batch of invoice copies is sent from the billing department to the accounts receivable department, a list of the invoices may be prepared on an adding-machine tape. The batch is then entered in a sales journal or posted by a machine that accumulates the total automatically. The total in the sales journal or in the machine register may then be compared with the original list to see whether or not an error was made.

Another sound practice is to have someone other than the accounts receivable bookkeepers, perhaps someone from the credit department, remove the

APPLICATION FOR CHARGE ACCOUNT

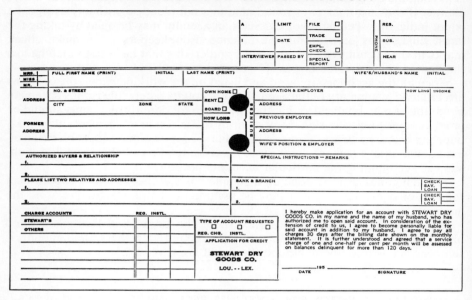

statements from the ledger at the end of the month, checking to see that the ledger accounts and statements agree, and mail the statements to the customers. This recommendation assumes that the statements and ledger accounts are prepared concurrently by means of carbon paper. This practice prevents a bookkeeper who may wish to conceal a fraud—say a theft of a customer's remittance—from covering it up by sending the customer a statement that differs from the ledger record.

MANAGEMENT PROBLEMS IN EXTENDING AND COLLECTING CREDIT

Three problems are discussed in the following sections:

1. Identifying customers whose credit is acceptable
2. Collection of accounts receivable
3. Credit policy—what financial strength will be required of customers

IDENTIFYING RETAIL CUSTOMERS HAVING ACCEPTABLE CREDIT

Financial and other information about the prospective customer comes from three sources: the customer himself, the references he gives, and credit agencies. Credit agencies are organizations formed to gather credit information as a service that they can sell to concerns who need it or, in the case of cooperatives, that they issue to their members.

In retail trade a customer who applies for credit is usually asked to fill out an application. This provides for information about the applicant's financial status as reflected by his occupation, whether or not he owns his home, and what bank accounts he has. It also inquires about charge accounts at other stores, from which his paying habits may be learned. It includes a contract in which the applicant agrees to the credit terms. The accompanying illustration shows a credit application form used by a department store. Retail stores in metropolitan areas are often organized in a credit information association, which issues to its membership a book of credit ratings based on reports of the stores. It lists the customers' names and reports their paying record. For example, the book may include this entry: "Adams, O. B., 6P, 2M, 1S." This code means that six stores have reported that O. B. Adams pays promptly; two, that he pays moderately promptly; and one, that he is slow. Other symbols may be used to report special information.

Recently a system of credit based on credit cards issued by a central agency has been widely developed. The central agency examines the applicant's credit, using traditional methods, before it issues a card. It then pays the cooperating business concerns for merchandise or services given to cardholders who have used the cards, and bills the cardholders.

IDENTIFYING WHOLESALE CUSTOMERS HAVING ACCEPTABLE CREDIT

Information on a wholesale customer may also come from the prospective customer, in which case it is likely to be in the form of a financial statement.

KEY TO RATINGS

ESTIMATED FINANCIAL STRENGTH			COMPOSITE CREDIT APPRAISAL			
			HIGH	GOOD	FAIR	LIMITED
Aᴀ	Over	$1,000,000	A1	1	1½	2
A+	Over	750,000	A1	1	1½	2
A	500,000 to	750,000	A1	1	1½	2
B+	300,000 to	500,000	1	1½	2	2½
B	200,000 to	300,000	1	1½	2	2½
C+	125,000 to	200,000	1	1½	2	2½
C	75,000 to	125,000	1½	2	2½	3
D+	50,000 to	75,000	1½	2	2½	3
D	35,000 to	50,000	1½	2	2½	3
E	20,000 to	35,000	2	2½	3	3½
F	10,000 to	20,000	2½	3	3½	4
G	5,000 to	10,000	3	3½	4	4½
H	3,000 to	5,000	3	3½	4	4½
J	2,000 to	3,000	3	3½	4	4½
K	1,000 to	2,000	3	3½	4	4½
L	Up to	1,000	3½	4	4½	5

CLASSIFICATION AS TO BOTH
ESTIMATED FINANCIAL STRENGTH AND CREDIT APPRAISAL

FINANCIAL STRENGTH BRACKET			EXPLANATION
1	$125,000 to	$1,000,000 and Over	When only the numeral (1, 2, 3, or 4) appears, it is an indication that the estimated financial strength, while not definitely classified, is presumed to be within the range of the ($) figures in the corresponding bracket and that a condition is believed to exist which warrants credit in keeping with that assumption.
2	20,000 to	125,000	
3	2,000 to	20,000	
4	Up to	2,000	

NOT CLASSIFIED OR ABSENCE OF RATING

The absence of a rating, expressed by the dash (—), or by two hyphens (- -), is not to be construed as unfavorable but signifies circumstances difficult to classify within condensed rating symbols and should suggest to the subscriber the advisability of obtaining additional information.

SEE REFERENCE BOOK FOR EXPLANATION OF ABSENCE OF A LISTING AND ADDITIONAL SYMBOLS USED IN REFERENCE BOOK

Dun & Bradstreet, Inc.

Banks are prominent as references. Although the financial data constitute the bulk of the material, the honesty of the persons involved is obviously of prime importance too. In the wholesale field the commercial credit agency plays an especially prominent role. The leading agency publishes a reference book that lists financial ratings of 3,000,000 business organizations in the United States. The same agency prepares reports on the individual businesses that are available to the agency's customers, and it renders other services. Frequently the only action taken in deciding whether or not to extend credit to a business is to look up its rating in the reference book of this agency.

COLLECTION OF ACCOUNTS RECEIVABLE

Many concerns pay valid invoices sent to them without further notice; but some have to be urged or forced to pay. Regular procedures are therefore set up to assure that slow accounts are noticed and acted upon. Sometimes "flags" are attached to ledger accounts to indicate the condition of the account. In one system, small tabs or flags of different colors are clipped to the top of the ledger card, much as a paper clip might be. The color indicates the age of the oldest part of the balance. Another system uses a plastic slide that runs along the top or bottom of a ledger card and indicates by its position the age of the oldest part of the balance. These devices are moved as payments come in or as time passes. They permit a person to run through the cards quickly and to spot accounts that need attention. In smaller organizations a list of open balances—the regularly prepared schedule of the accounts receivable ledger—may be all a manager needs to note trouble spots, since he is familiar enough with the transactions to recognize old balances. In more complex cases an aging of the accounts may be prepared for the manager's scrutiny.

The steps taken when an account is slow include a series of letters, often so designed as to make the appeal for payment more and more pressing; as time passes, calls are made by telephone or in person. If these fail, the concern may give the account to a collection agency. This agency will, of course, resort to a lawsuit if it thinks the action would be rewarding. The seller may take his own legal action, and will ordinarily do so for large accounts, because a typical collection agency fee is 50 percent of the amount collected. As a matter of policy, some concerns turn over to a collection agency all accounts that they consider hopeless. In any case management must keep a careful watch on the accounts receivable to avoid losses, which are sometimes very serious.

CREDIT POLICY

Credit policy determines what kind of credit risks will be accepted. One can hold bad debt losses to a bare minimum by selling on credit only to customers whose ratings leave no doubt that they can and will pay promptly. The trouble with this policy is that a great deal of business is done by concerns that are not so secure. In exchange for taking a few losses on bad debts, a firm may gain a considerable amount of sales. In theory, this problem should be solved by extending credit to concerns with increasingly poorer ratings until a certain point is reached. That point is reached when the expenses of obtaining the new business, including bad debt losses from the new group, are just equaled by the revenue actually collected from it. Beyond that point, losses would presumably exceed the additional revenue collected. This is a *marginal* calculation. It is an application of the same principle discussed in the chapter on sales, where the contribution of a class of sales was calculated as the revenue less the variable costs of obtaining that revenue. Any contribution improves the profit picture; any excess of revenue over the variable costs of obtaining it, including amounts lost as bad debts, improves profit. This reasoning may be clearer in the form of figures, as follows:

Calendar Year 1966		
Sales to the most risky groups.		$80,000
Less: bad debts with this group		20,000
Net sales.		$60,000
Variable costs of serving the group:		
Salesmens' commissions.	$10,000	
Cost of merchandise sold.	45,000	
Delivery and miscellaneous.	4,000	59,000
Addition to profit from this group.		$ 1,000

Note that no fixed costs are included in the foregoing calculation. These include depreciation, executive salaries, real estate taxes, insurance on buildings and equipment, and so on. This exclusion assumes that facilities with fixed costs are available to serve the group of customers added, with no increase in costs of the facilities. If new facilities had to be added to conduct the business and the cost of the additional facilities assignable to 1966 in the above case was $1,000, it would not be profitable to extend credit or to do the $80,000 of business involved.

In practice it is a work of fine art to predict the bad debts a business may incur in extending credit to the weaker concerns. However, the collection effort also affects the results. The point to which credit may be extended must be discovered through experiment and by application of judgment based on experience. Because of the possibility of increasing profit by carefully extending credit, it is said that "a good credit department is a profitable operation."

SUMMARY

Accounts receivable transactions include sales, sales returns and allowances, sales discounts, bad debts, and freight allowances. Sales discounts apply to the invoice price of the goods and are not increased by sales taxes or diminished by freight allowances. Bad debts preferably are recorded by an allowance method, but may be recorded on a direct writeoff basis. Bad debt recoveries are preferably recorded by first reversing the writeoff, but are sometimes recorded as a reduction of bad debts.

The Accounts Receivable ledger account is often kept in three-column form, the third column giving a running balance.

Statements are usually sent to customers monthly; these give a transcript of the account or, in a few cases, a summary of it or just the open charges.

Direct posting, from the invoice or cash receipt slip (remittance slip of the customer) to the ledger account, improves the distribution of work and gives a check on accuracy. Bookkeeping machines for posting accounts receivable and sometimes for writing the account, the statement, and the sales or the cash receipts journal at one operation are popular. They include automatic calculation of balances and automatic accumulation of journal totals. In computerized records, original records, such as the invoice and the customer's check, are used to prepare machine-processable cards or tapes; all summaries are then prepared internally by the computer, which prints them out as directed.

Estimation of the collectible amount of receivables strictly should include allowances for sales discount, returns and adjustments, and freight (where appropriate). These items are not important in most cases so the only allowance account commonly used is the one for doubtful accounts. This is set up by estimates based on prior experience of the percent of sales lost in writeoffs of accounts receivable or by judgment based on scrutiny of the accounts. This estimating is aided by aging the accounts.

Internal control is important for accounts receivable and requires separation of accounts-receivable bookkeeping from the credit department, sales, billing, cash receiving, and so on. Other useful control procedures and practices are noted in the text.

Managements' problems in extending and collecting credit, over and above its concern with the more typically accounting matters outlined above, are three in number: identifying customers whose credit is acceptable, collecting the receivables, and forming credit policy. The latter problem is best approached from the viewpoint of a calculation embracing marginal cost and marginal revenue. In practice the data must come from judgment and experimentation.

QUESTIONS

9.1 (1) In the year-end trial balance Allowance for Doubtful Accounts has a debit balance. Explain how the debit balance probably arose. Does the debit balance indicate that the allowance at the close of the prior fiscal year was inadequate?

(2) By what two basic methods may bad debts be estimated? Discuss the advantages and the disadvantages of each method.

(3) Explain how the computation of bad debts differs in the periodic adjustment of the accounts according to the two basic methods.

(4) Illustrate the difference by a numerical example.

9.2 (1) Present journal entries for five common transactions affecting Accounts Receivable or Allowance for Doubtful Accounts.

(2) Listed below are the balances of Accounts Receivable and Allowance for Doubtful Accounts of the Zippo Co., with a partial explanation of the change in those accounts for the year. One item of explanation has been omitted for each account. Compute the cash recovered from accounts written off in prior years.

Accounts Receivable: Opening balance, $24,246; closing balance, $23,659; collections on account, $118,166, less cash discounts $2,145; sales, $120,126.

Allowance for Doubtful Accounts: Opening balance, $6,125; closing balance, $7,657; provision for bad debts, $3,467.

9.3 The Helm Company buys 1,000 units of merchandise at $3 each. The invoice specifies that $200 freight paid by the buyer on the shipment may be deducted, and that a 2 percent cash discount may be taken if the bill is paid in ten days. A sales tax of 4 percent is added to the invoice. (1) How much is the cash discount? (2) How much will Helm Company remit if the invoice is paid on time? (3) What entries should be made by Helm Company to record the purchase, payment of freight, and settlement within the discount period?

9.4 Zenobia, Inc., sent to a customer an invoice for merchandise billed at $1,200. It provided for 2 percent discount, and a $48 charge for sales tax was added. The customer took 2 percent off the $1,248 total and remitted $1,223.04 within the discount period. (1) Did the customer take the proper discount? (2) What entry should Zenobia, Inc., make for collection of this account?

9.5 (1) Explain how a cash discount is calculated when it is allowed on a partial payment.

(2) Compute the discount on a check for $1,900 to apply on account, if the company allows discounts on customers' partial payments. The check was received within the discount period on an invoice marked "5/10 e.o.m."

(3) Should a company allow cash discounts for customers' accounts settled by notes? Would it make any difference if the notes were interest bearing?

9.6 The Roller Manufacturing Co. ships $4,160 of goods to Dwan & Co. on terms 2/10 n/30, $510 freight allowed. Dwan is billed for the invoice price, plus 4 percent state sales tax and 10 percent federal excise tax. Dwan pays $500 freight on the shipment. Later, Dwan returns goods with an invoice price of $200 and pays the remainder of the bill. (1) Suggest the journal entries that might be made to record these transactions on the books of The Roller Manufacturing Co. and Dwan & Co. (2) Discuss possible alternatives.

9.7 On July 13 A Co. sold $420 of merchandise to B Co. The terms of sale were bill of lading attached to a sight draft for the amount of the sale less a 2 percent cash discount. B Co. paid the sight draft on July 15, received the bill of lading, and obtained the goods from the freight depot. A Co.'s bank credited the proceeds of $411.60 to the company on July 17. Give dated journal entries for both companies. What is the purpose of the sight draft?

9.8 (1) Describe the process of aging accounts receivable. How does aging assist in estimating bad debts?

(2) What precaution is necessary in going through the debits in an account to prepare an aging of it?

9.9 What are bad debt recoveries? Suggest two ways of recording them. Give the advantages and the disadvantages of each method.

9.10 A firm frequently receives inquiries over the telephone from customers asking "How much do I owe?"

(1) What form of ledger account for the subsidiary accounts receivable ledger would you recommend to this firm?

(2) Describe briefly two methods of keeping customers' accounts that are designed to reduce the effort and cost of this work.

(3) What is direct posting? Describe its application to accounts receivable.

9.11 You have received the following letter from the comptroller of L Co.:

Dear Sir:

Our company has recently met the following problem on which I should appreciate having your comments and opinions.

As you know, our credit terms in the past have been net/30 days. Recently, however, we decided to grant a 2 percent discount on all payments made within ten days and find that most of our customers are taking advantage of this discount.

Because a large portion of the company's current assets consists of accounts receivable, do you think that we should make a provision for cash discounts in preparing the year-end financial statements? I feel that because discounts on 90 percent of the year-end receivables will undoubtedly be allowed, the amounts involved are significant.

Yours truly,
T
Comptroller

Outline the points you would cover in reply to T. Give reasons to support opinions and suggestions.

(ICAC—adapted)

9.12 The total balance due from customers of a television production company as shown by the controlling account in the general ledger is less than half the total debit balances shown by a list taken from the customers' ledger. What does this indicate? How should the facts be shown on the balance sheet?

9.13 The Accounts Receivable account of Helmholdt, Inc., at December 31, 1966, consists of the following items:

Debit balances from certain customers less amounts owing to other customers for returns and advances.

Advance payments to creditors on purchase of merchandise.

Unissued capital stock of the company, which the directors plan to dispose of in the very near future.

Installments on a mortgage from sale of land, due after December 31, 1967.

Accounts known to be worthless.

Debit balances from officers, due in six months.

How should these items be shown on the balance sheet?

9.14 Suggest some internal control devices that are useful in protecting the accounts receivable records from error and fraud.

9.15 (1) What are the sources of information that permit identification of customers to whom one wishes to extend credit in a retail business?

(2) What type of information is available about the credit of prospective customers among business concerns?

(3) In theory, how should a concern determine how far to go in extending credit to firms of differing financial strength?

9.16 The sales manager of the XYZ Company estimates that the annual sales volume could be increased $120,000 by making credit sales to class C credit risks, who are now on a c.o.d. basis. The business is currently operating below capacity.

The bookkeeper has prepared an analysis to assist in arriving at a decision whether or not this kind of credit risk should be accepted. It is of the following form:

Sales to most risky group		$xxx
Less: Bad debts with this group		$xxx
Net sales		$xxx
Allocated costs (based on percentage of sales):		
Cost of merchandise sold	$xxx	
Delivery and miscellaneous	xxx	
Depreciation of building and equipment	xxx	
Executive salaries	xxx	
Salesmen's commissions	xxx	xxx
Addition to profit from this group		$xxx

Discuss.

EXERCISES

9.1 The trial balance of the A Co. at December 31, 1966, contains the following balances:

Accounts Receivable $52,000
Allowance for Doubtful Accounts 300
Sales. $600,000
Sales Returns and Allowances 30,000

Present the journal entry to record the estimated bad debts for the year, assuming (1) the loss is estimated on the basis of 1 percent of net sales, (2) the allowance is increased to $5,200 on the basis of an aging of accounts receivable.

9.2 The following account balances appear in the ledger of the Sundeck Sales Corporation on December 31, 1966:

	Debit	Credit
Accounts Receivable	$75,000	
Allowance for Doubtful Accounts		$ 200
Sales.		130,000
Bad Debts	—	
Sales Returns and Allowances	5,000	

Provision for losses on doubtful accounts is made on the basis of ½ percent of net sales.

Required:

1. The journal entry for bad debts on December 31.
2. The journal entry to write off the following accounts on December 31: R. E. Robinson $200, F. L. Wepfer $300.
3. The journal entry to record the collection of Wepfer's account on January 30, 1967.

9.3 The B Co. has been using the direct writeoff method on bad debts. Losses for the past three years have been recorded as follows:

	In 1964	In 1965	In 1966
From 1964 sales	$200	$900	$2,400
From 1965 sales		400	1,000
From 1966 sales			1,700

It is estimated that additional losses of $500 will be incurred on 1964 accounts, $900 on 1965 accounts, and $2,400 on 1966 accounts. The reported net income and stockholders' equity for the company was as follows:

	1964	1965	1966
Income for the year	$ 30,000	$ 40,000	$ 50,000
Stockholders' equity, 12/31.	360,000	400,000	450,000

Revise the net income and the stockholders' equity to match bad debts with revenues by year of sale.

9.4   Journalize the following transactions:

Oct. 5   Sold merchandise to Capri Lodge, $4,000 plus 5 percent sales tax; terms 2/10 n/30, f.o.b. destination.

14   Received payment from Capri Lodge in full of account less freight allowed, $300.

17   Issued a credit memo for merchandise returned by Capri Lodge, $1,000 plus 5 percent sales tax.

20   Sold merchandise to Capri Lodge, $3,000 plus 5 percent sales tax; terms 2/10 n/30, f.o.b. destination.

30   Received payment from Capri Lodge in full of account less freight allowed, $250.

31   Received within the 2 percent discount period a check from Village Mart for $4,900 to apply on account. It is the company's policy to allow discounts on customers' partial payments.

9.5   Prepare an aging of the account of C Co. at December 31, 1966, following the form illustrated on page 288; terms are 2/10 n/30.

C CO.

Date	Explanation	Debit	Credit	Balance
1966				
July 5		(a) 525		525
15		190		715
Aug. 20			190	525
Sept. 10		420		945
18		380		1,325
25			420	905
Oct. 5		(a) 250		1,155
25			(a) 775	380
Nov. 15		612		992
Dec. 25		38		1,030

9.6   Indicate by letter from the statement sections below where each numbered item would be shown.

Balance Sheet
(A) Current assets
(B) Fixed assets
(C) Current liabilities
(D) Fixed liabilities
(E) Stockholders' equity

Income Statement
(F) Gross margin
(G) Expenses
(H) Other income
(I)   Other deductions

(1)   Notes receivable
(2)   Allowance for doubtful accounts
(3)   Merchandise inventory (ending)
(4)   Allowances for depreciation – buildings
(5)   Sales returns and allowances
(6)   Discounts taken
(7)   Interest charges on bonds
(8)   Unexpired insurance
(9)   Rent received in advance
(10) Interest earned on investments
(11) Discounts allowed
(12) Depreciation – delivery equipment
(13) Capital stock
(14) Bonds payable
(15) Allowance for sales discounts
(16) Accrued bond interest payable
(17) Unfilled paid orders
(18) Accrued interest receivable
(19) Loss on sale of fixed assets
(20) Freight out

9.7   A summary of the activity in Accounts Receivable of Security Diamond for 1964-1966 is as follows:

	1964	1965	1966
Opening balances	$ —	$ 20,000	$ 25,000
Sales	240,000	300,000	370,000
Totals	$240,000	$320,000	$395,000
Collections.	$219,000	$292,600	$362,200
Writeoffs	1,000	2,400	2,800
Totals	$220,000	$295,000	$365,000
Closing balances	$ 20,000	$ 25,000	$ 30,000

Recoveries of bad debts were: 1964 — $200, 1965 — $600, 1966 — $800. The company maintains its allowance for bad debts at 10 percent of accounts receivable.

Required:

1. Prepare schedules showing by years the activity in the Allowance for Bad Debts account for 1964 to 1966 under the assumption that (a) recoveries of bad debts are included in income in the year of recovery and (b) the recoveries of bad debts are not included in income in the year of recovery.
2. Do the alternative assumptions in 1 have any affect on net income? Would your answer differ if bad debts were estimated as a percentage of sales?

9.8   The balance of the Accounts Receivable controlling account of the D Co. was $199,285 at December 31, 1966. It consisted of the following items:

Accounts not due (after deducting credit balances of $1,535)	$111,465
Accounts 1–30 days past due	31,500
Accounts 31–60 days past due	18,120
Accounts 61–90 days past due	9,200
Accounts over 90 days past due	6,100
Accounts due from officers and employees	7,500
Refund from U. S. Internal Revenue Service for net loss carryback	2,200
Consignment accounts	12,000
Interest receivable on notes	500
Rebates for purchase returns and allowances	700
Total	$199,285

(1) The accounts due from officers and employees are being repaid by payroll deductions, which will clear the balances by December 31, 1967.
(2) The consignment accounts represent the billed piece of merchandise shipped by the company to an agent at cost plus 20 percent. Title to the goods remains with the company until the agent sells the items, at which time he will remit the billed price less his commission.
(3) The Allowance for Doubtful Accounts, prior to adjustments at December 31, 1966, had a credit balance of $1,200; it should be adjusted on the basis of the following expected losses:

Accounts not due 1%
Accounts 1–30 days past due 5%
Accounts 31–60 days past due 10%
Accounts 61–90 days past due 20%
Accounts over 90 days past due 50%
No provision need be made for nontrade items.

Required:

1. Prepare necessary adjusting entries.
2. Prepare the balance sheet section for receivables.
3. Discuss the classification of any of the above amounts not shown in 2.

9.9 Accounts Receivable were reported on the balance sheet of F Co. at December 31, 1965, as follows:

Accounts Receivable		$92,000
Less: Allowance for Doubtful Accounts	$3,900	
Allowance for Sales Discounts	1,100	5,000
Net		$87,000

The following transactions were completed during 1966:

Collections on account (net of $11,080 cash discounts) $791,230
Uncollectible accounts written off 4,560
Collections on accounts written off in prior years 550
Sales on account . . . . ?

An aging of accounts receivable with estimated percentages uncollectible at December 31, 1966, is as follows:

Classification	Amount	Estimated Loss
Current	$10,500	5%
1–60 days	2,500	10%
61–90 days	2,100	30%
Over 91	3,000	50%

It is anticipated that sales discounts at 2 percent will be taken by 80 percent of the current accounts.

Prepare T accounts for Accounts Receivable, Allowance for Doubtful Accounts, Sales, Bad Debts, Sales Discounts, and Cash, and record the foregoing directly in the accounts.

9.10 Cyert and Trueblood estimate the allowance for doubtful accounts on the basis of a sample aging of accounts receivable. Of 100,000 customers' accounts, 15,000 are classified as follows:

	Amounts	Loss Expected
Current	$330,000	5%
0–4 months	60,000	10%
4–6 months	30,000	15%
6–10 months	20,000	30%
Over 10 months	10,000	70%
Total	$450,000	

The Accounts Receivable control amounts to $3,000,000. Prepare the entry to adjust Allowance for Doubtful Accounts, which has a ledger balance of $120,000.

9.11 The Furniture Mart has been selling quality furniture to cash customers or customers whose contracts were acceptable by the bank. The manager estimates that sales could be increased $120,000 annually if the store held house accounts from customers whose contracts were not bankable. It is estimated that credit losses from this group will amount to 5 percent of sales and that the cost of additional record keeping, interest on capital, and collection effort attributable to these accounts will amount to $10,000. No increases in inventory, floor space, or equipment will be required for the additional volume.

The bookkeeper has prepared the following statement:

Sales	100%
Cost of Goods Sold	60
Gross Margin on Sales	40%
Expenses:	
Salesmen's Commissions	10%
Depreciation	10
Rent and Other Fixed Charges...............	10
Total Expenses	30%
Net	10%

Additional volume from credit business	$120,000
Percent above..............................	10%
	$ 12,000

Less:		
Bad Debts (5% × 120,000)..........	$ 6,000	
Additional Record Keeping, etc.......	10,000	16,000
Expected loss from Selling to Poorer Credit Risks		$ (4,000)

The bookkeeper advises against expanding volume by selling to the poorer credit risks. Do you agree?

PROBLEMS

9.1 Record the following transactions in general journal form.
   (1) In the past three years the company has had $16,000 of bad debts on $800,000 of sales. Sales for September 1966 were $30,000. Estimate and record an allowance for bad debts for the month.
   (2) Cash is received in payment of an invoice for merchandise of $16,000 and sales tax of $640. A cash discount of 2 percent is allowed.
   (3) A payment is received for an invoice showing $6,000 for merchandise, subject to a freight allowance of $300 and a cash discount of $1\frac{1}{2}$ percent. Payment is made within the discount period, and the discount is taken.
   (4) An account for $320 is found to be uncollectible and is written off. The allowance method is used.
   (5) An account written off three years ago is paid in full in the amount of $85. The allowance method is used.
   (6) An account for $640 is determined to be uncollectible. Record the writeoff by the direct method.
   (7) Cash is received in payment of an invoice showing $14,000 for merchandise plus $420 for sales tax. It is subject to a freight allowance of $200 and to a cash discount of 1 percent. Record the receipt; the discount is properly taken.

(8) A year ago an account for $525 was written off by the direct writeoff method. A check is received for the whole amount. Record the receipt.

(9) At the end of the year the accounts are aged. Of the total, $9,600 are found to be over ninety days past due; $17,200 are sixty to ninety days past due, and $36,000 are thirty to sixty days past due. It is decided that the allowance for doubtful accounts should cover 60 percent of the balances over ninety days past due, 30 percent of those sixty to ninety days past due, and 10 percent of those thirty to sixty days past due. The allowance now has a credit balance of $8,000. Give any adjusting entry needed.

9.2 Prepare an aging at June 30, 1966, of the accounts of Andale Feed Co. and Ulysses, Inc., using the same periods as those in the illustration on page 288. Terms given by the seller are 1/10 n/30.

	Andale Feed Co.					Ulysses, Inc.			
Date	Explanation	Debit	Credit	Bal.	Date	Explanation	Debit	Credit	Bal.
1966					1966				
Jan. 1	Balance			80 60	Jan. 1	Balance			144 00
14		92 00		172 60	20		132 00		276 00
Feb. 9			80 60	92 00	30		80 00		356 00
25		64 00		156 00	Feb. 8			200 00	156 00
Mar. 8		52 00		208 00	27		110 00		266 00
24		75 00		283 00	Mar. 4			200 00	66 00
31			116 00	167 00	17		196 00		262 00
Apr. 11		88 00		255 00	31		144 00		406 00
28		61 00		316 00	Apr. 15		96 00		502 00
May 12		80 00		396 00	22			400 00	102 00
27			141 00	255 00	May 5		158 00		260 00
June 10		130 00		385 00	20		168 00		428 00
25		38 00		423 00	June 3		90 00		518 00
					24		115 00		633 00

9.3 Triton Products, located in San Francisco, is a wholesale distributor of hardware, housewares, sporting goods, and electrical appliances. During November and December of 1966 it completed the following transactions relating to accounts receivable.

Nov. 1 Sold merchandise to Giant Value Stores, Inc., of St. Louis for $3,000; terms 2/10 n/30, f.o.b. destination. (By agreement, Giant Value will pay the freight bill and deduct it from the invoice.)

7 Sold merchandise to Redi-Wares Co. of Seattle for $6,000; terms 5/10 n/30, f.o.b. shipping point. As a convenience for the buyer, Triton prepaid the freight of $300 and added it to the invoice.

9 Received from Giant Value a check accompanied by a $200 freight bill, in full of November 1 invoice.

10 Sold merchandise of $5,000 plus 4 percent sales tax to Basic Homes, Ltd., of Los Angeles; terms 5/10 e.o.m.

11 Issued a credit memo to Redi-Wares for $1,000, the invoice price of merchandise returned.

16 Received a check from Redi-Wares in full of account.

20 Wrote off San Pablo Sales Co. account of $1,200.

30 Estimated November bad debts at ½ percent of sales net of returns (sales discounts are not deducted in computing the estimated bad debts).

Dec. 9 Received a check from Basic Homes in full of account.
     12 Received $1,000 cash from the creditors committee for Norman Metals Products Co., a customer whose account had been written off. The enclosed notification stated that the entire amount of $2,500 originally due will be paid as assets are realized.
     14 Sold merchandise to Giant Value, $4,000; terms 2/10 e.o.m., f.o.b. destination.
     16 Sold merchandise to Redi-Wares, $8,000; terms 5/10 n/30.
     23 Received a check from Giant Value less discount and $250 freight allowed.
     26 Received a check from Redi-Wares for $3,800 to apply on account. The company's policy is to allow discounts on customers' partial payments.
     31 Adjusted Allowance for Doubtful Accounts to a balance of $4,000; the balance on November 1 was $2,000.

Prepare journal entries to record the above transactions. The company records sales discounts when checks are received.

9.4 Norsco, in business for four years, has used the direct writeoff method for bad debts. The following statistics are available.

Year	Sales	Accounts Written Off and Year of Sale			Recoveries and Year of Sale
1963	$ 50,000	1963 – $500			
1964	200,000	1963 – $2,000	1964 – $2,000		1963 – $100
1965	250,000	1963 – $600	1964 – $7,000	1965 – $2,200	1964 – $500
1966	500,000	1964 – $3,500	1965 – $4,600	1966 – $5,000	1965 – $800

An aging of accounts receivable at December 31, 1966, indicates additional losses as follows:

	Accounts Receivable	Estimated Loss
1965 sales................	$ 20,000	$ 4,000
1966....................	180,000	20,000
	$200,000	$24,000

Required:

1. Prepare a schedule showing sales and net losses by year of sale. Compute the rate of net loss to sales, using the aggregate data for the four-year period.
2. Prepare an adjusting entry to set up the Allowance for Doubtful Accounts at December 31, 1966, charging Retained Earnings for the loss attributable to sales prior to 1966.

9.5 Following are the trial balance of a hardware supply company and data for adjustments for the eleven months ended November 30, 1966. The accounts were last adjusted at December 31, 1965. Prepare working papers.

CRANE SUPPLY COMPANY
ELEVEN MONTHS ENDED NOVEMBER 30, 1966

Cash in Bank	$ 6,641	
Accounts Receivable	5,400	
Allowance for Doubtful Accounts		$ 72
Allowance for Sales Discounts	630	
Merchandise Inventory	6,928	
Prepaid Advertising	120	
Unexpired Insurance	360	
Supplies on Hand	—	
Furniture and Fixtures	3,000	
Accrued Depreciation—Furn. and Fixt.		800
Notes Payable		5,000
Accounts Payable		622
Advances from Customers		—
Interest Payable		—
Sales Tax Payable		206
Payroll Taxes Payable		180
Contracts Payable		1,945
J. L. Crane, Capital		9,735
Sales		44,078
Bad Debts	—	
Sales Discounts	—	
Purchases	29,052	
Freight In	1,220	
Cost of Sales	—	
Advertising	136	
Depreciation	—	
Insurance	—	
Rent	2,200	
Salaries	5,600	
Supplies	508	
Repairs	103	
Taxes	179	
Utilities	460	
Unclassified	21	
Interest Expense	80	
	$62,638	$62,638

Data for adjustments:

(1) The balance of the Sales Tax Payable account represents the actual sales tax collected on charge sales for the past two months of the current quarter. An analysis of the Sales account reveals the following data for the past two months:

Charge sales:		
Sales for resale—nontaxable		$15,000
Taxable sales:		
City		4,200
Out of city		2,000
Cash sales plus tax (at $3\frac{1}{2}\%$)		2,277
Total		$23,477

The state sales tax rate is 3 percent on all sales less exempt items; the city levies an additional ½ percent tax on city sales. The company credits Sales for the revenue from charge sales and credits the tax to Sales Tax Payable; but on cash sales the total sales plus tax is credited to Sales and adjusted when necessary.

(2) Bad debts are estimated at 2 percent of sales, before deduction for sales discounts.

(3) An analysis of the accounts receivable ledger at November 30, 1966, discloses the following:

$$\begin{array}{lr}
\text{Customers' debit balances} & \$8,000 \\
\text{Customers' credit balances — advances} & 3,100 \\
\text{Net} & \$4,900
\end{array}$$

The difference between the subsidiary and the control represents an account sent to the attorney for collection, which should have been removed from the control at November 30.

(4) It is anticipated that all customers will pay within the discount period, taking their 5 percent cash discount. All these accounts arose from sales exempt from sales taxes.

(5) The estimated inventory of merchandise on hand at November 30 is $7,000.

(6) Depreciation is taken on furniture and fixtures at 10 percent a year. An analysis of the Furniture and Fixtures account discloses that the balance of the account at January 1, 1966, was $1,800, and an addition costing $1,200 was made on July 1, 1966.

(7) The balance of the Prepaid Advertising account represents the cost of a 6-month contract with radio station KSMO for spot commercials beginning November 1, 1966.

(8) The Unexpired Insurance account represents a 2-year premium on a single policy dated May 1, 1966.

(9) The balance of Notes Payable represents a single 3-month note dated October 1, bearing 6 percent interest.

(10) Supplies on hand November 30 are $208.

9.6 The Bruxton Printing Company is a proprietorship owned by Robert Bruxton, who asks you to prepare interim financial statements for the six months ended June 30, 1966. He provides the following schedule:

	January 1, 1966	June 30, 1966
Cash	$ 1,650	$ 2,039
Note Receivable	0	600
Accounts Receivable	1,300	1,700
Inventory	2,370	3,140
Prepaid Insurance	315	?
Equipment (original cost)	8,600	10,200
Total Assets	$14,235	$?
Accounts Payable	$ 890	$ 1,100
Accrued Expenses	55	100
Total Liabilities	$ 945	$ 1,200

You are able to accumulate the following information:

(1) The cash balance of $2,039 was taken from the bank statement. The checkbook reveals the following:

Deposits:

Collections from customers $25,385
Loan from bank ($2,000 4-month note due September
    30, 1966, with interest at 6% per annum) 2,000
        $27,385

Withdrawals:

Payments to suppliers $20,996
Insurance premiums   264
Purchases of equipment 1,600
Withdrawn by Bruxton 2,700
Miscellaneous expenses 1,436
        $26,996

(2) A check for $450 was received from a customer on June 30, 1966, and mailed to the bank on that day. The payment was deducted from the accounts receivable as of June 30 but was not recorded in the checkbook or by the bank until July 2.

(3) The note receivable is a 6 percent note due on September 1. It was accepted on May 1 from a delinquent account receivable.

(4) New equipment costing $1,600 was installed on April 1. The equipment on hand at January 1, 1966, was purchased on that date; prior to that time all machinery was rented. Equipment has an estimated life of ten years and zero salvage value.

(5) An examination of insurance policies reveals the following:

Policy No.	Acquired	Term (years)	Premium	Unexpired Dec. 31, 1965
2479	Jan. 1, 1965	3	$360	$240
C2160	June 1, 1965	1	180	75
831	Apr. 1, 1966	1	72	
C2380	June 1, 1966	1	192	
			$804	$315

(6) The accrued expenses are miscellaneous public utility charges, which you verify to be $100 at June 30.

(7) The June 30, 1966, accounts receivable includes an account for $150 known to be uncollectible. In addition, 10 percent of the balance are doubtful.

Required:

Prepare a work sheet showing:

1. Beginning balance sheet accounts
2. Adjustments to the beginning balance sheet
3. Cash transactions for the six months ended June 30, 1966
4. The financial position of the company at June 30, 1966
5. The results of the company's operations for the six months then ended on an accrual basis

(AICPA — adapted)

9.7 The Conroy Company is exploring the possibility of increasing its net income by extending credit to concerns considered somewhat risky. Its survey shows that an additional $200,000 of sales could be made per year if this business was accepted, but that 34 percent of it would turn out to be uncollectible, on the average. The additional cost of goods sold involved would be $112,000; additional costs of $10,000 for delivery and $14,000 for postage, clerical work, and miscellaneous items would also be incurred. In the past the company has incurred fixed costs equal to 10 percent of sales.

Would the company increase or decrease its net income before income taxes by accepting this additional business? How much would income before taxes be increased or decreased?

10

Merchandise Inventory

Merchandise inventory is often the largest asset a business has, except for land, buildings, and equipment. It is subject to physical decay and damage, to declines in value because of changing market conditions, and to theft. It therefore requires careful control if needed goods are to be on hand in good condition when they are required and if excessive stocks are to be avoided. Furthermore, different methods of pricing inventory have different effects on the net income figure arrived at for the period. Since inventory is a large asset, this effect may be large. This chapter is concerned with the basic accounting records and procedures by which inventory is controlled, with the pricing methods that may be used for it, with internal control for it beyond the basic accounting records, and with the management problem of determining how much of each kind of stock to be bought and to be kept on hand.

PERIODIC INVENTORY

The simplest accounting procedure for merchandise inventory is the periodic inventory method. This consists, first, of counting and listing each item of stock, pricing the items, multiplying quantities by prices ("extending"), and adding the extensions to get the inventory figure. Secondly, the figure is recorded by an adjusting entry. The entries to record cost of goods sold by this method, given previously, and assuming that no Cost of Goods Sold account is desired, are again illustrated by the transactions of the Raymond Company for 1966. The company had an inventory on January 1, 1966, of $18,200; it had purchases during the year of $67,500, with no returns, allowances, discount, or other adjustments; it had $17,600 of merchandise on hand at December 31, 1966. Its entries for these figures at December 31, 1966 are:

Profit and Loss..............................	$18,200.00	
Merchandise Inventory...................		$18,200.00
(to close opening inventory to Profit and Loss)		
Profit and Loss..............................	$67,500.00	
Purchases............................		$67,500.00
(to close Purchases to Profit and Loss)		
Merchandise Inventory.........................	$17,600.00	
Profit and Loss.......................		$17,600.00
(to record Dec. 31, 1966 inventory)		

These entries result in a net figure of $68,100 in the Profit and Loss account for cost of goods sold. If there had been any returns and allowances, freight in, or purchases discount, they would have been closed to Profit and Loss along with the Purchases figure. If the company had desired, it might have used a Cost of Goods Sold account to accumulate this information and then have closed out that account to Profit and Loss. This procedure is commonly carried out once a year but may be done more often if accurate statements are desired more often.

PRICING PERIODIC INVENTORY

The primary basis for pricing inventory is cost, and this section is concerned with the determination of cost in a periodic inventory. The problem arises because different lots of goods are frequently purchased at different prices. Four methods of determining the particular cost prices to be placed on the inventory are described in the following sections:

1. Identified-unit cost
2. First-in, first-out (*fifo*)
3. Last-in, first-out (*lifo*)
4. Average cost

IDENTIFIED-UNIT COST

An inventory for a particular item may be priced at the specific amount paid for that item. This procedure requires some means of identifying the price of the item, and is called the method of identified-unit cost. It can be used easily where each item is unique, as in an inventory of fine gem stones kept in separate envelopes with separate identifying numbers. It can be done easily when units of merchandise are tagged, as in a furniture store or a dress shop. It is not practical where units of merchandise are intermingled and lose their identity, as in the case of wheat in a single elevator bin. The method is ordinarily used only in the special cases where the units of merchandise are unique or at least quite distinct from each other.

FIRST-IN, FIRST-OUT

First-in, first-out is a very popular method of assigning cost prices to units of inventory. It is based on the assumption that the first units received are the first ones used and that the ones still on hand are the last ones received. The assumption does not have to be true as a physical fact, but most concerns try to handle their merchandise in this way to avoid deterioration of the older portions. In applying the method in a periodic inventory procedure, the accountant looks up the invoices for purchases of a particular item—say commercial-grade Douglas fir 2 × 4's—and works back until he has invoices for a sufficient quantity to cover the inventory. For example, suppose that there are 64,800 board feet[1] of this material on hand. Assume that the following purchases, at various prices per thousand board feet, were made during the year:

---

[1] A board foot of lumber is one square foot one inch thick. It is measured when the lumber is in the rough state (sawed but not planed). Various actual dimensions are translated into this unit.

	Board Feet	Price per M	
Feb. 3	16,400	$105.00	$ 1,722.00
April 22	18,000	103.00	1,854.00
July 19	19,000	102.00	1,938.00
Oct. 14	23,000	100.00	2,300.00
Nov. 7	18,500	98.00	1,813.00
Nov. 24	21,000	96.00	2,016.00
Dec. 19	20,000	99.00	1,980.00
Totals	135,900		$13,623.00

The inventory is then priced on a first-in, first-out basis as follows:

From the purchase of:	Units	Price	Amount
Dec. 19	20 M	$ 99.00	$1,980.00
Nov. 24	21 M	96.00	2,016.00
Nov. 7	18.5M	98.00	1,813.00
Oct. 14	5.3M	100.00	530.00
Total inventory	64.8M		$6,339.00

LAST-IN, FIRST-OUT

The method of last-in, first-out may be said to proceed on the assumption that the last units received are always the first ones used. This assumption almost never corresponds with the physical facts, and the real purpose of the method is to match recent purchase prices with current revenue in the income statement. The method is ordinarily applied on an annual basis. If the inventory quantity is larger at the end of the year, the first units received during the year are taken as the addition to the beginning inventory to get the ending inventory. If the ending inventory quantity is smaller than the beginning, the last units added to the beginning inventory in a prior year are assumed to be the ones used. For example, assume that the January 1, 1966 inventory of Douglas fir 2 × 4's of the company whose purchases are listed in the preceding paragraph had an opening inventory of 49,000 units, made up on a last-in, first-out basis as follows:

Date Purchased	Units	Price	Amount
April 18, 1954	32M	$40.00	$1,280.00
May 16, 1959	8M	60.00	480.00
July 10, 1963	4M	80.00	320.00
Jan. 16, 1964	5M	95.00	475.00
Total inventory	49M		$2,555.00

Assume that the inventory at December 31, 1966, contains 64,800 board feet. It would be priced on a last-in, first-out basis as follows:

Balance from Jan. 1, 1966 inventory.....................49.0M	$2,555.00
Add—increase in quantity during the year, at $105.........15.8M	1,659.00
Inventory Dec. 31, 1966................................64.8M	$4,214.00

The addition is priced as if it came from the earliest acquisition of the year, that is, February 3. As a result, the other 0.6M board feet purchased on that date and all the remaining purchases of the year go into cost of goods sold for the year. If the ending inventory had been smaller than the beginning inventory, the reduction would have been made from the lot purchased January 16, 1964, until it was exhausted, then from the lot purchased July 10, 1963, and so on.

AVERAGE COST

An average cost method may be used with a periodic inventory, but is much less often used for this kind of inventory than for a perpetual inventory. There is more than one way to compute an average. A common one is computed by taking the weighted average of the cost of the units in the beginning inventory and the purchases for the year. Assume that the January 1, 1966, inventory of the concern whose figures are given in the two preceding paragraphs (computed on an average cost basis) was 49,000 board feet at $100 per thousand, or $4,900. The purchases for the year were as given above. The ending inventory of 64,800 board feet is priced on an average cost basis as follows:

49,000 BF	$ 4,900
135,900 BF	13,623
184,900 BF	$18,523

The average cost is thus

$$\frac{\$18,523}{184.9} = \$100.18 \text{ per 1,000 board feet}$$

and the ending inventory is then

$$64.8 \times \$100.18 = \$6,491.66$$

PERPETUAL INVENTORY METHOD

The perpetual inventory method records purchases and issues currently so that the quantity and dollar amount of goods on hand are continuously shown. The entries in general journal form to record the transactions under this method are:

```
Merchandise . . . . . . . . . . . . . . . . . . . . . . . . . . . . . .$18,000.00
        Accounts Payable (or Vouchers Payable or
            Cash, etc.) . . . . . . . . . . . . . . . . . . . . . . .              $18,000.00
        (purchases—recorded in purchases book or simi-
        lar journal)


Profit and Loss (or Cost of Goods Sold) . . . . . . . . . . .$14,000.00
        Merchandise. . . . . . . . . . . . . . . . . . . . . . . . . .              $14,000.00
        (cost of goods sold—recorded in general journal)
```

Any purchase adjustments are entered directly to the Merchandise account. For example, a return of $40 is recorded by this entry:

Accounts Payable (or Vouchers Payable, etc.) . . . . . . $ 40.00
            Merchandise . . . . $ 40.00
        (recorded in general journal)

Because of the inconvenience of changing unit prices, which are needed in a perpetual inventory account, any cash discount should be deducted before the purchase entry is made.

In any but the simplest perpetual inventory systems a subsidiary ledger is needed to record the transactions in each separate item of stock. The Merchandise account in the general ledger is the control account. The subsidiary ledger is often called a *stores ledger*. Debit postings to the stores ledger are made from suppliers' invoices or the related receiving reports. Credit postings are made from copies of the sellers' invoices or from requisition slips by which stock is withdrawn. Special transactions are posted from the general journal. The problem of determining the cost price of the units in inventory exists in the perpetual inventory exactly as in the periodic inventory. Since the procedure in keeping a stores ledger account varies somewhat according to the pricing method used, the procedure is illustrated separately for the first-in, first-out and for an average cost method below.

STORES LEDGER ACCOUNT ON A FIRST-IN, FIRST-OUT BASIS

An example of a stores ledger account kept on the first-in, first-out basis is shown in the accompanying illustration.

STORES LEDGER ACCOUNT ON A FIRST-IN, FIRST-OUT BASIS

Date	√	Received			Issued			Balance		
		Units	Price	Amount	Units	Price	Amount	Units	Price	Amount
1966										
Jan. 2								400	1.00	400 00
4		200	1.01	202 00				600		602 00
12		150	1.02	153 00				750		755 00
15					280	1.00	280 00	470		475 00
19					120	1.00 }	200 80	270		274 20
					80	1.01 }				
21					75	1.01	75 75	195		198 45
25		300	1.03	309 00				495		507 45
27					45	1.01 }	101 55	395		405 90
					55	1.02 }				
29					50	1.02	51 00	345		354 90

The transactions recorded in the account are the following:

```
Balance:
    Jan.  1, 1966      400 units at $1.00 = $400.00
Receipts:
    Jan.  4            200 units at $1.01
          12           150          1.02
          25           300          1.03

Issues:
    Jan. 15            280 units
          19           200   "
          21            75   "
          27           100   "
          29            50   "
```

Note that the price in the opening balance is used until the quantity in that balance is used up, and so on through each lot received. Note also that an issue must sometimes be priced in two or more parts according to the number of lots it is drawn from. When this method is used, the amount in the balance can be identified as consisting of certain lots. The balance of $354.90 in the example is accounted for as follows:

```
Received Jan. 25     300 at $1.03 = $309.00
Received Jan. 12      45 at  1.02 =   45.90
     Totals          345             $354.90
```

The 45 units in the balance are all that remain of the lot of 150 received on January 12; the others were issued on January 29 (50 units) and on January 27 (55 units). This analysis of the balance of units on hand gives an easy way to find the lot from which the next issue is to be taken: simply go back through the last receipts until they provide enough units to cover the balance. Another method is to check off the receipts as they are issued; in this case it will be convenient to write in the check column the number issued when only part of a lot is issued.

STORES LEDGER ACCOUNT ON AN AVERAGE COST BASIS

The second stores ledger account illustrated here shows the account kept on a commonly used average cost basis. A running average is used; each time a new lot is received it is averaged in with the balance previously on hand and a new price for the new balance is calculated. This price is used for all issues until a new lot is received at a different price, at which time the averaging process is repeated. The amount of the balance may be checked at any time by multiplying the quantity by the price. This computation is likely to be a few cents off, because the unit prices cannot be conveniently carried to enough places to give accuracy to the cent. In the average cost example shown, the multiplication of 345 units by the price of $1.0208 gives $352.18. The difference between this and the figure of $352.20 obtained in the account by subtraction is due to dropping small fractions. The average cost method gives results like those of the first-in, first-out method, except that the changes do not occur as fast. In other words, inventory figures follow price trends with some holding back due to the averaging process.

STORES LEDGER ACCOUNT ON AN AVERAGE-COST BASIS

Date		Received			Issued			Balance		
		Units	Price	Amount	Units	Price	Amount	Units	Price	Amount
1966										
Jan.	1							400	1.0000	400 00
	4	200	1.010	202 00				600	1.0033	602 00
	12	150	1.020	153 00				750	1.0066	755 00
	15				280	1.0066	281 85	470	1.0066	473 15
	19				200	1.0066	201 33	270	1.0066	271 82
	21				75	1.0066	75 50	195	1.0066	196 32
	25	300	1.03	309 00				495	1.0208	505 32
	27				100	1.0208	102 08	395	1.0208	403 24
	29				50	1.0208	51 04	345	1.0208	352 20

OTHER METHODS FOR STORES LEDGER ACCOUNTS

Although identified-unit cost may be used in stores ledger accounts, it is not done often. Last-in, first-out can be applied to a stores ledger account but is not applied, because it tends to defeat the purpose of the method. The purpose is to take *all* the latest receipts of the year into the cost of goods sold for the year. If the method is applied in a stores ledger account and a new receipt comes in before an older one is used up, the next issue would come out of the new receipt. This issue might leave a part of the older receipt in the account permanently, and the same thing could happen several times a year. The ending balance would then include parts of various lots received during the year, but the object of lifo is to make additions to the inventory, if any are required, only from the first receipts of the period. Concerns that wish to use the superior control offered by a stores ledger system and also to use last-in, first-out as a basis for calculating cost of goods sold do one of two things. They may keep the stores ledger accounts by one of the other methods and adjust the control figure to a last-in, first-out basis at the end of the year without changing the stores accounts, the adjustment being reversed at the beginning of the next year. Or they may keep stores accounts in units but not in dollars. In either case the ending inventory figure is calculated as it is in the periodic inventory method.

ADVANTAGES OF PERPETUAL INVENTORY

A perpetual inventory permits the preparation of financial statements at any time without the trouble and expense of a physical inventory. It is a superior control device in three respects:

1. Knowing the quantities on hand at all times permits more accurate planning and a smaller investment in inventory.

2. Having a record of what is supposed to be on hand permits disclosure of theft or improper handling. Even though a perpetual inventory is kept, it is necessary to count the stock physically from time to time. Any discrepancy between the actual quantity of an item on hand and the record of what should be on hand can be investigated and needed action taken.

3. Physical inventory may be taken more easily and economically. As was noted in the preceding paragraph, a physical check cannot be dispensed with entirely, even when perpetual records are used. However, when a perpetual inventory is maintained, the work of taking a physical inventory may be done in installments at intervals. This is possible because the perpetual inventory shows what should be on hand for each item, so a few items may be counted when it is convenient to do so, and the record can be adjusted for the items counted without regard to the others. A count is not needed in order to prepare financial statements, since the perpetual records give the required figures. Incidentally, any discrepancy is adjusted by changing the record, as the physical facts cannot usually be changed. For example, if a store finds that the physical inventory is short of the book record by thirty dresses at $5.60 each, this entry would be made:

Dr. Inventory Shrinkage (or Cost of Goods Sold)............$168.00
    Cr. Merchandise................................ $168.00

INVENTORY PRICING IN GENERAL

The foregoing sections have described methods of determining the particular costs to be used when cost is the basis for the final inventory figure. We shall now summarize the effects on net income given by the different cost methods, and point out the generally accepted methods of inventory pricing that depart from cost. The process of determining what figure shall be used for an asset, as noted in the chapter on Accounts Receivable, is referred to as *valuation* of the asset. It must be remembered that accounting valuation is not a market valuation but a selection of accounting principles appropriate to the particular asset and their application.

SUMMARY OF EFFECTS OF DIFFERENT COST METHODS OF INVENTORY PRICING

If prices were always perfectly stable, there would, of course, be no difference in the effects of the several cost methods of inventory pricing. Since prices change — sometimes radically — the effects of the different methods on the figures for ending inventory, net income, and cost of goods sold are different. A table lists the effects of fifo, average cost, and lifo on these figures.

It is possible to get mixed effects when prices change direction. First-in, first-out and average cost are the older methods. Last-in, first-out came into prominence in the United States in the 1930's. At that time concerns in some lines of trade, particularly mining and ore processing, had wide swings in profits as selling prices changed. On a first-in, first-out basis the costs of goods sold would be high for a while after sales revenue dropped, and a large loss would appear. The reverse happened as prices rose. The result was that income taxes were levied on the profits with no compensating refund for the losses, so that, over a period of years, companies with this pattern of profits paid a higher per-

EFFECTS OF DIFFERENT COST METHODS OF INVENTORY PRICING

Cost Method	Figures Affected	Effect under Different Price Movements[a]	
		Rising Prices	Falling Prices
First-in, first-out	Ending inventory and net income Cost of goods sold	Highest Lowest	Lowest Highest
Average cost	Ending inventory and net income Cost of goods sold	High Low	Low High
Last-in, first-out	Ending inventory and net income Cost of goods sold	Lowest Highest	Highest Lowest

[a] Assumes that the method was started when prices were moving in the direction indicated, and that they have contined in that direction.

cent of tax than those with steady profits. Last-in, first-out was devised to match current acquisition costs with current sales revenue. It has the effect of smoothing out profits, provided that prices do not change direction suddenly and violently and that the level of inventory does not change greatly.

Since the 1930's the United States income tax laws have been changed to permit the carry-forward and carry-back of corporate losses for a limited period of years. These permit losses in one period to deducted from profits in another, thus reducing the tax or even resulting in a refund of past tax. Carry-forward and carry-back remove some of the incentive for last-in, first-out, but lifo still has some advantage in reducing a current profit and thus postponing indefinitely a certain amount of income tax. It has therefore increased in popularity and is used even by department stores. It has the disadvantage of showing a very outdated inventory figure on the balance sheet. Many accountants dislike last-in, first-out on the grounds that it does not put the flow of costs through the accounts in the way that the physical goods flow through the concern, but accountants and businessmen use it for its tax advantages.

INVENTORY PRICING THAT DEPARTS FROM THE COST BASIS

There are two situations in which departures are commonly made from the cost basis of inventory pricing: when a specially organized market virtually eliminates the selling problem and when there is evidence that the earning power of inventory has declined. The former situation is discussed below under the heading Market Price Method and the latter under the heading Cost or Market, Whichever Is Lower.

MARKET PRICE METHOD

The selling problem is eliminated in the markets for many farm products, such as wheat and cattle. These products are traded on highly organized markets; prices are quoted hourly; a producer needs only to haul his cattle or wheat to the nearest dealer to get the published market price. Like the producers, the dealers who handle grain can always sell it at the current market quotation. A similar situation exists in the production of gold. Under United States law the use of gold is controlled by the federal government. In connection with this regulation the government fixes the price of gold and agrees to take all that is produced and to pay the established price. The producer therefore has only to get the gold to the government's receiving office; once he has produced it he has, for all practical purposes, earned his profit.

Some other basic commodities are handled on the same basis. In these circumstances market prices are used for inventories. This method has the effect of taking into account, before the product is actually sold, any profit earned by producing or handling it; but the evidence that the profit has been effectively earned is so strong that an actual sale is not required to prove it. The method also takes into account any loss created by market forces. Market price valuation could not be applied in the production or distribution of dresses; no one is sure that a profit will be earned on them until they are sold — the trade may not like the style and no profit may be earned.

Products inventoried at market may be recorded by means of the same entries and accounts as are periodic cost basis inventories. The inventory is simply priced at the market quotation less any delivery expense. It then reduces the cost of goods sold more than a cost basis inventory would do and so makes the net income for the period higher. Many concerns that have inventories priced at market use a "merchandising" account. This is an account in which all sales and all figures for cost of goods sold are entered. Purchases, purchase adjustments, and beginning and ending inventories go into it, as they would in a Cost of Goods Sold account. The balance of the account is merchandising profit, which corresponds to gross margin on sales except that gain or loss on the market value of inventories is also included.

COST OR MARKET, WHICHEVER IS LOWER

A traditionally popular method of inventory pricing is to compare the actual cost and the replacement cost or "market" price of each item, then use the lower one as the inventory price of that item. Some units accordingly are taken at cost and some at market. The market price referred to here is a replacement or purchase cost price, not the price in the market in which the unit will be sold. It is therefore not the market price of the market price method. The purpose of the cost-or-market method is to recognize declines in the earning power of the merchandise. It records the loss in the period in which the market forces that bring it about are operating. The effect is to give a better picture of the results of each period. The cost-or-market method may also be applied group by group or on an over-all basis rather than item by item. Determination of the amount of an inventory by the cost-or-market method is illustrated on page 317 for a part of the inventory of a shoe store. The illustration shows the item by item, group by group, and over-all methods for the same inventory.

MODERN APPLICATION OF THE COST-OR-MARKET RULE

The cost-or-market rule has been used somewhat indiscriminately in the past. At present there is more inclination to apply it only where its purpose is served by the application. For example, a manufacturing concern may use a small quantity of copper in its product. If the market for copper declines so the copper on hand could be replaced at a lower price, some would apply the cost-or-market rule to the inventory of copper. But if the price of the concern's finished product and its opportunity to use the copper in earning its income are not affected, there is no need to apply the rule and it is not appropriate to do so. The rule was devised on the assumption that a decline in replacement cost would be accompanied by a decline in the selling price of the product. This is true of most merchandising businesses; competition causes sales prices to follow purchase prices. If the assumption is not correct for a given case, the rule should not be followed.

THREE APPLICATIONS OF THE COST-OR-MARKET METHOD

Item-by-item application:

Item	Quantity	Price Cost	Price Market	Lower	Inventory Amount
Style 482	10	$5.00	$4.00	$ 4.00	$ 40.00
Style 467	18	6.00	5.00	5.00	90.00
Style 428	24	7.50	8.00	7.50	180.00
Style 431	26	6.10	6.15	6.10	158.60
Style 318	13	8.00	8.50	8.00	104.00
					$572.60

Group-by-group application:

Item	Quantity	Price Cost	Price Market	Amount Cost	Amount Market	Inventory
Street shoes						
Style 482	10	$5.00	$4.00	$ 50.00	$ 40.00	
Style 467	18	6.00	5.00	108.00	90.00	
Style 428	24	7.50	8.00	180.00	192.00	
				$338.00	$322.00	$322.00
High-style shoes						
Style 431	26	6.10	6.15	$159.90	$158.60	
Style 318	13	8.00	8.50	104.00	110.50	
				$263.90	$268.60	263.90
						$585.90

Over-all application:

Item	Quantity	Price Cost	Price Market	Amount Cost	Amount Market	Inventory
Style 482	10	$5.00	$4.00	$ 50.00	$ 40.00	
Style 467	18	6.00	5.00	108.00	90.00	
Style 428	24	7.50	8.00	180.00	192.00	
Style 431	26	6.10	6.15	159.90	158.60	
Style 318	13	8.00	8.50	104.00	110.50	
				$601.90	$591.10	$591.10

The traditional rule is modified in another respect in modern usage. The choice now is not simply between cost price or replacement cost price. The choice is a range of prices. The highest acceptable price is the selling price of the goods less any direct cost of selling, if that price is lower than original cost. The lowest acceptable price is the sales price less the normal gross margin. The use of this price permits a partial decline in earning power to be recognized. For example, goods costing $200 and normally selling for $300 become available at $100. They can now be sold for $250. It is necessary to price the inventory no lower than $150, since the normal gross margin will be realized on this figure.

APPRAISAL OF THE COST-OR-MARKET RULE

Some accountants prefer to recognize net income of a period only by comparing the sales and cost price of each unit sold in the period, less expenses incurred. They cannot, of course, insist on this comparison for items that are never sold but have to be given away or thrown away. The question then is, what evidence should be taken into account in determining the net income of a period? The cost-or-market rule reflects loss of earning power as indicated by reduced prices in the period in which the decline appears. It has the advantage or preventing some manipulation of results by managers who might postpone disposing of a stock of goods on which a loss would have to be taken, since it does not require a sale to record the loss. It also has the advantage of showing the loss in the period in which the determining forces are operating and thus improving appraisal of the performances of different periods. It might be that different managers were in charge in different periods; the mistakes of one might be attributed to another if loss of earning power of inventory were not recognized until the goods were sold.

The cost-or-market rule has been criticized for recognizing declines but not increases. This criticism is more applicable to the item-by-item approach than to the group-by-group or over-all approaches. In the latter two, some items in the smaller total will be higher than cost. See, for example, Style 428 in the illustration on page 317. In general, accountants are "conservative" in requiring very strong evidence to justify recognition of an increase in value or an income, while requiring less certain evidence to justify a writedown. This attitude is due in large part to centuries of experience in which business promoters have often been unduly, and sometimes even fraudulently, optimistic about values of business assets. When the evidence is strong enough, as in the case of grain or cattle, accountants have been willing to record increases in value or income before sales are made. It is also true that accountants have refined their concepts increasingly in the last two or three decades and are less inclined than before to be conservative for the sake of conservatism.

With regard to the cost-or-market rule and its modern refinements one more point should be mentioned: When an inventory is "written down" by use of the rule, a part of its cost is normally charged to Cost of Goods Sold. Literally it is not true that this is a cost of goods "sold"; it is a cost associated with keeping goods for sale. If the amount is large it would be better to enter the closing inventory this way:

```
Merchandise Inventory.........................$18,000.00
Decline in Inventory Replacement Cost............  2,000.00
        Cost of Goods Sold (or Profit and Loss)....            $20,000.00
(to  record  closing  inventory  costing  $20,000.00,
priced at $18,000.00)
```

The figures would then be appropriately shown in the income statement as follows:

Sales..		$108,000.00
Less Cost of Goods Sold:		
Inventory Jan. 1............................	$16,500.00	
Purchases—net............................	56,000.00	
	$72,500.00	
Less Inventory Dec. 31 at Cost.................	20,000.00	52,500.00
Gross margin on sales........................		$ 55,500.00
Less Decline in inventory replacement cost...		2,000.00
Gross Margin Less Inventory Decline..........		$ 53,500.00

OTHER INVENTORY METHODS

The amount of an inventory may be obtained by three methods in addition to the periodic physical inventory and the perpetual inventory. These are:

1. By estimate
2. By the gross profit method
3. By the retail inventory method

ESTIMATED INVENTORIES

Estimates may be made in many ways, and some kinds of estimates are often involved in ordinary physical inventory taking. For example, wheat is inventoried by weight (a bushel is defined as 60 pounds). It may have to be "counted," however, by measuring the bin it is in and converting the cubic feet to equivalent pounds, which will vary for different grades. Recently a method of estimating an inventory from a sample of it by means of scientific sampling principles has received prominent use. In this method a sample is planned in accordance with statistical principles to give an estimate within a certain degree of precision, say plus or minus 3 percent, and with a certain degree of confidence, say 95 percent. The latter figure means that the estimate can be expected to be more than 3 percent over or under the actual figure only five times in one hundred. By adjusting the plan one can change these figures. The calculations are based on probability formulas. This procedure should be used only in cooperation with someone well grounded in statistical-sampling principles. Properly used it will save much time and expense in taking large physical inventories.[2]

GROSS PROFITS METHOD

An ending inventory may be computed by the gross profits method, which proceeds on the assumption that the percent (ratio) of gross margin on sales is known. "Gross profit" is an older term for which "gross margin" is now recommended. The method is useful when the inventory is destroyed by fire or otherwise and an estimate of its amount is needed for insurance purposes. It may also be used as a check on other methods. The computation may

---

[2] The principles and formulas involved are described in Vance and Neter, *Statistical Sampling for Auditors and Accountants*, John Wiley & Sons, Inc.

be made by setting up the information for a regular income statement with the figures for ending inventory, cost of goods sold, and gross margin missing. The gross margin is then filled in by applying the given percent to sales, and the remaining figures are computed by working back from gross margin. The following table indicates the steps for a concern that normally sells on a 30 percent gross margin. In this case the inventory was destroyed on March 18.

	Data Available	Gross Margin Calculated	Cost of Goods Sold Calculated	Ending Inventory Calculated
Sales—Net	$9,000	$9,000	$9,000	$9,000
Cost of Goods Sold:				
Inventory Jan. 1	$2,000	$2,000	$2,000	$2,000
Purchases—Net	6,400	6,400	6,400	6,400
	$8,400	$8,400	$8,400	$8,400
Inventory Mar. 18	—	—	—	2,100
Cost of Goods Sold	—	—	6,300	6,300
Gross Margin—30%	—	$2,700	$2,700	$2,700

RETAIL INVENTORY METHOD

This method, also called simply the "retail method," requires a continuous record of purchases and purchase returns and allowances at both cost and selling price. The beginning inventory and each invoice received are entered in a book with columns for these figures. Any increases in prices (markups) or decreases (markdowns) must also be entered. The percent (ratio) of cost to sales price is then computed for the total goods available for sale to any date in the year. The inventory at selling price or at retail can be found by deducting the recorded sales from the total sales value of goods acquired. The inventory at cost can be computed by applying the percent of margin or "markon" to the inventory at selling price. The method is demonstrated by the following calculation:

	Cost	Retail	Percent (Ratio) of Cost to Retail
Inventory Jan. 1..............................	$ 20,000	$ 28,000	
Purchases.....................................	100,000	142,000	
Freight In....................................	6,925	—	
Purchase Returns..............................	(4,000)[a]	(5,500)	
Markups......................................	—	1,200	
Markdowns....................................	—	(1,800)	
Total Goods Available for Sale................	$122,925	$163,900	75
Sales..		146,000	
Inventory at Retail..........................		$ 17,900	
Inventory at Cost (75 percent of Retail).........	$ 13,425		

[a] Parentheses indicate deductions.

The retail method may be handled so as to reduce ending inventory for a decline in earning power. In doing so, it is assumed that normal percents of markon should be earned on all goods and that goods that have to be marked down have lost some of their expected earning power. The normal markon percent is then calculated with the markdowns omitted. This calculation produces a smaller percent (ratio) of cost to selling price and a smaller inventory. As made on the same data used above, it is:

	Cost	Retail	Percent (Ratio) of Cost to Retail
Total Goods Available for Sale, Excluding Markdowns.	$122,925	$165,700	74.2
Sales.		$146,000	
Markdowns.		1,800	
Total Deductions.		$147,800	
Inventory at Retail.		$ 17,900	
Inventory at cost or less (74.2 percent of retail).	$ 13,282		

As the name implies, the retail method was developed for retail stores and is especially popular in department stores and retail chain stores. It gives a book inventory without the detail or expense of a perpetual inventory kept in units and amount for each item of stock. It is also used by some wholesalers. The method must be supplemented with a periodic physical count, as in the case of any book inventory.

INTERNAL CONTROL FOR INVENTORY

Certain organizational arrangements and practices are important in protecting merchandise and the merchandise records from loss due to error, carelessness, or fraud. Devices recommended previously, but important in connection with inventory, are:

1. Use separate departments for warehousing the stock, shipping it, and accounting for it.
2. Separate the handling of merchandise from the handling of cash receipts.
3. Use shipping orders prepared as duplicates of the customer's invoice.
4. Use inventory control; that is, keep records that show what quantities should be on hand (as a perpetual inventory or retail inventory system does).

Additional steps not previously mentioned are:

5. Keep the storeroom under lock and key and have one person responsible for the issuing of merchandise from it.
6. Use cost and ratio analysis as a check on goods used.

In a manufacturing concern the cost per unit of product of different materials can be computed and the result compared with what should be used. In a merchandising or manufacturing concern the ratio of sales to average inventory for a period (sales divided by average inventory) or the percent of gross margin realized can be computed. These figures can be compared with prior experience or with budgets, and differences investigated.

Control procedures to assure an accurate count when a physical inventory is taken require special attention. The following suggestions apply to a complete count of stock. Some of them are equally important in a partial count:

1. Plan the whole process of inventory taking—time to start, personnel to use, assignment of teams to areas, for example.

2. Arrange the stock for counting. This means segregating different items in separate piles or bins, removing junk, marking stock held for others and not the property of the firm, for example.

3. Tag the stock and see that all stock has been tagged. One system provides for entering the count on the tag and leaving it there until the counting is complete. Another provides for placing only the inventory takers' names on the tags to show that they have counted that stock. In this case they record the count on a separate sheet.

4. Prenumber and account for all tags and inventory sheets.

5. Provide for checking the count. Many concerns use two counts, one team counting the stock once and a second team counting it a second time. Simplify comparison of the counts, while preventing the second team from copying the count of the first team. This may be done by using three-copy tags—one copy is brought in by the first team with its count, another is brought in by the second team with its count, and the third remains on the stock as a record of the fact that the lot was counted. Comparison is made still easier when the tag consists of an envelope with a stub. The first team records its count on the stub and seals the stub inside the envelope. The second team records its count on the outside of the envelope. When the envelopes are brought in, no sorting is necessary before the comparison is made.

6. Provide for recording receipts and issues after the count and before the closing time, or, if the count must be made in part after the closing time, for receipts and issues between closing time and the count. This record permits the actual count to be adjusted to bring it up to the exact moment at which the inventory is taken. This information is ordinarily entered on the tags.

7. Supervise the inventory taking. Someone should be available to solve problems as they arise in the counting.

8. Go through the stock before leaving the job to see that all tags indicate that the count has been made.

9. Compare the two counts, if two are made, and re-count any items showing wide discrepancies.

To complete the physical inventory, the counts are finally sorted, listed, priced, extended, and footed.

MANAGEMENT PROBLEMS WITH INVENTORY

Inventory management is of prime importance for many reasons, but for two in particular: (1) excess stocks require an excess capital investment, and are subject to extra losses from deterioration and price changes; (2) an understocked condition can lead to loss of sales and customer good will. The question of what items to stock was briefly considered in the chapter on sales. We are now concerned with the problem of deciding how much stock should be maintained. The next section briefly describes some traditional approaches to this problem, and the succeeding one indicates the kind of solution possible by means of operations research. Both methods depend upon accounting data and techniques.

TRADITIONAL INVENTORY QUANTITY CONTROLS

The controls described in this section are:

1. Inventory purchase budget
2. Stock-to-sales ratios
3. Minimum and maximum levels
4. Turnover ratios

An inventory purchase budget is a plan for purchasing a certain amount of stock in a certain period. It is derived from the sales budget, which gives the amount expected to be sold, and depends upon the amount of inventory the firm wishes to have left on hand at the end of the period. As purchases are made, they are deducted from the budget total; the remainder gives the amount that can still be purchased in the period. In department stores this amount is called "open to buy."

The ratio of stock to sales is obtained by dividing the retail value of the inventory at the beginning by sales for a period (sometimes the ending inventory is used, or the average may be used). It is useful in planning when a complete budget is not made up. For a budget or a less formal plan the *expected* sales are multiplied by the ratio obtained from past experience, and the result gives the amount to buy.

Minimum and maximum levels for various items or groups may be established on the basis of experience and judgment. The inventory is not allowed to fall below the minimum, and if the maximum is reached, no further orders for the item may be placed until the level is worked down. This system usually includes a "reorder" point, a level at which a new order is placed to avoid having the stock fall below the minimum.

A turnover ratio is the number of times the stock is sold during a period. Ideally it would be computed for a particular item by dividing the average inventory of the item into the number of items sold during the period. The average may be computed by adding the beginning inventory to the ending inventory and dividing by 2. Usually the ratio is calculated by dividing the dollar amount of the average inventory into the cost of goods sold. When this ratio is a basis for stock control, the turnover desired is given to the responsible executives as a guide and they are supposed to keep within the limit so established.

OPERATIONS RESEARCH APPROACH TO INVENTORY MANAGEMENT

Operations research techniques apply advanced mathematical methods to operational problems. They are able to take into account many more cost factors than the traditional methods do. They also apply much more sophisticated mathematical tools to the solution of the resulting equations. For example, one application to inventory management takes into account the following costs: carrying costs, costs of new orders, out-of-stock costs, and costs of special expediting of emergency orders.

The carrying costs consist of interest on the investment in stock and the costs of storing it, including insurance and taxes.

Costs of placing new orders are those of the purchasing department and include salaries, supplies, postage, and so on.

Out-of-stock costs are the amounts lost because a sale cannot be made and the cost of disappointing a customer. The latter cost is the only one named that has to be estimated; the others are all obtainable from the accounting records.

The costs of placing emergency orders include the extra expense of long distance telephone and telegraph messages as well as salaries, supplies, and so on.

In this application the mathematics take into consideration the fact that there is variability in the time to receive an order and in the demand for issue of the goods (a "statistical" or probability factor). The equations are solved to give the order quantities and reorder points for each article that would minimize the total annual variable costs.

Once quantitative decision rules have been developed, inventory control becomes a fertile field for the application of electronic data processing. A computer can revise estimates of demand continually based on information about units issued. It can review the status of each item in the inventory and can automatically print out reorder requests. High-speed computers have made possible a complete systems approach to the control of inventories.

SUMMARY

Inventory figures may be obtained for the accounting statements by a periodic inventory that requires a physical count of stock or by a perpetual record that gives a running balance. In either method a choice of means of determining what cost figures to be used must be made. Alternatives include first-in, first-out (fifo), last-in, first-out (lifo), average cost, and identified-unit cost.

Fifo produces the highest inventory amount in periods of rising prices, and lifo the lowest. Lifo tends to smooth out net income, especially where large inventories are carried over long periods when wide swings in prices occur.

Inventory-pricing methods that depart from cost include the market price method used in farming and some other basic industries, and cost or market, whichever is lower. The latter may be applied in different ways; it should not be applied where its purpose would not be served. Its purpose is to reflect in the net income of a period the loss of earning power that occurs then, rather than wait for the goods to be sold.

Inventory figures may also be obtained by estimates, in which case scientific sampling is recommended, or by the gross profit or the retail inventory method.

Internal control for inventory requires the usual departmental segregation of duties and related devices; special attention to control devices is needed in taking physical inventory.

Managements' problem in determining what level of inventory to carry may be approached by traditional or the operations research method.

QUESTIONS

10.1   (1) What are the twin dangers confronting a business from an inventory that is not adequately controlled?

      (2) Wade Corporation is a distributor and processor of cable and related com-

munication products. A major proportion of its capital is invested in inventories. Management is concerned about the proper levels for its various inventories and, as a preliminary step in the analysis of the problem, has tentatively listed the following costs as relevant to the determination of optimum inventory levels:

Holding Costs	*Order Costs*
Obsolescence	Labor and paper cost of
Interest on investment	placing orders
Occupancy cost	Quantity discounts lost on
Personal property taxes	small orders
Insurance	Margin on lost sales
	Airfreight on out-of-stock items
	Loss of customer goodwill

For each item, discuss whether or not the cost would be accumulated in the accounting records. If it would not, indicate how the cost might be estimated.

10.2 (1) Distinguish between periodic inventory and perpetual inventory; indicate the kind of records required for each.
(2) What are three advantages of perpetual inventories?
(3) Why is the last-in, first-out method of inventory pricing generally not applied to a stores ledger account?

10.3 A wholesaler completed the following transactions in an electrical appliance:

1/1	Inventory	100 @	$20 per unit
1/10	Sold	50 @	50 per unit (selling price)
1/20	Purchased	100 @	18 per unit
1/29	Sold	80 @	49 per unit (selling price)

(1) Compute the January 31 inventory under the periodic inventory system by (a) first-in, first-out pricing and (b) last-in, first-out pricing.
(2) Give all journal entries required for the January 29 sale, using fifo under (a) the perpetual inventory system and (b) the periodic inventory system.

10.4 Indicate what pricing method is being used in each of the following cases. All represent procedures used in periodic inventories.
(1) The number of each article is listed on a sheet, and the invoice for it is looked up and the price inserted on the sheet.
(2) The ending inventory quantities are compared with beginning inventory quantities. The increases are priced at the earliest purchases of the year and the ending inventory consists of these plus the beginning inventory figures.
(3) All purchases of each article for the year are added up and the total divided by the number bought. The price thus computed is used in pricing the ending inventory.
(4) Invoices are pulled from the files representing the latest purchases, and the prices on them are used for the inventory.

10.5 Specific identification is sometimes said to be the ideal method for assigning cost to inventory and to cost of goods sold.
(1) List arguments for and against the above statement.
(2) First-in, first-out, weighted average, and last-in, first-out methods are often used instead of specific identification. Compare each of these methods with the specific identification method. Include in your discussion an analysis of the effect of each method on the determination of income and asset valuation.

(AICPA – adapted)

10.6 State how each of the following cost pricing methods, relative to other cost pricing methods, cause the item named to be high, low, highest, or lowest under the general economic conditions indicated.

Method	Economic Condition (movement of prices)	Item Affected
(1) Average cost	Rising	Ending inventory
(2) Lifo	Falling	Cost of goods sold
(3) Fifo	Rising	Net income
(4) Average cost	Falling	Net income
(5) Lifo	Rising	Ending inventory
(6) Fifo	Falling	Cost of goods sold
(7) Average cost	Falling	Cost of goods sold
(8) Fifo	Rising	Ending inventory
(9) Lifo	Rising	Net income

10.7 (1) Under what normal circumstances are accountants willing to use selling prices as the inventory price?
(2) Give examples of this practice.
(3) When is income realized when inventories are valued at selling price? What accounting principle justifies the method of income measurement applied in these circumstances?

10.8 (1) What "market" is referred to by the "cost or market, whichever is lower" inventory pricing method?
(2) Does one apply the cost-or-market rule on an item-by-item basis, a group-by-group basis, or an over-all basis? What is the rationale for each basis?

10.9 Palmer Electric Co. makes electrical home appliances. It has a sizable stock of rheostats on hand at December 31, 1966, purchased at an average cost of 80 cents. A recent price reduction in the electronics industry makes the item replaceable on December 31, 1966, at 75 cents, but the change in the price of rheostats will not change the selling prices or the volume of Palmer Electric products. Assuming that the company believes in the principle of cost or market, what price should it use for rheostats in its December 31, 1966, inventory?

10.10 (1) When the replacement cost of inventory has declined and a loss of revenue on its sale will result, the modern interpretation of the cost-or-market rule permits a writedown within a range of prices, depending upon the circumstances. What is this range?
(2) Indicate the unit inventory price in the following cases according to the modern interpretation of the cost-or-market rule:

	Cases				
	1	2	3	4	5
Cost	$2.00	$2.00	$2.00	$2.00	$2.00
Net realizable value	1.30	2.05	1.80	2.40	1.90
Net realizable value less normal profit	1.10	1.85	1.60	2.20	1.70
Market (replacement cost)	1.20	2.10	1.85	2.15	1.60

10.11 (1) Babar Company completed its first year of business on December 31, 1966. Operations for the year resulted in sales, $200,000; purchases, $140,000; and operating expenses, $100,000. The correct ending inventory is $50,000. Because of an error, this inventory had initially been computed at $60,000. What effect would this error have on the December 31, 1966, balance sheet and the income statement for the year then ended? Prepare a comparative income statement for 1966 showing in adjoining columns the net income resulting from the correct ending inventory and from the overstated one. Assume a combined federal and state income tax rate for 1966 of 30 percent.

(2) Operations of the Babar Company for 1967 resulted in sales, $220,000; purchases, $150,000; and operating expenses, $63,000. The December 31, 1967, inventory is $55,000. Prepare a comparative income statement for 1967 showing the net income, using the correct and overstated January 1, 1967, inventories. Assume a combined federal and state income tax rate for 1967 of 25 percent. Discuss the effect of the inventory error on the aggregate net income for the two-year period 1966-1967.

10.12 (1) The gross profit method of computing a closing inventory depends upon one basic assumption. What is that assumption?

(2) The entire merchandise inventory of the ABC Store was destroyed by fire on October 1, 1966. The following information was taken from accounting records saved from the fire:

	Year Ended December 31			Nine Months Ended
	1963	1964	1965	9/30/66
Net sales....	$600,000	$700,000	$800,000	$500,000
Gross profit..	270,000	315,000	360,000	

Merchandise purchases for the period January 1, 1966, to September 30, 1966, were $350,000. The merchandise inventory at December 31, 1965, was $400,000.

Compute the estimated cost of the merchandise inventory lost in the fire.

10.13 (1) Don Wilson owns three women's clothing stores with diversified stocks. Perpetual inventories would be too expensive because of the large volume of low unit-price merchandise handled. Wilson asks if you can recommend any other kind of inventory control. What is your recommendation? Describe the elements of the system.

(2) Businessmen and accountants commonly wish to reduce the figure for ending inventory below cost if there is evidence that its earning power has declined. What evidence of a decline in earning power is likely to exist in a department store? How can the inventory reduction be made if the retail inventory method is in use?

10.14 Eastern Soya, Inc., purchased merchandise at a cost of $30,000 and sold half of the units purchased for $25,000. The replacement cost of this merchandise declined, so that the value of the remaining half of the units purchased on a cost-or-market basis was only $10,000.

(1) Prepare a comparative income statement showing in adjoining columns the results of operations on a basis of (a) the decline in inventory replacement cost included in cost of goods sold and (b) the decline reported after gross margin.

(2) Compute the percent of gross margin to sales for both alternatives. Discuss.

(3) Give the entry to record cost of goods sold, using a Decline in Inventory Replacement Cost account.

10.15 (1) Suggest internal control devices of use in the day-to-day control of merchandise or supplies.

(2) Discuss control procedures to assure an accurate count when taking a physical inventory.

10.16 When raw materials are ordered by a medium-sized manufacturing concern, a duplicate copy of the purchase order is sent to the receiving department. As materials are received, the receiving clerk checks the quantities against the purchase order copy, initials the quantities as being correct or makes such changes as he finds necessary, and forwards the copy to the accounting department. The copy is compared to the supplier's invoice, which is used only to support the charge to material purchases. As materials are transferred into stores, quantities are recorded on bin cards in the storeroom by the stores clerk.

(1) Point out existing weaknesses in the system of internal control.
(2) Outline the errors or fraudulent manipulation that might arise as a result o
such weaknesses.
(3) Suggest changes that will overcome such weaknesses.

(ICAC — adapted

10.17 (1) List four traditional methods of controlling stock levels. Explain how eacl
operates.
(2) How do operations research techniques improve stock control?
(3) Tropical Industries imports canned pineapple, which it uses in constan
amounts throughout the year in the manufacture of a specialty food product
During 1966, the company used 6,000 cases at an average cost of $10 pe
case. It estimates the cost of placing a purchase order (including clerica
costs, stationery, postage, and incidentals) at $30 per order. Storage (in-
cluding insurance, property taxes, and warehouse rent) has been estimated
at an annual cost of $4 per case.

The following schedule of total costs for various alternative order sizes has been
prepared by management:

Order Size	No. of Orders	Annual Costs		
		Order	*Storage*	*Total*
200	30	$900	$ 400	$1,300
300	20	600	600	1,200
400	15	450	800	1,250
500	12	360	1,000	1,360

The company operates in a rented warehouse. The annual rent for 25,000 square
feet is $100,000, or $4 a square foot. Storage of 1,000 cases requires 500 square
feet of warehouse space. At no time during the past five years has more than 75
percent of the capacity of the area been utilized; and under current plans, apart
from possible use for pineapple, increased utilization in 1967 appears unlikely.
The purchasing agent suggests that the provision in the above tabulation for
storage cost is overstated by the improper inclusion of a charge for rent. He
recommends that rent be eliminated from the storage costs, and that pineapple
be ordered in larger lot sizes than that indicated by the tabulation. Do you agree?
Discuss briefly.

10.18 The management of M Co. is considering expanding the company's warehouse
facilities in order to accommodate a larger stock of the raw material components of its products and thereby to take advantage of quantity discounts offered by suppliers on bulk deliveries. Because of limited storage space at
present, only two weeks' requirements can be kept on hand, and as a result
suppliers deliver weekly. Payments to suppliers are made on the tenth of the
month following delivery.

Discussions with major suppliers have disclosed that a 15 percent contract
quantity discount would be available if materials were purchased in quantities
sufficient to provide for three months' production and if deliveries were made by
suppliers every three months. The raw materials are not perishable, but one
type may require minor processing before use if stored for a long period.

Management estimates that the cost of expanding the facilities to provide
adequate space for taking advantage of the quantity discounts offered by suppliers would be $120,000.

Outline the factors management should consider before making a decision on the
proposed expansion to the warehouse.

(ICAC — adapted)

10.1 On December 31, 1966, Strout and Co., dealers in industrial detergents, completed its first year of business. The results of operations for the year then ended, with the inventory priced at first-in, first-out cost, is presented in the income statement below.

STROUT AND CO.

INCOME STATEMENT

Year Ended December 31, 1966

Sales.		$600,000
Cost of Goods Sold:		
Purchases	$530,000	
Less: Inventory, December 31, 1966 . .	50,000	
Cost of Goods Sold		480,000
Gross Margin on Sales		$120,000
Expenses		90,000
Net Income		$ 30,000

The price of a particular detergent was reduced drastically in late 1966, and management has decided to drop it from the product line. The December 31, 1966, inventory would have been $40,000, valued on a cost-or-market basis because of this price reduction. What would be the effect of using a cost-or-market inventory valuation on net income for 1966 and 1967?

10.2 The B and G Sales Company uses the perpetual inventory system. One Model 360 tape recorder, purchased at a cost of $300, was in the store on December 1; a second Model 360 was purchased at $400 on December 15.

Present journal entries to record the December 20 cash sale of a Model 360 for $500, pricing the cost of goods sold by (1) first-in, first-out and (2) last-in, first-out.

10.3 The inventories and invoices of Associated Wholesalers show the following quantities and prices for cases of Ocean Spray Cranberry Sauce, size 6/10, during 1966:

Date	Quantity	Price
Inventory, 1/1/66	20	$7.00
Purchase, 3/15/66	60	7.50
Purchase, 11/20/66	20	8.00
Inventory, 12/31/66	30	

Compute the extended cost of this item at December 31, 1966, and the cost of goods sold for the year then ended by each of the following methods: first-in, first-out, last-in, first-out, and average cost.

10.4 The January 1 inventory of item X consisted of 400 units at $20 per unit. During the year 600 units were bought at $15. Under three different methods of pricing, the December 31 inventory of 500 units amounted to (1) $9,500, (2) $7,500, and (3) $8,500.

Identify the pricing methods.

10.5 The Clipper Boat inventory at December 31, 1966, consisted of the following items:

	Quantity	Unit Price Cost	Unit Price Market
Motor boats:			
Model No. M 100	10	$ 1,000	$ 800
Model No. M 200	20	12,000	10,000
Sail boats:			
Model No. S 100	10	1,000	800
Model No. S 200	5	15,000	17,500

Compute the inventory at the lower-of-cost-or-market, applying the method on an item-by-item basis, a group-by-group basis, and an over-all basis.

10.6   B Co. began operations January 1, 1965. Sales and purchases for three years are given below, accompanied by closing inventories valued under two alternative bases:

	1965	1966	1967
Sales	$100,000	$120,000	$150,000
Purchases	70,000	82,000	100,000
Inventories, 12/31			
First-in, first-out cost	10,000	20,000	30,000
Cost-or-market	8,000	16,000	29,000

1. Prepare the gross margin sections of the 1965–1967 income statements, valuing the inventories on the basis of first-in, first-out cost and cost or market, whichever is lower.
2. Discuss the effect of these alternatives with respect to their conservatism in determining income by years.

10.7   Purchases and sales of the C Co. for January, February, and March of 1966 are given below:

	Purchases	Sales
January	$ 3,000	$10,000
February	12,000	20,000
March	7,000	15,000

The inventory at January 1, 1966, was $6,000. The gross profit is 40 percent of sales. Estimate the inventories at the end of January, February, and March.

10.8   A fire in the early morning hours of May 1, 1966, destroyed all the inventory and most of the accounting records of M. Styx and Company. However, the following information has been obtained:

	As of 1/1/66	As of 5/1/66
Cash	$ 7,610	$ 150
Inventory	22,600	
Purchases		16,940
Freight in		360
Sales		52,000
Salesmen's commissions . . .		1,700
Retained earnings	65,100	

M. STYX AND COMPANY
INCOME STATEMENT
Year Ended December 31, 1965

Sales	$196,000
Cost of Goods Sold	112,700
Gross Margin on Sales	$ 83,300
Expenses:	
Selling $38,300	
Administrative 20,000	58,300
Net Income before Taxes	$ 25,000
Income Taxes	5,500
Net Income	$ 19,500

Estimate the cost of the inventory loss in the fire.

10.9 From the data below compute the February 28, 1966, inventory for the glove department of Renton's, Inc.:

Inventory, 3/1/65:
  Cost $18,590
  Retail 28,600
Purchases:
  Cost 48,410
  Retail 65,400
Additional markups 6,000
Sales 70,000

10.10 Day Sales Co. maintains a retail inventory system. Data for 1966 are given below. Calculate the December 31, 1966, inventory at retail and cost with cost not reduced for markdowns and with cost reduced for markdowns.

	Cost	Retail
Inventory, 1/1/66	$17,100	$22,500
Purchases	43,800	55,300
Freight in	4,300	
Purchase returns	5,200	6,800
Markups		9,000
Markdowns		5,000
Sales		50,000

10.11 An examination of the accounting records of the D Co. for the year ended December 31, 1966, revealed the following errors:

(1) Three sheets were omitted from the recapitulation of the December 31, 1966, periodic inventory. The omission resulted in an inventory understatement of $5,400.

(2) An invoice for $3,600 of merchandise was omitted from the December invoice record. The merchandise was received before December 31 and was included in the ending inventory.

(3) Merchandise purchased f.o.b. shipping point on December 26 in the amount of $2,700 was in transit on December 31 and was not included in the inventory. The invoice was not recorded as of December 31, 1966.

(4) Merchandise purchased f.o.b. destination on December 27 in the amount of $1,875 was in transit on December 31 and was not included in the inventory. The invoice was not recorded as of December 31, 1966.

(5) A December 28 charge sale of $2,000 plus 4 percent sales tax had been recorded for merchandise costing $1,600, which the company had not ordered from the supplier at December 31, 1966.

Give correcting entries at December 31, 1966. Accounts have been adjusted but not closed. The company adjusts inventories through a Profit and Loss account.

10.12 L. Saxton and Co., a wholesale grocer, sells 10,000 cases of canned salmon a year at the rate of 40 cases per day in the company's 250-day business year. (Assume the sales are made at a constant rate throughout the year.) Annual storage, interest, and other carrying costs amount to $1 per case. The clerical and handling costs of placing an order amount to $10 per order.

Prepare a schedule with columns for Order Size, Annual Storage Cost, Annual Order Cost, and Total Annual Cost. Compute the total annual costs resulting from the alternative policies of ordering in 200-, 300-, . . . 1,000-case lots. What is the most economic lot quantity?

PROBLEMS

10.1 The income statement of the Antioch Furniture Mart for the year ended December 31, 1966, as prepared by the bookkeeper, is presented below.

ANTIOCH FURNITURE MART
INCOME STATEMENT
Year Ended December 31, 1966

Sales		$170,000
Cost of Goods Sold		
Inventory, January 1	$ 16,900	
Purchases	118,300	
Total	$135,200	
Inventory, December 31	14,700	
Cost of Goods Sold		120,500
Gross Margin on Sales		$ 49,500
Expenses:		
Salaries	$ 22,700	
Rent	7,200	
Advertising	6,900	
Taxes	3,200	
Utilities	2,800	
Miscellaneous	1,100	43,900
Net Income		$ 5,600

After this statement had been prepared, the following errors were discovered:

(1) An invoice had not been recorded at December 31, 1966, for $2,100 of merchandise purchased from Mission Furniture Company; however, the goods had been received and were included in the periodic inventory.

(2) An invoice in the amount of $1,800 from Bervan Carpets for goods shipped f.o.b. shipping point had been received and recorded on December 27; however, the goods had not been received as of December 31 and were not included in the ending inventory.

(3) An invoice from Carolina Mills, Inc., in the amount of $3,200 for a December 20 shipment, terms f.o.b. shipping point, had not been recorded at December 31. This merchandise was not included in the ending inventory.

(4) An invoice in the amount of $1,400 had been received and recorded from Lightolier for goods shipped f.o.b. destination on December 26; however, the goods had not been received as of December 31 and had not been included in the ending inventory.

(5) A page had been omitted from the total of the January 1, 1966, inventory, resulting in its understatement by $1,700.

Required:

1. Revise the income statement.
2. Revise the current ratio. Computed from the balance sheet as prepared by the bookkeeper, at December 31, 1966, it was

$$\frac{32,100}{12,200} = 2.6 \text{ to } 1.$$

3. For each item above, indicate whether income for 1967 would be understated or overstated if the error is not corrected.

10.2 Manning Bros. took a physical inventory on December 31, 1966. The following data on three articles of merchandise are available. Calculate the inventory by each of the following pricing methods: first-in, first-out, and last-in, first-out.

	Article 1	Article 2	Article 3
Inventory, Jan. 1, 1966:			
Quantity	400	350	280
Amount.	$2,400	$2,800	$2,800
Purchases during the year:			
Feb. 4.	100 at $6.00	100 @ $ 8.10	
Oct. 11.		80 @ $ 8.20	40 @ $10.00
21.		200 @ $ 9.00	
31.	500 at $6.40	100 @ $ 9.00	
Nov. 10.			60 @ $11.00
23.		150 @ $10.00	
Dec. 16.			110 @ $11.00
29.			90 @ $12.00
Inventory, Dec. 31, 1966:			
Quantity	440	360	240

10.3 Enter the following transactions of the Peabody and Co. in a stores ledger account, using the first-in, first-out price basis and the average cost price basis (carry unit prices to four decimal places). The opening balance and transactions are as follows:

	Units	Price	Issues	Units
Balance, July 1	800	$1.20	July 5	200
Receipts:				
July 7.	200	1.25	8	700
12.	300	1.30	15	150
21.	400	1.50	19	200
26.	350	2.00	28	300

10.4 The periodic inventory of Clupak Co. includes the items listed below. Calculate the inventory value of these items on a cost or market whichever is lower basis, using an item-by-item method and a group-by-group method.

	Quantity	Unit Price Cost	Market
Group 1:			
1	300	$0.55	$0.60
2	145	1.00	1.20
3	200	1.05	1.00
4	800	0.75	0.78
Group 2:			
A	200	$0.80	$0.75
B	140	0.60	0.65
C	100	1.20	1.16
D	400	1.18	1.15
E	300	0.40	0.30

10.5 Lylton & Co. suffered a fire on April 19, 1966, that completely destroyed its merchandise inventory. Its records show that its inventory on January 1, 1966, was $96,000; that its sales for the period were $800,000; and that it made purchases during the period of $600,000, of which $16,000 were returned. During the past three calendar years it has had a gross margin on sales of 25 percent. Calculate the amount of the inventory destroyed on April 19, 1966.

10.6 Divco, Inc., maintains a retail inventory system. Data for 1966 are given below. Calculate the December 31, 1966, inventory at cost and retail, with cost not reduced for markdowns and cost reduced for markdowns. Carry percents to two decimal places and other figures to the nearest dollar.

	Cost	Retail
Inventory, Jan. 1, 1966 ...	$35,800	$45,100
Purchases	42,000	58,400
Freight in	2,200	—
Purchase returns	4,000	5,200
Markups	—	1,700
Markdowns	—	5,000
Sales.................	—	75,000

10.7 The errors listed below are discovered during the 1966 audit of the Leisey Co. The company follows periodic inventory procedures.

(1) Merchandise bought for $1,000 f.o.b. destination was recorded as a purchase in December 1966 but was not included in the December 31, 1966, inventory, since it was received on January 9, 1967.

(2) Merchandise costing $2,000 was received in 1966 and included in the ending inventory; however, the purchase was recorded on January 4, 1967, when the invoice was received.

(3) One hundred units of item X costing $4 each were entered in the December 31 inventory at $40.

(4) Merchandise costing $6,000, sold for $9,000 f.o.b. shipping point, and shipped on December 31, 1966, was not included in the December 31, 1966, inventory; however, the sale was not recorded until January 5, 1967.

(5) An invoice for merchandise costing $5,000 purchased f.o.b. destination was received and recorded on January 15, 1967. The invoice was dated December 30, 1966, when the goods were placed in the hands of the carrier. This merchandise was not included in the December 31, 1966, inventory.

Required:

1. Open a T account for Profit and Loss and enter the net income of $10,000 per general ledger for 1966. Enter the adjustments for items 1 to 5 and compute the adjusted net income.

2. Draft adjusting journal entries required to correct the balance sheet and income statement accounts at December 31, 1966.

10.8 Ramsell Securities & Co. deals in over-the-counter securities for its own account and others. It completed the following transactions in Consolidated Truckers Co. during 1966:

	Shares	Purchases Price per Share	Shares Sold
Jan. 15	100	$12	
June 20	100	18	
Oct. 5	200	20	
Total sales for year			300

(1) The bid price of Consolidated Truckers Co. at December 31, 1966, was $18 per share.
(2) The company priced its inventory on a specific identification basis prior to January 1, 1966. The inventory on January 1, 1966, consisted of 100 shares at $10 per share.
(3) During 1966, the company placed various securities, including Consolidated Truckers Co., with another broker in street name, and the company is considering a change in its inventory pricing basis. To determine the effect of alternative valuation methods, the company has requested its accountant to prepare a statement showing gross profit for 1966 transactions, assuming alternative methods of inventory valuation. The accountant has prepared the following statement:

	Inventory Pricing Basis			
	A	B	C	D
Sales	$6,000	$6,000	$6,000	$6,000
Cost of sales	4,000	5,800	4,800	4,400
Gross profit	$2,000	$ 200	$1,200	$1,600

Required:

Identify the inventory valuation method designated by each letter, and present computations to establish the identity of each method.

10.9 During the five years ended December 31, 1967, National Metals purchased and sold scrap steel as follows:

Year	Purchases (tons)	Price (per ton)	Sales (tons)	Price (per ton)
1963	50,000	$26	40,000	$36
1964	40,000	37	40,000	47
1965	40,000	26	40,000	36
1966	40,000	15	40,000	25
1967	40,000	26	40,000	36

Required:

1. Prepare a schedule showing inventories and gross profits by years under the fifo and the lifo bases of valuing ending inventories.
2. "Carrying a given physical inventory quantity under conditions of changing prices results in an inventory profit or loss equal to the increase or decrease in the book value of that quantity of inventory." (a) What was the inventory profit in the December 31, 1964, inventory priced at fifo? (b) Which inventory valuation basis would you find most useful as manager of the company?

3. (a) Which inventory valuation basis would produce the lowest tax if prices trended upward? Why? (b) Which inventory valuation basis would result in the most favorable current ratio if prices trended upward? Why? (c) Which inventory valuation basis would you find most useful as a general creditor of the company? (Assume that the inventory in the financial statements is disclosed only under one method of inventory pricing.)

10.10 Regional Bolt Works has accumulated statistics over the years which show that the annual sales of stock B-471 average 100 cases per year, distributed evenly throughout the year. The inventory is kept in a bonded warehouse at an annual cost of $10 per case. Analyses prepared by the company show that it costs $10 for labor, fringe benefits, and paper work to place an order for stock B-471, regardless of the size of the order.

Required:

Prepare a table with columns for Order Size, Annual Cost, Annual Order Cost, and Total Annual Cost, and complete the table for orders of 5, 10, 15, 20, 25, and 30 cases. (The annual storage cost for a policy of ordering in lots of five cases is $5 \times \frac{1}{2} \times \$10 = \$25$. The annual order cost is $[100/5] \times \$20 = \$400$). What is the optimum order size?

Fixed and Intangible Assets

Fixed assets consist of land, buildings, and equipment. Intangible assets include patents, copyrights, trademarks, franchises, goodwill, and organization costs. Leaseholds and leasehold improvements are classed as fixed assets by some accountants and as intangible assets by others. Some accountants prefer to designate all these assets as fixed assets. The distinction between fixed assets and intangible assets is usually observed in practice. The essential difference is that fixed assets are useful for their physical qualities, whereas intangible assets do not depend on physical qualities for their usefulness. From this viewpoint leaseholds and leasehold improvements should be classed as fixed assets, since they represent possession and use of land and physical structures on it. In present practice leaseholds result in asset accounts only if the rents are paid for a substantial period in advance, or if they are, in effect, a purchase.

This chapter is concerned with the accounting principles and procedures applicable to fixed and intangible assets, including the amounts chargeable to them, depreciation or depletion on them, and their retirement. It also takes up related internal control devices and managerial problems to the solutions of which accounting can contribute. Managerial problems of importance here are decisions of when to purchase new assets and when to replace old ones and problems caused by changing price levels (which have a major impact on long-lived assets.) Chapter 24, Capital Budgeting, carries this subject further.

ACCOUNTING FOR ACQUISITION OF FIXED AND INTANGIBLE ASSETS

Fixed and intangible assets are carried at cost less any amounts recognized as depreciation ("depletion" in the case of natural resources and "amortization" in the case of intangibles). The assets are long-lived and are held for use, not for sale. Fluctuations in their "actual" or "salable" value, if that could be determined, are not considered in accounting for them, because they will ordinarily be used in the business, not sold. Furthermore, adherence to the cost basis permits comparison of the income earned with the investment and gives some indication of the efficiency of management, although a current value would do this better.

All costs necessary to put a newly acquired asset into use are properly charged to the asset account. These include costs of investigating the title to land and of removing an old structure from it. The cost of erecting a machine, as well as the freight and drayage paid to bring it to the site, is chargeable to the machine. The cost of defending a patent in court is considered a legitimate part of the investment in the patent, since litigation is often necessary to establish the validity of the patent.

After an asset has been in use for some time, additions may be made to it. At such times repairs are also often made. In many cases it is difficult to determine how much of the expenditure is repairs and how much represents an improvement in or addition to the asset. The principle, however, is clear: Any amount spent to improve the total productivity of the asset as originally installed is an addition, and any amount spent to maintain the asset in condition to produce what it was originally created to produce is a charge to repairs. The additions are chargeable to the asset account. Repairs is an expense account that is deducted from current revenue in the income statement. For example, suppose that a truck costing $12,000 was expected to last six years. At the end of five years it is decided to install a new motor costing $2,000; this extends the life of the truck three years to a total of nine years. This addition is chargeable to the asset account. If the old motor had been overhauled so the truck would run another year as originally expected, the charge would be to Repairs.

This distinction between asset charges and repair or maintenance charges is referred to as "capital" versus "revenue" expenditures. The asset is a capital, or productive, asset lasting more than one period; the repair expense is a charge against current revenue. Some accountants prefer to charge to the Accumulated Depreciation account rather than to the asset account additional investments in an asset that extend its usefulness beyond the original amount or period. This preference seems to be based on a reluctance to show a higher cost for the asset when it is no bigger physically. However, the economic facts are the important ones, and the charge to the asset account presents them well, showing in that account all that was invested, and in the Accumulated Depreciation account what was written off.

PLANT LEDGER ACCOUNTS

Subsidiary ledgers are needed when fixed or intangible assets are numerous. The most common subsidiary ledger is that for machinery and equipment, called a plant ledger. Buildings may be included in it. Similar ledgers for office furniture and equipment are also common. The subsidiary ledger accounts provide a history of the asset, including the name of the supplier, amounts invested, expected life, and amounts written off to depreciation. The depreciation entries, subtotaled period by period, furnish a subsidiary record for the Accumulated Depreciation account. A plant ledger account is shown on the following page. The form used is one sold by commercial stationers; the term "Depreciation Reserve" is the older term for "Accumulated Depreciation."

NATURE AND RECORDING OF DEPRECIATION

In accounting the term "depreciation" refers to the process of writing off to expense the cost of buildings, machinery, and similar improvements. The causes of the eventual loss of usefulness of these assets are:

1. Wear and tear due to use
2. Action of the elements – weathering and decay
3. Obsolescence
4. Inadequacy

Obsolescence occurs when technical progress in general makes the asset uneconomical or unsuitable for further use. For example, the only product that a specialized machine can make may be superseded by another. Inadequacy occurs when equipment in a particular plant can no longer render the service or production demanded of it. It is a kind of intramural obsolescence.

The purpose of the depreciation entries is to assign the amount invested in the asset to the periods in which it is being used and presumably producing or helping produce revenue. The recording of depreciation is a matter of matching costs and revenues. The entries, already familiar from a prior chapter, are illustrated below.

Depreciation of Building........................$8,000.00		
Accumulated Depreciation—Building.........		$8,000.00
Depreciation of Machinery.......................$6,200.00		
Accumulated Depreciation—Machinery.......		$6,200.00

FALLACIES ABOUT DEPRECIATION

People sometimes think, or speak as though they think, that making entries for depreciation (or depletion or amortization) assures recovery of the cost of the asset depreciated; it does not. Good accounting is an essential guide to management and investors, but it does not assure that a concern will earn enough revenue to cover all its expenses. *If* the concern does cover all its expenses in revenue, it will receive back from customers the amounts invested in the assets that are used up in the process.

It is sometimes assumed that this achievement assures that funds will be on hand to replace the worn-out assets when they are retired. They may not be. Businessmen usually prefer to use for expansion, if possible, the cash that is not needed immediately in maintaining the current level of operations. If they do, then when the old fixed assets must be retired, the cash that represents recovery of investment in them may be tied up in additional fixed assets or in expanded inventory or accounts receivable. Proprietors may withdraw funds that are not currently needed; rising price levels may make it impossible to replace worn-out assets with the cash recovered at lower price levels during their lifetime. It is proper, therefore, to think of depreciation accounting as a process of matching costs and revenue to calculate net income, not as an element of financial management.

Sometimes cash or securities are set aside in a special fund to be used to construct buildings or to replace machinery, but this segregation is unusual. If the segregation is made, it is quite independent of the depreciation accounting and involves the management of funds (or assets), not the calculation of expense. Furthermore, depreciation is not a means of "valuing" the asset in the sense of market value, but only of showing what part of the investment has been recognized as expense.

CALCULATION OF DEPRECIATION

Two general methods of assigning the cost of depreciable assets to expense may be noted:

1. Service units method
2. Periodic method

In the service units method, an estimate is made of the units of service the asset

EQUIPMENT RECORD

NAME OF ASSET *Drill Press*

ASSET NO. 14-1.20 CLASS NO. A ACCT. NO. 3146

THE TODD COMPANY, INC. - CHARLES R. HADLEY DIVISION PRINTED IN U.S.A. —

EQUIPMENT RECORD

MADE BY *B. J. L.*

PURCHASED FROM *Stewart Tool Co.* PURCHASE GUARANTEE *5 years*

MANUFACTURER'S SERIAL NO. *18-433*

YEAR *1962* TYPE *M* MODEL *H - LX* SIZE *3/4 "* H. P. GENERATED OR REQUIRED *5*

ESTIMATED LIFE *12 YEARS* DEPRECIATION RATE *8 1/2* % OR $ PER

ESTIMATED RESIDUAL VALUE $ *100.00*

INSURANCE CARRIED *1500.00*

WHEN APPRAISED

APPRAISED BY

APPRAISED VALUE $ 19

LOCATION

PLACE *Dept A*

BUILDING *Shop*

FLOOR *1st*

DEPARTMENT *Machine*

CONNECTED WITH CENTER

FLOOR SPACE OCCUPIED *30 sq. ft.*

APPRAISAL REPORT REFERENCE

DATE	DESCRIPTION	POSTING REF.	COST		
			DEBIT	CREDIT	BALANCE
1 1 62	*Vertical drill press*	V870	1800 40		1800 40

DEPRECIATION RESERVE		NET ASSET VALUE
YEAR	ANNUAL AMT.	TO DATE
1962	144 53	144 53
1963	144 53	289 06
1964	144 53	433 59
1965	144 53	578 12
1966	144 53	722 65

340

will produce in its lifetime. For truck tires this is miles operated; for aircraft engines it is flying hours; for a stamping machine it is number of stampings. Then depreciation is recorded at so much per service unit. When this kind of estimate can be made with reasonable accuracy, it gives a superior basis for depreciation; the costs are written off in proportion to the amount of usage and presumably in proportion to the revenue earned in a period.

In the periodic method, an estimate is made of the number of years the asset will be useful. Depreciation is written off over this period. Three methods of calculating the periodic depreciation entry are discussed in the following sections. These are:

1. Straight line
2. Double declining balance
3. Sum of the years' digits

One other estimate may be needed: the amount of any salvage or trade-in value at the end of the assets' life. If this is a significant amount, it is deducted from cost to obtain depreciable value. If it is uncertain or insignificant, it may be ignored.

STRAIGHT LINE DEPRECIATION

"Straight line" means an even distribution of the charges over the years. Suppose that a machine costing $12,000 has a salvage value of $560 and a life of ten years. Its depreciation per year is computed on a straight line basis in this way:

$$\frac{\text{cost} - \text{salvage}}{\text{years of life}} = \frac{\$12,000 - \$560}{10} = \frac{\$11,440}{10} = \$1,144 \text{ per year}$$

The rate per year on the depreciable amount in this case is 10 percent.

DOUBLE DECLINING BALANCE DEPRECIATION

This calculation has enjoyed popularity in the United States since the U.S. Internal Revenue Code was amended in 1954 to permit its use for income tax purposes. Similar methods have been used in Great Britain and in Europe for many years. The calculation is made by applying twice the straight line *rate* to the undepreciated cost of the asset each year. For the machine noted above, this calculation is made as follows:

Year	Undepreciated Cost	Rate	Depreciation	Accumulated Depreciation
1	$12,000	20%	$2,400	$ 2,400
2	9,600	"	1,920	4,320
3	7,680	"	1,536	5,856
4	6,144	"	1,229	7,085
5	4,915	"	983	8,068
6	3,932	"	786	8,854
7	3,146	"	629	9,483
8	2,517	"	503	9,986
9	2,014	"	403	10,389
10	1,611	—	1,051	11,440

Note that the amount written off during the last year is the undepreciated amount ($1,611) less the salvage value ($560). This remainder must be written off to have all the depreciable amount charged to expense at the end of the life of the asset. The tax law permits the taxpayer to switch at any time from this method to straight line depreciation for the remaining years. In other words, the remaining depreciable amount may be written off on a straight line basis beginning with any year. In the case given above, if the switch were made in the sixth year, the straight line calculation would be:

$$\frac{\text{remaining cost} - \text{salvage}}{\text{remaining years}} = \frac{\$3,932 - \$560}{5} = \frac{\$3,372}{5} = \$674$$

The influence of the tax law leads to the double rate being applied to the full cost of the asset without regard to salvage until a shift is made to straight line depreciation.

SUM-OF-THE-YEARS'-DIGITS DEPRECIATION

Another declining balance method spreads all the depreciation over the life of the asset in a steadily declining amount with no adjustment required. Each year's charge is determined by a fraction of the depreciable cost in which the denominator is the sum of the digits representing the years of life and the numerators are the individual digits taken in reverse order. In the case of the $12,000 machine with $560 salvage and $11,440 depreciable amount, the calculations for the whole period are as follows:

Year	Fraction	Depreciation	Accumulated Depreciation
1	10/55	$2,080	$ 2,080
2	9/55	1,872	3,952
3	8/55	1,664	5,616
4	7/55	1,456	7,072
5	6/55	1,248	8,320
6	5/55	1,040	9,360
7	4/55	832	10,192
8	3/55	624	10,816
9	2/55	416	11,232
10	1/55	208	11,440
55			

SELECTION OF A DEPRECIATION METHOD

Many businessmen assert that a new fixed asset is most productive in the early part of its life and much less useful thereafter. On this basis, more depreciation should be taken in the early years as a charge against the larger part of the revenue that falls in that period. It is also contended that repairs increase as assets get older, and that higher depreciation charges in the early years tend to make the whole cost of using the asset more uniform. This theory assumes that a uniform charge to revenue over the years is appropriate. Ideally, the method used should be selected to give as good a matching of cost and revenue as possible. If the pattern of revenue attributable to particular assets can be identified, the depreciation method can be fitted to it, but often the pattern cannot. The preferred method in the United States during recent decades has been straight line, and in the absence of satisfactory knowledge of revenue patterns this at least has the merit of systematically assigning the cost over the life of the asset.

NATURE AND CALCULATION OF DEPLETION

The exploitation of many natural resources results in the physical removal of the valuable material. The traditional term for these resources is "wasting assets." Such assets include mines, oil wells, quarries, and timber stands.[1] In these cases the amount invested in the resource is eventually used up. This expense is accounted for as depletion. Entries are like those for depreciation; for example, the entry to record depletion of $180,000 on a mine for a year is:

Depletion. $180,000
    Accumulated Depletion—Mine. $180,000

The traditional term for Accumulated Depletion is Reserve for Depletion; Allowance for Depletion is also used.

Depletion is calculated by dividing the cost of the resource by the number of units of material in it. The unit differs with the resource; oil is measured by the barrel, ore in tons, and timber in thousands of board feet. The amount available is determined by engineering surveys. Residual values must be considered here, as in the case of depreciable assets.

Depreciable assets are often installed on a wasting asset. Roads and buildings are constructed on timberland; holes are drilled and tanks and pipes are installed in oil land; roads and ore-handling and -processing equipment are built in or near mines. This situation may affect the accounting for the depreciable fixed assets in one way: by placing another limit on the life of the asset. If the exploitation of the natural resource will be over before the depreciable asset is worn out, and if the depreciable asset cannot be used elsewhere, it must be depreciated over the time that the natural resource is being worked. This is the only period that will receive any benefits from the investment in the depreciable assets under the circumstances stated.

AMORTIZATION OF INTANGIBLE ASSETS

Common intangibles that have a strictly limited life are:

1. Patents
2. Copyrights
3. Franchises (usually)

Intangibles that have an indefinite life are:

1. Trademarks
2. Goodwill
3. Organization costs

[1] Unless they are "farmed"—logged selectively and replanted continually.

Those with a definitely limited life must be written off to expense during the period of their usefulness. This process is called *amortization*. The writeoff is almost always on a straight line basis. The credit is commonly made directly to the asset account; no "accumulated" credit account is used, as in the case of fixed assets. The entry for amortization of a patent for a year, assuming the amortization to be $2,000 per year, is:

```
Amortization of Patent.........................$2,000.00
        Patent.................................          $2,000.00
```

Intangible assets are recorded at cost, as are fixed assets. They often prove to be of little or no value, so accountants and others are reluctant to charge an asset instead of an expense with costs of experimentation, for example, that result in a patent, or with the cost of organizing a business that may or may not prove profitable. The decision depends on having sufficient objective evidence that the cost will actually benefit future periods. Thus, these assets are shown, as a rule, only in balance sheets of concerns that have bought them from someone else; an arm's-length purchase is convincing evidence of future usefulness.

PATENTS

In the United States a patent, giving the owner exclusive right to manufacture a mechanical invention, runs for seventeen years and is not renewable. Most patents, in spite of a few spectacular successes, are not valuable for seventeen years. One must estimate the *economic* life of the patent in obtaining a period for amortization. Costs of experimentation or research are often very hard to trace to specific results. When a patent is obtained on a useful discovery, it may be a wholly unexpected result of research directed at something else. Though there are exceptions, most concerns do not attempt to set up asset accounts for patents they develop. The research costs are simply charged to expense as they occur. Purchase of a patent from someone else is quite another matter, and is the chief source of asset charges for patents. Patents are issued, after application and official investigation of the claim, by the United States Patent Office.

COPYRIGHTS

A copyright is the exclusive right to reproduce a work of literary, musical, or other art. In the United States it runs for twenty-eight years and is renewable for another twenty-eight. In England it runs for the lifetime of the author or artist creating the work and for fifty years after his death. It is obtained in the United States by depositing with the Copyright Office the required copies of the work bearing suitable notice and paying a small fee. Most copyrights also prove to have a useful life much shorter than the legal one, and amortization calculations are based on estimates of economic life. For the same reasons as in the case of patents, copyrights are only rarely recorded in asset accounts.

FRANCHISES

A franchise is the legal right to operate a public service. It usually provides a monopoly within the area covered and is subject to regulation by the public authority granting it. Electric power and light companies, bus lines and street railways, and radio and television broadcasting companies are examples of franchise holders. Franchises should be amortized over their legal life. If this is perpetual, they need not be written down unless a decline in their value is evident. For example, if half a street railway is abandoned and earnings fall proportionately, a similar writedown of any unamortized franchise is necessary.

TRADEMARKS

A trademark is obtained by invention and use; it may be registered, but in the United States, registration is only an additional precaution. The trademark is legally valid as long as it is used. If an asset value is established by purchase or by such a cost as a legal defense, it need not be amortized unless evidence of declining usefulness appears.

GOODWILL

Goodwill is the value of earning power in excess of that attributable to the other assets. It appears on the books when one concern purchases another and pays more than a reasonable market price for the other assets. Goodwill arises from the reputation of the concern and the customer loyalty it has gained. It need not be amortized unless there is evidence that it is declining.

ORGANIZATION COSTS

Statutory fees and lawyer's fees are incurred in forming companies. Many concerns find that they must operate at a loss for a time in order to get the business established. Both these costs are theoretically assets in that they are investments made to create an organization useful over a future period. The future usefulness is a prediction subject to error and optimism, perhaps to willful overoptimism. Because of the impossibility of making an objective and reliable calculation of the amount that benefits future periods, charges to organization costs are restricted to direct costs such as statutory and legal fees. Because of the aura of doubt that surrounds the asset, these also are customarily charged to expense, but they need not be unless there is evidence that the expected economic benefits will not develop or continue.

LEASEHOLDS AND LEASEHOLD IMPROVEMENTS

A leasehold is the right to possess and use real estate (including buildings) that is derived from a contract with the owner. It commonly involves rent to be paid monthly. If rent is paid in a lump sum in advance, an asset is created. This is amortized over the period of the prepayment. Frequently the tenant (lessee) erects buildings on land leased for a long period, or he may erect partitions, install signs, and otherwise improve a leased building. At the end of the lease all structures revert to the landlord (lessor), so the tenant must depreciate his improvements over a period no longer than the life of the lease. The lease is often the limiting factor in the life of such assets. Depreciation entries for leasehold improvements are made like other depreciation entries.

If rents have been paid in advance, the asset "leasehold" is created, and must be written off or "amortized" over the period of prepayment. The annual amortization entry for a 20-year lease for which $40,000 was paid in advance is:

```
Rent.........................................$2,000.00
        Leasehold...........................          $2,000.00
```

BALANCE SHEET PRESENTATION OF FIXED AND INTANGIBLE ASSETS

Fixed and intangible assets are desirably shown as follows:

Fixed assets:			
Land....................................		$ 40,000.00	
Buildings........................	$250,000.00		
Less: Accumulated Depreciation.....	86,000.00	164,000.00	
Machinery and Equipment.........	$618,000.00		
Less: Accumulated Depreciation.....	272,000.00	346,000.00	
Office Furniture and Equipment.....	$ 28,000.00		
Less: Accumulated Depreciation.....	7,100.00	20,900.00	
Leaseholds..............................		82,000.00	$652,900.00
Intangible assets:			
Patents.................................		$ 44,000.00	
Goodwill...............................		182,000.00	226,000.00
Other assets: Land held as future building site..................			28,000.00

Note that assets not used in the regular conduct of the business are listed as "other assets" at the bottom of the balance sheet.

REVISION OF DEPRECIATION OR DEPLETION

Estimates of useful life or recoverable resources may prove inaccurate. If such an error is apparent before the asset is disposed of, the rate of depreciation or depletion should be revised. In order to obtain a proper matching of cost and revenue, the correction for past periods' expense should go to the Retained Earnings account and future expense entries should be made at the rate indicated by the new estimate of useful life. For example, a machine costing $18,800 and with salvage value of $800 was expected to last eighteen years. Depreciation was recorded at $1,000 per year for ten years. It was then realized that the machine would last only five years more. The newly determined life of fifteen years indicates that $1,200 instead of $1,000 per year should have been recorded. The correction for the past ten years is made as follows:

```
Retained Earnings.............................$2,000.00
        Accumulated Depreciation—Machinery.......          $2,000.00
        (to correct past depreciation on machine #88 now esti-
        mated to have 15, not 18 year life)
```

It is a common practice to avoid adjusting prior periods' results by writing off the remaining depreciable amount over the remaining life as revised. This practice leaves the remaining periods with an erroneous rate and is therefore objectionable. One reason for its popularity is that it may be used for income tax purposes, and its use in the regular accounts means that there will be fewer items of difference between the regular accounts and the income tax return. In this case preparation of the return is easier.

RETIREMENT OF FIXED AND INTANGIBLE ASSETS

Retirement of fixed and intangible assets may occur in any of these three forms:

1. Abandonment
2. Sale
3. Trade-in

At time of retirement, care must be taken to see that depreciation is recorded up to date. For example, machine #72 costing $12,400 with expected salvage of $400 is scrapped after eight and one-half years of an expected 10-year life. Depreciation has been recorded annually on December 31; on August 31, 1966 (the day of retirement), the Accumulated Depreciation account shows $9,400. Before other entries are made for the retirement, the depreciation for the eight months ended August 31, 1966 is recorded as follows:

```
Depreciation—Machinery....................$   800.00
       Accumulated Depreciation—Machinery.....        $   800.00
```

Entries for each type of retirement are presented in the following section, with the figures for the machine referred to in this section furnishing the basic data.

ABANDONMENT

When an asset is abandoned no consideration is received and the asset is removed from the record, any loss being recorded. For the machine noted above, the entry is:

```
Accumulated Depreciation—Machinery...........$10,200.00
Loss on Retirement of Fixed Assets...............   2,200.00
       Machinery...........................              $12,400.00
```

Note that the debit to Accumulated Depreciation is for the amount accumulated to August 31, 1966, the retirement date.

SALE OF FIXED ASSET

Assume that the machine noted above was sold on August 31, 1966, for $2,800 cash. Depreciation for the eight months to retirement date having been recorded, the retirement entry is:

```
Cash......................................$ 2,800.00
Accumulated Depreciation—Machinery............ 10,200.00
       Gain on Retirement of Fixed Assets........        $   600.00
       Machinery...........................              12,400.00
```

If the "sale" had been only for scrap value, the same entry would have been made except that the amount received would probably have been smaller, and a loss instead of a gain might have resulted.

TRADE-IN OF FIXED ASSETS

When an asset is traded in on another, the allowance on the old asset is the consideration received on the sale of the old machine. Assume that the machine discussed above was traded in on a new one costing $14,000, and that an allowance of $3,000 was made on the old machine. This transaction may be recorded in two steps as follows:

```
Allowance on Trade-in......................$ 3,000.00
Accumulated Depreciation—Machinery............  10,200.00
    Gain on Retirement of Fixed Assets........              $    800.00
    Machinery.............................              12,400.00
(to record retirement of machine #72)


Machinery..................................$14,000.00
    Allowance on Trade-in..................              $ 3,000.00
    Vouchers Payable......................              11,000.00
(to record purchase of machine #89)
```

These entries may be combined into one, in which case the Allowance on Trade-in account may be eliminated. Sometimes allowances in excess of the actual value of the old asset are given. These are really price cuts on the new asset. Where they are known to exist, they should be deducted from the price of the new asset; this revision of the price also reduces the amount of gain that otherwise would be shown on the old asset. For example, if the old asset in the preceding illustration had been worth only $1,200 instead of $3,000, the entries should have been as follows:

```
Allowance on Trade-in......................$ 1,200.00
Accumulated Depreciation—Machinery............  10,200.00
Loss on Retirement of Fixed Assets..............   1,000.00
    Machinery.............................              $12,400.00
(to record retirement of machine #72; allowance of
$3,000.00 received, of which $1,200.00 is value of
machine #72 and $1,800.00 is price concession on
new machine)


Machinery..................................$12,200.00
    Allowance on Trade-in..................              $ 1,200.00
    Vouchers Payable......................              11,000.00
(to record purchase of machine #89)
```

TAX RULE ON TRADE-INS

Under the United States Internal Revenue Code no gain or loss is recognized when one asset is traded in on a substantially similar asset. However, any undepreciated amount remaining on the old asset is added to the cost or other consideration given for the new asset to get the depreciable amount or "cost" of the new asset. Some concerns use the tax method in order to avoid the need to make separate calculations of depreciation for the tax return, though most accountants disapprove of the tax method as a matter of accounting principle. Efforts are being made continually to bring tax rules into closer conformity with generally accepted accounting principles. Under the tax method, the entry for the trade-in described in the preceding section (assuming the $3,000 allowance to be a valid market price for the old machine) is:

Machinery (new machine)	$13,200.00	
Accumulated Depreciation—Machinery	10,200.00	
Machinery (old machine)		$12,400.00
Vouchers Payable		11,000.00

INTERNAL CONTROL FOR FIXED AND INTANGIBLE ASSETS

Most fixed assets are not easily misplaced or stolen, and managers therefore often neglect to use any special internal control devices for them. Some internal control practices are nevertheless important for fixed and intangible assets. The following practices are recommended.

Use a plant ledger. A plant ledger provides information about the units in use. It permits a review of the age of the equipment; this is helpful in anticipating the need for replacements. It is useful in determining the amount of insurance that should be carried, in anticipating the need for repairs and planning a repair program, in checking on the firm's experience with equipment acquired from different makers, and in other ways.

Use acquisition controls. It is a common experience to find that a plant has been overbuilt, or contains unnecessary facilities, when fixed asset additions are left to the discretion of individual plant managers. It also often happens that an addition expected to cost $10,000 turns out to cost $15,000. Because of the amounts involved, mistakes in planning or constructing fixed assets can be very expensive. Acquisition controls tend to prevent these mistakes and consist of two parts:

A SYSTEM OF AUTHORIZATION. This often consists of a special committee of executives that must approve each project in writing before it can be begun. A common term for the document that describes the project and provides space for the signatures is "Appropriation for Expenditure" or "AFE," but other forms, including some that specify no cost for the project, may be used.

A BUDGET FOR EACH PROJECT. A specific amount should be authorized for each project, which may not be exceeded without special permission. This not only provides pressure to keep within the budget but gives opportunity to revise the plans if the original ones are proving too expensive.

Issue small tools and similar assets only on requisition from a locked storeroom. Small tools are the special prey of persons who like to borrow but neglect to return. A written requisition makes the user accountable for the return of the tool.

Control maintenance and repair expenditures as acquisitions are controlled. Authorization and budgeting are useful in controlling repair expenditures, just as they are in controlling acquisitions.

Keep such title documents as letters patent, copyright certificates, leaseholds, and so on, in a safe deposit box with access only by two authorized persons acting together. These are not likely to be the object of theft, but if they are lost by fire or otherwise, trouble and expense may result.

MANAGEMENT DECISIONS ON FIXED AND INTANGIBLE ASSETS

Important management decisions on fixed and intangible assets in which accounting has an important role are:

1. Whether or not a major new investment should be made in facilities.
2. Whether or not a particular asset should be replaced.
3. Price-level problems: changing price levels affect the interpretation of net income under conventional accounting methods. Decisions that are affected include dividend payments, asset replacement financing, setting of sales prices, and insurance coverage of assets.

MAJOR NEW INVESTMENTS

The decision to make a major new investment involving long-lived buildings and equipment must be made on the basis of a careful forecast of revenue and a careful calculation of costs.

The revenue estimate involves the probability of continued demand for the type of merchandising or service contemplated or for the product to be made. It also must inquire into the need for additional service or production as indicated by growth of population and by trends in national and regional income.

The cost calculation must include all costs of producing the revenue, including depreciation on the fixed assets required.

Many other factors are involved, such as the present and expected availability of a good labor supply and the availability of economical transportation for materials and finished products. A complete summary of the data would give a budgeted income statement for the new operation. If this should indicate that a satisfactory net income would not be earned on the investment, it presumably would not be made.

Since it is obviously not possible to anticipate all conditions over a long period, some people invest only when it appears that the amount invested can be recovered in a limited period—three, five, or ten years. This idea is illustrated in the following section. In any case, a careful decision on a major new facility requires the assembling of all the cost and revenue data available on it.

PAYOUT PERIOD

The time in which the investment in a new asset can be recovered is called the "payout" or "payoff" period. Assume that a distributor is considering building a branch warehouse in a new territory. This facility would cost $28,000 and last twenty years. The following figures show the annual cost of operating such a warehouse, excluding depreciation and the cost of merchandise:

Labor	$12,000.00
Taxes	1,200.00
Delivery expense	6,000.00
Other sales expense	8,000.00
Miscellaneous	3,000.00
	$30,200.00

Annual gross margin from the new territory is estimated at $42,000, and the company pays income taxes at approximately 50 percent of net income. The payout calculation for this case is:

Annual gross margin...		$42,000.00
Expenses:		
Depreciation.............................	$ 1,400.00	
Other.....................................	30,200.00	31,600.00
Net operating income..		$10,400.00
Income tax at 50 percent.......................................		5,200.00
Net income..		$ 5,200.00
Add back depreciation...		1,400.00
Annual recovery of funds.......................................		$ 6,600.00

$$\text{Payout period} = \frac{\$28,000}{\$6,600} = 4.24 \text{ years}$$

Depreciation is added back because it requires no funds once the fixed asset has been paid for.

After 4.24 years the investors will have their money back and can look forward to earning a profit.

REPLACEMENT OF A PARTICULAR ASSET

Many assets are replaced before they are physically worn out, because their continued use is uneconomical. An asset is uneconomical when the *out-of-pocket* cost of operating it is greater than the *out-of-pocket* cost of buying and operating a replacement, if the output is assumed to be the same in the two cases so that revenue will not be changed by the replacement. Note that only out-of-pocket costs are considered. These are the amounts that must be spent currently to get the goods or services that the asset — say a machine — can produce.

The depreciation on the old machine is not considered, because it no longer has to be paid out of pocket. However, the cost of the new machine *is* an out-of-pocket cost if one considers a change, so depreciation on the new machine must be included. Furthermore, any resale or salvage value that the old machine has is considered, because this would reduce the out-of-pocket cost of the new one if the change were made. The following tabulation shows the cost comparison; in this case the old machine has no trade-in or salvage value:

	Annual Costs	
	Old Machine	New Machine
Depreciation........................	—	$2,000
Labor...............................	$4,000	3,000
Power...............................	1,600	1,000
Repairs.............................	3,000	2,000
Taxes, insurance, and sundry...........	400	800
	$9,000	$8,800

In the case illustrated it would pay to replace the old machine. This calculation can be refined by use of compound interest, as discussed in Chapter 24.

THE PRICE LEVEL PROBLEM

Cost is the basis for the accounting related to fixed and intangible assets. These assets are long lived, and price levels sometimes change considerably over ten or twenty years. The result may be that an amount for depreciation or amortization, based on costs that prevailed many years ago, is deducted from the amount of revenue received in current dollars. This discrepancy distorts net income. Suppose that a warehouse built in 1946 for $300,000 to last thirty years is in use in 1966. It is rented to tenants who pay rent and also pay the taxes, repairs, and insurance. Suppose also that during the 1946–1966 period the price level has at least doubled and that the rentals and the out-of-pocket expenses have followed suit. To get a net income figure that is realistic and is expressed in 1966 dollars, the depreciation expense should also be doubled. This adjustment is illustrated in the following partial income statements of the owners:

	Conventional Statement 1946	Conventional Statement 1966	Adjusted Statement 1966
Rental income	$42,000	$84,000	$84,000
Depreciation	$10,000	$10,000	$20,000
Sundry expenses	2,000	4,000	4,000
Total expenses	$12,000	$14,000	$24,000
Net operating income	$30,000	$70,000	$60,000

In general, a 1946 dollar is approximately the same in purchasing power as two 1966 dollars; this ratio is recognized above in the fact that rents here doubled and so have the sundry expenses. The net income is also expected to double, and it has done so in the adjusted statement. The conventional statement for 1966 shows the distorted income that is computed under ordinary accounting procedures in which the old prices remain in the depreciation figures.

This distortion has many ramifications. Net income is overstated when prices are rising, and understated when prices are falling. Income taxes are levied on the fictitious profits that appear when prices are rising. Dividends may be paid in excess of a reasonable amount if management is not aware of the problem. On the higher price level, assets cannot be replaced at the figures at which they appear in the accounts, so special care is needed in planning replacements. Many concerns finance replacements under these conditions by retaining more income in the business than they otherwise would do. Sales prices must be set (if they can be set) in the light of the current price level during periods of rising prices if the purchasing power invested in long-lived but exhaustible assets is to be recovered from customers. When sales prices are set with reference to costs, the costs must be expressed in current dollars if the results are to be satisfactory.

The problem of financing replacements at higher price levels has an accompanying problem of maintaining adequate insurance coverage of the assets. An asset cannot be replaced on a higher price level with the same number of dollars in insurance that were adequate on the lower price level. The effects are reversed when prices are declining, but they have not declined on a general scale during the last twenty years.

The best solution for the accounting side of these problems is to adopt price level adjustments as normal accounting procedure. The accounts can be adjusted systematically with a general price index, but the method is not generally accepted practice as yet. Note that price level adjustment is not a departure from the cost basis, but only a means of expressing the costs from various price levels in dollars of the same purchasing power.

SUMMARY

This chapter has dealt with the acquisition, writeoff, and retirement of fixed and intangible assets. These include land, buildings, equipment, patents, trademarks, copyrights, goodwill, organization expense, and leaseholds and leasehold improvements. Fixed and intangible assets are carried at cost in the accounts. The cost of using them up (trademarks, goodwill, and organization expense do not necessarily lose their usefulness) is recorded by periodic entries to depreciation, amortization, or depletion. Accounts for accumulated depreciation and depletion are customarily carried. Internal control for these assets is often neglected, but desirably should be given attention. Managements' decisions involving them include whether to invest in a major new facility and when to replace a particular asset. Management must also notice the effect of changing price levels on net income and replacement costs and take adequate account of this effect in declaring dividends, providing for replacements, setting sales prices, and providing insurance coverage.

QUESTIONS

11.1 You receive a call on New Year's Eve from a friend who owns a small business. He tells you that an automobile salesman has just convinced him that he should buy a new car before midnight so he "can deduct it on his income tax return." Your friend, who is not averse to the pleasures of a new car, asks your advice.

(1) What is your reply, based on general accounting principles?

(2) How should your friend decide when to replace his automobile?

11.2 (1) What valuation basis is generally employed in the reporting of depreciable assets? Why are fluctuations in market values generally ignored? What accounting principles justify this procedure?

(2) Which of the following expenditures incident to the purchase of real estate are properly charged to a fixed asset account?

(a) Title insurance fees

(b) Payments of delinquent property taxes

(c) Current real estate taxes

(d) Termite inspection costs

(e) Annual fire insurance premiums paid in advance as required by mortgage

(f) Payments of mortgage principal

(g) Payments of interest charges on mortgage

(3) Why should the cost of buildings and land not be comingled in a single account?

11.3 The problem of "capital versus revenue expenditures" has been called one of the fundamental problems of accounting.

(1) Explain briefly what is meant by the problem.

(2) What general criteria are available for distinguishing capital from revenue expenditures?

(3) Indicate whether the following are capital or revenue expenditures. State assumptions where necessary.

(a) A stone building was sandblasted to remove dirt.

(b) A neon sign was erected on the face of a building.

(c) A large diesel engine was installed to turn the generator that provides light and power for the building; a steam engine had been used before.

(d) Two of the elevators in the building were overhauled.

(e) The roof of the building was re-covered with tar and gravel, as is done every ten years.

(f) The basement of the building was partitioned and lights were installed so that storage space could be rented to tenants.

(g) Windows of the building were washed by a window-cleaning company.

(h) An air-conditioning system was installed in the building.

11.4 (1) What is the principle for deciding whether an expenditure relating to equipment should be charged to an asset or an expense account?

(2) Classify the following as charges to an asset or an expense account:

(a) The cost of safety guards installed on 3-year-old equipment.

(b) Engineering costs for testing and installing new equipment.

(c) Expenditures for insurance on machinery purchased while the machinery is in transit.

(d) Costs of installing an automatic fire alarm system in a plant, as required by the fire commissioner.

(e) Costs of moving and reinstalling equipment from one location in the plant to another.

(f) Carrying charges paid in connection with the acquisition of depreciable property.

(g) Costs of a rebuilt engine and new differential placed in a secondhand truck on its acquisition.

(h) Fees paid to attorneys and to the state relative to incorporation.

(i) Expenditures for promotional and institutional advertising which the sales manager says will be returned by increased revenues next year.

(j) Cash discounts lost on purchase of equipment because of failure to pay invoices within the discount period.

11.5 (1) What control accounts may be supported by a plant ledger?

(2) What are some of the reasons for use of a plant ledger?

11.6 (1) What is meant by the term "depreciation" in accounting?

(2) Suggest causes for the fact that fixed assets (other than land used as a site) eventually lose their usefulness.

(3) How is the "book value" of plant and equipment related to "market value"? Is depreciation designed to measure changes in market value?

11.7 Criticize the following statements about depreciation from an accounting point of view: (1) "Industry should spend its depreciation reserves for new equipment to help relieve unemployment in this time of depression." (2) "We showed a larger net income this year because we decided not to deduct as much depreciation as before." (3) "Our machines are kept in excellent condition by a planned repair program so we do not have to record any depreciation on them."

11.8 (1) Contrast the service units method of calculating depreciation with the periodic method.

(2) Explain what is meant by the following terms in connection with depreciation: straight line, double declining balance, sum of the years' digits.

(3) As stated in the text, straight line was the generally accepted method of depreciation in the United States prior to the 1954 Internal Revenue Code. The declining balance method was allowed for the purpose at that time, and since then there is some evidence indicating a switch to this method by corporations in their annual reports. Can you suggest reasons why financial accounting should not be governed by the requirements of tax accounting?

11.9 An asset is acquired at a cost of $10,000 with an estimated life of four years and residual value of $2,000. What portion of the cost would be written off under the straight line method by the end of the second year? under the double declining balance method? under the sum-of-the-years'-digits method?

11.10 (1) Compare and contrast the following terms: depletion, depreciation, and amortization.

(2) Which term is customarily used with each of the following assets?

(a) Oil wells   (d) Bridges
(b) Patents   (e) Copyrights
(c) Automobiles   (f) Quarries

11.11 (1) What kind of legal and economic lives may the following assets have?

(a) Patents   (d) Franchises
(b) Trademarks   (e) Copyrights
(c) Goodwill   (f) Organization costs

(2) The Evans Co. purchased another company three years ago and paid market prices for such assets as merchandise, buildings, and land, and an additional $100,000 for the goodwill of the other business. Evans has not amortized any of this investment in goodwill and states that it does not consider it necessary because it sees no diminution in the patronage it continues to get from the loyal customers of the old firm. Is this accounting policy acceptable?

(3) What factors other than satisfied customers give rise to goodwill?

11.12 (1) What rights does a leasehold confer? (2) How can a leasehold result in an asset account? (3) What are leasehold improvements? (4) Should leasehold improvements be classified as fixed assets or as intangibles? (5) How does the leasehold affect the accounting for leasehold improvements?

11.13 The management of Jewell Stores, Incorporated, is considering two alternatives for the acquisition of a new building. The building can be purchased for $736,000, with $136,000 down and the balance payable in ten annual installments of $81,540, which include interest at 6 percent per year on the unpaid balance. The building can also be leased for ten annual payments of $100,000, at the end of which time the company can take title to the building for one dollar. (The present worth of ten payments of $100,000 at 6 percent is $736,000.) The building will be constructed on leased land which has a term of ten years with no renewal option.

(1) How will the accounting differ under the alternatives if the building is not recorded under the leasing plan?

(2) Evaluate these differences.

11.14 A truck with a book value of $800 is traded in on a new truck with a list price of $10,000. The trade-in allowance is $2,000, and the balance is paid by cash.

(1) How much cash is paid on the new truck?

(2) What is the loss or gain on the trade, assuming the $10,000 is a firm price?

(3) What is the loss or gain, assuming the $10,000 is not a firm price and the

$2,000 allowance constitutes a payment of $800 for the old truck and a price concession of $1,200 on the new truck?

(4) What is the depreciation on the new truck for the first year at the rate of 20 percent, if the transaction is recorded as in 2?

(5) What will be the depreciation for the first year on the new truck at the rate of 20 percent if the transaction is recorded as in 3?

11.15 The Equipment account and its related Accumulated Depreciation before adjustment on December 31, 1966, appear below:

Equipment		Accumulated Depr. — Equipment	
6/30/65	2,400	12/31/65	120
1/2/66	800		
6/30/66	1,200		

(1) What entry would be made on December 31, 1966, to record depreciation by the straight line method, using a life of ten years and no residual value?

(2) The debit of $2,400 to Equipment on June 30, 1965, represents the cost of a bookkeeping machine. This machine is sold for $1,800 cash on March 31, 1967. What entries are required to record the transaction?

(3) Assume the same facts as in 2, except that the machine is traded in on a new one. The new machine costs $2,800 and the allowance on the old is $1,800; the balance is paid by check. Discuss the alternative entries that might be made.

11.16 The Oceanic Transport Co. bought a steamship on January 2, 1961, for $2,000,000. The ship was expected to have a useful life of twenty years and a residual value of $200,000 for the service in which it was placed. During early January 1966 the company decided that the vessel will be used only fifteen years in all, with no change in residual value.

(1) Explain and illustrate two alternative sets of journal entries the company can make for 1966.

(2) Under what circumstances might each be proper?

11.17 Two fixed assets and related accumulated depreciation accounts are presented below:

Machine A		Accumulated Depr. — Mach. A	
1/1/65	10,000	12/31/65	1,500
		12/31/66	1,500
		12/31/67	1,500
		12/31/68	1,500
		12/31/69	500
		12/31/70	500

Machine B		Accumulated Depr. — Mach. B	
7/1/66	60,000	12/31/66	3,000
		12/31/67	6,000
		12/31/68	6,000
		12/31/69	15,600
		12/31/70	15,600

The residual value is estimated at 10 percent of cost for each machine.

(1) What life was used in the original computation of depreciation for each machine?

(2) What was the total life for each machine based on the depreciation of 1969 and 1970?

11.18 (1) List five internal control devices for fixed and intangible assets.

(2) It has been suggested that the concept of internal control should be extended from one of mere asset safekeeping to include all effective managerial cost and profit controls. Name several categories of management decisions in which fixed assets are especially involved.

(3) Discuss briefly three management decisions that must be made with the effects of changing general price levels in mind. Give a concrete example illustrating the kind of error that may result from a failure to recognize the price level problem.

EXERCISES

11.1 A Co. purchased a 1966 Chevrolet truck on January 5, 1966. The contract showed the following:

Price of truck	$3,180.69
Extra charges for special tires, painting company name on truck, and special hitches	80.42
Total	$3,261.11
Sales tax, 4%	130.44
Total	$3,391.55
Insurance for 1966	143.00
Motor vehicle registration and license for 1966	35.62
Total	$3,570.17
Cash payment	1,000.00
Difference	$2,570.17
Carrying charges, ½% a month for 24 months	308.42
Balance due – contract payable	$2,878.59

Required:

1. What is the cost of the truck?
2. Present the entry to record the acquisition of the truck.
3. Compute the depreciation for 1966 by the straight line method, using a life of three years and scrap value of $300.

11.2 A businessman, having heard about various methods of depreciation but understanding little of their practical effect, asks you to demonstrate the difference between them for an asset costing $10,000 with an expected life of three years and scrap value of $1,000. Prepare a schedule showing the annual depreciation and book value at the end of each year by each of the following methods: straight line, sum of the years' digits, and double declining balance (depreciation in the third year to reduce the asset to salvage value.)

11.3 E Co. paid $120,000 on January 1, 1966, for ore reserves estimated to contain 30,000 tons. A total of 18,000 tons was mined and sold during the three years ended December 31, 1968. According to a geological survey in early January 1969, it was then estimated that 22,000 tons remain; that is, 40,000 tons were actually purchased on January 1, 1966.

Required:

1. Submit the journal entry to record depletion for 1966 based on 5,000 tons mined.
2. Submit the journal entry for January 1969 to adjust the Accumulated Depletion account to the amount it would have contained if depletion had originally been based on the estimates, which seem to be correct in 1969, and to base subsequent depletion charges on the revised estimates.

3. Submit the journal entry to record depletion for 1969 based on 4,000 tons mined.

11.4 The Machinery account of C Co. includes a vertical drill press purchased July 1, 1960, for $3,600. Depreciation has been recorded on December 31 of each year on the straight line basis, estimated life ten years, and estimated residual value $400. On October 1, 1966, the company finds it has no further use for this machine.

Required:

1. Present the entry to record the depreciation for the nine months ended September 30, 1966, before the asset is retired.
2. Present the entry to record the disposal of this machine assuming: (a) it is abandoned; (b) it is sold for $1,000 cash; (c) it is traded in on a new machine costing $6,000, an allowance of $1,600 is made on the old machine, and the balance is paid by check.

11.5 D Co. purchased a truck on January 2, 1963, at a cost of $7,200. At the time of purchase, the useful life was estimated to be six years, the residual value zero, and the asset was depreciated by the straight line method. Three years later, on January 2, 1966, a new truck was purchased for $8,000; the old truck was traded in for $2,500 of the purchase price, and the balance was paid by check.

Give journal entries (1) to record the retirement (including the elimination of the accumulated depreciation account) and (2) to record the purchase of the new truck for each of the following assumptions: (a) the old truck had a fair market value of only $1,000 at the date of trade in; (b) the old truck was worth exactly the trade-in allowance of $2,500; (c) the old truck was worth exactly book value; that is, the company recognized no gain or loss. (Record each transaction in two entries, one for retirement of the old truck and one for purchase of the new truck. Charge an Allowance on Trade-in account for the assumed value of the truck in each retirement entry.)

11.6 Newport Chemicals, Inc., is considering the establishment of a branch plant in a new territory. The plant would cost $240,000 and would last twenty years. The best evidence available indicates that at present price levels $272,000 of goods per year could be sold from the new location. The goods would cost $148,000 per year (including depreciation on the plant) and would involve selling expenses of $52,000 and administrative expenses of $24,000 per year. The officers feel that they should expect earnings of at least 10 percent per year after taxes on the initial plant investment (disregarding working capital) in view of the risks in this line of business. Assume that income taxes will average 50 percent of income before taxes. Do the figures given indicate that the investment should be made? Show your calculations.

11.7 The Mautz Company is considering replacement of a heavy machine that has no trade-in or salvage value. The annual cost of operating the old machine and the possible new one are as follows:

	Old	New
Depreciation	$1,000	$2,600
Labor	2,400	1,100
Power	1,200	800
Repairs	2,000	1,100
Sundry out-of-pocket costs	600	800
	$7,200	$6,400

As far as the foregoing figures can indicate, should the replacement be made? If the new machine was available on a trade-in basis that would reduce the amount paid so that depreciation would be $2,300, not $2,600 per year, what would your answer be? Give your reasons.

11.8 The Fiber Company is considering building a new factory in California, where it has a new market. The factory would cost $800,000 and would last twenty years. An additional $200,000 of working capital would have to be used in connection with the plant. The best estimates indicate that annual sales of $950,000 can be made; that cost of goods sold will be $500,000; that selling expenses will be $200,000; that administrative and general expenses will be $100,000 per year (the foregoing figures include depreciation). Federal and state income taxes are estimated at 50 percent of income before tax. Management is interested in making the investment if the payout period on the investment in the factory building, exclusive of working capital, will be seven years or less. (1) On this basis, will the investment be made? Show your calculations. (2) Comment briefly on some of the deficiencies in this approach to plant feasibility analysis.

11.9 Give entries to correct the following errors in the records of the H Co. for 1966:

(1) Truck 41 was acquired on January 6, 1966, for $8,200; terms, $1,000 cash, the balance payable in thirty-six monthly installments. Carrying charges of $\frac{1}{2}$ percent per month were added, making a total contract of $8,496 ($7,200 balance plus $1,296 carrying charges). The down payment and eleven monthly payments of $236 were debited to Motor Vehicles during 1966.

(2) A trailer for truck 41, pchased on January 7 at a cost of $500, was debited to Purchases.

(3) On July 2, truck 43, a used vehicle, was purchased for cash and was properly debited to Motor Vehicles; however, the $600 cost of a major overhaul, including a new motor and rebuilt transmission, was charged to Repairs Expense.

(4) Payment of $3,856 for truck 45 on July 14 was debited to Motor Vehicles. The payment consisted of the following items:

Price of truck	$3,400
One-year service contract	250
Sales tax, 4% × $3,650	146
Licenses and taxes for remainder of 1966 . .	60
Cash paid	$3,856

(5) The bookkeeper recorded depreciation at 25 percent of the year-end balance of Motor Vehicles. There were no additions or retirements, other than those cited above. Depreciation should have been computed to the nearest whole month on a straight line basis, using a life of four years and no residual value.

11.10 The Centerville Electric Company is a municipally owned electric utility. It calculates its net income in the same way that private business concerns do, following conventional accounting principles. It does not try to make a substantial profit, but wants at least to cover all costs. It has a plant that cost $1,200,000 sixteen years ago and was expected to last twenty-five years. Its net income in 1966 was $16,000. Since the plant was built the general price level has doubled, but few increases in rates have been made by the utility. There is a controversy in the city on the question of whether or not rates are high enough. What is your opinion? Give your reasons and show any calculations.

11.11 G Co. can acquire a C−360 electrostatic copier by purchase or lease. The machine can be purchased for $1,200 on terms of $200 down and the balance in four semiannual installments of $250 plus interest at 8 percent per year on the principal repaid. (The first payment is $260, the next $270, and so on.)

Alternatively, the machine can be leased for a period of two years for an initial payment of $100 plus a semiannual charge of $220. The company can take title to the copier at the end of the 2-year contract for $400.

Repairs and maintenance are the responsibility of the company under either arrangement. The copier has an estimated useful life of five years with no residual value.

It has been suggested that the lease is economically equivalent to ownership in this instance. Management is interested in how a formal record of the rights and obligations with respect to the machine might be included in the accounts regardless of the plan under which it is acquired.

Required:

1. Present entries to record acquisition of the copier, semiannual payments, and annual depreciation by the straight line method for the first two years, assuming the machine is bought.
2. Present entries to record acquisition of the copier, semiannual payments, and annual depreciation, assuming the machine is leased and treating the "lease" as, in economic reality, a purchase.
3. Is it better for the company to purchase or to lease the copier? Why?

11.12 An offer has been made to acquire the business of the F Co. In this connection, goodwill is defined as the value of the business in excess of the net tangible assets. The value of the business will be computed by capitalizing the normal earnings for the last year at 10 percent. (A return is capitalized by dividing it by the rate of return. The quotient is the present value of the perpetuity. For example, $12,000 capitalized at 8 percent is $150,000, which capital provides a perpetual income of $12,000 at 8 percent.) Net income for last year was $480,000 after the following debits and credits:

Gain on sale of land adjoining plant $30,000
Depreciation of plant and equipment 90,000
Amortization of patents 10,000

The tangible net assets of the company amount to $4,000,000. Compute goodwill.

PROBLEMS

11.1 Following is a summary of receipts and disbursements of Rochdale Properties, Inc., for the year ended December 31, 1966:

Receipts:
    Issuance of Capital Stock $30,000
    Rents Received 30,000
        Total Receipts $60,000

Disbursements:
    Payments for Properties $25,000
    Taxes 5,000
    Insurance 1,000
    Mortgage Payments:
        Principal . . . . $ 1,250
        Interest 15,000   16,250
    Miscellaneous 750
        Total Disbursements $48,000

    Cash Balance, December 31, 1966 . . . . $12,000

The company was formed on January 2, 1966, to acquire and operate rental properties; at that date it purchased real estate at a cost of $250,000, of which $25,000 was the assigned value of the land. The company elects to depreciate the building, having a useful life of forty years, by the double declining balance method.

Required:

1. Prepare an income statement for the year ended December 31, 1966.
2. Assuming rent receipts, mortgage payments, and operating expenditure are the same in 1967, as in 1966, what will be the amount of excess of cash receipts over disbursements for 1967? How will this compare with the net income (or loss) for the year, assuming the interest portion of the mortgage payments declines $100 and the principal portion increases $100?
3. At December 31, 1967, the president of the company cannot understand why the accounts fail to show an "earned surplus." He points out that in addition to the cash in bank and the repayment of the mortgage, the property has appreciated 6 percent compared to its price on January 2, 1966. Discuss briefly.

11.2 Included in the ledger of Berkwood Industries is an account called Real Estate, which contains the following debits and credits for 1967:

Debits

Jan.	1	Cost of land and buildings acquired as a plant site	$ 60,000
	15	Fees for title search	600
June	30	Payments to building contractors	200,000
July	1	Real property taxes to 7/1/67, date of building completion . .	4,000
	1	Insurance on improvements during construction	2,000
	10	Architects' fees on construction	14,000
	15	Assessments made by city for road construction	1,400
			$282,000

Credits

Feb.	1	Proceeds from sale of salvage materials in old building	$ 2,000
Dec.	31	Depreciation at 2 percent per year from completion of construction	2,800
	31	Balance	277,200
			$282,000

Required:

1. Prepare a schedule with columns for Date, Description, Total, Land, Buildings, and Other, and reclassify debits and credits erroneously combined in the foregoing account. Credits may be written in parentheses to distinguish them from debits.
2. Prepare journal entries to distribute debits and credits in the Real Estate account and to correct the charge for depreciation. Closing entries for 1967 have not been made.

11.3 Prepare journal entries to record the following transactions of Miller Construction Co., Inc.:

(1) Received an invoice of $800 for reinforcing the frame and body of a truck so it could carry heavier loads.
(2) Received an invoice of $400 from Holland Garage for overhauling the motor of a truck. Truck motors are overhauled after each 25,000 miles of operation; overhauls do not prolong the lives of the trucks and are not included in the charges for depreciation.
(3) Antismog arresters are installed on all trucks at a total cost of $1,000.

(4) The administrative offices are painted at a cost of $400. Sections of the buildings are painted each year.

(5) Depreciation is recorded on the trucks for the month. It amounts to 8 cents per mile on the 1,800-mile run.

(6) Depreciation is recorded on the office furniture and fixtures for the month. It is computed by the straight line method on a depreciable amount of $28,800, using an estimated life of twenty years.

(7) Depletion of the quarry is recorded for the month. The quarry cost $52,000, and $18,000 was spent removing dirt from the top of the rock. When operations were begun it was estimated that 350,000 tons of rock were available. During the month 7,000 tons were removed.

(8) Ten years ago the company purchased a patent for $36,000 that still had twelve years to run. Record the amortization for the month.

11.4 Newport Co. owned four trucks on January 1, 1966, as listed below.

Truck No.	Acquired	Cost	Accumulated Depr.
1	7/1/64	$ 3,000	$ 900
2	1/1/65	3,600	720
3	1/1/65	4,800	960
4	7/1/65	5,000	500
		$16,400	$3,080

Trucks are depreciated by the straight line method over a life of five years with no residual value.

The following transactions relating to trucks were completed in 1966 and 1967.

1966

Jan. 2 Truck 1 was totally destroyed. The loss was uninsured.
July 1 Truck 5 was purchased for $6,000 cash.
Dec. 31 Annual depreciation.

1967

Jan. 31 Truck 2 was sold for $2,000 cash.
July 1 Truck 3 was traded for an allowance of $3,000 on the $7,200 list price of truck 6; the balance was paid by check. (Use the income tax method.)
Dec. 31 Annual depreciation.

Required:

1. Prepare journal entries.
2. Prepare a schedule of trucks showing cost and accumulated depreciation at December 31, 1967.
3. Submit alternative entries for the last two transactions in which loss or gain is recorded on the exchange.

11.5 The Manet Company purchased a large truck on January 1, 1966, for $25,000. Trade-in value at the end of five years is expected to be $2,500. The president of the company has heard of depreciation being calculated by straight line, double declining balance, and sum-of-the-years'-digits methods. Prepare a comparative schedule in columnar form showing the depreciation each year under the three methods. Switch to straight line depreciation in the fourth year of the double declining balance method. Include figures to show how each of the declining balance methods is computed.

11.6   Listed below are the fixed assets of the J. M. Riddle Co. at December 31, 1966.

Asset	Date Purchased	Cost	Expected Life (years)	Expected Salvage
Autos:				
No. 1.	6/30/65	$4,400	4	$400
No. 2.	3/31/65	5,200	4	400
Office equipment:				
Adding machine	1/1/60	800	10	0
Cooler	1/1/60	1,200	8	0
Other equipment	1/1/60	2,000	10	200

The company records depreciation by the straight line method on December 31 of each year, unless there is reason to record it earlier on a particular asset.

Required:

Journal entries for the following transactions. Entries are required only at the dates mentioned. Record depreciation for a fraction of the year at disposal.

(1) On April 30, 1967, the cooler is given to the junk collector.
(2) The adding machine is sold on March 3., 1967, for $300.
(3) Auto 1 is destroyed in an accident on June 20, 1967. The insurance company is liable for the market value of the car, $2,500.
(4) Depreciation is recorded on the assets owned at December 31, 1967.
(5) On March 31, 1968, auto 2 is traded in on a new car. The allowance is $2,000 and the price of the new car is $6,000. (Record the loss or gain on the exchange.)
(6) Record the trade-in of auto 2, using the tax method.
(7) Record the trade-in of auto 2, assuming the $2,000 trade-in price really represented a $300 price-cut on the new car and $1,700 actual market value of the old car.

11.7   A schedule of the fixed assets of Berkshire, Ltd., at December 31, 1966, is given below:

Asset	Date Purchased	Cost	Declining Balance Rate
Motor vehicles:			
Chevrolet truck	1/1/65	$ 6,000	40%
Ford truck	7/1/65	5,000	40%
Office equipment:			
Printing calculator	7/1/66	4,000	20%
Bookkeeping machine.	1/1/65	12,000	20%

Depreciation is recorded on December 31 of each year by the double declining balance method, unless there is reason to record it earlier.

1. Prepare journal entries for the transactions and adjustments at the dates listed below. Depreciation on disposals should be recorded for a fraction of the year. (Round all amounts to the nearest dollar.)

1967

Dec. 31   Annual depreciation.

1968

Mar. 31   The Ford truck was stolen. The insurance company will reimburse the company $2,000 on the loss.

Dec. 31 As a result of a systems study, the company plans to introduce an electronic data processing system, which will make the bookkeeping machine obsolete by December 31, 1970. Record depreciation on the bookkeeping machine, switching to the straight line method and writing off the remaining depreciable value over the remaining useful life. (Entries for depreciation of other assets need not be submitted.)

1969

June 30 The bookkeeping machine is sold for $3,000.
Dec. 28 The Chevrolet truck is traded in on a new Dodge costing $7,000. The allowance on the Chevrolet is $1,000, and the balance is paid by check. (Loss or gain on the trade-in is recorded.)

2. Record the trade-in (a) by the tax method and (b) by assuming the allowance of $1,000 consists of a discount of $600 on the Dodge and payment of $400 for the Chevrolet.

11.8 The Garrett Company bought a lathe for $24,000 on January 1, 1966. Its useful life was estimated at ten years, with a residual value of $1,800. Depreciation by the straight line method is recorded on December 31 of each year.

Required:

1. Give the entries for 1966.
2. In 1970 additional data became available indicating a probable over-all life of fifteen years for the lathe. Make the proper adjustments and the depreciation entry for 1970 in such a manner that the depreciation cost will be correctly stated in 1970 and subsequent years.
3. On December 31, 1977, the lathe was replaced by a newer model. The new lathe costs $40,000 and was acquired on the following terms: $20,000 in cash; $6,000 allowance in trade for the old lathe; and a $14,000 note payable. Give entries, assuming the allowance represents the fair market value of the old lathe.

11.9 On October 1, 1966, the Olefins Company bought a truck chassis for $4,500 and put on it a tank which cost $1,200. It was estimated that the chassis would last four years with an estimated turn-in value of $500 and that the tank would last six years with no scrap value. The entire unit is carried under the title of "Automobiles" and only one account is used to record the accrued depreciation. The company records depreciation by the straight line method at December 31 and whenever an asset is retired.

Required:

1. Give the entry to be made on December 31, 1966.
2. Give the entry to be made on December 31, 1967.
3. On June 30, 1970, the old chassis is turned in on a new one. The price of the new chassis is $5,000 and an allowance of $600 is given on the old one. Give the journal entries that would be made at this time. Disregard income taxes.
4. Give the entry on December 31, 1970. The estimated life of the new chassis is four years and the estimated turn-in value is $600.
5. On June 30, 1971, the truck is destroyed by fire. On account of the high rate, no insurance was carried, and $100 was paid to have the truck removed from the highway. Give the journal entries to be made at this time.

11.10 The following debits and credits appear in the Equipment account of the Tonga Co. for 1966:

Jan. 2 A bill for $1,000 freight on equipment purchased f.o.b. shipping point was debited to Freight In.
Mar. 31 Annual maintenance of $400 was debited to Equipment.

July   1   A payment of $12,800 debited to Equipment is detailed as follows:

List price of machine. $25,000
Sales tax, 4%   1,000
Interest, 2 years @ 6%   1,800
Total $27,800
Less: Note due in 2 years   15,000
Cash paid $12,800

Sept. 30   A payment of $39,600 on the trade-in of an old unit debited to Equip-
ment is detailed as follows:

Contract price of new equipment $39,400
Cost of removal of old equipment   1,000
Installation of new equipment   2,700
Freight in—new equipment   1,500
Freight out—old equipment   1,000
Total $45,600
Trade-in allowance—old equipment   6,000
Cash paid $39,600

The old equipment was acquired January 2, 1960, at a cost of
$28,000.

Depreciation at 10 percent was computed on the year-end balance of
the Equipment account.

Submit correcting entries, assuming the nominal accounts have not been closed
to Profit and Loss for 1966. Equipment is properly depreciated by the straight
line method at 10 percent per year. Disregard income tax considerations, and
assume the trade-in allowance represents the fair market value of the old equipment.

11.11 The Eastman Company shows net income for 1966 of $180,000, computed by
conventional accounting methods. The company proposes to pay a dividend of
$100,000 out of 1966 net income, and asks you whether or not this amount may
be excessive. Your investigation reveals that the company has working capital
of $300,000 and fixed assets purchased fifteen years ago for $1,750,000, with an
expected life of twenty years. During the last fifteen years the general price level
has doubled. The company does not plan to expand by reinvestment of income,
but does expect to maintain the current level of facilities and activity. What is
your answer?

Sometimes the ordinary open book account (recorded in Accounts Receivable or Accounts Payable) is not satisfactory to creditors. They are usually not willing to extend credit on open book account when:

1. The term for repayment is longer than the usual thirty or sixty days.
2. The creditor wants a contract that is easier to enforce, if necessary.
3. The creditor wishes to be able to sell the receivable easily.
4. The creditor desires specific security for the loan.
5. The creditor wishes to charge interest on the debt.

In these circumstances promissory notes, bonds, or mortgages are commonly used. This chapter deals with some of the legal characteristics and accounting requirements of these instruments. It also considers the internal control and some of the managerial problems surrounding their use.

DEFINITIONS

A *promissory note* is a written promise

1. to pay a certain sum of money
2. on demand or on a fixed or determinable future date
3. to the bearer or to the order of a designated person
4. signed by the maker

A promissory note is a negotiable instrument. This means that it can be transferred from one person to another so that the person who takes it without notice of any defect in the title gets a good and enforceable title to it, except for such absolute defenses as forgery. For example, if A gives B a promissory note for an automobile and B sells the note to C, who does not know that B has not delivered and has no intention of delivering an automobile to A, C can collect from A. By the same token, a note may be enforced in court without proving that a debt exists, as one would have to do to enforce an ordinary account receivable. The note may or may not provide for the payment of interest in addition to the face amount of the note. If provision for interest is made, it is an *interest-bearing* note; if no provision is made, it is a *noninterest-bearing* note. Interest is customary in transactions involving notes, but it may be provided for by making the note for a larger amount than the purchase or loan. Interest is not customary on open book accounts (ordinary accounts receivable), and neither is provision of special security for the debt. When these things are desired, the creditor usually asks for a note. A promissory note is illustrated here.

366

$ 800.00   August 1   19 66

60 days *after date, (without grace)* 1 *promise to pay to the order of* Bank of Rochester

Eight hundred - - - - - - - - - - - - - *Dollars for value received with interest of* 4 *per cent per* annum *from* Aug. 1, 1966 *until paid, both principal and interest payable only in* LAWFUL MONEY OF THE UNITED STATES.

Payable at Rochester, Minnesota

No. 1427 *Due* Sept. 30, 1966   *Albert L. Pinkson*

Bonds are elaborate, formal, subdivided promissory notes. They are subdivided so that many different people can furnish funds as creditors. Because of the scattered ownership, a *trustee* represents the bondholders in dealings with the debtor. The trustee is usually a trust company. The contract that sets out the rights and duties of the parties is called a *trust indenture*. This may be a very long document. For example, some railroad bond indentures are fat printed books because of the necessity of describing each parcel of land that forms part of the security for the bond. The illustration on page 369 shows a bond certificate registered in the name of the person to whom it was issued. Such a bond is called a "registered" bond; other bonds, payable to "bearer," are called "bearer" bonds.

A *mortgage* is a document giving a creditor the right to take designated property of the debtor if the repayment terms of the debt are not met. Usually the language of a mortgage includes a promissory note for the debt out of which the mortgage grew. Bond indentures often include a mortgage.

CALCULATION OF INTEREST

Interest is usually expressed as a certain percent of the principal of the debt per year. For example, the interest on a 5 percent 1-year note for $1,000 is $1,000 × 5% × 1 = $50. Fractions of a year may be "exact" or "ordinary." The interest on a note for $500 at 6 percent running twenty-eight days is computed as 28/365 × $30 = $2.30 if exact, and 28/360 × $30 = $2.33 if ordinary.

The ordinary method is satisfactory for accruals and is used in this text. It permits calculation by the 6 percent 60-day method. This method takes advantage of the fact that 6 percent per year for 60 days is 1 percent of the principal if we assume 360 days in the year (60 is 1/6 of 360; 1 percent is 1/6 of 6 percent). Since 1 percent is computed by moving the decimal point two places to the left, this simplifies many computations. When the rate is different from 6 percent or the time different from 60 days, we start with this rate and time and adjust the result for any different rate or time or both. For example, the interest at 6 percent on $1,200 for 90 days by this method is:

$1,200.00 at 6% for 60 days	$12.00
$1,200.00 at 6% for 30 days (½ of $12.00)	6.00
$1,200.00 at 6% for 90 days	$18.00

Interest on $1,400 at 7 percent for 86 days may be computed:

```
$1,400 at 6% for 60 days.............................$14.00
$1,400 at 1% for 60 days (⅙ of $14.00)................  2.33
$1,400 at 7% for 60 days.............................$16.33
$1,400 at 7% for 20 days (⅓ of $16.33)...............  5.44
$1,400 at 7% for 6 days (1/10 of $16.33).............  1.63
$1,400 at 7% for 86 days.............................$23.40
```

Sometimes it is more convenient to subtract, as the case of 7 percent for 87 days on $1,400 indicates:

```
$1,400 at 6% for 60 days.............................$14.00
$1,400 at 1% for 60 days (⅙ of $14.00)................  2.33
$1,400 at 7% for 60 days.............................  16.33
$1,400.00 at 7% for 30 days (½ of $16.33)............  8.17
$1,400.00 at 7% for 3 days (1/10 of $8.17)............(  .82) (deduction)
$1,400.00 at 7% for 87 days..........................$23.68
```

In determining the period for calculating interest the following rules will be used for work in this text:

1. If exact interest is specified, the exact number of days should be counted and that number divided by 365 should be used as the fraction of a year. The days from January 10 to July 9, 1966, for example, may be counted as follows:

```
January: 31 − 10 = 21
February.......... 28
March............. 31
April............. 30
May............... 31
June.............. 30
July.............. 9
   Total...........180
```

In a similar way, the due date of a note due in a certain number of days may be determined. The maturity date of a note dated January 10, 1966, and due in 180 days is determined as in the preceding computation, the number of days needed in the last month to make the total required being the date on which the note is due.

2. If exact interest is not specified and the term of the note is given in days, ordinary interest may be used. The fraction is the number of days given divided by 360 and the computation may be made by the 6 percent 60-day method.

3. If the time is given in months, ordinary interest may be used and a month may always be considered to have thirty days. Thus two months is 1/6 of a year, three months 1/4, four months 1/3, and six months 1/2. The due date in this case is the same day of the month in which the note comes due as the day on which the note is dated. A 3-month note dated May 15 is due on August 15

by this rule. If the note is dated on the 31st of a month and falls due in a month with fewer days, it is due on the last day of that month.

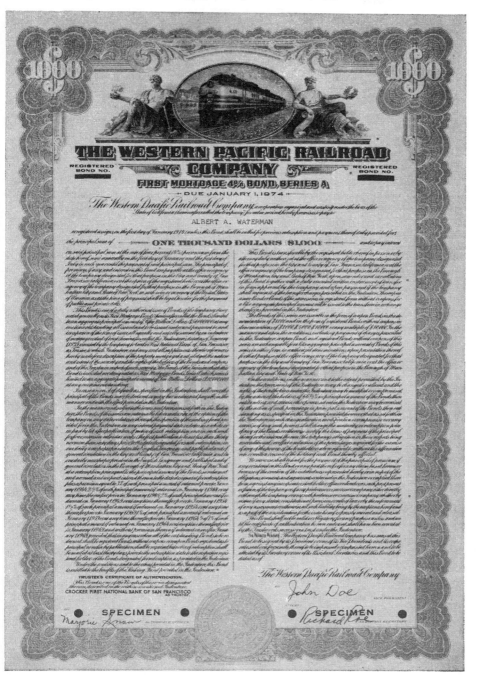

NOTES PAYABLE

Notes are sometimes issued for cash loans, sometimes for purchases of merchandise, and sometimes to convert a debt to the note form. On the books of the maker the note is a liability; if a 4 percent 9-month note dated May 10, 1966, is issued for a bank loan of $6,000, the entry on the borrower's books is:

```
Cash........................................ $6,000.00
    Notes Payable..........................              $6,000.00
```

If the borrower closes his books on June 30, 1966, ordinary interest accrued on the note to June 30 may be recorded as follows:

```
Interest Expense............................... $   34.00
    Accrued Interest Payable..................          $   34.00
```

The interest is computed by the 6 percent 60-day method as follows:

$6,000.00 at 6% for 60 days............................ $60.00
$6,000.00 at 2% for 60 days (⅓ of $60.00).............. (20.00)
$6,000.00 at 4% for 60 days............................ $40.00
$6,000.00 at 4% for 9 days ($\frac{1\frac{1}{2}}{10}$ of $40.00)............. (6.00)
$6,000.00 at 4% for 51 days (31 − 10 + 30 days)........ $34.00

NOTES RECEIVABLE

If a note is taken when goods are sold, say for $8,000, the entry is:

```
Notes Receivable.............................. $8,000.00
    Sales....................................              $8,000.00
```

In wholesale trade it is rare to use notes in this way; they usually result from ordinary accounts receivable that are slow of collection. The creditor will ask for a note in this case and the debtor gives it to avoid more drastic demands. For an $1,800, 5 percent 6-month note dated June 16, 1966, taken on an open account, the entry on the creditor's books is:

```
Notes Receivable.............................. $1,800.00
    Accounts Receivable......................              $1,800.00
```

If the firm closes its books for the quarter ended September 30, 1966, the accrued interest is recorded as follows:

```
Accrued Interest Receivable...................... $   26.50
    Interest Income..........................          $   26.50
```

The interest was computed by the 6 percent 60-day method as follows:

$1,800.00 at 6% for 60 days	$18.00
$1,800.00 at 1% for 60 days (⅙ of $18.00)	(3.00)
$1,800.00 at 5% for 60 days	$15.00
$1,800.00 at 5% for 40 days (⅔ of $15.00)	10.00
$1,800.00 at 5% for 6 days ($\frac{1}{10}$ of $15.00)	1.50
$1,800.00 at 5% for 106 days	$26.50

DISCOUNTING NOTES PAYABLE

Money is sometimes borrowed on noninterest-bearing notes. The lender obtains his interest by giving less cash than the face of the note. This practice is called *discounting*. The *discount rate* is the percent deducted from the face of the note; the amount deducted is the *discount* and the cash loaned is the *proceeds*. Exact and ordinary discount are computed in the same way as exact and ordinary interest. Consider a $5,000 note due in three months, dated and discounted at the bank on May 3, 1966, at 5 percent. The discount is computed on the ordinary basis as $5,000 × 0.05 × 1/4 (of a year) = $62.50. The entry on the borrower's books is:

Cash	$4,937.50	
Discount on Notes Payable	62.50	
Notes Payable		$5,000.00

The discount becomes expense as time passes. Assume that the borrower closes his books for the quarter on June 30, 1966. The following adjusting entry recognizes the interest expense incurred from May 3 to June 30:

Interest Expense	$ 40.28	
Discount on Notes Payable		$ 40.28

The interest for these fifty-eight days was calculated by the 6 percent 60-day method as follows:

$5,000.00 at 6% for 60 days	$50.00
$5,000.00 at 1% for 60 days (⅙ of $50.00)	(8.33)
$5,000.00 at 5% for 60 days	$41.67
$5,000.00 at 5% for 2 days ($\frac{1}{30}$ of $41.67)	(1.39)
$5,000.00 at 5% for 58 days	$40.28

At the maturity of the note any remaining discount will be written off to Interest Expense. The entries required at that time are:

Notes Payable	$5,000.00	
Cash		$5,000.00

Interest Expense	$ 22.22	
Discount on Notes Payable		$ 22.22

DISCOUNTING NOTES RECEIVABLE

One of the advantages of promissory notes is that they are readily salable. If a creditor wishes to get his money out of a note he "discounts" it with a bank or some other note buyer. The banker first computes what he will collect at maturity—the maturity value—and then discounts this at whatever rate is agreed upon. If the note is noninterest bearing, the maturity value is face value. If it is interest bearing, maturity value is face value plus the interest. For example, suppose that a merchant took a 4 percent 90-day $4,000 note from a customer on July 19, 1966, the date of the note. On July 31 the merchant discounted the note at the bank at 5 percent. The maturity value of the note is:

Principal...	$4,000.00
Interest (¼ of a year × 4% × $4,000.00)...............	40.00
Maturity value...................................	$4,040.00

Discount for seventy-eight days is calculated on the ordinary basis as follows:

$4,040.00 at 6% for 60 days..........................	$40.40
$4,040.00 at 6% for 18 days (³/₁₀ of $40.40).............	12.12
$4,040.00 at 6% for 78 days..........................	$52.52
$4,040.00 at 1% for 78 days (⅙ of $52.52)..............	(8.75)
$4,040.00 at 5% for 78 days..........................	$43.77

The merchant receives $4,040 minus $43.77, or $3,996.23. The entry on his books is:

Cash...	$3,996.23	
Interest Expense...............................	3.77	
Notes Receivable.........................		$4,000.00

If there had been accrued interest receivable on the merchant's books for this note, that account would have been written off when the note was discounted. The difference between the amount received and any accounts representing principal or interest receivable on the note is the interest expense or income of the seller. For example, The Aster Co. held a note receivable for $8,000 on which $46 of accrued interest had been recorded at the last closing date. The company decided to discount the note and received $8,052 for it. Its entry is:

Cash...	$8,052.00	
Notes Receivable.........................		$8,000.00
Accrued Interest Receivable................		46.00
Interest Income..........................		6.00

The proceeds will be more or less than the amounts recorded for the note on the sellers' books, depending upon the relative size of the interest and discount rates and the length of time since any accrual was recorded.

CONTINGENT LIABILITY ON NOTES RECEIVABLE DISCOUNTED

It is possible to endorse a note "without recourse" and so avoid guaranteeing the eventual payment of it. However, as a buyer will rarely take a note with such an endorsement, notes are usually transferred with the seller's guarantee automatically attaching to the note. Notes that have been sold are accordingly *contingent liabilities* of the seller until they are paid. Generally accepted accounting principles require that contingent liabilities be reported when balance sheets are issued. The usual practice is to describe them briefly in a footnote to the balance sheet.

DISHONORED NOTES RECEIVABLE

A note not paid at maturity is *dishonored.* Nonpayment, of course, casts doubt on the collectibility of the note, although dishonored notes are often paid later. Merchants customarily charge a dishonored note to an ordinary Accounts Receivable account, together with any accrued interest that has been recorded on it and any other charges. The entry required is illustrated by a $6,000 5 percent 5-month note dated April 28, 1966. The holder closes his books quarterly, and on June 30, 1966, had accrued interest of $52.50. On September 28, 1966, the note was dishonored. The entry on the holder's books at this time is:

```
Accounts Receivable............................$6,052.50
     Notes Receivable........................          $6,000.00
     Accrued Interest Receivable..............             52.50
```

Actually, $125 of interest is due, but in view of the doubtful status of the debt, no additional accrual is made.

If the note has been discounted by the original holder, it will come back to him when dishonored with a protest fee added. The "protest" must be made to hold any endorsers liable for the amount due. It is a notarized statement that the note was presented for payment on the date due and that it was not paid. Assume that the note mentioned just above had been discounted at the bank by the merchant who originally took it. When it was dishonored, the bank protested it and charged it back to the merchant's deposit account. The entry at that time on the merchant's books is:

```
Accounts Receivable........................$6,127.50
     Cash......................................          $6,127.50
```

The amount is calculated as follows:

```
Principal........................................$6,000.00
Interest ($\frac{5}{12}$ × 5% × $6,000)..................    125.00
Protest fee.......................................      2.50
     Total........................................$6,127.50
```

KINDS OF BONDS

Bonds may be classified in various ways; some of the classifications follow:

1. According to security:
   (a) Debenture bonds (no special security — a general obligation.)
   (b) Mortgage bonds (usually secured by real estate mortgage. They may be first-, second-, third-, (and so on) mortgage bonds according to the number of mortgages placed on the property by bond issues.)
   (c) Equipment-trust bonds (secured by equipment such as railroad cars, to which a trustee takes "title.")
   (d) Collateral-trust bonds (secured by deposit of other securities with a trustee.)
2. According to method of payment of interest:
   (a) Coupon bonds (Coupons are attached, one for each interest date; they are detached and presented by the holder at a bank or other paying agency.)
   (b) Registered bonds (Holders are registered and receive interest payments by mail.)
3. As to payment of principal:
   (a) Registered.
   (b) Bearer (Anyone in possession of the bond may present it for payment. Coupons are also payable to bearer.)

A bond issue customarily matures at one date, but *serial* bonds are issued, which mature in installments over a period of years. They are favored by state and local governments. Various other special features may be included in bond contracts; for example, *convertible* bonds may be exchanged for the stock of the issuing company at specified ratios. Bonds are usually issued in units of $1,000, but $500 and $100 certificates are sometimes used. United States savings bonds are issued in denominations as small as $25.

ISSUE OF BONDS

Many elaborate preparations go into the issuance of bonds. In large issues arrangements must be made for legal advice and for audit of the concern's accounts, so that financial statements with a certified public accountant's opinion may be presented to prospective buyers and to the Securities and Exchange Commission. Arrangements must be made with the securities dealers who will sell the bonds: The certificates must be printed. A trustee must be engaged. It is usually not possible to predict the exact price at which the bonds can be sold sufficiently far in advance to have the contract and certificates drawn up for the interest rate that will be acceptable to the market and which would allow the bonds to be sold at face value. Any difference between the rate of interest provided in the bond contract and the rate at which buyers are willing to take the bonds is adjusted by changing the price at which they sell. (Bond prices are expressed as a percent of par or face value.) If the bonds are sold at a *discount*, the price is lower than par (face or maturity value). In this case, the interest paid periodically is supplemented by the difference between the price paid and the face value received at maturity. The discount thus increases the yield rate over the face or contract rate. If the bonds are sold at a *premium*, the price is more than par. In this case some of the interest to be received periodically is, in effect, given back before it is received. The premium thus reduces the yield rate below the face or contract rate.

RECORDING DISCOUNT ON BONDS PAYABLE

The entry for a 10-year 4 percent bond issue of $100,000 par value, selling at 98½, is:

Cash.	$ 98,500.00	
Discount on Bonds Payable.	1,500.00	
Bonds Payable.		$100,000.00

As time passes, the discount becomes expense and is amortized at the same time that cash interest is accrued or paid. Bonds usually pay interest semiannually. Assume that the issue recorded above was sold on September 30, 1966, and that the issuer closes its books annually; on December 31, 1966, this entry is made:

Interest Expense.	$ 1,037.50	
Discount on Bonds Payable.		$ 37.50
Accrued Interest Payable.		1,000.00

The discount is spread over the 10-year life in straight line fashion, and for the quarter ended December 31, 1966, 1/40, or $37.50 of it is written off. On March 31, 1967, when the first semiannual interest payment is made, this entry is used:

Interest Expense.	$ 1,037.50	
Accrued Interest Payable.	1,000.00	
Discount on Bonds Payable.		$ 37.50
Cash.		2,000.00

When the second interest payment is made on September 30, 1967, no accrual has been recorded and the entry is:

Interest Expense.	$ 2,075.00	
Discount on Bonds Payable.		$ 75.00
Cash.		2,000.00

RECORDING PREMIUM ON BONDS PAYABLE

The entry to record a $100,000 4 percent 10-year bond issue selling at 102 is:

Cash.	$102,000.00	
Premium on Bonds Payable.		$ 2,000.00
Bonds Payable.		100,000.00

Assume that this issue also is sold on September 30, 1966, that it pays interest semiannually, and that the issuer closes its books annually on December 31. The entry on December 31, 1966, is:

```
Interest Expense...........................$    950.00
Premium on Bonds Payable...................      50.00
        Accrued Interest Payable.............             $  1,000.00
```

The amortization of the premium (1/40 of $2,000) has the effect of reducing the interest expense. The entry on March 31, 1966, the date of the first interest payment, is:

```
Interest Expense...........................$    950.00
Premium on Bonds Payable...................      50.00
Accrued Interest Payable...................   1,000.00
        Cash................................              $  2,000.00
```

The entry for the second payment on June 30, 1966, is:

```
Interest Expense...........................$  1,900.00
Premium on Bonds Payable...................     100.00
        Cash................................              $  2,000.00
```

INVESTMENTS IN BONDS

On the books of the buyer, a bond is an asset. It may be recorded in accounts similar but opposite to those used by the issuer. For example, a buyer of $1,000 of the 10-year 4 percent $100,000 bond issue sold at $98\frac{1}{2}$ and referred to above might make the following entry on September 30, 1966:

```
Bond Investment...........................$  1,000.00
        Discount on Bond Investment...........            $     15.00
        Cash................................                   985.00
```

It is common practice not to record the par value and discount or premium separately when a bond investment is made. If this alternative is followed, the above entry would become:

```
Bond Investment...........................$    985.00
        Cash................................              $    985.00
```

For the sake of uniformity the discount and premium accounts will be used in this text. Accrued interest income is recorded for the above purchase on December 31, 1966, as follows:

```
Accrued Interest Receivable.................$     10.00
Discount on Bond Investment.................       0.38
        Interest Income.....................              $     10.38
```

The entries for other dates and for investments made at a premium may be worked out along these same lines.

BONDS PURCHASED BETWEEN INTEREST DATES

When a bond is purchased between interest dates, the only convenient way for the seller to collect his accrued interest is to get it from the buyer, who will collect the next full payment. On the books of the buyer the entry for a 6 percent $1,000 bond bought at par with accrued interest of $10 is:

Bond Investment...........................	$ 1,000.00	
Accrued Interest Purchased..................	10.00	
Cash..............................		$ 1,010.00

When the next semiannual interest payment is received, the entry is:

Cash.....................................	$ 30.00	
Accrued Interest Purchased............		$ 10.00
Interest Income.....................		20.00

On the books of the seller the corresponding entries (assuming the bond was issued by the selling company) are:

Cash.....................................	$ 1,010.00	
Accrued Interest Sold................		$ 10.00
Bonds Payable.....................		1,000.00
Accrued Interest Sold........................	$ 10.00	
Interest Expense...........................	20.00	
Cash..............................		$ 30.00

Any premium or discount on bonds sold between interest dates applies to the period from the date of sale to maturity, and is amortized accordingly.

DISCOUNT AND PREMIUM IN THE BALANCE SHEET

Discount and premium accounts arise because of the custom of recording in the accounts the par value of obligations, which is the maturity or future value of the debt and may be very different from the present value. For example, a $1,000 noninterest-bearing note due in five years is worth only $747.26 today if interest at 6 percent compounded annually is required. In a sense, the $1,000 is not owed today; it is owed five years from now. To show it in the balance sheet at $1,000 and to compare it there with assets that will have five years to grow before they are called upon to meet the obligation is misleading. The best way to show debts incurred on a premium or discount basis in the balance sheet is to show the maturity value and premium or discount together. This combination gives the present value of the debt. It is illustrated as follows:

Notes payable................................	$ 8,000.00	
Less discount................................	420.00	$ 7,580.00
Bonds payable................................	$100,000.00	
Add premium.................................	2,000.00	102,000.00

Although many concerns have adopted the practice presented above, a majority still follow the older practice of showing discount on notes or bonds payable as a deferred charge on the asset side of the balance sheet. This practice suggests that the interest has been prepaid, but it is impossible to prepay anything by making a contract to pay back more than was borrowed. Those who show discounts as assets show premiums as deferred credits, and while this latter practice is better (they are liabilities), it is preferable to show them with the related debt. The same conclusion applies to investments in notes and bonds as to payables.

SINKING FUNDS

Bond indentures often require that some funds be deposited with a trustee either to pay off the bond issue or to enable some bonds to be retired periodically. The latter procedure aids the bondholders by assuring at least a limited market for their bonds. Sometimes a concern will establish a separate fund of assets to pay off a debt on its own initiative. These funds are called sinking funds. The entry to record payment of $10,000 cash to a trustee for a sinking fund is:

```
Sinking Fund.............................$10,000.00
    Cash................................              $10,000.00
```

Transfer of any other assets to a sinking fund is similarly recorded. If the trustee uses $2,000 of the fund to buy in bonds of the issue for which it is established, the entry on the books of the issuer of the bonds is:

```
Bonds Payable...........................$ 2,000.00
    Sinking Fund........................              $ 2,000.00
```

MORTGAGES PAID ON THE INSTALLMENT PLAN

It is a popular practice to pay off principal and interest of mortgages by uniform periodic payments, especially in the financing of homes. The payments are often calculated so the mortgage will be paid off in a specified time — 20, 25, or 30 years. Each payment consists of two parts: interest on the principal outstanding after the last payment, and the remainder, which reduces the outstanding principal. As time passes, the interest portion of each payment gets smaller and the principal payment gets larger. The process can be observed in an amortization schedule. This may be recorded in a passbook, which the borrower presents with each payment. An amortization schedule is shown here for a mortgage of $10,000 to be paid off in five annual installments with interest at 4 percent. The payment required each year in this case is $2,246.27, except that the last payment must be 1 cent more to adjust for dropping fractions of a cent. The interest for each year is 4 percent of the principal balance at the beginning of the year. If installments were paid monthly, the interest would be 4/12 percent each month. The amount of the payment to be made each period is obtained from interest tables.

AMORTIZATION SCHEDULE FOR MORTGAGE

($10,000.00 due in five annual installments with interest at 4%)

Date	Total	Interest	Principal	Balance of Principal
Jan. 1, 1966				$10,000.00
Dec. 31, 1966	$2,246.27	$400.00	$1,846.27	8,153.73
Dec. 31, 1967	2,246.27	326.15	1,920.12	6,233.61
Dec. 31, 1968	2,246.27	249.34	1,996.93	4,236.68
Dec. 31, 1969	2,246.27	169.47	2,076.80	2,159.88
Dec. 31, 1970	2,246.28	86.40	2,159.88	—

INTERNAL CONTROL FOR NOTES AND BONDS

Notes and bonds held as assets require the same kind of internal control that title documents require in the case of fixed assets. They should be kept in a safe deposit box with access permitted only to two persons acting together. If access to notes receivable must be frequent, they are kept in the office of the concern holding them, in a safe that should be as fire-resistant as possible. Investment in bonds is an unusual transaction for most concerns, and authority to make such an investment is usually reserved to the board of directors. For concerns that are investing companies by virtue of the character of their business, such as life insurance companies, a committee of officers often selects the issues to be purchased.

The authority to borrow modest sums on notes payable may be delegated to a financial officer or to an executive committee, but in almost all companies the incurring of large debts is reserved to the board of directors. The funds received from such loans are safeguarded by the internal control procedures used for cash receipts in general. The handling of periodic payments on them for interest or principal is safeguarded by the methods applicable to other cash disbursements. One internal control device deserves special emphasis at this point: The returned note or bond certificate received when the debt is paid must be canceled effectively so that it cannot fall into the hands of an innocent purchaser and give rise to another demand for payment. The documents are usually canceled by a perforating machine that spells the word "CANCELED" in small holes. Trustees customarily burn redeemed bonds and send the issuer a "cremation certificate" attesting to this fact.

MANAGEMENT PROBLEMS RELATING TO NOTES RECEIVABLE AND BOND INVESTMENTS

Merchandising and manufacturing businesses usually prefer not to hold notes receivable, and take them only when an open book account becomes slow. Notes receivable are thus a part of the general credit policy of the concern. The decision to ask for a note, or to accept an offer of one, when a customer has not been able to pay his account at the proper time, or, alternatively, to attempt to force payment requires information on the customer's financial condition and the prospects of his business. A balance sheet and a recent income statement may be requested, and general information on the industry the customer is in may be obtained. From the accounting information one can decide whether or not an extension of the credit will probably enable the customer to pay, or whether immediate action to salvage what can be gotten is better.

Accounting data are of similar importance in choosing bonds for investment. The ratio of bonds payable to the amount invested in the land, buildings, and equipment that are mortgaged or are available to secure the bonds will be computed. Income statements will be examined to see how the interest requirements of the issue compare with income available to pay the interest (in many cases, this is the net operating income figure). Other accounting comparisons will be made and additional information about the debtor's reputation and general ability and prospects will be assembled. If the issue seems likely to be paid and corresponds with the rate of return and type of risk the investor is willing to take, it will be bought; otherwise, it will be refused. The higher the risk of nonpayment, the higher the interest return required.

MANAGEMENT PROBLEMS RELATING TO NOTES PAYABLE

Notes payable are a prominent feature of the short-term financing of many concerns. The concerns having a substantial seasonal fluctuation in inventory often borrow enough to build up the stock to its seasonal peak and repay the loans as the merchandise is sold. For example, the operators of large grain elevators typically borrow heavily when the crop is being harvested. Some short-term loans may also be carried because the firm does not have a sufficient minimum working capital of its own or because it can borrow at a lower rate than the owners are willing to take on their own capital. In this sort of borrowing the firm must furnish the kind of accounting information required by the lender. It is therefore important for the debtor to maintain a good accounting system and staff, or he may have to get the data by hiring public accountants to come in and prepare financial statements and forecasts when a loan is negotiated. In the more important loans a formal opinion on the fairness of the accounts from a public accountant who has examined the records will be required.

An important problem with short-term loans is the management of cash and the scheduling of maturities so that notes falling due may be paid. The scheduling is largely a matter of avoiding the bunching of maturities; it can usually be arranged satisfactorily as long as the problem is kept in mind. The management of cash is best approached through a cash budget. As was explained earlier, this consists in computing, from the best estimates and planning available, what cash will be received and what paid out over the budget period. Prospective difficulties can thus be foreseen and solved before they cause real trouble.

MANAGEMENT PROBLEMS RELATING TO BONDS PAYABLE

Two factors of opposite effect are most prominent in management's decision on the use of bonds payable. One is the financial safety of the concern and the other is the possibility of improving the rate of return to owners by using long-term loans. The safety of the concern is affected because the interest on bonds, as well as their principal, is a debt that must be paid regardless of earnings; default can bring foreclosure in either case. If sales and earnings drop, the concern may not be able to pay interest. The management must therefore look at its own balance sheet and income statement as would an outsider who was considering buying its bonds, and the amount of bonds payable that it can safely use must be determined in the light of its assets and earnings. In favor of using bonds payable is the fact that money can usually be obtained in this way at lower rates than are earned on all the funds of the concern. The excess increases the rate of return to owners. This principle is called *leverage*; it may be demonstrated as follows:

LEVERAGE

Case 1		Case 2	
Current liabilities............	$ 80,000,000	Current liabilities............	$ 80,000,000
Proprietorship..............	200,000,000	Bonds payable—4%.........	100,000,000
		Proprietorship..............	100,000,000
Total assets and financial		Total assets and financial	
interests................	$280,000,000	interests................	$280,000,000
Earnings before interest.......	$ 28,000,000	Earnings before interest.......	$ 28,000,000
Interest....................	—	Interest (4% × $100,000,000)..	4,000,000
Earnings before income tax....	$ 28,000,000	Earnings before income tax....	$ 24,000,000
Income tax at 50%..........	14,000,000	Income tax at 50%..........	12,000,000
Net income to owners........	$ 14,000,000	Net income to owners........	$ 12,000,000

Rate of return on proprietorship:

$$\frac{\$14,000,000}{\$200,000,000} = 7\%$$

Rate of return on proprietorship:

$$\frac{\$12,000,000}{\$100,000,000} = 12\%$$

The ratio of owner and creditor capital to be employed is a matter for careful judgment. In the forming of this judgment, accounting data will play a major role. There is a special advantage to proprietors of a corporation in financing with bonds in the fact that interest is deductible in calculating income for income tax purposes.

SUMMARY

A promissory note is a written promise to pay a certain sum of money on demand or on a fixed or determinable future date to the bearer or to the order of a designated person, signed by the maker. It is a negotiable instrument. Bonds are elaborate, formal, subdivided promissory notes. A mortgage is a document giving a creditor the right to have property sold if the debt is not paid.

Interest is customary with these instruments. It may be calculated on an exact or ordinary basis. The ordinary basis permits use of the 6 percent 60-day method of calculation.

Notes payable are often discounted in borrowing; notes receivable may also be discounted by the holder. In either case the discount is computed on the maturity value of the note, including any interest. A note receivable discounted and not yet paid is a contingent liability to the person who discounted it. Premiums or discounts on notes and bonds are amortized to interest expense or interest income, and any unamortized balance is desirably shown in the balance sheet as a deduction from or addition to the par value of the obligation.

Sinking funds may be established for the purchase or retirement of bonds or other debt. Mortgages are often paid by uniform installments; an amortization schedule shows the payments and the portion of each constituting interest and principal.

Internal control for notes and bonds is similar to that for title documents in the case of assets; in the case of liabilities it is chiefly a matter of fixing authority. Proper destruction of redeemed debt instruments is especially important.

Managements' problems with notes and bonds include credit policies in connection with notes receivable, analysis of financial statements of debtors in connection with both notes receivable and bond investments, scheduling of maturities and cash budgeting in connection with short-term notes payable, and considerations of financial safety and possibilities of leverage in the use of long-term bonds payable.

QUESTIONS

12.1 (1) Why are special physical safeguards required for negotiable instruments?

(2) What is a "cremation certificate"? Who issues it? Why is it used?

12.2 (1) The Adler Co. buys an automobile and signs a promissory note to be paid off in installments of $88.50 per month. How does the creditor provide for interest in this transaction?

(2) Describe the entries made by the company for the purchase of the automobile and for the payments on the note.

12.3 (1) Explain the difference between "discounting a company's own note" and "discounting a customer's note."

(2) In which case does the company incur a contingent liability? How is it reported in the financial statements?

(3) Compute the proceeds on the following notes:

    (a) A $5,000 noninterest-bearing note due December 31, discounted December 1 at 6 percent.

    (b) A $10,000 6 percent 90-day note, dated September 1, discounted at 6 percent on October 1.

12.4 A $10,000 6-month 6 percent note issued by a company is dated August 1, 1966.

(1) What is the amount of accrued interest payable on the note as of December 31, 1966?

(2) What adjusting entry would be made for accrued interest on the note if the company closed its books annually on December 31?

(3) How would the entry be made on December 31 if the company did not use reversing entries and closed quarterly? monthly?

(4) How would the entry be made on December 31 if the company used reversing entries and closed quarterly? monthly?

12.5 (1) Explain the 6 percent 60-day method of computing interest.

(2) How can it be applied to a 6 percent note which runs sixty-six days?

(3) Is there a 4 percent 90-day method?

(4) Is "exact interest" larger or smaller than interest computed on the basis of a 360-day year?

12.6 (1) When is a note said to be dishonored?

(2) Describe the entries to be made by the payee (a) if he has held the note, (b) if he has discounted the note.

12.7 A gives B a 6 percent 6-month $10,000 note on May 1 and is given credit for the face value of the note. B endorses the note to C on August 1, at which date the note is applied on account at its face value plus accrued interest. The note is paid at maturity.

(1) Describe the entries made by A, who closes annually.

(2) Describe the entries made by B, who closes quarterly.

(3) Describe the entries made by C, who closes monthly.

12.8 (1) What are "bonds" when used in the term "bonds payable"?

(2) What is a trust indenture used in connection with bonds?

(3) What is the function of a trustee for a bond issue?

12.9 Suggest two kinds of bonds for each of the following characteristics: security, method of interest payment, method of payment of principal.

12.10 (1) How can bonds be sold when the buyer requires an interest rate higher than the fixed contract and the printed certificates provide?

(2) What is the effect of a premium on the interest expense of the issuer of bonds as compared with the face rate?

(3) It has been contended that discount on bonds payable is equivalent to pre-paid interest and should be shown as a deferred charge on the balance sheet. Criticize this position and suggest an alternative presentation.

12.11 (1) Bonds typically pay interest semiannually. What is done to divide an interest payment between a buyer and a seller when a bond is sold between interest dates?

(2) At times bonds are issued other than on the date printed on the bonds. Over what period should premium, or discount, be amortized? Why?

12.12 A trucking company purchased two trailers on September 30, 1966. The purchase contract specified a total price of $15,752 and a down payment of $5,000. The balance was covered by a "noninterest-bearing" installment note to be paid in twenty-four monthly installments of $448. The first payment was due on October 31, 1966. Included in the total price was an interest and finance charge of $1,152.

The purchase was recorded by the following entry:

Trailers	$14,600	
Deferred Interest and Finance Charge	1,152	
Cash		$ 5,000
Installment Note Payable		10,752

(1) In journal entry form, record the October 31, 1966, payment and adjustment of the deferred interest and finance charge account. Use the straight line method of amortization.

(2) Give arguments for and against the straight line method of amortizing the deferred interest.

(3) The company wishes to show the deferred interest as a deduction from the installment note payable on its balance sheet. Give arguments for and against this treatment.

(AICPA — adapted)

12.13 (1) What is a sinking fund?

(2) The sinking fund of the X Co. is invested in AAA bonds listed on the New York Stock Exchange. These bonds were bought at a discount. A dispute has arisen as to whether these bonds should be reported at cost, cost plus amortization of discount, or market value. What is your opinion?

12.14 (1) Suggest an internal control procedure for handling documents such as notes receivable or bonds (investments) that can be kept in a safe deposit box.

(2) What internal control step is especially important in connection with the payment of note or bond obligations?

12.15 (1) How do accounting statements contribute to management decisions regarding the acceptance of a customer's note? a bond investment?

(2) What kind of planning should a concern do that uses notes payable to a large extent?

12.16 (1) What two opposing factors are important in deciding whether or not to use bonds as a source of funds?

(2) Two companies are financed as follows:

	A	B
4% bonds payable.	$ 200,000	$ 600,000
Common stock – $100 par	800,000	400,000
Total investment	$1,000,000	$1,000,000

At what rate of return on the total investment will the net income per share be the same for both companies? What will the net income per share be if the company earns $100,000? if it earns $10,000?

(3) How do income taxes affect the decision whether or not to finance a capital project by the issuance of bonds?

12.17 Some businesses acquire land and plant by buying them and financing the purchase price by long-term debt. Others acquire the use of such assets by leasing them.

The usual practice of disclosing long-term lease commitments by a footnote in financial statements is thought by some persons to be inadequate to show the two basically similar transactions on a comparable basis. The alternative is to reflect the long-term lease in the financial statements as though an asset had been acquired by means of debt financing.

(1) Discuss the similarities and differences between the purchase and the lease of assets from the point of view of the nature and financial implications of each type of transaction.

(2) Illustrate the results of the usual statement presentation for the purchase of an asset as compared to the leasing of an asset.

(3) List the problems inherent in the alternative presentation of long-term leases.

EXERCISES

12.1 On November 1 Aubert's Diamond Palace requires additional goods for the Christmas season at a price of $100,000, terms 2/10 n/70. This merchandise can be financed from any of the following sources:

(1) Pay sixty days after expiration of the cash discount period with monies received from customers.

(2) Pay within the discount period with funds borrowed on a promissory note at 8 percent per year. The bank requires the company to leave in the checking account a balance of 20 percent of the amount borrowed.

(3) Sell securities bearing interest at 5 percent per year. Brokerage commission is ½ percent of the amount sold and ½ percent of the amount bought. (Other loss or gain on the sale and repurchase may be ignored.)

Required:

1. For each source of financing what is the effective interest cost in dollars and in annual rate percent if the full $98,000 is obtained for seasonal expansion?

2. How would each method of financing affect the company's current ratio at December 31, assuming it is to be 200,000/100,000, or 2 to 1, without recognition of the inventory expansion?

12.2 Calculate the due date and interest payable at maturity for each note listed below.

No.	Face	Dated	Term (days)	Rate
1	$10,000	6/1/66	30	6%
2	5,000	12/1/66	90	6%
3	3,600	5/17/66	33	7%

12.3 (1) Simplex Co. borrowed $10,000 from Finance Factors on October 1, 1966, giving the following note:

October 1, 1966

Sixty days after date we promise to pay Finance Factors, or order, $10,000.00 with interest at the rate of 6 percent per annum payable at maturity.

Simplex Company

(a) Present the entry to record the issuance of the note by the Simplex Company.

(b) Present the entry to record the payment of the note by the Simplex Company.

(c) Present the entries for Finance Factors.

(2) Suppose the note were payable in sixty days "without interest" and $9,900 were received from Finance Factors on October 1, 1966.

(a) Present the entry to record the borrowing.

(b) Present the entry to record the repayment.

12.4 The Apex Pump Co. borrowed $60,000 on September 1, 1966, from its bank, giving a note bearing interest at 6 percent per year due in six months. The fiscal year of the company ends on December 31.

Required:

1. Give the adjusting entry at December 31, 1966.
2. Give the entry to record payment of the note at maturity assuming (a) the company uses reversing entries, (b) the company does not use reversing entries.

12.5 On March 2, 1966, the Michigan Machine Company received a $10,000 promissory note from A. Carlson & Co., a customer, to apply on the latter's account. The note was dated March 1, 1966, was due on September 1, 1966, and bore interest at 6 percent per year, payable at the maturity of the note. The customer's account is credited with the face value of the note. At September 1, 1966, A. Carlson & Co. paid the interest and $6,000 on the principal of the note, signing a new 3-month 6 percent note for $4,000.

Required:

1. Give entries from March 2, 1966, through September 30, 1966, on the books of the Michigan Machine Company, which closes its books quarterly at March 31, June 30, September 30, and December 31. Reversing entries are not used.
2. Set up T accounts for the interest accounts used in 1. Show all entries, including closing entries.

12.6 Give entries for the following transactions on the books of Meyers and Co., whose fiscal year ends June 30:

1966

May 1   Sold merchandise on account to Colonial Stores, Inc., $12,600; terms 4/15 n/90.

16   Accepted a 60-day 6 percent note for $4,800 from Colonial Stores on account, less discount.

June 30   Interest is accrued on the note.

July 1   The note is discounted at 4 percent.

15   The note is dishonored. The bank issued a debit memo against the company's checking account for the maturity value of the note plus charges of $10.

Oct. 1   The balance due from Colonial Stores is written off.

1967

Apr. 1   The Colonial Stores account is collected less 50 percent attorney's fees.

12.7 Two companies are financed as follows:

M Fabricators, Inc.

4% mortgage bonds	$ 200,000
Common stock, 8,000 shares at $100 per share	800,000
Total	$1,000,000

G Gasco, Inc.

4% mortgage bonds	$ 600,000
Common stock, 4,000 shares at $100 per share	400,000
Total	$1,000,000

Assume net income is taxed at 40 percent. Compute the net income per share after taxes for each company if the net income before interest is $60,000, $100,000, $20,000.

12.8 The Golden Gate Company's balance sheet at January 1, 1966, showed Bonds Payable of $500,000 and a balance of $5,000 in the Discount on Bonds account. The bonds are due on January 1, 1976. Interest of 4 percent per year (on the face value) is paid on June 30 and December 31. Give journal entries for the following transactions:

1966

Mar. 31   The books are closed quarterly. Record the accrued interest and amortization of discount.

June 30   Record the payment of interest and amortization of discount. Reversing entries are not used.

July 1 $100,000 (face value) of the bonds are purchased from a holder for $95,000. The bonds are retired.

Sept. 30   Prepare the necessary adjusting entry for the bonds.

12.9 The L. P. Stevens Company issued $3,000,000 of 4 percent convertible debentures on September 1, 1966, at 98.85 and accrued interest from April 1, 1966. Interest is payable semiannually on April 1 and October 1, and bonds are due April 1, 1976. The company adjusts its books monthly and closes as of December 31 each year. Present journal entries as follows:

1966

Sept.   1   To record the issuance of the bonds.
Sept. 30   To accrue interest and amortize discount.
Oct.   1   To record payment of the bond coupon.

1967

July   1   To record purchase and retirement of $1,000,000 face amount of
            bonds at 99 and accrued interest.
Dec. 31   To record the closing of the bond interest account for the year.

12.10 On January 2, 1966, Y Corporation paid for a lathe costing $24,000 by giving
three noninterest-bearing notes for $10,000 each. The notes mature on January
2, 1967, January 2, 1968, and January 2, 1969, respectively. Give entries
through December 31, 1967, for the lathe and the notes. Y's fiscal year ends on
December 31. Depreciation is recorded at the double declining balance rate of
25 percent.

12.11 The M Co. purchased equipment for $12,000 on January 2, 1966, on terms
of $2,000 cash and chattel mortgage for $10,000. Mortgage payments of $3,741,
which include interest at 6 percent on the unpaid balance, are due on December
31 of 1966, 1967, and 1968.

Required:

1. Prepare an amortization schedule for the mortgage. (Round amounts to nearest dollar).
2. M Co. sold the equipment on January 2, 1968, for $9,000. The buyer as-
   sumed the mortgage, and the balance was received in cash. Show all entries
   relating to the equipment and mortgage through January 2, 1968. M Co.
   uses the double declining balance method of depreciation and a life of ten
   years for the equipment.

PROBLEMS

12.1 Burke & Co. had the following transactions in notes receivable. Prepare journal
entries to record them, using a 360-day year. The company does not use reversing entries.

1966

Apr.   1   Received a 6-month 4 percent note dated April 1, 1966 for $5,000,
           and credited the customer for the face of the note.
      15   Received a 12-month 6 percent note dated March 1, 1966 in the face
           amount of $10,000. The note, which had been received by the
           customer from someone else, was accepted at the face plus accrued
           interest.
June 30   Recorded accrued interest on the April 1 note.
      30   Recorded accrued interest on the March 1 note.
Aug.   2   Discounted the April 1 note at the bank on a 6 percent basis. The
           bank charged discount for sixty days.
Dec. 31   Discounted the March 1 note at the bank on a 6 percent basis. The
           bank charged discount for sixty days.

1967

Mar.   1   The March 1 note was dishonored and charged back to the company
           by the bank, with a $10 protest fee. The company charged it back to
           the customer.

12.2 The KSB Company prepared a bond issue dated March 1, 1966, to run twenty
years to March 1, 1986. Par value was $1,000,000; interest at 6 percent per

year was payable March 1 and September 1. Prepare journal entries for the following transactions involving this issue. Reversing entries are not used.

1966

Mar. 1 Sold $200,000 par value of the bonds at 97.

Sept. 1 Paid interest on the bonds sold on March 1, 1966, and recorded interest expense.

Dec. 1 Sold $400,000 par value of the bonds at 102.31 plus accrued interest from the last interest date, which was September 1.

31 Recorded accrued interest and interest expense on the bonds sold on March 1 for the December 31 closing.

31 Recorded accrued interest and interest expense on the bonds sold on December 1 for the December 31 closing.

31 Made a sinking fund deposit of $10,000.

1967

Mar. 1 Paid interest on all bonds outstanding.

1 Recorded amortization of discount on bonds issued March 1, 1966.

1 Recorded amortization of premium on bonds issued December 1, 1966.

Sept. 1 Paid interest and recorded amortization on bonds outstanding.

12.3 On June 1, 1966, the Sonoma Company borrowed $9,784 on a mortgage, agreeing to pay $3,660 at the end of each of the next three years, which payments will discharge the debt with 6 percent interest.

Required:

1. An amortization schedule. (Round to the nearest dollar.)
2. Journal entries for the first two payments.

12.4 Pacific Builders, Inc., had the following transactions in notes during 1966:

Sept. 1 A customer, B. S. Lee, turns in a note on his account, which he received from the maker, E. A. Allen. The note is dated July 31, is due November 30, and is noninterest bearing. The face value is $5,000. Lee is given credit for the present value of the note. The discount rate used is 6 percent per year. (Credit Discount on Notes Receivable for the discount.)

15 $10,000 is borrowed at the bank on a 2-month 6 percent note payable.

30 The books are closed. Make the necessary interest and discount adjustments.

Oct. 31 The Lee-Allen note is discounted at the bank at 6 percent per year.

31 The books are closed. Record the accrued interest on the note payable.

Nov. 15 The note payable to the bank is renewed. A check is drawn for the interest.

30 Record the accrued interest.

Dec. 2 The Lee-Allen note is not paid when it is due and a check is drawn to the bank for the face value plus protest fee of $10. The amount is charged to B. S. Lee's account.

5 Lee sends a new note for $3,000 and a check for the balance.

Required:

Dated journal entries.

12.5 On October 1, 1966 the Hilo Land Company bought a motel, including the fee to the land, for $200,000. Payment was made as follows:

(1) An existing 6 percent first mortgage of $80,000 due July 1, 1976, with interest payable each January 1 and July 1 was assumed.

(2) Delinquent taxes of $1,200 were assumed.

(3) A second mortgage of $50,000, which bears interest at the rate of 8 percent per year payable on October 1 and April 1 of each year, was given to the vendor. This mortgage also provides for a payment of $1,000 of the principal at each interest date in addition to the interest.

(4) A check was written for the balance. The company closes its books annually on December 31. Reversing entries are not used. The assessed value of the land is $10,000 and of the buildings, $40,000. Depreciation is provided by the double declining balance method to the closest whole month, with an estimated life of twenty years on the building.

Required:

Journal entries for (1) October 1, 1966, purchase of property; (2) December 31, 1966, adjusting entries; (3) January 1, 1967, payment of interest on first mortgage; (4) April 1, 1967, payment on second mortgage; (5) July 1, 1967, payment of interest on first mortgage; (6) October 1, 1967, payment of principal and interest on second mortgage; (7) December 31, 1967, adjusting entries.

12.6 The following trial balance is taken from the books of Tabco, Inc., at December 31, 1966. The accounting period is the calendar year.

Accounts Receivable . . . . $	82,000	
Accumulated Depreciation – Buildings		$ 100,000
Accumulated Depreciation – Equipment		32,000
Bond Sinking Fund	105,000	
Buildings	1,000,000	
Capital Stock		200,000
Cash in Bank	3,400	
Certificate of Deposit	30,000	
Cost of Goods Sold	3,100,000	
Debenture Bonds Payable		600,000
Equipment	50,000	
Expense Control (allow 2 lines)	1,036,000	
Interest Expense	21,500	
Interest Income (allow 3 lines)		1,200
Interest Payable (allow 2 lines)	–	
Land	100,000	
Merchandise Stock	240,000	
Mortgage Receivable	3,000	
Notes Payable		20,000
Notes Receivable	10,000	
Premium on Bonds Payable		39,000
Rent Income		3,600
Rent Receivable	–	
Retained Earnings		340,700
Sales		4,400,000
Supplies on Hand	–	
Taxes Payable		6,000
Unearned Interest Income	–	
Unearned Rent		800
Unexpired Insurance	5,200	
Vouchers Payable		42,800
	$5,786,100	$5,786,100

Adjustments:

(1) The certificate of deposit, dated November 1, 1966, due in 180 days, bears interest at the rate of 4 percent per year payable at maturity.

(2) The note payable of $20,000 bears interest at the rate of 6 percent per year payable at maturity. The note is dated September 1, 1966, and is due September 1, 1967.

(3) The note receivable of $10,000 is a noninterest-bearing note dated July 1, 1966, due July 1, 1967, accepted from a customer at a discount of 6 percent. The discount is included in Interest Income.

(4) The unexpired insurance at December 31, 1966, is $2,000.

(5) The inventory of supplies at December 31, 1966, is $5,000.

(6) A section of the building is rented for $400 a month. The balance in the Unearned Rent account is the result of a 2-months' adjustment made at December 31, 1965. Collections of rent during the year have been credited to Rent Income.

(7) Depreciation is to be recorded for the year by the double declining balance method. The estimated useful lives are: buildings, forty years; equipment, ten years. There have been no additions or retirements during the year.

(8) The Bond Sinking Fund account was properly adjusted as of December 31, 1965. During 1966 semiannual deposits of $10,000 were made on July 1 and December 31. Interest credited to the account during 1966 by the sinking fund trustee at the rate of 4 percent per year has not yet been recorded.

(9) The debenture bonds were issued on March 1, 1963, at 110, and are due March 1, 1973. Interest at 6 percent per year is payable semiannually on March 1 and September 1.

(10) The balance in the Mortgage Receivable account comprises the following:

Sale of land, 12/31/65		$5,000
Cash collections		
6/30/66	$1,000	
12/31/66	1,000	2,000
Balance per ledger, 12/31/66		$3,000

Collections were erroneously credited in full against the Mortgage Receivable account. They include interest at the rate of 4 percent per year.

Required:

1. Work sheet. The company is not subject to income taxes.
2. Balance sheet.

12.7 The South Pacific Development Company began business on January 2, 1966, with $500,000 from the issuance of 5,000 shares of $100 par common stock. On that date, the company acquired a hotel for $800,000 by (1) assuming an existing 4 percent first mortgage of $200,000 and accrued interest from April 1, 1965, (2) giving a 6 percent second mortgage of $100,000, and (3) paying the balance by check. The first mortgage required payment of interest on April 1 of each year and payment of the principal on April 1, 1970. As a condition of assuming this mortgage, the company agreed to make semiannual deposits of $10,000, beginning April 1, 1966, into a sinking fund earning 3 percent per year. The second mortgage required semiannual payment on June 30 and December 31 of $4,326, which amount includes interest at the rate of 6 percent per year on the unpaid balance of the mortgage.

The hotel was turned over to a management company, which operated the property for a percentage of the gross receipts. The management company paid all expenses except interest. Net amounts received from the management company were $80,000 on December 31, 1966, and $88,000 on December 31, 1967. The assigned value of the land is $200,000. Depreciation is computed on a straight line basis, life forty years, residual value 10 percent. The company closes annually on December 31. It is not subject to income taxes.

On January 2, 1968, the stockholders are considering the formation of another corporation to acquire like property. An additional $500,000 will be required to finance the acquisition. Four proposals are under consideration.

Proposal A. Issue 5,000 shares of common stock at $100 per share.

Proposal B. Issue 4,000 shares of common stock at $100 per share and borrow $100,000 on 20-year debentures with interest at 6 percent.

Proposal C. Issue 2,500 shares of common stock at $100 per share and borrow $250,000 on 20-year debentures with interest at $6\frac{1}{2}$ percent.

Proposal D. Issue 2,000 shares of common stock at $100 per share and borrow $300,000 on 20-year debentures with interest at 7 percent.

Receipts from the new venture are more uncertain than from the old. The developers feel there is a good chance that annual receipts will be $67,210; however, they may be as high as $87,210 or low as $31,210.

Required:

1. Journal entries reflecting all transactions and adjustments for the two years ended December 31, 1967. (Round amounts to the nearest dollar.) Closing entries are not required.
2. A statement of cash receipts and disbursements for the years ended December 31, 1966 and 1967.
3. An income statement for the years ended December 31, 1966 and 1967.
4. A schedule showing the expected net income per share of common stock for 1968 under each of the four proposals, assuming receipts of $67,210.
5. A schedule showing the expected net income per share of common stock for 1968 under each of the four proposals, assuming receipts of $87,210.
6. A schedule showing the expected net income per share of common stock for 1968 under each of the four proposals, assuming receipts of $31,210.
7. Discuss briefly the desirability of the four alternative financing proposals.

Payroll and Income Taxes

Government expenditures represent roughly 25 percent of the national income in the United States, and most of the revenue is raised in taxes. A substantial part of the income of each individual and each business is taken in taxes. Income tax and other tax laws require that records adequate for computing the taxes be kept. It is also necessary to maintain good records of transactions that affect taxes and to consider the tax effect of proposed transactions to avoid paying more than is required. In prior chapters the accounting for sales and property taxes was presented. This chapter presents the accounting involved in taxes based on payrolls and gives some fundamentals of income taxes. Internal control procedures useful in these areas are noted and some of the basic management decisions stemming from tax problems are outlined.

NATURE AND PURPOSES OF PAYROLL TAXES

Taxes are levied on payrolls to finance the social security programs of the United States, which consist primarily of (1) old age and survivors' insurance; (2) unemployment insurance (in rare cases a state disability insurance program is also provided for); and (3) health insurance for the aged (medicare). The first pays old age pensions to retired persons, provides disability payments for disabled persons, and pays benefits to dependents of insured workers who are disabled or die. The tax for these purposes and for medicare is collected under authority of the Federal Insurance Contributions Act and the Self-Employment Contributions Act, and is known as the F.I.C.A. tax or the social security tax. This program is frequently referred to as the social security program, although this, the unemployment program, medicare, and nine other programs (such as aid to the blind and child welfare services) are all part of the federal social security program. The old age program is operated entirely by the federal government and is financed by taxes levied on *both* employers and employees. The taxes are a certain percent of the first $6,600 earned in a year by each employee. Almost all workers in the country are covered by the program; the main exclusions are (1) state and local government workers who have not elected to come under the program, and (2) railroad and certain federal government workers who are covered by other plans. Casual work not in the regular course of the employer's business is also excluded. Self-employed persons pay taxes for old-age and survivors' insurance and medicare at rates approximately one and one-half times those paid by employees or employers alone.

Similar exclusions apply to the unemployment program, which is administered by the states. In most states it is financed by a tax on employers only, the greater part of the tax going to the states and a small part of it going to the federal government to finance the Social Security Board. Also, in most states

392

it is measured by the first $3,000 of earnings by each employee in a year, but some have established a higher base for this tax. California, for example, uses $3,800. The rates are shown in summary form in the accompanying table. They are subject to over-all changes at the will of Congress, which has revised the program several times since it was enacted. The table also takes note of the withholding of income taxes on employees, which the federal government requires.

TAX RATES

Tax	Paid by		Tax Returns Made
	Employer (Accrued)	Employee (Withheld)	
Federal income tax withholding	—	Per withholding table	Quarterly
Federal Insurance Contributions Act (old-age or F.I.C.A. and medicare) tax	4.2% of the first $6,600 of each employee's wages each year[a]	4.2% of the first $6,600 of each employee's wages each year[a]	Quarterly
State unemployment and disability taxes	0 to 2.7% of the first $3,000 of each employee's wages each year depending upon merit ratings[b]	none[c]	Quarterly
Federal unemployment tax	0.4% of the first $3,000 of each employee's wages each year[d]	none	Annually

[a] Rates in effect 1966. Rate is scheduled to go to 4.4% in 1967 and 1968; to 4.9% in 1969–1972; to 5.4% in 1973–1975; to 5.45% in 1976–1979; to 5.55% in 1980–1986; to 5.65% in 1987 and thereafter.

[b] Basic rate is 2.7 percent. Merit-rating plans in some states permit various lower rates to be paid by employers whose labor turnover is low.

[c] A very few states have disability insurance plans requiring deduction from employee's wages, or require employee contributions for unemployment purposes.

[d] This rate will be higher in cases where the state has borrowed unemployment funds from the federal government in order to repay the funds; some states have increased the basic rate also.

ENTRIES FOR PAYROLL TAXES

Entries required to record salaries and wages and the taxes relating to them are summarized as follows:

Recording salaries and wages and taxes withheld:

```
Salaries and Wages.................................$xxx.xx
      Vouchers Payable.........................         $xxx.xx
      Federal Income Tax Withheld................         xx.xx
      F.I.C.A. Tax Withheld......................         xx.xx
      (entered in the voucher register)
```

Note: In states levying unemployment or disability taxes on employees, another account would be needed.

When the accounting system provides for more than one salary or wage account, as it does in the larger concerns, debits are made to the different accounts in the voucher register.

Paying salaries and wages:

```
Vouchers Payable...............................$xxx.xx
        Cash.....................................        $xxx.xx
(entered in check register)
```

Recording employer's payroll taxes:

```
Payroll Taxes....................................$xxx.xx
        F.I.C.A. Tax Accrued.........................        $xxx.xx
        Federal Unemployment Tax Accrued...........        xxx.xx
        State Unemployment Tax Accrued..............        xxx.xx
(entered in general journal)
```

Paying the taxes:

```
Federal Income Tax Withheld.......................$xxx.xx
F.I.C.A. Tax Withheld.............................. xxx.xx
F.I.C.A. Tax Accrued.............................. xxx.xx
Federal Unemployment Tax Accrued.................. xxx.xx
State Unemployment Tax Accrued.................... xxx.xx
        Vouchers Payable.........................        $xxx.xx
(entered in voucher register)

Vouchers Payable...............................$xxx.xx
        Cash.....................................        $xxx.xx
(entered in check register; separate vouchers are made to the Federal and State
authorities)
```

The figures for the foregoing entries come from payroll sheets, where the names of individuals, the wages earned, and the deductions made are listed, or from calculations made from the payroll data. They are entered in total in the voucher register, check register, and general journal. If a voucher system is not used, a single entry in the cash disbursements book records the payroll and its payment.

CALCULATION OF WITHHELD TAXES

Payroll taxes may be calculated by applying the proper percentage to the wages. In the case of income tax withheld, the rate is 14 percent of the wage over the amount of withholding exemptions ($667 for each exemption per year). The taxes may be read from tables, and for income taxes the tables are especially time-saving. A recent official federal income tax withholding table for weekly payments over $50 is shown on page 395; the rates change at the will of Congress, and tables must be changed accordingly.

INCOME TAX WITHHOLDING TABLES

Weekly *Payroll period—Continued*

And the wages are—		And the number of withholding exemptions claimed is—										
At least	But less than	0	1	2	3	4	5	6	7	8	9	10 or more
		The amount of income tax to be withheld shall be—										
$50	$51	$7.10	$5.30	$3.50	$1.70	$0	$0	$0	$0	$0	$0	$0
51	52	7.20	5.40	3.60	1.80	0	0	0	0	0	0	0
52	53	7.40	5.60	3.80	2.00	.20	0	0	0	0	0	0
53	54	7.50	5.70	3.90	2.10	.30	0	0	0	0	0	0
54	55	7.60	5.80	4.00	2.20	.50	0	0	0	0	0	0
55	56	7.80	6.00	4.20	2.40	.60	0	0	0	0	0	0
56	57	7.90	6.10	4.30	2.50	.70	0	0	0	0	0	0
57	58	8.10	6.30	4.50	2.70	.90	0	0	0	0	0	0
58	59	8.20	6.40	4.60	2.80	1.00	0	0	0	0	0	0
59	60	8.30	6.50	4.70	2.90	1.20	0	0	0	0	0	0
60	62	8.50	6.70	5.00	3.20	1.40	0	0	0	0	0	0
62	64	8.80	7.00	5.20	3.40	1.60	0	0	0	0	0	0
64	66	9.10	7.30	5.50	3.70	1.90	.10	0	0	0	0	0
66	68	9.40	7.60	5.80	4.00	2.20	.40	0	0	0	0	0
68	70	9.70	7.90	6.10	4.30	2.50	.70	0	0	0	0	0
70	72	9.90	8.10	6.40	4.60	2.80	1.00	0	0	0	0	0
72	74	10.20	8.40	6.60	4.80	3.00	1.20	0	0	0	0	0
74	76	10.50	8.70	6.90	5.10	3.30	1.50	0	0	0	0	0
76	78	10.80	9.00	7.20	5.40	3.60	1.80	0	0	0	0	0
78	80	11.10	9.30	7.50	5.70	3.90	2.10	.30	0	0	0	0
80	82	11.30	9.50	7.80	6.00	4.20	2.40	.60	0	0	0	0
82	84	11.60	9.80	8.00	6.20	4.40	2.60	.90	0	0	0	0
84	86	11.90	10.10	8.30	6.50	4.70	2.90	1.10	0	0	0	0
86	88	12.20	10.40	8.60	6.80	5.00	3.20	1.40	0	0	0	0
88	90	12.50	10.70	8.90	7.10	5.30	3.50	1.70	0	0	0	0
90	92	12.70	10.90	9.20	7.40	5.60	3.80	2.00	.20	0	0	0
92	94	13.00	11.20	9.40	7.60	5.80	4.00	2.30	.50	0	0	0
94	96	13.30	11.50	9.70	7.90	6.10	4.30	2.50	.70	0	0	0
96	98	13.60	11.80	10.00	8.20	6.40	4.60	2.80	1.00	0	0	0
98	100	13.90	12.10	10.30	8.50	6.70	4.90	3.10	1.30	0	0	0
100	105	14.40	12.60	10.80	9.00	7.20	5.40	3.60	1.80	0	0	0
105	110	15.10	13.30	11.50	9.70	7.90	6.10	4.30	2.50	.70	0	0
110	115	15.80	14.00	12.20	10.40	8.60	6.80	5.00	3.20	1.40	0	0
115	120	16.50	14.70	12.90	11.10	9.30	7.50	5.70	3.90	2.10	.30	0
120	125	17.20	15.40	13.60	11.80	10.00	8.20	6.40	4.60	2.80	1.00	0
125	130	17.90	16.10	14.30	12.50	10.70	8.90	7.10	5.30	3.50	1.70	0
130	135	18.60	16.80	15.00	13.20	11.40	9.60	7.80	6.00	4.20	2.40	.60
135	140	19.30	17.50	15.70	13.90	12.10	10.30	8.50	6.70	4.90	3.10	1.30
140	145	20.00	18.20	16.40	14.60	12.80	11.00	9.20	7.40	5.60	3.80	2.00
145	150	20.70	18.90	17.10	15.30	13.50	11.70	9.90	8.10	6.30	4.50	2.70
150	160	21.70	19.90	18.10	16.30	14.50	12.70	10.90	9.10	7.30	5.50	3.80
160	170	23.10	21.30	19.50	17.70	15.90	14.10	12.30	10.50	8.70	6.90	5.20
170	180	24.50	22.70	20.90	19.10	17.30	15.50	13.70	11.90	10.10	8.30	6.60
180	190	25.90	24.10	22.30	20.50	18.70	16.90	15.10	13.30	11.50	9.70	8.00
190	200	27.30	25.50	23.70	21.90	20.10	18.30	16.50	14.70	12.90	11.10	9.40
		14 percent of the excess over $200 plus—										
$200 and over		28.00	26.20	24.40	22.60	20.80	19.00	17.20	15.40	13.60	11.80	10.10

PAYROLL RECORDS

Payroll records are of three kinds:

1. Records of work done
2. Payroll summary (payroll sheet or payroll book)
3. Supplementary records:
   (a) Employee's individual earnings record
   (b) Withholding statement

Other records, such as application forms, may be used, but the foregoing list gives the essential types.

RECORDS OF WORK DONE

When workers are paid by the hour, a *timecard* or *time report* is used. A timecard may be filled out by hand, but in the preferred arrangement a time clock automatically stamps the time "in" and "out" when the card is inserted in the machine. The daily time may be entered on a payroll sheet or summarized on the timecard and the wage computed there. The accompanying illustration shows a common form of timecard. A time report may be made by each employee, but in many concerns it is made by a foreman or a supervisor. It is used, for example, by construction crews and also by professional people to record time spent on jobs for different clients. Employees on monthly salary usually do not make out timecards or reports; a list of salaried employees is kept by a payroll clerk, and checks are made for the people on the list until a change notice is received from the proper executive. In some manufacturing plants, workers are paid on a piecework basis and turn in piecework tickets detached from the lots of product they have worked on.

PAYROLL SUMMARY

The payroll for each period is summarized on a *payroll sheet*. The sheets are often bound into a *payroll book*. The payroll sheet gives the employee's name, his number, time data such as hours worked (if needed), amount earned, deductions made, and amount and number of the payroll check. The deductions include:

1. Deductions required by law:
   (a) Federal income tax withheld
   (b) F.I.C.A. tax withheld
   (c) State or local income or payroll taxes withheld (in a few localities)
2. Deductions made by agreement: (in addition to those listed, others may be agreed upon)
   (a) Union dues
   (b) Hospital or medical plan dues
   (c) Group insurance premiums
   (d) Bond or stock savings plan deposits
   (e) Repayment of advances on pay
   (f) Retirement plan deposits

TIMECARD

NAME B. L. Garry   NO. 49

PERIOD ENDING July 16, 1966

DEDUCTIONS		RATE	HOURS	EARNINGS	
$_____	REG. 2.50	40	$ 100, 00		
F.I.C.A $ 3.23	O.T. $ 3.75	2	$ 7.50		
INC. TAX $ 12.40			$_____		
_____ $_____			$_____		
_____ $_____	TOTAL HOURS 42	TOTAL EARNINGS $ 107.50			
MISC. ___ $_____ (DESCRIBE BELOW)	$_____ $_____	TOTAL DEDUCTIONS $ 15.63			
		NET PAY $ 91.87			

	R E G U L A R				E X T R A		
HRS.	IN	OUT	IN	OUT	IN	OUT	HRS.
8	8:00	12:00	12:30	4:30			
8	8:01	12:00	12:29	4:31			
8	8:00	12:00	12:30	4:30	5:30	7:30	2
8	8:00	12:00	12:30	4:30			
8	8:02	12:00	12:30	4:33			

PAY BASIS $ 2.50   PER **hour**

CHARLES R. HADLEY CO., PATHFINDERS, LOS ANGELES, SAN FRANCISCO, NEW YORK, CHICAGO — (3)
PRINTED IN U.S.A.   STANDARD TIME CARD   FORM C588

The illustration on page 399 shows a weekly payroll sheet for a group of workers paid on an hourly basis. Note that time over forty hours in one week is paid at time and a half, that is, at a premium of 50 percent over the regular rate. The overtime premium, or extra cost of the overtime work, is separately shown so that management may know the amount of this excess cost. The payroll sheet usually serves as a check register for the payroll checks. If the payroll checks are drawn on the regular bank account, the total from the payroll sheet may be entered in the regular check register under Payroll and the numbers of the checks given. In the case of the payroll sheet illustrated, the numbers would be shown as "420–428." Frequently a separate bank account for payroll checks is kept so that they form a separate series; one check is drawn on the general bank account for the total pay and deposited in the payroll bank account. The payroll sheets then form a check register for the payroll bank account. In this case no general ledger account is kept for the payroll bank account, because it never has any balance. This system is assumed in the entries that follow.

ENTRIES FOR THE PAYROLL IN THE ILLUSTRATION

The following entries record the data of the illustrated payroll sheet:

Salaries and Wages	$1,045.40	
Vouchers Payable		$881.20
Federal Income Tax Withheld		97.80
F.I.C.A Tax Withheld		43.90
Savings Plan Deposits Withheld		15.00
Group Insurance Premiums Withheld		7.50
(recorded in voucher register)		
Vouchers Payable	$ 881.20	
Cash		$881.20
(entry in check register for check on general bank account deposited in payroll bank account. Payroll bank account checks are entered on payroll sheet only)		
Payroll Taxes	$ 69.00	
F.I.C.A. Tax Accrued		$ 43.91
Federal Unemployment Tax Accrued		4.18
State Unemployment Tax Accrued		20.91
(recorded in general journal; state unemployment tax calculated at 2%)		

The figure entered for F.I.C.A. Tax Accrued is a cent more than that for F.I.C.A. Tax Withheld because of rounding fractions to the cent on the individual withholdings. The final liability is calculated on the total wages. The state unemployment tax liability in the foregoing entry is calculated at 2 percent, on the assumption that the employer operates in a state with a merit-rating system that entitles him to this rate.

PAYROLL SHEET

Payroll period March 6 to March 12, 1966   Sheet no. 88

| Employee | | Hours worked | | Gross Earnings | | | | Deductions | | | Payment | |
Name	No.	Reg-ular	Over-time	Rate	At regular rate	Over-time pre-mium	Total	In-come tax	F.I.C.A.	Other*	Amount	Check No.
Ben Foster	81	40	6	3.00	138 00	9 00	147 00	13 50	6 17	A 5 00	122 33	420
Robert Moore	44	40		2.80	112 00		112 00	8 60	4 70	B 2 50	96 20	421
H. G. Parker	39	40	4	2.80	123 20	5 60	128 80	12 50	5 41	A 5 00	105 89	422
A. Gormly	82	40		2.70	108 00		108 00	6 10	4 54		97 36	423
Bertha Gould	93	40	2	2.40	100 80	2 40	103 20	12 60	4 33	B 2 50	83 77	424
H. Sharkey	61	40	2	2.40	100 80	2 40	103 20	9 00	4 33		89 87	425
Hazel Shalk	55	40		2.60	104 00		104 00	10 80	4 37		88 83	426
Dorothy Carroll	38	40	8	2.60	124 80	10 40	135 20	17 50	5 68	A 5 00	107 02	427
R. G. Vincent	42	40		2.60	104 00		104 00	7 20	4 37	B 2 50	89 93	428
					1,015 60	29 80	1,045 40	97 80	43 90	22 50	881 20	

* Indicate type by symbol: A = savings plan; B = group insurance.

EMPLOYEE'S INDIVIDUAL EARNINGS RECORD

The federal law requires that a record of each individual's earnings and other employment data be kept. The record used is called an individual earnings record and is illustrated on page 401. This form may be prepared, as the payroll is written, by means of a carbon tape or paper. The individual earnings record is inserted beneath the payroll sheet as that employee's data are being entered on the sheet. The individual earnings record can also be used for personnel administration; for example, a distribution of ages of the work force can be made from the records. The "Soc. Sec. account no." designation on the form is for the social security account number assigned by the Federal Social Security Board and identifies this worker on its records.

OTHER INDIVIDUAL EMPLOYEE FORMS

Each employee must file an *employee's withholding exemption certificate* with his employer. This is a federal form and indicates the number of income tax exemptions to which the employee is entitled (one for himself and one for each dependent, as a rule). The employer is then required to give each employee at least once each year a receipt for the amounts he withholds as taxes; most employers give such a statement with each payroll check. It is usually made out on a stub attached to the payroll check and is called a *statement of earnings and deductions*. At the end of the year the employer prepares a *withholding tax statement* for each employee, showing the total paid and the amount of federal income tax withheld during the year. One copy goes to the Internal Revenue Service and gives it information with which it can check the employee's tax return; another copy provides the employee with data for making out his tax return.

INTERNAL CONTROL FOR PAYROLL

Internal control is especially important in this area. A favorite fraud involves "padding the payroll" with extra names; the embezzler obtains the pay for the extra names. The following six procedures are recommended to assure the accuracy and honesty of payroll records and payments.

1. *Use central or centrally controlled hiring.* This is done by means of a personnel department. It assures adherence to the company's hiring policies and provides a central record of names admitted to the payroll and the authorized rates of pay for them.

2. *Keep timekeeping separated from payroll preparation.* A timekeeper who prepares the payroll sheet or a payroll clerk who keeps time records has added opportunity to falsify the record.

3. *Keep distribution of the pay to workers separate from timekeeping and payroll preparation.* Ideally, the person who takes the pay checks from the payroll clerk should compare them with the payroll sheet, if an intermediate person does not do it (see 6 below).

4. *Pay workers with checks rather than currency and coin.* If currency and coin must be used, get a signed receipt from each worker.

5. *Use checks good for a limited amount.* This amount may be $200 or $250 when the payroll is weekly. The limitation, being printed on the check, reduces the opportunities for raising the amount.

INDIVIDUAL EARNINGS RECORD

Name: *Ben Foster*   Telephone: *AL 3-0421*   Soc. Sec. account no. *569-46-1810*   Birth date: *1-18-15*   Date reaches 65: *1-18-80*

Address: *1816 Pike St., Denham, Mass.*   Male √ Female   Married √ Single   Dependents other than spouse: 2   No. of income tax exemptions claimed: 4   Exempt from Soc. Sec. tax: no

Employment began: May 11, 1959   Compensation rate: $3.00   hourly daily weekly   Type of work: *Machinist*

Employment terminated: 19—   Reason: Remarks:

For period ended 1966	Gross Earnings			Deductions			Payment		For period ended 19—
	At regular rate	Overtime premium	Total	Income tax	F.I.C.A.	Other	Amount	Check No.	
3–12	138 00	9 00	147 00	13 50	6 17	A 5 00	122 33	420	

For period ended 19—	Gross Earnings			Deductions			Payment	
	At regular rate	Overtime premium	Total	Income tax	F.I.C.A.	Other	Amount	Check No.

6. Use two signatures on checks; the first signer may be the payroll clerk, the second an executive who should compare the checks with the payroll sheet as he signs them.

FEDERAL INCOME TAXES

The largest source of federal revenue is income taxes. They are levied on *net* income, that is, gross income less various deductions. Each individual, estate, trust, and ordinary business corporation is subject to the tax. Partnerships and sole proprietorships are not taxed as distinct units; the income earned in a partnership or a proprietorship is the income of the partners or the proprietor. Each person with income from such concerns reports his share of the income on his individual income tax return and pays the tax on it; it does not matter how much he did or did not withdraw. The stockholders of a corporation, on the other hand, are persons legally separate from the corporation, and do not report the corporation's income as their own. They are taxed on income received from it in dividends, not on what it earns. Recently the law was changed to allow the owners of certain corporations (those having not more than ten shareholders and meeting other requirements) to agree among themselves to report as personal income their shares of the corporation's income, whether or not paid, and thus avoid the tax on corporations. Also, some proprietorships and partnerships may elect to be taxed as corporations. Partnerships must file information returns showing the income accruing to the partners, who pay tax on it individually. In general, individuals having a yearly income of $600 or more must file a federal tax return.

CASH VERSUS ACCRUAL BASIS

Accounting that takes into consideration income earned but not collected and expenses incurred but not paid is *accrual* accounting. It is the kind of accounting with which this book is concerned and that is usually needed for meaningful statements. The *cash* basis of accounting takes as income only the revenue collected in cash and as expenses only those paid in cash. The general rule in the tax law is that the taxpayer must use whatever method of accounting will properly reflect his income. As a result, concerns handling merchandise, which may be sold before the purchase is paid for, must use accrual accounting. Almost all individual taxpayers report on the cash basis, since for them this gives the same or almost the same result as would an accrual method. They must report as income any income *constructively* received, that is, available to them, whether or not they actually received it. One cannot postpone an item of income to the next year by neglecting to pick up his December pay check until January. Interest on a savings account credited on December 31 by the bank is another example. Depreciation may be deducted even though the cash method is used; for example, an apartment-house owner will ordinarily be on the cash basis but will deduct depreciation. The actual method in many cases is therefore a modified cash method. Although individuals may elect to pay income taxes on a fiscal-year basis, almost all individuals pay on a calendar-year basis. Corporations often pay on the basis of a fiscal year corresponding to their regular closing date.

OUTLINE OF COMPUTATION OF PERSONAL INCOME TAX

The income tax calculation for an individual takes the following form:

Gross income..	$xx,xxx.xx
Less deductions from gross income	x,xxx.xx
Adjusted gross income	$xx,xxx.xx
Less deductions from adjusted gross income ("itemized deductions")	x,xxx.xx
Balance after deductions..............................	$xx,xxx.xx
Less exemptions......................................	x,xxx.xx
Taxable income..	$xx,xxx.xx
Tax at applicable rates...............................	$ x,xxx.xx

CONTENT OF GROSS INCOME

Gross income includes such items as the following:

Wages, salaries, bonuses, and commissions
Dividends, interest, royalties, and rents
Net income from a business or a profession
Tips, prizes, and gambling winnings
Gains on the sale of property (But no gain or loss is recognized for tax purposes on a trade-in of one asset on a similar one.)

Certain items are excluded from gross income and do not have to be reported. These include:

Accident and health insurance proceeds, including workmen's compensation insurance
Interest on bonds of a state, city, or political subdivision, and on most federal securities issued prior to 1941
Sick pay, within limits
Social security benefits
Veterans bonuses, disability pensions, and grants
Life insurance proceeds paid because of death of the insured
Gifts and inheritances
Noncompetitive awards, such as the Nobel prize

DEDUCTIONS FROM GROSS INCOME

Deductions from gross income are business expenses incurred in order to earn the income. These include all the ordinary kinds of business expenses of a person who owns a business. Most such expenses are deducted from business revenue in a special schedule in the tax return and the resulting "profit or loss from business" is shown in the gross income section of the return. Sundry others are deducted from the gross income total. Some "business" expenses are deductible by an employee. For example, if an outside salesman has to entertain customers of the firm out of his own pocket, the entertainment expense is deductible. Expenses in this category deductible by employees are limited, but they include travel expenses, including meals and lodging when the employee is away from home on business, business-transportation expenses other than commuting to and from work, and any similar expenses if those other expenses are reimbursed by the employer. Any reimbursement by the employer in this case must be counted as income. The costs of moving family and household because of a transfer of employment or because of employment with a new employer are deductible from gross income. Costs of operating rental properties, including depreciation, are deductible in this section, as are losses on the sale or exchange of property held for "business" or income-earning purposes. Thus, loss on the sale of a store building is deductible; loss on the sale of one's own residence is not.

DEDUCTIONS FROM ADJUSTED GROSS INCOME ("ITEMIZED DEDUCTIONS")

Deductions from adjusted gross income may be characterized as non-business deductions, although some of them are incurred to earn an income. They are allowed because of congressional policy. The following categories, in general, are deductible:

Charitable contributions (generally limited to 30 percent of adjusted gross income)

Taxes paid (but not social security, inheritance, gift, federal income, or estate taxes)

Interest incurred for nonbusiness purposes (business interest is deductible from gross income)

Losses from casualty, such as fire or accident, or from theft, occurring to the taxpayer's property in excess of $100

Medical expenses in excess of 3 percent of adjusted gross income, within limits

Child-care expenses under certain conditions

Alimony paid

Miscellaneous — includes certain expenses incurred by employees, such as union dues, cost of uniforms, fees for obtaining employment, professional dues and subscriptions to professional journals, some educational expenses, cost of attending conventions, and any other "ordinary and necessary" expenses incurred for business purposes. These include expenditures for investment counsel and preparation of tax returns. Similar expenses, incurred by a merchant or a professional man in his practice, would be deductible as a business expense from gross income to arrive at adjusted gross income.

The adjusted gross income figure and the distinction between deductions from gross income and the deductions from adjusted gross income are important. The reason is that certain deductions are limited in relation to adjusted gross income (see charitable contributions and medical expenses in the list above) and because a standard deduction may be taken from adjusted gross income instead of detailing actual deductions. In most cases the standard deduction is 10 percent of the adjusted gross income up to a total deduction of $1,000. (Furthermore, the minimum standard deduction is $200 plus $100 for each personal exemption, except for married persons filing separate returns.) If allowable deductions for actual expenditures are less than 10 percent, the standard deduction should be taken. It is available on tax returns showing less than $5,000 of adjusted gross income only by use of the optional tax table, which not only avoids calculation of the tax by the taxpayer but automatically provides the standard deduction at approximately 10 percent of adjusted gross income.

NONDEDUCTIBLE EXPENDITURES

Personal living expenses that Congress has not specifically made deductible for tax purposes may not be deducted. These include rent of a dwelling, the cost of food and clothing (some uniforms required at work are deductible), the expense of traveling from home to a place of work and back, and innumerable others.

EXEMPTIONS

Each individual is exempt from tax on $600 of net income each year, and is also exempt on $600 of income for each dependent. An additional $600 exemption is allowed each taxpayer who is sixty-five years old and another $600 is allowed to each blind taxpayer. Thus a man and wife, each of whom is sixty-five years old and blind, are entitled to $3,600 of exemptions. Dependents, in general, are close relatives, including some in-laws, who receive more than half their support from the taxpayer and have less than $600 gross income of their own in a year. A student may be a dependent even though he has a gross income of $600 or more and files his own tax return.

CAPITAL GAINS AND LOSSES

Certain assets are defined in the law as capital assets. Gains or losses on sale of these items receive special treatment, the most important feature being that the tax on gains from the sale of capital assets held for more than six months is limited to a maximum of 25 percent of the gain. The law is involved and space does not permit adequate description of it here. However, the reader should note that much tax planning is devoted to arrangements that permit a capital gain instead of ordinary income to be realized. This is important to many taxpayers who pay much higher rates than 25 percent on most of their income, as the following section shows.

FEDERAL INCOME TAX RATES

The federal rates are set up separately for single individuals, for married couples filing a joint return, and for unmarried or legally separated persons who qualify as head of a household. The rates in effect at this writing are shown on the next page. The rates for joint returns of married couples are set so that they pay the tax they would pay if the total income were divided equally between them and each one filed a return as a single person. This assumption prevents them from going as high in the progressive rates as a single person with the same total income would, and is known as the income-splitting benefit. A "head of a household" is an unmarried person who maintains as his home a household in which his child or descendent or any of certain other dependents lives. He gets about half the benefits available to married couples from income splitting.

The tax on business corporations has recently been set at 22 percent, plus 26 percent of all income over $25,000; thus the tax on income up to $25,000 is

22 percent and on income over $25,000 is 48 percent. The rates, like almost all elements of the income tax law, are subject to change at the discretion of Congress. Changes also come about from court decisions and administrative rulings. Unless one is continually conversant with the tax law, it is wise to check the law whenever an important decision affected by income tax is contemplated. Commercial tax services that keep their subscribers constantly informed of changes are a convenient source of tax law information.

FEDERAL INCOME TAX RATES

Individuals Filing Separate Returns			Head of Household Returns			Joint Returns for Married Taxpayers and Surviving Spouses		
Taxable Income	Tax on Amount in Column 1	% on Excess	Taxable Income	Tax on Amount in Column 1	% on Excess	Taxable Income	Tax on Amount in Column 1	% on Excess
$ 0	$ 0	14	$ 0	$ 0	14	$ 0	$ 0	14
500	70	15	1,000	140	16	1,000	140	15
1,000	145	16	2,000	300	18	2,000	290	16
1,500	225	17	4,000	660	20	3,000	450	17
2,000	310	19	6,000	1,060	22	4,000	620	19
4,000	690	22	8,000	1,500	25	8,000	1,380	22
6,000	1,130	25	10,000	2,000	27	12,000	2,260	25
8,000	1,630	28	12,000	2,540	31	16,000	3,260	28
10,000	2,190	32	14,000	3,160	32	20,000	4,380	32
12,000	2,830	36	16,000	3,800	35	24,000	5,660	36
14,000	3,550	39	18,000	4,500	36	28,000	7,100	39
16,000	4,330	42	20,000	5,220	40	32,000	8,660	42
18,000	5,170	45	22,000	6,020	41	36,000	10,340	45
20,000	6,070	48	24,000	6,840	43	40,000	12,140	48
22,000	7,030	50	26,000	7,700	45	44,000	14,060	50
26,000	9,030	53	28,000	8,600	46	52,000	18,060	53
32,000	12,210	55	32,000	10,440	48	64,000	24,420	55
38,000	15,510	58	36,000	12,360	50	76,000	31,020	58
44,000	18,990	60	38,000	13,360	52	88,000	37,980	60
50,000	22,590	62	40,000	14,400	53	100,000	45,180	62
60,000	28,790	64	44,000	16,520	55	120,000	57,580	64
70,000	35,190	66	50,000	19,820	56	140,000	70,380	66
80,000	41,790	68	52,000	20,940	58	160,000	83,580	68
90,000	48,590	69	64,000	27,900	59	180,000	97,180	69
100,000	55,490	70	70,000	31,440	61	200,000	110,980	70
			76,000	35,100	62			
			80,000	37,580	63			
			88,000	42,620	64			
			100,000	50,300	66			
			120,000	63,500	67			
			140,000	76,900	68			
			160,000	90,500	69			
			180,000	104,300	70			

ILLUSTRATION OF THE COMPUTATION OF THE INDIVIDUAL INCOME TAX

John and Mary Franklin had the following financial transactions in a recent year:

Receipts
Net income of appliance-repair business $8,000.00
Interest on savings deposit. 20.00
Health-insurance benefits 200.00
Radio-quiz-contest prize 100.00
Inheritance from Mary's uncle. 1,000.00
Expenditures (selected)
Contributions to charity 200.00
Real estate tax on home 175.00
Interest on real estate loan on home 240.00
Cost of John's trip to business convention 180.00
Medical expenses. 362.00
State gasoline tax 30.00
Cost of family vacation trip 210.00
State income tax 60.00

The Franklins have two young children. Their federal income tax for the year follows:

Gross income:
Net profit from business $8,000.00
Interest on savings deposit. 20.00
Contest prize. 100.00
                                                                          $8,120.00

Deduction from gross income:
Cost of trip to business convention 180.00
Adjusted gross income $7,940.00
Less deductions from adjusted gross income:
Contributions to charity $200.00

Taxes:
Real estate $175.00
State gasoline tax 30.00
State income tax. 60.00   265.00

Interest 240.00
Medical ($362.00 — [$7,940 × 3%]) 123.80   828.80
Balance after deductions $7,111.20
Less exemptions (4 at $600.00 each) 2,400.00
Taxable income. $4,711.20

Tax per joint-return schedule [page 406 in this book]:
First $4,000.00. . . . . $ 620.00
Next $711.20 × 19% 135.13
Total tax . . . . $ 755.13

If the Franklins had not had so many deductions as a result of their expenditures, they would have been entitled to take, as an alternative, a standard deduction from adjusted gross income. This is 10 percent of the adjusted gross income or $1,000, whichever is smaller, except that a married person filing a separate return is entitled to a maximum of $500. In the Franklins' case this would have been $794. Taxpayers who have salaries or wages subject to withholding deduct the amount from the total tax due and pay the difference if it is in favor of the government, or claim a refund if their tax has been overpaid.

ESTIMATED TAX

In order to put all individual taxpayers on a pay-as-you-go basis, the federal government requires estimates of tax and quarterly payments during the year to which the tax applies. Taxpayers who expect more than $5,000 (single) or $10,000 (married couple) of wages subject to withholding, and taxpayers who expect income from other sources in excess of $200 for the year are required to file estimates. The estimate shows the estimated total tax, the amount expected to be withheld, and any remainder. The remainder must be paid in four installments—on April 15, June 15, September 15, and January 15 of the following year. If the income prospects of the taxpayer change during the year, an amended declaration must be filed by the next payment date. There are penalties for failure to file an estimate and to pay estimated tax, but some leeway in making estimates is allowed. For example, if the estimated tax comes within 70 percent of the final tax there is no penalty for an underestimate.

CORPORATION INCOME TAX

The corporation income tax has many special features that cannot be discussed here, but some of its characteristics should be noticed. In general, corporations are required to compute net income by accounting methods adequate for the purpose. But the law, as a result of Congressional action, court decisions, or administrative ruling, has many special rules for the calculation of income for tax purposes. One result is that income for tax purposes and net income calculated on generally accepted accounting principles virtually never coincide in a substantial enterprise. For example, depletion is allowed the producers of minerals, including oil and gravel, at arbitrary percents of gross income if greater than the actual cost of depletion (provided it does not exceed 50 percent of taxable income from the property computed before depletion). This rate is $27\frac{1}{2}$ percent for oil and gas and 23, 15, 10, or 5 percent for various other minerals. In some cases income received in advance of the period in which it is to be earned (deferred income in regular accounting) is taxed as income in the year of receipt. Other differences arise from the fact that some interest income is exempt from taxation and that no gain or loss is recognized for tax purposes when equipment is traded in on new equipment of similar type. Furthermore, the Internal Revenue Service and the taxpayer may honestly disagree on the period for depreciating fixed assets, with one period being used in the accounts and another on the tax return. These and many other technicalities indicate why tax accounting is a specialty that occupies the time of a considerable number of persons.

DEFERRED INCOME TAXES PAYABLE

In order to postpone payment of taxes a company may elect tax accounting procedures which differ from financial accounting. For example, accelerated depreciation may be used on the tax return but not in the general ledger. The general ledger treatment reflects what the concern considers a proper calculation of net income for general purposes, regardless of tax law options. In such cases the aggregate income over the life of the fixed asset will be the same on the tax returns and financial reports, but the amount shown for individual years will differ. Some companies report income taxes in their published income statements at an amount determined by applying the tax rates to the reported income, even though they are paying more or less than this because of the different treatment of some items in the published statement and the tax return. Any excess of tax shown on the published statement is credited to Deferred Income Taxes Payable, and any overage is debited to the account.

A schedule showing the deferred tax liability for a depreciable asset costing $120,000 with a life of three years and producing annual net revenues (before depreciation) of $160,000 is shown below. Federal and state income taxes are provided at 50 percent. Straight line depreciation is used in the financial statements, but sum-of-the-years'-digits depreciation is used in the income tax returns.

	First Year	Second Year	Third Year
Financial Statements			
Net revenues before depreciation...........	$160,000	$160,000	$160,000
Depreciation—straight line	40,000	40,000	40,000
Net income before income taxes...........	$120,000	$120,000	$120,000
Income taxes	$ 60,000	$ 60,000	$ 60,000
Income Tax Returns			
Net revenues before depreciation...........	$160,000	$160,000	$160,000
Depreciation—sum of years' digits	60,000	40,000	20,000
Net income before income taxes...........	$100,000	$120,000	$140,000
Income taxes	$ 50,000	$ 60,000	$ 70,000
Deferred taxes—increase (decrease)	$ 10,000	—	$(10,000)

The entries to record income taxes for the three years are as follows:

End of first year

Income Taxes	$60,000	
Income Taxes Payable		$50,000
Deferred Income Taxes Payable		10,000

(to record income taxes based on recorded income; $10,000 of tax deferred because of accelerated depreciation)

End of second year

Income Taxes	60,000	
Income Taxes Payable		60,000

End of third year

Income Taxes	60,000	
Deferred Income Taxes Payable.................	10,000	
Income Taxes Payable		70,000

Deferred Income Taxes Payable is reported as a noncurrent liability at the end of the first year. This accounting procedure of allocating income taxes is consistent with the general principle of matching expenses with revenues; it shows a tax in the published statement consistent with that year's income.

INTERNAL CONTROL FOR TAXES

Internal control for taxes may be divided into two functions: day-to-day administration and tax planning.

The day-to-day function is concerned with making tax payments when due, with negotiating tax matters with public officers, and with reporting tax developments. Paying taxes on time is largely a matter of keeping a calendar carefully. Commercial tax services are published that provide calendars and other reminders of important tax dates. In a large concern with many local taxes as well as national and state taxes to keep track of, this activity is a sizable job. Assessors and tax examiners will require information when making assessments or auditing accounts in connection with returns; the tax specialist looks after this.

The function of tax planning attempts to minimize tax expense by arranging transactions in the most favorable way. For example, a concern operating in a state where a tax on money and credits is levied each year on the first Monday in March may buy United States government securities just before this assessment date so it will have less cash in the bank subject to the tax (such securities are exempt). Tax planning takes innumerable forms; it may involve a recommendation to locate a branch in one state instead of another because of higher taxes in one; it may involve a decision to use several small corporations instead of one to avoid the higher tax on corporation income over $25,000. If an existing corporation is to be split up, there must be a legitimate business reason for the split if the tax advantage is to be gained. However, corporations in a controlled group (80 percent owned by an individual, estate, trust, or another corporation) must either divide one $25,000 surtax exemption between them, take the $25,000 surtax exemption in each case but pay an additional 6 percent of tax on the $25,000, or file a consolidated return (a consolidated return permits only one $25,000 surtax exemption). With complicated tax laws and high rates of taxation, tax planning is very important. Large concerns have tax departments to look after tax administration and planning; smaller concerns can get similar service from public accountants, with whom larger concerns often consult.

The disbursement of tax payments is controlled as are other cash disbursements.

MANAGEMENT PROBLEMS RELATING TO TAXES

Many management decisions are involved with taxes, as indicated above in the reference to tax planning. The following items are listed as illustrative, both from the standpoint of the kinds of problems and because the accountant's computations of the consequences of different decisions are of prime importance in the decision.

Form of organization to be used. Corporations are subject to a special tax, but sole proprietorships and partnerships are not. However, several factors are involved: stockholders of a corporation cannot be held for the corporation's debts in case of failure; a general partner or a proprietor can be held for the debts of the business. Also, partners may make contracts for the business; stockholders may not; partners' contracts may be troublesome. If the owners are few enough they can get the protection of the corporate form and agree to be taxed as though they were partners. Also, owners of a small corporation may be able to take out virtually all its profits as salaries, thus avoiding corporate tax, provided the salaries are reasonable for the work done. On the other hand, the corporation may be advantageous with respect to taxation. If the main owner is in the 70 percent tax bracket already, any additional income from a new business would be taxed at that rate. He can invest in a corporation and if there is legitimate use for the profits to expand the business, he can leave the profits in the business subject to a tax of 22 percent plus 26 percent for any amount over $25,000 (48 percent on the income over $25,000). He may also be able to sell his stock at a profit that is subject only to the capital gains tax of 25 percent maximum, or transfer it to his heirs. The form of organization to use will depend upon the circumstances and objectives of the owners. The general advantages of corporation organization are given in Chapter 15.

One corporation or several. There is often a legitimate business reason apart from taxes for using different corporations to handle different parts of an activity that could be handled by one corporation. For example, different owners may bring different skills—one in manufacturing, another in selling. They may wish to separate the two kinds of risks and to give more shares in the selling activity to one owner and more shares in the manufacturing activity to another. Since corporate tax rates are higher on incomes over $25,000, tax may be saved by dividing up the activity and the income between corporations.

Location of the business. Taxes may influence the location both because of their impact on the business and because of their effect on its officers or employees. Some states do not levy income taxes; persons living in those states have a tax advantage. Business done in the state is not subject to a state income tax. However, business done in other states that do have income taxes may result in a liability to them for tax on income earned in those states.

Contracts for compensation of officers and others. Officers of large corporations may have very high earnings for a few years and then retire and have much less. The problem is even more acute for entertainers, who may be popular and have very high earnings for a few years and then get little. These people are subjected to extremely high tax rates when they are making a large income, and they need to be able to spread their income out, not only to keep it out of the higher tax brackets but also, in quite a few cases, to be more sure of having a satisfactory income in the later years. This tax problem gives rise to compensation contracts of special kinds. In corporations, part of an officer's compensation may be in the form of stock options (options to purchase stock) which, if properly written, permit gains to be realized in later years and often at capital-gains rates (25 percent). Corporations may also contribute to pension funds for officers with no tax to the officer being due until payments are received under the pensions. Officers may also be hired as consultants after their most active service is over. Entertainers have made contracts by which they render regular services for a limited time, but receive payments over a much longer time, often with a proviso for consulting or advisory service during that time. These arrangements spread the income and reduce the top rates of taxation on it.

SUMMARY

This chapter has described the accounting for payrolls, together with the taxes levied on or withheld from payrolls. These taxes include federal income tax and F.I.C.A. (old age insurance and medicare) tax withheld from employees, and F.I.C.A. and unemployment taxes levied on employers.

The chapter has also provided an introduction to federal income tax. This, for the individual taxpayer, involves gross income and deductions from gross income (of a business sort) to get adjusted gross income. Deductions from adjusted gross income (of a personal sort) are made to arrive at the remainder of income, which is further reduced by personal exemptions to give the taxable income.

The internal control for payrolls and for taxes was noted, and management's problems resulting from taxes, chiefly income taxes, were illustrated.

QUESTIONS

13.1 (1) What kind of benefits does the F.I.C.A. program provide?

(2) What taxpayers furnish the funds for the F.I.C.A. program?

(3) What taxpayers furnish the funds for the unemployment-insurance program?

(4) What deductions other than F.I.C.A. tax may be made from workers' pay?

(5) What kinds of records are needed in connection with payrolls?

13.2 (1) What is meant by time and a half for overtime?

(2) How may the amount of overtime premium be isolated for management attention?

(3) Employers Casualty Insurance Company charges $1.30 per $100 of payroll for workmen's compensation insurance based on total hours worked at the regular hourly rates, regardless of overtime, if payroll records clearly show the amounts of overtime premium paid. Americo, Inc., pays 100 workers an average of 200 overtime hours each during 1966 at the regular hourly rate of $2 an hour, time and a half for overtime. How much does Americo save by having its payroll records show the overtime premium pay?

13.3 (1) A. S. Baker, president and sole stockholder of Baker Metals, Inc., is paid a salary of $20,000 by a single annual check. The only withholdings are for income tax and F.I.C.A. Baker claims no income tax withholding exemption. What is the amount of the check? Explain how to record the payment to Baker and the related employer payroll taxes. (The company is exempt from F.U.I., since it employs fewer than four workers.)

(2) What is a withholding exemption certificate, and how is it used?

(3) What are income tax exemptions? What benefits do they provide, and to whom?

(4) Explain how to compute the amount of income tax to be withheld by the percentage method. How much income tax should be withheld on gross pay of $100 a week for a worker claiming one exemption. Compare with the table on page 395. Why is the difference not important?

13.4 (1) The total wages and salaries reported by the A Co. in its 1966 income statement amounted to $240,000. Payroll tax returns are filed on the basis of wages paid. Accrued wages and salaries amounted to $10,000 on December 31, 1965, and $20,000 on December 31, 1966. Payroll of $24,000 was exempt from F.I.C.A. tax, $30,000 from S.U.I. tax, and $40,000 from F.U.I. tax. Compute the employer payroll taxes for 1966 at the following rates: F.I.C.A., 4.2 percent; S.U.I., 2.0 percent; and F.U.I., 0.4 percent.

(2) D. C. Burry, CPA, has two employees, a statistical typist paid $400 per month and a staff accountant paid $800. S.U.I. taxes at 3 percent apply on $3,800 of wages per employee and F.I.C.A. taxes apply at 4.2 percent on the $6,600 of wages per employee. Burry pays no F.U.I. tax, since he employs less than four persons. State the amount of employer payroll taxes due for each quarter of 1966.

(3) Both of Burry's employees claim no income tax withholding exemption. Show the entry for the January payroll. What entry would be made to record the February remittance of withholdings and federal employer payroll tax? (The withheld income tax and 8.4 percent employer-employee F.I.C.A. tax are payable by the 15th of the month following payment of wages.)

13.5 (1) The owner of the Dixie Club objects to the employer tax and record keeping associated with the social security program. In the past, he has treated the band and vocalist at the club as employees. He proposes to classify these people as "independent contractors," and if the classification is accepted by the tax authorities, he would avoid payroll taxes. What do you think of his proposal?

(2) Indicate whether employer payroll taxes are payable for each of the following cases:

(a) Brown is engaged as a carpenter for A Co. to build some cabinets in the office. Brown furnishes his own tools. A Co. furnishes the lumber and other materials. Brown has never advertised in newspapers or elsewhere that he is in the carpentry business.

(b) Wilson and Jones are partners in a public accounting practice. The partnership pays each a salary of $1,000 a month.

13.6 (1) What persons, natural or legal, are subject to the United States income tax?

(2) Marsha Tandy is a full-time student at State College. She works during the summer as a swimming instructor and earns $800, but she receives over one half her support from her father. Should Marsha file a federal income tax return? What exemption can she claim? Is Mr. Tandy entitled to an exemption for Marsha?

(3) The M and N partnership earned $60,000 net income during 1966. M and N are equal partners. Each withdrew cash in the amount of $20,000 during the year. How much gross income must each partner report in his individual tax return?

(4) Ridge Corporation elects to be taxed as a partnership (under Subchapter S of the Internal Revenue Code). Carlson and Davis are the sole stockholders, each owning 50 percent of the stock. Each stockholder files a joint return with his wife. Each has nonbusiness income exactly equal to his deductions. How much must Ridge Corporation earn before Carlson and Davis should revoke their tax-option under Subchapter S if they desire to minimize taxes paid for the year? (It may be assumed that the partnership earns only ordinary income.)

13.7 (1) Distinguish between the cash and the accrual basis of accounting. What is a modified cash basis?

(2) Professor T. R. Wilson left Rutgers and accepted an appointment at the University of California beginning September 1, 1966. In 1967 he paid the bill for moving his family and household goods. Should Wilson claim a deduction for moving expenses in 1966 or in 1967?

(3) Why is the postponement of income for tax purposes often advantageous to the taxpayer? Suggest several tax accounting procedures to achieve this end.

(4) B, an insurance agent, files his tax return on the cash basis, although his accounting records are prepared on an accrual basis. His income statement shows revenues from commissions, $32,400. Related balance sheet items are:

	Jan. 1	*Dec. 31*
Accrued commissions............	$4,100	$6,200
Unearned commissions...........	3,400	1,600

What gross income should B include on his tax return for the year?

(5) T, who should have reported his income on an accrual basis but has been reporting on the cash basis for many years, finally switches to the accrual basis in 1966. If the taxpayer makes the change by himself, he must add the receivables plus inventories less payables at year end to his cash-basis income. If the IRS makes the change, the taxpayer adds the balances in the foregoing accounts less the corresponding balances in those accounts on January 1, 1954.

T's net income on a cash basis is $200,000 for 1966. The account balances required for the adjustment of income to the accrual basis are as follows:

	1/1/54	12/31/66
Accounts receivable	$16,000	$32,000
Inventories	8,000	20,000
Accounts payable	6,000	10,000

What is T's accrual-basis income for 1966 (a) if the change is made by T and (b) if the change is made by the IRS?

13.8 (1) Describe the relationship, under the federal income tax law, of gross income, adjusted gross income, and the remainder of income after deductions.

(2) What is the difference on taxable income if a given expenditure is a deduction from gross income or a deduction from adjusted gross income? Suggest several expenditures which might be either type of deduction depending upon the situation, and explain how the situation changes the tax nature of the expenditure.

(3) What standard deduction is generally allowed to a married taxpayer filing a joint return for an adjusted gross income of (a) $4,800, (b) $9,600, and (c) $12,000?

13.9 (1) What kind of items must be reported as gross income for tax purposes?

(2) Indicate which of the following constitute gross income for federal income tax purposes:

(a) Honorarium received by speaker at a conference
(b) Interest received on local government bonds
(c) Gift of cash from uncle
(d) State unemployment benefits received
(e) Directors' fees received in common stock of the corporation
(f) Apartment house received as a legacy
(g) Receipts by automobile owner in partial payment for gas and oil in transporting fellow employees to work
(h) Payment received in settlement of personal injuries in automobile accident
(i) Interest received on U. S. Savings bonds
(j) Gain on sale of municipal bonds

13.10 (1) Name some of the major deductions from adjusted gross income allowed by the federal tax law.

(2) Classify each of the following items as (A) deductible from gross income for computing adjusted gross income, (B) deductible from adjusted gross income, or (N) not deductible.

(a) Labor union dues
(b) Depreciation on an apartment building owned as an investment
(c) Travel expenses incurred away from home overnight
(d) Entertaining of customers by an employee who is not an outside salesman, required but not reimbursed.
(e) Cost of repairs to neighbor's automobile sideswiped by taxpayer when backing out of driveway

(f) Pension fund deduction from weekly pay
(g) Interest on nonbusiness loan on life insurance policy
(h) Accountant's fee for preparation of income tax return
(i) Contribution to nephew to help him through graduate school
(j) Contributions to a political campaign fund

13.11 (1) What place has the estimated tax in the taxation of individual incomes?
(2) John Smith, a stockbroker at Rollins and Co., received a W-2 form showing $300 of state income taxes withheld from his 1966 pay. He made additional payments on 1966 state income taxes as follows:

Date	Amount	Explanation
4/15/66	$200	On declaration of estimated tax
6/15/66	200	On declaration of estimated tax
9/15/66	200	On declaration of estimated tax
1/15/67	200	On declaration of estimated tax
3/15/67	100	With 1966 tax return

Smith paid no state income taxes on 1965 earnings.
What deduction may he claim for state income taxes on his 1966 federal income tax return?

13.12 (1) Give illustrations of the fact that net income calculated according to generally accepted accounting principles is likely to be different from taxable net income.
(2) Generally, a corporation is allowed a dividends-received deduction equal to 85 percent of dividends received from domestic corporations. Can you offer an explanation for the reasonableness of this procedure? Why are individual taxpayers not granted the same deduction?
(3) Frank Lee, owner of Frankie's Trucking, is single and takes the standard deduction in 1966. His net profit from operations for 1966 amounted to $60,000, which was twice the normal amount, because of a special job which he does not expect to get again.
On December 31, 1966, Lee is considering the purchase of a new truck for $20,000. He can trade in an old truck with a $10,000 book value for an allowance of $2,000, or he can sell the old truck for $2,000. Lee asks your advice. Explain the tax benefits of a sale rather than an exchange. How will taxable income for the next year be affected, assuming straight line depreciation and a 5-year life?

13.13 C Co. has purchased earth-moving equipment at a cost of $100,000 with an estimated useful life of four years and no residual value. The company adopts straight line depreciation per books and sum-of-the-years'-digits depreciation per tax returns. By what amount will the income tax liability differ from the tax on recorded income, assuming net income before depreciation of $30,000 for each of the four years and a corporate tax rate of 22 percent?

13.14 (1) What internal control functions may a tax department perform?
(2) Suggest important management decisions that depend considerably on tax considerations.

13.15 (1) One of the factors considered in a decision of whether or not to incorporate is the current outlay for federal income taxes. How great must taxable income be before the tax rate on a joint return exceeds the corporate normal tax rate?
(2) Philip Walker earns $32,000 a year doing business as Walker Enterprises. He files a joint return, taking the standard deduction. His income from interest and dividends exactly equals his personal deductions and exemptions. Compute the difference in 1966 taxes under the alternatives of

(a) incorporating and paying himself a $12,000 salary or (b) paying individual income taxes on the entire $32,000.

(3) What additional tax will Walker eventually pay if he incorporates and later wants to spend the income?

(4) Robert Victor's regular taxable income for 1966 is estimated at $100,000, which will place him at the top of the 60 percent tax bracket. He is the sole stockholder in Victor Enterprises, Inc., a corporation that has an annual income in excess of $25,000 after Victor's compensation. Victor expects to complete a special transaction during the year which will result in an additional $100,000 of ordinary income. Thus, he is faced with the choice of undertaking the transaction in the name of the corporation or on his own account. He is interested in the tax consequences of the two alternatives. Compute the taxes payable on this transaction if completed by Victor as an individual and if completed by Victor Enterprises, Inc. Ignore the income-averaging provisions. Assume the gain (net of corporate tax) distributed from the corporation at a 25 percent capital gains tax rate; assume furthermore that there are no collapsible corporation or other problems that would bar the use of the corporate entity.

13.16 Wade Corporation holds a 5-year lease on the Downtown Parking Lot. The corporation has received an offer of $300,000 for the remaining five years of the lease and must decide whether to hold or sell. The lease has a zero tax basis, or book value.

The parking lot shows earnings of $70,000 a year before taxes. What should the company do? Figure taxes at 55 percent on ordinary income and 25 percent on capital gains.

EXERCISES

13.1 Barr International, incorporated March 1, 1966, has one employee, A. S. Barr, who receives a gross salary of $1,000 payable at the end of each month. Barr is married and has four children. He is therefore entitled to a withholding exemption of $333 per month, and the balance of his pay is subject to income tax withholding at 14 percent. The company also withholds 4.2 percent of the first $6,600 of his annual salary for F.I.C.A. tax.

Tax returns are filed with the Internal Revenue Service and state department of employment on April 10. Attached to these returns are checks for employee's withholding and employer's taxes at the rate of 4.2 percent for F.I.C.A. and 2.7 percent for state unemployment tax. The company records the employer's taxes only at the time these taxes are paid.

Give dated journal entries to record the payment of Barr's salary and the payment of employer and employee taxes.

13.2 Prepare a payroll sheet and journal entries to record the following earnings for the week ended January 28, 1966, and related tax accruals:

Name	Hours Worked	Hourly Rate	Withholding Exemptions
B. Allen	40	$1.50	5
J. Borth	44	2.00	2
P. Carr	44	2.50	0
T. Davis	46	5.00	4

Employees are paid time and a half for hours worked in excess of forty per week. Income tax withholding figures can be obtained from the table on page 395. The employer is subject to state unemployment tax at 2 percent of payrolls and federal unemployment at 0.4 percent.

13.3   Draft the journal entry to accrue the employer's F.I.C.A., S.U.I., and F.U.I. tax for the month of December 1966, based on the payroll data given below.

Employee	Earned Year to Date 12/1/66	Gross Pay for December
A	$6,600	$600
B	4,400	400
C	3,700	400
D	6,600	400
E	2,900	300

The company is located in a state that imposes an unemployment insurance tax on the first $3,800 of wages paid to each employee during the calendar year. The S.U.I. tax rate for this company is 3.2 percent. Rates and amounts subject to F.I.C.A. and F.U.I. taxes are given on page 393.

13.4   Data relating to the 1966 income tax return of D. R. Smith are presented below.

Gross income.........................	$14,000
Deductions from gross income	2,000
Itemized deductions:	
Contributions to church...............	200
Interest on home mortgage	400
Real estate taxes.....................	300
Estimated tax payments	1,770

Smith is single and claims no dependents.

Required:

1. Calculate Smith's adjusted gross income, taxable income, tax (using rates on page 406), and tax due or refund.
2. How much tax would Smith pay if he were married, assuming other data remain unchanged?

13.5   Colonel Robert R. Brown, who files a joint return, is exactly at the top of the 50 percent tax bracket. He has just been granted the Fluidometer agency for twelve Western states, from which he expects to derive additional business income of $20,000 per year. The taxpayer is not interested in spending this income, but would like to plan his taxes so as to leave a maximum estate for his heirs. He is trying to decide whether or not to incorporate this new venture. Compute the difference in tax between the two alternatives.

13.6   David S. Burns is the sole proprietor of The Furniture Mart. One day he is visited by a manufacturer's representative who asks why he does not incorporate. "Look at the income tax advantages," says the representative. "General Motors is a corporation. Standard of California is a corporation. Why aren't you?"

Burns is married, has three children, and has no other exemptions. Operations for 1966 are expected to result in business income of $30,000. He has no other items includable in adjusted gross income and will take the standard deduction. Burns is primarily interested in minimizing 1966 income taxes, as he wants to expand by plowing income back into the business.

(1) What are his 1966 income taxes if he does not incorporate?
(2) What are his combined personal and corporate taxes if he incorporates and pays himself a salary of $16,000?
(3) How much does he save in 1966 taxes by incorporating?

(4) What is his aggregate tax liability over the years if he pays a capital gains tax of 25 percent on distribution of the corporate earnings retained in the business?

(5) Suppose Burns were single, but entitled to a deduction for five exemptions, and all the other facts remained the same. At what level of income would his tax liability for the year be minimized by incorporation?

13.7 Tay Banning, who is single with no dependents, began business as Tay's Jewelers on July 1, 1966. She has prepared the following statement for the year ended December 31, 1966, from her cash records:

Sales			$23,000
Less Costs and Expenses:			
Advertising	$	800	
Contributions		100	
Electricity and Telephone		400	
Furniture and Fixtures		10,000	
Purchases		10,500	
Rent		1,800	
Taxes		120	
Wages and Salaries		2,400	26,120
Net loss			$ 3,120

You have been asked to review the accounting records and supporting documents, and to prepare the 1966 federal tax return for Tay Banning. Your examination discloses:

(1) The statement agrees with the bank records, but does not include the merchandise inventory at December 31, 1966, which amounts to $2,100.

(2) A list of uncollected charge sales at December 31 totals $2,000.

(3) Total unpaid invoices to suppliers for merchandise at December 31 amounts to $900.

(4) Furniture and fixtures were acquired for cash on July 1, 1966. For federal income tax purposes, 20 percent of the cost of this property may be deducted as additional first-year depreciation. Unlike ordinary depreciation the additional first-year depreciation deduction is determined without regard to salvage value and is allowed in full even though the property is acquired during the year. Ordinary depreciation is then computed on the cost less additional first-year depreciation and less the salvage value. The estimated useful life is ten years and the estimated salvage value is $400. The straight line method is used.

(5) Wages and salaries consist solely of cash drawings by the owner, none of which qualify as deductions from adjusted gross income.

(6) The contributions consist entirely of church box offerings.

Prepare an income statement on an accrual basis and a tax computation, using the rates on page 406.

13.8 A taxpayer who files a joint return and who is at the top of the 64 percent tax bracket owns a building constructed on leased land. The lease has five years to run, at which time all property rights revert to the lessor. The property produces $10,000 a year after depreciation but before income taxes.

The taxpayer has received an offer to sell for $26,000. His cost less accumulated depreciation is $6,000. Any gain would be subject to a capital gains tax of 25 percent.

Compute the cash proceeds to the taxpayer under the alternatives of operating the property or selling it. Comment briefly on the relative desirabilities of each alternative.

13.9 Nova Marine, Inc., is formed on January 1, 1966, to operate a 1950 freighter, acquired at a cost of $1,000,000. The vessel has an estimated 5-year life, at the end of which it can be scrapped for $100,000.
Charter revenues less expenditures for operations and supervision will amount to $400,000 per year. The company is considering a choice between the straight line and sum-of-the-years'-digits methods of depreciation.

Required:

1. Prepare a schedule showing the income taxes by years for each method of depreciation. Provide for federal and state taxes at 50 percent of net income. Also include in the schedule a row showing the annual taxes deferred by use of the sum-of-the-years'-digits method of depreciation and another row showing the cumulative deferred taxes at the end of each year.
2. Compute the present value of the savings effected by the sum-of-the-years'-digits method of depreciation. Use a discount factor of 0.90; that is, a dollar due one year hence is worth 90 cents now; a dollar due two years hence is worth 81 cents; and so on.

PROBLEMS

13.1 Prepare a payroll sheet and journal entries to record the following payroll data of the Dart Co. and related tax accruals.

Name	No.	Hours Worked	Hourly Rate	No. of Income-Tax Exemptions	Sundry Deductions[a]
Helen Smith	18	40	$2.00	1	(A) 6.00
Mary Yee	22	40	2.00	0	(A) 6.00
Mae Deemer ...	24	44	2.50	2	(B) 10.00
Harry Wilson ...	31	40	2.50	3	(B) 10.00
John Jones	34	44	2.50	2	(A) 6.00
Peter Mcanly ...	42	46	3.00	4	(C) 8.00

[a](A) hospital plan dues; (B) hospital and medical plan dues; (C) savings bond deposits.

The payroll is for the week ended May 28, 1966. Employees are paid time and a half for all time over forty hours in one week. Obtain income tax withholding figures from the table on page 395. The company pays state unemployment taxes at 2 percent of payrolls.

13.2 The Bay Sales Co. payroll data for the month ended October 31, 1966, are given below.

Name	Number of Exemption	Prior Compensation	Gross Pay This Month
Florence Walker	1	$1,800	$200
Wendy Loo	0	3,200	300
Jean Tregalia.............	2	3,500	500
Martin Wilson	2	6,300	500
Donald Carwin	5	7,000	200

The following tax rates apply:
Employee—F.I.C.A., 4.2 percent on first $6,600
    Federal income tax, 14 percent of monthly pay in excess of $56 per exemption.
Employer—S.U.I., 2.0 percent on first $3,800
    F.U.I., 0.4 percent of first $3,000
    F.I.C.A., 4.2 percent on first $6,600

Required:

1. Journalize the payment of the monthly payroll
2. Journalize the employer taxes based on the monthly payroll
3. Journalize the remittance of the withheld income taxes and the employer and employee F.I.C.A. taxes

13.3 Calculate the 1966 federal income tax of Claude and Mary Horan, who have three children, aged four, six, and seven, and no other dependents. The Horans file a joint income tax return. Information supplied by them appear below:

Receipts:
Salary as vice president of T. Donnelly & Co.	$25,000
Interest on municipal bonds	3,000
Interest on corporation bonds	400
Consulting fee in lawsuit	500

Expenditures:
Contributions to qualified religious and charitable organizations	900
Taxes on residence	1,100
State income tax	500
Payments of life insurance	700
Interest on home mortgage	800
Trip to convention related to employment	600
Legal fees for patent application	400
Dues to professional society	100

13.4 Frank B. and Elizabeth Davis file a joint return for 1966. They have three children, two daughters and a son. The daughters live at home and have no income. The son lives at home when not attending the university. He earned $800 during the year, which, supplemented by $1,600 from his parents, was spent on his education.

The taxpayers furnish the following details of their receipts and disbursements for 1966:

Receipts:
Salary as comptroller of Computer Science Co. (Earnings, $30,000, less income tax withheld, $3,800, less F.I.C.A. tax withheld, $277)	$25,923
Interest on savings account	700
Interest on Monterey County bonds	400
Proceeds from sale of land*a*	10,000
Rents received from property	2,400
Drawings from Mary-Beth Studios, a copartnership in which Elizabeth Davis has a half interest. (The partnership reported a net income of $40,000 for the year)	6,000

Disbursements:
Moving expenses from San Francisco to New York	2,100
Mortgage payments on residence:	
Interest	1,200
Principal	800
Real estate taxes on residence	700

---

a The land, purchased July 1, 1950, for $6,000, was a long-term capital asset (held over six months.) Since this is the only capital asset transaction of the taxpayers, only one half of the gain is subject to tax. (Furthermore, the tax on the long-term gain cannot exceed 25 percent.)

Mortgage payments on rental units:

Interest	1,000
Principal	500

(Building cost, $30,000; life, 20 years)

Real estate taxes on rental units	500
Preparation of tax return	100
Church box collections	300
University of California donation	700
Community Fund disbursements	200
Medical bills	2,500
Miscellaneous personal living expenses	36,000
Sales tax on personal expenses	800
Payments during 1966 on estimated income tax	9,000

Required:

1. Computation of 1966 Federal tax liability.
2. Computation of balance due or refund.
3. At what level of earnings would the alternative capital gains tax of 25 percent be to the advantage of the taxpayers?
4. What is the rationale for taxing a gain on real estate at a lower rate than ordinary income?

13.5   Sherman and Mae Van Camp operate a retail poultry business as Van's Poultry. They file a joint return and have no dependents. Their business is operated in a stall rented in a large market. Prior to 1966, all operations were on a cash basis, with inventories sold off before the end of each year. During 1966 the owners expanded operations to include charge sales to restaurants and institutions, and installed refrigeration equipment to maintain an inventory at all times. The taxpayers realize that, as a result, they must change their tax accounting methods from a cash to an accrual basis, and ask you to assist them with their 1966 return. They submit the following summary of cash receipts and disbursements:

Receipts		$217,000
Disbursements:		
Merchandise creditors	$182,600	
Payroll	11,820	
Supplies	1,600	
Advertising	1,200	
Rent	12,000	
Utilities	600	
Insurance	1,600	
Refrigeration equipment	10,240	
Property taxes on business	200	
Business licenses	100	
Property taxes on residence	700	
Bank loan	10,100	
Doctors and hospital	1,200	233,960
Decrease in cash		$(16,960)

The following additional information is available:

(1) The receipts represent collections from customers, except for $10,000, which Van Camp borrowed from the bank and repaid during the year with interest. The Van Camps have taken $3,000 from cash collections during the year for personal expenses that are not deductible for income taxes.

(2) A summary of uncollected sales invoices at December 31 totals $30,000.

(3) A summary of unpaid creditors' invoices at December 31 totals $8,000.

(4) During the year the Van Camps have taken home $600 worth of poultry for personal consumption. Merchandise on hand December 31 amounts to $10,000.

(5) The disbursements for insurance comprise:

Policy	Date	Term (years)	Premium	Coverage
C-1264	1/1/66	3	$1,200	Comprehensive business liability
L-4247	1/1/67	1	400	Life insurance on Mr. Van Camp payable to Mrs. Van Camp

(6) Refrigeration equipment with a list price of $10,000 was purchased in early January on an installment contract. During the year checks for installments totaled $10,240, as shown in the foregoing summary. The final installment of $840 is payable January 1, 1967. The refrigeration equipment has an estimated useful life of ten years. Depreciation is claimed by the double declining balance method.

(7) The Van Camps have compiled the following information pertinent to 1966 from their check books and other sources:

Salary received from university extension as lecturer in marketing (net of income tax withheld $280)	$1,720
Cash received from partnership (distributive share of the net income for the year, $600).	100
Prize won in essay contest	200
Gift from Sherman Van Camp's father	5,000
Cashed 1958 U. S. Savings bonds during the year (cost $900), proceeds . . . . (difference taxable as ordinary income)	1,200
Proceeds from sale of land in Centerville (bought land 1/1/40 for $3,000; one half of gain includable in adjusted gross income)	5,000
Costs of traveling to university extension classes from regular place of business and returning	100
Community fund, cash contributions.	500
Republican Party, cash contributions	200
First Church, cash contributions	260
Payments to Sears for carrying charges on home furnishings	40
Payments to First National Bank on home mortgage: Principal . . . . $ 640 Interest 360	1,000
Taxes paid during 1966: State and local gasoline . . . . $ 50 General sales tax . . . . 250 Self employment tax (F.I.C.A.) for 1965. . 250 On 1966 declaration of estimated tax 6,000	6,550

Required:

1. Federal income tax return for 1966
2. Schedule of business income, with supporting computations

13.6   Owens, Peters, Rogers, Sanders, and Thomas each own 20 percent of the stock of the Western States Trucking Corporation. The corporation has been earning $400,000 before salaries of $30,000 each for the five stockholders.

The owners are considering a financial reorganization of the business. They ask your opinion regarding the tax consequences of two possibilities: They could elect to be taxed as a partnership under Subchapter S of the Internal Revenue Code. Alternatively, they could split up the existing corporation geographically into five equal parts operated by five new corporations, in which case each stockholder would draw a salary of $30,000 from his corporation.

All stockholders are married and file joint returns. Their income outside of salaries exactly equals their itemized deductions and exemptions. Assume that either reorganization would be approved by tax authorities and would effect no tax consequences other than the changes in sources of owners' incomes as outlined above.

Required:

1. Computation of over-all saving, or loss, for each owner if the company elects to file returns under Subchapter S.
2. Computation of over-all saving, or loss, for each owner if the company is split into five corporations.

13.7 A taxpayer whose personal income on a joint return puts him exactly at the top of the 48 percent federal income tax bracket has received an inheritance of $500,000 and is considering investing it. He is trying to choose between buying widely traded common stocks that pay 5 percent per year or forming a new corporation in which he would be the sole stockholder. The contemplated business would earn 5 percent and should appreciate at the same rate as the portfolio of common stock. The taxpayer is not interested in receiving the income from the new investment but wishes to preserve it for his heirs; however, he could draw a salary as an officer of the new corporation if he wished to do so.

Required:

Determine which alternative is best for the purposes expressed, and calculate the annual saving in income taxes resulting from the choice (ignore special provisions of the tax law such as the dividend exclusion). Assume that conditions and rates remain unchanged.

13.8 Arthur Adams owns a service station on leased land at the corner of Broadway and Twelfth Avenue. The lease expires in five years, at which time all rights in the property including improvements revert to the owner of the land. A syndicate has offered to buy the station for $30,000 cash. The station shows annual earnings of $10,000 and has a book value of $2,000 on January 1, 1966. If the station is sold, the gain is taxable to Adams at 25 percent capital gain rates. Adams is single and is exactly at the beginning of the 62 percent tax bracket. (It may be assumed that the tax rates and his other income will remain the same for the next five years.)

Required:

1. Prepare a schedule showing the aggregate net proceeds to Adams (a) if he sells and (b) if he does not sell.
2. The syndicate forms a corporation known as Banway, Ltd., which purchases the Broadway and Twelfth Avenue station. The owners of Banway, are trying to choose between sum-of-the-years'-digits or straight line depreciation. (The entire purchase price may be assumed to apply to the depreciable property with a 5-year life.) The syndicate can invest funds at the end of each year at 10 percent.
   Prepare a schedule showing the net income after taxes to Banway for each of the years 1966-1970 (a) if depreciation is computed by the sum-of-the-years'-digits method and (b) if depreciation is computed by the straight line method. Banway, Ltd., is taxable at 22 percent on the first $25,000 of taxable income. Assume the station will produce annual cash earnings of $10,000 before depreciation. Comment briefly on the comparison.

3. Prepare schedules showing the net cash available at the end of each year under the two depreciation methods. Calculate the compound amount at the end of the fifth year if funds are invested exactly at the end of each year. For simplicity, compute interest at 10 percent per year net after taxes. Compare the December 31, 1970, cash balances for the two depreciation methods, and comment briefly. (Round amounts to nearest dollar.)

4. How much cash will be available for stockholders of Banway if the company is dissolved on December 31, 1970, and the shareholders pay a capital gains tax of 25 percent (assuming sum-of-the-years'-digits depreciation?) Their cost is the original $30,000 invested.

5. Suppose Banway, Ltd., were owned by four officer-shareholders, who owned all the stock equally. They all file joint returns and are at the top of the 62 percent bracket. Would they be better off, or worse off, if Banway paid annual salaries of $1,000 to each of them?

6. Suppose the taxpayers are at the top of the 32 percent bracket, would an annual salary of $1,000 then be advisable? Comment. (The capital gains tax under this assumption would be at the rate of $1/2 \times 32\%$, or 16%.)

PART IV

Problems of
Particular Organizations

A partnership is "an association of two or more persons to carry on as co-owners a business for profit."[1] This chapter deals with the accounting for formation of a partnership and the distribution of earnings among the partners. It also presents the managerial considerations basic to the decision to use the partnership form of organization and important in operating it.

LEGAL CHARACTERISTICS OF PARTNERSHIPS

A partnership is not a separate legal entity for most purposes, although property can usually be held in the partnership name. The partners act as individuals joining together to conduct a business, and this relation has consequences different from those affecting stockholders in a corporation. In a partnership the following conditions exist:

Unlimited liability. Each partner is responsible for the debts of the partnership. If the organization fails, creditors can take property belonging to the partners to satisfy the business debts even though it was not connected with the business. Special kinds of partnerships, called limited partnerships, permit limited or "silent" partners to invest in a partnership without assuming liability for its debts. In these organizations there must always be one or more general partners who are personally liable for the debts of the organization. Limited partnerships can be formed only under special statutes.

Mutual agency. Each partner in a general partnership has the power to make contracts for the business, and thus is an agent of all the other partners. A limited partner in a limited partnership does not have this power unless he takes part in the management of the business, in which case he also becomes liable as a general partner. Hence the "silent" partner. The mutual agency existing in a partnership should be borne in mind in accepting a person as a partner; if the person makes an unwise contract the other partners are bound by it.

Limited life. The incapacity, death, or withdrawal of a partner automatically ends the partnership. Sale of a partner's interest or admission of a new partner ends the old partnership. The partner or his estate has the right to withdraw his interest in the partnership, which may considerably disrupt the business. If a partner withdraws in violation of the partnership agreement the other partners may recover damages, but this compensation may not enable the business to be preserved.

Flexible division of net income. The partners may agree to divide net income in any way they desire. If they make no agreement about dividing net income or

[1] Per the Uniform Partnership Act.

427

"profits" and later disagree about the division, the courts will assume they intended to share the net income equally. If they make no agreement about losses, the courts assume that they intended to share losses in the same way they share net income, and if there is no agreement about either losses or net income, that losses were intended to be shared equally.

Easy withdrawal of funds. Partners may withdraw assets from the business as they wish. In this privilege they are different from stockholders in a corporation, who receive dividends only when they are declared by the directors. However, partners should have an agreement as to how much each one may withdraw.

Exempt income tax status. Since partnerships are not recognized as legal entities separate from their owners, they are not subjected to an income tax. This characteristic and its implications were discussed in the preceding chapter.

FORMATION BY CASH INVESTMENT

If E. A. Wilkins and C. O. Clyde form a partnership by investing $10,000 and $15,000 respectively, the entry is:

Cash	$25,000.00	
E. A. Wilkins, Capital		$10,000.00
C. O. Clyde, Capital		15,000.00

FORMATION FROM PRIOR PROPRIETORSHIP

Assume that H. F. Wells has operated as a sole proprietor for a number of years, and has the following balance sheet:

H. F. WELLS
Balance Sheet
June 30, 1966

Cash	$ 500.00	Notes Payable	$ 2,000.00
Accounts Receivable, less		Accounts Payable	3,000.00
Allowance	2,000.00	Mortgage Payable	8,000.00
Merchandise	4,000.00	H. F. Wells, Capital	11,050.00
Supplies	200.00		
Prepaid Expense	350.00		
Land	3,000.00		
Building, less Accumulated Depreciation	14,000.00		
	$24,050.00		$24,050.00

Wells agrees with E. A. Wilkins and C. O. Clyde to form a partnership that will continue and expand the business Wells formerly conducted as a sole proprietorship. Wilkins is to invest $10,000 and Clyde $15,000 in cash, and Wells is to contribute the assets of his old business. The partners agree to assume the debts of the old proprietorship. However, they agree that Well's accounts receivable should be valued at only $1,500 ($2,200 gross less allowance for doubtful accounts of $700), and that the supplies are worth only $150.

The other assets are to be taken over at the figures given in Well's balance sheet, except that Wells will not transfer any cash to the partnership. The entries to begin the new partnership are:

Accounts Receivable	$ 2,200.00	
Merchandise	4,000.00	
Supplies	150.00	
Prepaid Expense	350.00	
Land	3,000.00	
Building	14,000.00	
Allowance for Doubtful Accounts		$ 700.00
Notes Payable		2,000.00
Accounts Payable		3,000.00
Mortgage Payable		8,000.00
H. F. Wells, Capital		10,000.00

(to record contribution of H. F. Wells to form partnership of Wells, Wilkins and Clyde)

Cash	$25,000.00	
E. A. Wilkins, Capital		$10,000.00
C. O. Clyde, Capital		15,000.00

The agreement of the partners on the values at which assets shall be taken into the partnership is important. The asset values determine the capital credit of the partner contributing them, and this determines the proportion of the assets that he is entitled to receive on dissolution of the firm (but not necessarily the proportion of profit he will receive).

DRAWING ACCOUNTS

The net income of a partnership is the net income of the partners from that business. Since there is no legal distinction between the firm and its owners, anything earned or lost by the firm is the earning or loss of the owners in a legal as well as an economic sense. It follows that the owners do not incur an expense if they take out funds to live on or "pay themselves a salary," as they may say. They are only transferring funds from one pocket to another. The amounts taken out are known as drawings, or withdrawals; they are recorded in Drawing accounts. The entry to record a regular monthly withdrawal of $500 by H. F. Wells is:

H. F. Wells, Drawing	$ 500.00	
Cash		$ 500.00

A withdrawal of some other asset would be credited to that asset (merchandise withdrawals are credited to Purchases unless a perpetual inventory is used). The Drawing account is closed to Capital at the end of the accounting period; it serves to accumulate the amount of withdrawals during the period so it can be used in statements, and to prevent the Capital account being so cluttered with entries as to require analysis when a statement of capital for the period is prepared. The Drawing account is also called "Personal" account. Note that any "salary" or "interest" calculation made by the partners in dividing net income is not an expense in the statements of the partnership, but only a calculation made for the purposes of dividing net income among the partners.

DIVISION OF NET INCOME

Net income may be divided in any way the partners wish. As was noted above, if they do not make their intentions clear the courts will assume that they intended to divide the net income equally. If their intentions about net income are clear but nothing is said about losses, the courts assume that losses were intended to be divided in the same way as net income or profits. In practice the partners may arrange to divide net income so as to compensate different partners for their differing contributions. Some may contribute more capital than others; some may spend more time in the business than others; and some may have a greater skill and experience or a reputation that attracts business. The reflection of these differences in schemes for dividing net income appears in the following paragraphs. The illustrations are from the firm of Wells, Wilkins, and Clyde, whose opening entries were given above. Net income of this firm for the year ended June 30, 1967, was $28,000, and the illustrations concern that year.

DIVISION OF NET INCOME ON FIXED RATIOS

The partners may agree to divide net income in, say, shares of $4/10$ for Wells and $3/10$ each for Wilkins and Clyde. In this case the entry to distribute the net income is:

Profit and Loss............................. $28,000.00		
H. F. Wells, Capital...............................		$11,200.00
E. A. Wilkins, Capital................................		8,400.00
C. O. Clyde, Capital................................		8,400.00

(to distribute net income for the year ended June 30, 1967)

Some accountants prefer to credit the shares of net income to the drawing accounts of the partners on the theory that they are withdrawing current income. However, they are not restricted to income that is earned currently, or even to past accumulations—they may dip into their original capital. Furthermore, it is convenient to be able to see the opening balance of capital, the credit for net income or debit for loss, the debit for drawings, and any special additional investments in the Capital account for the year.

DIVISION OF NET INCOME ON OPENING CAPITAL BALANCES

If the partners agree to divide net income in ratio to their opening Capital balances each year, the division for 1967 would be as follows:

	Total	Wells	Wilkins	Clyde
Opening Capital.............	$35,000	$10,000	$10,000	$15,000
Ratios.....................	7/7	2/7	2/7	3/7
Net Income.................	$28,000	$ 8,000	$ 8,000	$12,000

It would be important when dividing profits in the ratio of the opening balances to agree to a fixed limit on withdrawals, since arbitrary withdrawals could considerably change the relationship of the Capital balances. However, an agreement on withdrawals is important in any case.

DIVISION OF NET INCOME ON CLOSING CAPITAL BALANCES

The accounts below show the Capital transactions of the partners during the year ended June 30, 1967.

H. F. Wells, Capital

1967			2 000 00	1966 June	30		10 000 00
Mar.	31			Oct.	31		4 000 00

E. A. Wilkins, Capital

1966			1 000 00	1966 June	30		10 000 00
Sept.	30		1 000 00	1967			
Dec.	31			May	31		2 000 00

C. O. Clyde, Capital

				1966 June	30		15 000 00
				Dec.	31		3 000 00
				1967			
				Mar.	31		3 000 00

Distribution on ending capital balances (before adding net income to the balance) takes the following form in this case:

	Total	Wells	Wilkins	Clyde
Ending Capital balances.	$43,000.00	$12,000.00	$10,000.00	$21,000.00
Ratios.	43/43	12/43	10/43	21/43
Net Income.	$28,000.00	$ 7,813.95	$ 6,511.63	$13,674.42

In the foregoing distribution it is assumed that the withdrawals recorded in the Capital accounts are the only ones made during the year. If regular monthly withdrawals were made and charged to the Drawing accounts, they could also be deducted in calculating ending balances. The net income earned during the year and now being distributed is not considered, although it could be taken into account by means of algebra.

DIVISION OF NET INCOME ON AVERAGE CAPITAL BALANCES

The average-balance method gives effect to the actual investment maintained during the year by taking into consideration the time a particular balance was in existence. The average is a weighted average; the computations of the averages based on the accounts given in the preceding paragraph follow (averages are rounded to the nearest dollar):

Date	Balance	Time extant (in Months)	Extension	Average Balance (Extension ÷ 12)
H. F. Wells:				
6–30–66	$10,000 ×	4 =	40,000	
10–31–66	14,000 ×	5 =	70,000	
3–31–67	12,000 ×	3 =	36,000	
Totals		12	146,000	$12,167
E. A. Wilkins:				
6–30–66	$10,000 ×	3 =	30,000	
9–30–66	9,000 ×	3 =	27,000	
12–31–66	8,000 ×	5 =	40,000	
5–31–67	10,000 ×	1 =	10,000	
Totals		12	107,000	$ 8,917
C. O. Clyde:				
6–30–66	$15,000 ×	6 =	90,000	
12–31–66	18,000 ×	3 =	54,000	
3–31–67	21,000 ×	3 =	63,000	
Totals		12	207,000	$17,250

Division of net income is then calculated as before. In this case it is:

	Total	Wells	Wilkins	Clyde
Average Capital balances......	$38,334	$12,167	$8,917	$17,250
Ratios........................	100.00	31.74	23.26	45.00
Net Income...................	$28,000	$ 8,887	$6,513	$12,600

The allocation in this case is made to the nearest dollar.

DIVISION OF NET INCOME ON "SALARY," INTEREST, AND FIXED RATIO

Services rendered to a business by each partner often are more important than the capital investment of each. Furthermore, the contribution of each in skill and experience may be quite different. In such a case the partners may wish to specify that each one should get a certain "salary" out of profits. At the same time, different capital contributions may be compensated for by allocating part of the net income as though interest were being paid on the capital invested. Any remainder would then be distributed in an agreed ratio. Assume that Wells, Wilkins, and Clyde have agreed that "salaries" should be allowed out of profits in the amounts of $10,000 to Wells, $6,000 to Wilkins, and $5,000 to Clyde. Assume that they also agreed that each partner should be allocated 5 percent of his ending capital balance as compensation for use of the capital, and that remaining profits are to be divided equally. The distribution of the net income of $28,000 for 1967 under this scheme is as follows (ending balances are given in the accounts presented above):

	Total	Wells	Wilkins	Clyde
Salary	$21,000.00	$10,000.00	$6,000.00	$5,000.00
Interest	2,150.00	600.00	500.00	1,050.00
Remainder	4,850.00	1,616.67	1,616.67	1,616.66
Totals	$28,000.00	$12,216.67	$8,116.67	$7,666.66

The calculation of the interest factor could have been made on the opening balances of Capital or on the average balances as calculated above, or otherwise—for example, on the lowest balance of the year.

DIVISION OF NET INCOME WHEN IT IS LESS THAN SALARY AND INTEREST

It may happen that net income is less than the salary and interest considered necessary to compensate the partners for their services and for use of their capital. In this case the intent of the partners can be carried out only by distributing the net income as before except that the "remainder" in the distribution will be a negative figure. Taking the same profit-sharing agreement that was used in the preceding paragraph with the same ending Capital balances, but assuming a net income for the year of only $18,020, the calculation is:

	Total	Wells	Wilkins	Clyde
Salary	$21,000.00	$10,000.00	$6,000.00	$5,000.00
Interest	2,150.00	600.00	500.00	1,050.00
Remainder	(5,130.00)	(1,710.00)	(1,710.00)	(1,710.00)
Totals	$18,020.00	$ 8,890.00	$4,790.00	$4,340.00

STATEMENT OF CAPITAL ACCOUNTS

It is useful to include in the balance sheet a brief summary of the changes in the Proprietorship account or accounts for the year. In a partnership, with a Capital account for each partner, this is likely to be too cumbersome. A separate statement of Capital accounts will supply the need for such a summary in more appropriate form. The statement is illustrated below with data from the following sources: (1) transactions during the year from the accounts presented above for calculation of ending and average capital balances and (2) the distribution of net income presented in the preceding section where net income was too small to cover the agreed salary and interest allocations.

WELLS, WILKINS AND CLYDE
Statement of Capital

Year Ended June 30, 1967

	Total	H. F. Wells	E. A. Wilkins	C. O. Clyde
Balances July 1, 1966	$35,000.00	$10,000.00	$10,000.00	$15,000.00
Additional Investments.	12,000.00	4,000.00	2,000.00	6,000.00
	$47,000.00	$14,000.00	$12,000.00	$21,000.00
Withdrawals.	4,000.00	2,000.00	2,000.00	—
	$43,000.00	$12,000.00	$10,000.00	$21,000.00
Net Income.	18,020.00	8,890.00	4,790.00	4,340.00
Balances June 30, 1967	$61,020.00	$20,890.00	$14,790.00	$25,340.00

PARTNERSHIP REORGANIZATION AND DISSOLUTION

Admission of an additional partner, or withdrawal of a partner where remaining partners continue, need not disrupt the business. But any change of partners technically dissolves the old partnership and a new one must be created to carry on. The books of the old partnership are contined in these cases, with adjustments being made to recognize the new capital structure and any changes in asset values that the new agreement establishes. When the business of a partnership is liquidated after dissolution of the partnership, its assets are sold, its liabilities paid, and the net proceeds distributed to the partners. The calculations and entries involved in these transactions are the subject of the following paragraphs.

ADMISSION OF AN ADDITIONAL PARTNER

A new partner may acquire his interest in the following ways:

1. Purchase of an interest from another partner.
2. Contribution of assets to the partnership, in which:
   (a) Amount of assets contributed equals amount of the interest acquired.
   (b) Amount of assets contributed is greater than the amount of the interest acquired.
      (1) Bonus adjustment is made.
      (2) Goodwill adjustment is made.
   (c) Amount of assets contributed is less than the amount of the interest acquired.
      (1) Bonus adjustment is made.
      (2) Goodwill adjustment is made.

In some firms, especially in the professional fields such as public accounting or law, a new partner may come in with no capital ownership and have a share in net income only. In these cases he is often expected to leave some of his share of net income in the firm and so to build up a capital interest.

PURCHASE OF AN INTEREST FROM ANOTHER PARTNER

A new partner may acquire his interest by buying all or part of another partner's interest. Of course, the admission of the new partner must be acceptable to the remaining partners. The purchase price is paid to the selling partner and its amount is a personal matter between buyer and seller. The books of the old partnership are converted to the use of the new one simply by transferring the proper amount from the Capital account of the old to the Capital account of the new partner. Suppose that J. E. Osgood purchases for $18,000 one half of E. C. Perry's $28,000 Capital interest in the Esterman Company. The entry to record the transaction on the partnership books is:

    E. C. Perry, Capital...........................$14,000.00
            J. E. Osgood, Capital................... $14,000.00

No notice has to be taken on the partnership books of the price Osgood paid Perry, but because a new partnership is being formed, adjustments to state the assets at values indicated by the price paid for a 20 percent interest could be made.

CONTRIBUTION OF ASSETS IN AMOUNT EQUAL TO THE INTEREST OBTAINED

Suppose that J. E. Osgood is to be admitted to the partnership of Jones, Scully, and Scammon. The capital of the old partnership is $80,000, and Osgood is to contribute $20,000 in cash. This gives him the 20 percent interest in the new total capital of $100,000 that the partners have agreed upon, and his admission is very simply recorded as follows:

    Cash......................................$20,000.00
            J. E. Osgood, Capital................... $20,000.00

Presumably in this case the partners are satisfied that the assets as carried on the books are sufficiently close to current values to require no adjustment.

CONTRIBUTION OF ASSETS IN GREATER OR LESSER AMOUNT THAN THE INTEREST OBTAINED

Frequently the accounts will not reflect current asset values, because they are kept on a cost basis and changing conditions will raise or lower actual as compared with ledger asset values. Furthermore, a concern may enjoy goodwill as a result of effective work or it may suffer a decline below its original value because of deteriorating management. When actual values are higher than book figures and when goodwill has arisen, a new partner will be required to invest more for a given percent of the capital interest than the book figures of the old organization would indicate. If values have declined, he can acquire his percent of the capital interest for a smaller investment than the books would seem to indicate. As was noted earlier, the proportion of capital each partner has determines his right to assets in case of liquidation, so any agreement about the proportion of the capital a partner is to have should be reflected in the Capital accounts. Otherwise there may be confusion as to the actual intentions of the partners. Accordingly, an investment by a new partner will require some kind of adjustment of the Capital accounts if it is at more or less than the amount that his percent of interest would be on the basis of the existing Capital accounts.

This adjustment traditionally takes either of two possible forms. These are known as the *bonus method* and the *goodwill method*. In the bonus method, the necessary adjustment is made between the partners' Capital accounts when the new partner's investment is recorded; the asset accounts are not affected. In the goodwill method, the asset Goodwill is recorded and the proper partners' Capital accounts are credited in order to give those accounts the proper relationship. If it were known that a particular asset was responsible for the increase in value—say a strategically located piece of land used as the site of a store—that asset should be debited instead of Goodwill. Similarly, if a particular asset is known to be overvalued in the ledger, it should be written down and the Capital accounts debited. In the following sections, as a matter of convenience, only the Goodwill account will be used. Note that the ratio of capital ownership we are concerned with now is not necessarily the same as the ratio for dividing net income among the partners.

ADMISSION OF NEW PARTNER—BONUS METHOD

Bonus to old partners. When the new partner's investment is more than the old accounts would indicate as necessary, the old partners are credited with part of the new partner's investment; they receive a bonus. Suppose that Forman and Cooke, who share net income and losses equally and have the Capital balances shown below, admit F. M. Osgood. Osgood pays in $50,000 for a 33⅓ percent interest in the new partnership. The figures are tabulated as follows:

H. A. Forman, Capital	$ 30,000.00
C. D. Cooke, Capital	40,000.00
Total of old Capital balances	$ 70,000.00
New investment by Osgood	50,000.00
Total of new Capital balances	$120,000.00
Osgood's 33⅓% interest in new Capital balances	$ 40,000.00
Excess of new investment over credit to new partner—bonus to old partners	$ 10,000.00

The old partners share the bonus in their profit-sharing ratio. The bonus represents values created since the organization of the partnership and is therefore in the nature of an earning. The entry to record Osgood's investment is:

Cash	$50,000.00	
H. A. Forman, Capital		$ 5,000.00
C. D. Cooke, Capital		5,000.00
F. M. Osgood, Capital		40,000.00

Bonus to new partner. Assume that Forman and Cooke had admitted Osgood with an investment of only $20,000 for his 33⅓ percent interest. The bonus would then go to Osgood, as follows:

Total of old Capital balances. $70,000.00
New investment by Osgood. 20,000.00
      Total of new Capital balances. $90,000.00
Osgood's 33⅓% interest. $30,000.00
Excess of credit to new partner over his investment—bonus to new
   partner. $10,000.00

The bonus is debited to the old partners' Capital accounts in their profit-sharing ratio; and the entry to record the admission of the new partner is:

Cash. $20,000.00
H. A. Forman, Capital. 5,000.00
C. D. Cooke, Capital. 5,000.00
    F. M. Osgood, Capital. $30,000.00

ADMISSION OF NEW PARTNER—GOODWILL METHOD

Goodwill to old partners. If the old partnership has created goodwill that the new partner recognizes in making his investment, this may be recorded in a new Goodwill asset account with credits to the old partners' capital accounts. Some other asset should be debited if its value, in excess of the recorded amount, is the reason for the higher rate of contribution by the new partner. One can determine whether the old partners or new partner will get credit for the goodwill by observing whether or not the new investment exceeds the new partner's share of the old Capital balances plus the new investment. When Osgood was admitted to the firm of Forman and Cooke with an investment of $50,000, the old Capital balances plus the $50,000 totaled $120,000. One third of this is $40,000. This indicates that Osgood's investment recognizes that the firm's value is higher than that of its assets as recorded, and that the credit for goodwill accrues to the old partners. Under the goodwill method, no partner's investment is reduced in favor of another partner. If the old partners' accounts get the goodwill credit, the new partner's credit will be the full amount of his investment. The goodwill may then be computed as follows in the case of the admission of Osgood with a $50,000 investment:

Investment by Osgood for 33⅓% interest. . . . .$ 50,000.00
Total capital value when $50,000 is ⅓ (that is, $50,000.00 ÷
   ⅓). $150,000.00
Capital value exclusive of goodwill:
   Old partners. $70,000
   New investment. 50,000   120,000.00
Goodwill. . . . .$ 30,000.00

Goodwill that arose after the old partnership was formed is also in the nature of an earning, and is shared by the old partners in their profit-sharing ratio (equal in this case). The entries required to record the admission of the new partner and to adjust the accounts in this case are:

```
Cash.......................................$50,000.00
        F. M. Osgood, Capital...................        $50,000.00
Goodwill....................................$30,000.00
        H. A. Forman, Capital...................        $15,000.00
        C. D. Cooke, Capital...................         15,000.00
```

Goodwill to new partner. If the old partners are willing to admit the new partner with a higher capital credit than his cash investment indicates, it may be that they recognize that he brings goodwill into the business. In this case the goodwill method records the goodwill with a credit to the new partner. In this case the *old* partners' balances will be unchanged and the new capital and the goodwill may be computed with reference to them. In the case in which Osgood was admitted with an investment of $20,000 for a $33\frac{1}{3}$ percent interest in Forman and Cooke, the goodwill method is applied as follows:

Investment of old partners—to be a 66⅔% interest.........$70,000.00

Capital balance of new partner required for a 33⅓% interest

$$(\$70,000.00 \times \frac{33\frac{1}{3}}{66\frac{2}{3}} \text{ or } \$70,000.00 \times \frac{1}{2}) ....\$35,000.00$$

Investment by new partner..........................   20,000.00

Goodwill of new partner.............................$15,000.00

The entry to record Osgood's admission in this case is:

```
Cash.......................................$20,000.00
Goodwill....................................  15,000.00
        F. M. Osgood, Capital...................        $35,000.00
```

WITHDRAWAL OF A PARTNER

When a partner withdraws and the other partners wish to continue the business, provision must be made for paying out the withdrawing partner's interest. Different payouts may be arranged as follows:

1. Withdrawing partner takes assets at ledger figures to the recorded amount of his Capital.

2. Withdrawing partner takes less than his recorded Capital balance. The difference may be a bonus to the old partners, or it may indicate that some assets are worth less than the ledger figures.

3. Withdrawing partner takes more than the recorded balance of his Capital. The difference may result from unrecorded increases in asset values including goodwill, or it may result from a willingness on the part of the old partners to pay the retiring partner a bonus to get out, as they might after a dispute.

The illustrative entries for these possible settlements are drawn from the firm of Hixon, Cass, and Fish, who have capital and share net income as follows:

	Capital	Share of Net Income
D. X. Hixon	$25,000	40%
O. L. Cass	32,000	40%
F. E. Fish	20,000	20%

WITHDRAWING PARTNER TAKES HIS RECORDED CAPITAL BALANCE

The entry to record the withdrawal of Fish on this basis, and assuming that cash is paid, is:

F. E. Fish, Capital..............................$20,000.00
    Cash................................. $20,000.00

In this case the recorded capital is paid out with no adjustment. Presumably the partners are agreed that the assets as stated on the books are actual values.

WITHDRAWING PARTNER TAKES LESS THAN HIS RECORDED CAPITAL

If the business is not worth as much as the recorded capital balances indicate, the withdrawing partner, realizing this fact, may take less than his ledger balance. If the decline in value can be identified with specific assets, they should be written down, and the Capital accounts would then show what the retiring partner should expect to receive. However, if the decline is not associated with particular assets, but with bad conditions in the industry or some other general cause, the partners may not wish to revise the asset record. Furthermore, the retiring partner may be willing to pay the bonus in order to be allowed to withdraw without liquidation of the business, which might involve losses due to forced sale. In this case the retiring partner's Capital balance in excess of the assets withdrawn is shifted to the other partners. In this situation, Hixon, Cass, and Fish, assuming that Fish agrees to take only $15,000 on withdrawal, will record the transaction as follows:

F. E. Fish, Capital..............................$20,000.00
    Cash................................. $15,000.00
    D. X. Hixon, Capital.....................   2,500.00
    O. L. Cass, Capital......................   2,500.00

WITHDRAWING PARTNER TAKES MORE THAN HIS RECORDED CAPITAL

In the third case the actual asset values presumably are in excess of the recorded ones; some assets may have increased in value, or the firm may have built up goodwill. On the other hand, the old partners may pay a bonus to get rid of the retiring partner without liquidation of the business. If specific assets that account for the higher values can be identified, they should be adjusted to their actual values and the Capital accounts credited. The retiring partner's Capital account will then show what he can withdraw. The revaluation would not be considered good practice except in a reorganization. In the case of the partnership, the new organization, although continuing the old business and retaining the old books, is entitled to record the assets at their actual values at the time they are taken over by the new organization. The fact that the values are established in connection with retirement of a partner and that payments are made to him based on these values gives considerable protection against arbitrary valuations. If specific assets that account for the higher values cannot be identified, goodwill may be recorded. Suppose it was agreed to allow Fish to withdraw $25,000, the extra $5,000 representing his share of the goodwill. The entries required are:

Goodwill...................................	$25,000.00	
D. X. Hixon, Capital....................		$10,000.00
O. L. Cass, Capital.....................		10,000.00
F. E. Fish, Capital......................		5,000.00
F. E. Fish, Capital............................	$25,000.00	
Cash.................................		$25,000.00

Total goodwill is $25,000 if Cass's 20 percent interest in it is worth $5,000. Some accountants would prefer to record only the $5,000 of goodwill allowed to Cass, but a more accurate and complete record is presented when all of it is entered.

If the continuing partners wish to retain the assets at their original ledger values and do not wish to record goodwill, they can use a bonus method of adjustment. For the case just presented the bonus method requires this entry:

F. E. Fish, Capital............................	$20,000.00	
D. X. Hixon, Capital..........................	2,500.00	
O. L. Cass, Capital...........................	2,500.00	
Cash.................................		$25,000.00

This is especially appropriate when the bonus is paid to persuade Fish to withdraw without liquidation of the business or litigation over the value of his interest. Such difficulties should be avoided by providing explicitly in the partnership agreement for the method of determining what a retiring partner shall receive.

LIQUIDATION OF A PARTNERSHIP

When a partnership business is liquidated the following steps are taken:

1. Assets are sold.
2. Gains or losses on realization of the assets are distributed to the partners' Capital accounts in their ratio for sharing net income.
3. Liabilities are paid.
4. Cash (or other assets, if desired) is distributed to the partners in the amounts of their Capital balances.

The process may be summarized for the case of Moore, Bonner, and Gold, who share profits in the ratio of 0.4, 0.4, and 0.2, respectively, as follows:

	Cash	Other Assets	Liabili-ties	Capital Moore	Capital Bonner	Capital Gold
Balances.................	$ 5,000	$75,000	$20,000	$20,000	$18,000	$22,000
First sale of assets.........	40,000	(60,000)	—	(8,000)	(8,000)	(4,000)
New balances.............	$45,000	$15,000	$20,000	$12,000	$10,000	$18,000
Second sale of assets......	18,000	(15,000)	—	1,200	1,200	600
New balances.............	$63,000	—	$20,000	$13,200	$11,200	$18,600
Payment of liabilities......	(20,000)	—	(20,000)	—	—	—
Cash to be paid to partners.	$43,000	—	—	$13,200	$11,200	$18,600

Note that the first sale of assets was made at a loss of $20,000 ($60,000 = ledger value of assets sold, $40,000 = cash received), and that this loss was distributed to the partners' Capital accounts in their profit-and-loss ratio. On the second sale of assets a gain of $3,000 was realized and this was similarly distributed. In practice it is useful to have an account for "Gain or Loss on Realization of Assets" in which the gains or losses are accumulated prior to distribution to the partners' accounts.

LIQUIDATION WHEN A PARTNER HAS A DEFICIT

A general partner is liable for the debts of the firm and he is liable for his share of the firm's losses. If losses chargeable to him exceed his capital, he may be forced to pay in the difference. However, if he has no personal assets, the loss will be shifted to any other general partners. This event is illustrated in the case of Adam, Blake, and Towne, as follows (they share profits and losses equally):

	Cash	Other Assets	Liabili-ities	Capital Adam	Capital Blake	Capital Towne
Balance.................	$ 4,000	$62,000	$14,000	$22,000	$18,000	$12,000
Sale of assets............	23,000	(62,000)	—	(13,000)	(13,000)	(13,000)
New balances............	$27,000	—	$14,000	$ 9,000	$ 5,000	$(1,000)
Distribution of Towne's deficit..............	—	—	—	(500)	(500)	1,000
New balances............	$27,000	—	$14,000	$ 8,500	$ 4,500	—
Payment of liabilities......	(14,000)	—	(14,000)	—	—	—
Cash to be paid to partners indicated...........	$13,000	—	—	$ 8,500	$ 4,500	—

MANAGEMENT CONSIDERATIONS IN FORMING AND OPERATING A PARTNERSHIP

Fundamental management problems entailed in the partnership form of organization are discussed under the following headings:

1. Personal qualifications of partners
2. Content of the partnership agreement
3. Continuity
4. Availability of capital
5. Income tax status

PERSONAL QUALIFICATIONS OF PARTNERS

The mutual agency involved in a partnership makes it essential that one know any prospective partner very well and have full confidence in his character and ability before joining with him in a partnership. Honesty is essential, and in view of the small size of most partnerships and their dependence on the personal efforts of their members, industry and skill are also essential. Although it may seem rather mundane in connection with a relationship that often involves personal friendship and a certain amount of idealism, it is wise to consider even the health of a prospective partner. Bad health that prevented a partner from carrying his share of the work or that caused his withdrawal could be a serious handicap. The importance of knowing a prospective partner well is indicated, at the extreme, by police records. Police departments have much experience with a confidence game known as the "partnership racket," in which a confidence man persuades another to go into partnership and then absconds with the partnership assets. When a partnership is formed, most difficulties of a personal nature can be well provided for by explicit agreement. For example, one can provide for adjusting the division of net income if a partner cannot do his share of the work. Caution in selecting partners is nevertheless important.

CONTENT OF THE PARTNERSHIP AGREEMENT

The partnership contract, called *articles of copartnership*, should be in writing and as complete as possible. It is desirably drawn with the aid of a lawyer experienced in such matters. It should cover at least the following eleven subjects:

1. Names of the partners, name of the firm, and its location.
2. Date, and, if the business is to run for a specified time, the period covered.
3. Kind of business to be conducted.
4. Duties of each partner in conducting the business, including anything each one is *not* to do. (Although a partner may legally bind the others by making a contract he has agreed with his partners not to make, they may have a right of damages against him.)
5. The amount of capital to be contributed by each partner, the form in which it is to be paid in, and the time when it is to be paid in. The agreement should specify the values at which any assets other than cash are to be taken onto the partnership books. Of course, any liabilities to be assumed in connection with the assets contributed should also be specified in detail.
6. The determination and distribution of net income. This involves the accounts to be kept, the accounting principles to be followed (for example, cash or accrual methods, fiscal year to be used), and the way net income is to be divided. Provision for absence or illness of a partner and its effect on net income division may be specified.
7. Rights and limitations of the partners on drawings.
8. Pricing of sales of the firm's merchandise to partners. One of the advantages some people get out of being in business is the opportunity to purchase at wholesale, but other partners may not be willing to provide the related services of the firm involved in such purchases at no charge.

9. Provision for withdrawal of a partner's capital on his death. Provision may be made for waiting until the next regular closing date to compute net income, with the portion of the year that the deceased partner was alive determining his share. It may take the form of allowing a specified period for orderly liquidation of assets. It may take the form of allowing the remaining partners to buy the deceased partner's interest, and should then specify how the accounts shall be kept to determine the amount and whether or not anything additional should be paid for goodwill. If the remaining partners expect to buy a deceased partner's interest in order to continue the business, the partners may need to take out life insurance on each other's lives in order to have funds to make the purchase.

10. Provision for liquidating the business or buying out a withdrawing partner; the considerations are similar to those in provision 9.

11. It is wise to provide for arbitration of disputes, since it is impossible to anticipate every possible event, and litigation is costly.

CONTINUITY OF THE PARTNERSHIP

One of the disadvantages of the partnership form of organization that is frequently emphasized is its vulnerability to dissolution by withdrawal or death of a partner. This is to a considerable degree a disadvantage of all small organizations and is due also to the failure to provide for contingencies rather than a disadvantage solely of the partnership form. Although a partnership is technically dissolved by death or withdrawal of a partner or admission of a new one, such a dissolution need not harm the business or the interests of the old partners or the estate of a departing partner. Large partnerships such as the nationally organized public accounting firms and large law offices, which have dozens of partners, change the composition of the partnership frequently, but provision is made for determination of the amounts to be withdrawn and their orderly withdrawal by departing partners; thus the business is not usually disrupted when there are many partners to carry it on. This stability may be contrasted with the condition of a small organization, say one that consists chiefly of two men, one who is an effective salesman and the other an effective production specialist. If one of these men dies the organization has a serious problem, whether it is a corporation or a partnership. (A small corporation that cannot replace a key man may be forced to liquidate, and a small corporation owned equally by a surviving key man and the heirs of a deceased key man may be greatly disrupted by a quarrel over liquidation or continuation.) Persons participating in small partnerships as well as large ones should therefore provide for orderly liquidation or for buying out the interest of a departing partner as indicated in the section on the partnership agreement.

AVAILABILITY OF CAPITAL

It is often said that a partnership is less able to raise capital than is a corporation. This again is often a characteristic of small size rather than of organizational form. Large banking partnerships have no trouble obtaining adequate capital. Large group medical practices are able to obtain needed capital although organized on a partnership basis. A corporation in which the success of the business depends upon the skill of one or two persons has the same difficulties in raising capital as does the same business organized as a partnership; the real difficulty is that the enterprise depends too much on the life and health of one or two persons. However, it is true that the partnership form becomes much too cumbersome for the operation of most very large businesses, and in most lines of business individuals are not willing or able to take the risk of being held responsible for the organization's debts. With the exception of such specialized lines as investment banking, large organizations are not ordinarily created in the partnership form.

INCOME TAX STATUS

The difference in income tax status of partnerships and corporations was outlined in the preceding chapter. In the last two or three decades many closely held corporations have been converted to partnerships to avoid the income tax on corporations. Tax considerations are often the major basis for deciding on the form of organization for operating a business. They are quite complex, and involve the fact that a limited partnership may be taxed as a corporation in some cases, that small corporations may elect to avoid the tax on corporations, that some small businesses may elect to be taxed as corporations, and so on. The problem can be adequately solved only with an expert knowledge of the tax rules and a consideration of the circumstances of the individuals concerned.

SUMMARY

Partnerships are associations of two or more persons for doing business as co-owners for a profit. They involve unlimited liability of the members (except limited partners in a limited partnership), mutual agency, and limited life. They are formed by investments of cash or other assets; the latter should be valued by agreement of the partners.

Current withdrawals of the partners are recorded in Drawing or Personal accounts and closed at the end of the accounting period to the partners' Capital accounts.

Net income of the partnership is divided according to the partnership agreement; this may provide for "salary," "interest," and remainder to compensate partners for differing contributions. All such payments are distributions of the net income to the partners, however, and not expense of the partnership.

A statement of partners' capital shows opening and closing Capital balances with transactions during the year in summary form.

Admission of an additional partner into a partnership that continues a pre-existing business may involve an investment by the new partner that exceeds or falls short of the proportion of the capital interest that he is to receive. In these cases the Capital accounts may be adjusted by a bonus method that leaves the ledger assets undisturbed or by a goodwill method that records the asset Goodwill. If some other asset is identifiable as having a higher value than the record shows, it may be increased instead of, or along with, the recording of goodwill.

Similar problems arise on the withdrawal of a partner when the business is being continued by the remaining partners, and the same solutions may be used.

When the business of a partnership is liquidated, assets are sold, debts are paid, and the cash that results is paid out to the partners. Losses and gains on the realization of the assets are distributed to the partners' accounts. If a partner has a deficit he is expected to pay in that amount (except for a limited partner); if he cannot do so, the deficit is charged against the other partners.

Managerial considerations in the formation and operation of a partnership include personal qualities of prospective partners, content of the partnership agreement, continuity of the organization, availability of capital to it, and income tax status of the partnership and its owners.

QUESTIONS

14.1 (1) Three men are pooling their resources to go into the orchid and garden-supply business. They are trying to choose between forming a corporation or a partnership. What legal characteristics does a partnership have that are important in deciding what form of organization to use? *427-8*

(2) A and B agree with C, who is sole proprietor of a flourishing business, to furnish capital to expand the business and to join C as partners. Do you think that A, B, and C would be wise to carry over the accounting figures on C's proprietorship books to the new partnership accounts? Why?

(3) M. Barton and P. Carter form a partnership in which Carter contributes equipment with a cost of $50,000 and accumulated depreciation of $30,000. How should the equipment be recorded in the partnership accounts if Barton and Carter agree it is worth $40,000?

(4) Suppose Carter contributes customers' accounts carried on his books at $25,000 less an allowance of $1,000, but the partners agree that probably only $20,000 will be realized on collection of the receivables. How should the receivables be recorded?

14.2 (1) Ackerman and Thomas are considering the formation of a partnership to conduct a general insurance agency. Ackerman will invest $40,000 and Thomas $10,000. Ackerman will devote full time and Thomas half time to the business. In the absence of a specific agreement, how will net income be divided?

(2) Zimmerman and Carr are dealers in fats and oils. They buy commodities on their own account and as brokers for others. Although their business is highly speculative, they both have substantial capital credits. They are considering the admission of a bright young employee, John Hinman, as a partner in the firm. He is to make no investment, but is expected to allow his share of income to accumulate as capital. Would Hinman be correct in assuming that in so far as he has made no investment, he stands no risk of loss?

14.3 (1) M, N, and L form a partnership to operate a clothing store. M has been earning $10,000 a year as manager of the men's ready-to-wear department in a local department store, and N and L have been working as men's-clothing salesclerks in other stores, each for a salary of $5,200 per year. M has $5,000 to invest in the new partnership, N has $20,000, and L has $10,000. Suggest a method of dividing the net income of the M, N, and L partnership that will compensate the three partners for their distinct contributions; all three will spend full time in the new business.

(2) The Peters Bros. Co., a partnership, has three employees whose annual salaries total $18,000. The two partners together take out $21,000 per year for living expenses. What figure for salary expense appears on the annual income statement of the partnership? Explain.

14.4 (1) What account appears in the closing process in a partnership that is not used in corporation accounting? What is its purpose?

(2) The articles of copartnership of Sears and Tall provides that Sears is entitled to a monthly payment of $750 and Tall is entitled to a monthly payment of $1,000. At the end of their first year of operations, the partners find they disagree on how to divide the net income of $25,000. Give two interpretations of the articles and state the distributive net income belonging to each partner for each interpretation.

(3) The articles of copartnership of Lum and Fair contains the following provisions in regard to the sharing of profits and losses:

(a) Each partner will be credited with a salary allowance of $3,000.

(b) Each partner will be credited with interest on his average capital investment at the rate of 6 percent per year.

(c) The balance of the profit or loss will be divided equally.

The partners' capital accounts were as follows:

A. R. Lum, Capital				J. A. Fair, Capital	
3/31/66	1,000	1/1/66	10,000	1/1/66	8,000
		9/30/66	3,000		

Determine the distributive shares of the partners for a net income of $7,000.

14.5 (1) Suggest major areas for management consideration in the decision to use or not to use the partnership form.

(2) The Custom Machine Shop was operated by two partners, Riley and Olson. Olson died and his heirs pressed for liquidation of Olson's interest. The assets consisted principally of land, building, and a few pieces of machinery. Most of the assets had to be sold to satisfy the claims of the estate, and Riley could not raise sufficient capital in time to pay off the estate without liquidating the partnership assets. What might Riley have done before Olson's death to avoid this difficulty?

14.6 (1) What matters should be covered in a partnership agreement?

(2) What personal qualifications are important in a partner?

(3) E, F, and G are equal partners, each having subscribed $5,000 to the partnership. E pays in $3,000, leaving $2,000 still due the partnership on his capital account. It is agreed that for the present this $2,000 may remain unpaid, provided E pays interest on it, which he does. Later a dispute arises as to how this interest shall be credited. E claims that it should be included with the other earnings of the business and be divided equally among the three partners. F and G claim that this interest should be divided between them only, as they have fully lived up to their obligations under the partnership agreement, while E has only partially done so. To what account should the interest on the deferred payment be credited?

14.7 Bayless and Corbin, as equal partners, formed an investment club on January 2, 1966. Bayless contributed $10,000 cash and Corbin contributed 100 shares of Communication Engineering Common. The stock sold on the New York Exchange at $100 a share on January 2, but had cost Corbin only $40 a share when he purchased it on November 1, 1960. The partnership sold Communications Engineering on May 1, 1966, at $120 a share. For income tax purposes, gain is not recognized to a partner on contribution of property to a partnership; but when the property is sold by the partnership, gain is measured by the difference between the sale price and the original cost of the property to the contributing partner.

(1) What gain on sale of the securities will be shown in the books of the partnership following general accounting procedures?

(2) What gain will be reported by Corbin on his individual tax return?

14.8 A statement of partners' capital accounts for Surrey and Warren is as follows:

	Total	Surrey	Warren
Beginning balances	$100,000	$50,000	$50,000
Net income	52,000	26,000	26,000
Totals	$152,000	$76,000	$76,000
Drawings	32,000	16,000	16,000
Ending balances	$120,000	$60,000	$60,000

Each partner files a joint return with the standard deduction and five exemptions; neither has outside income. (Use the tax table in Chapter 13.)

(1) Compute the income taxes paid for the year by Surrey and Warren.

(2) Compute the aggregate business and individual income taxes paid if the partners incorporate and take salaries equal to their drawings.

14.9 (1) May a business operated by a partnership be continued if a partner dies or withdraws? Explain.

(2) A new partner may acquire his interest either by *investment* or by *purchase*. How does the accounting differ for these two methods of acquisition?

14.10 (1) Why might a new partner be willing to pay more for his interest in a firm than the Capital accounts of the old partners show that they invested for the same share? Why might he be allowed to pay less?

(2) Arthur and Brooks wish to admit Ivey as a partner. They realize that the building occupied by the business is in a deteriorating neighborhood and that it will have to be sold for less than its ledger value. A new location will be needed to put the business back on a vigorous basis. They offer to admit Ivey to a one-half interest in the capital for an investment of less than their combined capital accounts. What sort of adjustment of the accounts should be made when Ivey is admitted?

14.11 Austin and Bradford are partners. They share profits equally and have equal investments. The partnership's net assets are carried on the books at $20,000. Crane pays $9,000 cash into the partnership for a one-third interest in profits and net assets. Prepare journal entries to show three possible methods of recording the admission of Crane. State the conditions under which each method would be appropriate.

(AICPA – adapted)

14.12 The balance sheet of E at December 31, 1966 shows:

Assets . . . . $10,000   E, Capital $10,000

X has been invited to join E as a partner by an investment of $15,000 for a one-half interest in assets and a one-fourth interest in profits. This amount is based in part on the goodwill created by E.

E and X have been told that there are two methods of accounting for the admission of an incoming partner: the bonus method and the goodwill method. They are interested in the effect, if any, of the alternatives on the amounts they will eventually receive on dissolution of the partnership.

(1) On what ratio will the realization of goodwill be credited to the partners, if it is not recorded on formation of the partnership?

(2) Prepare journal entries to record: (a) the admission of X by the bonus method and (b) the subsequent dissolution of the firm for $30,000, assuming partnership income had been distributed as earned. Compare the cash distribution with that which results from the recording of goodwill.

(3) Would the choice between the goodwill and the bonus methods matter if the shares in assets and profits were the same?

14.13 (1) What possibilities can you suggest for paying out the capital of a retiring partner to achieve equity, assuming the other partners will continue the business?

(2) A. S. Ward, of Ward, Adams, and Ball, has reached retirement age and wishes to withdraw his investment from the firm. The business earns considerably more than is usual on assets of the type and value that appear on its balance sheet. These high earnings are due to the reputation built up over the years by the partners; it is expected to continue indefinitely even though Ward retires. As a result, it is agreed he will take $20,000 from the business in addition to the balance of his Capital account. What should be charged when this $20,000 is credited to Cash? Should any other entry be made as a result of this payment?

14.14 (1) What steps are taken in liquidating the business of a partnership and arriving at the amounts to be paid to the partners?

(2) A and B have equal investments but share profits in the ratio of 4 to 1. The balance sheet of the firm exhibits assets of $45,000 and liabilities of $25,000 when the partnership is dissolved. The assets bring $40,000 at a forced sale. What is the loss on realization? How should it be divided between A and B? How should the cash remaining after payment of liabilities be divided between A and B?

14.15 Aubert and Granat have been liquidating their jewelry business. The losses on realization are so large that Aubert's Capital account has a debit balance of $18,000 after all assets are sold. Granat's account shows a $22,000 credit.

(1) What will be required of Aubert if his assets outside the firm exceed $18,000? What amount will Granat then get out of the business?

(2) What will happen if Aubert has no assets?

14.16 M, N, and O decide to liquidate. Their balance sheet is as follows:

Cash	5,000	Liabilities	25,000
Noncash Assets	40,000	M, Capital	10,000
		N, Capital	6,000
		O, Capital	4,000
	45,000		45,000

The noncash assets are sold for $29,500. Prepare a statement summarizing the liquidation.

14.17 The capital balances of X, Y, and Z are $3,000, $4,000, and $5,000, respectively, on December 31, 1966. They share profits and losses in the ratio of 3:2:1. The partners plan to liquidate. After selling the assets and paying the liabilities, they have $5,400 of cash remaining. Partners have no assets outside of the business. How should the cash be divided?

14.18 P has recently been invited to purchase a one-half interest in the firm of V and S for $54,000. This amount would be paid privately to S, who is at present sole owner. Information relating to the firm is as follows:

(1) Year Ended May 1	Profits before Partners' Salaries and Interest	Average Net Tangible Assets Employed
1966	$30,000	$89,200
1965	26,000	84,800
1964	27,000	85,600
1963	24,400	81,200
1962	25,200	80,400

(2) The former senior partner, V, died during 1966, and S had purchased V's interest from his estate.

(3) S considers that his services could command a salary of $10,000 elsewhere if he gave up the business.

Information relating to P is as follows:

(1) He is presently employed by a business in competition with V and S, at an annual salary of $9,000 with a promise of an additional $2,000 per year starting in 1967.

(2) He owns securities purchased in 1965 for $40,000, which earn $1,800 per year. Present market value of the securities is $36,000.

(3) He can readily borrow up to $30,000 by a first mortgage on his home for purposes of entering into this venture.

On the basis of the above information, discuss the financial aspects P should take into consideration in making a decision.

EXERCISES

14.1 Evers and Hazard formed a law partnership on January 1, 1966, sharing income and expenses equally after partners' salaries. Evers contributed $10,000 in cash; Hazard contributed a law library and office equipment. The partners agreed that the property invested by Hazard had a fair market value of $25,000; but they were not concerned about how this contribution was recorded, because they said "it was only a matter of mere bookkeeping and they felt they would always be able to work everything out." The partners collected $100,000 in fees during 1966 and paid $85,000 for expenses, including partners' salaries. Hazard was killed in a skiing accident on December 31, 1966. In conformity with the articles of copartnership, the firm is to pay Hazard's widow his capital credit at December 31, 1966.

What is the amount to be paid to her (1) if the law library and office equipment were recorded at $10,000 and (2) if the law library and office equipment were recorded at $25,000? Fixed assets depreciate at 10 percent.

14.2 R. L. Bell and S. T. Clay agree to form a partnership. Clay is credited with a cash contribution of $11,000. Bell is credited with his contribution of the assets less liabilities of his business. A balance sheet prepared from the accounting records of R. L. Bell Co. at November 1, 1966, follows:

R. L. BELL CO.
BALANCE SHEET—AS OF NOVEMBER 1, 1966

Assets

Cash		$ 2,000
Accounts Receivable	$2,400	
Less: Allowance for Doubtful Accounts	100	2,300
Merchandise		3,700
Equipment	$6,000	
Less: Accumulated Depreciation	1,800	4,200
		$12,200

Liabilities and Proprietorship

Accounts Payable	$ 4,400
Accrued Payables	800
R. L. Bell, Capital	7,000
	$12,200

After reviewing the foregoing statement of financial condition, Bell and Clay agree to the following revisions: (1) the allowance for doubtful accounts should be increased to $240; (2) the inventory should be priced at $4,200; (3) the equipment should be stated at its fair market value of $5,000; (4) accrued payables should be increased by $160; and (5) goodwill of $3,000 should be credited to Bell.

Required:

1. Draft the journal entries to record the admission of Clay and the revision of Bell's accounts, assuming Bell's ledger is to be continued by the partnership.
2. Prepare the balance sheet of the Bell and Clay copartnership as of November 1, 1966. (The accumulated depreciation account is not carried forward.)

14.3 The capital accounts of R and S are presented below:

R, Capital	
	1/1/66 Balance 20,000

S, Capital	
	1/1/66 Balance 40,000
	10/1/66 Additional
	investment 40,000

Prepare computations showing the distribution of $16,800 net income for 1966 for each of the following agreements:

(1) The net income is to be divided in the ratio of the partners' capital at the end of the year.
(2) Interest at 10 percent is to be allowed on partners' capitals at the beginning of the year and the balance is to be divided equally.
(3) The net income is to be divided in the ratio of the partners' average capitals.
(4) Interest at 10 percent is to be allowed on partners' average capitals; the balance is to be divided equally.
(5) Interest at 10 percent is to be allowed on average capitals; salaries R, $9,000; S, $6,000; the balance is to be divided equally.

14.4 M and N are partners, sharing profits on a 60–40 basis after a monthly salary of $500. Each partner's Drawing account was debited $6,000 for payments made during the year.

What entries are necessary to close the 1966 Profit and Loss account if operations result in (1) $22,000 net income, (2) $10,000 net income, and (3) $8,000 net loss? The entries to close the Drawings accounts may be omitted in (2) and (3).

14.5 A's balance sheet at July 1, 1966, shows:

Assets. $60,000	Liabilities $20,000
	A, Capital 40,000
$60,000	$60,000

B is to be admitted as a partner, and A and B agree that A's business has unrecorded goodwill in the amount of $10,000.

Journalize the admission of B for each of the following cases: (1) B buys a one-half interest from A, paying him $25,000 personally. Goodwill is not recorded. (2) B invests $50,000 in the business for a one-half interest. Goodwill is not recorded. (3) B invests $50,000 in the business for a one-half interest. Goodwill is recorded.

14.6 The capital accounts of X and Y had balances of $30,000 and $10,000 on July 1, 1966. They share profits in the ratio of 60 to 40. Z is to be admitted as a partner, with a one-half interest in the capital.

Journalize the admission for each of the following cases: (1) Z buys his interest from X for $25,000. No new assets are to be recorded on the partnership books. (2) Z invests $40,000 in the business for his interest. (3) Z invests $50,000, and the partners agree that no asset increases other than cash will be recorded. (4) Z invests $50,000, and the partners agree to record the goodwill implied by his investment. (5) Z invests $30,000; no new assets other than cash are recorded. (6) Z invests $30,000; goodwill is to be credited to Z.

14.7 B is to retire from the firm of P, R, and B. The Capital account balances and profit and loss ratios at the date of retirement are as follows:

	Capital	Profit and Loss
P	$16,000	20%
R	24,000	30
B	40,000	50
	$80,000	100%

Journalize B's retirement for each case listed below. (Adjustments to the capital account of P and R are to be shared on the ratio of 20 to 30.)

(1) B is paid $40,000.
(2) B is paid $50,000; the excess over book value paid to B is considered a bonus.
(3) B is paid $50,000, after goodwill in the amount of $20,000 is recorded on the partnership books.
(4) B is paid only $35,000, because he is eager to leave the partnership.
(5) B is paid only $35,000, because it is recognized that goodwill recorded on the books is overstated $10,000.

14.8 The following balance sheet of R, S, and T shows the partners' Capital balances and profit and loss ratios at December 31, 1966:

Cash	$ 5,000	Liabilities	$10,000
Other Assets	50,000	R, Capital, 50%	15,000
		S, Capital, 30%	15,000
		T, Capital, 20%	15,000
	$55,000		$55,000

Prepare a schedule, with columns for Cash, Other Assets, Liabilities, and R,S,T, showing the dissolution of the firm, assuming (a) $60,000 is realized on the sale of the noncash assets and (b) assuming $12,000 is realized on the sale of noncash assets. None of the partners has any assets outside the business.

14.9 The articles of copartnership of M and N Co. provide that the first $20,000 of net income is to be divided in the ratio of 4 to 1 and the remainder is to be divided equally. The net income per books was $12,000 in 1965 and $30,000 in 1966.

An examination of the accounting records discloses:

(1) Merchandise inventories were understated $3,000 at December 31, 1965, and $1,000 at December 31, 1966.
(2) Invoices for merchandise in the amount of $4,000 received in 1965 were recorded when paid in 1966.
(3) Invoices for merchandise received in 1966 and included in the year-end inventory in the amount of $2,000 were not journalized as of December 31, 1966.
(4) Equipment purchased on July 1, 1965, at a cost of $8,000 was charged to Repairs.
(5) Equipment is depreciated by the straight line method over a life of four years.

Required:

1. A schedule to correct the net income for 1965 and 1966 and the balance sheet accounts at December 31, 1966. The following column headings are suggested: Explanation; Net Income—1965: Dr., Cr.; 1966: Dr., Cr.; Balance Sheet Accounts—Amount, Dr., Cr., Name.
2. A journal entry to correct the partners' Capital accounts, assuming the 1966 Profit and Loss account has been closed.

14.10 F and G are forming a company with a fiscal year ending June 30. Each will have a one-half interest in assets and profits. They are comparing the relative tax advantages of doing business as a partnership with doing business as a "tax option" corporation. If they elect the tax-option corporation, each stockholder will report cash distributions on his personal income tax return in the year when the distributions are received; any undistributed earnings will be reported in the year the corporation closes its books. If they elect the partnership, each partner will be taxed on his distributive share of earnings in the year the partnership closes its books, regardless of when such amounts are distributed.

Income received by F and G from outside sources fluctuates considerably from year to year, so they are interested in a form of business organization that permits them some discretion as to when they must report business income on their individual returns. They both file joint returns, claiming the standard deduction and five exemptions.

Following are data on income and distributions for 1966 and 1967:

```
F and G Co. income:
    Fiscal year ended 6/30/66 . . . . . . . . . . . . . . . . . . $10,000
        Distribution: none
    Fiscal year ended 6/30/67 . . . . . . . . . . . . . . . . . .  60,000
        Distribution: 12/1/66 . . . . . . . . . . . . . $50,000
F's other business income:
    Year ended 12/31/66 . . . . . . . . . . . . . . . . . . . . . .  20,000
    Year ended 12/31/67 . . . . . . . . . . . . . . . . . . . . . .  45,000
```

Compute the 1966 and 1967 income taxes for F (a) if the business is organized as a partnership and (b) if the business is organized as a tax-option corporation. Assume the tax rates continue as shown in Chapter 13. Comment.

14.11 The balance sheet of A at January 1, 1966, is as follows:

A CO.

BALANCE SHEET—

January 1, 1966

Assets		*Liabilities and Capital*	
Cash	$ 5,000	Accounts Payable	$ 3,000
Accounts Receivable	8,000	A, Capital	10,000
	$13,000		$13,000

For a cash investment of $30,000, B is admitted for a one-half interest in the net assets and a one-quarter interest in net income.

Results of operations for 1966:

(1) Revenues billed on account, $120,000.
(2) Collections on account, $125,000.
(3) Expenses incurred on credit, $60,000.
(4) Paid on account, $63,000.

As of December 31, 1966, A and B receive an offer of $23,000 for the noncash assets. They sell and dissolve the partnership.

Required:

    1. Assume that goodwill was recorded on admission of B. Open T accounts for the opening balances. Post the admission of B, operating transactions for 1966, and dissolution.

    2. Assume that goodwill was not recorded on the admission of B; that is, A was credited with a bonus. Open T accounts for only A, capital, and B, capital. Record all transactions through dissolution. Enter brief explanations for each entry.

    3. Explain why the cash received by A in 1 differs from the amount received in 2.

14.12 N and S formed a partnership on January 1, 1966, by contributions of $10,000 and $40,000 respectively. During 1966 N withdrew $4,000 and S withdrew $12,000. No accounting records were maintained. On December 31, 1966, they decided to dissolve the partnership. They sold all the noncash assets, paid off all the debts, and were left with $44,000 cash to distribute between them. How should the $44,000 be divided between N and S?

PROBLEMS

14.1 W. A. Thomas, a sole proprietor, had the following balance sheet at January 1, 1966:

W. A. THOMAS CO.

BALANCE SHEET

January 1, 1966

Assets

Cash		$ 3,200
Notes Receivable	$ 8,000	
Accounts Receivable	12,000	
	$20,000	
Less: Allowance for Doubtful Accounts..	2,400	17,600
Merchandise		25,000
Equipment	$32,000	
Less: Accumulated Depreciation	7,200	24,800
		$70,600

Liabilities and Proprietorship

Notes Payable	$ 6,000
Accounts Payable	16,000
Equipment Contract Payable	10,000
W. A. Thomas, Capital	38,600
	$70,600

J. S. Rodgers and T. Q. Smith join the business as partners, with Rodgers contributing $35,000, and Smith $25,000 cash, capital on January 1, 1966. They agree that Thomas will contribute all the assets of his going business and that the liabilities of his business will be assumed by the new partnership. They also agree that the allowance for doubtful accounts on Thomas' books must be increased $600; that the merchandise is to be valued at $30,000; and that Thomas is to be credited with goodwill of the old business, which is not recorded on its books, in the amount of $10,000.

Required:

    Journal entries to record the capital contributions to the new partnership of Rodgers, Smith, and Thomas.

14.2   Davis, Evans, and Fox share net income as follows:

	Davis	Evans	Fox
Salary	$12,000	$13,200	$10,800
Interest on opening capital	6%	6%	6%
Balance	40%	30%	30%

On January 1, 1966, they had Capital balances of $25,000, $30,000, and $20,000. Drawing accounts had the following debit balances at December 31, 1966: Davis, $7,200; Evans, $6,400; Fox, $6.200.

Required:

1. Schedules showing net income credited to each partner for (a) net income of $50,500, (b) net income of $40,000, (c) net loss of $9,500.
2. Journal entries to close Profit and Loss and Drawings. The entries to close Drawings may be omitted in parts b and c.
3. State amount of income or loss each partner should include on his individual tax return for part c.

14.3   Capital accounts for 1966 of Hay, Isham, and Lowrey are as follows:

D. I. Hay				P. L. Isham				O. T. Lowrey			
6/1	3,000	1/1	21,000	7/1	3,000	1/1	17,000	6/1	3,000	1/1	16,000
10/1	7,000	3/1	3,000	9/1	4,000	2/1	2,000	10/1	10,000	4/1	3,000

Net income for 1966 was $60,000. The partners share profit and losses in the ratio of average capital investments.

Required:

Calculate the distribution of net income to Hay, Isham, and Lowrey.

14.4   F. E. Allen and M. O. Barnes admit P. H. Jones to the partnership. Allen has capital of $28,000 and Barnes has $56,000. They have divided net income one third to Allen and two thirds to Barnes. Jones will have a one-quarter interest in the capital of the new firm. Journalize the admission of Jones for each of the following cases:

(1) Jones buys his interest from Barnes for $25,000.
(2) Jones invests $28,000 in the business.
(3) Jones invests $32,000, and the partners agree that any required adjustment will be made only in the Capital accounts.
(4) Jones pays in $32,000, and it is agreed that any goodwill implied in this price will be recorded.
(5) Jones invests $24,000, and the partners agree that no new asset other than the cash will be recorded.
(6) Jones invests $24,000, and the partners agree that Jones has brought goodwill into the business, which will be recorded on the books.

14.5   E. A. L. Davis is retiring from the firm of Davis, Rogers, and Smith. Davis has a capital balance of $100,000; Rogers, $60,000; and Smith, $40,000. They share income in the ratio 5:3:2. Journalize the retirement of Davis under each of the following agreements:

(1) Davis withdraws $100,000.
(2) Davis withdraws $105,000; goodwill is not recorded.
(3) Davis withdraws $105,000; goodwill is recorded.
(4) Davis withdraws only $90,000; the assets of the firm are properly valued.
(5) Davis withdraws only $90,000; it is recognized that land owned by the firm is worth less than the ledger amount.

14.6   Arcus, Baker, and Charles decide to liquidate. At the beginning of the liquidation process on June 30, 1966, the firm had the following balances: cash, $10,000; other assets, $60,000; liabilities, $20,000; Arcus, Capital, $26,000; Baker, Capital, $16,000; Charles, Capital, $8,000. The partners share profits and losses equally. None of the partners has any assets outside the business. On July 6, 1966, $40,000 of the assets were sold for $22,000. On July 8, 1966, the liabilities were paid. On July 28, 1966, the remaining noncash assets were sold for $8,000.

Required:

Prepare a schedule showing the opening balances, the several transactions, the balances after each transaction, and the final amounts paid to partners.

14.7   The trial balance of the Cobb-Douglass Company at the close of the year 1966 is shown below.

Accounts Receivable	$ 18,052	
Accrued Social Security Taxes		$ 560
Advances by Customers		3,120
Acceptances Payable		4,000
Accounts Payable.		5,320
Allowance for Bad Debts		457
Allowance for Depreciation		3,693
Bad Debts	1,160	
Cash in Bank	32,651	
C. Cobb, Capital		19,908
D. Douglass, Capital		9,200
Delivery Supplies, Repairs, etc.	1,100	
Depreciation	2,096	
Furniture and Equipment	15,520	
Leasehold	7,200	
Merchandise Inventory, Jan. 1, 1966. . . .	15,000	
Purchases.	114,820	
Purchase Discounts		2,280
Rent Expense.	2,200	
Sales		197,796
Unexpired Insurance	600	
Wages and Salaries	36,500	
Withheld Income and F.I.C.A. Taxes . . .		565
	$246,899	$246,899

Data for adjustments:

(1) The merchandise inventory at December 31, 1966, is $16,000.

(2) The inventory on January 1, 1966, was overstated $800.

(3) Accrued salaries of $600 at December 31, 1965, and $1,000 on December 31, 1966, were not recorded.

(4) The unexpired insurance represents the premiums paid January 1, 1965, on a single 3-year policy.

(5) Advances by customers at January 1, 1966, was understated $2,000, but the December 31, 1966, balance is correct.

(6) The cost of an $8,000 addition to furniture and equipment on July 1, 1965, paid for by Cobb out of his personal funds, is not reflected in the foregoing trial balance. The estimated life of this addition is ten years.

(7) The partners' automobiles used in the business are not recorded in the partnership accounts. Supplementary records show their automobile expenses for 1966 were $2,400 for Cobb and $3,000 for Douglass. (Partners' Drawings are to be credited for these amounts.)

(8) Drawings during the year, charged to Wages and Salaries, were as follows: Cobb, $400 a month; Douglass, $500 a month.

(9) Prior to January 1, 1966, profits were divided on a 50–50 basis. From January 1, 1966, on it was agreed to allow a salary of $6,000 to each partner and divide the remaining profits on a 40–60 basis.

Required:

1. Entries to correct the partnership accounts for the data presented. It is suggested that adjustments to income and expense prior to January 1, 1966, be debited or credited to a Correction of Prior Years Profits account. After all adjustments are recorded, this account can be closed to the partners' Capital accounts.

2. Entries to close the accounts for 1966. The entries to close individual revenues and expense accounts to Profit and Loss may be omitted.

3. A statement of the partners' Capital accounts for 1966, showing unadjusted balances at January 1, adjustments, income, drawings, and December 31 balances.

15

Corporations: Formation and

Capital Stock

DEFINITION AND NATURE OF CORPORATIONS

The classic definition of a corporation was given over a century ago by John Marshall, Chief Justice of the United States Supreme Court, in these words: "A corporation is an artificial being, invisible, intangible, and existing only in contemplation of the law." There are many kinds of corporations, but we are concerned here only with the private business corporation. Most business in the United States is conducted by corporations as a result of these advantages:

Limited liability. The owners — stockholders — of a corporation are not personally liable for the corporation's debts, so their possible losses are limited to the amounts they have invested in it.

Transferable shares. Stockholders may buy or sell shares of ownership in the corporation freely without interfering with the management of the business.

Separation of the functions of ownership and management. The corporation is managed by directors who are elected by the shareholders; the directors may or may not own any shares, and if they are required to do so the holding may be only a single share each. Owing to the separation of functions, the owners need not conduct the business. Many persons may contribute capital to a corporation, whereas it would be highly impractical to bring many persons into a partnership, so very large businesses may be conveniently organized as corporations. A disadvantage to the individual small stockholder is that separation gives him relatively little voice in the management of the business.

Continued existence. The corporation is independent of its owners, and its life is set in its charter. The deaths of any owners or the sale of their holdings does not affect it, as would be the case with a partnership. The corporation may have a limited life, which is renewable, or a perpetual one by virtue of its charter.

Legal entity. Being a legal person separate from its owners, the corporation may own property in its own name, sue and be sued, and make contracts. Being an entity offers many conveniences, but it has one great disadvantage: the corporation is taxed as a separate person. With recent federal income tax rates on corporations of 48 percent on all income over $25,000 per year, this feature is extremely important. However, certain corporations may elect to avoid this tax, as discussed in Chapter 13.

This chapter is concerned primarily with the proprietorship transactions and accounts of corporations, because they are the ones affected by the peculiar nature and legal status of corporate organizations. It is also concerned with certain managerial problems and opportunities resulting from use of a corporate organization.

ORGANIZATION OF A CORPORATION

Persons wishing to form a corporation apply to the proper officer of a state government for a charter. Statutes typically require that they specify the name of the corporation, the kind of business it is to do (this is expressed very broadly as a rule), the amount of capital stock authorized to be issued, names and addresses of incorporators, subscribers to stock, the first directors, and the amount and kinds of payments made or to be made by the subscribers. A fee is usually required. When all requirements are met, the charter (*articles of incorporation*) is filed with the county clerk in the county containing the principal office of the corporation, and the corporation is empowered to operate.

The directors of a corporation are in charge of its management. The directors are elected annually by the stockholders, sometimes for staggered terms so that the board will always have some continuing members. Day-to-day management of the corporation is typically delegated by the directors to the officers, who are the president, secretary, and treasurer, with such vice presidents and assistant secretaries and treasurers as are desired. In some companies the controller (comptroller) is an officer elected by the directors.

The directors or stockholders adopt bylaws that set out the authority of the officers and establish rules for the conduct of the business. Corporations often obtain their charter in a state that permits considerable freedom of action, even though their main office and business is elsewhere. They obtain a permit to do business in other states as a "foreign" corporation.

PROPRIETORSHIP IN A CORPORATION

Two requirements determine the accounts used in the proprietorship section of a corporate balance sheet;

1. The need to show the sources of the financing
2. Statutory requirements for designating capital that is to be retained in the business

Investors need to know the sources of existing financing to make decisions about buying or selling shares in the corporation. For example, the existence of a substantial proportion of capital resulting from retained earnings is considered favorable. Statutes frequently require that a capital stock figure be declared for shares issued. This is recorded with the state authorities, and if it is to be changed, proper legal steps must be taken so that interested persons will have notice of the action. This requirement is designed to protect creditors; the declared figure for capital stock issued indicates what amount of assets the owners declare that they have permanently invested in the business—the amount that can absorb losses without reducing the total assets below the amount owed creditors. The basic rule of law in this connection is that dividends may not be paid to stockholders that would reduce net assets (total assets less liabilities) below the designated or "stated" capital. However, some states permit dividends to be declared out of profits earned in a year even though a deficit was previously built up.

Proprietorship accounts in a corporation consist of these three types:

1. Capital Stock (this records the stated "value" or amount of capital; there may be several classes of stock)
2. Paid-in Surplus (this consists of capital paid in by stockholders or others, over and above the declared amount of any capital stock issued)
3. Retained Earnings

The amount of capital stock authorized may be recorded in the offsetting memorandum accounts Capital Stock Authorized and Capital Stock Unissued, but this practice is not common.

The proprietorship section of a corporation balance sheet should disclose the number of shares authorized and the number issued, as well as the declared or stated value of the stock. This section may have the following appearance:

Capital		
Capital Stock: 10,000 shares authorized,		
of which 9,000 are issued and outstand-		
ing—stated value................	$450,000.00	
Paid-in Surplus....................	75,000.00	
Retained Earnings.................	671,000.00	$1,196,000.00

KINDS OF CAPITAL STOCK

Characteristics of capital stock with which we are concerned are indicated as follows:

1. Preferred versus common stock
2. Classes of preferred or common stock
3. Par versus no-par stock

Shares of stock are evidenced by certificates. A stock certificate is usually an engraved or similarly decorated document giving the following information: number of the certificate, name of the corporation, state of incorporation, date issued, number of shares represented by the certificate, any par value or the fact that the stock has no par value, authorized capital, the fact (normally) that the shares are fully paid and nonassessable, and sometimes the rights of the holder. It carries the corporate seal and is signed by an officer of the corporation and perhaps by a registrar and a transfer agent. The registrar authenticates shares issued and the transfer agent records their ownership. Registrars must be used by corporations listing shares on the stock exchanges. They are usually trust companies. On the back of the certificate is a form for signing over the ownership to someone else. Note that a stock certificate, under the terms of the Uniform Commercial Code, has some of the qualities of a negotiable instrument and must be guarded as such. A stock certificate is shown on page 460.

PREFERRED VERSUS COMMON STOCK

Preferred stockholders have a preference; almost invariably this is the right to receive dividends before the common stockholders are paid a dividend. Preferred stockholders are also often entitled to receive assets, in case of liquidation, up to a certain figure (usually what was paid for the stock or a little more) before the common stockholders get any.

Preferred stock may be *cumulative*, which means that the specified dividend for each year must be paid before the common stockholders get any dividend in any year. In other words, the right to receive dividends before the common stockholders receive them accumulates each year. The stock may be *noncumulative*, in which case missing a dividend in one year does not result in a right to any more than the normal annual dividend in any later year. Noncumulative preferred stock is not often seen, because it is not attractive to investors; it is more likely to arise from a reorganization in which this type of stock is considered a fair settlement of a particular class of claims.

Preferred stock may be *participating* or *nonparticipating*. Participating preferred stock may receive dividends in excess of the normal or expected amount in any year. The extra amount is paid after common stockholders receive a dividend and is a participation in more-than-normal distributions. The amount of participation is usually limited. Nonparticipating preferred stock lacks the participating feature and is the most common type.

Preferred stock does not ordinarily have the right to vote, but provision is often made for election of one or more directors by preferred stockholders if preferred dividends fall in arrears.

Common stock has the residual rights; that is, all the rights of stockholders not specially assigned to another group. Unless preferred stock is fully participating with common, which is rare, the common stockholders own all the net income after preferred dividends are met. This right means that their gains may be high but that they are the first to suffer when net income declines.

CLASSES OF STOCK

Both preferred and common stocks may be divided into classes. Thus a corporation could have Preferred Stock, Series I, with a dividend of $4 per share per year, and Preferred Stock, Series II, with a dividend of $5 per share per year. The rights of each class are set out in the bylaws and constitute a contract between the corporation and the holders of the stock. Common stock may be designated class A and class B, for example. Some corporations have created two classes of common, one having voting rights and the other not, otherwise with the same rights. The purpose in this plan is to restrict control of the corporation by selling only the nonvoting stock to new stockholders.

PAR VERSUS NO-PAR STOCK

Par value is a figure established for stock in the corporation's charter. Historically, stock of $100 par value per share has been popular. Assets equal in value to the par value of the stock issued for them are required to be received for the stock, par value being credited to the Capital Stock account. If the stock is issued for a lesser amount, it is said to be issued at a discount and the holders are liable to creditors of the corporation for the amount of the discount. Most states now prohibit issuance of stock at a discount. Stock issued at a discount is now largely an historical phenomenon. Stock issued for assets in excess of the par value is issued at a premium.

Par-value stock has often confused unsophisticated investors, who thought that the actual value could not be less than par. Par-value stock, especially the $100 par value, also may present a problem when a corporation wishes to issue more stock after a period of time. The corporation's record will then influence what investors will pay for new issues, and if it has not earned enough to justify a price of $100 per share it will not be able to sell more stock at that price.

No-par-value stock was invented to meet these problems. States that have authorized the issue of no-par stock have usually required either that a *stated value* (or declared value) be used as a substitute for the par value or that a minimum amount be received for issue of the shares. The directors are usually free to declare any stated value they wish for no-par stock. No-par stock requires the investor to consider the assets behind the stock. It avoids the problems of discount and of fluctuating prices obtainable for the stock. In recent years stock of very low par values—$1, $5, or $10 per share—has become popular because of federal and state issue and transfer taxes. These taxes have been based on par value of $100, no-par shares being treated as though they were shares of $100 par value. However, the federal rates have now been changed to apply to actual values regardless of par or no par. Concerns using low par values at the present time often have a declared value, much higher than the par value, that is closer to the actual asset values given for the stock. In this case capital paid in above the amount of stated capital may also be present. It is treated as it would be with no-par stock.

PAID-IN SURPLUS

The term "paid-in capital" refers to all amounts paid in for stock or as donations. "Paid-in surplus" refers to that part of the payment in excess of the par or declared value. The par or declared value is recorded in the Capital Stock account; the excess may be credited to Premium on Capital Stock if par value stock is used, or to *Paid-in Surplus*, to Contributed Capital, or to Excess of Capital Paid-in over Declared (or Par) Value when either par or no-par stock is used.

Some states restrict the amount received for no-par shares that can be designated as paid-in surplus, and a few permit none of the payment to go to paid-in surplus. Any contributions to the corporation for capital purposes for which stock is not issued are credited to Paid-in Surplus. For example, a corporation may receive free land from a city, county, or state to get it to locate a plant there. It may receive assets donated by promoters in order to get it established. Sometimes stockholders donate shares to the corporation for sale to others in order to raise more capital. It is usually considered desirable to record these special contributions (after the shares are sold) in a separate account called Donated Capital. Accounts for paid-in capital over and above the capital stock figure have traditionally been called Capital Surplus or Paid-in Surplus. These terms are still widely used, but in view of the popular misinterpretation of the word "surplus" it is better not to use them in published statements. Although several accounts may be kept to record paid-in capital from different sources, they are usually shown in one figure on published balance sheets. Accountants are very concerned to see that proprietorship accounts resulting from funds paid in by stockholders are not confused with retained earnings, especially in connection with dividends. They are also concerned to see that actual values are placed on assets that are received for stock, such as land, buildings, or patents, so that the corporation's financial condition is not misrepresented.

ENTRIES FOR ISSUE OF STOCK

The following eight cases illustrate the entries made for different kinds of stock at various prices.

Case 1. Common stock is issued for cash; 1,000 shares of a par value of $100 are issued for $100 per share:

```
Cash......................................$100,000.00
    Common Stock.......................          $100,000.00
```

Case 2. Common stock of $100 par value is issued for $105 cash per share. The issue is 1,000 shares.

```
Cash......................................$105,000.00
    Common Stock.......................          $100,000.00
    Premium on Common Stock............            5,000.00
```

Case 3. Common stock of no par value is issued for cash of $55 per share. The issue is 500 shares and the directors place a declared value of $55 per share on it.

Cash.................................	$ 27,500.00	
Common Stock......................		$ 27,500.00

Case 4. Common stock of no par value is issued for $80 cash per share. The issue is 600 shares. The directors place a declared value of $60 per share on the stock.

Cash.................................	$ 48,000.00	
Common Stock......................		$ 36,000.00
Paid-in Surplus—Common.............		12,000.00

Case 5. Preferred stock, series I, par value $100 per share, is issued for $103 cash per share; 1,000 shares are issued.

Cash.................................	$103,000.00	
Preferred Stock, Series I..............		$100,000.00
Premium on Preferred Stock...........		3,000.00

Note that accounts for premiums on stock or for paid-in capital may be kept for each class of stock that involves a premium, if desired.

Case 6. Preferred stock, series II, no par value, is sold for $90 cash per share. The directors place a declared value of $75 per share on the 800 shares issued.

Cash.................................	$ 72,000.00	
Preferred Stock, Series II..............		$ 60,000.00
Paid-in Surplus—Preferred.............		12,000.00

Case 7. Common stock of a par value of $5 per share is issued for $80 cash per share. The directors place a declared value of $50 per share on the 1,000 shares issued.

Cash.................................	$ 80,000.00	
Common Stock......................		$ 50,000.00
Paid-in Surplus—Common.............		30,000.00

(In states that require par value to be stated value, all the excess over par value would have to go to paid-in surplus.)

Case 8. Land, building, and patent are taken in exchange for stock. The directors place a value of $40,000 on the land, $100,000 on the building, and $60,000 on the patent. They issue 1,000 shares of $100 par value preferred stock and 1,000 shares of no-par common stock for the properties. They use the par value of the preferred stock as its declared value and record the common with a declared value of $75 per share.

```
Land...................................... $ 40,000.00
Building..................................   100,000.00
Patent....................................    60,000.00
        Preferred Stock.....................                    $100,000.00
        Common Stock.......................                       75,000.00
        Paid-in Surplus—Common.............                      25,000.00
```

SUBSCRIPTIONS TO CAPITAL STOCK

In some cases the corporation may not need at once all the assets agreed to be paid in for stock, and may call for them in installments as they are needed. This arrangement is likely to be satisfactory only for small corporations. When it exists, accounts for subscriptions are needed. The entry to record subscriptions to 500 shares of common stock at $50 per share on which the declared value is $40 per share follows:

```
Subscriptions Receivable—Common............... $25,000.00
        Common Stock Subscribed................              $20,000.00
        Paid-in Surplus—Common ...............                5,000.00
```

The account for stock subscribed takes the place of the regular stock account until the shares are paid for and issued. The Common Stock Subscribed account is shown immediately after the regular Common Stock account in the balance sheet. The Stock Subscribed account for any other class of stock would appear just after the regular stock account for that class. Payment of one-half the price on the subscription entered above is recorded as follows:

```
Cash...................................... $12,500.00
        Subscriptions Receivable—Common.........              $12,500.00
```

Payment of the other half of the price and issue of the stock certificates is recorded in the following entries:

```
Cash...................................... $12,500.00
        Subscriptions Receivable—Common.........              $12,500.00

Common Stock Subscribed....................... $20,000.00
        Common Stock.........................                 $20,000.00
```

The excess over the declared value of the stock subscribed is not traditionally entered in a temporary account to indicate that the related shares have not been issued. Subscribers to capital stock have the same rights as stockholders whose shares are issued, with the obligation to pay in the subscription price when it is required. A subsidiary subscribers ledger, like an accounts receivable ledger, may be needed.

DEFAULTS ON SUBSCRIPTIONS TO STOCK

The rights of a subscriber who cannot pay his subscription differ between states. He may forfeit anything he has paid in; he may be entitled to the issue of shares for what he did pay in; or he may be entitled to a refund. The refund is calculated after the corporation sells the shares in question. The corporation keeps the amount originally subscribed to and any amount needed to cover the expense of the sale, and refunds any excess to the subscriber. For example, A. B. Dunlop subscribed to 100 shares of Z Corporation common at $100 per share, paid in $35 per share, and then defaulted. The corporation sold the shares at $90 each and incurred a sale expense of $40. Under the refund rule the entries are:

Common Stock Subscribed	$10,000.00	
Subscriptions Receivable—Common		$ 6,500.00
Due to A. B. Dunlop		3,500.00
(to close out defaulted subscription and to credit Dunlop with his payments)		
Cash	$ 9,000.00	
Due to A. B. Dunlop	1,000.00	
Common Stock		$10,000.00
(to record sale of defaulted subscription stock at 90 and to charge Dunlop with the loss on subscription price)		
Due to A. B. Dunlop	$　40.00	
Cash		$　40.00
(to charge Dunlop with cost of selling defaulted stock)		
Due to A. B. Dunlop	$ 2,460.00	
Cash		$ 2,460.00
(to record refund on defaulted subscription of A. B. Dunlop)		

If the local rule requires forfeit of all that was paid in by the subscriber, the amount shown as refunded to A. B. Dunlop in the preceding illustration would be credited to Paid-in Surplus instead.

If Dunlop was entitled by the local law to shares for the amount he had paid in, and the remainder of the subscription was canceled, the entry would be:

Common Stock Subscribed	$10,000.00	
Subscriptions Receivable—Common		$ 6,500.00
Common Stock		3,500.00

TREASURY STOCK

Treasury stock is stock that has once been issued and is reacquired by the issuing corporation and not canceled. It may be reacquired by donation or by purchase. If donated, no entry is necessary in the double-entry system; only a memorandum of the shares held in the company's treasury need be made. This treasury holding will be disclosed in the proprietorship section of the balance sheet as in the following example (it could be disclosed in a footnote instead):

Capital

Preferred Stock, $100.00 par value, authorized, and
outstanding, 5,000 shares. $500,000.00

Common Stock, no par value, authorized and issued,
10,000 shares, of which 500 are held in the corporation's treasury; stated value, $45.00 per
share. 450,000.00

Paid-in Surplus:
Premium on Preferred Stock. . . $50,000.00
Paid in on Common Stock. 25,000.00   75,000.00

Retained Earnings. 671,000.00 $1,696,000.00

If the donated shares are canceled, the caption for the Common Stock in the foregoing illustration may simply be altered to read "10,000 shares of no par value authorized, of which 9,500 are outstanding."

Sale of the denoted treasury shares, of course, requires entries in the accounts. Assume that the 500 treasury shares shown above are sold for $55 per share. The entry is:

Cash $27,500.00
    Donated Capital $27,500.00

The common stock section of the balance sheet would thereafter read, in part: "10,000 shares authorized and issued; stated value, $45 per share . . . . $450,000."

TREASURY STOCK PURCHASED

When a corporation buys in its own shares, it is in effect returning the investment of some stockholders. Of course, it may return more or less than was originally invested. The shares purchased are not an asset and should not be shown on the asset side of the balance sheet. Some accountants argue that the asset showing is appropriate if the shares are expected to be sold promptly, but shares that had never been issued and were expected to be sold shortly would have as good a claim to asset status as this, and no one argues for it. One cannot create an asset by giving money back to stockholders. Treasury stock should therefore be deducted in the proprietorship or capital section of the balance sheet, as it usually is. Assume that the 500 shares of treasury stock discussed in the prior section had been bought by the corporation for $50 per share. The following entry would record the purchase:

Treasury Stock. $25,000.00
    Cash. $25,000.00

The general rule in corporation statutes is that treasury stock may not be purchased unless there is paid-in surplus ("capital surplus") or retained earnings equal to the cost of the stock. Dividends are not permitted to reduce the declared value of stock issued even though some of it has been reacquired by the company. It is desirable to call attention to this restriction; accountants usually consider that it should be applied against retained earnings. This may be shown, for the case previously suggested, as follows:

Capital

Preferred Stock, $100.00 par value, authorized and outstanding, 5,000 shares		$500,000.00
Common Stock: 10,000 shares of no par value, of which 500 are held in the corporation's treasury; stated value, $45.00 per share		450,000.00
Paid-in Surplus:		
Premium on Preferred Stock	$ 50,000.00	
Paid-in on Common Stock	25,000.00	75,000.00
Retained Earnings:		
Restricted by purchase of treasury stock	$ 25,000.00	
Unrestricted	646,000.00	671,000.00
Total		$1,696,000.00
Less Treasury Stock		25,000.00 $1,671,000.00

RESALE OF TREASURY STOCK PURCHASED

The entries for resale of the 500 shares of treasury stock purchased at $50 per share ($25,000) are given for three different possible prices as follows:

Case 1. Sold at the purchase price of $50 per share:

Cash	$25,000.00	
Treasury Stock		$25,000.00

Case 2. Sold for more than the purchase price, at $60 per share:

Cash	$30,000.00	
Treasury Stock		$25,000.00
Paid-in Surplus from Sale of Treasury Stock		5,000.00

Case 3. Sold for less than the purchase price, at $40 per share. This case presents the problem of where to charge the amount representing the price decline. It is considered undesirable to reduce any capital paid in by shareholders of other classes with a "loss" on treasury stock. If a paid-in surplus has arisen from transactions in treasury stock of this class, that account may be charged; or if there is paid-in surplus from the original issue of shares of this class, it may be used. Otherwise a debit to Retained Earnings is suggested. Arguments about where to place the debit, in the absence of any clear-cut legal requirement on it, may easily be overworked: there may be some inequality of treatment between individual shareholders even when the charge is against capital paid in by shareholders of the same class. This inequality arises because the new members of the class are allowed to get the same interest per share at a lower cost than the old ones. However, such matters cannot be determined on the basis of ledger values alone; presumably conditions have

changed that justify the change in price, and the present payment by the new stockholders is equal to the actual present value of the per share contributions of the old ones. This conclusion may apply as between classes of stockholders also. The entries are:

If a suitable source of paid-in surplus is present:

```
Cash.......................................$20,000.00
Paid-in Surplus...............................  5,000.00
     Treasury Stock........................              $25,000.00
```

If a suitable source of paid-in surplus is not present:

```
Cash.......................................$20,000.00
Retained Earnings.............................  5,000.00
     Treasury Stock........................              $25,000.00
```

Some accountants would assign the cost of treasury shares, on acquisition, to Capital Stock and Paid-in Surplus, with any excess going to Retained Earnings. They would show a deduction directly from Capital Stock and from Paid-in Surplus in presenting the figures in the balance sheet.

The presentation described in the preceding paragraphs is widely used in practice. It appeals to the authors as more in keeping with the spirit of the statutes that prohibit purchase of treasury shares unless the price is covered by retained earnings, since it leaves the original total declared value intact even though the number of shares is reduced.

SPECIAL CORPORATE RECORDS

The records special to corporations are:

1. Stock certificates
2. Capital stock ledger
3. Capital stock journal
4. Minute book

Stock certificates may be bound in pads or books like pads of checks. In this case they have stubs on which are recorded the name of the person to whom the shares are issued and the number of shares. Space is also provided for recording the name of any predecessor holder of the shares. A stock certificate was shown on page 460. In small corporations with few stockholders the stock certificate book is the only detailed stock record required; its stubs readily give the list of stockholders and their holdings. Certificates returned for cancellation and issue of new certificates may be perforated or marked "canceled" and pasted to the old stub as a record. Federal stock-transfer tax stamps are pasted to the canceled certificates.

When the list of stockholders becomes too long for convenient reference to the certificate stubs for information about individual stockholdings, a stockholders ledger is used. This is a book of accounts, one for each stockholder, showing the number of shares acquired by him (credit), the number transferred by him (debit), and the balance. It is kept in number of shares, not in dollars. If transactions are not very frequent it is satisfactory to post the stockholders ledger from the stock certificate stubs.

A larger number of stock transactions requires the addition of a stock journal, or stock transfer record. This takes the form of an ordinary general journal except that number of shares is entered instead of dollars. Separate ledgers or ledger sheets and separate journals are advisable for different classes of stock.

Stock exchanges require the use of a registrar in connection with issues of stock. Trust companies do this work. The registrar puts an authenticating signature on each certificate and sees that only the authorized amount of stock is issued and that only genuine certificates are registered. A transfer agent may also be used; he maintains the record of stockholders. When the number of stockholders is large — it is over 1,000,000 in one case in the United States — the work is done with mechanical tabulating or electronic equipment.

The corporate minute book contains minutes of the directors' and stockholders' meetings. It is an extremely important record because it is the official record of all major decisions. Although the minutes are signed by the corporation's secretary, they may be prepared with the aid of an attorney because of the need for legal impregnability.

MANAGEMENT PROBLEMS IN DECIDING WHETHER OR NOT TO USE THE CORPORATE FORM OF ORGANIZATION

Major considerations in a decision on using the corporate form of organization were noted at the beginning of this chapter in connection with the advantages of the corporation. The major disadvantage is that the corporation is subject to a special tax. This disadvantage was developed more fully in Chapter 13, and mentioned in Chapter 14. In this connection, it should be borne in mind that a limited partnership may be taxed as a corporation, that small corporations may elect to avoid the tax on corporations, and that some small noncorporate businesses may elect to be taxed as corporations. Other management considerations are the following:

1. Leverage through use of preferred stock
2. Possible loss of control
3. Advantageous executive-compensation plans
4. Tax on accumulated earnings
5. Minor problems

LEVERAGE THROUGH USE OF PREFERRED STOCK

Leverage in financing refers to the possibility of increasing the rate of return to some securities by using securities with a priority or preference that yield a lower rate than is earned over all. They can be sold on the lower yield basis because of the greater certainty of a return due to their priority. This point was made previously in connection with borrowing on notes or bonds; it applies equally to the use of preferred stock. This is demonstrated in the following tabulation, which shows the effect of preferred stock paying 6 percent where 8 percent on the whole proprietorship is earned. The results, of course, differ as the proportions of preferred and common investment change and as the preferred dividend rate and over-all rate of return vary.

Capital Investments		Amount of Investment	Share of Net Income	Rate of Return
Preferred stockholders—6% stock............		$200,000	$12,000	6%
Common stockholders:				
Stock.......................	$200,000			
Retained earnings............	50,000	250,000	24,000	9.6%
Totals................................		$450,000	$36,000	8%

Note that use of securities with priorities—"senior securities"—increases the risk that the "junior securities" will get a very small return or no return in a given year.

POSSIBLE LOSS OF CONTROL

Unless a stockholder owns a majority of the voting shares of a corporation, he runs some risk of losing control of his investment. If a partner disagrees with his partners, he has a right to withdraw his capital from the business; a stockholder can only sell his stock, perhaps at a loss if there is not a ready market for it. Furthermore, if a stockholder who is also an executive of the corporation disagrees with the majority of the stockholders, or if the majority stockholding changes hands, he is likely to lose his job and the salary that goes with it. Some people have made a practice of buying large blocks of stocks in corporations in which they believe they can acquire control, sometimes with the intent of improving the management but sometimes with the intent of "raiding" the corporation for their own benefit. Raiding cannot occur in a partnership.

ADVANTAGEOUS EXECUTIVE-COMPENSATION PLANS

As was noted in Chapter 13, one of the problems of the more highly paid executives is that their incomes may be very high only for a few years of active service in a high position. As a result, high income tax rates are applied to a large part of their total income. They can spread out their total compensation by accepting part of it in the form of a right to a pension from an employee's trust created and paid for by the corporation. The executive pays no tax on the amounts contributed to the trust by the corporation until he receives payments from the trust. He then reports the payments as income. Since he receives this income after his period of highly paid service is over, it falls in lower tax brackets.

Another device of similar effect is the granting of stock options to executives. These permit the executive to buy stock of the corporation over a long period at a specified price. If the stock increases in value over a period of years the executive can exercise the option and receive substantial compensation from it. If the terms of the option are properly drawn, the gain is taxed as a capital gain at only 25 percent. This device often serves as an incentive to the executives to increase the profitability of the corporation; it does not provide extra compensation if the value of the corporation's stock does not rise, assuming that the option price was close to the market price when the option was granted.

TAX ON ACCUMULATED EARNINGS

Investors already in very high personal income tax brackets may wish to use the corporate form in order to accumulate the income in the corporation subject only to the corporation income tax. This device is useful and effective as long as the accumulation can be justified by a legitimate business use of the funds in the corporation. If the funds have no such use, but are allowed to pile up in cash or in investment securities, they become subject to the federal tax on accumulated earnings. This tax is designed to prevent stockholders from avoiding personal income taxes by refraining from paying themselves dividends they presumably otherwise would pay. In recent years the rate has been 27½ percent on the first $100,000 of "accumulated taxable income" and 38½ percent of the remainder. These rates are in addition to the regular corporation income tax rates. An exemption of $100,000 is allowed.

MINOR PROBLEMS

Corporations are subject to more regulation than are partnerships or proprietorships, and this consumes time and involves expense. Statutes regulating the sale of securities must be complied with, including registration of securities with the United States Securities and Exchange Commission for sufficiently large issues sold in interstate commerce. Some states require a permit to issue stock in addition to the authorization in the charter; this permit is designed to prevent issues that do not have a substantial value behind them. More formality is involved in keeping minutes and in using stock certificates. Some of these disadvantages would result from large size in any case, but they may influence a decision on the form of organization to use.

SUMMARY

A corporation is a legal person separate from its owners, with advantages and disadvantages that this status provides, including limited liability of stockholders and additional taxation.

Proprietorship in a corporation is evidenced by certificates representing shares of ownership. In the accounts it appears in three categories: Capital Stock, Paid-in Surplus, and Retained Earnings.

The Capital Stock account records the declared value established by the directors in response to statutes. It designates the amount of owner investment that is expected to be kept in the business as a buffer against losses that otherwise might fall on creditors.

Paid-in Surplus is the excess of amounts paid in by stockholders (or by others for capital purposes) over the declared value.

Stock may be preferred or common, and it may be issued in several classes. Par-value stock has at least a minimum declared value established by the corporation charter; no-par stock has none.

Subscriptions to stock may be recorded if assets are not to be paid in promptly.

Treasury stock consists of shares reacquired by the issuing corporation; it may be donated or purchased.

Special corporate records include the stock certificates, the stock ledger, the stock journal or transfer record, and the minute book.

Management decisions on the question of whether or not to use the corporate form of organization involve, in addition to the major advantages and disadvantages of corporations such as limited liability of stockholders and extra taxation, possible loss of control in a corporation, the advantageous executive-compensation plans possible, the federal tax on accumulated earnings, and minor problems of greater formality and regulation.

QUESTIONS

15.1 (1) What fundamental legal characteristic does a corporation have that gives it a variety of advantages?

(2) Name some of the advantages that flow from the legal character of a corporation.

(3) Suggest disadvantages of the corporation as a form of organization for business.

15.2 (1) What document discloses the general powers of a corporation?

(2) What document or record discloses the duties and limitations of its officers?

15.3 (1) List the three general types of proprietorship accounts for a corporation. Give at least one example of each kind, and suggest a transaction out of which it could arise.

(2) What two requirements determine the types of proprietorship accounts used in corporation accounting?

15.4 (1) Distinguish between preferred stock and common stock.

(2) What kind of preferences does preferred stock usually have?

(3) Distinguish cumulative from noncumulative preferred stock.

(4) Distinguish participating from nonparticipating preferred stock.

15.5 (1) Distinguish par from no-par stock.

(2) What is stated or declared value? What is its purpose?

(3) How is stated value related to par value—historically and necessarily?

15.6 (1) What is paid-in surplus? What are its legal and economic significances?

(2) Suggest sources of paid-in surplus.

(3) Suggest terminology that is appropriate to describe paid-in surplus in an annual report to stockholders.

15.7 (1) Technically, any agreement to buy the stock of a corporation that is in the process of formation, or to buy shares in a new issue being brought out, may be said to be subscription to the stock. Under what circumstances are accounts with subscriptions advisable, and under what circumstances are they not?

(2) Under what circumstances might it be appropriate to show subscriptions receivable as a deduction from the gross capital of a corporation?

(3) What possibilities exist for settling defaulted subscription contracts among the various state laws?

(4) In what account should a corporation show amounts retained as a result of a forfeited stock subscription when stock is not issued to the defaulting subscriber?

15.8 (1) What is treasury stock?
(2) How may it be acquired?
(3) What legal restraint is commonly placed on the purchase of treasury stock?
(4) Is treasury stock an asset? Explain.
(5) How may treasury stock be shown in the balance sheet?

15.9 What ledgers, journals, and other accounting records are peculiar to corporations in comparison with partnerships and sole proprietorships? What are their functions?

15.10 According to the bylaws of the Norton Corporation any shares on which subscriptions are in default over ninety days must be resold at the best price obtainable in the judgment of the directors. The amount collected from the subscriber, less any loss on resale of the defaulted shares, is to be refunded to the original subscriber. Submit illustrative journal entries to record a default, resale of stock, and refund to the subscriber.

15.11 Distinguish between (1) subscriptions receivable and capital stock subscribed; (2) premium on preferred stock and premium on subordinated debentures.

15.12 Audrey Company, a newly formed corporation, issued 10,000 shares of its $10 par common in exchange for unimproved real estate. Discuss the problems arising from the accounting for this transaction and the importance of them.

15.13 Redifusion, Inc., is formed by the residents of a suburban community in which television reception is cut off by surrounding terrain. The company has erected a receiving tower on a nearby mountain and is transmitting signals over direct wire to customer-stockholders for a fee set to cover operating costs and to provide a small reserve. Unforeseen capital expenditures make it necessary to assess each stockholder (customer) for a substantial percentage of his original capital contribution. Should the assessment be credited to revenue or to paid-in capital? Discuss.

15.14 How will the income statement of a business operated as a sole proprietorship differ from the income statement for the same business if it is incorporated — all capital stock being held by one stockholder?

15.15 The Hanalei Corporation was authorized on January 1, 1966, to issue 5,000 shares of $4.75 Series Preferred Stock, no par value. Seven hundred shares were issued at $105 a share, on which the directors assigned a stated value of $100 a share.

During 1966, 400 shares were reacquired at a cost of $110 a share; subsequently, 100 of these were resold at 115. The company was also authorized to issue 35,000 shares of $1 par-value common stock; 16,000 shares have been issued at $18, to which the directors assigned a stated value of $10 a share. Of these shares, 5,000 were donated to the company during 1966; 2,000 have been resold at $20, and the remaining 3,000 are held in treasury at December 31, 1966. The net income for 1966 was $800,000. How should the proprietorship section appear at December 31?

15.16 On June 1, 1966, Watanabe, Yim, Kaaako, and Haole formed Pacific Thermal Power Company, Inc., to exploit geyser properties on the island of Hawaii. The developers each held a one-quarter undivided interest in the properties until incorporation. They exchange the properties with the company for 40,000 shares of common stock issued at its par value of $10 a share; each stockholder received 10,000 shares.

Because the company needed working capital, each stockholder donated 2,000 shares of his stock to the company and the stock was resold at $8.

(1) What was the total capital of the corporation before the donation, assuming par value to be the best evidence of value?
(2) What was the book value per share before the donation?
(3) What was the total book value of the ownership equity for an individual stockholder before donation?

(4) What was the book value per share outstanding after the donation but before the donated stock was resold?

(5) What was the aggregate book value of a stockholder's equity after donation but prior to resale?

(6) Assuming, contrary to (1) above, that the resale price of the donated shares is the best indication of value, what was the total capital after the donated stock was resold?

15.17 (1) Should the excess of resale prices over the purchase prices of a corporation's own common stock be reflected in retained earnings (either directly or through the income account), or should the difference be reflected in a capital surplus account? Give reasons for your conclusion.

(2) How would your answer differ, if at all, if the resale price were less than the purchase price?

15.18 The Prosperous Co. issued $1,000,000 of Convertible 10-year Debentures on July 1, 1965. The debentures provide for 6 percent interest payable semiannually on January 1 and July 1. Discount on the issue was $18,000, which is being amortized monthly on a straight line basis.

The debentures are convertible after one year into seven shares of the Prosperous Co.'s $100 par-value common stock for each $1,000 of debentures. On August 1, 1966, $100,000 of debentures were turned in for conversion into common. Interest has been accrued monthly and paid as due. At the time of conversion any accrued interest on debentures being converted is paid in cash. Give the journal entries to record as of:

(1) August 1, 1966, the payment of accrued interest in bonds converted and issuance of stock in exchange for debentures.

(2) August 31, 1966, the accrual of coupon interest and amortization of discount on debentures remaining outstanding.

EXERCISES

15.1 American Flight Service, Inc., has total assets less current liabilities of $600,000, $200,000 represented by 6 percent cumulative preferred stock and $400,000 by common stock. Compute the rate of return to preferred and common stockholders if the rate of net income after taxes on total ownership is 8%, 20%, 1%, assuming all earnings are currently distributed to stockholders as dividends.

15.2 Murphy Corporation was organized March 1, 1966, authorized to issue 40,000 shares of $100 par 5 percent cumulative preferred stock and 60,000 shares of no-par-value common stock.

The company issued shares as follows during March:

(1) March 2   10,000 shares of preferred at $105 a share, for cash.

(2) March 10   20,000 shares of common at $110 a share, for cash; the directors assigned a stated value of $100 a share to the common stock.

Prepare the proprietorship section of the company's balance sheet at March 31, assuming earnings of $50,000 for the month and no dividends.

15.3 The Machine Tool Company obtained authorization on July 1, 1966, to issue 10,000 shares of $3 par-value common stock. On July 5, 1966, the company issued for cash 5,000 shares at $10 a share. On July 14, the company issued 4,000 shares at $10 a share for land worth $25,000 and a building worth $35,000, assuming an outstanding mortgage of $20,000 against the real estate. On July 30, the company paid $2,000 for legal fees and related costs of incorporation. Give journal entries to record these transactions, and draft the July 31, 1966, balance sheet.

15.4 Supergyro, Inc., obtained authorization on March 1, 1966, for 10,000 shares of $100 par-value preferred stock and 40,000 shares of no-par common stock.

The directors placed a stated value of $20 a share on the common stock. The following transactions occurred during March:

(1) Issued 4,000 shares of preferred stock at $108 a share for cash.
(2) Issued 50 shares of preferred stock to attorneys in payment of incorporation charges.
(3) Issued 10,000 shares of common stock in exchange for the assets and liabilities of Warren and Sweeny, a partnership. These items comprise: accounts receivable (face value, $30,000) worth $25,000; materials and supplies (cost, $70,000) worth $75,000; buildings on leased land (cost, $500,000 on which the partnership had accumulated depreciation of $400,000) valued at $330,000; equipment (cost, $300,000 less accumulated depreciation $150,000) valued at $100,000; and accounts payable in the amount of $30,000.
(4) Received 3,000 shares of common stock donated to the corporation by Warren and Sweeny.
(5) Sold 2,000 of the donated shares for $50 cash per share.

Required:

1. Prepare journal entries to record the foregoing transactions.
2. Present the proprietorship section of the March 31 balance sheet.

15.5 The Aerospace Corporation was organized on May 1, 1966, with an authorization of 2,000 shares of $30 par 4 percent preferred stock and 8,000 shares of no-par common. The directors assign a stated value of $1 a share to the common. Transactions for May were:

(1) Received subscriptions for 1,000 shares of preferred at $50 a share.
(2) Received subscriptions for 5,000 shares of common at $20 a share.
(3) Collected cash for the entire subscription price of the preferred and issued the certificates.
(4) Collected one-half the subscription price from all common stock subscribers.

Required:

1. Give journal entries for the transactions.
2. Present the May 31 balance sheet.

15.6 The balance sheet of Thermal Power, Inc., at December 31, 1966, shows:

Common Stock, par value $100 a share, authorized 1,000 shares
    issued 900 shares, less 300 shares held in treasury (note) . . . . $ 90,000
Capital in Excess of Par Value:
    Premium on Common Stock   9,000
      Total paid in capital . . . . $ 99,000
Retained Earnings:
    Restricted by Purchase of Treasury Stock $24,000
    Unrestricted   78,000   102,000
                                                          $201,000
Less: Cost of 200 Shares of Treasury Stock Purchased at $120
    a Share   24,000
Total Capital $177,000

The company purchased 200 shares at $120 a share, which it carries at cost. An additional 100 shares have been donated to the company, which are held in treasury at no cost.

Required:

1. Compute the book value per share of common stock on December 31, 1966. The following transactions occurred in January, 1967:

(a) Sold the 100 shares that had been donated to the company for $150 a share.

(b) Sold 100 of the treasury shares that had been purchased for $150 a share.

2. Journalize the foregoing transactions.

3. Compute the book value per share after the transactions, assuming no other changes in proprietorship.

4. Present the proprietorship section of the balance sheet, reflecting the December 31 balances and foregoing January transactions.

15.7 The National Beverage Company has 5,000 shares of $100 par-value 4 percent preferred stock and 15,000 shares of $100 par-value common stock outstanding. Dividends have been distributed during the four years 1966–1969 as follows:

	1966	1967	1968	1969
Dividends	$100,000	$5,000	$135,000	$50,000

What is the total amount received by preferred and common shareholders each year, if the preferred is (1) noncumulative and nonparticipating, (2) cumulative and nonparticipating, (3) cumulative and participating equally with common? Dividends on preferred have been paid through December 31, 1965.

15.8 The Lillith Corporation received a subscription for 1,000 shares of its $10 par common stock at $15 a share. After the subscriber paid one-half the subscription price he defaulted. The 1,000 shares were subsequently resold at $12 a share.

Give the entries to record the default by the subscriber and the subsequent resale of the defaulted shares assuming (1) the amount paid in on the defaulted subscription less the price reduction on resale is returned to the original subscriber; (2) the full amount paid in on the defaulted subscription is forfeited; and (3) shares equal to the number paid for in full according to the original agreement are issued to the defaulting subscriber (and 500 remaining shares are sold at $12 a share.)

15.9 A new corporation has ledger accounts with footings as shown below.

Cash		*Subscriptions Rec.—Preferred*	
172,000	23,000	420,000	105,000

Subscriptions Rec.—Common		*Preferred Stock—$100 par*	
110,000	55,000		100,000

Common Stock—$100 Stated Value		*Preferred Stock Subscribed*	
	150,000	100,000	400,000

Common Stock Subscribed		*Premium on Preferred Stock*	
50,000	100,000		20,000

Paid-in Surplus		*Treasury Stock—Common*	
	10,500	23,000	11,500

Submit a set of journal entries, with explanations, that will account for these footings.

15.10 The Pietch Metal Company is contemplating a change in its capital structure with a view to reducing the charge for dividends on its 7 percent preferred stock. The capitalization of the company at July 1, 1966, was as follows:

	Authorized	Issued
7% Cumulative Preferred Stock, par value $100 per share	$500,000	$300,000
6% Preferred Stock, par value $50 per share	250,000	100,000
Common Stock, par value $20 per share	500,000	200,000

Two alternatives have been suggested for financing the elimination of the 7 percent preferred stock:

(1) Issuance of $300,000 20-year 5 percent first mortgage bonds at 92.
(2) Offering common stockholders the right to purchase one and one-half shares of common stock for each share now held at par.

The common stock is on a $2 annual dividend basis, and should any new common stock be issued, the rate is expected to remain unchanged. The annual net profits of the company before deducting federal income taxes have averaged $90,000; and considering the inelasticity of the business, it is estimated that in the future there will be no radical variations. You may assume that the federal income tax will remain at 22 percent on the first $25,000 and 48 percent on the remainder of net income.

The directors of the company ask you to prepare a statement showing the effect of these projected changes on the earnings applicable to common stock. If they are satisfied that a saving can be effected, they will call the necessary directors' and stockholders' meetings and secure the proper authorization from the Secretary of State so that the new capitalization may take effect as of January 1, 1967.

Required:

1. Prepare such a statement.
2. Discuss briefly additional factors the directors should consider in arriving at their decision.

15.11 Berkwood Electronics, Inc., has been capitalized with $60,000 of common stock representing the entire personal wealth of the founders. The company requires another $60,000 for working capital and specialized equipment. While the company has not been successful in securing a loan from a commercial bank, it can obtain the $60,000 from a small business-investment company. The SBIC will invest this amount (half the equity capital) for a quarter share of the net income. As a condition of their investment, the SBIC wants 6 percent a year before anything is paid to the founders. On dissolution, the SBIC investment will be paid before that of the founders.

Required:

1. Can you work out a capitalization for the corporation consisting of common and preferred shares such that the SBIC will receive one quarter of the profits, but in any event will be sure of 6 percent to the extent it is earned?
2. Draft a *pro forma* balance sheet showing the financial position of the company six years hence, assuming the net assets have doubled after paying 18 percent each year to the common stockholders. How would net assets be paid to the founders and SBIC on liquidation at this date?
3. How much have the founders earned by the leverage provided by the SBIC funds? (Compare the earnings to the founders on $120,000 of capital with the earnings on $60,000.)

PROBLEMS

15.1 Arnold Corporation is authorized to issue 10,000 shares of $100 par value preferred and 20,000 shares of no-par common. It issued capital stock as follows:

(1) Two thousand shares of $100 par-value preferred stock for $110 cash per share.

(2) Fifteen hundred shares of no-par-value common stock for $80 cash per share. The directors placed a stated value of $50 per share on this stock.

(3) The directors arranged with the partners in the firm of Hall and Knight to take over their business in exchange for stock. The assets transferred and liabilities assumed, together with the values agreed upon were as follows: accounts receivable, $20,000, less allowance for doubtful accounts, $1,000; merchandise, $50,000; land, $30,000; building, $129,000; notes payable, $20,000; accounts payable, $18,000. Issued 1,000 shares of preferred stock and 1,000 shares of common. The directors specify that the preferred stock was issued at a 10 percent premium and that the stated value on the common was $50 per share.

Required:

1. Journal entries.
2. Proprietorship section of balance sheet.

15.2 Kirch, Inc., is authorized to issue 10,000 shares of $100 par-value preferred stock and 10,000 shares of $1 par-value common stock. It has the following capital transactions:

(1) Accepted from R. Hargrove subscriptions for 1,000 shares of preferred at $105 per share.

(2) Accepted from B. Jerome subscriptions for 1,000 shares of common at $110 per share. The directors decide to place a stated value of $100 per share on the common stock.

(3) Accepted from J. Eastman subscriptions for 500 shares of common at $110 per share.

(4) Received payment in full for subscription from Hargrove and issued his stock.

(5) Received payment of one-half the subscription of Jerome.

(6) Received payment in full for subscription of Eastman and issued his stock.

(7) Received remaining amount of Jerome's subscription and issued the shares.

(8) Purchased at $105 per share 200 shares of the common originally issued to Eastman.

(9) Received 300 shares of common from Jerome as a donation to the corporation.

(10) Sold 100 of the common shares purchased at $102 per share.

(11) Sold 200 of the common shares received as a donation at $102 per share.

Required:

1. Prepare entries in general journal form to record the foregoing transactions.
2. Prepare the proprietorship section of the balance sheet reflecting the foregoing transactions. Assume that the company had accumulated $50,000 of retained earnings by the time the balance sheet was prepared.

15.3 The Kensington Corporation has issued 5,000 shares of $100 par value preferred stock out of 10,000 shares authorized at par. The company has purchased 200 of these shares at $92 per share, which it carries at cost as treasury stock— preferred. Common stock of no-par value is authorized for 10,000 shares, of which 4,000 shares have been issued. The proceeds were credited to Common Stock in the amount of $200,000 and to Paid-in Surplus—Common in the amount of $20,000. Of the common shares issued, 100 have been donated to the company and are held in treasury without entry. Another 100 purchased for $65 per share are carried at cost as treasury stock—common. After the foregoing balances were established, the company had the following transactions:

(1) Accepted a subscription for 200 shares of preferred stock at $100.
(2) Sold the 100 shares of common that were donated to the company. The price obtained was $60 a share.
(3) Accepted a subscription for 500 shares of common at $60. The directors placed the same stated value on these shares as on the common shares previously issued.
(4) Collected one-half the amount of the subscriptions noted in (1) and (3) above.
(5) Sold 100 of the preferred shares held in the treasury for $110 per share.
(6) Sold the 100 purchased shares of treasury common at $75.

Required:

1. Journal entries.
2. The proprietorship section of the balance sheet. The retained earnings was $42,000 at the balance sheet date.

15.4   The proprietorship section of the balance sheet of the Wellesley Corporation as of December 31, 1966, follows:

Class A Preferred Stock – 8%	$300,000
Class B Preferred Stock – 6%	200,000
Common Stock	500,000
Retained Earnings	80,000

All shares have a par value of $100. The Class A Preferred is cumulative and nonparticipating. The Class B Preferred is noncumulative and participating at the same rate as paid to the common after the common is paid 6 percent. Dividends are payable to Class B Preferred stockholders only after Class A Preferred stockholders are paid in full.

Required:

1. The directors plan to distribute cash equal to the retained earnings. What amount will be distributed to each class of stockholders if:
(a) Dividends are unpaid for the current year only?
(b) Dividends are unpaid for two years?
(c) Dividends are unpaid for three years?
2. Suppose that dividends are unpaid for only the current year. What is the total cash required for all dividends if the directors want to pay a dividend of 10 percent on the common stock?

15.5   Burr and Carter, who share profits in a 3 to 2 ratio, decide to incorporate on July 1, 1966. Their balance sheet at that date is as follows:

THE DECORATING CENTER

BALANCE SHEET

July 1, 1966

Assets

Current Assets:		
Cash		$ 10,800
Accounts Receivable		60,000
Merchandise		72,000
		$142,800
Fixed Assets:		
Equipment	$24,800	
Less: Accumulated Depreciation	7,200	17,600
		$160,400

Liabilities and Capital

Current Liabilities:
Accounts Payable .... $ 25,400

Capital:
Burr, Capital $85,000
Carter, Capital 50,000   135,000
                                         $160,400

The business is incorporated as The Decorating Center, Inc., with an authorized capital stock of 100,000 shares of common stock, par value $10 a share. The corporation takes over the assets and liabilities of the partnership at book figures as above, except an allowance for doubtful accounts is established at 10 percent of accounts receivable, the equipment is restated at depreciated replacement cost of $19,200, and accrued expense of $600 is recorded.

The partners are paid for their capitals as follows:

(1) $25,000 of 6 percent 10-year promissory notes are issued to each partner.
(2) The remainder is issued in common shares at par.

One hundred shares of stock were issued to William A. Bentley, attorney at law, for services rendered regarding incorporation. Of the remaining shares, 10,000 were subscribed for by a group of investors at $12 a share, and one-half the subscription price per share was paid in cash.

Required:

1. Prepare the entries to record the incorporation on the partnership books. New books are not opened for the corporation (charge Organization Expense [asset] for the stock issued to the attorney).
2. Prepare a balance sheet for the corporation. All the above transactions were completed on July 1.

15.6   Helex, Inc., completed its first year of operations on December 31, 1966. The trial balance as prepared by the bookkeeper appears below.

Cash	$112,500	
Treasury Stock	10,000	
Accounts Receivable	70,000	
Inventories	90,000	
Equipment	126,000	
Accumulated Depreciation		$ 12,100
Accounts Payable		23,500
Income Taxes Payable		5,200
Debentures Payable		100,000
Preferred Stock		10,200
Common Stock		232,000
Surplus		25,500
	$408,500	$408,500

An examination of the accounting records and supporting documents discloses:

(1) Authorized capital stock consists of 1,000 shares of no-par-value $4.40 cumulative convertible preferred stock and 60,000 shares of $10 par common.
(2) Subscriptions were received for 500 shares of preferred stock at $102 a share. Collections of $10,200 have been received and credited to Preferred Stock, but no certificates have been issued. No entry has been made to

record the amount receivable from the subscribers. The directors placed a stated value of $50 a share on the preferred stock.

(3) Certificates have been issued for 11,600 shares of common stock paid for at $20 a share.

(4) During the year, the company purchased 500 of its common shares for $9,000. The bookkeeper credited Surplus for the difference between the price paid by the company and the original issue price of these shares.

(5) Six percent debentures of face value $100,000, due July 1, 1976, were issued July 1, 1966, at a discount of $10,000, which was charged to Surplus.

(6) No interest has been paid on the debentures.

Required:

1. Prepare a work sheet to adjust the accounts for the above data. (Ignore changes in the income tax liability.) Suggested column headings:

Name of Accounts	Per Books Dr.	Cr.	Adjustments Dr.	Cr.	As Adjusted Dr.	Cr.

2. Prepare a balance sheet at December 31, 1966.

15.7 The Hale Lahaina, whose balance sheet at December 31, 1966, is presented below, has been growing steadily. Management is attempting to secure an additional $40,000 of risk capital. It is expected that additional net revenues can be generated through plant expansion with these additional funds such that total assets will be doubled in five years—after payment of $2,400 a year, or 6 percent on the $40,000 of funds provided.

BALANCE SHEET—December 31, 1966

Assets . . . . . $40,000   Common Stock—$10 par $40,000

The First State Small Business Investment Company (SBIC) agrees to provide $40,000 of funds on 6 percent convertible debentures. Each $1,000 debenture is convertible in five years into a block consisting of 25 shares of common stock at $10 a share and a $750 8 percent note payable in twenty-four months.

Required:

1. Prepare a condensed balance sheet five years after securing the SBIC loan, assuming the net assets have doubled since December 31, 1966.
2. Give the journal entry on December 31, 1971, to record the conversion of all debentures into common stock.
3. Prepare a condensed balance sheet reflecting the capitalization after conversion of the debentures.
4. What is the total 5-year cost of the SBIC financing to the original shareholders?
5. How much did the promoters benefit by the leverage of the SBIC financing, assuming the original net assets would have doubled without issuance of the debentures?

Corporate proprietorship, it will be recalled, is divided into three general categories: capital stock, paid-in surplus, and retained earnings. This chapter is concerned with the accounting for retained earnings and dividends, with some related transactions such as stock splits and with the attendant legal rules and managerial problems.

NATURE OF RETAINED EARNINGS

Retained Earnings or Earned Surplus is a proprietorship account reflecting the growth of assets from net income earned, the assets being left in the business or used to reduce debt. If accumulated losses exceed gains, the account has a debit balance and is called Deficit. The term "retained earnings" is often used to refer to the assets that come into the business, and this use of the term sometimes leads to confused thinking. For example, people may say that "the X Company should pay out some of its retained earnings." One can pay out assets, but not an account representing a financial interest. One must be careful to determine whether a statement containing the term refers to the assets or to the proprietorship account. The assumption is often made, for example, that a balance in Retained Earnings means that a cash dividend can be paid. Actually, it means only that a dividend would be legal; a need to use the assets obtained through earnings for expanding the business may make it impractical to pay a dividend.

All net income and gains and losses from unusual sources, such as the sale of a factory building, but not from transactions in the concern's own capital stock, are reflected in the Retained Earnings account. Reference was made previously to the two concepts of the income statement: the current-operating concept versus the all-inclusive concept. If the current-operating concept is adopted, large gains or losses that are not part of the regular activities of the concern, such as a large loss from fire, or revisions of past periods' income calculations, such as corrections for accruing too little tax, will be carried directly to the Retained Earnings account. Otherwise (clean-surplus concept) they will go into that account as part of the regular net income figure. The other major sources of entries to Retained Earnings are appropriations of retained earnings, and dividends.

482

APPROPRIATIONS OF RETAINED EARNINGS

An appropriation of retained earnings is a segregation of part of the account in a separate account. The purpose is to call attention to the fact that some special use of the assets that came into the business as earnings is intended. For example, a bond contract may require that a certain sum be accumulated to pay off the bonds; in other words, that a sinking fund be established. When assets are set aside in the sinking fund, management may wish to segregate a portion of the Retained Earnings account under the title Appropriation for Sinking Fund or (traditionally) Reserve for Sinking Fund. Appropriations of retained earnings may arise from any of these three sources:

1. Legal restriction (the restriction arising from purchase of treasury stock is the only one)
2. Contractual obligations (for example, bond sinking funds)
3. Policy of the management

Examples of the last category include Reserve for Contingencies and Reserve for Self-Insurance. The former account may be set up when an actual contingency is present, such as a lawsuit, or it may be created simply to express the management's intention to retain earnings as a general safety measure. The Reserve for Self-Insurance account is an indication of intent to retain earnings so that any casualty or other insurable losses can be absorbed without reducing the regular Retained Earnings account. Although the term "reserve" is popular in titles for these appropriation accounts, it is objectionable, because it suggests that assets are set aside, while in fact the "reserve" accounts are often set up when nothing whatever is done about the assets.

ENTRIES FOR APPROPRIATIONS OF RETAINED EARNINGS

The entry to create an appropriation for a sinking fund of $18,000 is:

Retained Earnings	$18,000.00	
Appropriation for Sinking Fund		$18,000.00

An appropriation for contingencies of $50,000, made because of a pending lawsuit, would be recorded thus:

Retained Earnings	$50,000.00	
Appropriation for Contingencies		$50,000.00

Settlement of the lawsuit for $40,000 could be recorded as follows:

Retained Earnings	$40,000.00	
Cash		$40,000.00
Appropriation for Contingencies	$50,000.00	
Retained Earnings		$50,000.00

The last entry assumes that a current-operating concept of the income statement is being used; otherwise the charge for the $40,000 payment should be made to an expense or loss account that would go through Profit and Loss.

Entry of the payment is made in the same account that would be used if there had been no appropriation. The purpose is to make the figure appear in the normal place in the company's statements and not be hidden in an appropriation account.

A curious result occurs when an appropriation for sinking fund, for example, is made and, the debt being paid, the appropriation is reversed. The appropriation was designed to indicate that a particular use was to be made of that amount of earnings, but after the assets are so used no record of the use appears in the proprietorship accounts. The only solution to this difficulty is to describe *all* the Retained Earnings account in terms of the intended or actual use of the assets that gave rise to it. This procedure is impractical and is not attempted. Furthermore, the practice of setting up appropriations for only a part of retained earnings (usually a small part) tends to suggest that all the rest represents assets that could be used for any desired purpose, including dividends. Actually the assets may nearly all be invested in permanent facilities or used as working capital so that they could not be used for another purpose without contracting the size of the business. In view of these facts it is recommended that appropriations arising from contractual obligations and from managerial policy be omitted and the same information given as footnotes to the balance sheet. In some states the law seems to require accounting recognition of the restriction on retained earnings for purchase of treasury stock.

STATEMENT OF RETAINED EARNINGS

Information on the transactions in Retained Earnings during a year is of importance to investors and others who analyze changes in the balance sheet. This is especially true if an unusual loss or gain has been taken directly to the Retained Earnings account. The retained earnings statement on page 485 illustrates the possibilities. Note that the statement presents the transactions in Retained Earnings for the year in summary form. Where Retained Earnings has been divided into two or more accounts, as in this example, these balances are listed individually in the balance sheet at the same point where the single balance would otherwise appear. A restriction on retained earnings from purchase of treasury stock may be recorded in an appropriation account, or, if not, the amount may nevertheless be shown separately in the balance sheet, in which case the figure comes out of the unappropriated balance.

KINDS OF DIVIDENDS

The following kinds of dividends may be distinguished:

1. Ordinary dividends
2. Dividends of wasting-asset companies
3. Liquidating dividends
4. Stock dividends

ORDINARY DIVIDENDS

Dividends are ordinarily distributions of earnings and are debited to Retained Earnings. State laws differ in the restrictions placed on the sources

THE CALDOR CORP.
Statement of Retained Earnings
Year Ended December 31, 1966

Appropriation for Sinking Fund

Balance January 1, 1966	$ 18,000.00	
Add—additional appropriation	6,000.00	
Balance December 31, 1966		$ 24,000.00

Appropriation for Self-Insurance

Balance January 1, 1966	$ 62,000.00	
Add—additional appropriation	12,000.00	
	$ 74,000.00	
Deduct—returned to unappropriated retained earnings	42,000.00	
Balance December 31, 1966		$ 32,000.00

Appropriation for Contingencies

Balance January 1, 1966	$120,000.00	
Deduct—returned to unappropriated retained earnings	120,000.00	

Unappropriated Retained Earnings

Balance January 1, 1966	$162,000.00	
Add:		
Net income for the year	74,000.00	
Returned from self-insurance appropriation	42,000.00	
Returned from contingency appropriation	120,000.00	
	$398,000.00	
Deduct:		
Appropriation for sinking fund	$ 6,000.00	
Appropriation for self-insurance	12,000.00	
Windstorm loss	42,000.00	
Settlement of lawsuit	100,000.00	
Dividends on preferred stock	18,000.00	
Dividends on common stock	26,000.00	$204,000.00
Balance December 31, 1966		$194,000.00
Total retained earnings December 31, 1966		$250,000.00

of dividends. The most common requirement is that dividends may be paid only out of the excess of net assets over stated capital. In terms of accounts, this restriction means that dividends can usually be paid out of assets that gave rise either to Paid-in Surplus or to Retained Earnings, but not to Capital Stock. Of course, individual assets are not usually identifiable with any of the proprietorship accounts, but the presence of assets arising from transactions recorded in those accounts is indicated by the balances in them. Some states restrict dividends to the amount of retained earnings, usually with an exception for dividends on preferred stock and for special circumstances. In some states dividends may also be paid out of earnings made during six months or a year even though stated capital is impaired by a deficit. The law is designed to protect creditors by prohibiting disbursements to stockholders that would reduce net assets (total assets less total liabilities) below the stated capital. It is concerned to some extent also with the protection of stockholders, and therefore sometimes requires that the source of any dividend not paid out of retained earnings be disclosed. Accountants are especially concerned to see that stockholders do not receive dividends that represent a return of paid-in surplus under the impression that they are a distribution of earnings; hence the emphasis on maintaining accounts for the different kinds of proprietorship in a corporation and on reporting clearly the transactions in each part.

SIGNIFICANT DATES FOR DIVIDENDS

Three dates are important in the legal and accounting treatment of dividends; these are:

1. Declaration date
2. Date of record
3. Payment date

The declaration date is the date on which the directors adopt a resolution to pay a dividend. This action establishes a liability for payment of a dividend; a legally declared dividend cannot be revoked. The declaration will specify a dividend of so many dollars per share, or, in the case of par-value stock, it may specify a certain percent of that value.

The date of record is the date which determines the list of stockholders who will receive the dividend. It is set to fall sometime beyond the declaration date, especially in large, widely held companies, so that persons who have bought the stock may get it registered in their names to receive the dividend.

The payment date is the date on which the dividend is to be disbursed. It is set to fall beyond the record date to give time to prepare the checks. Dividends are not paid on treasury stock; treasury stock is the equivalent of unissued stock for payment of dividends.

ENTRIES FOR ORDINARY DIVIDENDS

The simplest method for recording a cash dividend is to credit Cash and to debit Retained Earnings. However, if a balance sheet date will intervene between the declaration and the payment, a liability account will be needed. Also, it will be a convenience to have a separate account to accumulate the charge for dividends if they are paid quarterly, as they often are. Use of these accounts produces the following entries:

Dividends...	$xx,xxx.xx	
Dividends Payable.....................		$xx,xxx.xx
(to record dividends declared)		
Dividends Payable...........................	$xx,xxx.xx	
Cash.................................		$xx,xxx.xx
(to record payment of dividends)		
Retained Earnings...........................	$xx,xxx.xx	
Dividends............................		$xx,xxx.xx
(to close dividends at year-end)		

Separate Dividends accounts for preferred and common stock may be advisable. Assume that The Weltex Company has 1,000 shares ($100,000 par value) of 6 percent participating preferred stock and 5,000 shares of no-par-value common stock. The preferred participates equally with common on a share-by-share basis in distributions beyond $3 per share of common up to $7 per share of preferred, at which point participation stops. Regular quarterly dividends of $1.50 (or 1½ percent) on preferred and 75 cents on common are recorded as follows:

Preferred Dividends	$ 1,500.00	
Common Dividends	3,750.00	
Dividends Payable		$ 5,250.00

The fourth quarterly dividend for last year included an extra distribution of $8,000. Of this, $1,000 is sufficient to bring the preferred stock to its extra $1-per-share limit, leaving $7,000, or an extra $1.40 per share, for common. The entry for this last quarter was:

Preferred Dividends	$ 2,500.00	
Common Dividends	10,750.00	
Dividends Payable		$13,250.00

The entry to close the dividends accounts for the year is:

Retained Earnings	$29,000.00	
Preferred Dividends		$ 7,000.00
Common Dividends		22,000.00

NATURE OF THE LIABILITY FOR DIVIDENDS

A dividend becomes a debt only when legally declared. It therefore does not accrue. This statement is true of preferred as well as of common stock dividends. However, the passing of a preferred dividend when the stock is cumulative (the usual case) means that it must be paid in another year along with the dividend of that and any intervening years before the common stockholders can receive a dividend. This requirement is important for stockholders and prospective stockholders. It may, if the situation continues, result in election of one or more directors by preferred stockholders under provisions of the preferred stock contract. The fact that dividends have been passed must therefore be reported in the financial statements. The disclosure may take the form of a parenthetical note after the caption for preferred stock or the caption for retained earnings in the balance sheet, or as a footnote to the balance sheet. In either case it may read simply, "Cumulative preferred stock dividends in arrears, $xxx.xx."

FINANCING OF DIVIDENDS

The corporation's cash position is important in considering whether or not to declare a dividend, but it does not follow that a corporation cannot or should not declare a dividend if the cash required is not on hand. If cash that might have been used to pay a dividend was used for some permanent improvement, it would be appropriate to arrange a loan that would finance the improvement and release cash for a dividend. Cash may have been temporarily tied up in a seasonal inventory or in an unusual purchase, in which case a short-term loan would be appropriate to finance the stock and to release cash for a dividend.

Dividends are sometimes paid in "scrip," that is, promissory notes. The use of scrip enables the corporation to postpone the disbursement of cash while allowing the stockholder to get cash if he wishes to discount the note. In this case, assuming that Scrip Dividends Payable or Dividends Payable has been credited at the time of declaration, Scrip Payable or Notes Payable is credited, and the Dividend liability debited, when the scrip is issued.

Dividends may also be paid in property, that is, some asset other than cash. Such payment is cumbersome unless there are few stockholders or the distribution can be made in the form of a marketable security, such as common stock of another company, that can be issued in fractional shares.

DIVIDENDS OF WASTING-ASSET COMPANIES

A wasting-asset company exploits a natural resource that is exhaustible, such as a mine, an oil well, a timber tract that will not be replanted, or a gravel pit. In the process of producing and selling the product, the resource is depleted. The law ordinarily allows a corporation in this field to pay dividends that reduce net assets below stated capital, since it is believed that stockholders in these companies expect to get their capital back as the resource declines and that creditors also understand this expectation. Traditionally, such enterprises were not large and their owners did not expect to continue the same organization when the particular resource was gone. The assumptions are no longer as valid as before, since there now are large corporations in these fields that continue their existence and explore for and invest in new deposits as old ones are exhausted. Nevertheless, they may pay out capital in dividends. In declaring dividends the directors should indicate what portion is intended to be a distribution of earnings and what is intended to be a distribution of capital. For example, a dividend of $5 per share may be declared "$3 payable from earnings and $2 from capital." If there are 10,000 shares, the entry for this declaration is:

Dividends	$30,000.00	
Dividends Paid Out of Capital	20,000.00	
Dividends Payable		$50,000.00

The Dividends account is closed to Retained Earnings as usual. The Dividends Paid Out of Capital account is not closed but is shown in the balance sheet as a deduction from Capital Stock and Paid-in Surplus. The reader can thus see what the original capital was and how much has been returned. This presentation is illustrated as follows:

Capital

Capital Stock: 5,000 shares of no-par-value authorized and issued	$200,000.00	
Paid-in Surplus	110,000.00	
	$310,000.00	
Less—Dividends Paid out of Capital	50,000.00	
	$260,000.00	
Retained Earnings	42,000.00	$302,000.00

LIQUIDATING DIVIDENDS

Liquidating dividends accomplish the distribution of assets to stockholders when the business is partially liquidated or completely wound up. In so far as there are undistributed earnings when the liquidation of the corporation is begun, these may be dividends that include both earnings and capital. The same treatment suggested for wasting-asset dividends applies here; the directors should designate the source of the distribution, and the ordinary Dividends account should be charged for any distribution of earnings. The amounts that represent a return of capital stock or paid-in surplus may be charged to an account titled Liquidating Dividends, Capital Returned, or the like. If the process of liquidation is drawn out, it may be desirable to issue a balance sheet now and then to inform the stockholders of the progress. In this case the account for Liquidating Dividends is deducted from Capital Stock and Paid-in Surplus, just as the account for Dividends Paid Out of Capital was in the preceding paragraph.

STOCK DIVIDENDS

A stock dividend is the issue of additional shares to existing stockholders accompanied by a transfer from the Retained Earnings account to the Capital Stock account. It is used when directors wish to give stockholders tangible evidence of their earnings but wish to retain the earnings in the corporation for expansion. If the dividend were paid in cash and the stockholders were offered the opportunity to buy additional stock, the amount they could reinvest would be greatly reduced by income taxes; stock dividends are not subject to the tax. The stockholders may, if they wish, obtain cash by selling some of their stock. The procedure has the merit of shifting from Retained Earnings to Capital Stock an amount that represents a permanent investment, thus indicating more clearly the use of the assets involved.

Opinions differ on the question of how much per share should be transferred from Retained Earnings when a stock dividend is issued.[1] However, the average amount paid in per share, which puts the new shares on the same basis as

---

[1] The American Institute of CPA's recommends that stock dividends which are a small percentage of the shares outstanding be entered as a charge against Retained Earnings and a credit to Capital and Paid-in Surplus at the current market price of the shares. They base this recommendation on the ground that the stockholder is likely to think that earnings in the amount of the market value of the shares have been distributed, and this method would reduce retained earnings accordingly.

the old ones, seems appropriate. Assume that a corporation has outstanding 10,000 shares of no-par-value common stock with a stated value of $65 per share and that $10 per share additional was paid in on these shares when they were issued. The directors declare a stock dividend of one share for every twenty shares held. On the basis suggested above, the entry for the dividend is:

Retained Earnings.............................$37,500.00		
Capital Stock.........................	$32,500.00	
Paid-in Surplus........................	5,000.00	
(to record issue of 500 shares as stock dividend with		
stated value of $65.00 per share and paid-in sur-		
plus of $10.00 per share)		

If a balance sheet date intervenes between the declaration and the issue of a stock dividend, a note describing the declaration should be appended to the balance sheet.

Fractions of a share may be settled in cash, in which case a "warrant" entitling the bearer to cash may be issued for the fractional shares. In that case an account for Fractional Share Warrants Payable may be added to the above entry, and the credits to Capital Stock and Paid-in Surplus correspondingly reduced. One kind of stock may be issued as a dividend on another kind.

STOCK SPLIT-UP

A transaction that may be confused with stock dividends is the stock split-up. In a stock split-up the number of shares outstanding is increased without any transfer from Retained Earnings to Capital Stock.[2] The stock certificates may be called in and new ones issued if the certificates carry a par or stated value on their face, or stickers showing the change may be issued. Changing the certificates is desirable in any case to avoid confusion about the number of shares a certificate represents. Par or stated values must of course be reduced when the number of shares is increased without changing the figure in the Capital Stock account. Stock splits require no entry in the double-entry system, but the number of shares shown for each stockholder in the stockholders ledger must be changed. The purpose of a stock split usually is to reduce the market price per share of the stock. Stocks that sell at high prices are less favored by the smaller investors. Having a stock selling at a low figure per share enables a corporation to get wider distribution of its stock, which makes for stability. A stock split also may be used to continue a dividend at a fixed number of dollars per share when management wants to increase the total amount of dividends paid.

QUASI REORGANIZATION

A quasi reorganization is an accounting reorganization. It involves chiefly the proprietorship section of the balance sheet, but may also involve the assets. It is typically undertaken to remove a deficit from the books that evidently can-

[2] In current usage a stock dividend that is quite large relative to the shares previously outstanding may be called a stock split-up. It no doubt has the same motivation but the use of the wrong name is regrettable.

not be made up and that prevents dividends from being paid. In the case of a large decline in the value or supposed value of an asset, the asset account is written down to a current value. Suppose, for example, that The Overton Mining Company acquired a mining property by issuing stock to the owners. The ore deposit was estimated to be worth $1,750,000, and capital stock was issued with a stated value of $1,500,000 and Paid-in Surplus was credited with $250,000. After two years of operations a deficit of $300,000 had been accumulated and it was also obvious that the deposit was now worth only $800,000. A quasi reorganization was undertaken on the basis of the following calculations:

Mining property per ledger	$1,750,000.00
Less Allowance for depletion per ledger	125,000.00
Net	$1,625,000.00
Present value of mining property	800,000.00
Writedown of mining property	$ 825,000.00
Deficit	300,000.00
Total Reductions	$1,125,000.00

The reduction is applied first against any retained earnings, then against any paid-in surplus, and finally against capital stock. These entries were accordingly made:

Revaluation Clearing	$825,000.00	
Allowance for Depletion	125,000.00	
Mining Property		$ 950,000.00
(to write down mining property to $800,000.00)		
Revaluation Clearing	$300,000.00	
Deficit		$ 300,000.00
(to write off deficit)		
Capital Stock	$875,000.00	
Paid-in Surplus	250,000.00	
Revaluation Clearing		$1,125,000.00
(to reduce stated value of stock and paid-in surplus in connection with quasi reorganization)		

The Revaluation Clearing account is used as a convenience in collecting the various writedowns and credits.

The quasi reorganization, also called informal or accounting reorganization, is to be distinguished from a legal reorganization that changes the rights of creditors and stockholders under supervision of a court. The only legal steps required in a quasi reorganization are whatever steps the state requires in connection with the reduction in stated value of capital stock. However, regulations of the United States Securities and Exchange Commission and good accounting standards require the following:

1. Consent of a majority of stockholders must be obtained.
2. Writedowns are to be applied first against any retained earnings, then against any paid-in surplus, and finally against capital stock.

3. Retained Earnings account is to be dated as of the reorganization.
4. Effective date of the reorganization must not be prior to the last closing date before stockholder approval was obtained.
5. Full disclosure is to be made in financial statements of the year in which the reorganization is effected.

These requirements, except 1, are designed to prevent misleading data from being circulated. If a Retained Earnings account appears after the reorganization, for example, people might think that earnings had been enjoyed throughout the corporation's history if the account did not indicate that they had accumulated only since the reorganization date. The correct impression is accomplished by giving the figure a caption such as "Retained earnings accumulated since October 31, 1966." The SEC requires this dating practice to be continued three years; the American Institute of Certified Public Accountants suggests continuing it as long as it is significant, which they think should rarely be longer than ten years.

APPRAISAL CAPITAL

In rare circumstances it may be necessary to appraise an asset and to record this appraisal in the accounts. For example, suppose that a farm is purchased for $40,000 with the expectation of raising cattle on it. Two years later oil is discovered on the property and its value rises to $4,000,000. The cost of the land is so far out of line with the actual value that financial statements would be less useful to creditors and others than they should be. In such a case the Land account may be debited and Appraisal Capital, Revaluation Capital, Revaluation Surplus, or an account with a similar title credited. The traditional term is Appraisal Surplus. In general, accountants adhere to historical cost and do not approve of appraisals, because they are subject to wide differences of opinion and to deliberate misrepresentation. In the very unusual case where the entry of an appraisal is acceptable, full disclosure of the facts is essential.

The problem of revising accounting figures as general price levels change is different from the appraisal problem just described. It is not due to an unusual event that affects only a certain property or a certain company, but to general changes in the purchasing power of the unit of money. It can best be approached by applying price indexes to the historical cost figures to get an expression of them in terms of the current price level; the resulting figure does not depart from cost but only expresses the costs in terms of one price level. Although this procedure has been authoritatively recommended for statements to supplement the ones given on the conventional basis, it has not yet been generally adopted or required in the United States.

MANAGERIAL PROBLEMS AND DIVIDENDS

Managerial problems may be summarized under the following headings:

1. Management of cash
2. Attracting or obtaining permanent investment funds
3. Legal and contractual restrictions
4. Liability for illegal dividends

MANAGEMENT OF CASH

Although dividends may be paid by borrowing or by scrip, eventually they must be met out of the regular cash flow of the business. They must be planned in the light of seasonal needs for cash (large inventories or accounts receivable may have to be carried in some months, for example) and in the light of needs for replacement or expansion of assets. This planning can best be done by drawing careful budgets, both short and long term. The accounting records and accounting skills will be of prime importance in constructing a good budget.

ATTRACTING OR OBTAINING PERMANENT INVESTMENT FUNDS

If a concern is to attract new stockholders, it needs to pay out what investors consider adequate dividends as well as to earn a satisfactory return in its operations. A very few widely held companies have been able to get by with frequent small stock dividends or with stock split-ups and no cash dividends for a long period, but this is not considered practicable for all companies. At the same time, reinvestment of earnings by the corporation is a very economical method of obtaining additional permanent investment needed to meet increased opportunities. Management must therefore effect a compromise between retaining earnings and paying dividends that is suited to the circumstances of the particular concern.

LEGAL AND CONTRACTUAL RESTRICTIONS

Reference has already been made to legal restrictions on dividends. Further, contracts with certain creditors may provide that no dividends are to be paid if working capital falls below a certain figure, for example. Failure to meet the contractual terms may result in automatic maturity of the debt, which could lead to foreclosure or reorganization. Where such restrictions exist, avoidance of difficulties leads to emphasis on the cash and other budgets and on the accounting records, and constant reference to them.

LIABILITY FOR ILLEGAL DIVIDENDS

State laws generally prohibit dividends that would reduce net assets below stated capital or that would make the corporation unable to meet its debts as they mature. Directors who declare a dividend in violation of these rules are made personally liable under the law for repayment of the dividend to the corporation. In a large corporation this may be a very large sum. A director who votes against an illegal dividend is not held for any illegality in the declaration. Directors may also be guilty of negligence, in which case they may be sued for damages. The duties of a director should therefore not be taken lightly.

SUMMARY

The Retained Earnings account represents the owners' financial interest in assets that come into the business as the result of operating at a profit. The account must be distinguished from the assets to avoid confusion. Management sometimes segregates part of the Retained Earnings account in an "appropriation" or "reserve" account to indicate that a certain amount of the assets represented by Retained Earnings is expected to be used for some special purpose. Use of "appropriation" accounts is of doubtful value. A statement of retained earnings summarizes the transactions in the Retained Earnings account for the year, including any portions of it carried as "appropriations."

There are ordinary dividends, dividends of wasting-asset companies, liquidating dividends, and stock dividends. Ordinary dividends, once legally declared, are a liability of the corporation; they may be paid in cash, in some other asset, or in scrip, which is a promise to pay later.

A stock split-up is an increase in shares without an increase in total stated value of stock.

In a quasi reorganization, proprietorship accounts may be restated, after changes in asset values, if necessary and if proper steps are taken.

Appraisals may be recorded only in extraordinary circumstances.

Managerial problems connected with retained earnings and dividends include the management of cash, attracting or obtaining permanent investment funds, legal and contractual restrictions on retained earnings, and the liability for illegal dividends.

QUESTIONS

16.1 In the two quotations below, the term "retained earnings" is used with different meanings.

"The X Company should pay out some of its retained earnings."

"The purpose of stock dividends is to capitalize a portion of the Y Company's retained earnings."

Explain the difference between the two meanings.

16.2 (1) From what three sources may the decision to set up an appropriation of retained earnings come? Give an example of each.

(2) Explain how a large flood loss would be recorded if the company had set up an appropriation for contingencies to provide for such an event, assuming the company follows the current-operating concept.

16.3 Indicate (a) whether or not each of the following would be reported in a statement of retained earnings and (b) if it would be reported, whether it would be an addition, a deduction, or both (except for addition of final balances in the last column).

(1) Additional appropriation for contingencies for the year.

(2) Large loss by fire; the clean-surplus viewpoint is taken.

(3) Dividends declared on preferred stock.

(4) An extra amount is paid as a dividend on preferred stock because it is a participating stock; the current-operating concept is followed.

(5) Appropriation for sinking fund is canceled during the year.

(6) Windstorm loss is charged to unappropriated retained earnings; an equal amount of the self-insurance "reserve" account is transferred to the unappropriated section.

(7) Net income for the year.

(8) A new appropriation for treasury stock purchased is set up.

(9) A $100,000 life insurance policy on the president is taken out because the appropriation for self-insurance was not intended to cover this risk.

16.4 (1) Name the kinds of dividends, and describe each briefly.

(2) What is the general rule of law that restricts the payment of ordinary dividends by a corporation?

(3) What are the significant dates in connection with ordinary dividends, and why is each one important?

16.5 The Near East Trading Company has $100,000 of 6 percent cumulative preferred stock outstanding. The company has been unable to pay dividends for three years. What is done about this situation in the accounts and the statements?

16.6 (1) On what theory are wasting-asset companies permitted to pay dividends out of capital currently? What criticism can you offer of the theory? How does the reporting of dividends for a wasting-asset company differ from the reporting of dividends for other companies?

(2) Compare and contrast the accounting for dividends paid by a company in liquidation with the accounting for dividends paid by a wasting-asset company.

16.7 (1) Distinguish a stock split from a stock dividend.

(2) How may one determine what amount to transfer out of Retained Earnings when a stock dividend is issued? Where may it be credited?

16.8 A corporation may resort to a quasi reorganization to restate its proprietorship accounts and perhaps to reduce some asset valuations. In doing so, what steps should it take to satisfy good accounting standards and other requirements?

16.9 A board of directors discussed paying a dividend; it developed that there was some doubt the corporation could pay the dividend without endangering its ability to meet its debts as they matured. Most of the directors decided to declare the dividend anyway, but one of them asked that the secretary be instructed to record that he voted against it. Why did the dissenter want his position recorded?

16.10 The balance sheet of RS, Inc., at December 31, 1966, follows:

Cash	$200,000	Capital Stock—$10 par	$100,000
Other Assets	300,000	Retained Earnings	400,000
	$500,000		$500,000

The 10,000 outstanding shares are owned equally by R and S. The corporation declares a 100 percent stock dividend.

(1) How does the stock dividend affect the book value per share?

(2) What is the effect on the equity of each shareholder?

(3) "A stock dividend is really not a dividend at all." Discuss.

(4) How would total assets of each shareholder be affected by distribution of a $200,000 cash dividend?

16.11 The December 31, 1966, balance sheet of the Tropical Fruit Company contained a Reserve for Foreign Business Risks in the amount of $5,000,000. The president's letter stated: "The company's foreign business always has been profitable, but today involves greater risk than domestic business. To give proper recognition to these risks, it was decided after careful study to establish a reserve for foreign business risks amounting to $5,000,000."

(1) What is the direct effect on cash of establishing the reserve? on working capital?

(2) What is the effect on retained earnings and possible dividend declarations?

(3) What is the effect on book value per share of common stock?

(4) Will the existence of the Reserve for Foreign Business Risks account mitigate the financial effects of an expropriation of the company's foreign assets?

16.12 In the past a "reserve" was any of three kinds of accounts: valuation accounts, estimated liabilities, and appropriations of retained earnings. Listed below are the titles of eight reserves taken from published reports. Indicate the classification of each, and name the account debited when each one was set up.

(1) Reserve for Depreciation
(2) Reserve for Maintenance
(3) Reserve for Sinking Fund
(4) Reserve for Preferred Stock Dividends
(5) Reserve for Product Warranties
(6) Reserve for Possible Future Inventory Price Decline
(7) Reserve to Reduce Inventory to Lifo
(8) Reserve for Self-insurance

16.13 (1) Tidal wave insurance is so expensive, at a $15,000 premium per year, that the XYZ Co. in Hilo, Hawaii, is a self-insurer. The treasurer of the company suggests setting up a liability reserve for self-insurance with charges to expense. The vice president argues that no expense or liability has been incurred, and since a tidal wave might not occur, no entry should be made. Discuss.

(2) At a meeting of the board of directors of the Magnatherm Corporation, the establishment of a bond sinking fund is discussed. The vice president — Finance moves that semiannual deposits be made with the State Trust Company and that a reserve for sinking fund be appropriated from retained earnings each year equal to the increase in assets held by the trust company. The vice president — Marketing objects, stating that setting up of both the sinking fund and the sinking fund reserve constitutes a double charge on the earnings of the business. Comment.

16.14 Indicate the effect of each of the following transactions on (a) the balance in the Unappropriated Retained Earnings account, (b) the total retained earnings, (c) the total paid-in capital, and (d) the total stockholders' equity.

(1) $10,000 is deposited in a sinking fund.
(2) $10,000 is added to the sinking fund reserve.
(3) A flood loss of $5,000 not covered by insurance is charged against Reserve for Contigencies.
(4) Fully depreciated machinery is written off.
(5) A scrip dividend is declared and issued.
(6) Additional common stock with a par value of $50 per share is sold for $55 cash per share.
(7) A bond issue of $50,000 for which a sinking fund reserve of $50,000 is on the books is paid off. (See 8.)
(8) The sinking fund reserve mentioned in 7 is disposed of by a stock dividend.
(9) New plant is constructed at a cost of $50,000 in cash financed out of the reserve for plant expansion.
(10) A stock split-up is voted by the directors. Par value is reduced from $100 to $20 a share, and each shareholder is given five new shares for each old share.

16.15 Indicate the effect of each of the following unrelated transactions upon the book value per share of common stock. Explain each answer clearly. Illustrate with journal entries.

(1) Declaration of a cash dividend, payment to be made one month later.
(2) Issuance of a dividend in common stock to the common stockholders.

(3) A stock split-up in reverse; that is, one share of new common stock is issued to replace each four shares of old common stock.

(4) Setting up of a reserve for preferred stock dividends in arrears.

(5) Purchase at $95 per share of 100 shares of outstanding preferred stock, originally issued at its par value, $100 per share.

(6) Sale of the company's own bonds at a discount.

(7) Setting up of a reserve for estimated income taxes.

(8) Purchase by a corporation of 10 percent of its own common shares at a price below book value.

(9) Payment of $10,000 principal of outstanding serial bonds.

(10) Issuance of additional shares of common at par ($100) when their book value is $110.

EXERCISES

16.1   The 1,000 shares of Berkwood Industries capital stock are owned equally by A. Garner and C. Daimler. A condensed balance sheet of the company at June 30, 1966, shows:

Cash	$ 80,000	Capital Stock — $10 par . .	$ 10,000
Noncash Assets.	20,000	Retained Earnings	90,000
	$100,000		$100,000

The stockholder-officers are considering two alternative possibilities: (a) distributing a cash dividend of $20,000; (b) repurchasing 200 shares of stock from each stockholder at $50 a share.

(1) What is the ultimate economic effect of these two possibilities on the shareholders and their company?

(2) In view of your answer to part 1, how would you expect the repurchase of treasury stock by the corporation to affect the shareholders for income tax purposes?

(3) Suggest reasons why the corporation laws of some states treat the alternatives as legally identical. How should the resale of the treasury shares be accounted for?

(4) Can you think of circumstances under which the acquisition of treasury shares by a corporation might be treated differently? Discuss.

16.2   On October 1, 1966, Ramco, Inc., declared its regular quarterly dividend of 20 cents a share on its 1,300,000 outstanding shares of common stock. The dividend is payable November 1 to holders of record October 18.

Required:

1. Present dated journal entries, as required, to record the above transactions on the books of the company. Discuss briefly the significance of each date.

2. On what date would an investor generally recognize income from the dividend? Why?

16.3   The balance sheet of S and M, Inc., whose stock is owned equally by Sanders and Moore, shows:

Cash	$ 5,000	Common Stock — par $10 . .	$10,000
Noncash Assets	55,000	Retained Earnings	50,000

The corporation proposes a 2-for-1 stock split, which will change par value to $5 a share.

Required:

    1. How many shares does each stockholder own before and after the split? What is the book value per share before and after the split? What is the book value of each stockholder's equity before and after?

    2. Assume that instead of a stock split the company issues a 100 percent stock dividend; answer the questions in 1.

    3. Present the journal entries, as necessary, for the stock split and the stock dividend.

16.4   Give journal entries, as required, for the following transactions of Consolidated Products, Inc.

1966

June 1   Declared and issued a scrip dividend of $1 per share on 5,000 shares of common stock.

Dec. 1   Paid the scrip dividend, with interest at 6 percent per year.

1967

June 1   Declared and issued a property dividend of 10 shares of Eclipse Common for every 100 shares of the company's 5,000 common shares outstanding. Eclipse has been carried on the books at its cost of $2 a share.

1968

June 1   Declared and issued an 8 percent stock dividend on the 5,000 shares of $5 par-value common stock. The stock was originally sold at $10, and the dividend is to be charged at that price.

16.5   The capital accounts of The Canberra Corporation at January 1, 1966, are shown below:

```
Common Stock, $10 par value,
    10,000 shares authorized, 5,000 shares issued . . . . .  $ 50,000
Additional Paid-in Capital . . . . . . . . . . . . . . . . . .    50,000
Retained Earnings:
    Appropriated for sinking fund . . . . . . . .  $ 20,000
    Appropriated for contingencies . . . . . . .    80,000
    Unappropriated . . . . . . . . . . . . . . . . .   300,000      400,000
    Total  . . . . . . . . . . . . . . . . . . . . . . . . . . . . . .  $500,000
```

During 1966 the following transactions occurred:

(1) Net income for the year was $57,000.

(2) On January 15 a dividend of one additional share of common stock was issued for each ten shares of the 5,000 previously outstanding. The common stock has consistently sold at $20 a share.

(3) An additional $10,000 was appropriated for the sinking fund.

(4) Paid $75,000 damages in a lawsuit against the company. The appropriation for contingencies had been established in anticipation of the settlement of this case, and is now eliminated. The company follows the current-operating concept of income statement.

(5) On December 15 a cash dividend was declared of $4 a share to stockholders of record December 26, payable on January 20, 1967.

Required:

Prepare (1) a statement of retained earnings, (2) a statement of additional paid-in capital, and (3) the capital section of the December 31, 1966 balance sheet.

16.6 Journalize the following transactions completed by Feldix, Inc.:

1966

Dec. 31 Issued $1,000,000 of 10-year 6 percent sinking fund bonds at par.

1967

Dec. 31 Deposited $100,000 cash in a bond sinking fund.
    31 Appropriated $100,000 of retained earnings to equal the assets invested in the sinking fund.

1968

Dec. 31 Received $5,000 income on the sinking fund, which income was left with the sinking fund trustee.
    31 Deposited an additional $95,000 cash with the sinking fund trustee.
    31 Increased the appropriation for the sinking fund by $100,000.

1976

Dec. 31 Paid the bonds out of the sinking fund.
    31 Eliminated the sinking fund appropriation.

16.7 The account balances of the Valley Inn at December 31, 1966, are as follows:

Current Assets	$1,000,000	
Plant and Equipment	3,000,000	
Liabilities		$ 500,000
Common Stock, $20 a share		2,000,000
Paid-in Surplus		2,300,000
Deficit	800,000	
	$4,800,000	$4,800,000

Because of a change in traffic patterns following construction of new freeways, it is determined that plant and equipment should be more properly valued at $1,500,000. As part of a plan of quasi reorganization, it is decided to write down the fixed assets from $3,000,000 to $1,500,000 and to eliminate the deficit of $800,000. Additional paid-in surplus is to be created to accommodate the reduction in asset values and elimination of the deficit by a reduction in the stated value of common stock from $20 a share to $10 a share.

Required:

1. Journalize the quasi reorganization. During the two years ended December 31, 1968, the company operated at a profit net of depreciation on the revised plant and equipment, accumulating earnings of $500,000. No dividends were paid.
2. Prepare the capital section of the balance sheet at December 31, 1968, at which date 100,000 shares are authorized and outstanding.

16.8 The following journal entries appear on the books of M Co.:

(1)

Cost of Goods Sold	$10,000	
Reserve for Contingencies		$10,000

(the board of directors resolved "In view of possibility of future increases in merchandise prices, it is suggested that a reserve be established equal to 20 percent of the cost of the physical inventory")

(2)

Retained Earnings	3,000	
Reserve for Bad Debts		3,000

(provision for estimated loss on accounts receivable at ½ percent of credit sales)

(3)

Sinking Fund	10,000	
Reserve for Sinking Fund		10,000

(to record transfer of cash between accounts at First National Bank as required by the bond indenture)

(4)

Reserve for Contingencies	4,000	
Patents		4,000

(to recognize as worthless the costs incurred in obtaining the patent on the Hilavator door closer; loss of suit in State Superior Court)

(5)

Cash	12,000	
Treasury Stock		10,000
Retained Earnings		2,000

(resold 1,000 shares of treasury stock at $12 a share, cost $10 a share)

Required:

Prepare adjusting entries, as required, to state the accounts in accordance with the explanations. Include complete explanations with the adjusting entries. The company follows the all-inclusive concept of income statement.

16.9 Financial data of the S Co. include the following:

	December 31	
	1967	1966
Preferred stock, par $100	$ 75,000	$100,000
Common stock, par $10	150,000	100,000
Additional paid-in capital	40,000	30,000
Retained earnings	53,000	20,000

During early 1967 the company distributed a 50 percent stock dividend to the common stockholders. Later in the year, it retired 250 preferred shares at 120, of which $8 a share was charged to Paid-in Surplus. Cash dividends paid during the year amounted to $12,000. Goodwill in the amount of $15,000 was written off to Retained Earnings. What was the net income for 1967?

16.10 The M Insurance Company's annual report for December 31, 1966, disclosed a stockholders' equity section as follows:

Stockholders' Equity

Common Stock, par value $10, authorized 2,000,000 shares, outstanding, 500,000 shares	$ 5,000,000
Premium on Common Stock	2,000,000
Other Paid-in Capital	9,000,000
Retained Earnings	8,000,000
Total	$24,000,000

For each of the following actions taken in early 1967, separately and independently, explain the effect (amount of dollar increase or dollar decrease), if any, on each of the individual accounts in the stockholders' equity section:

(1) On January 15, 1967, the company split its stock two-for-one (two shares of $5 par value were given for each share of the $10 par shares).

(2) On February 1, 1967, the company issued a 10 percent stock dividend to its stockholders. The stock was priced at $20 a share.

(3) On April 11, 1967, the company sold an additional 200,000 of the new $5 par-value shares to its stockholders for $25 per share. At the time of this action the shares were selling in the open market for $30 per share.

(4) On April 15, 1967, the company issued 150,000 of the new $5 par-value shares on a share-for-share basis in exchange for all the common stock of the N Insurance Company. At the time of the exchange, N Company stock had a book value of $27 per share and M Company stock was selling for $30 per share.

(CPCU—adapted)

PROBLEMS

16.1   The Jay-Vee Company had 10,000 shares of $100 par-value preferred stock authorized and outstanding on January 1, 1966. It also had 20,000 shares of $50 par-value common stock authorized and outstanding. It had one Retained Earnings account on that date with a balance of $210,000. Transactions involving retained earnings during 1966 follow:

(1) Net income of $800,000 was earned for the year.

(2) A 4 percent dividend was paid on the preferred stock.

(3) A 10 percent dividend was paid on common stock.

(4) An appropriation for self-insurance of $100,000 was made.

(5) A fire loss of $40,000 was recorded. The company follows the current-operating concept of the income statement.

Required:

Prepare a statement of retained earnings for the year.

16.2   Prepare dated journal entries, where necessary, to record the following events:

(1) A dividend of $10 per share on 10,000 shares outstanding is declared on October 15, 1966, payable on January 16, 1967, to stockholders of record December 15, 1966.

(2) The stockholders ledger is closed on December 15, 1966, and a schedule taken off for preparing the dividend checks declared in (1) above.

(3) The dividend declared in (1) is paid on January 16, 1967.

(4) A scrip dividend is declared on March 15, 1966, payable on April 30, 1966, to stockholders of record March 31, 1966, on 10,000 shares of capital stock outstanding at the rate of $2 per share.

(5) The scrip is issued on April 30, 1966.

(6) A dividend is declared on May 31, 1966, on 6 percent cumulative preferred, par value $100 per share. There are 10,000 shares outstanding and no dividend was paid last year. At the same time, a dividend totaling $150,000 was declared on the common stock.

(7) A company declares a total of $100,000 of dividends on March 31, 1966. The preferred is participating, $100 par, and carries a 5 percent dividend rate; 5,000 shares are outstanding. There are no dividends in arrears. The participation is equal per share on all shares on any distribution over $5 per share up to a total of $8 for the preferred. There are 7,000 common shares outstanding, $100 par value a share.

(8) The ZB Company, in liquidation, has paid all liabilities and is now paying cash to the stockholders as it becomes available. On June 30, 1966, a total of $200,000 is disbursed to the stockholders, at which date Retained Earnings had a debit balance.

(9) On May 31, 1966, directors of the Lady Luck Mining Company declare a dividend of $5 per share on the 105,000 shares of capital stock outstanding "payable on June 30, 1966, to stockholders of record on June 15, 1966, $2 from capital and $3 from earnings."

(10) A stock dividend is declared on April 12, 1966. It provides for one share to be issued for every fifty shares outstanding. As of April 12 there are 100,000 shares outstanding, with a stated value of $50 per share and a market value of $60 per share — which was the consideration received when the 100,000 shares were issued. The dividend is issued on May 15 to stockholders of record April 30.

(11) The stock dividend declared in (10) is issued on May 15, 1966.

16.3 The directors of Fraser Development, Inc., believing that certain land bought in Alberta, Canada, contained oil, bought 4,000 acres for $4,000,000. After running up a deficit of $800,000 exploring for oil, the directors abandoned the search and dedicated the land to cattle grazing. A quasi reorganization of the company was effected on July 1, 1966, and the land was appraised at $400,000 for ranch purposes.

Required:

1. Prepare journal entries to record the quasi reorganization. Prior to the quasi reorganization, capital stock was $5,000,000 and paid-in surplus was $1,000,000.
2. Prepare the capital section of the balance sheet as of December 31, 1966. Net income for the six months ended December 31, 1966, amounted to $40,000.

16.4 The ledger accounts of the Island Sugar Company had the following balances on February 28, 1966, after closing:

Accounts Payable	$ 2,400
Accounts Receivable	7,600
Bonds Payable	30,000
Cash	4,100
Common Stock	15,000
Dividends Payable	1,500
Donated Surplus	2,000
Earned Surplus	2,300
Inventories	6,200
Limestone Quarries	40,700
Organization Costs	1,000
Plant and Equipment	61,900
Preferred Stock	15,000
Premium on Bonds Payable	500
Premium on Preferred Stock	1,200
Premium on Sale of Treasury Stock	800
Taxes Payable	1,000
Reserve for Additional Payments to Beet Growers (applicable to sales from fiscal year ended February 28, 1966, crops)	4,600
Reserve for Bond Retirement	5,000
Reserve for Doubtful Accounts	600
Reserve for Depreciation	21,500
Reserve for Depletion	20,100
Reserve for Treasury Stock — Common	2,700
Treasury Stock — Common	2,700
Treasury Stock — Preferred	2,000

The company has an authorized capitalization consisting of 1,500 preferred shares of $10 par value per share and 2,000 common shares of no-par value per share. As of February 28, 1966, 1,500 of the preferred shares were issued, of which 200 had been donated back to the company; and 1,500 of the common shares were issued, of which 300 were held as treasury shares at a cost of $9 per share. The company is organized in a state in which retained earnings available for dividends are restricted by the cost of capital stock held in treasury.

Required:

Prepare a classified balance sheet, using contemporary terminology. The Donated Surplus was credited for the par value of the preferred shares acquired by donation and held in treasury at February 28, 1966,

16.5   The ledger accounts of the Aerospace Company had the following balances on December 31, 1967, after closing:

Accounts Payable	$12,200
Accounts Receivable	26,500
Buildings	91,600
Cash	18,000
Common Stock	50,000
Common Stock Subscribed	20,000
Earned Surplus	50,000
Inventories	55,400
Income Taxes Payable	20,100
Land	49,500
Machinery and Equipment	91,400
Organization Costs	800
Patents and Trademarks	3,100
Preferred Stock	60,000
Premium on Common Stock	65,000
Premium on Preferred Stock	10,000
Reserve for Depreciation—Buildings	24,200
Reserve for Depreciation—Machinery and Equipment	19,500
Reserve for Doubtful Accounts	700
Reserve for Income Taxes	4,200
Reserve for Possible Future Losses on Disposition of Assets	12,000
Reserve for Treasury Stock	8,000
Sinking Fund	30,000
Subordinated Convertible Debentures, 5%	40,000
Subscriptions Receivable	21,600
Treasury Stock	8,000

The company's authorized capital stock consists of 2,000 shares of $30 par-value preferred and 80,000 shares of $1 par-value common.

The preferred stock is required to be redeemed at specified percentages (5 to 10 percent) of such shares outstanding on June 15 in each of the years 1978 through 1987, and in anticipation thereof the company has established a sinking fund. In the opinion of the company's counsel, the existence of the redemption requirement and sinking fund imposes no restriction on surplus. A total of 50,000 of the common shares are issued, of which 45,000 are outstanding and 5,000 have been repurchased at $1.60 per share and are held in treasury.

Reserve for Income Taxes of $4,200 represents deferred income taxes relating to reported income, which was greater than taxable income. The subordinated convertible debentures are being retired in installments; $1,200 is payable within one year from December 31, 1966.

Required:

Prepare a classified balance sheet using contemporary terminology.

16.6 Capital accounts of the Radio Materials Company at January 1, 1966, were as follows:

Cumulative Convertible Preference Stock, 5% par value
$50 per share, 20,000 shares authorized, 8,000 shares
issued and outstanding $400,000

Common Stock, par value $1 per share, 30,000 shares
authorized, 20,000 issued less 1,000 reacquired and
held in treasury 19,000

Additional Paid-in Capital:

Excess of proceeds over par value of 20,000 shares of
common stock issued $480,000

Less: Amounts charged with respect to 1,000 shares
reacquired 22,000   458,000

Appropriation for Notes Payable[a] 550,000

Appropriation for Contingencies 500,000

Unappropriated Retained Earnings 150,000

The following transactions occurred during 1966:

(1) The company changed its method of accounting for treasury shares to reflect the cost of such shares as a reduction in capital rather than as a charge against common stock ($1,000) and additional paid-in capital ($22,000). This change conforms to the 1966 law of the state in which the company is organized, which requires that paid-in capital is not to be reduced on purchase of treasury stock. Furthermore, the directors resolve "to establish an appropriation of retained earnings equal in amount to the cost of shares held in treasury so that present and potential shareholders will be on notice through the published financial statements of the restriction on retained earnings available for dividends."

(2) It is discovered early in 1966 that $20,000 of equipment bought on January 2, 1964, had been charged to Maintenance Expense. Such equipment is being depreciated by the company over ten years by the straight line method.

(3) The company sold the equipment of its Brass Metals Division for $12,200. This equipment, which cost $65,400, had a net book value of $51,300. The directors resolve that "the loss on disposal of the equipment in the brass metals subsidiary be absorbed by the appropriation for contingencies." The company follows the current-operating concept of income statement.

(4) Notes payable to the insurance company in the amount of $50,000 were paid.

(5) Two thousand preferred shares were redeemed at $60 a share; the excess paid over par is to be charged to Retained Earnings.

(6) During the year the company issued to employees as compensation 600 of its treasury shares, valued at $25 a share.

(7) On December 31, 1966, cash dividends were declared of $1 a share on common and $2.50 a share on preferred, payable January 15, 1967.

(8) Net income for 1966 amounted to $420,000.

Required:

1. Journalize transactions (1) through (7).
2. Prepare a statement of retained earnings for 1966.
3. Prepare the capital section of the balance sheet at December 31, 1966.
4. Can you explain any differences in the accounting for acquisition and retirement of preferred stock and the acquisition of common as treasury shares?

[a]Under provisions of the notes payable to an insurance company, retained earnings is restricted in this amount and is unavailable for payment of cash dividends or purchases of common stock.

PART V

Cost Controls
and Accounting

Responsibility and Departmental Accounting

NATURE OF RESPONSIBILITY ACCOUNTING

The term "responsibility accounting" refers to a system of organizing and reporting accounting data according to the responsibilities of individuals.[1] Its object is to present information about the results obtained in each unit of the enterprise over which a responsible executive has control, and to exclude (or to recognize separately) figures that reflect conditions for which the executive cannot be held responsible. It involves a set of reports which begins with the foreman or supervisor in charge of only a few workers and continues with reports at each higher level that incorporate the figures of more and more underlying reports as the pyramid rises. An executive at any level can then review the results obtained by each level under him, including those in his immediate office.

To a considerable degree the emphasis in responsibility accounting is on costs, although it is often extended to cover revenues also, especially in the selling division of a concern.

BASES FOR EFFECTIVE USE OF RESPONSIBILITY ACCOUNTING

Two fundamental principles must be adhered to if responsibility accounting systems are to work effectively:

1. Organizational lines (responsibilities and authority) must be clearly drawn without overlap.
2. Controllable and noncontrollable costs must be clearly separated in the reports.

These principles are necessary in order to identify with reasonable certainty the costs (or revenues) for which any executive may be fairly held responsible. They are needed to avoid having one executive held to answer for decisions made by another; for example, a plant superintendent may be held responsible for cost of material used. The quality of materials bought for processing is a matter of judgment and affects the cost. If the purchasing is done by the president of the company, the plant superintendent may properly say that it is not

---

[1] Conceivably, the term can also be applied to group responsibilities.

fair to hold him responsible for the cost of materials since he does not have control over the purchasing.

The second principle — that controllable and noncontrollable costs be clearly distinguished — must be noticed because we commonly associate all the costs of performing a function with it regardless of the managerial opportunity to control all those costs. For example, the cost of operating a factory includes depreciation of the building, real estate taxes on the building and land (or rent), insurance on the building, and the same costs on the machinery used. Ordinarily the building and the machinery will have been acquired by a decision of the president or board of directors, and the plant superintendent will therefore have no opportunity at all to control the amount of depreciation expense. He will have no chance to control real estate taxes as a rule, and the insurance cost is usually a matter of top-management policy also. The plant superintendent will be able to control the power cost by efficient use of the equipment; he will be able to control wastage of materials and amount of labor required to turn out the product. The latter costs are therefore _controllable_ with reference to the superintendent; the ones mentioned above are not. Practice differs in reporting noncontrollable costs between omitting them entirely in reports up to the point where all figures are presented to the president or board of directors, on the one hand, or in showing them in each report as a separate group for which the various executives below the top level are not responsible, on the other. The merit of the latter procedure lies in showing the executive that his controllable costs are not the only concern of the enterprise and in letting him know how important the facilities and equipment he works with are.

ILLUSTRATION OF ORGANIZATIONAL AND REPORTING RELATIONSHIPS

The accompanying organization chart for a manufacturing concern shows the lines of responsibility in the firm on which a responsibility accounting system may be based. Such a system involves reports for all units of the organiza-

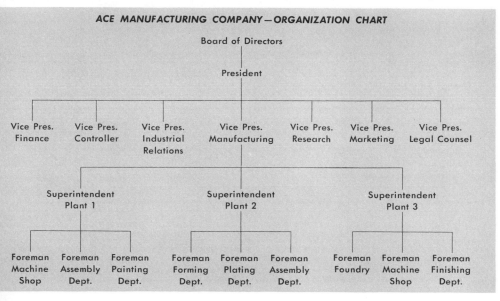

ACE MANUFACTURING COMPANY — ORGANIZATION CHART

tion, beginning at the bottom of the chart and proceeding to the top. The reports shown here to illustrate the content of responsibility accounting reports are those for the units beginning with the assembly department of plant 1 and for each step above it to the president. Although only this line of reports is illustrated, observation of the organization chart will disclose that a report will be prepared for each foreman and that each plant superintendent will receive a report combining the results of each of his foremen. The various vice-presidential officers will each have subsidiary units with a similar structure of reports. The president and the board of directors will have complete statements of the concern, including the conventional balance sheet and income statement. The organization chart has been kept simple for this exposition by showing only the manufacturing structure below the vice-presidential level. Each vice president will have some organization under him, although in such a case as that of the vice president for legal counsel, it will usually be a small one. Also, many more details and organizational units will appear in the case of an actual manufacturing concern of substantial size and complexity. Many other kinds of reports will also be used in complex situations.

Note that cost totals are usually difficult to interpret unless they can be related to some other significant information such as the number of units of product produced, hours worked, or revenue earned. Actual totals are also often compared with budgeted (planned) totals or with standard costs (precomputed costs) for the work done. The cost reports illustrated here show budgeted figures. Note that the total of cost incurred can be traced from each report to the next higher one. The terms "direct labor" and "indirect labor" in the reports refer to labor used directly on the product or for adjunct work such as maintenance, supervision, training, or watchman service.

ACE MANUFACTURING COMPANY
Cost Report

Department: Assembly, Plant 1
Officer: H. S. Clark, Foreman   Period: July 1966

	Actual	Budget	Actual Over (Under) Budget
Controllable costs:			
Materials used	$ 68,400	$ 67,300	$ 1,100
Direct labor	127,800	129,600	(1,800)
Indirect labor	13,600	12,950	650
Power	1,280	1,270	10
Supplies	1,690	1,720	(30)
Other	2,275	2,148	127
Total controllable	$215,045	$214,988	$ 57
Noncontrollable costs:			
Depreciation	$ 14,800	$ 14,800	—
Insurance	2,188	2,108	80
Property taxes	1,730	1,730	—
Total noncontrollable	$ 18,718	$ 18,638	$ 80
Total costs	$233,763	$233,626	$ 137

ACE MANUFACTURING COMPANY
Cost Report

Department: Plant 1
Officer: M. B. Olwan, Superintendent   *Period:* July 1966

	Actual	Budget	Actual Over (Under) Budget
Controllable costs:			
Superintendent's office:			
Salaries.........................	$ 4,474	$ 4,519	$ (45)
Other	398	402	(4)
Machine shop.......................	340,287	340,200	87
Assembly department	215,045	214,988	57
Painting department	89,445	88,876	569
Total controllable	$649,649	$648,985	$ 664
Noncontrollable costs:			
Depreciation	52,400	52,400	—
Insurance	7,140	7,310	(170)
Property taxes	5,700	5,700	—
Total noncontrollable................	$ 65,240	$ 65,410	$(170)
Total costs.........................	$714,889	$714,395	$ 494

ACE MANUFACTURING COMPANY
Cost Report

Department: Manufacturing Division
Officer: H. S. Ridley, Vice President   *Period:* July 1966

	Actual	Budget	Actual Over (Under) Budget
Controllable:			
Office of Vice President, Manufacturing:			
Salaries	$ 7,244	$ 7,266	$ (22)
Other.......................	3,100	3,000	100
Plant 1	649,649	648,985	664
Plant 2	877,940	870,860	7,080
Plant 3	572,182	569,030	3,152
Total controllable................	$2,110,115	$2,099,141	$10,974
Noncontrollable costs:			
Depreciation.......................	53,050	53,050	—
Insurance.......................	7,210	7,400	(190)
Property taxes.......................	5,785	5,785	—
Total noncontrollable	$ 66,045	$ 66,235	$ (190)
Total costs	$2,176,160	$2,165,376	$10,784

ACE MANUFACTURING COMPANY
Cost Report

Department: All
Officer: V. S. Markey, President   Period: July 1966

	Actual	Budget	Actual Over (Under) Budget
Controllable:			
President's office:			
Salaries	$ 26,000	$ 26,500	$ (500)
Other	13,710	12,680	1,030
Finance	11,400	12,000	(600)
Controller	142,000	139,000	3,000
Industrial relations	40,621	42,500	(1,879)
Manufacturing	2,110,115	2,099,141	10,974
Research	184,978	176,500	8,478
Marketing	302,066	300,050	2,016
Legal counsel	9,750	9,450	300
Total controllable............	$2,840,640	$2,817,821	$22,819
Noncontrollable:			
Depreciation...................	74,960	73,400	1,560
Insurance.....................	12,620	13,000	(380)
Property taxes.................	11,744	12,000	(256)
Total noncontrollable	$ 99,324	$ 98,400	$ 924
Total costs	$2,939,964	$2,916,221	$23,743

A CASE ILLUSTRATION OF RESPONSIBILITY ACCOUNTING[2]

Greater appreciation of the principles and the potentialities of responsibility accounting may be seen in the case of a large flour milling organization for which responsibility accounting was prescribed and installed. The company has several flour mills, each of which had its own (conventional) profit and loss statement. Centralized services were (and are) provided and their cost was charged to the several mills on a basis considered equitable. The mill profit and loss statements were the basis for evaluating the performance of management at each plant, and bonuses were calculated as a percent of the net income shown for each one. However, managers complained that the profit and loss statements did not properly measure their results.

Investigation of the company's organization and practices disclosed that sales figures represented shipments made at each mill, but that all except a few local sales resulted from orders taken by the central sales department, the selling prices being based on the daily quotations of wheat prices. The central sales department assigned the shipments to the mills so as to minimize freight costs, but almost all export sales were allocated to one mill that has export shipping facilities. Export sales carry a low margin. Wheat is purchased in central markets, sent to mills so as to minimize freight costs, and charged to mills at its actual cost. A mill might well end up with the highest wheat prices and lowest sales prices. A significant portion of operating expenses were the items incurred by the central offices and allocated to the mills. Under the circum-

[2]Originally reported by Clifford E. Graese in *The Accounting Review*, XXXIX:2, p. 387.

stances it became obvious that the mill profit and loss statements did not reflect adequately the activities that were really under the control of the managers. The thing they could control was the milling costs incurred at the local mill and the yield of flour from the wheat used. Mill profit and loss statements were accordingly abandoned and a mill conversion cost report substituted.

Sales prices are the responsibility of the central sales department, and a report was designed to compute the daily gross margin over out-of-pocket wheat cost. This report is supported by similar reports for each salesman, so the margin contributed by each one can be seen. Another report was designed to reflect the performance of the grain purchasing department. This report shows the actual cost of wheat purchased in comparison with the market price of the wheat required by sales orders accepted (wheat market prices are published on the basis of transactions on organized exchanges, just as capital stock prices are).

Allocations of central office costs were abandoned and a single profit and loss statement for the whole company is now the only one prepared. Use of the new responsibility accounting reports ended the preoccupation of the mill managers with the sales orders and wheat purchases sent to them, and caused them to concentrate on conversion costs. The sales office became concerned with the profitability of the business accepted and with the selling costs involved. It also reconsidered some types of business it had accepted uncritically before. The top management changed its attitudes toward the mills; some that had been considered for shutdown on the basis of the mill profit and loss statements were found to be satisfactory. Of course, management can now evaluate each performance effectively.

This case not only illustrates the effectiveness of responsibility accounting, but also indicates that it can be used in connection with revenue as well as costs, and it emphasizes again that the system must be tailored to the particular organization.

DEPARTMENTAL ACCOUNTING

"Departmental accounting" refers to the calculation of results by departments. It may be contrasted with responsibility accounting in that it is not necessarily concerned with the performance of an individual executive, and it does not necessarily focus on controllable costs. In a case where a department is under one executive and the departmental results are not carried beyond the deduction of controllable expenses, the two procedures coincide. A "department" may represent only an accounting classification, rather than a distinct organizational unit; for example, "departmental" accounting may be conducted for different product groups not all of which are handled in one organizational "department" of a business.

GENERAL OBJECTIVES OF DEPARTMENTAL ACCOUNTING SYSTEMS

The possible objectives of departmental accounting systems are:

1. Gross margin on sales by departments
2. Gross margin less selling expenses by departments
3. Net operating income by departments
4. Contribution by departments (gross margin less variable expenses)

If the objective is to get net operating income by departments, the first two objectives will be automatically included. The fourth objective requires that variable expenses be separated from fixed expenses to calculate the contribution made by the department to cover the over-all fixed expenses and to make a profit. This is the same kind of calculation discussed previously in Chapter 5.

DEPARTMENTAL ACCOUNTS

If departmental data are to be compiled continuously, the most convenient procedure is to use separate accounts for each revenue or expense for each department. For example, The Model Mode Shop, a ladies' ready-to-wear store with three departments, might keep the following ledger accounts for sales:

Sales — Dresses
Sales — Lingerie
Sales — Shoes

A similar group of accounts will be needed for sales returns and allowances. The determination of cost of goods sold requires the following accounts in this store:

Purchases — Dresses
Purchases — Lingerie
Purchases — Shoes
Freight In — Dresses
Freight In — Lingerie
Freight In — Shoes
Purchase Discounts — Dresses
Purchase Discounts — Lingerie
Purchase Discounts — Shoes
Purchase Returns and Allowances — Dresses
Purchase Returns and Allowances — Lingerie
Purchase Returns and Allowances — Shoes
Merchandise — Dresses
Merchandise — Lingerie
Merchandise — Shoes

Accounts for each kind of expense may be similarly set up, if desired.

FORMS OF LEDGER ACCOUNTS

Three types of ledger organization for departmental accounts may be found:

1. Separate general ledger accounts for each kind of departmental data
2. Controlling accounts in the general ledger with departmental accounts supporting them in subsidiary ledgers
3. General ledger accounts with distribution columns

The first type is the one described in the preceding section. It is satisfactory if there are few departments. In a large enterprise with twenty or thirty departments the general ledger control account with a subsidiary ledger carrying an account for each department is better. Placing the departmental accounts in a subsidiary ledger permits one person to post them from original documents while another works on the general ledger. For concerns with a moderate number of departments the general ledger account with distribution columns is simple and effective. The account in this case has the usual columns for debits and credits, with additional columns for departments. It is often designed with the regular account on the left page and the distribution columns on the right (facing) page. Such an account is shown on page 514, where the sales account of The Model Mode Shop for March through July 1966 is given. Note that the distribution columns show deductions recorded in parentheses (or they may be entered in red ink). More subsidiary accounts than are here illustrated are provided by inserting extra sheets with distribution columns on both sides.

JOURNALS FOR DEPARTMENTAL ACCOUNTS

Departmental accounts kept on a continuous basis require special provision in the journals. Postings to departmental accounts may be provided for in four ways:

In journals:
1. Column totals
2. Analyses of column totals
3. Sundry column entries
   From original documents:
4. Direct posting

Column totals are posted to departmental accounts when general ledger accounts for departments are used. The illustration on page 516 (part A) shows a sales journal with departmental Sales account columns. This system requires a column in some journal for each departmental ledger account that has many entries.

Analyses of column totals as a basis for posting is illustrated (part B) on page 517. This shows a cash receipts book with a sales column. The total of the sales column is analyzed and the result written below the total. The posting to departmental accounts is made from the detail given in the analysis. This technique can be used in any journal where the number of columns is restricted. It can be used to post general ledger departmental accounts, general ledger accounts with distribution columns, or control and subsidiary accounts. In the case of the distribution column account the column total from the journal is posted to the regular ledger account column and the details in the analysis are posted to the distribution columns of the account. When a control account is used, the column total is posted to that account, and the details are posted to the subsidiary ledger accounts. The analysis may be made from sales slips or from detail in the column (if detail is entered in the journal), or taken from cash register tapes that record cash sales by classes.

Sundry column entries appear in the sundry column of a special journal or in the general journal. They usually represent a single transaction with one person or concern. They can be posted to a general ledger account with distribution columns and also carried into the proper distribution column on the basis of information in the journal or from the original document entered in the journal. If a subsidiary ledger is involved, entries in the sundry column are posted

General Ledger Account with Departmental Distribution Columns

Account:

Date	Ref.	Debit	Credit	Dresses	Lingerie	Shoes
Mar. 31	S6		6050 00	3300 00	980 00	1770 00
31	C18		4410 00	2030 00	1070 00	1310 00
Apr. 30	S7		6420 00	3116 00	1840 00	1464 00
30	C22		2480 00	1208 00	810 00	462 00
May 31	S8		8430 00	5120 00	2200 00	1110 00
31	C26		4240 00	1870 00	1220 00	1150 00
June 22	J27	40 00		(40 00)		
30	S9		9100 00	6008 00	2010 00	1082 00
30	C30		4450 00	1400 00	1280 00	1770 00
July 31	S10		7500 00	4200 00	2600 00	700 00
31	C34		4300 00	1200 00	1600 00	1500 00
		40 00	57 380 00	29 412 00	16 610 00	12 818 00

57,840.00

Sales

Distribution

Left page

Right page

once to the general ledger control account and then to the subsidiary ledger account. Where subsidiary ledger postings are numerous, it is convenient to have separate columns for the subsidiary ledger entries in the general journal. Part C on page 517 shows such a general journal.

Direct posting, which means posting from the original document instead of the journal, is useful when there are many subsidiary ledger accounts for posting to those accounts.

INCOME STATEMENT WITH DEPARTMENTAL GROSS MARGIN FIGURES

Substantial benefits can be obtained from a knowledge of the gross margin earned in each department even though the departmental figures are carried no farther. To get this information either departmental accounts for the sales and cost of goods sold items must be maintained, or these figures must be analyzed departmentally from other records. The income statement of The Model Mode Shop for July 1966, with departmental gross margin figures, is shown on page 518.

DISTRIBUTION OF EXPENSES

Accounts for accumulation of data on revenue and cost of goods sold are readily maintained, but distribution of operating expenses by departments involves more effort. To set up a system for distributing expenses, four things must be considered; these are:

1. Direct and indirect expenses
2. Bases for distribution of indirect expenses
3. Selling and service departments
4. Ledger treatment of expenses

DIRECT AND INDIRECT EXPENSES

When the amount of an expense can be readily and definitely identified with a particular department, the expense is a *direct* expense of that department. When the amount of an expense cannot be readily and definitely identified with a particular department, the expense is *indirect* with reference to that department. For example, the salary of a sales person who works in one department all the time is a direct expense of that department. At the same time, the department uses space in the building that involves depreciation, real estate taxes, and heat and light. These expenses are indirect expenses of the department, because the amount of each of them that applies to the department is not readily and definitely indentifiable with the department. Other examples of direct departmental expenses are supplies used in the department, depreciation of counters and fixtures used in it, and separate advertising run for it. Other indirect expenses include advertising that covers several departments or the store as a whole and the salary of the manager who looks after all departments.

In order to assign a portion of an indirect expense to a department, some measure of the relationship between the amount of expense incurred and the requirements or activity of the department must be used. This is called a

JOURNALS FOR DEPARTMENTAL ACCOUNTS

A. SALES JOURNAL WITH DEPARTMENTAL SALES ACCOUNT COLUMNS

Sales Journal   page 6

Date		Customer	Ref.	Debit — Accounts Receivable	Credit — Sales Tax Payable	Credit — Sales—Dresses	Credit — Sales—Lingerie	Credit — Sales—Shoes
1966								
Mar.	1	Mrs. H. E. Jenks		40 51	1 56	38 95		
"	1	E. J. Franke		17 56	68			16 88

Cash Receipts Book

page 18

Date	Received from:	Ref.	Debit		Credit			
			Cash	Sales Discount	Accounts Receivable	Sales	Sundry Amount	Sundry Account
1966						4410 00		

Dresses   2,108.00
Lingerie 1,810.00
Shoes   492.00
          4,410.00

C. GENERAL JOURNAL WITH SUBSIDIARY LEDGER COLUMNS

General Journal

page 27

Date	Explanation	Subsidiary Ledger			General Ledger		
		Ref.	Debit	Credit	Ref.	Debit	Credit
1966 June 22	Sales—Dresses..........				27	40 00	
	Accounts Receivable				6		40 00
	E. S. Hyat.........	✓		18 00			
	A. F. Wright........	✓		22 00			
	(to correct overcharges)						

distribution base or *basis for distribution*. For example, the rent of a building may be distributed to the departments in it in proportion to the square feet of floor space occupied by each one. It could be distributed in ratio to the cubic space occupied or in ratio to the value of the space occupied (first-floor loca-

INCOME STATEMENT WITH DEPARTMENTAL GROSS MARGIN FIGURES

THE MODEL MODE SHOP
Income Statement

Month of July, 1966

	Total	Dresses	Lingerie	Shoes
Sales............................	$11 800 00	$ 5 400 00	$ 4 200 00	$ 2 200 00
Less returns and allowances.......	400 00	160 00	180 00	60 00
Net sales..................	$11 400 00	$ 5 240 00	$ 4 020 00	$ 2 140 00
Cost of goods sold:				
Merchandise July 1, 1966.......	$25 000 00	$11 000 00	$ 6 000 00	$ 8 000 00
Purchases....................	5 000 00	2 200 00	2 000 00	800 00
Freight in....................	400 00	200 00	100 00	100 00
Purchase returns and allowances..	(300 00)	(140 00)	(80 00)	(80 00)
Purchase discounts............	(80 00)	(60 00)	(20 00)	—
	$30 020 00	$13 200 00	$ 8 000 00	$ 8 820 00
Merchandise July 31, 1966......	23 000 00	9 010 00	6 800 00	7 190 00
Cost of goods sold...	$ 7 020 00	$ 4 190 00	$ 1 200 00	$ 1 630 00
Gross margin on sales...........	$ 4 380 00	$ 1 050 00	$ 2 820 00	$ 510 00
Selling expenses:				
Sales salaries.................	$ 2 000 00			
Sales supplies...............	60 00			
Depreciation of fixtures.........	48 00			
Rent........................	320 00			
Advertising....................	125 00			
Delivery service..............	90 00			
Delivery salaries.............	310 00			
Miscellaneous selling exp........	172 00			
Total selling expense..........	$ 3 125 00			
General expenses:				
Office salaries...............	400 00			
Office supplies...............	40 00			
Insurance....................	55 00			
Payroll taxes.................	165 00			
Miscellaneous general expense...	113 00			
Total general expense.........	$ 773 00			
Total operating expense......	$ 3 898 00			
Net operating income...........	$ 482 00			
Interest expense................	100 00			
Net income....................	$ 382 00			

tions are more valuable than second floor, for example). The fact that various distribution bases are possible shows why the amounts of indirect expenses cannot be readily and definitely assigned to a particular department. One should select the base that seems most realistic for the particular case.

SELLING AND SERVICE DEPARTMENTS

The departments that offer merchandise to customers in a store are *selling* departments. In any sizable establishment there are likely to be other departments, such as *service* departments. These departments are essential to the operation but they do not make sales. They have a facilitating function; they render a service to the selling departments. In a large organization there may be many service departments, such as credit office, personnel office, accounting department, maintenance department, and so on. The final objective of departmental accounting in the case of a store is to analyze revenues and expenses by selling departments and thus to see how much net operating income comes from each source. Another objective is to analyze the expenses by departments, selling as well as service, so that it can be seen how much it costs to do the different kinds of work and whether or not it is done efficiently. The latter objective is served by distributing expenses to departments. To achieve the first objective, the service department expenses (department totals) must be distributed among the selling departments they serve. This distribution is exactly like the distribution of indirect expenses to departments; each service department may be considered another kind of indirect expense to the selling departments. Thus there are two distributions: a *primary* distribution of expenses to departments and a *secondary* distribution of service department expense to selling departments. Such distribution is illustrated for The Model Mode Shop on page 521, which shows a work sheet for distribution of expenses to departments; it must be prepared before the income statement that shows income by departments can be made up.

BASES FOR DISTRIBUTION OF INDIRECT EXPENSES

All operating expenses are listed in the work sheet on page 521, although some of them require no special distribution base. These are the direct expenses. For example, the salaries represent workers assigned to a particular department; the supplies used are recorded on slips that show what department received them when they were issued. The bases listed in the illustration represent the best measures of the relationship between the amount of expense incurred and the requirements of activity of the departments that can be obtained in this case. Note that information on the activity of the departments must be accumulated in order to distribute the indirect expenses. Sometimes the measure of requirements or activity can be a relatively permanent one, such as square feet of floor space occupied. In other cases it must be recorded continuously; for example, the number of sales transactions, which is obtained from the number of sales slips used, less any slips canceled. Activity figures for the departments are not given in the illustration, but the figures on rent are given here to illustrate the computations made in preparing it. Rent was distributed as shown on page 520:

Department	Floor space (in sq. ft.)	Rate per Square Foot	Amount
General office.................	150	$0.20	$ 30.00
Delivery......................	100	0.20	20.00
Dresses.......................	600	0.20	120.00
Lingerie......................	400	0.20	80.00
Shoes........................	350	0.20	70.00
Totals....................	1,600		$320.00

The rate per square foot was calculated by dividing the total expense ($320) by the total square feet (1,600). Miscellaneous selling expense is distributed on the number of sales transactions as follows:

Department	Sales Transactions	Rate per Transaction	Amount of Misc. Sell. Exp.
Dresses.................	320	$0.172	$ 55.04
Lingerie................	480	0.172	82.56
Shoes..................	200	0.172	34.40
Totals.............	1,000		$172.00

The general office expense was distributed to the other departments on the basis of the number of employees in the other departments, because the general office work is believed to vary in volume and in cost with the number of persons who must be supervised. The delivery department expense is spread on the basis of the number of packages handled. The delivery department handles the packages at the store; actual delivery is done by a delivery service, whose charges appear under Delivery Service. In distributing the service department expenses it is customary to begin with the service department that gets the least service from other service departments and to distribute its expense to the others, and then to ignore any service they may return to it.

SALES REVENUE AS A BASIS FOR DISTRIBUTION OF EXPENSES

Expenses are sometimes distributed in ratio to sales revenue. The effect of this procedure is to show the same ratio of the particular expense to sales for each department as appears on the over-all income statement. Unless there is good reason to believe that a genuine cause-and-effect relationship exists between the number of sales *dollars* and the amount of the particular expense incurred (an unlikely situation), this procedure begs the question. It tells nothing about the relationship of what was earned separately in the various departments to the individual departmental cost of earning it. In selecting bases for distribution of expenses it is important to look for valid relationships between the activity of the department and the amount of expense involved.

DEPARTMENTAL INCOME STATEMENT

The illustration on page 522 presents the departmental income statement of The Model Mode Shop based on the expense distribution on page 521

WORK SHEET FOR DEPARTMENTAL EXPENSE DISTRIBUTION

THE MODEL MODE SHOP

Month of July, 1966

Kind of Expense	Basis for Distribution	Total Amount	Service Departments		Selling Departments		
			General Office	Delivery	Dresses	Lingerie	Shoes
Sales Salaries	Direct	2 000 00	—	—	990 00	670 00	340 00
Sales Supplies	Direct	60 00	—	—	12 00	10 00	8 00
Depreciation of Fixtures	Direct	48 00	8 00	4 00	15 00	10 00	11 00
Rent	Floor space	320 00	30 00	20 00	120 00	80 00	70 00
Advertising	Newspaper space	125 00	—	—	70 00	25 00	30 00
Delivery Service	No. of packages	90 00	—	—	30 00	40 00	20 00
Delivery Salaries	Direct	310 00	—	310 00	—	—	—
Miscellaneous Selling Expense	No. of sales transactions	172 00	—	—	55 04	82 56	34 40
Office Salaries	Direct	400 00	400 00	—	—	—	—
Office Supplies	Direct	40 00	40 00	—	—	—	—
Insurance	Value of merchandise	55 00	—	—	23 00	15 00	17 00
Payroll Taxes	Percent of payrolls	165 00	45 65	38 36	38 97	21 32	20 70
Miscellaneous General Expense	No. of sales transactions	113 00	—	—	36 16	54 24	22 60
Totals		3 898 00	523 65	402 36	1 390 17	1 008 12	573 70
Redistribution of Service Department Expenses:							
General Office	No. of employees		(523 65)	74 81	224 42	149 61	74 81
			0	477 17	1 614 59	1 157 73	648 51
Delivery Dept.	No. of packages			(477 17)	159 06	212 07	106 04
Totals		3 898 00		0	1 773 65	1 369 80	754 55

and the departmental gross margin figures on page 518. Note that the common segregation of expenses into selling and general without dividing any of them between the two categories involves some inaccuracies. For example, when rent as shown on page 521 is related to the use of the space, it is found

THE MODEL MODE SHOP
Departmental Income Statement
Month of July, 1966

	Selling Departments			
	Dresses	Lingerie	Shoes	Total
Sales..................	$ 5 400 00	$ 4 200 00	$ 2 200 00	$11 800 00
Less Returns and Allowances.....	160 00	180 00	60 00	400 00
Net Sales.............	$ 5 240 00	$ 4 020 00	$ 2 140 00	$11 400 00
Cost of goods sold:				
Merchandise July 1, 1966......	$11 000 00	$ 6 000 00	$ 8 000 00	$25 000 00
Purchases.................	2 200 00	2 000 00	800 00	5 000 00
Freight In.................	200 00	100 00	100 00	400 00
Purchase Returns and Allowances.................	(140 00)	(80 00)	(80 00)	(300 00)
Purchase Discounts..........	(60 00)	(20 00)	—	(80 00)
	$13 200 00	$ 8 000 00	$ 8 820 00	$30 020 00
Merchandise July 31, 1966....	9 010 00	6 800 00	7 190 00	23 000 00
Cost of Goods Sold......	$ 4 190 00	$ 1 200 00	$ 1 630 00	$ 7 020 00
Gross Margin on Sales..........	$ 1 050 00	$ 2 820 00	$ 510 00	$ 4 380 00
Selling Expenses:				
Sales Salaries..............	$ 990 00	$ 670 00	$ 340 00	$ 2 000 00
Sales Supplies..............	12 00	10 00	8 00	30 00
Depreciation of Fixtures.......	15 00	10 00	11 00	36 00
Rent......................	120 00	80 00	70 00	270 00
Advertising.................	70 00	25 00	30 00	125 00
Delivery Service.............	30 00	40 00	20 00	90 00
Delivery Department Expense..	159 06	212 07	106 04	477 17
Miscellaneous Selling Expense..	55 04	82 56	34 40	172 00
Total Selling Expense.....	$ 1 451 10	$ 1 129 63	$ 619 44	$ 3 200 17
General Expenses:				
Insurance...................	$ 23 00	$ 15 00	$ 17 00	$ 55 00
Payroll Taxes...............	38 97	21 32	20 70	80 99
Miscellaneous..............	36 16	54 24	22 60	113 00
General Office Expense.......	224 42	149 61	74 81	448 84
Total General Expenses...	$ 322 55	$ 240 17	$ 135 11	$ 697 83
Total Operating Expenses.	$ 1 773 65	$ 1 369 80	$ 754 55	$ 3 898 00
Net Operating Income (loss).....	$ (723 65)	$ 1 450 20	$ (244 55)	$ 482 00
Interest Expense..............				100 00
Net Income..................				$ 382 00

that some of the rent is chargeable to the general office, although it is predominantly a sales expense. Note also that distribution of some expenses to service departments and their redistribution gives a different classification of expenses in the total columns from that in pages 518 and 521. The amount shown as general office expense under general expense in the departmental income statement ($448.84) is the total general office expense ($523.65) less the part assigned to the delivery department ($74.81) and thereby shown as a selling expense.

DEPARTMENTAL EXPENSES IN THE LEDGER

In most cases, it is possible to make the kind of analysis of indirect expenses shown on pages 521 and 522 when the expenses are recorded, and to charge them to departmental accounts at once. This procedure is cumbersome and is usually not followed. Instead, the expenses are commonly accumulated in accounts by object of expenditure—accounts with the names shown on page 518—and analyzed on a work sheet at the end of the period (page 521). Accounts for sales, purchases, and so on, that determine gross margin are more commonly kept by departments. Departmental accounts for sales, purchases, and so on, and any departmental expense accounts may be closed to Profit and Loss at the end of the period in the usual way.

DEPARTMENTAL CONTRIBUTION

The question of whether to continue or drop a department depends on the *contribution* it makes to the firm. The term "contribution" refers, as in Chapter 5, to the margin of revenue over variable expenses. In other words, it is the amount available to cover fixed expenses and make a profit. It is the nature of the fixed expenses to go on for a considerable period regardless of the activity of the business. Dropping a department, therefore, does not dispose of the fixed expenses associated with it. These include any fixed elements distributed to the department as indirect expenses. Determination of the contribution requires classifying the expenses into two groups: *fixed* and *variable*. The classification requires scrutiny of each item and asking: how much of this would go on if we dropped that part of the business in question? That part is fixed for purposes of the decision being considered. For example, a company has two departments that have been doing badly. Their results are shown in the following tabulation.

	Department 1		Department 2	
Gross Margin on Sales.............		$8,000		$4,000
Expenses:				
Salaries......................	$3,000		$1,000	
Advertising...................	1,000		1,100	
Depreciation of Building..........	4,000		2,000	
Insurance on Building............	300		200	
Taxes on Building...............	400		250	
Miscellaneous—Variable..........	220		118	
Miscellaneous—Fixed............	317	9,237	296	4,964
Net Operating Loss..............		$1,237		$ 964

Analysis of the expenses discloses that $1,000 of the salaries charged to Department 1 and $500 of the salaries charged to Department 2 are general office salaries that would go on even if Departments 1 and 2 were dropped. Depreciation, insurance, and taxes on the building are also fixed. The contributions being made by Departments 1 and 2 are calculated as follows:

	Department 1		Department 2	
Gross Margin on Sales.............		$8,000		$4,000
Less Variable Expenses:				
Salaries......................	$2,000		$ 500	
Advertising....................	1,000		1,100	
Miscellaneous.................	220	3,220	118	1,718
Contribution to Fixed Costs..........		$4,780		$2,282

If these departments were dropped, the company would be worse off by $4,780 + $2,282 = $7,062 until it found some other use for the facilities represented by the fixed costs.

INTERNAL CONTROL OF DEPARTMENTAL OPERATIONS

Basic applications of internal control principles to departmental operations are briefly discussed under the following headings:

1. Cash control
2. Inventory control
3. Separation of accounting and operations

Cash control is easily established by separating the handling of cash and sales or other transactions. In a retail store this may be done by setting up separate wrapper-cashier cages to serve two or more departments. Since the sales people cannot make change, they cannot easily appropriate cash. Furthermore, the cashier checks the sales slip to see that it properly records the merchandise she wraps. In other kinds of business no cash will be handled in the operating departments; all cash will be received or disbursed in the general office. Sometimes there is a "city desk" that may handle cash sales; if so, it should be manned by a cashier separate from the cashiers who handle the merchandise.

Inventory control is best accomplished by maintenance of perpetual inventory records kept outside the operating departments that show how much stock should be on hand at any time. When a physical inventory is taken and compared with the record, any excessive discrepancy can be investigated. The retail inventory method is especially recommended for a departmentalized organization in the merchandising field, either wholesale or retail.

Separation of accounting and operations is important for obtaining an accurate and unbiased report of the activities of the departments. In a small or medium-sized organization such a report is accomplished well by use of a separate accounting staff. In very large ones an internal auditing staff is also likely to be needed, because in these concerns some accounting data must be prepared in the operating departments, which may be remote organizationally or even physically from the central accounting office. The method and adequacy of preparation of data in these circumstances should be verified periodically.

SUMMARY

Responsibility accounting compiles information according to areas of responsibility. It concentrates on controllable costs so that confusion about the results obtained by an officer may be avoided. To be effective, responsibility accounting must be based on clear organizational lines.

A department handles a distinct class of merchandise or performs a distinct service. Departmental accounting systems may stop with gross margin by departments, or they may include selling expenses or all expenses, or they may be designed to obtain departmental contributions to cover fixed expenses and profit. Separate accounts may be kept for each revenue and expense element by departments in the general ledger, or control and subsidiary accounts or general ledger accounts with departmental distribution columns may be used. Journals may provide specially for departmental accounts in column totals, by analysis of column totals, or by direct posting. Where subsidiary accounts are used, a pair of columns for entry to them are useful in the general journal.

Income statements showing departmental gross margin figures are easily prepared when accounts for departmental revenues, purchases, and related items are kept. Preparation of departmental income statements through net operating income requires distribution of expenses to departments. This requires a distinction between direct and indirect expenses and the selection of distribution bases for the indirect expenses. It also involves the distinction between service and selling departments and the redistribution of service department expenses to selling departments.

Internal control for departmentalized concerns uses separation of cashiering from other work, inventory control such as the retail inventory method, the separation of accounting from other work, and perhaps internal audit of the departments.

QUESTIONS

17.1 (1) Define "responsibility accounting."

(2) Under a system of responsibility accounting, how do the figures on a factory supervisor's report differ from those of a shop foreman?

(3) Explain, in general, how costs are compiled in the reports for successive levels of management.

(4) Explain how the departmental income statement of the Model Mode Shop on page 522 would differ under responsibility accounting.

17.2 (1) What two fundamental principles must be adhered to if a responsibility accounting system is to work effectively?

(2) In a recent annual letter to the stockholders, the president of one of America's most famous old-line retailing firms stated: "Following a careful

survey of your company's internal systems and financial controls, a firm of certified public accountants undertook the installation of a responsibility accounting system last fall. This system is now operative and provides management with monthly operating data which makes possible much closer control of both merchandising and expense budgets." Give concrete examples of the two fundamental principles referred to in part 1 for a firm of this kind.

17.3 (1) "All costs are controllable by a person or a group at some point in time." Distinguish noncontrollable from controllable costs.

(2) Are payroll taxes controllable or noncontrollable? How should they be included in the cost reports?

(3) Give the arguments in favor of including noncontrollable costs in the reports of executives below the top level.

(4) The Maintenance Department of the M Co. repairs equipment throughout the plant. How should this maintenance expense be reported under responsibility accounting?

17.4 (1) "Cost totals usually are difficult to interpret unless they can be related to some other significant information." Suggest three different kinds of information against which costs may be compared.

(2) Indicate quantitative criteria that might be used to measure performance in each of the following cases:

(a) Clean-up solvents in the Finishing Department of a textile mill.

(b) Payroll in the Accounts Receivable Office of a department store.

(c) Bar stock used in the machine shop of an electrical products company.

(d) Payroll for the Refuse Collection Department of a municipality.

(e) Payroll in the English Department of a public secondary school.

17.5 Suggest four different objectives that might be sought in departmentalizing the accounts of a firm. Which objective requires that fixed expenses be separated from variable expenses?

17.6 You find that the business of a furniture store comprises major appliances, furniture, floor coverings, drapes, and small appliances; however, no separation of sales or cost of sales is made in the accounts. Comment on the importance for internal control of classifying gross profit by departments.

17.7 The management of a store with twenty departments plans to set up a departmental accounting system but does not want to use twenty pages for each item of revenue and expense. Describe briefly two possible general ledger designs that can be used.

17.8 A departmental accounting system is proposed for a company, but the bookkeeper complains that the system will create too many columns in the journals. How should the bookkeeper be answered?

17.9 Distinguish between direct and indirect expenses.

17.10 Expense accounts in the ledger of Peabody and Fitch, Inc., include:

Newspaper Advertising	Personal Property Taxes
Rent	Employee Newspaper
Payroll Taxes	Transportation In

What bases might be used for distributing these charges to departments? Why?

17.11 What are the objections to sales revenue as a basis for distribution of expenses to selling departments?

17.12 In some companies the cost of a repair and maintenance department is allocated to selling departments proportionately to sales. In other companies it is charged on the basis of hours of maintenance work done for the department. Contrast these methods with respect to the message received by the departmental manager.

17.13 How does a departmental "contribution" differ from the net operating income of the department?

17.14 Indicate in each of the following cases whether the item is probably fixed or variable with reference to discontinuing a particular selling department:

Sales supplies	Business license
Sales salaries	Depreciation of decorations
Depreciation of fixtures	Advertising
Property taxes on building	Salaries of accountants

17.15 The departmental income statement of the K Co. shows the data below for Department X:

Gross Margin		$60,000
Expenses:		
Fixed	$35,000	
Variable	55,000	90,000
Net Loss		$30,000

(1) How would the net loss for the enterprise change if Department X is eliminated? Assume that discontinuance will eliminate the variable expense but will not affect the gross margin of the other departments.

(2) For internal purposes, K Co. computed cost of capital at 10 percent. What relevance, if any, is the fact that $100,000 of inventory in Department X would no longer be required after the department is discontinued?

17.16 Suggest internal control devices for a departmentalized organization with reference to (a) cash, (b) inventory, (c) general supervision.

EXERCISES

17.1 Following is a statement of departmental revenues and expenses of Fab Co. for the year ended December 31, 1966.

	Department A		Department B	
Gross Margin on Sales		$25,000		$50,000
Operating Expenses:				
Salaries – Officers	$10,000		$20,000	
Salaries – Employees	8,000		15,000	
Advertising	2,000		4,000	
Rent	3,000		3,000	
Insurance	1,000		2,000	
Miscellaneous	2,000	26,000	4,000	48,000
Net Income (Loss)		$(1,000)		$ 2,000

The question of eliminating Department A has arisen. For the purposes of this analysis it may be considered that officers' salaries, rent, and departmental miscellaneous expenses would not be reduced if a department were eliminated; all other expenses would be reduced by the amount allocated to the discontinued department.

Required:

Prepare a schedule showing the effect of the elimination of Department A on net income. What other factors are relevant to the decision to discontinue Department A?

17.2 Management reports of National Products, Inc., are prepared on a responsibility accounting basis. A section of the organization chart showing the lines of responsibility from the foremen through the vice president — manufacturing is shown below:

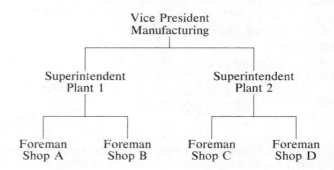

The ledger contains the following costs for January 1966:

	Shop A	Shop B	Shop C	Shop D
Controllable by foremen:				
Payroll	$20,000	$30,000	$15,000	$10,000
Other	12,000	20,000	8,000	6,000
Not controllable by foremen:				
Depreciation	10,000	15,000	12,000	8,000
Other	8,000	12,000	8,000	5,000

	Plant 1	Plant 2
Controllable by superintendents:		
Payroll	$ 3,000	$ 1,200
Other	2,000	500
Not controllable by superintendents:		
Depreciation	1,000	800
Other	500	400
Controllable by vice president — manufacturing:		
Payroll		2,400
Other		600
Not controllable by vice president — manufacturing:		
Depreciation		400
Other		200

Required:

Prepare cost reports for Shop A, Plant 1, and the Manufacturing Division clearly separating controllable from noncontrollable costs. Discuss briefly the types of figures against which the actual cost figures might be compared in reports prepared under responsibility accounting.

17.3 Consolidated Electronics Co. uses responsibility accounting. The budget of the Manufacturing Division for the month of August 1966 is shown below:

CONSOLIDATED ELECTRONICS CO.
BUDGET — MANUFACTURING DIVISION
August 1966

Controllable:
Office of Vice President, Manufacturing:

Salaries	$	14,400
Other		6,200
Aerospace Plant		948,600
Surface Equipment Plant		870,800
Industrial Controls Plant		567,200
Total Controllable		$2,407,200

Noncontrollable costs:

Depreciation	$	54,000
Insurance		7,200
Property Taxes		6,700
Total Noncontrollable	$	67,900
Total Costs		$2,475,100

Actual noncontrollable costs for August were recorded in the amounts budgeted, except for property taxes, which increased because of a reassessment of the company's properties. Actual property taxes for the Manufacturing Division in August were $300 over the budget.

Controllable costs by plants in August were as follows:

Aerospace	$949,000
Surface Equipment	879,000
Industrial Controls	570,300

A new electrostatic copier was added to the office of the vice president — manufacturing on August 1, 1966, at a monthly rental of $300. This machine enabled the divisional office to get along without hiring a replacement for one of the clerical workers, paid $400 a month, who resigned as of the same date. There were no other variations from the budget in the office of the vice president — manufacturing.

Required:

Prepare a cost report for August. Discuss briefly the reasons for including noncontrollable costs on that report.

17.4 The board of directors of the Audio Sales Co. are concerned over the poor showing of Department A during the past years. They are thinking of closing the department and leasing the space to a concessionaire. Income data for the year ended December 31, 1966, are presented below.

	Department A		*Department B*	
Gross margin on sales	$30,000		$70,000	
Operating expenses:				
Sales salaries	$20,000		$40,000	
TV advertising	1,500		3,500	
Rent	6,000		4,000	
Delivery expense	2,000		3,000	
Miscellaneous	1,000	30,500	1,000	51,500
Net operating income (loss)		$ (500)		$18,500

It is predicted that elimination of Department A will have the following effects:

(1) The space released will be occupied by a concessionaire, who will pay an annual rent of $3,600.
(2) Sales salaries and TV advertising chargeable to Department A will be eliminated.
(3) Twenty percent of the total delivery expense will be eliminated.
(4) Total miscellaneous expense will be reduced 10 percent.
(5) Additional customers brought in by the leased department who buy in Department B will offset customers lost from the discontinuance of Department A such that the change is not expected to affect the gross margin in Department B.

Should Department A be discontinued? Prepare a schedule to support your recommendations.

17.5 The Marina Shop has two selling departments and two service departments. Department 1 sells boating supplies; Department 2 sells clothing and accessories. The service departments consist of a General Office and a Receiving Department. Expenses for the month of May 1966 and the data for their distribution are presented below.

Expenses:

Salaries	$5,400
Advertising	250
Depreciation of fixtures	125
Rent	700
Payroll taxes and benefits	540
Miscellaneous	300
Total	$7,315

Bases for distribution:

Salaries — direct: General Office, $800; Receiving Department, $600; Department 1, $2,400; Department 2, $1,600.

Advertising — newspaper space: Department 1, 350 sq. in.; Department 2, 150 sq. in.

Depreciation of fixtures — direct: General Office, $10; Receiving Department, $15; Department 1, $80; Department 2, $20.

Rent — floor space: General Office, 600 sq. ft.; Receiving Department, 400 sq. ft.; Department 1, 3,000 sq. ft.; Department 2, 3,000 sq. ft.

Payroll taxes and benefits — payrolls.

Miscellaneous expense — number of employees: General Office, 2; Receiving Department, 1; Department 1, 3; Department 2, 6.

General Office — number of employees.

Receiving Department — receipts of merchandise: Department 1, 200; Department 2, 400.

Required:

Prepare a departmental expense distribution work sheet.

17.6 The Pacific Tire Company recaps tires for the trade. It has an annual plant capacity of 600,000 tires, but during recent years normal production has been running at only 400,000 tires. An offer has been received for sale of 100,000 additional tires at $3 each to a foreign customer. Annual fixed costs are $500,000, and variable costs are $2.50 a tire. The additional business will have no effect on the regular selling price of $5 a tire or on fixed costs.

Required:

Prepare a schedule showing whether or not the order from the foreign customer should be accepted, based solely on the estimates given. Discuss briefly other factors relative to the decision of whether or not to accept the foreign order.

17.7 Norsco, Inc., sells systems furniture imported from Norway partly to retailers and partly to wholesalers. The following data are available from the company's records for the year ended December 31, 1966:

	Wholesale	Retail
Sales......................	$2,000,000	$3,000,000
Cost of goods sold...............	1,600,000	1,800,000
Number of salesmen's calls	100	900
Number of invoice lines...........	600	3,000

Expense of sales solicitation distributable on the basis of the number of salesmen's calls was $330,000 for the period. Expense of inventory record keeping, order receiving and filling, billing, accounts receivable record keeping, and collecting was $273,000. These costs are distributable on the basis of the number of invoice lines. Advertising to the retail trade was $112,000 and to the wholesale trade, $56,000. Storage costs, incurred exclusively to service retailers, were $96,000.

Required:

1. What is the percentage of selling expenses to sales for each channel of trade? (Round percentages to nearest tenth of a percent.)
2. Assuming that the ratios would not change with increasing sales, in which channel should additional sales be promoted?

17.8 S Co. owns the patent rights on a certain type of radar unit. These units have been manufactured for S during 1966 by another company at $24 per unit. S Co. discovered that its patent rights had been infringed upon during 1966, and that the infringing company sold 20,000 units. You have been asked to assist S Co. in its lawsuit against the infringing company for loss of profits. The following data are available:

(1) S Co. sold 100,000 units in 1966 at $30 each.
(2) The selling expenses in 1966 were $2 per unit, and the general expenses were $1 per unit.
(3) S Co. had the capacity to sell up to 20 percent more units than had been sold. For each 4 percent increase in volume over the present level, total general expense would increase by 2 percent of the general expense for the entire output at the present level.
(4) Selling expenses vary directly with the number of units sold.
(5) S Co. would have to pay 50 cents per unit more on the entire number of radar units manufactured to obtain 120,000 units.

Required:

Prepare computations showing (1) net operating income resulting from the 100,000 units sold, (2) net operating income which would have resulted from sales including those sold by the company infringing on the patent, and (3) the profit lost by the patent infringement.

PROBLEMS

17.1 Following is a partial organization chart of Chemco, Inc.

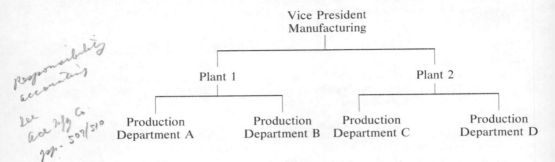

Controllable costs for the month of June 1966, classified by level of responsibility, are as follows:

	Superintendent Plant 1		Superintendent Plant 2	
Controllable at department level	Foreman Dept. A	Foreman Dept. B	Foreman Dept. C	Foreman Dept. D
Labor	$5,000	$10,000	$14,000	$3,000
Supplies	1,000	1,800	2,600	600
Power	800	1,500	2,000	500
Other	200	500	600	100

	Superintendent		
Controllable above department level	Plant 1	Plant 2	Manufacturing
Salaries	$1,200	$2,200	$3,000
Other	500	600	600

Certain other costs are noncontrollable by the individual responsibility units but are identifiable with them and are included on the departmental reports for the information of the respective supervisory personnel. These costs are as follows:

	Plant 1		Plant 2	
	Dept. A	Dept. B	Dept. C	Dept. D
Occupancy	$2,000	$2,800	$4,800	$1,200
Insurance	700	1,500	2,200	300
Other	300	800	1,000	100

Required:

1. Prepare a cost report for Production Department A following the procedures of responsibility accounting.
2. Prepare a cost report for Plant 1.
3. Prepare a cost report for the Manufacturing Division.
4. Comment briefly on the advisability of including noncontrollable costs in the report for Department A.

17.2 The departmental income statement of the Fairmont Shop for the month of July 1966 is presented below:

THE FAIRMONT SHOP
DEPARTMENTAL INCOME STATEMENT
Month of July 1966

| | Selling Departments | | | |
	Dresses	*Lingerie*	*Shoes*	*Total*
Sales	$5,400	$4,200	$8,200	$17,800
Cost of Sales	4,100	1,200	5,800	11,100
Gross Margin	$1,300	$3,000	$2,400	$ 6,700
Selling Expenses:				
Sales Salaries	$ 900	$1,680	$1,360	$ 3,940
Sales Supplies.	20	40	20	80
Depreciation of				
Fixtures	70	40	40	150
Rent.	100	60	40	200
Advertising.	200	100	100	400
Delivery Service.	150	300	160	610
Total Selling Expenses	$1,440	$2,220	$1,720	$ 5,380
General Expenses:				
Insurance	$ 70	$ 70	$ 60	$ 200
General Office	330	300	280	910
Total General Expenses . . .	$ 400	$ 370	$ 340	$ 1,110
Total Expenses.	$1,840	$2,590	$2,060	$ 6,490
Net Income (Loss).	$ (540)	$ 410	$ 340	$ 210

The company is organized with a buyer-manager responsible for each of the selling departments and an office-manager responsible for the general office. The board of directors is satisfied that the monthly income statements as currently prepared fairly state the results of operations for the company, but they are interested in simpler and more effective reports for internal control. In this regard, they are experimenting with reports to managers prepared in accordance with the principles of responsibility accounting. The budgeted profit contribution report which follows is an example:

THE FAIRMONT SHOP
SHOE DEPARTMENT
Budgeted Contribution—July 1966

Sales	$8,000
Cost of Sales	6,000
Gross Margin	$2,000
Controllable Expenses:	
Sales Salaries	$1,300
Sales Supplies	25
Advertising	75
Delivery Service	135
Total Controllable Expenses	$1,535
Contribution to Noncontrollable Expenses and Profits	$ 465

Required:

1. Prepare the July profit contribution report for the Shoe Department in accordance with the principles of responsibility accounting. Compare actual to budget.
2. What advantages does the responsibility accounting report offer to the manager of the Shoe Department in comparison with the old form of departmental income statement?
3. Management is concerned about the July loss on dresses, and asks whether they should close the department. Comment.

17.3 The departmental income statement of Parson's Pharmacy for the month of February 1966 is presented below.

PARSON'S PHARMACY
DEPARTMENTAL INCOME STATEMENT
Month of February 1966

	Drugs	*Fountain*	*Sundries*	*Total*
Sales	$30,000	$10,200	$59,800	$100,000
Cost of Sales	12,000	5,100	35,900	53,000
Gross Margin	$18,000	$ 5,100	$23,900	$ 47,000
Expenses:				
Advertising	$ 100	$ 200	$ 300	$ 600
Depreciation of Fixtures	600	400	1,000	2,000
Heat, Light, and Telephone	200	200	400	800
Insurance	50	50	100	200
Office	900	300	1,800	3,000
Payroll	2,000	1,000	1,500	4,500
Payroll Taxes	200	100	150	450
Rent	1,000	1,500	1,500	4,000
Repairs and Maintenance	300	200	500	1,000
Supplies	900	850	1,000	2,750
Taxes and Licenses	220	100	510	830
Total Expenses	$ 6,470	$ 4,900	$ 8,760	$ 20,130
Net Income	$11,530	$ 200	$15,140	$ 26,870

The management of Parson's Pharmacy is satisfied that the foregoing presents fairly the over-all results of operations, but feels that improvements are possible for reporting to department managers. To that end, they have reviewed the expenses and have classified them in terms of the responsibilities of the managers, with a further designation of each item as controllable or noncontrollable at the departmental level. A budget for February reflecting operations of the fountain on a responsibility accounting basis is presented below:

Sales	$10,000
Cost of Sales	5,000
Gross Margin	$ 5,000
Controllable Expenses:	
Payroll	$ 1,000
Payroll Taxes	100
Supplies	900
Repairs and Maintenance	175
Heat, Light, and Telephone	225
Total Controllable Expenses	$ 2,400
Noncontrollable Expenses:	
Advertising	$ 200
Depreciation of Fixtures	400
Insurance	50
Rent	1,500
Taxes and Licenses	100
Total Noncontrollable Expenses	$ 2,250
Total Expenses	$ 4,650
Departmental Profits	$ 350

Required:

1. Prepare a statement showing the February results of operations for the fountain. Use the same format as the budget, and show the amount by which each revenue and expense is over or under budget.
2. Why was office expense not included in the responsibility accounting report to the manager of the fountain?
3. Comment briefly on the pros and cons of including noncontrollable expenses in the departmental reports.
4. Why is advertising classified as noncontrollable and payroll taxes as controllable?
5. Discuss briefly the advantages that the company can expect from the responsibility accounting approach.

17.4 For some time, the R and S Sales Company has kept records to disclose the gross margin on sales by departments, but it has carried the departmental accounts no further. A dispute has arisen as to the net operating results of the two departments, and you are called in to calculate the net income by departments. Prepare a schedule showing the total and departmental details of net income for 1966, using the following information:

Gross margin in Department 1 was $49,000 and in Department 2, $60,000. Operating expenses and bases for their distribution were:

Expense		Basis for Distribution	Department		
				1	2
Salaries	$60,000	Direct	Salaries	$25,000	$35,000
Supplies	3,500	Direct	Supplies.....	2,600	900
Depreciation of buildings	4,000	Floor space	Floor space ..	2,000	3,000
Advertising	24,000	Square inches	Square inches.	14,000	10,000
Taxes on building ..	8,000	Floor space	See above		
Payroll taxes	4,800	Payrolls	See above		
Miscellaneous.....	3,600	No. of employees		4	5

17.5 The Seaward Company has two departments, M and N. Sales have not been satisfactory in N, and one of the owners thinks the firm would be better off if the operations in N were dropped and the space used for M. The additional space would not bring any additional sales in M. The other owner thinks that N should be retained. The owners present the following schedule for the year ended December 31, 1966:

	Department M		Department N	
Gross margin on sales............		$20,000		$10,000
Operating expenses:				
Salaries of salesmen	$9,000		$6,000	
Advertising..................	4,000		2,000	
Rent.......................	2,500		2,500–	
Miscellaneous	4,000	19,500	2,000	12,500
Net operating income (loss)........		$ 500		$ (2,500)

(handwritten margin note: Departmental Contribution p. 524)

Your inquiries reveal that rent is paid under a long-term lease that cannot be sold, and half the miscellaneous expenses charged to each department represent fixed expenses. What is your advice? Prepare a schedule to support your recommendation, if it would differ from the one given above.

17.6 The Jewelry Department of Gemco Stores, Inc., has been operating at a loss, as shown in the schedule below:

THE GEMCO STORES, INC.

SCHEDULE OF NET OPERATING INCOME

JEWELRY DEPARTMENT

Year Ended February 28, 1966

Gross Margin on Sales		$39,000
Operating Expenses:		
Salaries and Commissions	$24,500	
Advertising......................	4,000	
Store Supplies	3,000	
Depreciation	7,000	
Miscellaneous	1,000	39,500
Net Operating Loss		$ 500

It is proposed that the Jewelry Department be replaced by a Fur Department, which it is expected can realize $49,000 of gross margin a year if the following costs are incurred: $29,000 for sales salaries and commissions, $5,000 for store supplies, $8,000 for advertising, $7,000 for depreciation, and $1,000 for miscellaneous items. The miscellaneous items are all variable for the proposed department as well as for the present department.

Required:

1. Prepare a schedule showing the contribution to fixed costs and profit by the proposed and present departments.
2. Should the Jewelry Department be replaced by the Fur Department?

17.7 The Custom Appliance Co. has two selling and two service departments. Selling Department 1 sells major appliances and Department 2 sells small appliances. The service departments comprise a General Office and a Receiving Department. The expenses for October 1966 and the data on their distribution are presented below:

Kind of Expense		*Basis for Distribution*
Selling expenses:		
Salaries	$6,000	Direct
Advertising.	1,200	Square inches of newspaper space
Supplies	700	Direct
Depreciation of equipment	600	Direct
Miscellaneous selling expense	600	Number of sales transactions
General expense:		
Payroll taxes	480	Payrolls
Personal property taxes.	200	Value of equipment and merchandise
Insurance	100	Value of equipment and merchandise
Miscellaneous general expense . . .	120	Number of employees

Data for distribution of the expenses are summarized as follows:

	General Office	*Receiving Department*	*Department 1*	*Department 2*
Salaries—direct per payrolls. . .	$ 1,000	$ 500	$ 1,800	$ 2,700
Advertising—newspaper space (sq. in.)	–	–	14,000	10,000
Supplies—direct per asset record	$ 60	$ 40	$ 350	$ 250
Depreciation of equipment—direct per asset record	$ 154	$ 190	$ 110	$ 146
Miscellaneous selling expense—number of sales transactions .	–	–	3,000	5,000
Payroll taxes—payrolls (see salaries above)				
Personal property taxes—value of equipment and merchandise	$12,000	$12,000	$30,000	$46,000
Insurance—value of equipment and merchandise (see personal property taxes).				
Miscellaneous general expense—number of employees	2	1	3	6

The accounts provide the following data on sales and cost of sales:

	Department 1	Department 2
Sales	$130,500	$582,000
Sales Returns	4,200	3,800
Merchandise, October 1, 1966	42,200	60,100
Purchases	94,940	527,600
Freight In	11,800	41,000
Purchase Returns	2,100	3,400
Purchase Discount	840	1,200

Merchandise at October 30, 1966, was $41,800 in Department 1 and $62,400 in Department 2. There was interest income of $1,400 during the month. General Office expense is distributed to the other departments in ratio to the number of employees in these other departments (see "miscellaneous general expense" in the distribution data above). Receiving Department expense is distributed to the selling departments in ratio to the number of receipts of merchandise for each one; this was 200 for Department 1 and 400 for Department 2 during the month. Expense of the service departments is classified as general expense in the departmental income statement.

Required:

1. Prepare a work sheet distributing the expenses for the month to departments.
2. Prepare a departmental income statement for the month.

17.8 N Co., a wholesaler of small motors, is organized into two departments, electric motor sales and gasoline motor sales.

The bookkeeper prepared the following operating statement for the month of January 1966:

N CO.
OPERATING STATEMENT
FOR MONTH OF JANUARY 1966

	Gasoline Motors	Electric Motors
Sales	$60,000	$40,000
Cost of Goods Sold	35,000	31,000
Gross Margin	$25,000	$ 9,000
Warehousing Expenses	$ 4,000	$ 4,000
Selling Expenses	9,000	8,000
Financial and Administrative Expenses	2,250	2,250
	$15,250	$14,250
Net Profit (Loss)	$ 9,750	$ (5,250)

The general manager feels that this statement does not reflect the true profits of each of the departments and has asked you to redraft it, making whatever changes are necessary. You ascertain that:

(1) During the month 800 gasoline motors and 1,000 electric motors were sold.
(2) The total cost of goods sold for the month was apportioned arbitrarily by the bookkeeper between gasoline and electric motors.
(3) The purchase price to N Co. of gasoline motors is one and one-half times that of electric motors.
(4) Individual gasoline and electric motors are of roughly the same weight and bulk.
(5) The average inventory consists of 3/5 gasoline motors and 2/5 electric motors by quantity.

(6) The company carries twice as many varieties of gasoline motors as of electric motors.

(7) The company's building is used as follows:

	Area	Value
Warehouse	80%	60%
Administration	10%	20%
Gasoline motor sales office	5%	10%
Electric motor sales office	5%	10%

(8) The company's advertising budget is based on the dollar value of departmental sales.

(9) Warehousing expenses for January were made up of the following:

Wages	$2,500
Employee benefits	500
Depreciation of building	1,500
Depreciation of warehouse equipment	2,000
Light, heat, and power	400
Insurance and taxes on building	300
Repairs and maintenance to warehouse equip.	405
Miscellaneous warehouse expenses	200
	$8,000

(10) Selling expenses for January were made up of the following:

	Gasoline Motors	Electric Motors
Salary and wages	$4,500	$4,000
Employee benefits	900	800
Traveling expenses	2,300	1,900
Advertising	1,000	1,000
Catalogues	300	300
	$9,000	$8,000

Salaries and wages, employee benefits, and traveling expenses were charged to the two departments on the basis of actual cost, while advertising and catalogues were apportioned by the bookkeeper.

(11) Financial and administrative expenses for January were made up of the following:

General manager's salary	$ 900
General office salaries	2,600
Employee benefits	700
Interest	200
Miscellaneous office expenses	100
	$4,500

(These are to be distributed on the basis of dollar sales.)

Required:

1. Prepare a corrected departmental statement of income and expenses for January 1966.
2. If the corrected departmental statement of income and expenses were to show a profit on gasoline motor sales and a loss on electric motor sales, does it follow that the company would have had a greater net income had there been no electric motor sales during the month? Explain.

(ICAC – adapted)

Manufacturing Accounts

Merchandising operations involve the following steps:

1. Acquisition of assets and services, including purchase of merchandise
2. Sale of merchandise for cash or on credit, and use of other assets and services in selling and administration
3. Collection of accounts receivable

The cycle is repeated continually as cash is collected from customers.

When manufacturing is carried on, another step is added to the cycle. It then takes this form:

1. Acquisition of goods and services
2. Conversion of some of the goods and services into new merchandise
3. Sale of the merchandise for cash or on credit, and use of other assets and services in selling and administration
4. Collection of accounts receivable

Additional accounts are needed to record the activity in the new step — the manufacturing activity. These accounts describe the creation of the new merchandise, called *finished goods*. This chapter describes and illustrates the accounting required to record manufacturing activity when periodic inventories are used.

NATURE OF PRODUCTION COST ACCOUNTS

The accounts that describe the various elements of cost in the manufacturing or production process are called *production cost accounts*. They describe what is being invested in the product. They are summarized at the end of a period and the total cost of product made is determined. They may have names like those of the expense accounts with which the reader is already familiar. For example, Factory Supplies Used is a production cost account, since factory supplies are consumed in making a product. Technically, such accounts represent assets — investments that have future usefulness. They never appear on a balance sheet, however, because they are summarized at the end of each period. Their asset character is in contrast to such an account as Office Supplies Used or Office Supplies Expense, which has no identifiable future usefulness. It is helpful to maintain the distinction between these two types of accounts; accordingly, production cost accounts are referred to in this text as cost or manufacturing accounts, and accounts representing current charges to revenue are referred to as *expense* accounts.

ELEMENTS OF PRODUCTION COSTS

Production costs are divided into three categories:

1. Direct materials
2. Direct labor
3. Factory overhead

The classification of cost elements given above involves the distinction between *direct* and *indirect* costs. The terms are used in this case with reference to the product being made. *Direct materials* are materials that are incorporated into the product physically. Their cost per unit of product can readily and definitely be established. They are often called *raw materials*, but since many finished and semifinished products are used as materials for still other products, the term "raw materials" is often inappropriate. In rare cases the category includes materials that are readily identifiable with the product as to amount used but which do not become a physical part of it.

Direct labor is labor performed in physical contact with the product. This means that the cost of direct labor per unit of product is easily and definitely identifiable also.

Factory overhead includes all the *indirect* costs of production. *Factory overhead* is also called *manufacturing expenses, burden, production overhead*, and so on. The amount of these costs assignable to a particular unit of product is not so clear as are the amounts of the direct costs. For example, each unit of product represents the using up of some part of the building in which the product is made, but the amount of building depreciation that should be charged to each unit of product is not certain. This uncertainty is due to the uncertain life of the building, to the uncertain total of products to be made during that life, and to the fact that a variety of products is usually worked on. A reasonable tracing of the amount may nevertheless be made on the basis of the use made of the facilities by the product.

MANUFACTURING ACCOUNTS USED

The type of manufacturing accounting that we are presently concerned with requires accounts to develop the cost of direct materials used, the cost of direct labor used, and the amount of factory overhead incurred during a period.

The cost of direct materials used is obtained in this system by keeping one account for *Materials Purchases* and another for *Materials* (inventory). At the end of the period the beginning inventory of materials plus purchases of them less ending inventory gives the amount used. Any accounts for *Materials Purchase Returns, Freight In on Materials* or *Materials Purchase Discounts* that are needed are also used. This method of determining direct materials used is exactly the same as the method of determining cost of goods sold in a merchandising concern. As in the case of a merchandising inventory, the amount of inventory is recorded at the end of each period by adjusting entry after a physical count of the stock.

The *Direct Labor* account is debited when payrolls are paid or are recorded as accruals. Provision should be made on the payroll sheet to classify the factory labor as direct or indirect. If workers always do one kind of work, the classification may be made by listing their names in separate groups; if they shift about during the period, separate columns may be set up for direct and indirect labor.

Factory overhead is recorded in a number of accounts showing each kind of cost included (or it may be recorded in a control account). The charges are made as bills are recorded or paid and as adjusting entries are made at the end of the period. The entries arise and are made in the journals in the same way that selling or general expense entries are handled. Some of the accounts commonly found in the factory overhead group are:

1. Indirect labor (foremen, stock clerks, custodians, other indirect labor)
2. Factory supplies used (indirect material)
3. Depreciation of factory building and equipment
4. Amortization of patents
5. Insurance (on factory building, equipment, and materials)
6. Property taxes (on factory building, equipment, and materials)
7. Payroll taxes (on factory payrolls—direct and indirect labor)
8. Maintenance and repairs (on factory)
9. Heat, light, and power (used in factory)
10. Water (used in factory)

MANUFACTURING INVENTORIES

Instead of the single account for merchandise used in a purely trading concern, the manufacturer has three accounts. These are:

1. Materials
2. Work in Process
3. Finished Goods

When the manufacturing accounts are based on periodic inventories, a count of each kind of stock must be made at the end of a period. Prices must be determined and the totals computed. The new figures are then entered by adjusting entries, as in the case of periodic merchandise inventories. All three kinds of inventory are current assets.

PLACE OF MANUFACTURING ACCOUNTS IN THE INCOME STATEMENT

Where a merchandising concern has "purchases" (of merchandise) in its income statement, a manufacturing concern has "cost of goods manufactured." So much information is included in cost of goods manufactured that it is not, as a rule, presented in detail in the income statement. Instead, it appears in a separate statement. Observe the summary figure for cost of goods manufactured in the income statement of Hall Manufacturing Company for 1966, on page 544.

STATEMENT OF COST OF GOODS MANUFACTURED

The illustration given below presents the statement of cost of goods manufactured of Hall Manufacturing Company for 1966. Note the computation of

HALL MANUFACTURING COMPANY
Statement of Cost of Goods Manufactured
Year Ended December 31, 1966

Direct Materials:		
Materials on Hand January 1, 1966...............	$ 7,400.00	
Materials Purchases............................	32,800.00	
	$40,200.00	
Materials on Hand December 31, 1966............	6,200.00	$ 34,000.00
Direct Labor......................................		31,000.00
Factory Overhead Cost:		
Indirect Labor.................................	$ 8,000.00	
Factory Supplies Used..........................	1,200.00	
Depreciation of Machinery and Equipment..........	14,500.00	
Depreciation of Building........................	2,200.00	
Patent Amortization............................	2,000.00	
Insurance.....................................	600.00	
Property Taxes................................	2,300.00	
Payroll Taxes.................................	1,950.00	
Miscellaneous Factory Overhead..................	2,950.00	35,700.00
Cost to Manufacture...............................		$100,700.00
Add—Work in Process January 1, 1966............		8,000.00
		$108,700.00
Deduct—Work in Process December 31, 1966.......		12,000.00
Cost of Goods Manufactured......................		$ 96,700.00

direct materials used in the statement. Note also the distinction between the amount of cost put into the manufacturing activity—cost to manufacture—and the cost of product turned out—cost of goods manufactured. The difference is the change in inventory of work in process during the year.

MANUFACTURING WORK SHEET

The manufacturing work sheet begins with a trial balance, adds any needed adjustments, and classifies the figures in columns for the statement of cost of goods manufactured, income statement, and balance sheet. It is illustrated on page 550 with data of Hall Manufacturing Company. This company records some accruals currently, but other accruals along with depreciation entries must be made by adjusting entries at the end of the year. Information on the adjustments follows:

(a) Wages are accrued at December 31, 1966, in the amount of $1,000 for direct labor and $200 for indirect labor.
(b) Payroll taxes on the accrued wages amount to a total of 5 percent.
(c) Depreciation of office furniture and fixtures is at 5 percent of cost with no scrap value expected.
(d) Depreciation of machinery and equipment is based on a life of fifteen years without scrap value.
(e) Depreciation of building is based on a life of fifty years and no salvage value.
(f) The patent had nine years of its useful life to run after January 1, 1966.
(g) Factory insurance in the amount of $600 has expired but has not been recorded at December 31, 1966.
(h) The materials inventory at December 31, 1966, is $6,200. (Note that the credit is a credit to Cost of Goods Manufactured. Note also that on the line for Materials the trial balance figure goes over as a debit to Cost of Goods Manufactured and that the debit for the new inventory in the Adjustment column goes to the Balance Sheet column.)
(i) The work in process inventory at December 31, 1966, is $12,000. (This is also a credit to Cost of Goods Manufactured; the beginning balance is a debit to that account.)
(j) The finished goods inventory at December 31, 1966, is $75,000. (This is a credit to Profit and Loss, and the beginning balance is debited there.)
(k) Income tax is calculated at 22 percent of the first $25,000 and 48 percent of the remainder of the pretax income.

HALL MANUFACTURING COMPANY
Income Statement
Year Ended December 31, 1966

Sales..			$200,000.00
Cost of Goods Sold:			
Finished Goods January 1, 1966..................		$ 72,000.00	
Cost of Goods Manufactured (page 543)..........		96,700.00	
		$168,700.00	
Finished Goods December 31, 1966..............		75,000.00	93,700.00
Gross Margin on Sales.....................................			$106,300.00
Operating Expenses:			
Selling Expenses:			
Sales Salaries..................	$14,000.00		
Advertising....................	12,000.00		
Miscellaneous Selling Expense.....	4,700.00	$ 30,700.00	
General Expenses:			
Office Salaries................	$12,000.00		
Depreciation of Furniture and Fixtures	2,100.00		
Miscellaneous General Expense....	11,500.00	25,600.00	56,300.00
Net Operating Income.....................................			$ 50,000.00
Income Taxes...			17,500.00
Net Income...			$ 32,500.00

This company rents quarters for its sales and general office, so all costs of the building are factory costs. Extension of the adjusted balances to their proper columns, together with the transfer of the net cost of goods manufactured to the Income Statement columns and the net income after provision for income tax to the Balance Sheet columns, completes the work sheet. The statement of cost of goods manufactured and sold made up from the work sheet (page 550) appears on page 543. The income statement appears on page 544.

ADJUSTING AND CLOSING ENTRIES FROM THE WORK SHEET

The data shown in the work sheet (page 550) give rise to the following adjusting and closing entries:

Adjusting entries:

(a)	Direct Labor.............................$	1,000.00	
	Indirect Labor..........................	200.00	
	Wages Payable..................		$ 1,200.00
(b)	Factory Payroll Taxes...................$	60.00	
	Payroll and Property Taxes Payable.		$ 60.00
(c)	Depreciation of Office Furniture and Fixtures..$	2,100.00	
	Accumulated Depreciation — Office Furniture and Fixtures		$ 2,100.00
(d)	Depreciation of Machinery and Equipment....$	14,500.00	
	Accumulated Depreciation — Machinery and Equipment		$ 14,500.00
(e)	Depreciation of Building.................$	2,200.00	
	Accumulated Depreciation—Building.		$ 2,200.00
(f)	Amortization of Patent...................$	2,000.00	
	Patent.........................		$ 2,000.00
(g)	Factory Insurance......................$	600.00	
	Prepaid Insurance..............		$ 600.00
(h)	Materials............................$	6,200.00	
	Cost of Goods Manufactured......		$ 6,200.00
(i)	Work in Process........................$	12,000.00	
	Cost of Goods Manufactured......		$ 12,000.00
(j)	Finished Goods.........................$	75,000.00	
	Profit and Loss.................		$ 75,000.00
(k)	Federal Income Tax.....................$	17,500.00	
	Income Tax Payable............		$ 17,500.00

Closing entries:

(a)　Cost of Goods Manufactured............$114,900.00

	Materials......................	$ 7,400.00
	Work in Process.................	8,000.00
	Purchases of Materials............	32,800.00
	Direct Labor.....................	31,000.00
	Indirect Labor...................	8,000.00
	Factory Supplies Used............	1,200.00
	Property Taxes..................	2,300.00
	Factory Payroll Taxes............	1,950.00
	Miscellaneous Factory Overhead...	2,950.00
	Depreciation of Machinery and Equipment.....................	14,500.00
	Depreciation of Building..........	2,200.00
	Amortization of Patent...........	2,000.00
	Factory Insurance................	600.00

(b)　Profit and Loss........................$ 96,700.00

　　　　　Cost of Goods Manufactured......　　$ 96,700.00

(c)　Sales................................$200,000.00

　　　　　Profit and Loss.................　　$200,000.00

(d)　Profit and Loss........................$145,800.00

	Finished Goods...................	$ 72,000.00
	Sales Salaries...................	14,000.00
	Advertising.....................	12,000.00
	Miscellaneous Selling Expense......	4,700.00
	Office Salaries..................	12,000.00
	Miscellaneous General Expense....	11,500.00
	Depreciation of Office Furniture and Fixtures......................	2,100.00
	Federal Income Tax..............	17,500.00

(e)　Profit and Loss........................$ 32,500.00

　　　　　Retained Earnings...............　　$ 32,500.00

BALANCE SHEET

The balance sheet of Hall Manufacturing Company, showing the inventories of materials, work in process, and finished goods as current assets is presented on page 547.

PRICING OF MANUFACTURING INVENTORIES

The pricing of materials presents no problems not previously met in merchandising inventories. Cost is the usual basis and this includes the supplier's invoice price, less any discount, plus freight in.

HALL MANUFACTURING COMPANY
Balance Sheet
December 31, 1966

Assets

Current Assets:

Cash	$ 9,100.00	
Accounts Receivable	18,400.00	
Materials	6,200.00	
Work in Process	12,000.00	
Finished Goods	75,000.00	
Prepaid Insurance	3,000.00	$123,700.00

Fixed Assets:

Office Furniture and Fixtures	$ 42,000.00		
Less Accumulated Depreciation	14,700.00	$ 27,300.00	
Machinery and Equipment	$217,500.00		
Less Accumulated Depreciation	87,000.00	130,500.00	
Building	$110,000.00		
Less Accumulated Depreciation	24,200.00	85,800.00	243,600.00
Patent			16,000.00
Total Assets			$383,300.00

Liabilities and Capital

Current Liabilities:

Notes Payable		$ 10,000.00	
Accounts Payable		12,000.00	
Payroll and Property Taxes Payable		2,022.50	
Wages Payable		1,200.00	
Income Tax Payable		17,500.00	$ 42,722.50

Capital:

Capital Stock: authorized and outstanding, 2,500 shares of $100.00 par value			$250,000.00
Retained Earnings:			
Balance 1–1–66		$ 74,077.50	
Add Net Income		32,500.00	
		$106,577.50	
Less Dividends		16,000.00	90,577.50
			340,577.50
Total Liabilities and Capital			$383,300.00

Work in process and finished goods are priced with a cost per unit obtained from information about the manufacturing process and the costs of carrying it on. The problem is approached by considering separately each of the three major elements of cost. Materials per unit of product can often be measured accurately, allowance being made for necessary waste in cutting, pouring, machining, and so on. One can also keep a record of the total quantity of material used over a period and of the quantity of product turned out, and divide to get a quantity of material per unit of product. Direct labor cost can be calculated by keeping a time record of the work as it is done, and dividing the labor time by the number of product units turned out. Considerable care is necessary for accurate results in this procedure, because a worker may speed up or slow down (consciously or unconsciously) when he is being observed; allowance must be made for rest periods, normal delays, and so on. Unless the time study is made by an expert, it is probably better to keep actual records of the time and production of a number of workers over a considerable period of regular production to get labor costs per unit of product.

Factory overhead cost per unit cannot be arrived at so directly. The simplest method is to find the relationship between total factory overhead cost and some common measure of the product turned out. The direct labor cost of the product is usually a good measure of amount of product for this purpose; more direct labor time means more use of factory facilities, and more overhead cost is accordingly applied to that product. For the Hall Manufacturing Company this relationship—called the "factory overhead rate"—for 1966 was:

$$\frac{\text{total factory overhead}}{\text{direct labor}} = \frac{\$35,700}{\$31,000} = 115.2\%$$

The inventory price of product A is calculated in this case as follows:

Product A:		
Materials: 1 lb. of X at $1.60 . . . . = $1.60		
3 lb. of Y at $0.80 . . . . = 2.40		
Packaging material 15	$ 4.15	
Direct Labor:		
2 hours of machining at $3.40 . . . . = $6.80		
½ hour of assembly at $2.80 . . . . = 1.40	8.20	
Factory Overhead:		
$8.20 × 115.2%	9.45	
Total	$21.80	

For work in process, the materials may not be complete and not all the labor will be performed. For a unit of product A that is through the machining but not assembled, the price would be made up as follows:

Product A in Process (through Machining):	
Materials—per above, less packaging	$ 4.00
Direct labor—per above, machining only	6.80
Factory overhead = $6.80 × 115.2%	7.83
Total	$18.63

SIMPLE MANUFACTURING ACCOUNTS AS A MANAGERIAL DEVICE

The accounting described in the foregoing pages serves the accounting needs by providing some information for the calculation of inventories of manufactured product. This information permits net income to be calculated, because it indicates how much of the costs incurred should be carried as assets on the balance sheet and how much should be an expense for cost of goods sold and thus deducted in the income statement. The method also provides summary figures of the various kinds of cost incurred. Management may compare these period by period to observe changes that require action; for example, an increasing materials cost may result in redesigning the product to use plastic for some of the metal. Budgets may be made on an over-all basis and compared with actual costs incurred.

The system is not sufficiently refined for complicated manufacturing situations. For example, if each job is different from all others, as jobs are in most shipyards, the accounts discussed here will not tell how much each job costs. Furthermore, the costs as here described are obtained only at the end of an accounting period, and this is often rather late to take effective managerial action on them. The more elaborate methods required to overcome these weaknesses are the subject matter of the next two chapters.

SUMMARY

Manufacturing operations add a new step to the operating cycle observable in merchandising concerns. This step is the production of finished goods, or merchandise. The accounts required when periodic inventories are used are inventory accounts for the balance sheet and cost accounts describing the manufacturing operations. The inventory accounts are Materials, Work in Process, and Finished Goods. Accounts with Purchases of Materials and such accounts as Freight In on Materials and Discount on Materials permit the computing of the cost of materials used. Other cost accounts are Direct Labor (used) and various accounts with the several elements of factory overhead cost.

The amount of direct material and direct labor can be readily and definitely identified with the physical units of product produced. Factory overhead costs are indirect costs; their amount cannot be readily and definitely identified with physical units of product.

Manufacturing accounts take the place of merchandise purchases in the income statement, but are not usually shown in detail in that statement. The total cost of goods manufactured appears in the income statement and its details are given in a separate statement.

The cost information may be assembled at the end of a period in a manufacturing work sheet, which has a pair of columns for cost of goods manufactured.

Pricing of the periodic inventories of work in process and finished goods requires an analysis of the cost elements entering into each product. This method of accounting for manufacturing operations is not adequate in complicated industries, and has the disadvantage of producing the cost data rather late, but it serves in the less complicated cases.

HALL MANUFACTURING COMPANY
Manufacturing Work Sheet
Year Ended December 31, 1966

	Trial Balance		Adjustments		Cost of Goods Manufactured		Income Statement		Balance Sheet	
	Debit	Credit	Debit	Credit	Debit	Credit	Debit	Credit	Debit	Credit
Cash	9 100 00								9 100 00	
Accounts Receivable	18 400 00								18 400 00	
Materials	7 400 00		(h) 6 200 00		7 400 00				6 200 00	
Work in Process	8 000 00		(i) 12 000 00		8 000 00				12 000 00	
Finished Goods	72 000 00		(j) 75 000 00				72 000 00		75 000 00	
Prepaid Insurance	3 600 00			(g) 600 00					3 000 00	
Office Furniture and Fixtures	42 000 00								42 000 00	
Accumulated Depreciation—Office Furniture and Fixtures		12 600 00		(c) 2 100 00						14 700 00
Machinery and Equipment	217 500 00								217 500 00	
Accumulated Depreciation—Machinery and Equipment		72 500 00		(d) 14 500 00						87 000 00
Building	110 000 00								110 000 00	
Accumulated Depreciation—Building		22 000 00		(e) 2 200 00						24 200 00
Patent	18 000 00			(f) 2 000 00					16 000 00	
Notes Payable		10 000 00								10 000 00
Accounts Payable		12 000 00								12 000 00
Payroll and Property Taxes Payable		1 962 50		(b) 60 00						2 022 50
Capital Stock		250 000 00								250 000 00
Retained Earnings		58 077 50								58 077 50
Sales		200 000 00						200 000 00		
Purchases of Materials	32 800 00				32 800 00					
Direct Labor	30 000 00		(a) 1 000 00		31 000 00					
Indirect Labor	7 800 00		(a) 200 00		8 000 00					
Factory Supplies Used	1 200 00				1 200 00					
Property Taxes	2 300 00				2 300 00					
Factory Payroll Taxes	1 890 00		(b) 60 00		1 950 00					
Miscellaneous Factory Overhead	2 950 00				2 950 00					
Sales Salaries	14 000 00						14 000 00			

Advertising	12 000 00							12 000 00
Miscellaneous Selling Expense	4 700 00							4 700 00
Office Salaries	12 000 00							12 000 00
Miscellaneous General Expense	11 500 00							11 500 00
	639 140 00	639 140 00						
Wages Payable					(a) 1 200 00			1 200 00
Depreciation of Office Furniture and Fixtures		(c) 2 100 00					2 100 00	
Depreciation of Machinery and Equipment		(d) 14 500 00	14 500 00					
Depreciation of Building		(e) 2 200 00	2 200 00					
Amortization of Patent		(f) 2 000 00	2 000 00					
Factory Insurance		(g) 600 00	600 00					
Cost of Goods Manufactured		(h) 6 200 00	6 200 00		6 200 00			
Cost of Goods Manufactured		(i) 12 000 00	12 000 00		12 000 00			
Profit and Loss		(j) 75 000 00	75 000 00			75 000 00		
		115 860 00	115 860 00		18 200 00			
Cost of Goods Manufactured				114 900 00	96 700 00		96 700 00	
				114 900 00	114 900 00		225 000 00	275 000 00
Income Tax							17 500 00	17 500 00
Net Income							32 500 00	32 500 00
							275 000 00	509 200 00

QUESTIONS

18.1 What will be the effect, if any, on the various assets and proprietorship balances at the end of the period if a manufacturing overhead cost is erroneously classified as an expense?

18.2 What are the steps in the manufacturing cycle?

18.3 A company was organized on July 1, 1966, and produced a new product for three months. No effort was made to sell the product during that time because it was necessary to build up an inventory before taking orders. Were the amounts spent to operate the factory assets or expense at September 30, 1966? In either case, what kind?

18.4 What are three basic categories of production costs?

18.5 Identify each of the following either as a production cost or as an expense:

(1) Factory supplies used
(2) Sales salaries
(3) Depreciation of welding equipment
(4) Direct materials
(5) Advertising

(6) Depreciation of office equipment
(7) Indirect labor
(8) Amortization of patent
(9) Postage and stationery

18.6 (1) Where do manufacturing costs appear in the income statement?
(2) If a separate statement is prepared for such costs, what is it called?

18.7 What is the effect on cost of goods manufactured when an ending inventory of work in process is larger than the beginning inventory — is the cost larger or smaller than otherwise? What is the effect when a beginning inventory of materials is larger than the ending inventory?

18.8 State whether or not each of the following errors will throw a manufacturing work sheet out of balance:

(1) The trial balance figure for materials is carried to the debit side of the Income Statement columns.
(2) Ending inventory of work in process is too large by $1,000 because of an error in addition on the inventory sheets.
(3) Factory Supplies Used is carried to the credit side of Cost of Goods Manufactured columns.
(4) Net Cost of Goods Manufactured is transferred to the Income Statement columns by an entry debiting Cost of Goods Manufactured and crediting Profit and Loss.
(5) Office Salaries is carried to the debit side of the Cost of Goods Manufactured column.

18.9 (1) Suggest managerial uses for the cost data described in this chapter.
(2) Under what circumstances is this kind of cost data inadequate?

18.10 Differentiate between "cost to manufacture" and "cost of goods manufactured." Make up a concrete example illustrating the difference.

18.11 During July, the Alma Co. purchased materials costing $30,000. It paid $40,000 for direct labor and incurred $30,000 of manufacturing overhead cost. Periodic inventories taken at the beginning and end of the month showed that materials on hand decreased $5,000, work in process increased $4,000, and finished goods decreased $3,000. What was the cost of goods manufactured and the cost of goods sold for July?

18.12 Explain how rent and other occupancy costs of a building might be handled on the work sheet of a manufacturing company if 10 percent of the building is used for administrative and sales offices and the rest is used for production.

18.1 The following account balances appear in the ledger of the Cross Manufacturing Company on December 31, 1966, the end of its fiscal year:

Accounts Payable	$ 10,500
Accounts Receivable	9,200
Accumulated Depreciation — Factory and Equipment	14,000
Advertising	12,000
Depreciation of Factory and Equipment	8,000
Direct Labor	16,000
Factory Supplies Used	1,000
Finished Goods, January 1, 1966	10,500
Indirect Labor	4,000
Insurance — Factory	1,200
Materials on Hand, January 1, 1966	3,700
Materials Purchases	16,300
Office Salaries	14,000
Payroll Taxes — Factory	1,600
Sales	125,700
Sales Salaries	18,300
Wages Payable	2,400
Work in Process January 1, 1966	4,200

Periodic inventories taken on December 31, 1966, indicate:

Materials on hand	$ 6,000
Work in process	5,000
Finished goods	7,000

Required:

Prepare a statement of cost of goods manufactured.

18.2 The trial balance of the Art Manufacturing Company at December 31, 1966, appears below.

Cash	$ 29,200	
Accounts Receivable	17,500	
Materials	6,200	
Work in Process	7,800	
Finished Goods	62,000	
Prepaid Insurance	4,800	
Office Furniture and Fixtures	36,000	
Accumulated Depreciation of Furniture and Fixtures		$ 14,800
Machinery and Equipment	185,200	
Accumulated Depreciation of Machinery and Equipment		62,700
Accounts Payable		15,500
Payroll Taxes Payable		2,400
Capital Stock		100,000
Retained Earnings		35,000
Sales		225,400
Purchases of Materials	32,600	
Direct Labor	31,400	
Factory Overhead	28,600	
Operating Expenses	14,500	
	$455,800	$455,800

The company uses control accounts for factory overhead and operating expenses. Adjustment data for the year ended December 31, 1966, are as follows:

(1) Wages are accrued at December 31, 1966, in the amount of $1,200 for direct labor and $800 for indirect labor.
(2) Payroll taxes on the accrued wages amount to a total of 8 percent.
(3) Depreciation of office furniture and fixtures is at 5 percent of cost.
(4) Depreciation of machinery and equipment is based on a life of ten years and a residual value of 10 percent of cost.
(5) Insurance of $1,200 has expired, of which 20 percent is an operating expense and 80 percent is a factory overhead cost.
(6) The materials inventory at December 31, 1966, is $8,400.
(7) The work in process inventory at December 31, 1966, is $15,000.
(8) The finished goods inventory at December 31, 1966, is $60,000.

Required:

Submit in journal form the entries that would appear on the December 31 year-end work sheet.

18.3 Prepare a statement of cost of goods manufactured for the Art Manufacturing Company of exercise 2.

18.4 Prepare an income statement for the Art Manufacturing Company of exercise 2.

18.5 The trial balance of the Baker Manufacturing Company at December 31, 1966, is as follows:

Materials, January 1	$ 6,000	
Finished Goods, January 1	40,000	
Plant and Equipment	100,000	
Accumulated Depreciation		$ 20,000
Prepaid Insurance	3,000	
Other Net Assets	145,000	
Capital Stock		100,000
Retained Earnings		130,000
Sales		150,000
Purchases of Materials	32,000	
Direct Labor	30,000	
Indirect Labor	8,000	
Payroll Taxes	500	
Office and Sales Salaries	35,500	
	$400,000	$400,000

The company records some accruals and adjustments of deferred charges currently, but other adjustments are made at the end of the year. Information for adjustments at December 31, 1966, follows:

(1) The materials inventory at December 31, 1966, is $8,000.
(2) The finished goods inventory at December 31, 1966, is $25,000.
(3) Depreciation of plant and equipment is $10,000.
(4) Insurance expired is $1,000.

Payroll taxes, depreciation, and insurance are to be allocated 20 percent to manufacturing and 80 percent to operating expenses. Income taxes are 25 percent of pretax income.

Required:

Prepare a work sheet.

18.6 The items described below were in the inventory of the Nunes Manufacturing Company on September 30, 1966. Calculate the cost to be used for each in the inventory at that date. Factory overhead is calculated for each item by applying the over-all ratio of factory overhead to direct labor cost.

The following expense and cost account balances appeared in the September 30 adjusted trial balances:

Direct Labor	$60,000
Direct Materials Used	90,000
Factory Supplies Used	10,000
Indirect Labor	20,000
Miscellaneous Factory Overhead	5,000
Miscellaneous General and Selling Expenses	2,000
Office Salaries	4,000
Office Rent	6,000
Taxes on Factory Property and Payrolls	1,000

The inventory items are described as follows:

Item	Materials	Labor
Finished Goods:		
A	X – 50 yd. at $2/yd. Y – 40 ft. at $0.50/ft.	1. Cutting: 6 hr. at $5/hr. 2. Sewing: 4 hr. at $4/hr. 3. Finishing: 2 hr. at $6/hr.
Work in Process:		
A-1	Materials X only	Cutting labor only
A-2	Materials X and Y only	Cutting and sewing labor only

Required:

Calculate the cost of each item of finished goods and work in process.

18.7 Indicate whether each of the following should be charged to (a) a cost account, (b) an expense account, or (c) some other account.

(1) Wages of machinists
(2) Salary of factory superintendent
(3) Salary of president
(4) Welding flux used during period
(5) Office stationery and supplies used
(6) Cartons used to ship products to customer
(7) Salary paid to night watchman at the plant
(8) Payroll taxes on night watchman's salary
(9) Freight charges on materials received and used
(10) Freight charges on materials shipped
(11) Wages paid a machinist to build a conveyer system in the plant
(12) Wages paid to factory workers for painting the sales office
(13) Depreciation on office equipment
(14) Depreciation on factory machinery and buildings
(15) Depreciation on equipment used in fabricating the conveyor system (see 11)

18.8 From the data for Dwan & Co. given below, prepare a statement of cost of goods manufactured and sold for the year ended December 31, 1966, showing the computation of materials purchased.

Cost of goods sold for the period was $214,000. Detailed cost records show that direct charges incurred in 1966 were:

Materials Used $68,000
Direct Labor. 60,000

Inventory balances at the beginning and end of the year were:

	January 1	December 31
Materials	$20,000	$14,000
Work in Process	12,000	16,000

There were no inventories of finished goods.

18.9 The following cost report was prepared for the foreman of Shop 105 of the Eastern Electric Company:

	This Month	Increase (Decrease) Over Last Month Amount	Percent
Controllable:			
Wages and salaries	$30,312	$ 3,485	11.5%
Rework.	5,483	6,338	115.6
Factory supplies	2,697	(1,402)	(5.2)
Employee benefits	3,114	339	10.9
Power.	19,421	19	0.1
Maintenance	3,946	(38)	(0.1)
Other controllable costs.	4,472	47	1.0
Total controllable.	$69,445	$ 8,788	12.4%
Noncontrollable:			
Depreciation	$20,789		
Taxes	3,732		
Head office	1,041		
Other	375		
Total noncontrollable	$25,937		
Total	$95,382		

Required:

1. Suggest possible explanations for the change in wages and salaries.
2. Suggest possible explanations for the change in rework.
3. What is your general opinion of the form of this report?
4. As the foreman of Shop 105, can you think of any other costs or information that would help you in controlling operations?

18.10 An examination of the accounting records of the Norman Metal Products Co. on December 31, 1966, discloses that the company never recorded depreciation for the three years it has been in business. It acquired $60,000 of machinery January 1, 1964, all of which was still in use December 31, 1966, except for one unit. This unit, costing $20,000, was sold July 1, 1965, for $10,000. The entire

proceeds were credited to Machinery. On the same date another unit was purchased for $40,000. All equipment had an estimated useful life of ten years.

The direct labor for the year ended December 31, 1966, amounted to $40,000,
and factory overhead cost before depreciation amounted to $20,000. There was
no inventory of work in process at the beginning or the end of the year. The
finished goods inventory at December 31, 1966, recorded by the company,
which was correct except for the omission of depreciation, amounted to $23,000,
consisting of materials, $8,000; labor, $10,000; and overhead, $5,000. There
were no finished goods on hand at January 1, 1966.

Required:

1. Show how retained earnings at December 31, 1966, and net income for the
   year then ended will be affected by the recognition of depreciation. Ignore
   income taxes.
2. Present journal entries to correct the accounts, assuming the books had not
   been closed for 1966.

PROBLEMS

18.1 The following data of Tropwood Manufacturing Company represent its manufacturing costs for the calendar year 1966. Prepare a statement of cost of goods
manufactured.

Inventory of materials at January 1, 1966, $32,000; materials purchases,
$120,000; freight in, $10,000; discount on materials purchased, $2,400; inven-
tory of materials at December 31, 1966, $29,600. Direct labor for the year
totaled $170,000.

Other costs were: indirect labor, $36,000; factory supplies used, $9,000;
depreciation of building, $24,000; depreciation of machinery, $32,000; heat,
light, and power, $8,000; maintenance and repairs, $18,200; taxes on property   ✴ 153,000
and payrolls, $16,300; miscellaneous factory costs, $9,500. Work in process at
January 1, 1966, was $42,000 and at December 31 was $35,000.

18.2 Using the data of Tropwood Manufacturing Company, in problem 1, prepare the
entries to adjust inventories and to close the accounts in so far as the data
permit.

18.3 The products described below were in the inventory of Tropwood Manufacturing Company on December 31, 1966. Calculate the cost price to be used for
each one. Factory overhead for each product is computed by applying the over-
all percent of factory overhead to direct labor cost. This percent may be obtained from the data in problem 2. The products are described as follows:

Product	Materials	Labor
Finished Goods:		
S	1. 30 ft. at $0.50/ft.	1. Molding: 2 hr. at $4.00/hr.
	2. 10 lb. at $0.80/lb.	2. Finishing: 3 hr. at $3.00/hr.
T	1. 10 sq. ft. at $1.00/sq. ft.	1. Shaping: 3 hr. at $4.00/hr.
	2. 8 lb. at $0.75/lb.	2. Plating: 2 hr. at $3.50/hr.
		3. Finishing: 1 hr. at $3.00/hr.
Work in Process:		
S	All materials	Molding labor only
T-1	Material 1 only	Shaping labor only
T-2	All materials	Shaping and plating labor only

18.4. Eastman Manufacturing Company, Inc., presents the trial balance shown below at the end of its fiscal year, August 31, 1966.

EASTMAN MANUFACTURING COMPANY, INC.
TRIAL BALANCE
August 31, 1966

Cash	$ 13,100	
Accounts Receivable	14,000	
Allowance for Doubtful Accounts		$ 1,800
Materials	10,200	
Work in Process	12,300	
Finished Goods	104,000	
Building	80,000	
Accumulated Depreciation — Building		20,000
Equipment	153,000	
Accumulated Depreciation — Equipment		52,500
Patent	24,000	
Notes Payable		8,000
Vouchers Payable		11,000
Taxes Payable		2,200
Capital Stock		150,000
Retained Earnings		53,900
Sales		210,000
Purchases of Materials	22,000	
Direct Labor	23,000	
Indirect Labor	5,400	
Factory Supplies Used	900	
Taxes on Factory Property and Payrolls	4,100	
Miscellaneous Factory Overhead	2,400	
Sales Salaries	11,000	
Advertising	9,200	
Miscellaneous Selling Expense	3,800	
Office Salaries	7,400	
Stationery and Postage	1,400	
Miscellaneous General Expense	8,200	
	$509,400	$509,400

Adjustments are required for the following items:

(1) The allowance for doubtful accounts is to be increased to $2,500.

(2) The life of the building is expected to be forty years with no salvage value. The building contains the factory, sales office, and general office. Sales and general office each occupy 5 percent of the space (debit their shares to Miscellaneous Selling Expense and to Miscellaneous General Expense).

(3) The life of the equipment is expected to be fifteen years with no salvage. All equipment is used in the factory.

(4) The patent is being amortized at $4,000 per year; no amortization has been recorded in the year to date.

(5) Materials inventory at August 31, 1966, was $17,300.

(6) Work in process inventory at August 31, 1966, was $9,000.

(7) Finished goods inventory at August 31, 1966, was $55,900.

(8) Income taxes are to be estimated at 50 percent of net income before taxes.

Required:

A manufacturing work sheet for the year ended August 31, 1966.

18.5 The Uniflow Manufacturing Company produces a single product at a cost of $12 per unit, which is paid at the time of production. It costs $6 to sell the product, which is paid for at date of sale. The sales price is $25 per unit; all sales are on credit.

The following results of operations are expected during the first two years:

	Units Produced	Sold	Dollars Collected from Customers
First Year	100,000	70,000	$1,500,000
Second Year	80,000	90,000	1,875,000

The management of the company understands that revenue might be recognized on several bases, and asks you to explain the effect of these alternatives.

Required:

1. Suppose revenue is recognized at the time of production. (a) State the effect on the various assets and proprietorship of producing one unit, selling one unit, and collecting $25. (b) What will the net income be for the first and the second years?

2. Suppose revenue is recognized at the time of sale. (a) State the effect on the various assets and proprietorship of producing one unit, selling one unit, and collecting $25. (b) What will the net income be for the first and the second years?

3. Suppose revenue is recognized at the time cash is collected from the customer. (a) State the effect on the various assets and proprietorship of producing one unit, selling one unit, and collecting $25. (b) What will the net income be for the first and the second years?

18.6 The Blue Lakes Creamery accounts for production in terms of pounds of butterfat. On July 1, 10,000 pounds of finished goods were on hand at a cost of $4,000.

During July direct materials with a cost of $90,000 were purchased and used. Direct labor cost for the month was $10,000, and manufacturing overhead was $5,000. Selling and administrative expenses were $30,000. All the costs and expenses were paid in July.

Production for the period was 300,000 pounds. There were no direct materials or work in process inventories at either the beginning or the end of the period. Sales of 290,000 pounds of product were made at $1 per pound; all sales were for cash.

The company accounts for its raw materials and finished goods by periodic inventories on a fifo basis, using the production cost for the month to price ending inventories. The company is not subject to income taxes.

Required:

1. Prepare journal entries to record the above items, including adjusting and closing entries.

2. Prepare an income statement for July, supported by a statement of cost of goods manufactured.

Cost accounting is the process of ascertaining and interpreting the cost of manufacturing a product, of rendering a service, or of performing any function or operation in an enterprise. Cost accounting systems are basically of two types: job order cost accounting and process cost accounting. The two systems represent different methods of assembling the data and are designed for different circumstances. The present chapter describes job order costs; process and standard costs are the subject of succeeding chapters.

Cost accounting may be looked upon as an extension of general or financial accounting. Ordinary accounts are kept in any case by a manufacturing concern; these show the costs incurred on an over-all basis. Cost accounting takes these and related data and makes a more detailed record from which the unit costs of different products and the costs of operating individual departments or processes can be more accurately obtained.

THE JOB ORDER METHOD

Job order costs are also called *production order, specific order*, or *job lot* costs. Job order costs are used when production is done on distinct jobs or lots of product; frequently several different lots will be going through a single plant at the same time. The job order method is used in shipbuilding, furniture manufacture, building construction, and in many other industries. A complete cost accounting system of any type operates on the perpetual inventory principle: a continuous record is provided in the accounts of Materials, Work in Process, and Finished Goods. The flow of costs in the general ledger accounts of a job order system is shown in the diagram given here. Note that the information about *costs incurred* is collected in three accounts: Materials, Factory Payroll, and Factory Overhead Cost. The Materials account is a perpetual inventory account. Payrolls paid are charged to Factory Payroll, and the other costs are charged to Factory Overhead Cost. The *usage* of the costs is recognized in the Work in Process account. As materials are issued for use on jobs — *direct* materials — they are credited to Materials and debited to Work in Process. The arrow running from Materials to Factory Overhead Cost indicates that some materials are used as supplies; these are *indirect materials*. The arrow from Factory Labor to Factory Overhead Cost indicates that part of the labor is also an indirect cost; only the direct labor goes directly to Work in Process. As jobs are finished, their cost is transferred from Work in Process to Finished Goods; when they are sold, it goes to Cost of Goods Sold.

560

GENERAL LEDGER ACCOUNTS FOR JOB ORDER COST ACCOUNTING

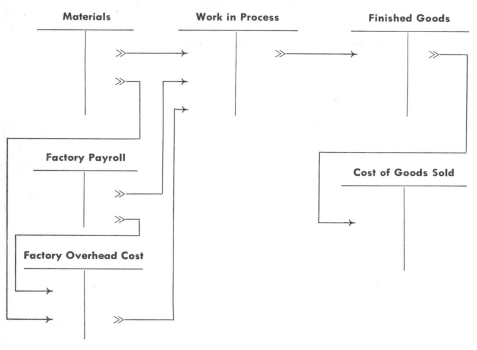

THE JOB COST SHEET

The cost of each job is assembled on a job cost sheet. Separate sections receive postings of materials, labor, and factory overhead cost. The postings are made from journals or directly from original records. Other information, such as the number of pieces ordered and the number produced, the name of the customer in the case of a special order, and unit cost of the work, are commonly included. The cost sheet is a subsidiary account supporting the Work in Process account in the general ledger. It may therefore be called a "job account." If the records are completely posted, a schedule of the balances can be taken from the job cost sheets and the total checked with the Work in Process control account balance. When the job is finished, the cost sheet is removed from the file and, with other sheets for finished jobs, summarized for the general journal entry crediting Work in Process and debiting Finished Goods. The sheets representing finished work are placed in a transfer file; they are an invaluable reference when bids on similar jobs are required or when management needs to know the cost of a product for some decision. A job cost sheet is shown on page 563.

MATERIALS

The Materials account in the general ledger is supported by a subsidiary stores ledger. This ledger contains an account for each item of materials handled. The stores ledger accounts record quantities and cost of units received, issued, and on hand. The stores ledger account for part No. 1812 is shown here.

Stores Ledger Account

Item: Part No. 1812									No.	41	
Date	Receipts				Issues				Balance		
	Ref.	Units	Price	Amount	Ref.	Units	Price	Amount	Units	Price	Amount
1966 7–1									400	2.00	800 00
10	V 11	100	2.00	200 00					500		1 000 00
15					R 88	55	2.00	110 00	445		890 00

Note the entry recording the issue of 55 units on July 15, 1966. These units were for job No. 422 and appear on its job cost sheet shown on page 563. The reference is R (requisition) 88. Requisitions are original records presented to the storekeeper as his authority to issue materials. Copies should be provided for the department requisitioning the materials, for the storekeeper, and for the accounting department. At the end of a period — desirably not over a month — the requisitions are summarized on an analysis sheet and the totals obtained for debiting Work in Process and Factory Overhead Cost and crediting Materials control account. The entry is made in the general ledger. The illustration on page 565 shows a stores requisition of the sort that can be purchased as a standard form from commercial stationers.

The basic general ledger entries associated with materials are:

```
Materials.......................................$xx,xxx.xx
         Vouchers Payable.......................             $xx,xxx.xx
(made in voucher register or equivalent journal to re-
cord purchases; details debited in stores-ledger sub-
sidiary accounts).
Work in Process...............................$ x,xxx.xx
Factory Overhead Cost.........................  x,xxx.xx
         Materials.............................             $ x,xxx.xx
(made in general journal from periodic summaries of
stores requisitions; details of the debit to Work in Proc-
ess entered on job cost sheet; details of credit to mate-
rials are credited in stores-ledger subsidiary accounts).
```

Job Cost Sheet
(Job Account)

For Stock _____   Date: Job No. 422
For customer: _____   Opened   7–15–66
_____   Closed   7–31–66   Article   Z-16
_____   Quantity   700   700
                                    Ordered   Completed

Material			Labor			Summary			
Date	Ref.	Amount	Date	Ref.	Amount				
1966			1966			Material..............		190	00
7–15	R 88	110 00	7–16	PA 27	48 00	Labor................		648	00
26	R 102	80 00	23	PA 28	286 00	Overhead............		583	20
			30	PA 29	314 00	Total..............	1	421	20
						Cost per unit.........		$2.0303	
						Memo			
			Total		648 00				
			Factory Overhead						
			Date	Ref.	Amount				
			1966						
			7–31	J 22	583 20				
Total		190 00	Total		583 20				

LABOR COST

In a manufacturing concern as well as in others, it is necessary to prepare payroll records to facilitate payment of wages and to comply with government requirements for records and tax returns. To get cost information it is also necessary to know how the time of each employee was spent. In a job order system the time spent on each job by each worker doing direct labor is required. This information may be compiled on a job timecard or on a time report. At the end of the month, or oftener if desired, these time records must be analyzed to get the labor cost for each job. The analysis may be made on a form

Week ended: 7–16–66		Payroll Analysis Sheet				No. 27
			Direct Labor			Debit Factory Over-head Cost
Employee or Card No.	Total Earnings	Debit Labor in Process	Job Accounts			
			420	421	422	
1842	80 00	80 00	32 00	32 00	16 00	
1848	80 00	80 00	32 00	32 00	16 00	
1861	80 00	80 00	32 00	32 00	16 00	
1875	75 00	75 00	30 00	45 00		
1880	75 00	75 00	30 00	45 00		
1892	90 00	90 00	40 00	50 00		
1900	72 00					72 00
1905	78 00					78 00
	630 00	480 00	196 00	236 00	48 00	150 00

like the one illustrated here. The data on the payroll analysis in this form give rise to the following general journal entry:

Work in Process	$480.00	
Factory Overhead Cost	150.00	
Factory Payroll		$630.00

(to record distribution of factory payroll for the week per payroll analysis sheet No. 27)

Note that the column totals for jobs are posted from the payroll analysis sheet to the job cost sheets. This process is illustrated by job 422; the labor charge of $48 may be seen in the job cost sheet on page 563 under date of July 16, 1966, and with the posting reference to PA (payroll analysis) No. 27.

Payment of the payroll results in a debit to Factory Payroll that offsets the credits week by week. However, payrolls made weekly do not coincide with the end of most months. To obtain a complete record to the end of the month a payroll analysis sheet is made up for the last few days even though the week is not over. Entering these figures in the accounts leaves a credit in the Factory Payroll account. This is the accrued payroll at the end of the month and is shown in the balance sheet as Wages Payable. At the end of the week another analysis sheet is made for the first few days of the new month. Payment of the payroll for the week that overlapped the two months automatically wipes out the credit balance. Payrolls and payroll analyses are now often prepared on electronic computers.

FACTORY OVERHEAD COST

As was noted in Chapter 18 on the manufacturing work sheet, some relationship between the product and the amount of factory overhead cost incurred must be found. Direct labor hours and direct labor cost are popular and defensible measures of product for this purpose. If wage rates do not vary much in the company, and especially if they do not vary much between people doing the same kind of work, the direct labor cost figure is preferred, owing to its ready availability (it must be obtained anyway). If wage rates differ considerably, as when apprentices and journeymen both turn out product, the different labor cost on different lots or jobs will not properly reflect usage of the plant. In this case direct labor hours may be used instead, but the hours will have to be accumulated for this purpose on the payroll analysis or elsewhere. In practice a variety of measures of product have been used, including materials cost and the total of materials and direct labor cost. Direct labor cost alone is definitely the most popular.

To obtain the rate for applying overhead to product, the *expected* factory overhead cost should be divided by the *expected* total of direct labor cost for the year. These figures are best developed in a carefully constructed budget. A concern that has a very steady volume of operations may be able to use the rate experienced in the preceding year, but this often proves quite inaccurate.

Factory overhead cost is computed on the job cost sheet at the end of each month. If a job is finished during the month, the overhead is computed then. At the end of the month all the overhead so applied is listed and totaled and a general journal entry made to record the applied overhead. The entry takes this form:

Work in Process............................$x,xxx.xx
        Factory Overhead Cost................... $x,xxx.xx
    (to record factory overhead applied for the month)

FACTORY OVERHEAD VARIANCE

The credits to Factory Overhead Cost for overhead applied to product are based on the estimate of the overhead to be incurred and the amount of

STOREROOM REQUISITION		Req. No. _9710_			
Storekeeper: Please furnish bearer with the following.		Date _Aug. 17_ 19_66_			
Charge Acct. No. ___ Dept. _Machine Shop_		Dept. No. _6_			
QUANTITY	ARTICLES	STOCK NO.	PRICE	AMOUNT	
30	A 780 Clips	1410	0.30	9	00
CHARGE JOB NO. _870_	ENTERED ON STOCK LEDGER Z.B.	ENTERED ON RECAP. Z.B.	Signed _Dudley Malone_		

work to be done for the year. At the end of a month there may be a balance in the Factory Overhead Cost account for either or both of two reasons. First, production may fluctuate seasonally, so that much overhead is applied in a month of high production and little in a slack month. The overhead cost is likely to be incurred more evenly over the year (some of it is depreciation, property taxes, salaries, and insurance that are recorded uniformly over the months). Production fluctuations tend to cause a credit balance in the account after a month of high production and a debit balance after a month of low production. Second, the estimates of cost to be incurred and product to be produced are not likely to be exactly right. This error may result in a balance in either direction. Whatever the source, the balance is called *factory overhead variance*, or it may be called *underabsorbed overhead* (debit balance) or *overabsorbed overhead* (credit balance). Within the year it may be carried as a balance sheet item at the end of any month; it will be shown as a deferred debit or credit. At the end of the year it is written off. Ordinarily all of it is debited or credited to Cost of Goods Sold, although, strictly speaking, some of it may really belong to the inventories of work in process and finished goods.

FINISHED GOODS

When a job is finished, it can be credited to Work in Process and debited to Finished Goods. The amount of the entry appears on the completed job cost sheet. Although an entry may be made whenever a job is finished, the entry for all jobs finished during a month is commonly made at the end of the month. If $142,000 of jobs are completed in a month, the entry is:

Finished Goods	$142,000.00	
Work in Process		$142,000.00

The Finished Goods account is supported by a finished goods ledger. This is exactly like a stores ledger (which supports the Materials account), but records finished products. The details of the amount debited to Finished Goods are debited to the individual stores accounts. The finished goods ledger may be posted directly from the completed job cost sheets.

When the goods are shipped to a customer, Finished Goods is credited and Cost of Goods Sold is debited. Details of the entry are posted as credits to the accounts in the finished goods ledger. This posting may be done from the office copies of the shipping orders or from the office copies of the invoices, but in either case the cost of the product shipped must be noted on the document. The general journal entry to record shipment of $161,000 of product is:

Cost of Goods Sold	$161,000.00	
Finished Goods		$161,000.00

ILLUSTRATION OF JOB ORDER COST ACCOUNTING

A more complete and unified, but condensed, illustration of job order accounting is given in the following paragraphs. The trial balance of Conroy Company on June 1, 1966, was as follows:

CONROY COMPANY
Trial Balance

June 1, 1966

Account	Debit	Credit
Cash...	22 000 00	
Accounts Receivable......................................	40 000 00	
Materials...	54 000 00	
Work in Process..	8 000 00	
Finished Goods...	47 000 00	
Prepaid Insurance..	2 900 00	
Building and Machinery...................................	417 000 00	
Accumulated Depreciation—Building and Machinery..............		162 000 00
Notes Payable..		30 000 00
Vouchers Payable...		28 000 00
Factory Payroll Accrued..................................		1 000 00
Capital Stock..		300 000 00
Retained Earnings..		69 900 00
	590 900 00	590 900 00

Materials consisted of the following:

Material O...	$20,000.00
Material N...	16,000.00
Material P...	18,000.00
	$54,000.00

Work in process consisted of one job with the following costs:

Direct materials..	$ 4,000.00
Direct labor...	2,000.00
Factory overhead cost..................................	2,000.00
Total in process, Job 81...............................	$ 8,000.00

Finished goods consisted of the following items:

Product H..	$14,000.00
Product J..	8,500.00
Product K..	24,500.00
Total...	$47,000.00

Transactions for June 1966 are given below. One total is given for each type of transaction. The transactions are posted to cost accounts, both general ledger and subsidiary, as shown in the illustration on pages 572-573. The other general ledger accounts appear in the illustration on pages 574 and 575.

1. Materials were purchased on credit for $46,000; of this, $14,000 was material O, $18,000 was N, and $14,000 was P.
2. Payrolls are vouchered in the following amount: factory, $70,000; selling expense, $10,000; and general expense, $12,000 (withholdings are ignored here).
3. Payrolls are paid in the amounts vouchered.
4. Expenses and costs incurred on credit are recorded as follows: factory overhead, $60,000; selling expense, $18,000; and general expense, $16,000.
5. Additional insurance is purchased on credit, $800.
6. Materials were used as follows: direct materials, $62,000; indirect materials, $2,000. The direct materials were used on these jobs:

> Job 81 $22,000.00
> Job 82   26,000.00
> Job 83   14,000.00

Materials used were:

Material N $24,000.00
Material O 18,000.00
Material P 22,000.00

7. Sales for the month total $312,000; all are on credit.
8. Cash is collected from customers in the amount of $288,000.
9. Vouchers are paid in the amount of $130,000.
10. Expired insurance in the amount of $300 and depreciation in the amount of $21,000 are recorded. The distribution is: factory overhead, $20,600; selling expense, $400; general expense, $300.
11. Factory wages earned during the month, including those not yet due to be paid, amount to $71,000. Of this, $68,000 is direct labor and $3,000 is indirect labor. The direct labor is distributed to jobs as follows:

> Job 81 $26,000.00
> Job 82   24,000.00
> Job 83   18,000.00

12. Factory overhead is applied to jobs at the rate of 125 percent of direct labor cost, as follows:

> Job 81 $32,500.00
> Job 82   30,000.00
> Job 83   22,500.00
> $85,000.00

13. Jobs 81 and 82 are finished and their cost is transferred to the Finished Goods account. Job 83 is still in process. The following cost totals appear on the job cost sheets:

> Job 81 $ 88,500.00
> Job 82   80,000.00
> $168,500.00

Job 81 is product H and Job 82 is product J.

14. Goods are sold during the month as follows:

Product H. . . . .$ 92,000.00
Product J. 84,000.00
Product K. 14,000.00
                                                                                            $190,000.00

Entries to record the transactions follow. All are given in general journal form, but the actual journal that would be used in practice is noted when it is different from the general journal.

1.	Materials. . . . .$ 46,000.00	
	Vouchers Payable.	$ 46,000.00

(entry in voucher register; details are:

	Material O	$14,000.00
	Material N	18,000.00
	Material P	14,000.00
		$46,000.00)

2.	Factory Payroll. . . . .$ 70,000.00	
	Selling Expense. 10,000.00	
	General Expense. 12,000.00	
	Vouchers Payable.	$ 92,000.00

(entry in voucher register)

3.	Vouchers Payable. . . . .$ 92,000.00	
	Cash.	$ 92,000.00

(entry in check register)

4.	Factory Overhead Cost. . . . .$ 60,000.00	
	Selling Expense. 18,000.00	
	General Expense. 16,000.00	
	Vouchers Payable.	$ 94,000.00

(entry in voucher register)

5.	Prepaid Insurance. . . . .$ 800.00	
	Vouchers Payable.	$ 800.00

(entry in voucher register)

6.	Work in Process. . . . .$ 62,000.00	
	Factory Overhead Cost. 2,000.00	
	Materials.	$ 64,000.00

(details of the entry are:

Work in Process		**Materials**	
Job 81	$22,000.00	O $18,000.00	
Job 82	26,000.00	N 24,000.00	
Job 83	14,000.00	P 22,000.00	
	$62,000.00	$64,000.00)	

7.   Accounts Receivable.........................$312,000.00

            Sales............................. $312,000.00

         (entry in sales book)

8.   Cash......................................$288,000.00

            Accounts Receivable................ $288,000.00

         (entry in cash-receipts book)

9.   Vouchers Payable.........................$130,000.00

            Cash.............................. $130,000.00

         (entry in check register)

10.   Factory Overhead Cost.....................$ 20,600.00

       Selling Expense...........................   400.00

       General Expense..........................   300.00

            Prepaid Insurance.................... $ 300.00

            Accumulated Depreciation—Building and

            Machinery.......................   21,000.00

11.   Work in Process..........................$ 68,000.00

       Factory Overhead Cost.....................   3,000.00

            Factory Payroll.................... $ 71,000.00

         (details of the debit to Work in Process are: Job 81,

         $26,000.00; Job 82, $24,000.00; Job 83, $18,000.00)

12.   Work in Process..........................$ 85,000.00

            Factory Overhead Cost.............. $ 85,000.00

         (details of the debit to Work in Process are: Job 81,

         $32,500.00; Job 82, $30,000.00; Job 83, $22,500.00).

13.   Finished Goods...........................$168,500.00

            Work in Process.................... $168,500.00

         (details of the entry are as follows:

Finished Goods		*Work in Process*	
Product H	$ 88,500.00	Job 81	$ 88,500.00
Product J	80,000.00	Job 82	80,000.00
	$168,500.00		$168,500.00)

14.   Cost of Goods Sold.......................$190,000.00

            Finished Goods..................... $190,000.00

         (goods sold were as follows:

H	$ 92,000.00
J	84,000.00
K	14,000.00
	$190,000.00)

The foregoing entries may be seen in the accounts in the illustrations on page 572 (cost accounts) and pages 574 and 575 (general accounts).

Entries to close the revenue and expense accounts are as follows (income tax is ignored in this illustration):

15.   Sales......................................$312,000.00
         Profit and Loss....................... $312,000.00

16.   Profit and Loss...........................$246,700.00
         Cost of Goods Sold.................. $190,000.00
         Selling Expense.....................   28,400.00
         General Expense....................   28,300.00

17.   Profit and Loss............................$ 65,300.00
         Retained Earnings................... $ 65,300.00

A statement of cost of goods manufactured may be made up from the data in the Work in Process account. This is presented in an illustration below. The income statement of Conroy Company for the month of June 1966 is also given below. The balance sheet at June 30, 1966, appears on page 576.

CONROY COMPANY
Statement of Cost of Goods Manufactured
Month of June, 1966

Direct Materials...$ 62,000.00
Direct Labor..   68,000.00
Factory Overhead Cost...................................   85,000.00
                                                         $215,000.00
Add—Work in Process June 1, 1966......................   8,000.00
                                                         $223,000.00
Deduct—Work in Process June 30, 1966..................   54,500.00
Cost of Goods Manufactured.............................$168,500.00

CONROY COMPANY
Income Statement
Month of June, 1966

Sales..$312,000.00
Cost of Goods Sold..................................... 190,000.00
Gross Margin on Sales..................................$122,000.00
Expenses:
   Selling.............................$28,400.00
   General............................. 28,300.00   56,700.00
Net Income...$ 65,300.00

Note that the underabsorbed overhead appears on the balance sheet as a deferred debit. As it is expected to be absorbed in the near future, it is a "prepaid" cost. Note also that the credit balance in Factory Payroll, representing the wages earned but not due to be paid at the closing date, appears in the balance sheet as Wages Payable.

COST ACCOUNTS OF CONROY COMPANY

Month of June, 1966

Materials

B.	54,000.00	(6)	64,000.00
(1)	46,000.00	B.	36,000.00
	100,000.00		100,000.00
B.	36,000.00		

Work in Process

B.	8,000.00	(13)	168,500.00
(6)	62,000.00	B.	54,500.00
(11)	68,000.00		
(12)	85,000.00		
	223,000.00		223,000.00
B.	54,500.00		

Finished Goods

B.	47,000.00	(14)	190,000.00
(13)	168,500.00	B.	25,500.00
	215,500.00		215,500.00
B.	25,500.00		

Cost of Goods Sold

(14)	190,000.00	(16)	190,000.00

Factory Payroll

(2)	70,000.00	B.	1,000.00
B.	2,000.00	(11)	71,000.00
	72,000.00		72,000.00
		B.	2,000.00

Factory Overhead Cost

(4)	60,000.00	(12)	85,000.00
(6)	2,000.00	B.	600.00
(10)	20,600.00		
(11)	3,000.00		
	85,600.00		85,600.00
B.	600.00		

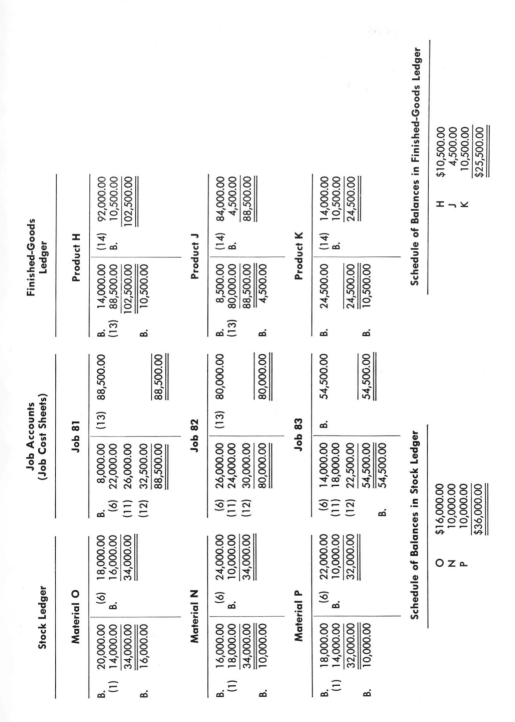

GENERAL ACCOUNTS OF CONROY COMPANY
(EXCLUDING COST ACCOUNTS)

		Cash						Notes Payable	
B.		22,000.00	(3)	92,000.00			B.		30,000.00
	(8)	288,000.00	(9)	130,000.00					
			B.	88,000.00					
		310,000.00		310,000.00					
B.		88,000.00							

		Accounts Receivable					Vouchers Payable		
B.		40,000.00	(8)	288,000.00	(3)	92,000.00	B.	28,000.00
	(7)	312,000.00	B.	64,000.00	(9)	130,000.00	(1)	46,000.00
		352,000.00		352,000.00	B.	38,800.00	(2)	92,000.00
B.		64,000.00					(4)	94,000.00
							(5)	800.00
						260,800.00		260,800.00
							B.	38,800.00

		Prepaid Insurance				Capital Stock	
B.		2,900.00	(10)	300.00		B.	300,000.00
	(5)	800.00	B.	3,400.00			
		3,700.00		3,700.00			
B.		3,400.00					

	Building and Machinery			Retained Earnings	
B.	417,000.00		B.	135,200.00	B.	69,900.00
					(17)	65,300.00
				135,200.00		135,200.00
					B.	135,200.00

	Accumulated Depreciation—B & M				Sales		
B.	183,000.00	B.	162,000.00	(15)	312,000.00	(7)	312,000.00
		(10)	21,000.00				
	183,000.00		183,000.00				
		B.	183,000.00				

Selling Expense				General Expense			
(2)	10,000.00	(16)	28,400.00	(2)	12,000.00	(16)	28,300.00
(4)	18,000.00			(4)	16,000.00		
(10)	400.00			(10)	300.00		
	28,400.00		28,400.00		28,300.00		28,300.00

Profit and Loss			
(16)	246,700.00	(15)	312,000.00
(17)	65,300.00		
	312,000.00		312,000.00

INTERNAL CONTROL FOR JOB ORDER ACCOUNTING

The internal control procedures especially helpful in job order accounting are discussed under the headings of materials control, factory payroll control, factory overhead control, and managerial reports.

Materials Control. Materials control is accomplished by the following three devices:

1. A PERPETUAL INVENTORY. This provides a continuous record of what is supposed to be on hand, which is useful in planning. It provides cost figures for materials used for entry in Work in Process and Factory Overhead and on the job cost sheets. It indicates what is supposed to be on hand so that short-ages can be discovered and investigated when a physical check is made.

2. USE OF A STOREROOM UNDER CONTROL OF A STOREKEEPER. A storeroom gives physical protection to materials. It also assures, if the storekeeper is properly instructed, that goods will be issued only for authorized purposes.

3. USE OF MATERIALS REQUISITIONS. These documents provide a record of the usage of the materials that is essential in keeping stores accounts and in getting proper cost records. It helps the storekeeper issue materials only for authorized uses by providing for an authorized signature.

The same measures apply to finished goods. In this case the storeroom is commonly called a finished goods warehouse and the shipping order takes the place of the materials requisition.

Factory Payroll Control. The controls suggested for payrolls in general in an earlier chapter apply here. The use of a timekeeper is of especial importance in manufacturing operations. His task, if well done, assures the preparation of an adequate record of the kind of work being done by each worker or crew, which is essential to a good record of cost. It also prevents unauthorized absences at the company's expense. If a separate timekeeper is too expensive, someone may watch as time in and out is being recorded in the morning and evening to see that a proper record of attendance is made (that no one punches two cards, for example), and timecards or reports may be initialed by foremen to attest to the accuracy of the report of time used.

Factory Overhead Cost Control. This is part of managerial control in general, rather than internal control in the narrower sense of protection of the ac-

CONROY COMPANY
Balance Sheet
June 30, 1966

Assets

Current Assets:

Cash	$ 88,000.00	
Accounts Receivable	64,000.00	
Materials	36,000.00	
Work in Process	54,500.00	
Finished Goods	25,500.00	
Prepaid Insurance	3,400.00	
Factory Overhead Deferred	600.00	$272,000.00

Fixed Assets:

Building and Machinery	$417,000.00	
Less: Accumulated Depreciation	183,000.00	234,000.00
Total		$506,000.00

Liabilities and Capital

Current Liabilities:

Notes Payable	$ 30,000.00	
Accounts Payable	38,800.00	
Wages Payable	2,000.00	$ 70,800.00

Capital:

Capital Stock	$300,000.00	
Retained Earnings	135,200.00	435,200.00
Total		$506,000.00

curacy and honesty of the records and physical protection of the assets. It involves all managerial efforts to minimize the amount of overhead cost incurred. It is most effectively approached through a well-drawn budget that permits comparison between well-planned costs and those actually incurred. Comparisons are also made between amounts incurred from one period to another, so that changes may be observed and corrected if possible. When reports on factory overhead are presented to executives, it should be remembered that some of the costs are controllable only by the highest officers. The amount of depreciation and real-property taxes, for example, depend upon the value of the over-all building and equipment provided, matters not usually under the control of department foremen or even of plant superintendents. In rendering reports to them on the overhead, only such *controllable* costs as supplies used, indirect labor, heat, light, and power used, and so on, may be shown.

Managerial Reports. In large organizations most executives must rely on reports for information required in making decisions. Certain general principles of effective reporting should be followed in preparing these reports. The principles are:

1. Design each report for the needs of the particular executive who is to use it.
2. Provide bases for comparison in the report.
3. Schedule the preparation of the report so as to make the information available as promptly as possible.

In connection with the first point, note that a report, no matter how skillfully drawn, will waste the time of an executive if it deals with matters in which he is not interested or cannot control, in addition to those with which he is directly concerned. Note also that reports for executives in immediate charge of workers, such as foremen, should be made at frequent intervals, daily or weekly, so any corrective action can be taken quickly. For example, a daily report of production by individual workers permits improper performance to be spotted quickly.

Bases of comparison are helpful in assessing the significance of changes. These bases may be budgeted figures, last month's or last year's figures, or some other reference. For example, the fact that a concern has earned a net income of $1,000,000 is not very informative in itself, but if it is accompanied by the information that this is 15 percent of proprietory investment it is much more significant.

Executives frequently complain that information gets to them too late to be used effectively. This problem can be overcome by careful scheduling and, in some cases, the substitution of well-formed estimates for actual figures.

MANAGERIAL DECISIONS AND COST ACCOUNTING

Most managerial decisions are made with costs in mind, so a cost accounting system can contribute to decisions of many kinds. The decisions may be outlined as follows:

Control of Operations. (1) USE OF DETAILED INFORMATION. For example, the number of pounds of material required to make a certain product will be available. From this it can be seen that a machine needs adjustment or a worker needs more training when the requirement of the product is exceeded.

(2) PERIODIC COST COMPARISONS. This permits trends to be observed and encouraged if they are good, corrected if they are bad.

(3) EFFICIENCY STANDARDS. Knowledge of costs to produce a certain product or provide a certain service enables management to scrutinize them and set standards of efficient use for the materials, labor and facilities involved.

Sales Decisions. (1) PRICE SETTING. Some companies are in industries where they have little control over the prices obtained. Many manufacturing concerns, however, make products that are distinctive, and thus have a fairly wide range of choice about the prices they will charge. In these cases prices are often based directly on the cost to manufacture the item.

(2) SELECTION OR ELIMINATION OF A PRODUCT, TERRITORY, CUSTOMER, SALESMAN, OR METHOD OF SELLING. In decisions of this kind the *contribution* involved (revenue in excess of the variable or out-of-pocket cost of getting it) is the basis for decision.

General Decisions. (1) Purchase of new plant and equipment. (2) Location of plant. (3) Choice between making and buying an article.

Some decisions, such as those involving the dropping of a product, require consideration of only the variable costs. Most cost accounting systems provide the total cost per unit, or "average total costs." The data must be analyzed to identify the variable elements when these are needed. The remarks made here about managerial decisions apply to other cost systems as well as to job order costs.

SUMMARY

Job order cost accounting is used to calculate the cost of producing product in distinct lots, or jobs. It employs perpetual inventories of materials, work in process, and finished goods if it is used in complete form. Subsidiary ledgers supporting these accounts are the stores ledger, job cost sheets or accounts, and finished goods ledger. Original records of special importance in job order cost accounting are the materials requisition to record material usage, and the job timecard, or time report, and payroll analysis to record and summarize labor cost.

Factory overhead cost is allocated to jobs on the basis of expected overhead and expected production. Production is most frequently measured by its direct labor cost, so that overhead is applied as a percent of the direct labor cost. At interim dates the overhead variance (over- or underabsorbed overhead) may be carried on the balance sheet, but at the year-end it is closed to Cost of Goods Sold.

A complete job order system provides internal controls through perpetual inventories, use of a storeroom under a storekeeper, requisitions, independent timekeeping, budget control of overhead cost, and managerial reports. Most managerial decisions involve costs, and a good cost accounting system is especially helpful in making numerous decisions.

QUESTIONS

19.1 Under what circumstances are job order cost methods appropriate?

19.2 What are the basic elements of manufacturing cost? How is each one identified with individual jobs?

19.3 What is the purpose of a payroll analysis sheet?

19.4 Under what circumstances is direct labor cost *not* a good measure of product for the purpose of applying factory overhead cost? What measure is preferred in this case?

19.5 Why are expected costs and production a better basis for applying factory overhead to product than the rate experienced last year?

19.6 Indicate whether each of the following circumstances would tend to produce a debit or a credit variance in factory overhead:
  (1) Production at a higher rate than expected
  (2) Production at a higher rate and cost incurred in a smaller amount than expected
  (3) More cost incurred than expected
  (4) Less production and more cost than expected

19.7 What should be done with a factory overhead variance in statements prepared at an interim date, assuming it is believed that the rate in use will prove to be accurate for the year as a whole?

19.8 Suggest internal control devices that tend to assure a proper accounting for materials in job order accounting.

19.9 (1) What device provides the best basis for factory overhead cost control?
  (2) What kind of factory overhead costs should be presented to any individual executive in reports designed for his action?

19.10 Suggest three principles for designing of cost reports.

19.11 Suggest some uses of cost data in managerial decisions.

19.12 The Fraser Manufacturing Company maintains job cost sheets to which direct labor charges are posted on the basis of time distributions prepared by the shop foreman. At the completion of each job the foreman lists the materials charged to the job. The materials are priced in the office, and the cost sheet is charged. General ledger entries are made as jobs are completed, and cost sheets are transferred from the in-process to the completed file. At the end of the year, the cost of goods sold is recorded on the basis of a physical inventory of finished goods priced at the sum of materials plus labor. Evaluate the accounting system used by the Fraser Manufacturing Company.

19.13 A factory overhead absorbed account is credited for the total overhead applied to production in some job order cost accounting systems. Can you explain why this account is added to the ledger? How would you dispose of a substantial difference between factory overhead and factory overhead absorbed at the end of the year if the difference was caused by errors in forecasting overhead and labor costs?

EXERCISES

19.1 The following costs were incurred by the Luther Manufacturing Company on job 521.

MATERIALS ISSUED

Date	Requisition	Amount
7/15/66	R 121	$500
7/20/66	R 135	120

LABOR

Date	Payroll	Amount
7/16/66	P 42	$100
7/23/66	P 43	300

Manufacturing overhead is applied to jobs by the company at a rate of 125 percent of direct labor.

Required:

Prepare a job cost sheet for job 521, showing the total cost of the job and the cost per unit. A total of 500 units was completed during the month.

19.2 The activity in the Work in Process account of the Baker Manufacturing Company for September 1966 is summarized below:

Balance September 1, 1966		$ 32,000
Debits:		
Materials	$48,000	
Direct labor	50,000	
Factory overhead cost	60,000	158,000
Total		$190,000
Credit—to finished goods		175,000
Balance, September 30, 1966		$ 15,000

Factory overhead costs incurred during September amounted to $62,000.

Required:

Prepare a statement of cost of goods manufactured. The company expects to absorb the overhead variance on future production.

19.3 The Hillivator Co. manufactures hillside elevators on special order and for stock. The activity in the Work in Process account for July 1966 is summarized below:

Balance July 1, 1966		$ 350,000
Add:		
Materials	$150,000	
Labor	200,000	
Factory overhead	300,000	650,000
		$1,000,000
Deduct:		
To cost of goods sold for job 401	$ 80,000	
To finished goods for job 403	65,000	145,000
Balance, July 31, 1966		$ 855,000

Factory overhead is applied to jobs on the basis of direct labor cost. Job 401 was made to order for a customer and had direct materials of $30,000. Job 403 was produced for stock and had factory overhead of $30,000.

Required:

1. How much direct labor was charged to job 403?
2. How much direct labor was charged to job 401?

19.4 The cost accounts of the Miller Manufacturing Company had the following balances at July 1, 1966:

Materials	$36,000
Work in Process	52,500
Finished Goods	26,600
Cost of Goods Sold	—
Factory Payroll	3,000 cr.
Factory Overhead Cost	500 dr.

Transactions affecting cost accounts completed during July are summarized below:

(1) Materials purchased on credit, $42,000.
(2) Payrolls paid, $82,000.
(3) Factory overhead incurred, $94,500.
(4) Materials issued during the month amounted to $58,000, of which $55,000 was charged to jobs and $3,000 to overhead.
(5) Factory wages earned during the month, including those not yet due to be paid, amount to $84,000, of which $80,000 was charged directly to jobs and the remainder was charged to overhead.
(6) Factory overhead is applied to jobs at a rate based on estimates of labor overhead for the year. The estimated labor cost was $400,000, and the estimated overhead cost was $500,000.
(7) Jobs completed and transferred to finished goods during the month cost $182,500.
(8) The cost of jobs sold amounted to $193,200.

Required:

1. Enter the opening balances in T accounts and post the transactions for the month.
2. Discuss the significance of the balances in Factory Payroll and in the Factory Overhead Cost accounts, and indicate how these balances would be reported in the financial statements.

19.5 Some of the general ledger accounts of Burton Fabricators on January 31, 1966, appear below:

Materials		Work in Process	
Jan. 1 Bal. 10,000	35,000	Jan. 1 Bal. 5,000	50,000
50,000		Materials 30,000	
		Labor 45,000	

Finished Goods		Cost of Goods Sold	
Jan. 1 Bal. 12,000	15,000		

Factory Overhead Cost		Factory Payroll	
		Jan. 1 Bal. 1,000	
		50,000	

Postings to the above accounts are incomplete; however, the following three additional facts are available:

(1) Factory overhead is being applied to jobs at 80 percent of direct labor cost.
(2) The only charge to Factory Overhead Cost, other than for indirect materials and indirect labor, was for $25,000 depreciation of plant and equipment.
(3) Accrued factory payroll on January 31 was $5,000.

Required:

1. What was the gross amount of factory payroll paid during January?
2. What was the January 31 balance of Finished Goods?
3. What was cost of goods sold?
4. What was the total amount of factory overhead cost actually incurred during the month?
5. What was the amount of over- or underabsorbed overhead for January?

19.6 The inventory accounts of the East Bay Machine Works on January 1, 1966, were as follows:

Materials $10,000
Work in Process 20,000
Finished Goods 30,000

The following costs and expenses were incurred during the year:

Materials purchased $120,000
Direct labor 100,000
Indirect labor 12,000
Depreciation of factory 20,000
Miscellaneous manufacturing costs 8,000
Salesmen's salaries 50,000
Office salaries 45,000
Miscellaneous selling and administrative expense 25,000

The inventory accounts on December 31 were as follows:

Raw Materials .... $ 8,000
Work in Process:
   Materials .... $ 2,000
   Labor 5,000
   Overhead 2,000   9,000
Finished Goods:
   Materials $12,000
   Labor 20,000
   Overhead 8,000   40,000

An examination of the accounting records reveals that $10,000 of miscellaneous selling and administrative expense should have been charged to Miscellaneous Manufacturing Costs.

Prepare a statement showing the cost of goods sold for the year, adjusted for the reclassification of this element of manufacturing overhead cost. Overhead was applied to jobs in the ratio of actual factory overhead to direct labor cost during the year.

19.7 Compute the missing amounts for each case below. (Overhead is applied as a percentage of direct labor cost.)

| | Estimated | | Actual | | Under or Over-Absorbed Overhead |
	Direct Labor	Manufacturing Overhead	Direct Labor	Manufacturing Overhead	
(1)	$200,000	$160,000	$250,000	$220,000	?
(2)	150,000	180,000	200,000	230,000	?
(3)	100,000	150,000	120,000	?	$20,000 under
(4)	160,000	?	200,000	300,000	50,000 under
(5)	?	200,000	150,000	250,000	25,000 over

19.8 La Salle Vintners produce table wines and champagnes. Paradoxically, while production of both items has increased during the past year and total costs have decreased, unit costs have increased. The production superintendent suspects that calculations made by the cost department are in error. The production of champagne requires a considerable amount of direct labor, but the production of table wines requires very little.

Following are two cost summaries. The summary prepared by the cost accountant shows fixed costs allocated to product lines on the basis of direct labor costs; the summary prepared by the plant superintendent shows fixed costs allocated on the basis of units of production. Total unit costs as prepared by the cost accountant increased. Total unit costs as prepared by the plant superintendent decreased.

Costs of production—as prepared by cost accountant:

	1965		1966	
	Amount	*Per Unit*	*Amount*	*Per Unit*
Champagnes:				
Wages and other variable costs ..	$ 400,000	$0.100	$ 300,000	$0.100
Occupancy and other fixed costs .	800,000	0.200	750,000	0.250
	$1,200,000	$0.300	$1,050,000	$0.350
Production	4,000,000 gal.		3,000,000 gal.	
Table Wines:				
Wages and other variable costs	$10,000	$0.010	$ 30,000	$0.010
Occupancy and other fixed costs . . .	20,000	0.020	75,000	0.025
	$30,000	$0.030	$105,000	$0.035
Production	1,000,000 gal.		3,000,000 gal.	

Costs of production—as prepared by plant superintendent:

	1965		1966	
	Amount	*Per Unit*	*Amount*	*Per Unit*
Champagnes:				
Wages and other variable costs ..	$ 400,000	$0.100	$300,000	$0.100
Occupancy and other fixed costs .	656,000	0.164	412,500	0.104
	$1,056,000	$0.264	$712,500	$0.204
Production	4,000,000 gal.		3,000,000 gal.	
Table Wines:				
Wages and other variable costs ..	$ 10,000	$0.010	$ 30,000	$0.010
Occupancy and other fixed costs .	164,000	0.164	412,500	0.104
	$174,000	$0.174	$442,500	$0.114
Production	1,000,000 gal.		3,000,000 gal.	

Required:

1. Comment on the advisability of showing noncontrollable costs in reports to the foreman.
2. Do you think occupancy and other fixed costs are correlated more closely with labor cost than with units of production?
3. If the winery is operating at less than full capacity in 1966, should it accept an order for 100,000 gallons of champagne at 25 cents a gallon? Why?
4. How would your answer change if the plant were operating at capacity?

PROBLEMS

19.1 The Heathware Company applies factory overhead cost to jobs on the basis of direct labor cost. The following figures are available from the Work in Process account for May 1966 and from the job cost sheets:

[handwritten left margin: factory overhead rate: $\frac{\$27,600 \text{ FO}}{46,000 \text{ DL}} = 60\%$*]*

Balance of work in process, May 1, 1966 .... $16,000
Debits to work in process:
Materials 40,000
Labor 46,000
Factory overhead cost 27,600
Credits:
To finished goods for job 188 40,000
To cost of goods sold for job 192 50,000

Job 188 was produced for stock and had direct labor of $16,000. Job 192 was made to order for a customer and had direct materials of $18,000.

Required:

1. How much factory overhead was charged to job 188? *[handwritten: $16,000 DL × 60% = 9,600]*
2. How much factory overhead was charged to job 192?

19.2 Prepare entries in general journal form for the following transactions of Haley Manufacturing Company for September 1966. The company uses a job order cost accounting system; it has control accounts in the general ledger for Selling Expense and General Expense.

(1) Purchased on credit materials costing $36,000.
(2) Issued materials as follows: for jobs, $27,900; as factory supplies, $2,400; to general office for use as stationery, $100.
(3) Vouchered payrolls, $57,000; of this total, $36,000 is factory payroll; $15,000 is sales department payroll, and $6,000 is general-office payroll. Withholdings are: federal income tax, $3,300; F.I.C.A. tax, $2,300.
(4) Factory payroll is distributed for the period as follows: direct labor, $34,000; indirect labor, $3,000.
(5) Depreciation is recorded on the building and equipment used in factory, selling, and general-office activities. The total is $11,700; of this, $8,400 is a factory cost, $2,100 is a selling expense, and $1,200 is a general expense.
(6) Sundry services purchased on credit are recorded. Factory costs account for $6,100 of these services, selling expense for $2,400, and general expense for $1,300.
(7) Factory overhead is applied to jobs at 75 percent of the direct labor cost.
(8) Jobs finished cost $81,000.
(9) Finished goods were sold on credit for $105,000.
(10) The finished goods sold cost $78,000.

19.3 Lawrence Manufacturing Company uses a job order cost accounting system. Opening balances of its perpetual inventory accounts, including subsidiary accounts, together with a summary of cost transactions for April 1966, are given below.

Required:

1. Prepare entries in general journal form for the transactions, including the detail for subsidiary accounts.
2. Set up T accounts for the general ledger and subsidiary ledger cost accounts (as in the illustration on pages 572 and 573), enter the opening balances, and post the entries. Other accounts are not required.
3. Prepare schedules of the subsidiary ledgers and see that they agree with the control-account balances.

The data follow:
Opening balances in perpetual inventories were:

Materials	Work in Process	Finished Goods
K $ 3,000	Job 101 $8,000	R $ 7,000
L 2,900	Job 102 1,500	S 6,000
M 4,100	$9,500	T 2,000
$10,000		$15,000

There was also a debit balance of $500 in the Factory Overhead Cost account. The transactions were:

(1) The following materials were purchased on credit:

$$
\begin{array}{ll}
K & \$\ 9,200 \\
L & 8,100 \\
M & \underline{5,500} \\
& \$22,800
\end{array}
$$

(2) Materials were issued as follows:

Materials		Used for	
K	$10,000	Job 101	$ 600
L	10,100	Job 102	14,000
M	8,700	Job 103	13,200
	$28,800	Supplies	1,000
			$28,800

(3) Payrolls are vouchered for the month, $30,000. Of this amount, $5,200 is withheld as income tax and $1,200 is withheld for F.I.C.A. tax.

(4) Labor is distributed for the month as follows:

$$
\begin{array}{lr}
\text{Job 101} \ldots\ldots\ldots\ldots & \$\ 1,600 \\
\text{Job 102} \ldots\ldots\ldots\ldots & 11,000 \\
\text{Job 103} \ldots\ldots\ldots\ldots & 14,400 \\
\text{Indirect labor} \ldots\ldots & \underline{4,000} \\
& \$31,000
\end{array}
$$

(5) Other costs are recorded as follows:

$$
\begin{array}{lr}
\text{Depreciation of plant and equipment} \ldots\ldots & \$\ 6,200 \\
\text{Services purchased on credit} \ldots\ldots\ldots\ldots & 6,100 \\
\text{Accrued liabilities} \ldots\ldots\ldots\ldots\ldots\ldots & \underline{6,600} \\
& \$18,900
\end{array}
$$

(6) Factory overhead is applied to jobs for the month at 90 percent of direct labor cost.

(7) Job 101 and job 102 were finished during the month. Job 101 is product R and job 102 is product S.

(8) Goods sold during the month are detailed as follows:

	Cost
Product R	$11,000
Product S	36,000
Product T	1,000
	$48,000

19.4 The Uris Manufacturing Company uses job order cost accounting. The ledger contains controlling accounts for Manufacturing Overhead and Operating Expenses. Transactions for July 1966 included:

(1) Materials purchased on credit, $80,000.

(2) Freight charges on materials purchased amounting to $6,000, paid by check.

(3) The payroll analysis shows charges for direct labor, $94,000; indirect labor, $12,000; and nonmanufacturing payroll, $15,000.

(4) Paid payroll, $125,000, less social security and income taxes withheld, $20,000.

(5) Materials issued amounted to $80,000 direct and $15,000 indirect.

(6) Employer payroll taxes accrue at 8 percent.

(7) End-of-the-month adjustments also included: depreciation of plant and equipment, $32,000; expired insurance, $6,000; and accrued property taxes, $2,000. All these charges are applicable to the factory.

(8) Factory overhead is applied to jobs on the basis of direct labor cost. At the beginning of the year it was estimated that direct labor cost for the year would be $400,000 and overhead for the year would be $240,000.

(9) The cost of jobs completed during the month amounted to $82,000.

(10) The cost of jobs sold amounted to $40,000. They were billed at $60,000.

Required:

Draft journal entries to record the foregoing transactions.

19.5 The trial balance of the Brown Manufacturing Company on December 31, 1966 is:

Cash	$ 6,000	
Accounts Receivable	12,000	
Materials	5,000	
Work in Process	17,000	
Finished Goods	33,000	
Plant and Equipment	125,000	
Accumulated Depreciation		$ 50,000
Accounts Payable		25,000
Capital Stock		50,000
Retained Earnings		53,000
Sales		180,000
Cost of Goods Sold	140,000	
Operating Expenses	20,000	
	$358,000	$358,000

An examination of the accounting records discloses that depreciation for the year was improperly omitted from the estimated and actual overhead. The plant and equipment is subject to depreciation at 10 percent, 80 percent of which is considered to be part of manufacturing overhead.

Production costs, as recorded for the year, consisted of:

Materials $60,000
Labor 40,000
Overhead 50,000

December 31 inventories of finished goods and work in process consisted of:

	Work in Process	Finished Goods
Materials	$8,000	$ 6,000
Labor	4,000	12,000
Overhead	5,000	15,000

Required:

Prepare journal entries to record depreciation, and adjust the inventories for the revised overhead rate.

19.6 The Lux Manufacturing Company, which uses job order cost accounting, had the following inventories on July 1:

Work in process $24,000
Finished goods   35,000

During July it completed the following transactions:
(1) Issued materials: direct, $47,000; indirect, $4,000.
(2) Incurred payroll: direct labor, $80,000; indirect labor, $12,000; selling and administrative salaries, $14,000.
(3) Other manufacturing overhead, $84,000.
(4) Selling and administrative expenses, $62,000.
(5) Applied manufacturing overhead, 120 percent of direct labor.
(6) The cost of goods completed during the month, $200,000.
(7) Sold goods for $321,000, which had a cost of $190,000.

Required:

1. Prepare an income statement for the month with a supporting schedule of the cost of goods manufactured. The overhead variance is to be carried forward as a balance sheet amount.
2. Was production during the month over or under that expected on the average for the year? Discuss briefly.

19.7 The Werner Manufacturing Company uses job order cost accounting. The July 1 balances of the inventory and overhead accounts were:

Material $10,000
Finished Goods   20,000
Factory Overhead Cost . . . .   500 (dr.)

The company incurred the following costs during July:

Direct materials issued $40,000
Indirect materials issued   4,000
Direct labor   50,000
Indirect labor   20,000
Depreciation   3,500
Insurance   2,000
Other manufacturing costs paid   10,000
Selling and administrative expense   12,000

The overhead rate is 80 percent of direct labor. On July 31, the finished goods, all of which had been started during the month, included materials $6,000 and direct labor $5,000. There were no work in process inventories at the beginning or at the end of the month. The inventory of raw material on July 31 amounted to $15,000.

Required:

1. Prepare journal entries to record the cost transactions for the period to the extent permitted by the foregoing data.
2. State the amount of under- or overabsorbed overhead. If overhead was incurred at the budgeted rate, was production above or below normal?

Process Cost Accounting

In process cost accounting the costs are collected by processes. This method is appropriate where the production is organized in processes in which all units of product get the same treatment. To get a cost per unit, the total cost of materials and labor used in the process plus its share of factory overhead is divided by the number of units produced. A process is usually equivalent to a department. For example, in canning peaches there will be a department or process for preparation, a department or process for canning, and one for cooking. Each has its own area in the plant and its own equipment. This separation is in contrast with job order conditions, where several jobs may be going on in the machine shop and in the assembly department at the same time. One could not collect the cost, including materials and labor, of operating the machine shop and divide this by units produced, to get a realistic cost per unit for the different products of the several jobs. Examples of process-type industries are flour milling, petroleum refining, meat packing, mining, and ore refining. Many chemical industries and those processing agricultural products fall in this class.

GENERAL LEDGER ACCOUNTS FOR PROCESS COSTS

The same cost elements recognized in job order accounts are the starting point for gathering costs for a process system. These are materials, labor, and factory overhead. The record of work in process, however, is different. It consists of an account for each process. The number of accounts used depends entirely upon the number of processes. Each process account is charged with the materials issued to it, the labor performed in it, and the factory overhead allocated to it. The following diagram shows general ledger accounts for a process system with two processes. This is called a *sequential* process system, because the product goes through each process in sequence. Other possibilities include (1) *parallel process costs*, in which two or more sequential groups exist in the same company, and (2) *selective process costs*, in which some products go through some of the processes and not others. Journal entries to record the flow of costs in a two-process sequential system take the following form.

```
Process A...................................$xx,xxx.xx
Process B...................................  x,xxx.xx
    Materials..............................           $xx,xxx.xx
(to record materials issued to processes)
```

DIAGRAM OF SEQUENTIAL PROCESS COSTS
General Ledger Accounts

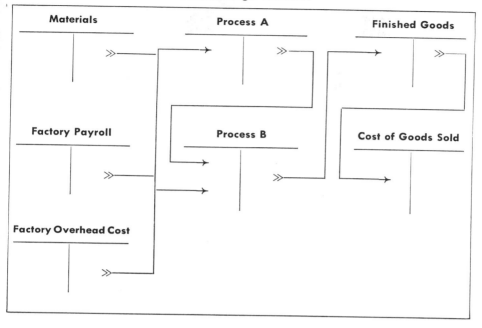

Process A....................................$xx,xxx.xx
Process B................................... x,xxx.xx
      Factory Payroll......................... $xx,xxx.xx
(to record distribution of wages earned for the period)

Process A....................................$xx,xxx.xx
Process B................................... x,xxx.xx
      Factory Overhead Cost.................. $xx,xxx.xx
(to record distribution of factory overhead cost to processes for the period)

Process B....................................$xx,xxx.xx
      Process A.............................. $xx,xxx.xx
(to record product transferred from process A to proc-
ess B)

Finished Goods...............................$xx,xxx.xx
      Process B.............................. $xx,xxx.xx
(to record goods finished)

Cost of Goods Sold...........................$xx,xxx.xx
      Finished Goods......................... $xx,xxx.xx
(to record cost of goods sold)

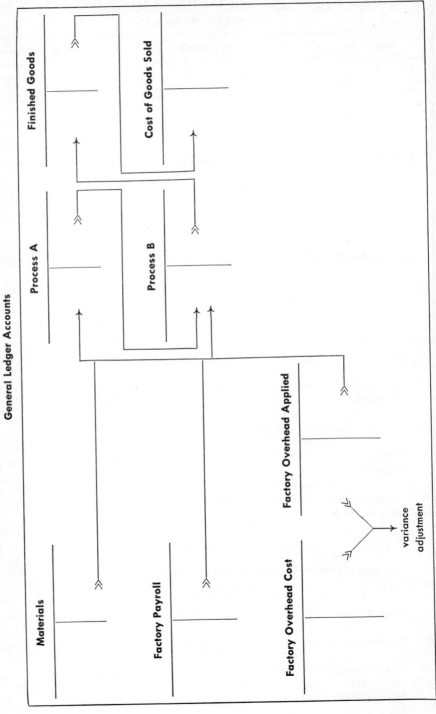

DIAGRAM OF PROCESS COSTS UNDER SEASONAL CONDITIONS

General Ledger Accounts

PROCESS COSTS UNDER SEASONAL PRODUCTION

The preceding discussion concerns a process industry that has no seasonal fluctuations in production. When production is steady through the year the factory overhead cost may be distributed to processes in the actual amounts incurred month by month. This approach applies, for example, to flour milling. If production fluctuates seasonally, more overhead must be charged to processes in months of high production than in months of low production. The plant capacity is presumably determined so that the highest seasonal peaks can be handled. The cost of maintaining this capacity during slack periods is part of the cost of producing at a high rate in the other periods. This approach applies to fruit and vegetable canning, an industry in which the plant may be shut down some of the time in the winter, but which is likely to run twenty-four hours a day in July and August. Under seasonal conditions, overhead is applied to each process by means of an overhead rate. The rate may be computed as follows:

$$\frac{\text{expected overhead of the process for the year}}{\text{expected operating hours of the process for the year}} = \binom{\text{overhead}}{\text{rate per hour}}$$

Note that this computation must be made for each process.

The entries required when a factory overhead rate is used in process cost accounting are diagrammed in the illustration on page 590. If the overhead rate is $20 per hour of operation for process A and $30 for process B, and A has run 160 hours in a month and B has run 300 hours, the entry to record the application of factory overhead is:

Process A	$ 3,200.00	
Process B	9,000.00	
Factory Overhead Applied		$12,200.00

During the year any variance (difference between the amount incurred and the amount applied) is carried on the balance sheet as a deferred debit in current assets or a deferred credit in current liabilities. At the end of the year it is written off, usually to Cost of Goods Sold. Strictly speaking, part of the variance at the year end should be applied to any inventory of work in process or finished goods that was made during the year, but the error from ignoring this variance is likely to be small.

PROCESS COSTS AND SERVICE DEPARTMENTS

Many industries operating under process cost conditions have service departments as well as process or producing departments. There may be a power plant, storeroom, factory office, first-aid department, cafeteria, receiving department, and so on. Distribution of factory overhead in these cases must be made in two steps: (1) distribution of the various elements of overhead to departments and (2) redistribution of the service department costs to processes. The kind of computations involved, together with a convenient work-sheet form, have been illustrated on page 521 (Work Sheet for Departmental Expense Distribution). Although that illustration deals with a merchandising concern, exactly the same principles apply to a manufacturing concern. The same computation is made with the *expected* factory overhead figures to get the overhead rates for the year. At the end of the year the distribution is made with the actual figures. By comparing the distributions made with expected and actual costs, management can see where actual performance varied from the expected or planned performance. Improvements in planning and in operations should result.

ORIGINAL RECORDS IN PROCESS COSTS

Materials are best accounted for by means of perpetual inventories in process as well as in job order conditions. Perpetual inventories imply use of materials requisitions that record the usage of materials. However, in many cases in process situations, given material is used in only one process. In these cases the periodic inventory method of determining the charge to a process for materials is often used.

Labor cost may be recorded with timecards or on time reports, as in job order accounting. It often happens that individual workers spend their time in only one department, in which case all their earnings are charged there without the need for a detailed time report. The analysis by processes can be made on the payroll sheet by columns or by listing the workers' names in groups by processes and taking subtotals. If workers are assigned to different processes during a week, a timecard or time report must be prepared and a payroll analysis sheet prepared as in job order cost accounting (see illustration page 564). Production reports showing the number of units finished, the number still in process, and the extent of completion of those in process are especially important in process cost accounting. They provide the data, together with the total costs charged into a process, for the computation of the unit cost of the product.

UNIT COST COMPUTATIONS

If there is no work in process, the unit cost of production in a process may be computed by dividing the total costs by the actual units produced. When work in process is present, the units worked on no longer represent a whole unit of work in all cases. It is then necessary to calculate the *equivalent units*, in order to get a figure that measures the work of the period to divide into total costs. *Equivalent units* expresses the work of a process for a period in terms of finished units. To get it, the number of unfinished units worked on must be translated into the equivalent number of finished units.

EQUIVALENT UNITS WITH ENDING WORK IN PROCESS

Suppose that 3,000 units of product are started in a process and that 2,700 are finished, 300 being in process at the end, one half complete. The calculation of equivalent units is:

	Units	Fraction	Equivalent Units
Finished	2,700	1	2,700
Work in process, ending	300	½	150
Totals	3,000		2,850

The units in the ending work in process inventory are multiplied by ½ because only half the work necessary to process a completely finished unit has been done on them. If this process had incurred costs of $5,700 (and if it is assumed that all the costs are applied to the units at a constant rate during the processing) the unit cost is obtained by dividing $5,700 by 2,850 units, and is $2 per unit.

EQUIVALENT UNITS WITH BEGINNING WORK IN PROCESS

Assume that 500 units are in process two-fifths complete at the start, and 2,000 units are started. All 2,500 are finished. The computation in this case is:

	Units	Fraction	Equivalent Units
Finished:			
From work in process, beginning..........	500	⅗	300
Started this period.....................	2,000	1	2,000
Totals.........................	2,500		2,300

Note that the work done during this period on the beginning inventory is the difference between what had already been done and a full unit of work.

EQUIVALENT UNITS WITH BEGINNING AND ENDING WORK IN PROCESS

Suppose that 800 units were in process at the beginning of the period, one-fourth complete. Another 4,000 units were started, and 600 units were in process at the end, one-third complete. In this situation it is helpful to set down the total number of units to be accounted for, as is done as a preliminary step in the computation that follows:

	Units	Fraction	Equivalent Units
Work in process, beginning.................	800		
Started......	4,000		
To be accounted for....................	4,800		
Disposition of product:			
Work in process, ending.................	600	⅓	200
Finished:			
From work in process, beginning.........	800	¾	600
Started this period....................	3,400	1	3,400
Totals......	4,800		4,200

MATERIALS COMPLETE WHEN STARTED

Materials cost is often complete as soon as the materials are started in the process. In other cases, materials are added as a last step, usually when a container is provided. For example, the tomatoes in a canning plant are complete when started in the preparation process; the cans in which they are packed are

100 percent present when started in the canning process. In contrast, sacks will be provided for stock feed (the feed will be "sacked") as the last step in processing the feed. In these cases the unit cost for materials must be calculated separately from the unit cost of labor and overhead. This operation requires that the equivalent units of production be separately calculated, as is illustrated in the following table. The figures in the table reflect the flow of product as follows: In process A, there was no work in process at the beginning of the period; 5,000 units were started of which 1,000 are one-half complete at the end of the period, the other 4,000 units going to process B. In process B, there were 800 units in process at the beginning, one-fourth complete, and 900 were in process at the end, one-third complete. In process A the materials are started at the beginning of processing and are complete when started; in B they are containers and are added just as the work is finished.

| | | Process A | | | | Process B | | |
| | | | Equivalent Units | | | | Equivalent Units | |
	Units	Fraction	Material	Labor and Overhead	Units	Fraction	Material	Labor and Overhead
Work in process, beginning...	—				800			
Started...	5,000				4,000			
To be accounted for...	5,000				4,800			
Disposition of product:								
Work in process, ending...	1,000	½	1,000	500	900	⅓	—	300
Finished:								
From beginning inventory...	—				800	¾	800	600
Started this period..	4,000	1	4,000	4,000	3,100	1	3,100	3,100
Totals...	5,000		5,000	4,500	4,800		3,900	4,000

The fractions indicate the proportion of work done, in terms of labor and overhead, on each segment of product during this period. The fact that materials are complete at the start of processing in A means that a whole unit of material is in each unit of ending work in process there, and that no material is added to beginning work in process inventory. The fact that materials are added as the last step in B means that any unfinished units at the end get no materials in that period and that a unit of material must be added to each unit of beginning inventory to finish it.

UNIT COST STATEMENT

The illustration below presents the unit cost statement of Bolton Manufacturing Company for June 1966. It is based on the units and equivalent units shown in the table of the preceding section. The following points should be noted.

BOLTON MANUFACTURING COMPANY
Unit Cost Statement

Month of June, 1966

	Process A		Process B		Total	
	Amount	Per Unit	Amount	Per Unit	Amount	Per Unit
Work in Process, beginning....	$ —	$ —	$ 3 378 00	$ —	$ 3 378 00	$ —
Materials.................	7 500 00	1.50	780 00	0.20	8 280 00	1.70
Labor....................	4 500 00	1.00	8 000 00	2.00	12 500 00	3.00
Overhead.................	3 375 00	0.75	6 000 00	1.50	9 375 00	2.25
Total................	$15 375 00	$3.25	$18 158 00	$3.70	$33 533 00	$6.95
Transferred in..............	—	—	13 000 00	3.25	—	—
Total................	$15 375 00	$3.25	$31 158 00	$6.95	$33 533 00	$6.95
Work in Process, ending.......	2 375 00	—	3 975 00	—	6 350 00	—
Transferred out.............	$13 000 00	$3.25	$27 183 00	$6.97	$27 183 00	$6.97

1. The unit price for materials in each process is obtained by dividing the materials cost by the number of equivalent units for materials of the process. The unit costs for labor and overhead are obtained by dividing their amounts by the equivalent units for labor and overhead.

2. The unit cost column is used to develop unit costs for operations this period; unit costs for beginning and ending inventories of work in process have no place in it.

3. Ending work in process in process A is calculated as follows (see the calculation of equivalent units for the units and fractions involved):

Material: 1,000 units × $1.50............................	$1,500.00
Labor and overhead: 1,000 × ½ × $1.75.................	875.00
Total...	$2,375.00

4. The units finished and transferred out of process are obtained by subtraction in the statement, but they can also be computed by using the units and unit costs. It is wise to make this latter computation because it indicates whether or not the methods used are consistent and the arithmetic correct. In this case it is:

$$4,000 \text{ units} \times \$3.25 = \$13,000.00$$

5. Ending work in process in process B is calculated as follows:

Cost from process A: 900 units × $3.25.....................	$ 2,925.00
Costs from process B (labor and overhead only, because materials are added in B only when the goods are finished): 900 × ⅓ × $3.50......................................	1,050.00
Total..	$ 3,975.00

6. The cost of work finished in process B is computed from units and unit costs as follows:

From beginning inventory:	
Balance at beginning of period.........................	$ 3,378.00
Material added: 800 × 1 × $0.20....................	160.00
Labor and overhead added: 800 × ¾ × $3.50...........	2,100.00
Total from beginning inventory......................	$ 5,638.00
From work started this period: 3,100 units × $6.95...........	21,545.00
Total......................................	$27,183.00

7. Figures in the total column are obtained by cross-footing, except, of course, that no figure for "transferred in" appears because that applies only to transfers from one process to another.

8. The unit cost of $6.97 shown on the line for "transferred out" for process B and in the total colmun is 2 cents more than the price arrived at just above it. This price of $6.97 is an average obtained by dividing the total amount transferred out by the units transferred ($27,183 ÷ 3,900). It differs from the price arrived at as the cost of operating the processes during this period because it includes a beginning inventory and this was processed in part during the last period at a different cost. The $6.97 will be used in the account in the finished-goods ledger.

JOURNAL ENTRIES FOR PROCESS COST ACCOUNTING

The costs shown in the unit cost statement on page 595 result from the following transactions, shown in summary and in general journal form (unless otherwise indicated, the entry would be made in the general journal):

Materials.....................................	$10,260.00	
Vouchers Payable......................		$10,260.00
(materials purchased; recorded in voucher register)		
Process A.....................................	$ 7,500.00	
Process B.....................................	780.00	
Materials............................		$ 8,280.00
(to record distribution of materials to processes)		
Factory Payroll................................	$11,800.00	
Vouchers Payable......................		$10,415.00
Federal Income Tax Withheld............		1,090.00
F.I.C.A. Tax Withheld		295.00
(payment of payrolls recorded in voucher register)		
Process A.....................................	$ 4,500.00	
Process B.....................................	8,000.00	
Factory Payroll........................		$12,500.00
(to distribute payrolls earned for the month)		

Factory Overhead Cost........................	$ 9,375.00	
Accumulated Depreciation...............		$ 1,100.00
Property Taxes Accrued.................		200.00
Sundry Accrued Liabilities..............		1,710.00
Prepaid Insurance......................		165.00
Vouchers Payable.....................		6,200.00

(factory overhead costs recorded in general journal and voucher register)

Process A.................................	$ 3,375.00	
Process B.................................	6,000.00	
Factory Overhead Cost.................		$ 9,375.00

(to distribute factory overhead cost for the month)

Process B.................................	$13,000.00	
Process A...........................		$13,000.00

(to record product transferred from process A to process B)

Finished Goods..............................	$27,183.00	
Process B...........................		$27,183.00

(to record goods finished)

Cost of Goods Sold..........................	$25,400.00	
Finished Goods........................		$25,400.00

(to record goods sold)

ACCOUNTS FOR THE ILLUSTRATION

The illustration on page 598 presents general ledger T accounts of the Bolton Manufacturing Company for June 1966. Only the cost accounts are given.

INTERNAL CONTROL FOR PROCESS COSTS

Internal control for process costs is the same as that recommended for job order costs (Chapter 19). In connection with reports, however, it should be noted that the production report is especially important in process cost conditions, because it is the only record of what is produced; there are no job cost sheets to indicate what was produced. Because production employees often dislike clerical work and do it badly, it is desirable to have an office employee designated a "production clerk," with responsibility for making a continuous record of production quantities.

MANAGERIAL PROBLEMS WITH PROCESS COSTS

Managerial decisions and cost accounting were discussed in Chapter 19 under the headings of Control of Operations, Sales Decisions, and General Decisions. That discussion applies to process cost conditions as well as to job order conditions.

PROCESS COST ACCOUNTS OF BOLTON MANUFACTURING COMPANY

Month of June, 1966

Materials

B.	2,400.00	(2)	8,280.00
(1)	10,260.00	B.	4,380.00
	12,660.00		12,660.00
B.	4,380.00		

Factory Payroll

(3)	11,800.00	(4)	12,500.00
B.	700.00		
	12,500.00		12,500.00
		B.	700.00

Factory Overhead Cost

(5)	9,375.00	(6)	9,375.00

Process A

(2)	7,500.00	(7)	13,000.00
(4)	4,500.00	B.	2,375.00
(6)	3,375.00		
	15,375.00		15,375.00
B.	2,375.00		

Process B

B.	3,378.00	(8)	27,183.00
(2)	780.00	B.	3,975.00
(4)	8,000.00		
(6)	6,000.00		
(7)	13,000.00		
	31,158.00		31,158.00
B.	3,975.00		

Finished Goods

B.	6,800.00	(9)	25,400.00
(8)	27,183.00	B.	8,583.00
	33,983.00		33,983.00
B.	8,583.00		

Cost of Goods Sold

(9)	25,400.00

SUMMARY

Process cost accounting is used when materials are put through the same operations in a process or a department. The general ledger accounts for materials, factory payroll, and factory overhead cost are used as in job order accounting, but the work in process record is different. It consists of a general ledger account for each process and there is no subsidiary record.

Under seasonal conditions factory overhead is applied to processes by means of a precomputed overhead rate. This may be based on hours of operation. If seasonal fluctuations are negligible, the overhead is distributed to processes each month in the amount incurred. If service departments are present in a process situation, the overhead is distributed in two steps: first to departments and processes, then from service departments to processes.

Unit cost calculations involve the conversion of partly finished product to the equivalent finished units. Separate computations of equivalent units for materials and for the other costs are necessary when materials go into process at the beginning or end of processing instead of being put in continuously. A unit cost statement displays the amounts of cost incurred in each process with the unit costs of product produced, together with any work in process inventories and the amounts transferred and finished.

Internal control and managerial decisions involve the same things in process cost situations as in other manufacturing conditions, except that the production report is especially important in the case of process costs.

QUESTIONS

20.1 Distinguish process cost conditions from job order cost conditions.

20.2 A certain company produces a metal specialty. It is first formed, then heat-treated, and finally goes through a finishing operation. What kind of general ledger record for work in process would you recommend for this concern? Be specific.

20.3 When production varies widely over the seasons, what step must be introduced into process cost accounting that is not required when production is stable?

20.4 What step is introduced into process cost accounting by service departments?

20.5 Indicate how information about each of the following costs is accumulated in a process cost system: (1) materials used in the several processes, (2) labor performed in the several processes. *time cards + payroll analysis*

20.6 What are "equivalent units"? How are they computed?

20.7 A certain process had 5,000 units started during a recent month. For each of the following cases, indicate whether the equivalent units for the process were larger or smaller than the 5,000 started.

(1) Work in process at the end was 50 units one-half complete; there was no beginning work in process. *smaller*

(2) Work in process at the start was 600 units one-third complete; there was no ending work in process. *larger*

(3) Work in process at the beginning was 1,000 units one-half complete, and at the end there were 800 units on hand one-fourth complete. *smaller*

(4) Work in process at the beginning was 400 units three-fourths complete, and at the end there were 900 units one-third complete. *S*

(5) Work in process at the beginning was 1,000 units one-fifth complete, and at the end there were 200 units one-half complete. *L*

20.8 In process X, materials are put into process only as the last step in the processing. During a recent month 2,000 units were finished in process X, of which 400 were on hand one-fourth complete at the beginning of the month. Also, 300 units two-thirds complete were on hand at the end. What are the equivalent units for material for the month? *2 000*

20.9 What report is especially important in process cost *production report* accounting? Why? What internal control may be advised for it in a concern large enough to afford it? *Cler*

20.10 It has sometimes been argued that the primary purpose of a good process cost accounting system is to determine unit cost figures for short-run pricing decisions. Do you agree? Discuss briefly.

20.11 How does the definition of direct labor in process cost differ from its definition in job order?

20.12 The Able Awl Company uses process cost accounting. Monthly charges for raw materials consumed are determined by physical inventories of stores on hand. Comment on this system.

20.13 The M Company and the N Company are each engaged in a similar manufacturing business and have approximately the same annual sales volume. Their condensed balance sheets at December 31, 1966, show the following condition:

	M	N
Cash	$ 65,000	$173,500
Receivables	81,500	77,000
Inventories	217,000	232,000
Plant and Equipment (net)	890,500	—
	$1,254,000	$482,500
Current Payables	$ 74,500	$ 61,500
Bonds Payable	750,000	—
Stock and Retained Earnings	429,500	421,000
	$1,254,000	$482,500

N is liable under a 10-year lease for $174,000 annual rental of plant and equipment used in its manufacturing operation.

Required:

Assuming that you have profit and loss statements and detailed operating figures available for both companies, state in what major ways you would expect to find the statements differing and explain how you would adjust the figures to obtain comparable manufacturing costs for the two companies.

(AICPA — adapted)

EXERCISES

20.1 Prepare general journal entries to record the following cost transactions completed by the P & F Canning Company during July 1966:

(1) Purchased $20,000 of materials on account.

(2) Issued $6,000 of materials to process A and $12,000 of materials to process B.

(3) Distributed payroll charges of $12,000 to process A and $24,000 to process B.

(4) Applied overhead to production at 150 percent of direct labor. (The company uses a Factory Overhead Applied account.)

(5) Transferred product costing $24,000 from process A to process B.

(6) Completed and sold from process B product costing $30,000.

20.2 The Far East Textile Company fabricates a single product in a nondepartmental-ized plant. There was no work in process on January 1, 1966. Costs incurred during January amounted to $4,000.

Production records for the month showed 8,000 units started and completed and another 4,000 units started and one-half completed with respect to material, labor, and overhead on January 31, 1966.

Required:

Compute (1) the equivalent units of production for the month, (2) the cost of the January 31 work in process, and (3) the cost of work completed during the month.

20.3 Harold Shein and Co. manufacture a single product in a nondepartmentalized plant. Work in process on January 1, 1966, consisted of 1,600 units one-fourth complete. Another 8,000 units were started, and 1,200 units were in process on January 31, 1966, one-third complete. Materials are added continuously, so the fractions refer to the degree of completion with respect to materials as well as labor and overhead.

Costs incurred during January amounted to $42,000, and the work in process on January 1, 1966, had a cost of $2,000.

Required:

Compute (1) the equivalent units of production for the month, (2) the cost of the January 31 work in process, and (3) the cost of work completed during the month.

20.4 There were 1,600 units one-fourth complete in process A of the M Co. on July 1, costing $5,000. Another 8,000 units were started during the month. On July 31 there were 2,000 units one-fourth complete. The fractions of completion refer only to conversion costs; materials are complete when units are started in the process. Costs for July were:

Materials	$16,000
Labor and overhead	38,500

Compute the equivalent units, giving separate figures for materials and for labor and overhead. Compute the cost of work in process on July 31, and the cost of units transferred out of process A.

20.5 At C Co., materials are added at the end of process O. Work in process on December 1 consisted of 1,600 units one-fourth complete, costing $2,500. Another 8,000 units were started during the month, and 1,800 units were on hand at the end of the month one-third complete. Costs for December were:

Materials	$39,000
Labor and overhead	40,000

Required:

Compute the equivalent units, giving separate figures for materials and for labor and overhead. Compute the December 31 cost of work in process and the cost of units transferred out of the process during December.

20.6 Process M is the third in a series of six processes used by the Superior Gadget Company in its manufacturing operations. The following data are for December:

(1) Inventory of work in process, December 1, none.
(2) Units transferred from the previous process at a cost of $20 per unit, 6,000.
(3) Costs added during the month:

Direct materials and supplies	$19,000
Direct labor	37,000
Other costs	18,250

Work in process, December 31, 1,500 units, 60 percent completed as to materials, labor, and overhead in process M.

Required:

What is the cost of the units completed in process M and transferred to the next process during December? Show all calculations. Carry calculations to nearest cent.

20.7 The following costs were charged to process 2 of the H Co. during July 1966:

Costs from process 1	$160,000
Materials	34,000
Labor and overhead	89,000

Production figures for the month were:

Work in process, July 1	2,000 pounds, 60% complete
Placed in process	20,000
Work in process, July 31	5,000 pounds, 40% complete

Materials are added at the end of the process. The work in process on July 1 had a cost of $22,500.

Required:

Compute the equivalent units, giving separate figures for materials and for labor and overhead. Compute the July 31 cost of work in process and the cost of units transferred out of the process during July.

20.8 Prepare a unit cost statement for the Weinberg Manufacturing Company from the data below.

	Process 1		Process 2	
	Units	Fraction Complete	Units	Fraction Complete
Work in process, July 1	—	—	1,000	3/4
Started in July	8,000		6,000	
Work in process, July 31	2,000	1/2	1,800	2/3

	Process 1	Process 2
Costs:		
Materials	$12,000	$1,300
Labor and overhead	13,300	5,085

Materials are complete at the beginning of process 1, but materials are added only at the end of process 2. The work in process on July 1 in process 2 amounted to $4,335.

20.9 The Unit Manufacturing Company manufactures a single product, but controls production by separate work orders. Costs and production for July were as follows:

	Job 701	Job 702	Job 703
Materials	$40,000	$48,000	$56,000
Labor	32,000	39,000	19,000
Units produced	8,000	10,000	12,000

Overhead is applied at 80 percent of direct labor. There were no inventories on July 1, and the only inventory on July 31 was job 703, complete as to material and one-half complete as to labor and overhead.

Required:

Compare the cost of work in process at the end of July under job cost accounting with the cost as computed by process cost accounting.

PROBLEMS

20.1 The following transactions were completed by the United Faucet Co. during September 1966:

(1) Purchased materials on credit, $24,000.

(2) Issued materials: Machining, $12,000; Assembly, $10,000.

(3) Vouchered payrolls: $30,000. Of this amount, $3,000 was withheld for income tax and $1,200 for F.I.C.A. tax.

(4) Wages earned for the month were $16,000 in Machining and $14,000 in Assembly.

(5) Insurance premiums expired on factory policies during September, $1,600.

(6) Depreciation on plant and machinery for the month was $5,000.

(7) An invoice is vouchered for repairs made by a maintenance company, $11,400.

(8) Factory overhead cost is distributed: $10,000 to Machining and $8,000 to Assembly.

(9) Product finished in Machining is transferred to Assembly, $32,000.

(10) Product completely finished cost $60,000.

(11) Product sold during the month cost $54,000.

Required:

Draft journal entries. The company uses a process cost system.

20.2 Prepare T accounts and enter the transactions of problem 1. Only the cost accounts are required (those shown in the illustration on page 590). Rule and balance the accounts where appropriate.

20.3 Calculate the equivalent units for each of the following:

(1) Units started, 20,000; work in process, ending, 4,000 units, one-half completed.

(2) Work in process, beginning, 4,000 units, three-fourths complete; started, 12,000 units; all units completed.

(3) Work in process, beginning, 5,000 units, one-fifth complete; started, 16,000 units; work in process, ending, 4,000 units, one-fourth complete.

(4) Work in process, beginning, 4,000 units, one-half complete; started, 16,000 units; work in process, ending, 2,000 units, three-fourths complete. Materials are complete when a unit is started in process. Show two computations of equivalent units, one for materials and one for labor and overhead.

(5) Work in process, beginning, 5,000 units, two-fifths complete; started, 20,000 units; work in process, ending, 4,000 units, two-fifths complete. Materials are added only as the last step in the processing. Show two computations of equivalent units, one for materials and one for labor and overhead.

20.4 The Bongo Company manufactures a product in two processes. In process A, all material is complete when units of product are started in process. In process B, materials are added as the last step in the processing. During September 1966, the company started 10,000 units in process A and completed 8,000, which were sent to process B. The remaining 2,000 were one-half complete in process A. There were 4,000 units three-fourths complete in process B at the beginning of the month; and at the end, 5,000 were on hand two-fifths complete. The following costs were incurred:

	Process A	Process B
Work in process, beginning	$ —	$35,500
Materials	20,000	1,000
Labor.	9,000	18,000
Overhead	13,500	12,000

Required:

(1) A calculation of equivalent units. (2) Unit cost statement for the month. (3) Calculations of work in process and of cost of goods finished in each process.

20.5   The Nelson Company manufactures a product in two processes: cooking and packing. Materials are complete when a product unit is started in cooking, but are added continuously in packing. During July 1966, the company started 15,000 units in cooking and had 3,000 of them one-third complete at the end of the month. The others went to packing, where there were 3,000 units one-third complete at the start of the month and 5,000 units three-fifths complete at the end. Costs were as follows:

	Cooking	Packing
Work in process, July 1 . . . $ —	$11,000
Materials 30,000	9,000
Labor 13,000	15,000
Overhead 6,500	12,000

Required:

(1) A calculation of equivalent units. (2) Unit cost statement for the month. (3) Calculations of work in process and cost of goods transferred out of each process.

20.6   Pan-Poly, Inc., manufactures a single product in five successive processes. In the first three listed below, materials as well as labor and overhead are introduced into the processing continuously. In the aging process, materials are complete when started, but in the packing process they are added at the end of the process. Production figures for July 1966 are:

First mix: units started, 14,000; work in process, ending, 4,000 units three-fourths complete.

Second mix: work in process, beginning, 5,000 units three-fifths complete; started, 10,000 units; no ending work in process.

Third mix: work in process, beginning, 4,000 units three-fourths complete; started, 15,000 units; work in process, ending, 3,000 units two-thirds complete.

Aging: work in process, beginning, 4,000 units one-fourth complete; started, 19,000 units; work in process, ending, 6,000 units one-third complete.

Packing: work in process, beginning, 5,000 units two-fifths complete; started, 23,000 units; work in process, ending, 3,000 units two-thirds complete.

Costs for the month were:

	First Mix	Second Mix	Third Mix	Aging	Packing
Materials.	$130,000	$80,000	$40,000	$38,000	$ 25,000
Labor and overhead. .	26,000	40,000	20,000	54,000	175,000

Required:

1. Compute equivalent units, giving separate figures for materials and for labor and overhead where appropriate.
2. Compute the cost of the work in process inventories.

Standard Cost Accounting

Standard costs are precomputed costs. If they are to serve as effectively as possible, they should be computed with great care and used as a measure of the actual performance. The general method of introducing standard costs into the accounts is shown in the following diagram:

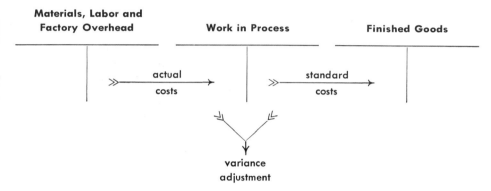

Standard costs may be applied in job order or process conditions. The method is to charge actual costs to Work in Process and to credit Work in Process with the standard cost of the product produced. A difference — a variance — is almost always left in Work in Process. At the end of the accounting period this variance is usually written off to Cost of Goods Sold. However, it should be first analyzed to find the causes of the variance. The information that this analysis gives about the actual performance permits management to find and correct inefficiencies. This, in the opinion of a large number of accountants, is the most valuable service rendered by standard cost data.

LIMITATIONS OF HISTORICAL COSTS

Up to this point we have discussed cost accounting systems that gave *historical* costs, that is, costs actually incurred as a historical fact. Historical costs have the following limitations:

1. In complicated cases their calculation is expensive.
2. The information becomes available too late for some decisions (for example, whether or not to accept a special offer to have work done at a special price).
3. They cannot anticipate changing conditions.

ADVANTAGES OF STANDARD COSTS

1. They are economical to compile (especially when manufacturing is for stock).
2. The data are available early—before the work is done.
3. They can take into consideration expected changes, such as price increases.
4. The proper preparation of standards involves a scrutiny of operations that may of itself detect inefficiencies.
5. They permit effective managerial review of actual costs.
6. Any actual costs due to inefficiencies are eliminated from the balance sheet when standard costs are used for inventory prices.

The possible economy in compiling costs arises when actual costs are recorded only in total. In this case total materials used, total labor cost, and total factory overhead incurred are charged into Work in Process with no analysis by jobs or processes. The credit is calculated by multiplying the units of product produced by the standard cost of each one. This procedure is economical, but it provides little opportunity to find out what jobs or what processes were responsible for the difference between total actual cost and total standard cost. The best managerial data are provided when actual costs are collected in detail in the usual way in addition to the standard costs. Some firms follow this practice; for example, one greeting-card manufacturer does so. This company prepares a standard cost calculation for each new greeting card made, and a large percentage of the jobs are new ones. Then the actual cost of the job is compared with the standard. This double costing gives the best control, but it is expensive, and most firms collect actual costs only in total when they use standard costs.

GENERAL LEDGER ACCOUNTS FOR STANDARD COSTS

A diagram of general ledger accounts for standard costs is shown below. Note that the same accounts are used to collect information about materials on hand, labor paid and accrued, and factory overhead cost as in a job order or process cost system. Note also that separate work in process accounts are set up for each of the three major divisions of cost, so that the variances between actual and standard cost can be recognized and analyzed more conveniently. The variance adjustment is usually made to Cost of Goods Sold, but some of it may properly belong to ending inventories of Work in Process and Finished Goods. For example, if a variance arose because materials used were higher priced than the standard cost allowed, it might be that the higher price is unavoidable and that the standard cost should be changed. In this case the ending inventories that contain these materials should be increased. The system diagrammed on page 607 has a Finished Goods account that is carried at standard cost. Using the standard cost in Finished Goods makes possible a simplified subsidiary ledger. The subsidiary ledger cards need show only the quantities of the product, with a notation in the heading of the card of the standard cost of the item. Since all units are carried at this cost, it is not necessary to multiply out the amounts of the receipts, issues, and balance on the card; no problem of choosing an issue price arises.

DIAGRAM OF GENERAL LEDGER ACCOUNTS FOR STANDARD COSTS

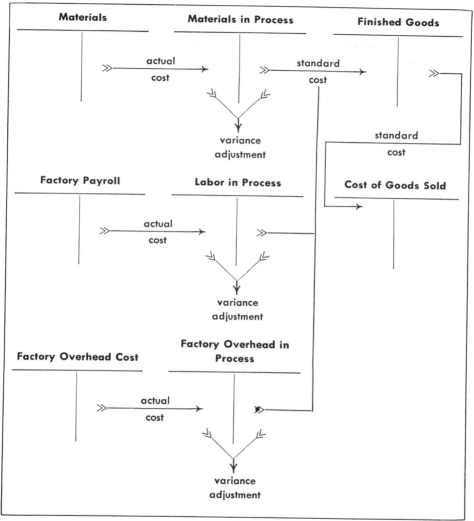

ORIGINAL RECORDS FOR STANDARD COSTS

Materials used may be accounted for by means of requisitions, as in other cost accounting systems. The advantages of a perpetual inventory and a storeroom under control of a storekeeper exist when standard costs are used, as they do in other cases. It is possible to calculate materials used on a periodic inventory basis when standard costs are used, and this method is likely to be used if only the total cost of materials used is wanted. Labor must ordinarily be recorded on timecards for payroll calculations in any case, and these cards or separate job cards or time reports may be used to record the kind of work done. Once again, the particular kind of work done may not be recorded if only the total of the actual labor cost is wanted. It should be noted that detailed records of materials used and labor performed must be kept if the analysis of variances is to be carried to such details as individual jobs. Factory overhead cost is recorded as payments are made and as accruals are recognized at the end of the period (in the usual way).

The Standard Cost Card. The standard cost cards are the fundamental documents in a standard cost system. They give the details of the materials and operations required to produce each product and the cost of each element, plus the factory overhead to be applied. In preparing them, every piece of direct material must be listed and each step of direct labor must be recorded. Establishing these data involves such things as determining how many pieces should be gotten out of the materials, which as a rule come in only certain sizes. In the labor section it involves determining proper but not excessive time for rest

---

THE AZURE NOVELTY COMPANY
Standard Cost Card

No. 427   Date made: 8–31–1966

Product No: 1818
   Name: ash tray   Costs are for 1,000 units
Card prepared by A. S. Glasman   Approved: O. F. Yates

Item	Quantity	Price or Rate	Extension
Materials:			
20 gauge sheet steel	250 square feet	0.10	25 00
Cleaning compound	30 ounces	0.05	1 50
Primer paint	1½ pints	0.50	75
Lacquer	2 quarts	2.00	4 00
Total materials			31 25
Labor:			
Cut blanks	0.50 hours	3.00	1 50
Forming	1.50 "	3.10	4 65
Smooth edges	1.00 "	2.80	2 80
Clean	0.25 "	2.40	0 60
Prime paint	0.33 "	3.00	0 99
Lacquer	0.50 "	3.30	1 65
Total labor			12 19
Factory overhead:			
Machine shop: Fixed costs	3.00 hours	2.00	6 00
Variable costs	3.00 "	1.00	3 00
Paint shop: Fixed costs	1.08 "	1.00	1 08
Variable costs	1.08 "	1.50	1 62
Total overhead			11 70
Total cost			55 14

periods and normal delays due to machine breakdown, failure of materials to arrive, and so on. The application of factory overhead cost is made, as in job order accounting, by dividing expected overhead by the measure of product expected to be produced. The same measures used in job order costs are used in standard costs, direct labor cost and direct labor hours being most popular. Use of direct labor makes the analysis of variance more understandable, and is the method adopted for illustrations in this chapter. The illustration on page 608 shows the standard cost card for a sheet-metal ash tray made by a novelty company. Note that factory overhead cost has been divided between the fixed and the variable portions. This division permits a more meaningful variance analysis. Many cost cards are considerably more elaborate than this one. If custom production is carried on, that is, if products are made to the customer's order and specifications, a standard cost card must be made for each job. Making it involves less extra work than may be imagined, owing to the fact that very careful cost estimates must be made in such cases before a satisfactory price can be quoted. The estimate can easily be turned into a standard cost card. In industries that manufacture for stock the standard cost cards will be useful over long periods. However, it is important that they be revised frequently, because prices, product designs, and working conditions are usually changing.

ILLUSTRATION OF STANDARD COST ACCOUNTING

Gale Manufacturing Company had the following postclosing trial balance on July 31, 1966:

GALE MANUFACTURING COMPANY
Trial Balance

July 31, 1966

	Debits	Credits
Cash	$ 4,800.00	
Accounts Receivable	16,200.00	
Allowance for Doubtful Accounts		$ 1,100.00
Materials	4,200.00	
Materials in Process	800.00	
Labor in Process	900.00	
Factory Overhead in Process	810.00	
Finished Goods	16,400.00	
Prepaid Insurance	710.00	
Land	8,000.00	
Building and Machinery	64,000.00	
Accumulated Depreciation—Building and Machinery		11,600.00
Patent	10,000.00	
Notes Payable		12,000.00
Accounts Payable		15,000.00
Accrued Payroll		800.00
Taxes Payable		1,400.00
Capital Stock		60,000.00
Retained Earnings		24,920.00
	$126,820.00	$126,820.00

Work in process balances consisted of ten units of product C that were complete as to materials and one-half complete as to labor and overhead.

The budget for August 1966 shows 6,600 direct labor hours to be worked and $17,820 of factory overhead cost to be incurred. Of this amount, $9,900 is variable cost and $7,920 is fixed cost. This $17,820 represents 110 units of product (6,600 hours at 60 hours per unit of product). It also represents an overhead cost of $1.50 per hour for variable costs ($9,900 ÷ 6,600), and $1.20 per hour for fixed costs ($7,920 ÷ 6,600).

The standard cost card for product C, the one product produced during August, is summarized as follows:

Standard Cost Card		
Product C		
Materials		
40 units at $2.00 per unit...		$ 80.00
Labor		
60 hours at $3.00 per hour..		180.00
Factory Overhead		
Variable: 60 hours at $1.50 per hour	$90.00	
Fixed: 60 hours at $1.20 per hour	72.00	162.00
Total...		$422.00

Transactions for August that affect the cost accounting are summarized as follows:

1. Materials purchased on credit cost $9,600.
2. Materials costing $8,320 (4,000 units at $2.08 each) were issued as direct materials, and materials costing $200 were used as indirect materials.
3. Payrolls paid totaled $19,800, of which $1,810 was withheld for income tax and $495 for old-age tax.
4. Wages earned for the period totaled $19,693, of which $18,693 (6,030 hours at $3.10 per hour) was direct labor and $1,000 was indirect labor.
5. Insurance premiums on factory coverage expired during the month in the amount of $150.
6. Depreciation on plant and machinery amounted to $2,000.
7. Various accrued costs chargeable to factory overhead amounted to $3,200.
8. Sundry obligations for repairs, power, and so on, were vouchered in the amount of $10,470.
9. Factory overhead was charged to Factory Overhead in Process in the amount incurred for the month.
10. During the month 100 units of product C were finished and transferred to the Finished Goods account (costs are on the standard cost card).
11. Goods carried at a standard cost of $46,430 were sold.
12. Variances remaining in the Work in Process accounts (after the work in process balances were computed at standard cost) were carried to Cost of Goods Sold. The work in process at the end consisted of five units of product complete as to materials, but two-fifths complete as to labor and overhead.

The foregoing transactions are recorded by the following journal entries (if the journal that would be used in practice is not named, it is the general journal):

1. Materials...................................$ 9,600.00
        Vouchers (or Accounts) Payable........... $ 9,600.00
    (purchases recorded in voucher register)

2. Materials in Process.........................$ 8,320.00
    Factory Overhead Cost........................   200.00
        Materials............................ $ 8,520.00
    (to record materials used)

3. Factory Payroll..............................$19,800.00
        Vouchers Payable..................... $17,495.00
        Federal Income Tax Withheld............   1,810.00
        F.I.C.A. Tax Withheld.................   495.00
    (payrolls recorded in voucher register)

4. Labor in Process.............................$18,693.00
    Factory Overhead Cost........................ 1,000.00
        Factory Payroll...................... $19,693.00
    (to record distribution of wages earned)

5. Factory Overhead Cost........................$ 150.00
        Prepaid Insurance.................... $ 150.00
    (to record expiration of insurance premiums)

6. Factory Overhead Cost........................$ 2,000.00
        Accumulated Depreciation—Building and Ma-
            chinery............................ $ 2,000.00

7. Factory Overhead Cost........................$ 3,200.00
        Accrued Liabilities.................... $ 3,200.00
    (to record accrued costs)

8. Factory Overhead Cost........................$10,470.00
        Vouchers (or Accounts) Payable........... $10,470.00
    (sundry obligations recorded in the voucher register)

9. Factory Overhead in Process..................$17,020.00
        Factory Overhead Cost................. $17,020.00
    (to transfer Factory Overhead Cost to Factory Over-
    head in Process)

10. Finished Goods..............................$42,200.00
        Materials in Process.................. $ 8,000.00
        Labor in Process......................   18,000.00
        Factory Overhead in Process...........   16,200.00
    (to record goods finished at standard cost)

11. Cost of Goods Sold..........................$46,430.00
        Finished Goods........................ $46,430.00
    (to record goods sold at standard cost)

12. Cost of Goods Sold............................$ 3,259.00
      Materials in Process.................... $ 720.00
      Labor in Process.......................   1,233.00
      Factory Overhead in Process............   1,306.00
   (to carry variances to Cost of Goods Sold)

The general ledger cost accounts reflecting the foregoing transactions are presented on page 613 (only the cost accounts are shown).

Note that the balances of the work in process accounts may be computed as follows:

Materials (5 × $80.00)...............................$400.00
Labor (5 × ⅖ × $180).............................. 360.00
Factory Overhead (5 × ⅖ × $162.00).................. 324.00

After the work in process balances are computed, the variances may be obtained by subtraction. If the variances are subsequently analyzed, this work will serve as a check on the computation of the balances and the variances.

ANALYSIS OF MATERIALS AND LABOR VARIANCES

The data of Gale Manufacturing Company for August 1966 permit an analysis of the variances. Materials and labor variances are analyzed to determine how much of the figure is due to prices different from those on the standard cost card and how much is due to the use of quantities different from those required by the standard. Part of the variance will be due to these two sources acting together in systems like the one illustrated here. The elements of the materials variance of $720 are presented in a calculation of the variance as follows:

	Price		Quantity		Amount
Actual.................	$2.08	×	4,000	=	$8,320.00
Standard..............	2.00	×	3,800	=	7,600.00
	0.08		200		$ 720.00

The standard quantity of materials (that presumably should have been used) is obtained by multiplying the equivalent units of production by the materials units specified by the standard cost card for one unit of product. In the present case the production may be summarized as follows (materials are complete when started in process in this case):

	Units	Equivalent Units	
		Material	Labor and Overhead
In process August 1.......	10 (½)		
Started in August........	95		
	105		
In process August 31......	5 (⅖)	5	2
Finished:			
From beginning inventory	10	–	5
Started this period.....	90	90	90
	105	95	97

Standard Cost Accounts of Gale Manufacturing Company

Month of August, 1966

Materials

	Debit		Credit
B.	4,200.00	(2)	8,520.00
(1)	9,600.00	B.	5,280.00
	13,800.00		13,800.00
B.	5,280.00		

Factory Payroll

	Debit		Credit
(3)	19,800.00	B.	800.00
B.	693.00	(4)	19,693.00
	20,493.00		20,493.00
		B.	693.00

Factory Overhead Cost

	Debit		Credit
(2)	200.00	(9)	17,020.00
(4)	1,000.00		
(5)	150.00		
(6)	2,000.00		
(7)	3,200.00		
(8)	10,470.00		
	17,020.00		

Materials in Process

	Debit		Credit
B.	800.00	(10)	8,000.00
(2)	8,320.00	(12)	720.00
		B.	400.00
	9,120.00		9,120.00
B.	400.00		

Labor in Process

	Debit		Credit
B.	900.00	(10)	18,000.00
(4)	18,693.00	(12)	1,233.00
		B.	360.00
	19,593.00		19,593.00
B.	360.00		

Factory Overhead in Process

	Debit		Credit
B.	810.00	(10)	16,200.00
(9)	17,020.00	(12)	1,306.00
		B.	324.00
	17,830.00		17,830.00
B.	324.00		

Finished Goods

	Debit		Credit
B.	16,400.00	(11)	46,430.00
(10)	42,200.00	B.	12,170.00
	58,600.00		58,600.00
B.	12,170.00		

Cost of Goods Sold

	Debit
(11)	46,430.00
(12)	3,259.00

As far as materials are concerned, production is equivalent to 95 finished units; 95 × 40 units of material = 3,800 units of material required for production at standard.

The analysis of the materials variance is:

Materials price variance:
   $0.08 × 3,800 . . . . $304

Materials quantity variance:
   200 × $2.00 400

Materials joint variance:
   $0.08 × 200 16

   Total $720

The formulas for this analysis are:

variation in price × standard quantity = materials price variance
variation in quantity × standard price = materials quantity variance
variation in price × variation in quantity = materials joint variance

The joint variance is the joint result or combined effect of having variations in both price and quantity and cannot be said to be due solely to one or the other.

The labor variance is analyzed in the same way. The labor variances are as follows:

	Rate	×	Hours	=	Amount
Actual	$3.10	×	6,030	=	$18,693.00
Standard	3.00	×	5,820	=	17,460.00
	$0.10		210		$ 1,233.00

The standard labor hours for the period were obtained by multiplying the equivalent units of production by the standard hours per unit of product given on the standard cost card. In the present case the computation is: 97 units × 60 hours = 5,820.

The analysis of labor variance is:

Labor rate variance:
   $0.10 × 5,820 . . . . $ 582.00

Labor efficiency variance:
   210 × $3.00 . . . . 630.00

Labor joint variance:
   $0.10 × 210 . . . . 21.00

   Total $1,233.00

The formulas for the labor variance analysis are like those for the materials variance; one simply has to recognize that "rate" is a price and that the "efficiency" variance is a quantity variance.

Once the variances are analyzed, management may take any steps indicated. The causes of using 200 units of material and 210 labor hours too many in the above case may be investigated and corrected. The causes of the higher prices may be investigated, and if they can be avoided (by substituting other materials, for example) such action may be taken. Furthermore, the analysis will indicate whether a particular variance due, say, to price, is large enough to justify any investigation, so that executives may avoid unprofitable inquiries.

ANALYSIS OF OVERHEAD VARIANCE

Factory overhead is commonly analyzed into three variances, namely:

1. Budget variance
2. Capacity variance
3. Efficiency variance

BUDGET VARIANCE

The budget variance is the difference between the actual overhead incurred and what the budget calls for. Where overhead costs are divided between the fixed and the variable elements, the budget may be adjusted at the end of a period to determine what level of cost should have been incurred for the level of activity actually reached. The fixed costs are incurred whatever the actual level of activity, but the variable costs are expected to vary according to the number of hours worked. For the case in hand the adjusted budget is:

```
Fixed costs...................................$ 7,920.00
Variable costs:
  6,030 actual hours × $1.50...................   9,045.00
Total adjusted budget.........................$16,965.00
```

The budget variance is then:

$$\$17,020 - \$16,965 = \$55$$

The formula for it is:

actual overhead − adjusted budget overhead = overhead budget variance

CAPACITY VARIANCE

If more or fewer hours are worked than the standard cost card contemplates, the fixed overhead will be over- or underabsorbed. The fixed overhead figure on the cost card given on page 608 is based on a production of 110 units of product, but the computation of equivalent units presented earlier shows that 97 units were obtained as far as labor and overhead were concerned. The difference of 13 units at $72 per unit gives unabsorbed fixed overhead of $936. In other words, the capacity variance is:

13 units short of budget × $72 per unit = $936

The formula for it is:

$$\left[\binom{\text{budgeted}}{\text{units}} - \binom{\text{actual}}{\text{units}}\right] \times \left[\begin{array}{c}\text{fixed overhead}\\\text{per unit}\end{array}\right] = \left[\begin{array}{c}\text{overhead capacity}\\\text{variance}\end{array}\right]$$

This may also be computed as:

$$\left[\binom{\text{budgeted}}{\text{hours}} - \binom{\text{standard hours}}{\text{for the product}}\right] \times \left[\begin{array}{c}\text{fixed overhead}\\\text{per hour}\end{array}\right]$$

$$= \left[\begin{array}{c}\text{overhead capacity}\\\text{variance}\end{array}\right]$$

This is

$$6,600 - 5,820 = 780 \quad \text{and} \quad 780 \times \$1.20 = \$936$$

The standard hours are the hours that should have been used according to the standard cost card—in this case $97 \times 60 = 5,820$.

OVERHEAD EFFICIENCY VARIANCE

The cost card provides $90 per product unit or $1.50 per labor hour for variable overhead costs. If the production actually required exactly the sixty hours per unit specified on the standard cost card, it would be expected that $90 of variable costs per unit of product would be incurred. If more hours are used, more variable cost is expected. The overhead efficiency variance reflects the cost of the extra hours. In this case it is:

$$\left[\binom{6.030 \text{ actual}}{\text{hours}} - \binom{5,820 \text{ standard}}{\text{hours}}\right] \times \left[\begin{array}{c}\$1.50 \text{ per}\\\text{hour}\end{array}\right] = \$315$$

The formula for it is:

$$\left[\binom{\text{actual}}{\text{hours}} - \binom{\text{standard}}{\text{hours}}\right] \times \left[\begin{array}{c}\text{variable overhead}\\\text{per hour}\end{array}\right] = \left[\begin{array}{c}\text{overhead efficiency}\\\text{variance}\end{array}\right]$$

The standard hours are obtained as in the preceding section, that is, (units of product obtained) × (hours needed per unit of product per the standard cost card). In this case it is 97 (equivalent units) × 60 = 5,820.

SUMMARY OF FACTORY OVERHEAD VARIANCE ANALYSIS

The foregoing overhead analyses are summarized as follows:

Overhead budget variance.	$ 55.00
Overhead capacity variance.	936.00
Overhead efficiency variance.	315.00
Total.	$1,306.00

No "joint" variance appears in the above figures as it did in the case of materials and labor because the budget variance computation removes the price element from the remaining computations. A variety of analyses of variances are possible, but the alternative computations are beyond the scope of this book. The variances shown above were all debit variances. They could have been credits, and some could have been credits while others were debits; the formulas given are expressed so that a positive figure is a debit and a negative figure is a credit. The usual rules of algebra apply; a positive times a positive gives a positive product, and so does a negative times a negative; but a positive times a negative gives a negative product.

SUMMARY

Standard costs are precomputed costs. They are best used as measures of performance, but they also can be used to economize on bookkeeping effort. In the standard cost accounting system described here, actual costs are charged into Work in Process and finished work is credited out at standard costs. The result is a variance that may be analyzed to discover its causes.

The system requires the usual record of materials, labor, and overhead, but it does not require a detailed record of each job or process. However, if the closest check on actual performance is desired, actual costs for each job or process must be collected and compared in detail with the standard costs.

Materials and labor variances are analyzed into price and quantity variances, with a joint variance emerging as the effect of the first two acting together. Factory overhead variance is analyzed into a budget, a capacity, and an efficiency variance.

QUESTIONS

21.1   Contrast historical costs with standard costs.

21.2   The manager of a small boat works tells you that he cannot use standard costs because many of his jobs are custom jobs done to the customer's specifications. Do you believe that this statement is true? Why?

21.3   What is meant by a variance in connection with standard costs? Illustrate.

21.4   What limitations do historical costs have that may be overcome by standard costs?

21.5   What advantages are attributed to standard costs?

21.6   What must be done in collecting actual costs and standard costs if management is to have the closest possible control over operations through cost accounting methods?

21.7   What simplification of the subsidiary ledger is possible when finished goods are carried at standard cost?

21.8   Describe in a general way the content of a standard cost card.

21.9   What is usually done in the ledger with the cost variances remaining at the end of the accounting period? What might be done with them if they were due to higher prices that could not be avoided?

21.10 Into what elements may materials and labor variances be analyzed?

21.11 State what causes each of the following variances: (1) overhead budget variance; (2) overhead capacity variance; (3) overhead efficiency variance.

21.12 In a departmentalized plant using standard costs it is generally considered unnecessary to classify material price variances by departments. Why?

21.1 Journalize the following transactions completed by the Day Co.:

(1) Issued direct materials at actual cost, $20,000. (The company uses a Materials in Process account.)

(2) Actual wages distributed consisted of $24,000 direct labor and $1,000 indirect labor.

(3) Actual factory overhead of $18,000 was transferred to Factory Overhead in Process.

(4) The standard cost of products finished comprised materials, $19,500; labor, $25,100; factory overhead, $19,200.

(5) Variances were transferred to Cost of Goods Sold as follows:

> Materials.................... $ 500 unfavorable
> Labor....................... 1,100 favorable
> Factory Overhead........... 1,200 favorable

21.2 The Parr Company uses a standard cost system. There was no work in process on June 1. The following data are available for June:

(1) Materials issued, $10,800.

(2) Labor distributed, $8,600.

(3) Actual factory overhead incurred, $6,500.

(4) Product finished and sold, 900 units at a standard cost per unit of $10 for materials, $8 for labor, and $6 for factory overhead.

(5) Variances were transferred to Cost of Goods Sold. Work in process on June 30 at standard comprised $1,000 for materials, $800 for labor, and $600 for factory overhead.

Required:

Open T accounts for Materials in Process, Labor in Process, Overhead in Process, and Cost of Goods Sold. Post the transactions to these accounts. Balance the in-process accounts for materials, labor, and overhead as of June 30, and transfer the variances to Cost of Goods Sold.

21.3 The cost card for product X shows:

> Materials A, 4 units at $5 .... $20
> Materials B, 6 units at $4 24
> Materials C, 10 units at $2 20
> Standard materials cost per unit of X $64

During the month 400 units of product X were started and completed. Materials issued were as follows:

> Materials A, 1,800 units at $5.00................. $9,000
> Materials B, 2,400 units at $4.10................. 9,840
> Materials C, 4,200 units at $2.10................. 8,820

Required:

Calculate and analyze the price, quantity, and joint variance for each material. Indicate for each variance whether it is favorable or unfavorable. Explain what action management should take.

21.4 The cost card for product Y shows labor cost as follows:

Operation R, 4.5 hr. at $4.00..................... $18.00
Operation S, 3 hr. at $3.50 .... 10.50
Operation T, 2 hr. at $4.00 .... 8.00
Standard materials cost per unit of Y $36.50

During the month 200 units of product Y were started and completed. The actual hours worked at actual wage rates were as follows:

Operation R, 950 hr. at $4.00 .... $3,800
Operation S, 600 hr. at $3.60 2,160
Operation T, 350 hr. at $4.20 1,470

Required:

Analyze the variances by operations. Indicate for each whether it is favorable or unfavorable. Explain what action management should take for each item.

21.5 Parker Manufacturing Company produced 400 units of product X during September 1966. The cost card for this product shows:

Variable, 40 hr. at $1.00 .... $ 40
Fixed (based on $27,000/450 units) 60
Total standard factory overhead per unit $100

During the month 17,000 labor hours were used on product X and factory overhead of $44,550 was incurred.

Required:

1. Calculate the total overhead budget based on the actual hours worked. How much of the total is fixed, and how much is variable?
2. Calculate the overhead budget variance. Explain the significance of this variance and indicate what action should be taken.
3. Calculate the overhead capacity variance by comparing the fixed costs absorbed (based on actual units produced) with the budgeted fixed costs as computed in requirement 1. Explain the significance of this variance and indicate what action should be taken.
4. Calculate the overhead efficiency variance by comparing the variable costs absorbed (based on standard labor hours) with the total variable costs as revised in requirement 1. Explain the significance of this variance and indicate what action should be taken.

21.6 The Hammond Company produced 800 units of product Y during July 1966. The cost card for this product shows:

Factory overhead:
Variable, 10 hr. at $2 .... $20
Fixed (based on $7,500/750 units) 10
Total standard factory overhead per unit $30

Factory overhead cost was incurred in the amount of $24,300. Labor hours totaled 8,100.

Required:

Analyze the variances and discuss their significance.

21.7 A fire occurred in the early morning hours of January 31 at the East Coast Plant of Styx Manufacturing Company, destroying most of the accounting records, including the cost reports and analyses of variances for the month. However, from the charred remains the following facts are available:

Standard material cost per unit of finished product,
10 lb. of A at $2 . . . . $20
Standard labor cost per unit of finished product,
30 hr. at $5 . . . . $150
Standard total overhead cost per unit of finished
product $110
Budgeted production for January . . . . 1,000 units
Actual production for January . . . . 800 units
Actual materials used . . . . 9,000 lbs.
Overhead efficiency variance . . . . $6,000 unfavorable
Fixed overhead for January $20,000
Variable overhead incurred in January $75,000
Variable overhead estimated for January $72,000

There were no inventories at the beginning or end of the month. Actual material and labor prices were exactly equal to the standard prices.

Required:

Prepare an analysis of all variances.

PROBLEMS

21.1 The following transactions were completed in August by the Polar Development Co., which uses a standard cost system:
(1) Materials issued for direct use on the product cost $17,000.
(2) Wages earned during the month consist of direct labor, $13,600, and indirect labor, $400.
(3) Actual factory overhead incurred is transferred to Factory Overhead in Process; it totals $8,000.
(4) Products with the standard unit costs shown were finished in the following quantities:

| | | Standard Cost per Unit | | |
Product	Units	Materials	Labor	Overhead
X	100	$60	$60	$30
Y	200	30	40	20

(5) Finished goods sold had a standard cost of $24,000.
(6) Variances were transferred to Cost of Goods Sold in the following amounts: materials, $200; labor, $300; overhead, $100. All are debit variances.

Required:

Draft journal entries to record the transactions.

21.2 The Anchor Co. manufactures a single product. The standard cost card for the product is summarized as follows:

Materials . . . . $ 8
Labor   5
Factory overhead cost   4
Total $17

The company completed the following transactions in August:
(1) Purchased materials on credit, $18,000.
(2) Issued materials, $16,610; of this amount, $16,240 was for direct use and $370 for indirect.

(3) Payrolls were vouchered for a gross amount of $10,600 less $1,200 withheld for income tax and $424 withheld for F.I.C.A. tax.

(4) Wages earned during the month consisted of $10,720 direct labor and $520 indirect labor.

(5) Depreciation of plant and equipment for the month, $3,000.

(6) Vouchered invoices for repairs, gas, electricity, and so on, $4,730.

(7) Transferred factory overhead costs for the month to Factory Overhead in Process.

(8) Finished 1,600 units during the month.

(9) Sold 1,000 units during the month.

(10) Closed variances to Cost of Goods Sold. On August 1 the company had 400 units on hand one-fourth complete as to labor and overhead but fully complete as to materials; at the end of August it had 800 units complete as to materials but three-fourths complete as to labor and overhead. During the month 2,000 units were started in process.

Required:

Draft journal entries.

21.3 Post the cost transactions of the Anchor Co. in problem 2 to T accounts (use the accounts shown on page 607). Rule and balance the appropriate accounts. August 1 balances were as follows:

Materials . . . . $25,000 dr.
Finished Goods . . . . 10,000 dr.
Factory Payroll . . . .   300 cr.

21.4 The following data give actual and standard prices and quantities for five cases. Calculate the variance for each case, and then analyze each variance. Designate the figures in the variance analysis as debits or credits ("dr." or "cr.")

	Price		Quantity	
	Actual	Standard	Actual	Standard
(1)	$0.55	$0.50	800	800
(2)	0.50	0.50	1,200	1,000
(3)	0.55	0.50	1,200	1,000
(4)	0.55	0.50	980	1,000
(5)	0.35	0.40	1,400	2,000

21.5 Jewell Manufacturing Company produced 400 units of product KDD during September 1966. The cost card for this product shows:

Materials: 8 units at $1 . . . . $ 8
Labor: 10 hr. at $3.50   35
Factory overhead:
    Variable, 10 hr. at $4 . . . . $40
    Fixed (based on 380 units) 10   50
Total $93

Costs incurred during the month were:

Materials: 4,000 units at $1.10 each
Labor: 4,200 hr. at $3.75 each
Factory overhead cost: $21,300

Required:

(1) Calculate the variances. (2) Analyze the variances.

Special Cost Analysis

The costs discussed so far are total costs. The unit costs calculated for manufactured product were approximately equivalent to the economists' *average total manufacturing costs*. In other words, all the manufacturing costs incurred during a period were identified with or charged to the product produced.[1] Such costs are the generally accepted basis for inventory figures, for the calculation of net income, and for decisions of long-run effect. For example, one would not decide to build a new factory to produce portland cement (the essential ingredient of concrete as we know it) if he were not confident that a profit could be earned after all costs of the product, including depreciation of the plant, were deducted from revenues. However, for certain decisions the total cost or average total cost per unit is not what is needed. In these situations it is usually the *variable* cost that is significant, and a proper decision depends upon distinguishing fixed from variable costs. Furthermore, this distinction is useful in determining how costs will behave as the volume of business increases or decreases. This chapter is devoted to the special decisions and calculations that use a special analysis of cost rather than the familiar total cost. The topics covered are:

1. Break-even analysis
2. Applications of the contribution theory
3. Differential cost and price discrimination
4. Variable vs. fixed cost and the decision to make or buy
5. Opportunity costs and the price level
6. Controllable vs. uncontrollable costs in reports

BREAK-EVEN ANALYSIS

The point at which a firm "breaks even" (just covers expenses with revenue) is important in planning. It is especially important in considering new equipment; management tries to avoid raising the break-even point because that makes the firm less able to stand reverses (losses occur at a higher volume of sales than before). Break-even analysis is most easily seen in the form of a "profit graph" or "break-even chart." This is a graph showing the fixed costs, the variable costs, and the revenue of a concern for a period—usually a year—for various possible levels of production and sales. Where the line for revenue crosses the total-cost line, the firm "breaks even"; below that it has a

---

[1] With exceptions for such special cases as unabsorbed overhead and standard cost variances not charged to product.

BREAK-EVEN CHART (PROFIT GRAPH)

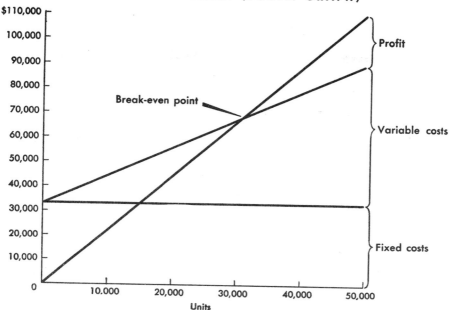

loss and above it a profit. A profit graph is illustrated here. Note that the units produced in a period are plotted on the horizontal, or *x*, axis and that the dollar amounts of cost and revenue are plotted on the vertical, or *y*, axis. The fixed costs, being a constant amount regardless of the volume of business, are represented by a horizontal line. In the illustration they amount to $35,000. The variable costs increase as the production level increases; in the illustration they are $1 per unit of product. Revenue in this case is $2.20 per unit of product. The break-even point is $64,169.[2]

DATA FOR THE BREAK-EVEN CHART

The revenue line on a break-even chart may be drawn by plotting the price of the product times the units for any level of operations; only one point need be plotted, since the origin (the zero point on the chart) plus any other point will define the line. The cost lines may be determined in various ways; two basic ones are:

1. Analyze the costs for a period (say a year), dividing them into fixed and variable portions, and plot the results.
2. Plot the total costs from several periods and fit a line to them. This line will cut the vertical axis at the level of fixed costs.

Use of the first method requires a close scrutiny of each element of expense. If expenses are not already broken down into many accounts, this breakdown may have to be done to separate the fixed from the variable elements. If some

---

[2]This is calculated by formula, which is discussed in this chapter in the section on Applications of the Contribution Theory.

accounts are set up on a functional basis, such as delivery expense, those accounts will have to be analyzed for their object-of-expenditure content. For example, delivery wages will presumably be a variable expense and depreciation of delivery equipment a fixed expense. Cost of goods sold is a variable element in a purely merchandising concern, but contains fixed elements in a manufacturing concern. It also includes an element of inventory change. To separate it into fixed and variable elements in a manufacturing concern one may analyze the "cost of manufacture" for the period and obtain from this the proportions of fixed and variable cost in the product. These proportions may then be applied to the figure for cost of goods sold. When the analysis is complete, it may be summarized in this form:

	Total	Fixed	Variable
Sales	$110,000		
Cost of Goods Sold	$ 45,000	$18,000	$27,000
Selling Expenses	22,000	9,000	13,000
General and Administrative Expenses	18,000	8,000	10,000
Total Operating Expense	$ 85,000	$35,000	$50,000
Net Operating Income	$ 25,000		
Units Sold	50,000		

The second method of constructing a profit graph requires total-cost data from more than one period—preferably several. However, it avoids the difficulty of analyzing expenses one by one to separate fixed from variable costs. It does this by arriving at a theoretical fixed cost where the total-cost line, fitted to the points for total costs of the several periods, cuts the vertical axis. If the several periods are comparable—that is, if prices and other conditions are not changing—this method will give a reliable figure.

The profit graph does not, as a rule, include income tax, since it does not apply below the break-even point. It can be inserted, if desired, by a line beginning at the break-even point and cutting off a portion of the profit. The same may be said of any expense based on net income, such as bonuses.

USES OF THE BREAK-EVEN CHART

The break-even chart helps visualize the following:

1. The break-even point. It is at a high production and sales level when fixed costs are high, lower when they are low.
2. Changes in profit as sales increase. Profit increases rapidly when variable costs per unit are small, slowly when they are large.
3. The effects of combinations of changes in fixed costs, variable costs and revenue. The effect of installing new machinery that increases fixed costs but which operates with lower unit costs is illustrated in the chart below. The solid lines are the same as those in the preceding illustration; the dotted lines show the new fixed-cost and total-cost positions. From this combination one can see the direction and extent to which the break-even point is shifted and the extent of possible additional profit as revenue increases. Other changes, such as increased selling prices, can be similarly shown. These changes can also be expressed in figures,

BREAK-EVEN CHART SHOWING EFFECT OF CHANGED COST STRUCTURE

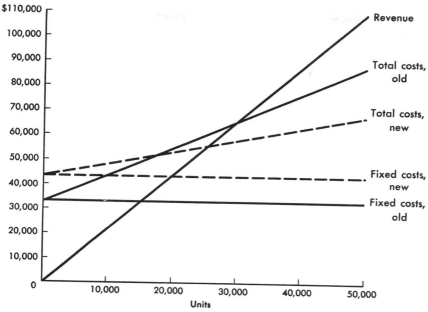

but the chart is helpful in discussing them, and especially so to people who are not sophisticated in accounting. It is also possible to draw charts for segments of a business, provided that the facilities reflected in the fixed costs are distinguishable for the separate parts. Different behavior of costs in the different divisions can then be observed.

LIMITATIONS OF THE BREAK-EVEN CHART

The break-even chart has these limitations:

1. The assumption that costs move in a straight line as volume of activity changes may not be true.
2. Basing the chart on data of one or a very few periods may give results that are not typical of the company's experience.
3. The chart is not well suited to firms that sell a variety of products, the proportions of which may change.

The criticisms apply to the simpler charts, but more elaborate charts can be constructed to overcome the limitations. For example, if fixed costs include the salaries of assistant foremen and if these assistants must be released at very low levels of production, the fixed-cost line may be drawn in steps instead of as a single horizontal line. Charts may be drawn for a variety of combinations of products; in fact, the basic advantage of the charts is their ability to show the effect of a variety of possibilities in advance. The danger of using data that are not typical of what has happened or can be expected is perhaps the most serious drawback.

APPLICATIONS OF THE CONTRIBUTION THEORY

The contribution theory considers the sales dollar to consist of two parts: the amount needed currently to produce or buy the unit sold (the variable cost) and the remainder. The remainder is the "contribution" made by that sales dollar to cover fixed costs and to yield a profit. As in the case of break-even analysis, the essential aspect of the theory is the distinction between fixed and variable costs or expenses. The break-even point is one of the things that can be computed when the "contribution" of each sales dollar and the total fixed cost are known. Applications of the contribution theory are discussed under the following headings:

1. Computation of the break-even point
2. Planning
3. Product selection
4. Appraising sales effort

COMPUTATION OF THE BREAK-EVEN POINT

Once fixed costs and variable costs are separated, the following formula can be applied:

$$\text{break-even point} = \frac{\text{fixed costs}}{1 - \dfrac{\text{variable costs}}{\text{sales}}}$$

or

$$\text{BEP} = \frac{\text{FC}}{1 - \dfrac{\text{VC}}{\text{S}}}$$

The denominator of the fraction is the contribution of each sales dollar; when this is divided into fixed costs, the number of sales dollars necessary to break even, or barely to cover fixed costs, is found. Sales dollars can then be converted into units of product if desired. To illustrate: A company has fixed costs of $82,000 and variable costs of $67,500 when sales are $225,000. The product sells for $5 per unit. Its break-even point in sales dollars is:

$$\text{BEP} = \frac{\$82,000}{1 - \dfrac{\$67,500}{\$225,000}} = \frac{\$82,000}{1 - .30} = \frac{\$82,000}{.7} = \$117,143$$

The break-even point in units of product is:

$$\frac{\$117,143}{\$5} = 23,429$$

THE CONTRIBUTION THEORY AND PLANNING

The effect of prospective or proposed changes can be worked out quickly when data on costs are divided between the fixed and the variable elements. This kind of appraisal is demonstrated in the following two cases.

Case 1. A concern has had fixed costs of $172,000 and a ratio of variable cost to sales of 42 percent. Owing to rising price levels, its fixed costs will be $180,000 next year and the ratio of variable costs to sales is expected to be 44 percent. What level of sales must be reached to provide a net operating profit of $18,000 next year?

The problem is solved by recognizing (1) that the contribution necessary to cover fixed costs and the desired profit is $180,000 + $18,000 = $198,000, and (2) that the number of sales dollars needed in these circumstances can be computed by dividing the desired contribution by the quantity one minus the ratio of variable cost to sales (that is, by the rate of contribution per sales dollar). The computation (to the nearest dollar) is:

$$\frac{\$198,000}{1 - 0.44} = \frac{\$198,000}{0.56} = \$353,571$$

Case 2. A company is considering the purchase of some rather elaborate equipment. The officers do not wish to buy the equipment unless the investment can be recovered in three years. The equipment costs $60,000; its product can be sold for $100,000 per year for at least three years; variable costs of 70 percent of sales must be incurred to manufacture the product.

The contribution here is $30,000 per year, that is:

$$[(1.00 - 0.70) \times \$100,000]$$

Some of this will be spent for property taxes and insurance on the equipment; this amounts to $3,000 per year. The remainder, or $27,000 per year, can be considered the return of the investment. At this rate the investment will be recovered in a little over two years.

CONTRIBUTION THEORY AND PRODUCT SELECTION

One way of improving net operating income is to eliminate or de-emphasize those products that yield a small contribution and to retain and promote those that give a large one. The same policy can be applied in selecting new products to make and sell. If a concern has unused capacity and is seeking new products, it is obvious that the product that gives the largest margin of revenue over its variable costs will add the most to net income. It will, in fact, add to the net income the total "contribution." In this situation, any new costs that must be incurred because the new product is added must be treated as variable costs. For example, consider a choice between the following three products for addition to the line:

	Product 1	Product 2	Product 3
Probable annual sales.......................	$80,000	$90,000	$100,000
Regular variable costs (materials, freight, etc.)...	40,000	40,000	50,000
Regular contribution.....................	$40,000	$50,000	$ 50,000
New fixed costs required (depreciation of special equipment, etc.).............	15,000	20,000	30,000
Addition to net operating income.........	$25,000	$30,000	$ 20,000

For purposes of this decision, product 2 is the best although product 3 has as large a contribution when it is figured in the usual way.

Two factors must be borne in mind when selecting products for emphasis or elimination on the basis of their contribution rates: (1) There must be unused capacity for producing or selling the additional product. If this is not true the fixed costs will not be "fixed"; they will have to be increased by acquisition of more equipment or more salaried people. Of course, the addition may still be profitable, but the added fixed costs must be considered before profitability can be determined. (2) A product may be important for good customer relations even though its contribution is not satisfactory. For example, if a concern did not carry replacement parts for its products it might find the regular product hard to sell. In other words, the "contribution" is not the only factor to be considered.

CONTRIBUTION THEORY AND APPRAISAL OF SALES EFFORT

Sales may be analyzed by salesmen or by sales territories and the "contribution" of the salesmen or the territory computed. Even though two salesmen bring in the same total of sales revenue, one will produce more net operating income if his sales contain a higher proportion of merchandise with a high "contribution" rate. This is a familiar fact in sales management; products that offer wider "margins" are always pushed. The accountant can prepare analyses of sales by salesmen or sales territories showing the "contribution" made by each one, and thus facilitate managerial review of the sales effort. Such an analysis may take the following form for a merchandising concern:

| | | | Territory | |
	Total	North	South	West
Sales	$600,000	$300,000	$160,000	$140,000
Cost of Goods Sold	310,000	160,000	80,000	70,000
Gross Margin	$290,000	$140,000	$ 80,000	$ 70,000
Other Variable Selling Expenses:				
Commissions	$ 30,000	$ 13,000	$ 7,500	$ 9,500
Travel Expense	42,000	11,000	8,000	23,000
Freight—Out	106,000	30,000	41,000	35,000
Sundry	21,000	8,000	7,000	6,000
Subtotal	$199,000	$ 62,000	$ 63,500	$ 73,500
Contribution	$ 91,000	$ 78,000	$ 16,500	$ (3,500)

DIFFERENTIAL COST AND PRICE DISCRIMINATION

Differential cost is the additional cost required to do an additional job. For example, a concern has been making 10,000 units of product a week at a total cost of $80,000 per week. In a certain week it made 10,500 units at a total cost of $81,000. The differential cost of the extra 500 units is $1,000. Differential cost in accounting is similar to "marginal cost" in economics. The economist defines marginal cost or "incremental cost" as the added cost necessary to get the last unit of product. Differential cost is not restricted to the cost of the last unit produced; it can be computed for a group of units or for any alternative. For example, if the fare from St. Louis to Minneapolis is $50, and the fare from St. Louis to Minneapolis by way of Kansas City is $75, the differential cost of going by way of Kansas City is $25. Differential costs are usually variable costs, but in some cases they may involve the addition of a fixed item. This was illustrated in the above section on product selection; all the added costs of the new product would be the differential cost of getting that product.

Differential costs are useful in decisions on price discrimination. Price discrimination is the practice of charging different prices to different customers. It does not refer to the practice of charging a different price to a wholesaler than to a retailer, for example, because the difference in that case is a normal arrangement providing a margin to the wholesaler so he can resell to retailers and earn an income. It exists when different prices are charged to different wholesalers or to different retailers. To be successful, price discrimination requires that the customers be ignorant of the prices charged to others, or that the customers be separated so that they cannot sell the product to each other. Otherwise, a customer who got a low price could sell the product to another of the customers at a profit and defeat the purposes of the manufacturer. The customers may be separated by tariff barriers or by a distance that imposes high transportation costs. The possibilities of increasing net income by means of price discrimination can be seen in the case of an electric power company. The company sells electricity to householders and small business concerns at established rates. A large industry proposes to build a plant in the territory of the electric company; it will buy current from the electric company if the company will establish a low industrial rate, but otherwise will build and operate its own private power plant. The electric company makes the following computation:

		Before Price Discrimination	Added by Price Discrimination
Sales:			
100,000,000 kwh at $0.05		$5,000,000	
10,000,000 kwh at $0.008			$80,000
Costs:			
Variable $0.0025 per unit	$ 250,000		25,000
Fixed	3,000,000	3,250,000	—
Operating margin		$1,750,000	$55,000

If the additional business is taken, the average total cost per unit of service will be $3,250,000 + $25,000 ÷ 110,000,000, which is $0.0298 per unit. This is more than the proposed industrial rate. Nevertheless, the electric company would be better off to establish the low industrial rate. Once again the decision is valid only if capacity exists to produce the extra service, or if any added fixed costs would also be covered and leave a margin.

Price discrimination may be practiced in exporting as against domestic sales. It may be practiced by altering the product so that it is suitable for one use but not another, and can then be sold at different prices in two markets.

For example, a metal may be alloyed for roofing material so that it cannot be economically used to make electric wire. In so far as these practices make it possible to use a product more widely, they are justifiable. The federal Robinson-Patman Act prohibits price discrimination between customers buying the same product in the same level of trade (retailers, for example) within the United States unless the difference in price is justified by a difference in the cost of supplying the particular customer.

VARIABLE AND FIXED COST AND THE DECISION TO MAKE OR TO BUY

The decision to make a product or to buy it from outsiders is another case in which fixed costs must be distinguished from variable costs. Consider the following product costs:

		Per Unit
Variable costs:		
Materials	$80.00	
Labor	28.00	
Sundry	14.00	$122.00
Fixed costs:		
Depreciation	$ 8.40	
Property Taxes	1.10	
Supervisory Salaries	6.40	
Other	2.50	18.40
Total cost per unit		$140.40

If this product can be purchased from outsiders for $130, the company should make the product, because it will spend less, currently ($122 in the above example), by making it. The fixed costs would be incurred whether or not the product was bought outside; they may be ignored if we assume that they represent facilities that cannot be used for any other purpose. If we change this assumption, we get a different answer. Assume that the facilities could be profitably used to make another product if this one were purchased outside. Then we must count the fixed costs; they represent the sacrifice of a valuable alternative. In that case the company should buy the product for $130.

If the product can be bought outside for $120, the company should presumably buy it even if there is no other use for the facilities reflected in the fixed costs. At $120, it costs the company less than would have to be spent currently ($122) to get the product out of its own production.

OPPORTUNITY COSTS AND THE PRICE LEVEL

An opportunity cost is the cost of the next-best alternative. In the section immediately above we assumed an opportunity cost for the use of the facilities when we said that they could be used to produce another product profitably. It could be said that the alternative to renting out a warehouse would be to sell it. In this case the sales value represents the value on which one would expect to base his rental charge if he preferred to keep the building. Opportunity costs change as the price level changes; one cannot establish prices on the basis of historical cost and expect to recover enough revenue to equal depreciation of current values. It is desirable to express costs in current price levels if they are to be used in setting prices or in calculating income. Suppose that the price level has doubled since the warehouse was built. The following figures show what is involved:

| | Condensed Income Statements | | |
	Conventional statement 25 years ago	Conventional statement; current year	Adjusted statement; current year
Rental income..............	$100,000	$200,000	$200,000
Expenses:			
Depreciation..............	$ 20,000	$ 20,000	$ 40,000
Current expenditures........	30,000	60,000	60,000
Total expenses...........	$ 50,000	$ 80,000	$100,000
Net operating income.........	$ 50,000	$120,000	$100,000

The rent revenue and the current expenditures for expense have doubled, along with other prices. In the conventional income statement, however, depreciation is still based on historical cost. This figure is not expressed in current dollars; it gives a misleading result in the statement. When it is adjusted to a current price level in the third statement, all the figures reflect the same price level. Note that the net operating income on an adjusted basis is twice what it was in the statement for "25 years ago." It represents the same purchasing power as the first (old) net income, but because of the rise in price levels, this now takes twice as many dollars. The conventional statement after inflation is misleading unless one takes notice of the effects of inflation on the conventional figures. Many accountants have advocated making adjustments of historical cost figures by means of a price index, but accountants in practice in the United States have not yet been willing to do so for the regular statements. The need must be borne in mind in setting prices based on costs and in interpreting income figures. This discussion should not be taken to imply that all prices or obligations move up uniformly in a period of inflation. They do not, and the differences are the source of most of the trouble that inflation causes. For example, the interest paid on an old loan does not change, and neither does the number of dollars of principal repayable on the loan; the lender therefore suffers a decline in purchasing power.

CONTROLLABLE VERSUS UNCONTROLLABLE COSTS IN REPORTS

To control operations, executives in large organizations must have reports. The transactions are too numerous, the locations and personnel too scattered, for control by personal observation. Even at low levels, the significance of events may often be seen more clearly in a summarized report. For example, the manager of a grocery store may get a better picture of his operations from a report showing his monthly inventory shortage (book figure less actual physical inventory) than he could obtain by looking at the shelves every day.

Many reports for management present cost or expense data. They are advisedly prepared with the distinction between *controllable* and *uncontrollable* costs in mind. These terms refer to a particular executive or level of management and describe costs as controllable or not controllable at this level. The manager of a single grocery store in a large chain cannot control the depreciation, the rent, or perhaps the salary of the assistant manager. He can control the heat, light, and power used, the inventory shrinkage, and the cost of some forms of labor used. Reports to him should at least segregate, and perhaps exclude, the costs he cannot control. They may only divert his attention from matters that he can do something about to ones that he cannot change. This principle applies at all levels of management, except that the highest officers are responsible for all costs. The principle must be applied by considering in each case what costs the manager can and cannot control by his decisions.

SUMMARY

Total costs or average total manufacturing costs per unit of product are the ones commonly computed by accountants. For many special decisions these are not the pertinent costs. As a rule, special decisions and related computations involve the distinction between fixed and variable costs. When this division is made, one can compute the break-even point and find how it shifts as costs change. One can compute the contribution made by revenue over the variable cost of earning the revenue and thus easily work out the effects of prospective changes. One may also select products and appraise sales effort on the basis of the "contribution" figures.

Other special-cost concepts are differential costs, useful in choosing between alternatives; opportunity costs, that help to show the need to adjust outmoded historical costs when setting prices; and controllable costs, that need to be distinguished in preparing reports for different levels of management.

QUESTIONS

22.1 Distinguish between the following types of cost: average total manufacturing costs per unit of product; fixed manufacturing costs; variable manufacturing costs.

22.2 What do the three lines on a typical break-even chart represent?

22.3 Should management be concerned if proposed new equipment would result in a higher break-even point? Why?

22.4 Is it possible to install new and more expensive equipment and at the same time lower the break-even point? Explain.

22.5 What two methods can you suggest for fixing the location of the fixed-cost line on a break-even chart?

22.6 Suggest uses of the break-even chart and its limitations. Assume the type of break-even chart shown in the text.

22.7 What is the "contribution" figure used in the contribution theory to analyze sales and cost data?

22.8 Suggest uses that may be made of the contribution theory in business management.

22.9 What cautions should be kept in mind in using the contribution rate as a basis for selecting products to adopt or to promote?

22.10 What is differential cost? How may it be used in deciding whether or not to accept an order at a special price?

22.11 Is it ever advisable to make a product in one's own plant at a higher average total cost per unit than would be paid to have the product made outside?

22.12 What effect do rising price levels have on the calculation of income where long-lived facilities are used? Explain. What can be done to compute a more realistic income figure?

22.13 A factory foreman has objected to direct labor being classified as a "controllable" cost. He has pointed out that he has absolutely no control over wage rates and the union grievance committee would take drastic steps if he tried to speed up production. Discuss whether or not the term "controllable" is being used appropriately in this situation.

EXERCISES

22.1 Fixed costs of the Marvadell Company amount to $120,000 a year. Variable costs are $2 per unit and the net selling price is $5 per unit. Calculate the break-even point. Draw a break-even chart with a horizontal scale running from 0 to 50,000 units of product.

22.2 The Marvadell Company (of exercise 1) can install new machinery that will increase fixed costs to $140,000 a year but will reduce variable costs to $1 per unit. Calculate the break-even point after installation of the equipment. Plot the new fixed- and total-cost curves on the graph prepared for exercise 1 and compare the break-even points.

22.3 Valley Forge, Inc., is considering the acquisition of special equipment for $175,000. If this equipment is purchased, additional product can be sold for $200,000 per year for at least three years. Variable costs of 60 percent of sales would be incurred to manufacture the product, and in addition property taxes and insurance of $5,000 a year would have to be paid. How long will it take the company to recover its investment in this equipment?

22.4 The Murphy-Pacific Company has unused plant capacity and is considering adding one of three products to its line. The following data are available:

	Product		
	X	Y	Z
Probable annual sales	$700,000	$600,000	$500,000
Regular variable costs			
(materials, labor, etc.)	400,000	300,000	250,000
Contribution.	$300,000	$300,000	$250,000
Additional fixed charges			
from adding product (super-			
vision, depreciation, etc.)	160,000	150,000	115,000
Difference	$140,000	$150,000	$135,000

Each project requires the same additional capital investment. If funds are currently available for only one project, which would you recommend? Why?

22.5 A condensed annual income statement for the Placer Manufacturing Company is presented below.

	Total	Product X	Product Y
Sales.	$190,000	$90,000	$100,000
Cost of Sales:			
Direct Materials.	$ 34,000	$22,000	$ 12,000
Direct Labor	41,000	16,000	25,000
Variable Overhead.	35,000	14,000	21,000
Fixed Overhead.	4,000	2,000	2,000
	$114,000	$54,000	$ 60,000
Gross Margin on Sales	$ 76,000	$36,000	$ 40,000
Selling and Admin. Expenses:			
Variable Expenses	$ 33,000	$13,000	$ 20,000
Fixed Expenses	40,000	18,000	22,000
	$ 73,000	$31,000	$ 42,000
Net Income	$ 3,000	$ 5,000	$ (2,000)

Required:

1. The company is currently operating at only 50 percent of capacity, but because of the losses shown above, it is thinking of abandoning product Y. Do you think the company should do so? Why or why not?
2. Suppose that production could be brought up to full capacity by opening a new sales territory at an annual expenditure of $40,000 (sales to be made in the same proportion of X to Y as heretofore). What action should be taken?
3. Which product should be emphasized to maximize profits?

22.6 The Kay Electronics Company is considering whether to make or buy a printed circuit for a new product X. The standard cost of the new circuit is $2.25 for direct materials, $5.80 for direct labor and variable overhead, and $2 for fixed overhead. The best bid from an outside supplier is $9 per unit.

Required:

1. Assume first that the company has unused capacity and would have no other use for the facilities. In this case, should the company make or buy the circuit?
2. How would your answer differ if the company were currently using the facilities for a sideline item on which it just covers its cost, including fixed overhead?

22.7 The Seven Seas Restaurant has recently been added to the Polynesian Hotel. The hotel pays for all electricity in the building, and the Seven Seas management has agreed to repay the hotel for electricity used by the restaurant.

At the end of the first month both parties agree the restaurant consumed 20,000 kws. of electricity, and the restaurant is billed $500. This represents half of the hotel's total electric bill, which was computed as follows:

First 10,000 kw. at $0.04	$ 400
Next 10,000 kw. at $0.03	300
Next 10,000 kw. at $0.02	200
Next 10,000 kw. at $0.01	100
Total 40,000 kw. at average of $0.025	$1,000

Comment on the equity of this cost computation.

22.8 The C. W. Wellman Company has been operating in recent years at 60 percent of capacity and has been selling its entire output in the domestic market. The results of operations for the past year are summarized below:

Sales (10,000 units)		$160,000
Cost and expenses:		
Variable	$100,000	
Fixed	44,000	
Income tax (25 percent)	4,000	148,000
Net income		$ 12,000

The company is considering an offer from a foreign customer for 2,000 units at $13 per unit or 4,000 units at $12 per unit.

Required:

Prepare computations showing which alternative will produce the highest net income after taxes.

PROBLEMS

22.1 The Michigan Company has fixed costs of $120,000 per year. Its variable costs are $12 per unit and its sales price is $20 per unit. It is considering the purchase of equipment that will increase the fixed costs to $132,000 per year, but will enable the company to reduce variable costs to $9 per unit.

Required:

1. Draw a break-even chart for the situation in which fixed costs are $120,000, covering a horizontal scale of 0 to 20,000 units of product. Then show with dotted lines the costs resulting from the purchase of the new equipment.
2. Compute the break-even point before and after the acquisition of new equipment by formula, giving it in both sales dollars and units of product.

22.2 Make the computations required in each of the following cases pertaining to the Summit Company:

(1) Fixed costs in the Western Division are now $178,000 per year. They are expected to increase to $214,000 next year. Variable costs will also go up from $2.25 to $2.40 per unit. The product sells for $6.00 per unit. How much sales revenue must be obtained to have a net operating profit of $26,000 next year?

(2) A new machine costing $108,000 is under consideration. The product it makes sells for $7 per unit and requires materials costing $1.50 per unit, direct labor of $1.80, and sundry variable costs of 70 cents. Sales of 12,000 units per year are assured. Over how long a period would this investment be recovered?

(3) The following cost and sales data refer to products made in separate departments, each with its own fixed costs and production conditions.

	Product	
	K	*L*
Sales price per unit	$ 4.00	$ 4.50
Variable costs per unit up to normal production capacity	$ 1.40	$ 2.00
Fixed costs	$ 40,000	$30,000
Normal production capacity (in product units)	100,000	50,000
Additional costs per unit for units over normal production capacity	$ 0.80	$ 0.60
Current production in units	85,000	40,000

Required:

1. Is it better to obtain an order for 5,000 additional units of K or for 5,000 units of L?

2. If actual present sales were 120,000 units of K and 50,000 units of L, which of the orders mentioned in 1 would be better?

3. If your answer in 2 was different from the answer in 1, explain why.

22.3 Roark, Inc., has the problems described in the following paragraphs. Prepare the required computations or recommendations.

Contribution theory
Case 1 p. 627

(1) The company is considering opening a branch in a location where not more than $190,000 of sales per year can be expected. A similar branch in a lower-cost location has fixed costs of $85,000 per year and variable costs of $5 per product unit. The new location will require $15,000 more per year of fixed costs and variable costs will be $1 per unit higher. The product sells for $15 per unit. Do these figures indicate that the new branch will be able to obtain a net operating income of $20,000 per year, which the management requires before investing?

(2) New equipment offered by a supplier has the following characteristics: cost, $243,000; depreciation per year, $24,300; property taxes and insurance, $1,000 per year; direct labor per unit of product, $4.20; direct material per unit of product, $2.80; sundry variable costs per product unit, 90 cents. The product will sell for $12 per unit and 20,000 units per year can be sold. In what period would an investment in the machine pay out?

(3) The company produces the following products with separate facilities. The products and facilities have the characteristics shown.

	Product	
	X	Y
Sales price per unit	$ 10.00	$ 9.00
Variable costs per unit up to normal production capacity	$ 8.10	$ 7.00
Fixed costs	$35,000	$38,000
Normal production capacity, units	40,000	35,000
Additional costs per unit for production over normal capacity	$ 1.30	$ 1.10
Current production, units	22,000	19,000
	42,000	36,000

Required:

1. Is it better to obtain an order for an additional 10,000 units of X or for an additional 10,000 units of Y?

2. If the current production was 42,000 units of X and 36,000 units of Y, which of the orders mentioned in 1 would be better?

3. If your answer in 2 is different from that in 1, explain why.

22.4 A. J. Trine Company asks your assistance in obtaining information about the following problems. Make the necessary computations and state your conclusions on the questions asked.

(1) One of the firm's products is being made at 80 percent of the normal capacity of 2,500 units. It sells for $100 per unit. The facilities used have fixed costs of $200,000 per year and the product requires $20 per unit of variable costs.

(a) The company has discovered a market for the product that can be kept separate from its regular market by altering the product without changing its cost. Can the company sell enough units in this market at $80 per unit to produce a profit on the whole operation without increasing its capacity? Show your computations.

(b) Assuming that the capacity could be doubled by increasing the fixed costs $95,000, how many units would have to be sold in the new market to provide a net operating income of $25,000 on the whole operation?

(c) Assuming that the special market referred to in (a) was not entered at all, what reduction in selling price could be made in order to obtain sales of 5,000 units in the regular market, after the increase in facilities referred to in (b) above, to have a net operating profit of $30,000?

(2) The company produces a product with the following unit costs:

Materials	$4.67
Labor	1.82
Depreciation	1.21
Sundry variable costs	.76
Sundry fixed costs	.44
Total	$8.90

Required:

1. Should the company have this product made outside if it can be obtained for $7.50, assuming that it would then have no use for the facilities represented by the fixed costs? Explain.
2. Should the company buy the product outside if there is an alternative profitable use for the facilities? Why?
3. Should the product be bought outside if the price is $7.00?

22.5 The Adler Company has to make decisions on the points described below. Make the necessary computations and give the figure or decision required in each case.

(1) The firm has a product that is now produced at 60 percent of the capacity of the related facilities. It sells for $50 and has variable costs of $10 per unit. The fixed costs are $36,000. The capacity of the facilities is 1,500 units. You are asked to answer the following questions: (a) How many units would have to be sold for export at $40 each to produce a net operating income of $20,000 on the whole operation? (b) How much could the company afford to spend on sales promotion to sell another 1,000 units in the domestic market and leave a net operating income of $5,000 on the 1,000 units (assuming that the promotion would result in selling the additional 1,000 units)? (c) What reduction in selling price could be made on sales of 2,000 units and still leave a net operating income of $14,000?

(2) The company makes a product that has the following unit costs:

Depreciation	$2.00
Property taxes	.47
Insurance	.35
Materials	4.27
Labor	1.51
Sundry variable costs	.30
Total	$8.90

Required:

1. Should the company accept an outside offer to make the product at $6.25 per unit, assuming that it would have no other use for the equipment now used for this product? Give your reasons.
2. Should the offer be taken if there is another profitable use for the facilities? Why?
3. Should the offer be taken if the outside price is reduced to $6?

22.6 At the present time, Rex Co. manufactures 900,000 units annually, which takes up 90 percent of the plant capacity. Fixed manufacturing expenses are $770,000, or 77 cents per unit manufactured, when operations are 100 percent of capacity.

The variable manufacturing expense rate is 50 cents per unit, while direct material costs $2 and direct labor costs $1.50 per unit. Each unit sells for $6.

An offer has been received from Savemore Stores, Inc., to purchase 200,000 units at $4.75 per unit. These units are to be marketed under the customer's own brand name at prices somewhat lower than the $6 charged by Rex Co.

To produce the additional 200,000 units, $80,000 must be invested in additional production facilities. Variable manufacturing expense at the new level of activity would be reduced to 48 cents per unit of total production.

The cost accountant has prepared the following statement concerning the offer:

ESTIMATED RESULTS FROM ACCEPTING SAVEMORE STORES, INC., ORDER

Sales . . . . 200,000 units at $4.75 . . . . $950,000
Cost of sales:
    Direct material . . . . . . 200,000 units at $2.00 . . . . $400,000
    Direct labor. . . . . 200,000 units at 1.50 300,000
    Variable mfg. exp. . . . . 200,000 units at .50 100,000
    Fixed mfg. exp. . . . . . . 200,000 units at .77 154,000   954,000
Loss on this order . . . . $ 4,000

Required:

1. Prepare a revised statement to show the net gain or loss on acceptance of the order from Savemore Stores, Inc.
2. What other factors should be considered before accepting the order?

(ICAC—adapted)

22.7 The W. L. Raby Company processes a single product in one department. On completion of the manufacturing operations the goods are transferred to a finished goods warehouse. Inventory records are maintained on a first-in, first-out basis. The inventories at January 1, 1966, were:

Finished goods . . . . 150,000 units at $1.10
Work in process . . . . 30,000 units
    Material. . . . . 80% complete
    Direct Labor and Factory Overhead Cost . . . . 40% complete

The following information applies to production at the present capacity:

        Material cost. . . . . $0.30 per unit
        Direct labor . . . . 0.20 per unit

	Fixed—per Quarter	*Variable*
Factory overhead cost. . . .	$45,000	$0.30 per unit processed
Selling expense	30,000	0.15 per unit sold
Administrative expense . . .	15,000	0.05 per unit sold

The sales manager has suggested that in order to increase sales the fixed selling expense be increased $10,000 per quarter. At the same time, selling prices should be decreased. It is estimated that this suggestion would produce the following results:

	3 Months Ended March 31	3 Months Ended June 30
Sales	200,000 units at $1.70	225,000 units at $1.60
Fixed expenses:		
Factory overhead cost. . . .	No change	Increase $7,640
Selling expense	$40,000	$40,000
Administrative expense . . .	No change	Increase $5,000
Variable – based on present capacity:		
Factory overhead cost. . . .	10% decrease	20% decrease
Selling expense	20% decrease	20% decrease
Administrative expense . . .	20% decrease	20% decrease
Production:		
Started in process	160,000 units	200,000 units
Work in process at end of month	40,000 units	50,000 units
Material	60% complete	40% complete
Direct labor and factory overhead cost.	30% complete	20% complete

Required:

Should the sales manager's recommendations be put into effect? Prepare estimated income statements for the quarters ended March 31, 1966 and June 30, 1966 to show the effect on operations, assuming the predictions are all realized.

(ICAC – adapted)

22.8 The Mity Tiger Company produces an item that it sells direct to consumers under its own brand name. The item sells at $20 per unit, which is a long-established price. Owing to a general decline in business activity, sales are currently being made at the rate of 10,000 units per month, which is only 40 percent of the normal capacity of the plant.

An analysis of the costs of the company for a recent month, during which only 10,000 units were produced and sold, shows the following:

Manufacturing Costs:		
Labor	$50,000	
Power	10,000	
Materials	39,000	
Depreciation	42,000	
Property taxes and insurance	11,000	
Social security taxes	4,000	
Miscellaneous fixed overhead	2,000	
Miscellaneous variable overhead	2,000	$160,000
Selling Expenses:		
Salaries	$26,000	
Travel	18,000	
Advertising	4,100	
Miscellaneous	800	48,900
Administrative Expenses:		
Salaries	$ 8,000	
Telephone	3,100	
Supplies	900	
Miscellaneous	600	12,600
Total		$221,500

An offer has been received from a national discount house to purchase 5,000 units a month of the product to be shipped and billed to the individual stores without change except for brand name. The items would be sold under the discount-house label and would be packed and shipped as directed by this customer at his expense; hence no additional selling expenses would be incurred by this proposed sale. The discount house offers $17 per unit unpacked on the basis of a one-year contract. The management of the Mity Tiger Company does not expect that there will be an improvement in the business within the next year, and there is no fear that the sale of the item to the discount house will reduce the present volume of sales to consumers.

The Mity Tiger Company does not believe it can afford to accept the order, as it is losing on its present price of $20; therefore, it appears that losses would be substantially increased by entering into the sales contract with the chain. The board of directors calls you in to prepare an analysis showing the result of accepting the order in comparison with the result of declining the order. In preparing the analysis you are to assume that depreciation, property taxes and insurance, and miscellaneous fixed overhead are completely fixed manufacturing costs and that the other manufacturing costs are completely variable. The administrative expenses will increase 50 percent if the new order is taken.

Required:

Prepare the analysis requested by the board of directors and comment on whether or not the new order should be accepted.

PART VI

Special Controls
and Analysis for
Management and Investors

23

Budgeting

A budget is a financial plan. It is an important device for managerial planning and control. *Planning* is made more exact when the specific quantities and amounts of merchandise, supplies, man-hours, and dollars are set down in a thoroughgoing budget. A complete budget summarizes all the transactions for a future period and produces budgeted financial statements. The process of working up the statements assures that the various parts are consistent with each other. *Control* is facilitated by comparison of the planned figures with the actual ones. If management wishes, it can require that each purchase order and each proposal to hire a person be checked against the budget before it is sent out, and thus prevent purchases that are different from those planned, or at least be able to decide whether or not to exceed the budget before any commitment is already made. This is the method used in governmental organizations, where it is illegal to spend money not appropriated in the budget. The advantages of budgeting may be cited as follows:

1. It forces planning on all levels.
2. It improves coordination of the various business activities.
3. It sharpens employee motivation.
4. It reduces costs by highlighting the areas where economies are possible.
5. It provides management with better tools for deciding on alternative courses of action.[1]

To these may be added futher advantages:

6. A standard of performance is established that helps management recognize good as well as poor performances.
7. Results of plans may be predicted before they are put into effect and unsatisfactory ones discarded.
8. Thoroughgoing preparation of a budget requires a careful scrutiny of the operations that often discloses opportunities for improvement even without further action.

Budgets are closely related to standard costs. As in setting individual cost standards, the budget should represent good but attainable performance. Budgets are commonly drawn in summary form for a year. The figures for the first quarter are then drawn up in greater detail and as each succeeding quarter draws near, its figures are developed in detail. In this way the final figures can take into account necessary changes in the plans.

[1] From *Budgeting for Profit in Small Business*, American Institute of Certified Public Accountants, New York.

Budgets may be *static* or *flexible*. A static budget contemplates just one level of activity. A flexible budget gives figures for a range of possible levels of activity. The flexible budget permits a more illuminating comparison of the actual expenses with those in the budget, because it shows what expenses should be incurred for the level of sales actually reached. The principles are the same; the flexible budget simply provides more figures. The discussion in this text is devoted to a static budget. It uses the transactions of a merchandising concern.

ORGANIZATION FOR BUDGETARY CONTROL

The following principles are recommended for effective preparation and use of a budget:

1. Participation of employees responsible for operations in setting the goals to be met
2. Classification of costs and expenses by lines of authority
3. Provision of review and enforcement procedure

People at the operating level have a detailed knowledge of the operations that is important in obtaining a realistic budget. Their sense of responsibility for its success is also necessary if it is to succeed, and this can be developed if they have a voice in making up the budget.

Reference was made in a preceding chapter to the distinction between controllable and uncontrollable costs or expenses. If a person is to be held responsible for the expenses incurred, he must be able to control them. Expenses should therefore be segregated along lines of authority. For example, if a concern has sales supervisors who are responsible for the selling expenses in different territories, there should be an analysis of sales expenses by territories.

Enforcement procedure should provide at a minimum for periodic statements comparing actual and budgeted sales and expenses. When these are reviewed, explanations for deviations from the budget may be obtained and any precautions needed for the future may be taken. The possibility of requiring that each purchase order be checked against the budget before its issue was noted above; this procedure gives the tightest control, but is not, as a rule, used by business concerns.

BUDGET LEVELS AND EMPLOYEE MOTIVATION

The effect of different possible levels of budgeted performance on the motivation of the employees should be considered in setting the budget. As in standard cost work, it is commonly believed that an extremely high standard of performance, which is very difficult to achieve, will discourage effort because the employees feel that they will fall short of the budget no matter how hard they try. It is also believed that setting a level of performance that can be achieved without doubt may cause people to work just hard enough to meet the goal, when they could do considerably better. However, these beliefs have not been based on any scientific investigation of the questions. In recent years scholars interested in the behavioral aspects of business administration have begun to investigate such questions as these, but as yet no very clear-cut results have been achieved on the problem of budget levels and motivation. More definite and reliable conclusions may appear as research proceeds, and in the future budget goals may be set with some assurance of their impact on employee motivation. In the meantime, careful managers will keep the motivation problem in mind and observe the reactions of their own employees and adjust their procedures to the conditions they find in their own organizations.

SALES BUDGET

The starting point for the budget of a business concern is the sales or other revenue to be obtained. Purchases of merchandise and incurrence of expenses depend upon the amount of sales that can be expected. The sales budget is both a plan and an estimate; it depends on what is possible as well as on the firm's efforts. Sales budgets are established after a review of (1) past performance; (2) indexes and forecasts of business conditions, and (3) special changes contemplated by the concern, such as a new product, more advertising, and other changes. Market studies may be used to obtain data on the demand for a particular product. A tentative decision will be made on sales prices, data on general conditions and past performance and expected changes will be summarized, and salesmen will be asked to estimate, in the light of the data, what they can sell in the budget year. These estimates will be revised by sales supervisors and higher executives to obtain a final sales budget, which shows the units, prices, and sales dollars for each product to be sold. Such a budget is illustrated in summary form below. This illustration is part of a series giving the whole budget of Hawthorne, Inc., for the calendar year 1966.

HAWTHORNE, INC.
Sales Budget
Year ended December 31, 1966

Product	Units	Price	Amount
A	121,000	$12.00	$1,452,000
V	88,000	16.00	1,408,000
C	92,000	9.00	828,000
Gross sales........................			$3,688,000

PURCHASES BUDGET

In a merchandising concern the products sold must be purchased. The quantities to be purchased depend not only on the level of sales but also on the inventory on hand at the start and the inventory desired at the end of the period. Hawthorne, Inc., believes that improved inventory controls it is installing will permit sales to be maintained with a lower average inventory than in past years. Its purchases budget, shown on page 646, accordingly shows an ending inventory level lower than at the start. This budget contains the unit data needed to compute budgeted freight in, so that is included as a memorandum item. It also makes use of inventory data, so it is convenient to compute the budgeted inventories in connection with the purchases budget. Note that the purchases budget gives purchases in terms of receipt and recording of the goods. They must be ordered sufficiently in advance to arrive in the period for which they are budgeted.

HAWTHORNE, INC.
Merchandise-Purchase Budget
Year ended December 31, 1966

	A	V	C	Total Purchases
Sales Requirements	121,000	88,000	92,000	
Ending Inventory Desired	12,000	9,000	9,500	
	133,000	97,000	101,500	
Less: Beginning Inventory	18,000	12,000	13,000	
Purchases, in Units	115,000	85,000	88,500	
Price per Unit	$ 7.00	$ 9.00	$ 5.00	
Purchases, in Dollars	$805,000	$765,000	$442,500	$2,012,500

Memo:

Freight-In, per unit	$ 0.30	$ 0.40	$ 0.15	
Freight-In, in dollars	$ 34,500	$ 34,000	$ 13,275	$ 81,775

Memo: Computation of budgeted inventories.

		Beginning			Ending		
Product	Units	Price	Amount	Units	Price	Amount	
A	18,000	$6.50	$117,000	12,000	$7.30	$ 87,600	
V	12,000	8.70	104,400	9,000	9.40	84,600	
C	13,000	4.80	62,400	9,500	5.15	48,925	
			$283,800			$221,125	

OPERATING EXPENSE BUDGETS

Selling and administrative expenses must be scrutinized one by one to determine what amount really needs to be increased or spent to maintain the proposed volume of business. This scrutiny and the resulting budget furnish the best control available for many administrative expenses. Since these are incurred by or under the immediate supervision of high executives, they can be controlled only by the self-discipline of these executives. A budget is the best aid to this self-discipline. The selling and the administrative expenses must be set with reference to many of the same factors that influence the sales figures. For example, increasing general prices will be reflected in salaries, travel expenses, cost of supplies, and cost of services such as advertising. Salesmen's travel expense will depend on the policy adopted as to coverage of the territory, and advertising expenditures will depend upon the plans for sales promotion. The operating expense budgets require, if they are to be well constructed, that all the activities be planned in detail. The selling and the administrative expense budgets of Hawthorne, Inc., are given here. These are summary budgets and would be supported in practice by budgets for each department, office, or territory involved.

SELLING AND ADMINISTRATIVE EXPENSE BUDGETS
HAWTHORNE, INC.
Selling Expense Budget
Year ended December 31, 1966

Sales Salaries	$218,000
Sales Commissions	42,000
Delivery Expense	95,600
Warehouse Rental	16,800
Sales Supplies	4,200
Travel	81,000
Advertising	134,500
Employment Taxes	10,400
Total	$602,500

HAWTHORNE, INC.
Administrative and General Expense Budget
Year ended December 31, 1966

Salaries	$ 87,000
Depreciation of Building	22,000
Depreciation of Furniture and Equipment	14,000
Stationery and Supplies	8,400
Telephone and Telegraph	12,600
Insurance	8,400
Legal and Auditing	18,000
Repairs	22,000
Postage	3,400
Property Taxes	10,800
Employment Taxes	3,500
Sundry	19,200
Total	$229,300

BUDGETED CASH RECEIPTS FROM CUSTOMERS

Cash receipts flow primarily from sales, but come also from borrowing or from investment by owners. They may arise from unusual transactions such as the sale of a fixed asset. The receipts from sales are calculated separately and combined with other sources of cash in the summary cash budget. Cash receipts from credit sales (usually the only source in wholesale trade) may be calculated from accounts receivable balances, with adjustment for returns and allowances, bad accounts, and sales discounts. The opening accounts receivable balance will not be available until the budgeted year actually begins, but it can be estimated with considerable accuracy, because the budget is drawn up in the last part of the old year. The simplest method of obtaining an estimate of the ending accounts receivable balance is to calculate the percentage of sales usually left in accounts receivable at the end of the year. An average of these is compiled over several years and may be modified for any new conditions, such as a change in credit policy. Similar percentages of returns and allowances, sales discounts, and bad debt writeoffs may be calculated, the reference being to sales or to average accounts receivable. The illustration below exemplifies these points with the calculation of budgeted cash receipts from customers of Hawthorne, Inc.

HAWTHORNE, INC.
Budgeted Cash Receipts from Customers
Year ended December 31, 1966

Accounts Receivable, Beginning		$ 284,000
Add: Gross Sales		3,688,000
		$3,972,000
Deduct:		
Accounts Receivable, Ending (8% of $3,688,000)	$295,040	
Sales Returns and Allowances (1% of $3,688,000)	36,880	
Bad Accounts Written Off (7.5% of Average Accounts Receivable)	21,714	353,634
Accounts Receivable Paid		$3,618,366
Deduct: Discounts Allowed (1½%)		54,275
Cash Receipts		$3,564,091

BUDGETED PAYMENTS ON MERCHANDISE PURCHASES

The cash paid for merchandise ordinarily follows the recording of the purchase by a month or less. Whatever the payment policy or requirements of the industry, the amount to be paid can be computed from opening and closing accounts payable balances adjusted for purchase discounts. Hawthorne, Inc., pays merchandise-purchase invoices in the month following receipt of the invoice. Purchase discounts average 1.6 percent of the invoice amounts in this company's experience. These facts are reflected in the budgeted payments on merchandise purchases, shown here.

HAWTHORNE, INC.
Budgeted Payments on Merchandise Purchases
Year ended December 31, 1966

Accounts Payable, Beginning		$ 152,000
Add: Purchases		2,012,500
		$2,164,500
Deduct: Accounts Payable, Ending (the last month's purchases)		143,000
Accounts Payable Paid		$2,021,500
Deduct: Discounts Taken (1.6%)		32,344
Cash Payments on Merchandise Purchases		$1,989,156

BUDGETED INCOME STATEMENT

When the budgets discussed above are complete, it is possible to draw up the budgeted income statement after computing a few additional figures. This will disclose whether or not the plans are satisfactory from an income point of view. If they are not, ways and means of changing them to get a satisfactory result must be sought. Some figures are calculated as the budgeted income statement is prepared. In the case of Hawthorne, Inc., three such figures are involved: bad debts expense, interest expense, and income tax for 1966. Bad debt *writeoffs* were computed in connection with budgeted cash receipts (page 648), but expense for the year, based on sales for the year, is estimated to be a little higher. The interest expense is based on the expected borrowings for the year; if this is not yet settled, the budgeted income statement will be a tentative one pending final determination of the plans for loans. The income tax figure is calculated at 22 percent of the first $25,000 and 48 percent of the remainder of net income before income tax. The budgeted income statement of Hawthorne, Inc., is shown here.

HAWTHORNE, INC.
Budgeted Income Statement
Year ended December 31, 1966

Sales			$3,688,000
Less: Sales returns and allowances		$ 36,880	
Bad debts		23,885	
Sales discounts		54,275	115,040
Net sales			$3,572,960
Cost of goods sold:			
Inventory January 1, 1966		$ 283,800	
Purchases	$2,012,500		
Freight-In	81,775		
	$2,094,275		
Less: Discounts	32,344	2,061,931	
		$2,345,731	
Less: Inventory December 31, 1966		221,125	2,124,606
Gross Margin on Sales			$1,448,354
Operating Expenses:			
Selling Expense		$ 602,500	
Administrative and General Expense		229,300	831,800
Net Operating Income			$ 616,554
Interest Expense			76,500
			$ 540,054
Taxes on Income			252,726
Net Income			$ 287,328

SUMMARY CASH BUDGET

Cash payments flow from the expense budgets and both receipts and payments arise from miscellaneous sources. If new financing is planned, the cash to be received from the lenders or investors is taken into account. Additions to plant and equipment require cash payments not reflected in the operating expense budgets, as do any payments of nonoperating expenses such as interest or income tax (disclosed in the budgeted income statement). All these sources of cash budget data are recorded with the cash payments required by the operating expense budgets to get a summary cash budget. In calculating the cash payments required by the operating cash budgets, consideration must be given to the items that are not paid currently. Insurance expense, for example, is commonly paid in advance for one, three, or five years. The cash disbursements budget must reflect the payment of the premium in this case, not the writeoff to expense. Property taxes are paid when the law requires, commonly twice a year. The disbursements budget shows the payments to be made in the period, not the accrual of expense in it. These remarks apply to supplies also, since they are not necessarily used in the period in which they are bought. However, unless the level of activity changes radically, the amount of supplies bought and the amount paid for in a year are likely to be almost equal. A summary cash budget for Hawthorne, Inc., for 1966 is given here. During 1966 the company plans a major expansion of its building, to be financed by a $2,000,000 mortgage. Receipt of these funds is recorded in the summary cash budget, as is the expenditure.

HAWTHORNE, INC.
Summary Cash Budget

Year ended December 31, 1966

Balance on Hand, Beginning		$ 92,000
Receipts from Customers		3,564,091
Proceeds of Mortgage		2,000,000
		$5,656,091
Disbursements:		
Merchandise Purchases	$1,989,156	
Selling Expense	602,500	
Administrative and General Expense *	174,100	
Freight-In	81,775	
Income Taxes †	318,000	
Insurance Premiums	9,400	
Property Taxes	10,100	
Addition to Building	2,000,000	
Dividends	200,000	
Interest ‡	51,500	
Payment of Notes Payable	150,000	5,586,531
Balance on Hand, Ending		$ 69,560

* $229,300 less depreciation $36,000, insurance $8,400 and property taxes $10,800.
† Includes payments on last year's higher tax.
‡ Other interest expense for the year is accrued.

The figure for disbursements on selling expenses is the same as the expense in this case, because the obligations for expenses of the last month paid in the next year are about equal to the same figure existing at the beginning of the year. Delivery expense is a cash expense paid to an outside delivery service. Employment taxes, although reported formally for a quarter of a year at a time, must be deposited month by month in government bank accounts (if over

$100 per month). Other selling expenses and their payments are also approximately equal for the year.

Two items of the budget for administrative and general expense require no current cash payments. These are the two depreciation expense items. The insurance expense arises from writeoff of insurance premiums; the cash budget therefore reflects only the payment of new premiums. Property taxes do not fall due month by month as they accrue, so the cash budget shows the payments to be made; in the case at hand, these include one payment on last year's tax and one payment on the 1966 tax. The other administrative expenses not paid at the end of the year are compensated for by the payment within the year of the corresponding item outstanding at the beginning of the year.

At this point all cash disbursements that have not been derived directly from the expense budgets or noticed in connection with special financing must be gathered into the cash budget. In the case of Hawthorne, Inc., several such items are present. Freight in was calculated in connection with the purchases budget but appears as a distinct item in the summary cash budget. Income taxes, which involve payments on last year's tax and payment of a portion of an estimated tax for 1966, are represented by these payments. Insurance premiums and property tax payments are similarly listed. Dividends proposed to be paid are shown here, as is interest. The expected payment of notes payable is included.

The immediately preceding budget is a summary cash budget for a year. It is often important to make up a cash budget for each month or even for shorter periods. The reason is that expenditures may run high in some months while receipts may run high in others. For example, an advertising campaign may have to be paid for before receipts resulting from the campaign come in. Or inventories may have to be built up considerably in advance of a heavy season, such as the Christmas season in retail trade, with receipts from this peak stock coming in two or three months later. In these cases, temporary borrowing may be necessary; a good budget anticipates the need and permits the most economical arrangements to be made, thus avoiding the difficulties of a cash shortage.

BUDGETED BALANCE SHEET

When the budgets through the income statement and summary cash budget are complete, it is possible to draw up a budgeted balance sheet. This is useful in determining whether or not a satisfactory financial condition will be maintained by the plans reflected in the budget. It is also useful as a means of assembling the budget figures and summarizing them so that they can be scrutinized for consistency. The most satisfactory procedure is to express the budgets in the form of journal entries and to post these to a work sheet. The opening figures are the actual postclosing balances of the year just before the budgeted year, except that some estimates of these figures have to be made if the budget is to be finished before the budget year begins. The journal entries for the budgets of Hawthorne, Inc., for 1966 are given on pages 655-656. The work sheet is presented on pages 652-653. The budgeted balance sheet taken from the work sheet is shown on page 654.

HAWTHORNE, INC.
Work Sheet for Budgeted Balance Sheet
Year ended December 31, 1966

	Trial Balance December 31, 1965 Debit	Trial Balance December 31, 1965 Credit	Transactions Debit	Transactions Credit	Income Statement Debit	Income Statement Credit	Balance Sheet Debit	Balance Sheet Credit
Cash	92 000		(3) 5 564 091	(5) 5 586 531			69 560	
Accounts Receivable	284 000		(11) 3 688 000	(3) 3 618 366 / (4) 58 594			295 040	
Allowance for Doubtful Accounts		18 000		(6) 23 885				20 171
Merchandise	283 800		(4) 21 714 / (11) 221 125		283 800		221 125	
Prepaid Insurance	8 200		(5) 9 400	(8) 8 400			9 200	
Land	180 000						180 000	
Building	1 100 000		(5) 2 000 000				3 100 000	
Accumulated Depreciation—Building		396 000		(7) 22 000				418 000
Furniture and Equipment	280 000						280 000	
Accumulated Depreciation—Furniture and Equipment		98 000		(7) 14 000				112 000
Notes Payable		150 000	(5) 150 000					—
Accounts Payable		152 000	(5) 2 021 500	(2) 2 012 500				143 000
Property Taxes Payable		6 400	(5) 10 100	(9) 10 800				7 100
Income Taxes Payable		204 000	(5) 318 000	(12) 252 726				138 726
Accrued Interest Payable		1 500	(5) 51 500	(10) 76 500				26 500
Capital Stock		850 000						850 000
Retained Earnings		352 100						352 100
	2 228 000	2 228 000						

Account	Dr Ref	Dr Amount	Cr Ref	Cr Amount	Income Statement Dr	Income Statement Cr	Balance Sheet Dr	Balance Sheet Cr
Sales			(1)	3 688 000		3 688 000		
Purchases	(2)	2 012 500			2 012 500			
Sales Discounts	(3)	54 275			54 275			
Sales Returns and Allowances	(4)	36 880			36 880			
Mortgage Payable			(3)	2 000 000				2 000 000
Selling Expense	(5)	602 500			602 500			
Administrative and General Expense	(5)(7)(8)(9)	174 100 / 36 000 / 8 400 / 10 800			229 300			
Freight-In	(5)	81 775			81 775			
Dividends	(5)	200 000					200 000	
Purchase Discount			(5)	32 344		32 344		
Bad debts	(6)	23 885			23 885			
Interest Expense	(10)	76 500			76 500			
Profit and Loss (closing inventory)	(12)	252 726			252 726			
Income Taxes			(11)	221 125		221 125		
		17 625 771		17 625 771	3 654 141	3 941 469	4 354 925	
Net Income					287 328			287 328
					3 941 469	3 941 469	4 354 925	4 354 925

HAWTHORNE, INC.
Budgeted Balance Sheet
December 31, 1966

Assets

Current assets

Cash			$ 69,560
Accounts Receivable	$ 295,040		
Less: Allowance for Doubtful			
Accounts	20,171	274,869	
Merchandise		221,125	
Prepaid Insurance		9,200	$ 574,754

Fixed assets

Land			$ 180,000
Building	$3,100,000		
Less: Accumulated Depreciation	418,000	2,682,000	
Furniture and Equipment	$ 280,000		
Less: Accumulated Depreciation	112,000	168,000	3,030,000
			$3,604,754

Liabilities and Capital

Current liabilities

Accounts Payable	$143,000	
Property Taxes Payable	7,100	
Income Taxes Payable	138,726	
Accrued Interest Payable	26,500	$ 315,326

Long term liability

Mortgage Payable	2,000,000

Capital

Capital Stock		$850,000
Retained Earnings:		
Balance Jan. 1, 1961	$352,100	
Net income, 1961	287,328	
	639,428	
Dividends	200,000	439,428
		1,289,428
		$3,604,754

JOURNAL ENTRIES EXPRESSING THE BUDGET

These "journal entries" are for work sheet purposes only; they are not part of the regular accounting record. The entries for the 1966 budget of Hawthorne, Inc., follow.

1. Accounts Receivable............................$3,688,000
        Sales.................................. $3,688,000
        (to record sales per sales budget)

2. Purchases....................................$2,012,500
        Accounts Payable...................... $2,012,500
        (to record purchases per merchandise-purchase budget)

3. Cash.......................................$5,564,091
        Sales Discounts............................. 54,275
            Accounts Receivable................... $3,618,366
            Mortgage Payable....................   2,000,000
        (to record cash receipts per budgeted cash receipts and summary cash budget)

4. Sales Returns and Allowances...................$ 36,880
        Allowance for Bad Debts....................... 21,714
            Accou   ..ivable.................... $ 58,594
        (to record returns and bad-debt writeoffs per budgeted cash receipts)

5. Accounts Payable...........................$2,021,500
        Selling Expense........................... 602,500
        Administrative and General Expense............. 174,100
        Freight-In................................. 81,775
        Income Taxes Payable........................ 318,000
        Prepaid Insurance.......................... 9,400
        Property Taxes Payable...................... 10,100
        Building................................. 2,000,000
        Dividends................................ 200,000
        Accrued Interest Payable..................... 51,500
        Notes Payable............................ 150,000
            Cash.............................. $5,586,531
            Purchase Discount.....................   32,344
        (to record cash disbursements per budgeted payments and summary cash budget)

6. Bad Debts..................................$ 23,885
        Allowance for Doubtful Accounts.......... $ 23,885
        (to record bad debts per budgeted income statement)

7. Administrative and General Expense.............$ 36,000
        Accumulated Depreciation—Building....... $ 22,000
        Accumulated Depreciation—Furniture and
            Equipment...........................   14,000
        (to record depreciation per budget for administrative and general expense)

8.	Administrative and General Expense............$	8,400		
	Prepaid Insurance.....................		$	8,400
	(to record insurance expense per budget for administrative and general expense)			
9.	Administrative and General Expense............$	10,800		
	Property Taxes Payable................		$	10,800
	(to record accrued property taxes per budget for administrative and general expense)			
10.	Interest Expense...........................$	76,500		
	Accrued Interest Payable...............		$	76,500
	(to record interest expense per budgeted income statement)			
11.	Merchandise Inventory.......................$	221,125		
	Profit and Loss......................		$	221,125
	(to record closing inventory per merchandise-purchase budget)			
12.	Income Taxes.............................$	252,726		
	Income Taxes Payable.................		$	252,726
	(to record income taxes per budgeted income statement)			

SUMMARY

A budget is a financial plan. It facilitates accurate planning and is an excellent control device. It permits results of plans to be foreseen before they are adopted; its preparation often discloses opportunities for improvement before any other action is taken; it creates a standard of performance that aids management in identifying good and poor performances.

There are *static* and *flexible* budgets. The former is drawn for only one level of operations, whereas the latter gives figures for a range of possible levels of operation.

Organization for budgetary control involves (1) the participation of employees responsible for meeting the goals that have been set, (2) classification of costs or expenses by lines of authority, and (3) provision of review and enforcement procedure. Consideration must be given to the ability of the performance level used in the budget to motivate the workers properly.

The budget begins with the sales budget, since other plans depend largely on the volume of sales anticipated. It is desirable to express the budget in memorandum journal entries and to post these to a work sheet. This procedure not only provides budgeted statements, but also permits an over-all scrutiny of the budget for consistency.

QUESTIONS

23.1 What is a budget? How does it enable anyone to control anything?

23.2 Suggest three major advantages of budgets.

23.3 Distinguish between static and flexible budgets. What advantage does a flexible budget have?

23.4 Suggest organizational matters that are important in the construction and use of a budget.

23.5 Suggest sources of information that may be used in drawing up a sales budget.

23.6 Answer the following questions about purchases budgets of the type described in the text:

(1) Does the purchases budget indicate just when to place an order for merchandise?

(2) Does the amount of budgeted purchases depend entirely on the amount of budgeted sales?

(3) Does the purchases budget show the amount of cash to be spent for merchandise in the budget year?

23.7 What kind of control can be devised for expenses incurred by or under the immediate supervision of top executives?

23.8 In connection with a cash receipts budget: (1) What items besides sales and accounts receivable balances must be considered in determining what will be collected from customers? (2) What other sources of cash may be involved?

23.9 The following items are cash disbursements captions from a summary cash budget. Designate them as falling into one of two groups: first, those for which cash is typically paid in the same month in which the expense or purchase or payable is recorded (or in the immediately following one); second, those for which the time of payment is quite different from the recording of expense or the original purchase or payable.

(1) Warehouse rental   (6) Insurance
(2) Bond payment   (7) Notes payable
(3) Stationery and supplies   (8) Interest
(4) Repairs   (9) Freight in
(5) Property taxes   (10) Income taxes

23.10 After budgets for sales, purchases, operating expenses, cash receipts from customers, and cash payments on merchandise are prepared, a budgeted income statement is made up. What new figures must be calculated for the budgeted income statement?

23.11 A home appliance distributor sets quotas for its salesmen, which when compared to actual sales determine the salesmen's bonuses. Different estimates of sales are used for general budgetary purposes. What do you think of this procedure? Discuss briefly the relationship between budget levels and employee motivation.

23.12 (1) List the principal categories that normally appear on a summary cash budget.

(2) How does the budgeted income statement differ from the summary cash budget? What type of control is provided by the budgeted income statement?

23.13 Each of the twelve regional offices of a large insurance company has been autonomous. For many years the financial controls over the regional offices consisted of an annual sales quota, a loss ratio based on the kinds of insurance in force in the territory, and an office expense ratio based primarily on previous performance, with occasional adjustment for changes in the volume or the nature of work done by the office.

A new controller wishes to lay out a budgetary control system for the regional offices. Managers of these offices have just been informed by the controller that budgets are soon to be prepared for the next year "with an aim to tightening controls and reduce costs." The regional managers are asked to attend a meeting at the home office, where the new system will be explained.

1. Several managers are unfavorably disposed toward the announced use of budgets. If you were trying to discover why the managers were unenthusiastic, list the possible causes you would want to investigate. Explain briefly why you think each cause might create a negative attitude.

2. In addition to the uses of budgets indicated above, what are the other purposes for which budgets may be introduced? Explain.
3. State three things that might be done at the meeting to create a more favorable attitude on the part of the managers toward the budget program.

(CPCU — adapted)

EXERCISES

23.1 From the data for 1966 given below prepare a statement of budgeted cash receipts from customers for the C Co.

Budgeted sales........................ $240,000
Accounts receivable:
    January 1, 1966   19,000
    December 31, 1966 .... 10% of 1966 sales
Uncollectable accounts .... 1% of sales

23.2 Prepare a statement of budgeted payments on merchandise purchases from the following data of the H Co. for 1966.

Budgeted sales at selling price........ $205,000
Percent of markup on sales price 40%
Accounts payable:
    January 1, 1966 .... $16,000
    December 31, 1966.............. 10% of 1966 purchases
Discounts taken.................. 2% of accounts paid

23.3 From the data below prepare a summary cash budget for the N Co. for February 1967. The trial balance reflecting January 1967 transactions shows:

Cash...........................	$ 26,600	
Accounts Receivable...............	20,000	
Merchandise.....................	32,000	
Equipment	60,000	
Accumulated Depreciation		$ 10,000
Rent Payable		2,000
Note Payable — 6% due 2/28/67........		20,000
Capital Stock		50,000
Retained Earnings..................		55,200
Sales		25,000
Cost of Sales	15,000	
Salaries.........................	6,000	
Rent............................	2,000	
Depreciation.....................	500	
Interest.........................	100	
	$162,200	$162,200

Additional information:
(1) Sales in February will be 20 percent greater than in January.
(2) Collections on account in February are forecast to be 80 percent of January 31, 1967, accounts receivable and 20 percent of February sales.
(3) A 5 percent salary increase will become effective February 1, 1967.
(4) Rent is payable at 8 percent of gross sales.
(5) Merchandise inventories will be decreased $2,000 during February.
(6) Equipment costing $5,000 will be purchased in February on terms of 20 percent down and the balance payable in thirty-six monthly installments.
(7) At February 28 it is expected that 5 percent of purchases will be unpaid.

23.4 The trial balance of the Custom Appliance Co. at December 31, 1966, is expected to be as follows:

Cash	$100,000	
Accounts Receivable	22,000	
Prepaid Insurance	2,400	
Equipment	50,000	
Accumulated Depreciation		$ 12,500
Other Expenses Payable		1,500
Capital Stock		20,000
Retained Earnings		11,600
Service Revenues		240,000
Salaries	80,000	
Depreciation	6,000	
Insurance	1,200	
Other Expenses	24,000	
	$285,600	$285,600

From the foregoing trial balance and the following additional information prepare the journal entries that would be used in preparing the budget work sheet for the quarter ended March 31, 1967.
Additional information:

(1) Sales of services for 1967 are expected to increase $60,000 over sales in 1966. Forty percent of the annual sales are made in the first quarter of each year. Accounts receivable at March 31, 1967, are expected to be $10,000 higher than on December 31, 1966.
(2) Salaries expense is half fixed and half variable.
(3) No insurance premiums will be paid in the three months ended March 31, 1967.
(4) The other expenses are variable. It is expected that $2,100 of other expenses will be accrued as of March 31, 1967.
(5) New equipment will be purchased for $5,000 cash on February 1, 1967. Depreciation will be calculated at 1 percent of cost per month.

23.5 Prepare a summary cash budget for the quarter ended March 31, 1967, for the Custom Appliance Co. of exercise 4.

23.6 Prepare a budgeted income statement for the quarter ended March 31, 1967, for the Custom Appliance Co. of exercise 4.

23.7 You are requested to prepare a cash budget for American Marine, Inc., showing details for July, August, and September 1966. In a conference with the owner, the accounting records for the past three years are reviewed and the following estimates are prepared for the four months June through September 1966.

	June	July	August	September
Charter Revenues Earned	$20,000	$25,000	$18,000	$21,000
Payroll	10,000	12,000	10,000	9,000
Travel Expense	4,000	5,000	4,000	5,000
Office Rent	800	800	800	800
Misc. Office Expense	2,000	3,000	4,000	2,000

Fifty percent of charter revenues are received in the month of the billing and 50 percent in the following month. Payroll and office rent are paid by check in the month shown. Travel expense and miscellaneous office expenses are paid by check—80 percent in the month shown and 20 percent in the following month. A mortgage payment of $8,000 must be paid in July 1966.

The cash balance is not to be permitted to fall below $6,000. When the expected balance is below this figure, a 30-day loan is to be secured from the bank in amounts of even thousands of dollars. This loan is increased or decreased each month to maintain a monthly opening cash balance in excess of $6,000. It is anticipated that the cash balance on July 1, 1966, will be $6,800.

23.8 On the basis of the data given below, prepare a cash budget for the Merlin Company, showing receipts and disbursements by month for March and April.

	February	March	April
Sales	$50,000	$100,000	$150,000
Purchases.................	50,000	60,000	150,000
Expenses	20,000	20,000	28,000

It is expected that 80 percent of the sales will be collected in the month of sale and a 2 percent cash discount is allowed on such collections; 20 percent of sales will be collected in the month following the sale, one half of these collections being entitled to the cash discount. Cash discounts of 2 percent are taken on all purchases. The discount period on purchases is thirty days, with one half of the purchases of any month paid for in the month of purchase, the remaining one half being paid for in the succeeding month. Depreciation of $8,000 is included in expenses. A bank loan of $10,000 is due on March 15. The Merlin Company's cash balance on March 1 is $25,000.

PROBLEMS

23.1 Underhill Company has budgeted sales at $620,000 for the calendar year 1966. Its accounts receivable (all sales are on credit) on January 1, 1966, are expected to be $48,000. At the year end it is expected that 10 percent of the year's sales will remain on the books. The company has regularly had sales returns and allowances of 2 percent of gross sales in a year, and it regularly has had to write off bad accounts equal to 10 percent of average accounts receivable in a year. It also offers sales discounts amounting on the average to 1 percent of the accounts paid.

Required:

Prepare a budget of cash receipts from customers.

23.2 Riverside Company closes its books and prepares its budget for the fiscal year ending March 31. Data on its cash budget for the year ended March 31, 1967, are given below. Cash on hand at April 1, 1966, is $162,500.

(1) All sales are for cash and are expected to total $1,989,900. Some returns are expected for which cash refunds must be given; these will amount to $2,400. The company has arranged to issue 5,000 shares of its capital stock for $100 cash per share. All the proceeds will be used during the year to erect a new store on land already owned by the company.

(2) Merchandise purchases will amount to $928,000. The company pays each month's purchases invoices in the next month, and records purchases net of discounts. Payables on April 1, 1966, are $85,000 and on March 31, 1967, are expected to be $72,000.

(3) Selling expenses will amount to $505,000. Cash payments will equal the expenses of the year except for depreciation of warehouse and delivery truck. Depreciation of warehouse and truck will amount to $20,000. Administrative and general expenses will total $495,000. Of this, $10,000 represents depreciation, $8,000 is insurance expense representing writeoffs of prepaid insurance, and $12,000 is property taxes that are accrued monthly throughout the year.

(4) Insurance premiums of $15,000 and property taxes of $21,000 will be paid during the year.

(5) Dividends of $60,000 are expected to be paid.
(6) Payments on income taxes will amount to $128,000.
(7) Expenditures of $500,000 on land and buildings will be made during the year.

Required:

Prepare a summary cash budget for the year.

23.3   Martin Warehouses, Inc., is preparing a summary cash budget for the calendar year 1966, and the data given below have been collected.

(1) Balance of cash on hand January 1, 1966, is $92,000. Rental income for the year will be $1,614,000. Most rents are collected in advance; the balance of deferred rent income on January 1 is $426,000 and on December 31 it will be $432,000.
(2) Office expense for the year is budgeted at $96,000. Of this, $8,000 is depreciation and $3,000 is insurance expense.
(3) Insurance expense on the warehouses will be $350,000. Most insurance is paid in advance. Prepaid premiums on January 1 are $295,000; on December 31 they will be $152,000.
(4) Property taxes of $280,000 will accrue during the year. Accrued property taxes at the beginning are $120,000; at the end they will be $128,000.
(5) Improvements to the warehouses will be made at a cost of $250,000.
(6) Interest on the company's $500,000 of 6 percent bonds payable will be paid in two installments on April 1 and October 1.
(7) Repairs will be made at a cost of $75,000, all of which will be paid to the contractors during the year.
(8) Dividends amounting to $500,000 will be paid. Payments on income taxes will total $250,000.

Required:

Complete the summary cash budget.

23.4   The Citadel Company prepared the cash budgets given below for the calendar year 1966.

BUDGETED CASH RECEIPTS FROM CUSTOMERS

Accounts Receivable, Beginning		$ 240,000
Add: Gross Sales		4,100,000
		$4,340,000
Deduct:		
Accounts Receivable, Ending	$245,000	
Sales Returns and Allowances	28,000	
Bad Accounts Written Off	15,700	288,700
Accounts Receivable Collected		$4,051,300
Deduct: Discounts Allowed		24,100
Cash Receipts		$4,027,200

BUDGETED PAYMENTS ON MERCHANDISE PURCHASES

Accounts Payable, Beginning	$ 95,000
Add: Purchases	2,025,000
	$2,120,000
Deduct: Accounts Payable, Ending	120,000
Accounts Payable Paid	$2,000,000
Deduct: Discounts Taken	20,000
Cash Payments on Merchandise Purchases	$1,980,000

SUMMARY CASH BUDGET

Balance on Hand, Beginning		$ 197,000
Receipts from Customers		4,027,200
Sale of Additional Capital Stock		500,000
		$4,724,200
Disbursements:		
Merchandise Purchases	$1,980,000	
Selling Expenses	796,800	
Administrative and General Expense	695,200	
Insurance Premiums	15,200	
Property Taxes	18,000	
Dividends	200,000	
Interest	36,000	
Income Taxes	228,000	
Payment of Mortgage	600,000	4,569,200
Balance on Hand, Ending		$ 155,000

Required:

Prepare the journal entries necessary to record on the company's work sheet all the transactions possible from the information given.

23.5 Certain journal entries prepared to record the budget of the Dodwell Company for the year ended March 31, 1966, are given below, together with certain opening and closing balances.

The balances available are:

	Beginning	*Ending*
Accounts Receivable	$121,000	$120,300
Accounts Payable	103,000	81,000
Cash (ending to be computed)	54,400	—

The journal entries available are:

(1)

Accounts Receivable	$1,820,000	
Sales		$1,820,000

(2)

Sales Returns and Allowances	$ 7,500	
Allowance for Doubtful Accounts	24,200	
Accounts Receivable		$ 31,700

(3)

Cash	$1,776,700	
Sales Discounts	12,300	
Accounts Receivable		$1,789,000

(4)

Purchases	$ 725,000	
Accounts Payable		$ 725,000

(5)

Accounts Payable	$ 747,000	
Purchase Discounts		$ 10,500
Cash		736,500

(6)

Cash	$ 900,000	
Mortgage Payable		$ 900,000

(7)

Selling Expense	$ 242,000	
Administrative and General Expense	131,000	
Freight In	15,400	
Prepaid Insurance	9,200	
Property Taxes Accrued	17,000	
Building	1,250,000	
Dividends	60,000	
Income Tax Payable	120,000	
Cash		$1,844,600

(8)

Bad Debts	$ 15,000	
Allowance for Bad Debts		$ 15,000

(9)

Administrative and General Expense	$ 42,000	
Allowance for Depreciation – Building		$ 26,000
Allowance for Depreciation – Furniture and Fixtures		16,000

(10)

Administrative and General Expense	$ 8,100	
Prepaid Insurance		$ 8,100

(11)

Income Taxes	$ 128,000	
Income Taxes Payable		$ 128,000

Required:

Prepare the following cash budgets for this company:

1. Budgeted cash receipts from customers.
2. Budgeted payments on merchandise purchases.
3. Summary cash budget.

23.6 Peter J. Flynn intends to open the Crossroads Bookstore on July 1, 1966. and asks you to assist him in the preparation of income and cash flow projections. He furnishes you with the following information.

(1) Sales for the year ended June 30, 1967, are expected to be $300,000. The cost of the merchandise at retail will be 60 percent of retail, or $180,000. Sales of $80,000 are expected in December, and sales of $20,000 per month are expected for the rest of the year. All sales are for cash.

(2) Opening inventory is expected to be $100,000 at retail. Payments to merchandise creditors each month will be made in an amount sufficient to maintain an inventory of the same size, except in December, when payments will increase for holiday business. Flynn expects that monthly payments for merchandise with a retail list price of $20,000 will be made from January to November, and payments for merchandise retailing at $80,000 will be made in December.

(3) Equipment costing $80,000 will be purchased on July 1, 1966; terms 30 percent cash, balance payable in fifty-six monthly installments beginning August 1, 1966. The equipment is expected to last ten years.

(4) Other monthly payments for operations and supervision are expected to be $7,000 from January to November and $22,000 in December.

Required:

1. Prepare a statement of projected income and expense by quarters for the year ended June 30, 1967. (The statement should have columns for Totals, Second Quarter 1966, Third Quarter 1966, First Quarter 1967, and Second Quarter 1967.)
2. Prepare a statement of projected receipts and disbursements by quarters for the year ended June 30, 1967.

23.7   Newport Yacht Sales Co., a local retailer of marine equipment, has requested bank assistance during the 1966 peak sales period. The bank manager has asked for a cash flow summary for the 1966 summer season. The following information is taken from company records as of April 30, 1966:

Cash in bank $27,000
Accounts receivable (arising from April sales)   4,950
Loan from the Small Business Administration—6% 30,000
Loan from Finance Factors, 6%—borrowed August 1, 1965   7,000

Additional information:

(1) Sales for April amounted to $5,500—$4,000 for boats and motors and $1,500 for parts and accessories.
(2) Sales estimates (the percentages shown below are increases or decreases from sales of each preceding month):

	Boats and Motors	*Parts and Accessories*
May	+ 300%	+150%
June	+ 100%	+ 120%
July.	+ 20%	+ 30%
August	− 40%	− 20%

(3) Collections are expected to follow this pattern:

Cash in month of sale 10%
Paid within the following month 50%
Paid within the second month 20%
Paid within the third month 15%
Bad debts 5%

(4) Purchase estimates:

Date Ordered	*Imported*	*Local*
April 10	$15,000	$10,000
May 5	20,000	16,000
June 15	21,000	22,000
July 17	14,000	6,000
August 8	—	3,000

Terms: Imported—F.O.B. Newport Yacht Sales Co., payable 10% with order and balance on delivery in three weeks.
Local—F.O.B. Newport Yacht Sales Co., payable net 30 days.

(5) Property taxes of $28 per thousand on an assessment of $45,750 are payable in July.
(6) The loan from Finance Factors is to be repaid on August 1, 1966, together with all interest, compounded semiannually.

(7) The loan from the Small Business Administration is to be repaid at the rate of $1,000 per month for the period May 1 to September 30 of each year. Interest is payable monthly on the balance at the end of the previous month.

(8) Salaries and general and administrative expenses are estimated at $2,000 for May and $3,300 monthly for June to September and are paid in the month incurred.

(9) Salesmen are paid commissions of 5 percent on all sales during the period of their employment—April 1 to September 30. Payment is made as cash is collected. However, salesmen are charged with 15 percent of bad debts expense, and the charge is made in the fourth month following sale.

(10) If the loan is granted, the bank will advance funds in multiples of $1,000 at the beginning of each month to meet anticipated requirements for the month. Interest at the rate of 6 percent per year will be charged at the end of each month on the amount of loan outstanding during the month. Repayment is to be made in multiples of $1,000 at the end of any month in which funds are available.

Required:

Prepare a cash budget summary for the months of May, June, July, and August 1966, assuming that the bank loan is obtained. Submit details of your calculations, which are to be made to the nearest dollar.

(ICAC—adapted)

23.8   Acme, Inc., and its wholly owned subsidiary, Fabco, are joint owners of patent rights on a certain type of component for computers. Subassemblies are manufactured by Fabco and sold only to Acme for assembly and sale of the finished units.

The companies discovered that their patent rights had been infringed upon during the years 1966 and 1967, and that the infringing company produced and sold 16,640 units during that time.

You have been asked to investigate the situation in order to assist Acme and Fabco in their lawsuit against the infringing company for loss of profits. You learn that:

(1) During 1966 and 1967 Acme sold 104,000 units at $36 each. Subassemblies were sold to Acme by Fabco at $16.20 each.

	Acme, Inc.	Fabco
(2) Gross profit per unit after including factory overhead costs of 25% of direct costs	$7.00	$2.80
Administrative and general expenses per unit	1.70	1.20
Selling expenses per unit	2.30	—

(3) Acme and Fabco could produce and sell 20 percent more units than had been sold. For each 4 percent increase in volume over the present level:

   (a) Total factory overhead costs would increase by 3 percent of the factory overhead costs of the entire output at the present level.

   (b) Total general and administrative expenses would increase by 2 percent of the general and administrative expenses of the entire output at the present level.

Selling expenses vary directly with the number of units sold.

Required:

Prepare a statement to show the full amount of profits lost by both Acme, Inc., and Fabco because of the components sold by the infringing company. Submit details of your calculations.

(ICAC—adapted)

23.9 In August 1966, the management of H. DeForest & Co., Inc., decided to embark on an expansion program. Marketing research has indicated that sales can be increased substantially if there is a reduction in sales price. Additional plant facilities are readily available to meet the increased production requirements. Management asked the accountant to prepare a budget for 1967, based on the new program, and provided him with the following information.

(1) Sales are estimated as follows:

	First Quarter Units	Second Quarter Units	Third Quarter Units	Fourth Quarter Units
1967 — at $8.50 per unit	3,000	7,000	7,000	7,000
1968 — at $8.00 per unit	7,000	10,000	10,000	10,000

(2) Inventories of finished goods at the end of each quarter are equal to the estimated sales of the next quarter.

(3) The conversion period from raw materials to finished goods is six months. All the raw materials are added at the beginning of the process, and labor and factory overhead costs are spread evenly over the production period.

The production is scheduled so that a batch, using all the raw materials in inventory, is put into process on the first day of each quarter. Thus the batch put into process on October 1 will use up all raw materials in inventory on September 30 and will be completed at the end of March. Similarly the batch put into process on January 1 will use up all raw material in inventory on December 31 and will be completed at the end of June.

(4) All inventories are priced on a first-in first-out basis.

(5) During the first seven months of 1966 the company sold 1,000 units per month at $9 each, which cost:

Raw materials	$1.50
Labor	1.50
Factory overhead cost	3.00
	$6.00

Management estimates that these levels of sales and costs will be maintained for the balance of the year. However, budgeted inventory requirements of finished goods, work in process, and raw materials as of December 31, 1966, will be met through production activities in the remaining period of 1966.

(6) Quantity discounts on purchases of raw materials are estimated at 4 percent on annual purchases of 30,000 or more units and 8 percent on annual purchases of 40,000 or more units.

(7) It is estimated that factory overhead cost will increase by 10 percent on January 1, 1967, but that labor costs will remain unchanged.

Required:

Prepare a budgeted statement of estimated gross margin by quarters for the year 1967, showing opening and closing inventories of materials, work in process, and finished goods.

(ICAC — adapted)

Capital Budgeting

Capital budgeting is that phase of budgeting concerned with the planning, evaluating, and controlling of asset additions, improvements, and replacements. A capital budget is a formal plan for securing and investing capital. Capital outlays range from the replacement of equipment to the establishment of a new division. They constitute large expenditures that affect the destiny of the organization for a major period of its life.

Capital budgeting decisions are the function of top management. These decisions, largely irrevocable by nature, set a pattern for the entire future development of the organization. The personal lives of the officers and employees of a company, and in many cases the economy of the community in which the company is located, depend on the capital budgeting decisions.

Common examples of such decisions follow.

1. The American Manufacturing Company has machinery and equipment which has been breaking down with greater and greater frequency. Maintenance costs are becoming excessive. An engineering study discloses that the old machinery and equipment can be completely reconditioned for $60,000, or it can be replaced by new, fully automatic equipment costing $300,000. The company must choose between the alternatives.
2. The P. G. Bates Company has decided to market its product through employee-salesmen instead of through manufacturer's representatives. As a result, it must choose between buying or leasing a fleet of fifty automobiles for its salesmen.
3. The Consolidated Oil Company is considering the establishment of a new service station. The financial analysts of the company have estimated the gross margin and operating expenses for the proposal, and management must decide whether the expected returns will justify the new station.

The steps in the capital budgeting process may be summarized as follows:

1. Operating personnel submit proposals for capital investments.
2. The proposals are analyzed and evaluated on the basis of expected costs and revenues.
3. An executive committee reviews the proposals and decides whether to accept or reject them. (Generally, authorization for asset expenditures of less than a specified amount are made at lower levels of management.)
4. Expenditures are approved and controlled as the project is implemented.
5. A postaudit and review is made of the project results.

This chapter is concerned primarily with the accounting information useful in comparing alternative investment opportunities and with the types of accounting controls that may be applied in the capital budgeting process.

The success of a company's capital budgeting program depends upon its having an excess of investment opportunities over the supply of available funds, so that it can ration its funds into the most profitable opportunities. Management is constantly searching for new investment proposals. Once a proposal is obtained, its profitability may be evaluated by a computation that considers the amount of the investment, the amounts and dates of the expected returns, and some measure of the time value of money. Four methods of varying precision for ranking proposals are discussed in the following sections. They are:

1. Payout period method
2. Rate of return on average investment method
3. Discounted cash flow method
4. Present value method

PAYOUT PERIOD

The payout period is the time required to recover the cash outlay on a project through net cash receipts. A $24,000 investment which produces an annual $8,000 cash return pays out in three years.

The payout period has been used for decisions on whether to repair or replace equipment. Suppose a company must choose between the alternatives of repairing or replacing a machine that has met with increasing breakdown and has required excessive maintenance. The cost of completely reconditioning the old machine is $8,100, which includes the addition of improved controls and a loading device. These improvements will eliminate one worker and reduce material handling. The price of a new machine is $22,000. The old machine, which is fully depreciated, will realize $2,000 in a tax-free exchange on the new machine. The new machine has features that will eliminate two workers and will reduce material handling. Annual operating costs for the alternatives are as follows:

	Present Method	Recondition Old Machine	Acquire New Machine
Direct labor....................	$11,000	$ 8,700	$3,000
Indirect labor	4,000	2,400	2,400
Payroll taxes	1,200	800	600
Maintenance and repairs...........	2,000	800	1,200
Totals	$18,200	$12,700	$7,200

Income taxes are computed at 50 percent. The economic lives of the reconditioned and new machines are three and ten years respectively, at the end of which time neither machine is expected to have any salvage value.

The payout periods are calculated as follows:

		Recondition Old Machine	Acquire New Machine
Investment. . . . .(a)		$8,100	$20,000
Annual cash recovery:			
Savings in operating costs		$5,500	$11,000
Less: Income taxes (see below)		1,400	4,500
Difference . . . .(b)		$4,100	$ 6,500
Payout period. . . . .(a)/(b)		2.0 yr.	3.1 yr.
Income taxes:			
Savings in operating costs		$5,500	$11,000
Added depreciation:			
Recondition old machine ($8,100/3)		2,700	
Acquire new machine ($20,000/10).			2,000
Increase in taxable income		$2,800	$ 9,000
Income taxes at 50%.		$1,400	$ 4,500

These calculations show that the $8,100 cost of reconditioning the old machine will be recouped in two years, while the $20,000 investment in the new machinery will not be recovered until three years. This information may be significant to management if there is a high probability that the new machine itself may become obsolete in a short time. In a world of uncertainty, the payout period calculations assist management in determining the probability that at least the capital invested in a project will be recovered; however, the payout period calculations do not measure profitability, since they ignore the streams of income beyond the payout periods.

RATE OF RETURN ON AVERAGE INVESTMENT

The rate of return on average investment is the average net receipts less depreciation divided by the average amount invested over the life of the project. For example, if average receipts less depreciation amount to $1,500 and the average investment amounts to $15,000, the rate of return on average investment is 10 percent.

The average investment is computed by adding the investment at the beginning of the first and last years and dividing this sum by two.[1] (For this purpose the investment is valued at cost less accumulated depreciation.) The average investment for a machine which costs $20,000 and has a 5-year life is $12,000; that is, ($20,000 + $4,000)/2. If net cash receipts are $7,000 per year, the average income would be $3,000; that is, $7,000 receipts less $4,000 depreciation. Thus the rate of return on average investment equals $3,000/$12,000, or 25 percent.

---

[1] This method of averaging is based on the assumption that a pro rata portion of the investment is recovered each year *at the end of the year*. For example, if $20,000 is invested for five years and $4,000 is recovered at the end of each year, $20,000 will be outstanding the first year, $16,000 the second, and $12,000, $8,000, and $4,000 the third, fourth and fifth years respectively. The sum of these amounts is $60,000, which, divided by five years, gives an average investment of $12,000, the amount obtainable by adding the opening balances of the first and last years and dividing by 2, as suggested in the text.

The rates of return on average investment can be computed for the repair-or-replace decision discussed in the preceding section on the payout period. The computation is as follows:

	Recondition Old Machine	Acquire New Machine
Average annual income:		
Annual net cash recovery...............	$4,100	$ 6,500
Less depreciation	2,700	2,000
Average annual income	$1,400	$ 4,500
Average investment:		
Recondition old machine		
($8,100 + $2,700)/2...................	÷ 5,400	
Acquire new machine		
($20,000 + $2,000)/2.................		÷ 11,000
Rate of return on average investment	25.9%	40.9%

These calculations show that although a faster payout is earned from reconditioning the old machine, the rate of return on reconditioning the old machine is only 25.9 percent compared to 40.9 percent from acquiring the new machine. Replacement rather than reconditioning is in order if no change in technology is foreseen during the next three years.

The rate of return on average investment provides a rough approximation to the true rate of return on capital expenditures for long-lived projects; however, it does not allow for differences in timing of outlays and receipts. A dollar to be received at the end of the first year is given the same value as a dollar to be received at the end of the fiftieth year. Only some present value calculation, which properly takes account of the equivalence of values at different points in time, provides a satisfactory measure of the profitability of various investment alternatives.

DISCOUNTED CASH FLOW

Under the discounted cash flow method a *rate of return* is computed at which the cash receipts expected during the life of a project are equivalent to the investment in the project. Sums of money due at different points in time are said to be equivalent when the choice between them is a matter of indifference for a given rate of return. For example, $100 now is equivalent to $106 due one year from now at the rate of 6 percent per annum.

If a dollar is invested at an annual rate r, it is equivalent to $(1 + r)$ at the end of the year. This amount $(1 + r)$ can be reinvested at r for another year, resulting in $(1 + r)(1 + r)$ or $(1 + r)^2$ at the end of the second year. Thus, one dollar invested at r results in a compound amount of $(1 + r)^n$ at the end of n years; and P dollars invested for n years at the rate r amount to $S = P(1 + r)^n$ at the end of n years.

Dividing by $(1 + r)^n$, the present value can be expressed as $P = S/(1 + r)^n = S(1 + r)^{-n}$. In other words, an investment of P dollars now is equivalent to S dollars n years from now at the annual rate of return of r percent. At the rate of 25 percent per year, $100 due one year from now is equivalent to $80 now; that is, $P = S(1 + r)^{-n} = 100/(1 + \frac{1}{4}) = 100 \times \frac{4}{5} = 80$. At the rate of 25 percent per year, the present value of $100 due in two years is $P = 100(0.8)^2 = 64$.

Values of $(1 + r)^{-n}$ are shown in Table I.

TABLE I, PRESENT VALUE OF $1.00

Years	1%	2%	3%	4%	5%	6%	7%	8%	9%	10%	11%	12%	13%	14%	15%	16%	17%	18%	19%	20%
1	.990	.980	.971	.962	.952	.943	.935	.926	.917	.909	.901	.893	.885	.877	.870	.862	.855	.847	.840	.833
2	.980	.961	.943	.925	.907	.890	.873	.857	.842	.826	.812	.797	.783	.769	.756	.743	.731	.718	.706	.694
3	.971	.942	.915	.889	.864	.840	.816	.794	.772	.751	.731	.712	.693	.675	.658	.641	.624	.609	.593	.579
4	.961	.924	.888	.855	.823	.792	.763	.735	.708	.683	.659	.636	.613	.592	.572	.552	.534	.516	.499	.482
5	.951	.906	.863	.822	.784	.747	.713	.681	.650	.621	.593	.567	.543	.519	.497	.476	.456	.437	.419	.402
6	.942	.888	.837	.790	.746	.705	.666	.630	.596	.564	.535	.507	.480	.456	.432	.410	.390	.370	.352	.335
7	.933	.871	.813	.760	.711	.665	.623	.583	.547	.513	.482	.452	.425	.400	.376	.354	.333	.314	.296	.279
8	.923	.853	.789	.731	.677	.627	.582	.540	.502	.467	.434	.404	.376	.351	.327	.305	.285	.266	.249	.233
9	.914	.837	.766	.703	.645	.592	.543	.500	.460	.424	.391	.361	.333	.308	.284	.263	.243	.225	.209	.194
10	.905	.820	.744	.676	.614	.558	.508	.463	.422	.386	.352	.322	.295	.270	.247	.227	.208	.191	.176	.162
11	.896	.804	.722	.650	.585	.527	.475	.429	.388	.350	.317	.287	.261	.237	.215	.195	.178	.162	.148	.135
12	.887	.788	.701	.625	.557	.497	.444	.397	.356	.319	.286	.257	.231	.208	.187	.168	.152	.137	.124	.112
13	.879	.773	.681	.601	.530	.469	.415	.368	.326	.290	.258	.229	.204	.182	.163	.145	.130	.116	.104	.093
14	.870	.758	.661	.577	.505	.442	.388	.340	.299	.263	.232	.205	.181	.160	.141	.125	.111	.099	.088	.078
15	.861	.743	.642	.555	.481	.417	.362	.315	.275	.239	.209	.183	.160	.140	.123	.108	.095	.084	.074	.065
16	.853	.728	.623	.534	.458	.394	.339	.292	.252	.218	.188	.163	.142	.123	.107	.093	.081	.071	.062	.054
17	.844	.714	.605	.513	.436	.371	.317	.270	.231	.198	.170	.146	.125	.108	.093	.080	.069	.060	.052	.045
18	.836	.700	.587	.494	.416	.350	.296	.250	.212	.180	.153	.130	.111	.095	.081	.069	.059	.051	.044	.038
19	.828	.686	.570	.475	.396	.331	.277	.232	.194	.164	.138	.116	.098	.083	.070	.060	.051	.043	.037	.031
20	.820	.673	.554	.456	.377	.312	.258	.215	.178	.149	.124	.104	.087	.073	.061	.051	.043	.037	.031	.026
21	.811	.660	.538	.439	.359	.294	.242	.199	.164	.135	.112	.093	.077	.064	.053	.044	.037	.031	.026	.022
22	.803	.647	.522	.422	.342	.278	.226	.184	.150	.123	.101	.083	.068	.056	.046	.038	.032	.026	.022	.018
23	.795	.634	.507	.406	.326	.262	.211	.170	.138	.112	.091	.074	.060	.049	.040	.033	.027	.022	.018	.015
24	.788	.622	.492	.390	.310	.247	.197	.158	.126	.102	.082	.066	.053	.043	.035	.028	.023	.019	.015	.013
25	.780	.610	.478	.375	.295	.233	.184	.146	.116	.092	.074	.059	.047	.038	.030	.024	.020	.016	.013	.010
30	.742	.552	.412	.308	.231	.174	.131	.099	.075	.057	.044	.033	.026	.020	.015	.012	.009	.007	.005	.004
35	.706	.500	.355	.253	.181	.130	.094	.068	.049	.036	.026	.019	.014	.010	.008	.006	.004	.003	.002	.002
40	.672	.453	.307	.208	.142	.097	.067	.046	.032	.022	.015	.011	.008	.005	.004	.003	.002	.001	.001	.001
45	.639	.410	.264	.171	.111	.073	.048	.031	.021	.014	.009	.006	.004	.003	.002	.001	.001	.001	.000	.000
50	.608	.372	.228	.141	.087	.054	.034	.021	.013	.009	.005	.003	.002	.001	.001	.001	.000	.000	.000	.000

This table gives the present value of $1 for various rates of return. For instance, a dollar due twelve years hence is worth 50 cents now at a rate of 6 percent. Table I can also be used to find the rate when the amount of a payment, the number of years, and present value are given. For example, if $1,000 is expected in eleven years from an investment of $350 now, the rate of return is found from Table I to be 10 percent.

A series of equal periodic payments made at the end of equal periods is called an *annuity*. The size of each payment is called the *rent*. For rents of $1 the present value of the annuity is

$$a = (1+r)^{-1} + (1+r)^{-2} + (1+r)^{-3} \cdots + (1+r)^{-n}$$

which can be written as

$$a = \frac{1 - (1+r)^{-n}}{r}.$$

Table II gives the present value of an annuity of $1 rents. At 10 percent, the present value of an annuity of three $100 rents is $249. The discounted value of these cash flows could also have been obtained by summing the present value of each $100 payment. This is shown in the diagram below.

In summary, Tables I and II show the present values, or discounted values, of future cash flows. Table I shows the present value of a single payment; Table II shows the present value of a series of payments.

The following example demonstrates how the rate of return is computed for a series of equal payments. The Falmouth Company can buy construction equipment for $250,000, which it will lease to an overseas contractor for three years at an annual rent of $100,000 payable at the end of each year. At the end of three years, the construction project will be completed and the equipment will be abandoned. To compute the rate of return, all amounts are divided by $100,000 to put the problem in terms of an annuity of $1 rents. Table II shows that three rents of $1 have a present value of 2.500 at a rate between 9 and 10 percent. Interpolation gives a rate of 9.7 percent.

Rate	P. V. of $1 per Year
9%	2.531
?	2.500
10%	2.487

$$r = 9\% + 31/44 \times 1\% = 9.7\%$$

The rate of return can be computed in a similar fashion for installments of unequal size. For example, suppose Cosmos Marine, Inc. is offered a used freighter for $500,000 which can be put out on charter and will produce receipts of $300,000 at the end of the first year, $200,000 at the end of the second

TABLE II, PRESENT VALUE OF ANNUITY OF $1.00 RENTS

Years	1%	2%	3%	4%	5%	6%	7%	8%	9%	10%	11%	12%	13%	14%	15%	16%	17%	18%	19%	20%
1	0.990	0.980	0.971	0.962	0.952	0.943	0.935	0.926	0.917	0.909	0.901	0.893	0.885	0.877	0.870	0.862	0.855	0.847	0.840	0.833
2	1.970	1.942	1.913	1.886	1.859	1.833	1.808	1.783	1.759	1.736	1.713	1.690	1.668	1.647	1.626	1.605	1.585	1.566	1.547	1.528
3	2.941	2.884	2.829	2.775	2.723	2.673	2.624	2.577	2.531	2.487	2.444	2.402	2.361	2.322	2.283	2.246	2.210	2.174	2.140	2.106
4	3.902	3.808	3.717	3.630	3.546	3.465	3.387	3.312	3.240	3.170	3.102	3.037	2.974	2.914	2.855	2.798	2.743	2.690	2.639	2.589
5	4.853	4.713	4.580	4.452	4.329	4.212	4.100	3.993	3.890	3.791	3.696	3.605	3.517	3.433	3.352	3.274	3.199	3.127	3.058	2.991
6	5.795	5.601	5.417	5.242	5.076	4.917	4.767	4.623	4.486	4.355	4.231	4.111	3.998	3.889	3.784	3.685	3.589	3.498	3.410	3.326
7	6.728	6.472	6.230	6.002	5.786	5.582	5.389	5.206	5.033	4.868	4.712	4.564	4.423	4.288	4.160	4.039	3.922	3.812	3.706	3.605
8	7.652	7.325	7.020	6.733	6.463	6.210	5.971	5.747	5.535	5.335	5.146	4.968	4.799	4.639	4.487	4.344	4.207	4.078	3.954	3.837
9	8.566	8.162	7.786	7.435	7.108	6.802	6.515	6.247	5.995	5.759	5.537	5.328	5.132	4.946	4.772	4.607	4.451	4.303	4.163	4.031
10	9.471	8.983	8.530	8.111	7.722	7.360	7.024	6.710	6.418	6.145	5.889	5.650	5.426	5.216	5.019	4.833	4.659	4.494	4.339	4.192
11	10.368	9.787	9.253	8.760	8.306	7.887	7.499	7.139	6.805	6.495	6.207	5.938	5.687	5.453	5.234	5.029	4.836	4.656	4.487	4.327
12	11.255	10.575	9.954	9.385	8.863	8.384	7.943	7.536	7.161	6.814	6.492	6.194	5.918	5.660	5.421	5.197	4.988	4.793	4.611	4.439
13	12.134	11.348	10.635	9.986	9.394	8.853	8.358	7.904	7.487	7.103	6.750	6.424	6.122	5.842	5.583	5.342	5.118	4.910	4.715	4.533
14	13.004	12.106	11.296	10.563	9.899	9.295	8.745	8.244	7.786	7.367	6.982	6.628	6.302	6.002	5.724	5.468	5.229	5.008	4.802	4.611
15	13.865	12.849	11.938	11.118	10.380	9.712	9.108	8.559	8.061	7.606	7.191	6.811	6.462	6.142	5.847	5.575	5.324	5.092	4.876	4.675
16	14.718	13.578	12.561	11.652	10.838	10.106	9.447	8.851	8.313	7.824	7.379	6.974	6.604	6.265	5.954	5.669	5.405	5.162	4.938	4.730
17	15.562	14.292	13.166	12.166	11.274	10.477	9.763	9.122	8.544	8.022	7.549	7.120	6.729	6.373	6.047	5.749	5.475	5.222	4.990	4.775
18	16.398	14.992	13.754	12.659	11.690	10.828	10.059	9.372	8.756	8.201	7.702	7.250	6.840	6.467	6.128	5.818	5.534	5.273	5.033	4.812
19	17.226	15.678	14.324	13.134	12.085	11.158	10.336	9.604	8.950	8.365	7.839	7.366	6.938	6.550	6.198	5.877	5.584	5.316	5.070	4.844
20	18.046	16.351	14.877	13.590	12.462	11.470	10.594	9.818	9.129	8.514	7.963	7.469	7.025	6.623	6.259	5.929	5.628	5.353	5.101	4.870
21	18.857	17.011	15.415	14.029	12.821	11.764	10.836	10.017	9.292	8.649	8.075	7.562	7.102	6.687	6.312	5.973	5.665	5.384	5.127	4.891
22	19.660	17.658	15.937	14.451	13.163	12.042	11.061	10.201	9.442	8.772	8.176	7.645	7.170	6.743	6.359	6.011	5.696	5.410	5.149	4.909
23	20.456	18.292	16.444	14.857	13.489	12.303	11.272	10.371	9.580	8.883	8.266	7.718	7.230	6.792	6.399	6.044	5.723	5.432	5.167	4.925
24	21.243	18.914	16.936	15.247	13.799	12.550	11.469	10.529	9.707	8.985	8.348	7.784	7.283	6.835	6.434	6.073	5.746	5.451	5.182	4.937
25	22.023	19.523	17.413	15.622	14.094	12.783	11.654	10.675	9.823	9.077	8.422	7.843	7.330	6.873	6.464	6.097	5.766	5.467	5.195	4.948
30	25.808	22.396	19.600	17.292	15.372	13.765	12.409	11.258	10.274	9.427	8.694	8.055	7.496	7.003	6.566	6.177	5.829	5.517	5.235	4.979
35	29.409	24.999	21.487	18.665	16.374	14.498	12.948	11.655	10.567	9.644	8.855	8.176	7.586	7.070	6.617	6.215	5.858	5.539	5.251	4.992
40	32.835	27.355	23.115	19.793	17.159	15.046	13.332	11.925	10.757	9.779	8.951	8.244	7.634	7.105	6.642	6.234	5.871	5.548	5.258	4.997
45	36.094	29.490	24.519	20.720	17.774	15.456	13.606	12.108	10.881	9.863	9.008	8.283	7.661	7.123	6.654	6.242	5.877	5.552	5.261	4.999
50	39.196	31.424	25.730	21.482	18.256	15.762	13.801	12.233	10.962	9.915	9.042	8.305	7.675	7.133	6.661	6.246	5.880	5.554	5.262	4.999

year, and $100,000 at the end of the third year (including the salvage value of the vessel). The rate of return on the investment can be computed as follows:

Year	Receipts (in thousands)	Present Value of $1.00		Present Value of Receipts (in thousands)	
		At 11%	At 12%	At 11%	At 12%
1	$300	0.901	0.893	$270.3	$267.9
2	200	0.812	0.797	162.4	159.4
3	100	0.731	0.712	73.1	71.2
				$505.8	$498.5

$$r = 11.0\% + 5.8/7.3 \times 1\% = 11.8\%.$$

Various rates of return are tried until the present value of the receipts brackets the amount of the investment. Interpolation gives the rate to the nearest tenth of a percent.

The true rates of return are computed below for the repair-or-replace decision discussed in the preceding two sections. The true rates of return are then compared to the rates of return on average investment to illustrate the error resulting from the use of the latter as an approximation of the former. The computation of the true rates of return is as follows:

	Recondition Old Machine	Acquire New Machine
Investment	$8,100	$20,000
Annual cash recovery	÷ 4,100	÷ 6,500
Present value of each $1 of annual payment	1.976	3.077
Economic lives	3 years	10 years
True rates of return	24.2%	34.2%
Rates of return on average investment..........	25.9%	40.9%

The rate of return on average investment method overstates the profitability of both alternatives — the overstatement being greater for the investment with the longer life. It can be shown that the error resulting from using the rate of return on average investment as an approximation to the true rate of return is always positive, and increases with the number of years, approaching 100 percent of the true rate as the number of years approaches infinity.[2]

The discounted cash flow method discussed in this section produces a rate of return which is generally a suitable index of a project's profitability, but the method has two limitations. First, it entails the assumption that all proceeds can be reinvested at the rate of return earned on the specific project. Second, it ranks projects according to their relative profitability, whereas, in the case of mutually exclusive projects, the crucial ranking is according to absolute profitability (assuming investment funds are available at an economical price).

This second limitation of the discounted cash flow method can be demonstrated by a numerical illustration. Suppose that a company has a choice be-

[2]Myron J. Gordon, "The Payoff Period and the Rate of Profit," *The Journal of Business,* October 1955, pp. 253–60.

tween two mutually exclusive investment alternatives. The absolute and relative rates of return expected are as follows:

	Proposal A	Proposal B
Investment.	$2,000,000	$1,000,000
Annual return	400,000	220,000
Rate of return	20%	22%

Suppose further that the company must pay 10 percent for its capital. Proposal A will return to the stockholders $200,000 ($400,000 − 10% × $2,000,000), while proposal B will return only $120,000 ($220,000 − 10% × $1,000,000). Using the rate of return method, proposal B would be ranked over proposal A; but proposal A actually produces the greater amount of profit for the stockholders.

PRESENT VALUE

Under the present value method of evaluating capital expenditures, the net cash benefits expected during the life of a proposal are discounted at an established cost of capital. The *cost of capital* is the minimum annual rate that a company must earn on proposed capital expenditures.

The present value of the expected benefits is the maximum amount a company can economically invest in the project. To illustrate the method, suppose that the cost of capital is 15 percent. Consider a project that is expected to return $1,000 a year for five years and which requires an immediate outlay of $4,000. The present value of the five installments at a cost of capital of 15 percent is

$$\$1,000 \times 3.352 = \$3,352.$$

This is $648 less than the required outlay; the project would be rejected. If the expected annual returns were $1,200, the present value would be

$$\$1,200 \times 3.352 = \$4,022,$$

and the project would be accepted, since this present value is $22 greater than the required investment.

The present value method can also be demonstrated by an example of a buy-or-lease decision. Suppose that an EDP 630 computer can be bought for a cash price of $750,000 and is expected to have a life of ten years with no scrap value. Alternatively, it can be leased for ten years at an annual rent of $100,000, payable at the end of each year. The company evaluates investment proposals, using a cost of capital of 10 percent. The calculation follows:

Cash price.	$750,000
Present value of rents ($100,000 × 6.145).	614,500
Saving by leasing	$135,500

On the basis of the figures given, the company should lease the computer.

Present value calculations are used to solve problems in the application of funds to repay debt as well as to solve problems in the application of funds to purchase fixed assets. The Royal Company has a $1,000,000 issue of 6 percent debentures outstanding, on which interest is payable at the end of each year. It can redeem the issue by paying a call premium of $50,000. Interest rates have dropped, and the company can sell a new 5 percent 10-year issue at par. The Royal Company can calculate the gain or loss on refunding by comparing the present value of its old issue at the effective interest rate of 5 percent with the present value of the cash outlay to refund the old issue. The computation is as follows:

Present value at 5% of payment due in 10 years on debentures ($1,000,000 × 0.614)	$ 614,000
Present value at 5% of annual payments on debentures ($60,000 × 7.722)	463,000
Total present value of debentures	$1,077,000
Cost of refunding debentures	1,050,000
Gain on refunding	$ 27,000

This shows that refunding is advantageous.

COMPARISON OF PRESENT VALUE AND DISCOUNTED CASH FLOW

The present value and the discounted cash flow methods may result in conflicting rankings of mutually exclusive proposals. This is due to the fact that the discounted cash flow approach implies that cash receipts are reinvested at the project rate of return; whereas the present value approach implies that receipts are reinvested at the cost of capital (generally a lower rate). A concrete example will make this conflict clear.

Capital Development Company is considering two mutually exclusive proposals. Both require a cash outlay of $100 million. Project A will produce $112.0 million at the end of one year. Project B will produce $133.1 million at the end of three years. The same risk is involved in either proposal. The company figures its cost of capital at 6 percent per year. The rates of return and the present values of the projects are as follows:

	Project A	Project B
Rates of return	12%	10%
Present values at 6 percent:		
$112.0 × 0.943	$106 mil.	
$133.1 × 0.840		$112 mil.

When the investments are ranked by rate of return, project A is superior; but when they are ranked by discounted cash flow, project B is superior.

The resolution of this paradox lies in an explanation of what happens to the $112.0 million returned on project A at the end of the first year. If the money can be reinvested at only 6 percent, project B is better because it keeps money at work throughout the three years at 10 percent. An investment in project A would average only 8 percent over the three years (one year at 12 percent, two years at 6 percent). On the other hand, project A is better than project B if cash received at the end of the first year can be reinvested at 12 percent.

The same conclusion is reached by comparing amounts at the end of three years for each proposition under the alternative assumptions regarding the rate of return on reinvested funds:

Assuming funds are reinvested at 6 percent:
Project A amounts to $112.0 × (1.06)² . . . . $125.8 mil.
Project B amounts to . . . .   133.1 mil.
Project B is better by . . . . $ 7.3 mil.

Assuming funds are reinvested at 10 percent:
Project A amounts to $112.0 × (1.10)² . . . . $135.5 mil.
Project B amounts to . . . .   133.1 mil.
Project A is better by . . . . $ 2.4 mil.

As stated before, the resolution of conflicting rankings between the discounted cash flow and the present value methods requires a determination of the expected rate of return on reinvested funds.

COST OF CAPITAL

The cost of capital is the minimum annual rate that must be earned on proposed capital expenditures. It is the sacrifice incurred by a company in obtaining funds for investment expenditures, including a margin to compensate the stockholders for risk. The cost of capital will differ between companies, and it will differ for the same company at different points in time.

When a company ranks projects by their rates of return, it constructs a demand schedule for funds. Increasing amounts of capital may be invested at successively lower rates of return. In a similar manner, management may visualize a supply schedule for funds showing increasing amounts of capital available at successively higher costs—on the assumption that these funds would have to be bid away from others in the capital markets. However, studies show that the marginal cost of capital is generally constant over the range of capital requirements. Thus, the average cost of capital is a good approximation to the marginal cost, and may be used for most capital budgeting problems.

The cost of capital is taken generally as an average of debt and equity funds based on an optimal capital structure. The use of the optimum debt-equity structure provides a long-term rate that serves as a more stable guide for capital budgeting than does the use of a specific rate for a particular year.

The cost of long-term debt can be obtained exactly from bond tables, or it can be approximated by simple arithmetic, as in the following example. The York Company has an issue of 10-year 6 percent debentures outstanding, which were sold at 90. The cost of long-term debt is computed as follows:

Average annual cost (per $100 of par value):
Annual coupon payment . . . . $ 6.00
Discount amortization ($10/10) 1.00
                                                                           $ 7.00
Average debt . . . .   ÷ 95.00
Approximate effective rate 7.4%

If the estimated returns on an investment proposal are stated net of income taxes, the cost of capital must also be stated net of income taxes. With income taxes at 50 percent, the after-tax rate becomes 3.7 percent in the example above.

Financial analysts are divided in their opinion on the proper method of determining the cost of equity[3] funds. One school of thought holds that expected

[3]"Equity funds" = stockholder or proprietary investment.

earnings are the ultimate source of value, and the cost of equity funds should be measured by the expected earnings-price ratio of the capital stock. For this purpose the "expected earnings" on a common stock may be quantified as the sum of expected dividends and the expected increases in the market price of the stock. The York Company stock has been selling at an average dividend-price ratio of 5 percent and the stock has been appreciating on the average at the annual rate of 6 percent; this makes the cost of its equity capital 11.0 percent.

The final step in the determination of the cost of capital consists of averaging the costs of debt and equity capital. Using an optimum debt-equity mix of 40 percent debt to 60 percent equity, the cost of capital for the firm in the previous illustration is 8.1 percent, as computed below:

	Cost of Capital	Fraction of Total Capital	Product
Debt	3.7%	0.40	1.5%
Equity	11.0%	0.60	6.6%
Total		1.00	8.1%

These calculations demonstrate one method of computing the cost of capital currently used by some companies. Other companies have developed minimum rates of return for capital proposals by starting with the historical rates actually earned on various investments relative to the degree of risk, and tempering these rates in consideration of their long-run goals. For example, an integrated oil company has accepted marketing proposals at a lower cutoff rate than production proposals because of its long-run goal of expanding the marketing division.

Any system for measuring the cost of capital must be viewed as only one of the quantitative measures to be used by management in making effective capital budgeting decisions. In summary, the cost of capital is that minimum rate which the management of a particular company stipulates must be earned on proposed capital expenditures.

ECONOMIC LIFE OF EQUIPMENT

The comparisons of investment proposals in the preceding sections have been based on the assumption that the economic lives of the plant and equipment utilized in these proposals are given. But the determination of these optimum replacement lives is itself an important and challenging subproblem of capital budgeting. Furthermore, an optimum replacement policy is essential for the general least-cost operation of the firm.

Fixed assets may be classified into two groups: (1) those which suddenly stop working, such as electric light bulbs, and (2) those which gradually deteriorate with age. This discussion is confined to the latter. The costs of repair and maintenance plus the costs from spoiled work and idle time increase for these assets with the passage of time. On the other hand, capital amortization cost diminishes as the price of the asset is spread over an increasing number of years. The determination of the economic life of equipment is a matter of balancing increasing maintenance and operating cost on the one hand against the decreasing cost of capital amortization on the other.

A simple example in which the cost of capital is omitted will illustrate the basic elements of the computation. A truck which costs $6,600 requires maintenance and operating expenditures of $600 at the end of the first year of operations, $1,200 at the end of the second year, and so on. To simplify the discussion, the salvage value of the truck will be ignored; thus the capital amortization cost resulting from a policy of replacing every year is $6,600. The capital amortization cost from replacing every two years is $6,600/2 = $3,300, and so on.

The annual maintenance and operating cost (referred to hereafter simply as maintenance) must be expressed on an annual basis so that it can be compared with capital amortization. The average maintenance for two years is ($600 + $1,200)/2 = $900; average maintenance for three years is ($600 + $1,200 + $1,800)/3 = $1,200, and so on.

The average annual costs are tabulated below:

Year	Capital Amortization per Year	Annual Maintenance	Average Annual Maintenance	Average Total Cost
1	$6,600	$ 600	$ 600	$7,200
2	3,300	1,200	900	4,200
3	2,200	1,800	1,200	3,400
4	1,650	2,400	1,500	3,150
5	1,320	3,000	1,800	3,120
6	1,100	3,600	2,100	3,200
7	943	4,200	2,400	3,343
8	812	4,800	2,700	3,512

This tabulation shows that the company should follow a policy of replacing such trucks every five years, because this policy results in the minimum average total cost of $3,120 per year.

As shown in this example, the determination of an economic life for equipment consists of balancing the diminishing capital amortization per year against the increasing average annual maintenance.

ACCOUNTING FOR CAPITAL BUDGETING DECISIONS

The accounting for capital budgeting consists of special investigations to produce reliable estimates of the investment expenditures to be made and the benefits expected to be received from an investment proposal. The investment can be measured with greater accuracy than the benefits, because it is based on facts that are reasonably well known rather than estimates of future levels of sales, production, and so on.

The investment is properly measured by all the resources the organization devotes to the project, whether in the form of cash or other property. The opportunity cost of an asset rather than its book value is its relevant cost. If the addition of a new product line uses warehouse space that otherwise would go vacant, the space is cost-free for the proposal. (Only the incremental costs, such as additional property taxes and property insurance, are relevant in this case.)

Most of the expenditures required by a project will be capitalized; but some, such as research and development, may be charged to expense. The tax accounting treatment is significant in that it determines the related cash flow because of income taxes associated with the project.

The investment, then, includes more than the current additions to plant and equipment: it includes working capital requirements plus estimates of future requirements for buildings and facilities to service the new project. For example, if the wiring and switch boxes in a plant are adequate to sustain the added load of new equipment, they need not be counted as part of the immediate investment. But if three years later, further expansion requires larger switch boxes and more wiring, then part of that expected outlay is properly part of the total investment in the original project.

A sample work sheet for estimating investment requirements follows.

	1967	1968	1969	Total
Project Investment:				
Asset:				
Land	$100,000			$ 100,000
Buildings		$ 200,000		200,000
Equipment............		800,000	$800,000	1,600,000
	$100,000	$1,000,000	$800,000	$1,900,000
Expense:				
Administrative		$ 50,000		$ 50,000
Relocations		10,000		10,000
Inventory loss..........		5,000		5,000
		$ 65,000		$ 65,000
Total project investment	$100,000	$1,065,000	$800,000	$1,965,000
Working Capital:				
Accounts receivable		$ 60,000		$ 60,000
Materials inventory		40,000		40,000
Containers inventory.......		10,000		10,000
Finished goods inventory....		30,000		30,000
Total working capital		$ 140,000		$ 140,000
Facilities:				
Warehouse (1,000 sq. ft. at				
$10/sq. ft.)			$ 10,000	$ 10,000
Additional power.........			20,000	20,000
Total facilities			$ 30,000	$ 30,000
Total investment	$100,000	$1,205,000	$830,000	$2,135,000

The investment expenditures are classified by date so they may be commuted to equivalent present values. Expense items, such as the $50,000 for administration, result in an immediate reduction in income taxes; capitalized amounts reduce income taxes through additional depreciation in subsequent years. These tax effects are summarized along with other data in the sample worksheet for estimating receipts and expenditures, which follows:

	(1) Projected Net Receipts	(2) Depreciation	(3) Net Income	(4) Income Tax At 50%	(5) = (1) − (4) Cash Flow Back
Year					
1968	$100,000	$ 84,000	$ 16,000	$ 8,000	$ 92,000
1969	300,000	164,000	136,000	68,000	232,000
1970	500,000	164,000	336,000	168,000	332,000
1971	500,000	164,000	336,000	168,000	332,000

(Remaining years omitted in this illustration)

Notice that depreciation is included solely to calculate the outlay for income taxes. Income taxes are deducted from the project earnings to get the "cash flow back."

It should also be kept in mind that the only relevant costs in a comparison of alternative investment proposals are the incremental costs occasioned by the project (see the discussion in Chapter 22). Some financial analysts have erroneously prorated total general overhead between new and old proposals without considering whether the new project actually caused an increase in total cost. When unused capacity exists, fixed overhead should not be applied arbitrarily as a percentage of direct labor cost. Those fixed overhead charges would be incurred whether the new proposal is accepted or rejected; they are not a sacrifice related to the immediate decision. The accounting records provide a good starting point for the assembly of the financial data required for effective capital budgeting decisions.

ADMINISTRATION AND CONTROL

The success of a capital budget depends on the administrative process for originating, evaluating, and authorizing investment proposals. These procedures will be discussed in terms of:

1. Appropriation request
2. Authorization of the appropriation
3. Postcompletion performance review

The first requirement of a well-administered capital budget is a written appropriation request for each proposal. This form includes (1) the name of the individual making the recommendation, (2) the purpose of the proposal, (3) a brief description of the project, (4) a detailed listing of the proposed expenditures, (5) an exposition of the reasons for accepting the project, (6) a schedule of expected savings and profits, and (7) space for approvals.

The request-authorization-review procedure is recommended for both of the broad classes of capital budgeting projects—those which increase profits or decrease costs, and those (an employee cafeteria, for example) considered necessary by management but impossible to justify on a profit and loss basis. (The postcompletion review of projects of the latter type must be verbal rather than quantitative.)

When the appropriation is accepted, a work order is assigned to the project and a corporate officer is given authority to approve expenditures against the work order up to a designated maximum. In general, costs are accumulated and a report on the total amount expended is prepared at the completion of the project.

Customarily, internal auditors review the expenditures soon after the project is completed. Later, a broader performance review can be made to evaluate the degree to which forecasted results were realized in terms of cost savings or revenues produced. Such a review includes these advantages:

1. Forecasting techniques may be improved by a comparison of actual and estimated amounts.
2. The originators of projects can be rated as to their accuracy in making estimates of the expected benefits and cost savings to be derived from proposals.

3. Junior executives are provided training in the art of reviewing investment opportunities. In reviewing past proposals they gain experience which should assist them when they come to approve projects themselves.

The postcompletion performance review has not been adopted by all companies, many of whom feel that changing economic conditions make such an inquiry worthless. Furthermore, some companies have avoided a postcompletion review, because they have felt it might discourage executives from submitting proposals if they knew they would be held responsible for those which failed to meet expectations. However, if the review is made in the spirit of helping the operating executive achieve better predicting methods, it should prove to be a valuable component of the capital budgeting process.

SUMMARY

A capital budget is a formal plan for the securing and investing of capital. Investment proposals have been ranked by various methods. The payout period method indicates how quickly cash is expected to be returned by the project, but it does not indicate the profitability of the project. The rate of return on average investment is an approximate measure of profitability; its computation includes the life of the project but omits the time value of money. The discounted cash flow method results in an internal rate of return at which the expected receipts are equivalent to the investment in the project. This method recognizes the time value of money and generally is a suitable ranking device. However, it entails the assumption that all proceeds can be reinvested at the project rate of return; furthermore, it may result in the selection of the less profitable of mutually exclusive projects. Under the present value method, expected cash benefits are discounted at the cost of capital, which is the minimum annual rate that a company must earn on proposed capital expenditures.

The comparison of investments in plant and equipment requires a prior determination of the optimum replacement policy for the equipment. Determination of that life consists of balancing the decreasing charges for capital amortization against the increasing maintenance cost as equipment ages.

Part of the accountant's role in capital budgeting is the assembly of the financial data required for effective capital budgeting decisions. The investment is properly measured by the opportunity cost of all resources devoted to the project, including working capital and future plant expansion. The costs relevant to projecting future net income are the incremental costs associated with the project. Depreciation is calculated solely to determine the cash flow for income taxes.

A well-organized administrative process for originating, evaluating, and authorizing investment proposals is essential to successful capital budgeting. Such a process involves (1) the use of written appropriation requests for all proposals, (2) a formalized procedure for authorizing appropriations, and (3) a systematic procedure for the performance review of projects after they have been completed and are in operation.

QUESTIONS

24.1 Give several examples of capital budgeting decisions.

24.2 Trace the steps in the life cycle of a successful capital budgeting proposal.

24.3 Explain four methods of ranking investment proposals. Evaluate each.

24.4 A company has two alternative investment opportunities. Project A shows a lower rate of return than project B, but project A has a faster payout than project B. Why might project A be selected rather than project B?

24.5 How is establishment of the optimum replacement life of equipment related to capital budgeting?

24.6 What are some items included in the investment in a capital budgeting proposal that are not properly charged to the cost of plant and equipment?

24.7 Explain how depreciation enters the present value computation for evaluating alternative investment proposals.

24.8 Under what circumstances would a pro rata share of building overhead cost be included in the computation of cost savings from new machinery?

24.9 List the principal items contained in an appropriation request.

24.10 Discuss the advantages and limitations of a postcompletion performance review.

EXERCISES

24.1 The East Bay Machine Works can expand its facilities by the purchase of an automatic bolt threader for $12,000, by the purchase of a turret lathe for $12,000, or the purchase of both machines for $24,000. The increase in annual revenues and costs expected from each machine is estimated as follows:

	Threader	Lathe
Revenues	$9,000	$7,500
Costs:		
Depreciation	$1,500	$1,000
Other	2,500	2,500
Totals	$4,000	$3,500
Net before income taxes	$5,000	$4,000
Income taxes	2,500	2,000
Net income	$2,500	$2,000

1. The company buys equipment only if it will pay out in three years or less. Should either of the machines be purchased?

2. Compute the total cash expected to be recovered over the entire life of each machine, and comment on how the payout rule may result in a spurious ranking of investment alternatives. (Cost estimates include straight line depreciation with no scrap value.)

24.2 The Dahl Lumber Company is considering the purchase of a semiautomatic lumber sorter that is expected to reduce annual costs by $20,000 a year. The lumber sorter costs $168,000 and is expected to have a useful life of twenty years with no salvage value. The company figures its cost of capital at 10 percent. Should it purchase the lumber sorter?

24.3 The Norton Company is considering the purchase of a machine for $55,000 that is expected to have a life of ten years and no residual value. The machine will save the company $10,000 a year. What is the rate of return computed by the discounted cash flow method?

24.4 The Lyons Company is comparing the cash cost of operating its own delivery truck with the cost of using a public express company. Lyons has determined that it will follow a policy of replacing the truck every five years, and has estimated the cash costs of the two alternatives as follows:

Payment at End of Year	Cash Operating Costs of Owning Truck	Cash Cost of Using Express Company	Advantage of Owning over Hiring
1	$6,500	$9,000	$2,500
2	7,000	9,000	2,000
3	7,300	9,000	1,700
4	7,600	9,000	1,400
5	7,800	9,000	1,200

The purchase price of the truck is $6,000, and its salvage value at the end of five years is expected to be $600.

Required:

Compute the rate of return on the investment by the discounted cash flow method.

24.5 The Capital Investment Company owes $1,000,000 on long-term notes due in ten years. Interest on the notes, at the rate of 5 percent, is payable at the end of each year.

Interest rates have dropped, and the company can now borrow money at an effective interest rate of 4 percent to refund the issue. The holders of the notes must be paid a call premium of $50,000 if the notes are retired at this time. Calculate the gain or loss from refunding.

24.6 The Acme Company has assembled the following data on trucks to determine how often they should be replaced.

Year of Operation	Operating Expense	Trade-in Value
1	$2,100	$3,900
2	2,900	3,000
3	3,600	2,300
4	4,200	1,700
5	4,700	800
6	5,200	500

The cost of a truck is $6,000. Compute the optimum replacement life. (Ignore income taxes and the cost of capital.)

24.7 The Downtown Bowl can buy or lease pin-setting equipment. The equipment can be purchased for a cash price of $45,000 and will have an economic life of five years with no salvage value. Alternatively, the equipment can be leased for five years for rents payable as follows:

End of Year	Rent Payable
1	$20,000
2	15,000
3	5,000
4	5,000
5	5,000

If the equipment is purchased, depreciation will be deducted from taxable income by the sum of the year's digits method. If the equipment is leased, the rent payments will be deducted from taxable income. Income taxes are estimated at the rate of 50 percent.

Required:

Compare the present values of the two alternatives at a cost of capital after income taxes of 20 percent. (If the equipment is leased, the net annual cash outflow is the rent payment less 50 percent thereof for the reduction in income taxes resulting from the rent deduction.)

24.8 The Solomon Development Co. is considering two mutually exclusive proposals for investment in East Asia. Both require a cash outlay of $100 million. Project X is expected to return $120.0 million at the end of one year. Project Y is expected to return $164.2 million at the end of three years. The same risk is involved in either proposal.

The company figures its cost of capital at 8 percent per year.

Required:

1. Rank the proposals by computing rates of return on the projects by the discounted cash flow method.
2. Rank the proposals by computing the present values of the projects discounted at the 8 percent cost of capital.
3. Show how much the company would accumulate under each proposal by the end of the third year if funds can be reinvested during the three year period (1) at 8% and (2) at 18%. Which proposal should the company choose? Why?

PROBLEMS

24.1 The Island Navigation Company can charter either of two ships. The S/S A. S. Colles is offered for three years at a price of $900,000 cash, while the S/S R. A. Bock is offered for four years at $900,000 cash. The company can invest in only one ship.

Annual revenues less annual expenditures for maintenance and operations will be $360,000 from the S/S A. S. Colles and $300,000 from the S/S R. A. Bock.

Disregard income taxes.

Required:

1. Compute the payout period for each ship.   2. 5   3
2. Compute the rate of return that will be earned on the average investment in each ship.
3. Which ship should be chartered? Why?

24.2 The International Development Co. can extract timber from properties it owns in Fiji in either of two ways. Plan A, which requires an investment of $1,000,000, will produce an annual cash recovery of $250,000 for five years. Plan B, which requires an investment of $1,250,000, will produce an annual cash recovery of $250,000 for ten years. In both cases terminal recovery values may be ignored, since it will not be feasible to remove equipment from Fiji. Also, ignore foreign and domestic taxes on income.

Required:

1. Compute the payout period for each plan.
2. Compute the rate of return that will be earned on the average investment for each plan.
3. Explain the difference in ranking of the plans under computations 1 and 2.

24.3 Louis A. Granat is considering a small computer for use in his chain of jewelry stores. The manufacturer will sell the computer for $100,000, 20 percent down and the balance payable in four equal annual installments of $20,000; or the manufacturer will lease the computer for ten years at an annual rental of $15,000 payable at the end of each year.

Required:

1. Compute the present value of buying or leasing at 6 percent. Ignore income taxes.
2. Compute the present value of buying or leasing at 20 percent. Ignore income taxes.
3. Consider income taxes at 80 percent, and compute the present value of buying or leasing at 20 percent after taxes. Use a 10-year life, no scrap value, and straight line depreciation.

Given:

Present value of series of $1 payments for	*At 6%*	*At 20%*
4 years	3.4651	2.5887
10 years	7.3601	4.1925

24.4 The Alii Trust has $60,000 to invest in a sale and leaseback agreement. Two propositions are presented to the trustees, each requiring an investment of $60,000. Proposition A will pay a rent of $6,000 at the end of each of fifteen years; proposition B will pay a rent of $5,000 at the end of each of twenty-five years.

Required:

1. Compute the rate of return on the average investment in each lease.
2. Compute the present value of the rents for each lease at 6 percent.
3. Compute the present value of the rents for each lease at 12 percent.
4. Which investment should the trust make if it normally earns 6 percent on its money? (Both investments are equally secure.)

Given:

Present value of annuity of 1 for	*At 6%*	*At 12%*
15 years	9.7122	6.8109
25 years	12.7833	7.8431

24.5 The Bowers Co. wants to replace existing welding equipment by either of two improved models. The semiautomatic model costs $10,000 more than the present equipment and is expected to produce a reduction in annual expenditures of $1,917. The fully automatic model costs $20,000 more than the present equipment and is expected to produce a reduction in annual expenditures of $3,522. Both machines are expected to have an economic life of ten years. The company wants help in deciding between the semiautomatic and the fully automatic model. It figures its cost of capital at 6 percent.

Required:

1. Compute the discounted cash flow rate of return for each alternative compared to replacement with the present equipment. (Answer to nearest percent.)
2. Compute the rate of return on the incremental investment required to acquire the fully automatic model compared to acquiring the semiautomatic model. (Answer to nearest percent.)
3. Comment.

Given:

TEN ANNUAL PAYMENTS EQUIVALENT TO $1

At an interest rate of. . . .	*6%*	*8%*	*10%*	*12%*	*14%*
Payments	0.1361	0.1490	0.1628	0.1761	0.1917

24.6 Culver Food Co. is considering the purchase of a new machine for $8,600; terms $2,600 down and the balance payable in three annual installments of $2,000. The new machine is expected to have an economic life of eight years and a scrap value of $600. It is expected to reduce annual operating and maintenance costs as follows:

				Year				
	1	2	3	4	5	6	7	8
Saving ...	$3,000	$2,700	$2,400	$2,100	$1,800	$1,500	$1,200	900

Depreciation will be computed by the straight line method; and income taxes are calculated at 50 percent of taxable income.

Required:

Compute the rate of return by the discounted cash flow method. Consider the annual cash recovery as the savings in maintenance and operations less income taxes on the savings net of additional depreciation. Express the rate to the nearest tenth of 1 percent.

24.7 Inter Island Air Lines anticipates the following monthly revenues and costs if it loads all flights to 100 percent of capacity:

Revenues	$400,000
Flight salaries	40,000
Ground salaries and administrative	172,000
Gross income tax	16,000
Rental on plane	86,000

All flight personnel are paid on a straight percentage of revenues; however, ground personnel receive a monthly salary. The gross income tax is based on revenues, and the plane rental is a fixed monthly payment.

Required:

1. Compute the break-even point.
2. What would the break-even point be if another plane were added, assuming no increase in ground personnel?
3. The company has three alternative investment opportunities for idle funds, which will yield returns as follows:

	Opportunities		
Year	A	B	C
1	$ 1,000	$ 2,500	$4,400
2	2,000	2,500	3,000
3	3,000	2,500	2,000
4	4,000	2,500	200
	$10,000	$10,000	$9,600

Compare these opportunities, using various capital budgeting tests. Each proposal requires an investment of $7,200 and has no scrap value. Net income is taxed at the rate of 50 percent.

24.8 The Morningside Corporation sells computer services to its clients. The company completed a feasibility study and decided to obtain an additional computer on January 1, 1966. Information regarding the new computer follows:
(1) The purchase price of the computer is $230,000. Maintenance, property taxes, and insurance will be $20,000 per year. If the computer is rented,

the annual rent will be $85,000 plus 5 percent of annual billings. The rental price includes maintenance.

(2) Because of competitive conditions, the company feels it will be necessary to replace the computer at the end of three years with a larger and more advanced one. It is estimated that the computer will have a resale value of $110,000 at the end of the three years. The computer will be depreciated on a straight line basis for both financial reporting and income tax purposes.

(3) The income tax rate is 50 percent.

(4) The estimated annual billing for the services of the new computer will be $220,000 during the first year and $260,000 during each of the second and third years. The estimated annual expense of operating the computer is $80,000, in addition to the expense mentioned above. An additional $10,000 of start-up expenses will be incurred during the first year.

(5) If it decides to purchase the computer, the company will pay cash. If it rents the computer, the $230,000 can be otherwise invested at a 15 percent rate of return.

(6) If the company purchases the computer, it can immediately reinvest the amount of the investment recovered during each of the three years at a 15% rate of return. All cash flows except the purchase price are assumed to be dated at the end of each year.

(7) The present values of $1 discounted at 15 percent are:

End of Year	Present Value
1	$0.87
2	0.76
3	0.66

Required:

1. Prepare a schedule showing the annual cash flows under the purchase plan and under the rental plan.
2. Prepare a schedule comparing the net present values of the cash flows under the purchase plan and under the rental plan.

(AICPA — adapted)

25

Branch and Consolidated Accounts
and Statements

Concerns with large numbers of employees and voluminous transactions, especially if operations are widespread geographically, may find it increasingly unsatisfactory or inefficient to conduct all business from a single office. Branches are established to meet the problems of maintaining warehouses at various locations, of furnishing customer service at many points accessible to the customers, of organizing sales forces to minimize travel time of salesmen and the difficulty of supervision from one location, and so on. Some of these problems on a larger scale, and still other problems, may be met by the use of separate corporations owned wholly or in part by the parent company. The existence of branches or subsidiary companies dictates the use of special accounting tools to record and control the branch transactions and to provide a summary of results and condition of the whole group of companies when a parent and subsidiary relationship exists. Because of a fundamental similarity in the accounting methods involved, branch accounts and the consolidated balance sheet are both discussed in this chapter.

DIVERSITY OF BRANCHES

The functions performed by a branch differ greatly between firms and between branches of one firm. Some branches are mere outposts of the home office, performing a single function such as warehousing stock, taking customer orders, or performing a repair service for customers. Other branches may combine several functions and enjoy some independence of decision within the firm's policies. In some cases the branch is a nearly independent manufacturing and merchandising unit with responsibility to the home office only for a satisfactory return on its investment. Very large concerns often set up this kind of organization, including competition between branches of the business, in order to encourage vigorous management in the branches and to stimulate the several parts to excel each other. This section is concerned with the fundamental accounting procedures necessary to the control of branch operations and with some of the other contributions accounting can make to the managerial decision to open or continue a branch.

DIVERSITY OF BRANCH ACCOUNTING SYSTEMS

In view of the variety of branches that exist, it is not surprising that branch accounting systems vary greatly. Four general types may be distinguished as follows:

Memorandum records only. In this case the branch makes out original records of its transactions and sends copies to the head office, where they are recorded in journals. A branch operating on this restricted basis usually handles only petty cash. A branch that warehouses merchandise and ships it as directed can be handled in this way, as can a branch that performs repair services for customers; the customers will be billed from the home office. The home office in this case pays the branch expenses and keeps records of the equipment it uses. This system is sufficient only for branches with very limited functions.

Memorandum and cash and accounts receivable records only. This system is popular because it retains a high degree of control in the home office while permitting the branch to perform a variety of functions. The branch can pay its cash expenses; it can handle sales to and collections from customers. It therefore keeps cash receipts and cash disbursements records, a sales book, and an accounts receivable ledger. Any other transaction, such as acquisition of a new machine, must be recorded by the home office on the basis of memoranda from the branch if the transaction does not originate in the home office. Furthermore, since the branch does not keep a general ledger, summaries of the cash and sales transactions must be sent to the home office for recording in the double-entry system there. These reports also serve as a basis for review of branch activities at the home office. They may consist of copies of the books kept by the branch or of summary figures only.

Incomplete general ledger at the branch. When the branch gets more independence, it needs a general ledger. In many cases the general ledger is incomplete; it will not, for example, have accounts for fixed assets or tax liabilities. The ledger may be incomplete for either or all of three reasons: the branch may not have sufficiently well-trained accounting personnel to handle all the accounts and transactions that affect it; the management may not want the branch personnel to know the complete results of branch operations; some transactions, such as income taxes, can be computed and entered only in combination with the same transactions of the rest of the company. The use of a general ledger, even though not complete, will permit the branch management to obtain better control over its expenses and to prepare statements from which operating efficiency can be better judged than is possible without it. The costs of maintaining salesmen in the field, for example, can more easily be compared with the sales produced. This system is probably the most popular for branches that carry on selling and even manufacturing activity and are authorized to incur a wide variety of expenses. The balances in the branch ledgers must be combined with those at the head office to get statements for the whole concern.

Complete general ledger at the branch. A branch that is independent of the home office except for very broad supervision over financial and other basic policies will have a virtually complete general ledger. All assets used by the branch will be carried in this ledger and even the branch's share of the company's income tax will be charged to the branch and recorded in its ledger. The value of any services rendered to the branch by the home office staff will also be charged to the branch. The only accounts lacking will be Capital Stock and Retained Earnings, unless what amounts to a branch is organized as a subsidiary corporation. The statements of the branch will then show its results completely, and its management will have all the accounting aids to effective control that it is willing to pay for. In some cases the home office and branch will deal with each other at market prices — as when selling merchandise or services to each other — so the results of each will not be influenced by any saving or inefficiency the other may have. Any profits in inventories resulting from this practice must be eliminated when balances of the branch accounts are combined for an overall company statement.

Each organization determines the procedures it will use in the light of its own policy on the degree of control to be exercised and the relative importance of home-office control and branch freedom to operate. Factors to consider in designing the system are distance from home office to branch, functions of the branch, type of personnel at the branch, volume of branch operations, and number of branches. The following discussion is based on a branch with an incomplete general ledger.

INTERBRANCH ACCOUNTS

The branch and home office ledgers are tied together by *reciprocal* accounts. The reciprocal account in the branch ledger is the Home Office account and in the home-office ledger it is the Branch Office account. If there are two or more branches, the home office will have accounts with St. Louis Branch, Cincinnati Branch, and so on. Use of the reciprocal accounts is illustrated by the following transactions:

1. The home office deposits $1,000 in a bank account for use at the branch:

Home-office books

Branch Office...................................	$1,000.00	
Cash....................................		$1,000.00

Branch books

Cash..	$1,000.00	
Home Office............................		$1,000.00

2. The home office pays a 3-year insurance premium of $500 for the branch:

Home-office books

Branch Office.................................	$ 500.00	
Cash.......................................		$ 500.00

Branch books

Prepaid Insurance.................................	$ 500.00	
Home Office............................		$ 500.00

Another kind of interbranch account is needed to record shipments of merchandise between the home office and the branch. These are needed so that they can be canceled one against the other when the accounts of the branches and the home office are consolidated to get company-wide statements. The accounts are Shipments to Branch and Shipments from Home Office. If shipments also move from branches to home office, accounts for Shipments to Home Office and Shipments from Branch will be needed. Shipments between branches are similarly handled. The shipment of $8,000 from home office to branch is recorded as follows:

Home-office books

Branch Office..................................	$8,000.00	
Shipments to Branch......................		$8,000.00

Branch books

Shipments from Home Office......................	$8,000.00	
Home Office.............................		$8,000.00

The Home Office account on the branch books may be thought of as a proprietorship account; the Branch Office account on the home-office books may be thought of as an investment in the branch.

ILLUSTRATION OF BRANCH ACCOUNTING

In the following illustration one branch is assumed and general journal entries are used throughout, although the usual special journals would be used in practice. Twelve transactions follow:

1. The home office deposits $15,000 to open the branch:

Home-office books

Branch Office.................................	$15,000.00	
Cash..................................		$15,000.00

Branch books

Cash...	$15,000.00	
Home Office...........................		$15,000.00

2. The home office ships merchandise costing $18,000 to the branch:

Home-office books

Branch Office.................................	$18,000.00	
Shipments to Branch....................		$18,000.00

Branch books

Shipments from Home Office.....................	$18,000.00	
Home Office...........................		$18,000.00

3. The branch paid freight of $190 on the merchandise shipment:

Home-office books—no entry
Branch books

Freight-in....................................	$ 190.00	
Cash...................................		$ 190.00

4. The branch sold merchandise to customers for $30,000:

Home-office books—no entry
Branch books

Accounts Receivable...........................	$30,000.00	
Sales...............................		$30,000.00

5. The branch purchased merchandise costing $14,000:

Home-office books—no entry
Branch books

Purchases...................................	$14,000.00	
Accounts Payable......................		$14,000.00

6. The branch collects $16,000 from its customers:

Home-office books—no entry
Branch books

Cash......................................	$16,000.00	
Accounts Receivable....................		$16,000.00

7. The branch pays $8,000 on its accounts payable and $9,000 of expenses:

Home-office books—no entry
Branch books

Accounts Payable.............................	$ 8,000.00	
Expenses....................................	9,000.00	
Cash......................................		$17,000.00

8. The branch remits $5,000 to the home office:

Home-office books

Cash..	$ 5,000.00	
Branch Office...........................		$ 5,000.00

Branch books

Home Office..................................	$ 5,000.00	
Cash...................................		$ 5,000.00

9. The branch records its closing inventory:

Home-office books—no entry

Branch books

Merchandise..................................	$15,000.00	
Profit and Loss.........................		$15,000.00

10. The branch closes its Sales account for the month:

Home-office books—no entry

Branch books

Sales..	$30,000.00	
Profit and Loss.........................		$30,000.00

11. The branch closes the other operating accounts for the month:

Home-office books—no entry

Branch books

Profit and Loss...............................	$41,190.00	
Purchases..............................		$14,000.00
Freight-in..............................		190.00
Shipments from Home Office.............		18,000.00
Expenses...............................		9,000.00

12. The branch closes Profit and Loss and reports its results to the home office:

Home-office books

Branch Office................................	$3,810.00	
Branch Profit...........................		$3,810.00

Branch books

Profit and Loss...............................	$3,810.00	
Home Office............................		$3,810.00

The accounts of the branch have the following appearance after they are ruled and balanced:

BRANCH LEDGER

Cash

(1)	15,000.00	(3)	190.00
(6)	16,000.00	(7)	17,000.00
		(8)	5,000.00
		Bal.	8,810.00
	31,000.00		31,000.00
Bal.	8,810.00		

Sales

| (10) | 30,000.00 | (4) | 30,000.00 |

Purchases

| (5) | 14,000.00 | (11) | 14,000.00 |

Accounts Receivable

(4)	30,000.00	(6)	16,000.00
		Bal.	14,000.00
	30,000.00		30,000.00
Bal.	14,000.00		

Freight-in

| (3) | 190.00 | (11) | 190.00 |

Shipments From Home Office

| (2) | 18,000.00 | (11) | 18,000.00 |

Merchandise

| (9) | 15,000.00 | | |

Expenses

| (7) | 9,000.00 | (11) | 9,000.00 |

Accounts Payable

(7)	8,000.00	(5)	14,000.00
Bal.	6,000.00		
	14,000.00		14,000.00
		Bal.	6,000.00

Profit and Loss

(11)	41,190.00	(9)	15,000.00
(12)	3,810.00	(10)	30,000.00
	45,000.00		45,000.00

Home Office

(8)	5,000.00	(1)	15,000.00
Bal.	31,810.00	(2)	18,000.00
		(12)	3,810.00
	36,810.00		36,810.00
		Bal.	31,810.00

The home office has the following accounts with the branch at this time (numbers refer to the numbered journal entries given above):

HOME OFFICE LEDGER

Branch Office

(1)	15,000.00	(8)	5,000.00
(2)	18,000.00	Bal.	31,810.00
(12)	3,810.00		
	36,810.00		36,810.00
Bal.	31,810.00		

Shipments to Branch

To P & L	18,000.00	(2)	18,000.00

Branch Profit

To P & L	3,810.00	(12)	3,810.00

The branch income statement for the month follows:

BRANCH OFFICE

Income Statement

Month of June, 1966

Sales			$30,000.00
Cost of Goods Sold:			
Purchases		$14,000.00	
Freight-In		190.00	
Shipments from Home Office		18,000.00	
		$32,190.00	
Inventory June 30, 1966		15,000.00	17,190.00
Gross margin on sales			$12,810.00
Expenses			9,000.00
Net income			$ 3,810.00

The branch also prepares the following balance sheet:

BRANCH OFFICE

Balance Sheet

June 30, 1966

Assets		Liabilities and Capital	
Cash	$ 8,810.00	Accounts Payable	$ 6,000.00
Accounts Receivable	14,000.00	Home Office	31,810.00
Merchandise	15,000.00		
Total	$37,810.00	Total	$37,810.00

COMBINED STATEMENTS

In order to obtain statements for the company as a whole, the balances on the branch ledger must be combined with those on the home-office ledger. This is a process of adding like balances. Interbranch accounts, such as the permanent reciprocal accounts Home Office and Branch Office, and the accounts representing shipments between offices are eliminated in this process. Since the corresponding accounts on the different ledgers have opposite balances, they cancel each other when they are brought together. It is necessary that they do so because they would represent double counting of some transactions if they were left in the statements. The process of combining the balances is most conveniently done on a work sheet. The accompanying exhibit gives the work sheet for combining the branch accounts illustrated above with the home-office balances.

Note that the interbranch accounts are eliminated by special entries in a pair of Elimination columns. Note also that the trial balances used in the work sheet are the trial balances taken before closing entries are made (see the accounts for Merchandise, Home Office, and Profit and Loss). Statements for the whole company may be made up from the work sheet in the usual way, including taxes on income, which were omitted in the illustration for simplicity.

MULTIPLE BRANCHES

Some concerns have many branches, notably chain grocery stores and other retail chains, but multiple branches are common in other industries also. Though the principles of branch accounting are not affected by the existence of a large number of branches, some special devices are needed to facilitate control and to obtain good accounting records. Internal control devices are described in the next paragraph. For obtaining good accounting data economically and for other purposes the branches are often grouped—typically, a chain grocery will have a zone office where most of the accounting for the stores in that zone will be done. The trial balance of the zone office will be combined with the trial balances of other zones and of the head office to get company-wide statements. In a very large chain, there will be divisional offices, each with control over several zones. In this case the process of combining the accounts will be made in two steps—combining one group of zones at each divisional office and combining the divisions at the head office.

INTERNAL CONTROL DEVICES FOR BRANCHES

Internal control practices especially useful in the control of branch activities are:

1. Imprest cash account for disbursements
2. Restricted deposit account
3. Retail inventory control
4. Review of reports
5. Internal audit

Work Sheet for Home Office and Branch Accounts

Month of June, 1966

	Home Office Debit	Home Office Credit	Branch Office Debit	Branch Office Credit	Eliminations Debit	Eliminations Credit	Income Statement Debit	Income Statement Credit	Balance Sheet Debit	Balance Sheet Credit
Cash	21 000 00		8 810 00						29 810 00	
Accounts Receivable	32 000 00		14 000 00						46 000 00	
Allowance for Doubtful Accounts		4 000 00		—						4 000 00
Branch Office	28 000 00		—			28 000 00				
Merchandise June 1, 1966	61 000 00		—				61 000 00			
Accounts Payable		20 000 00		6 000 00						26 000 00
Taxes Payable		6 000 00		—						6 000 00
Capital Stock		50 000 00		—						50 000 00
Retained Earnings		25 100 00		—						25 100 00
Home Office				28 000 00	28 000 00					
Sales		75 000 00		30 000 00				105 000 00		
Shipments to Branch		18 000 00			18 000 00					
Purchases	39 000 00		14 000 00				53 000 00			
Freight-In	2 100 00		190 00				2 290 00			
Shipments from Home Office	—		18 000 00			18 000 00				
Expenses	17 000 00		9 000 00				26 000 00			
Other Income		2 000 00		—				2 000 00		
	200 100 00	200 100 00	64 000 00	64 000 00	46 000 00	46 000 00	142 290 00	187 000 00		
Merchandise June 30, 1966	65 000 00		15 000 00					80 000 00	80 000 00	
							142 290 00	187 000 00	155 810 00	44 710 00
Net Income							44 710 00			
							187 000 00	187 000 00	155 810 00	155 810 00

BRANCH CASH CONTROLS

Cash disbursements at a branch may be made from an imprest fund. In this case the fund will probably be a deposit account in a bank. It will nevertheless be established for a specified amount, and when it is drawn down it will have to be reimbursed. The branch reports the checks drawn to the head office, which reimburses the branch for them. Under this system the branch personnel cannot spend more than the imprest amount without a review of the expenditures by officials in the head office. In some concerns customers are asked to remit to the head office, or their accounts are kept there completely. In cases in which the branch makes collections, the control of cash disbursements on an imprest basis requires a special treatment of deposits. The deposits are made in a special bank account from which only the head office can make withdrawals. This is a restricted deposit account. Amounts deposited are charged to Head Office on the branch books. Amounts reimbursed to the branch are credited to Head Office on the branch books and debited to Cash. This system is easier to operate when the ledger is kept only at the home office, but it can be applied when the branch keeps a ledger also.

OTHER BRANCH CONTROLS

Efficiency in handling merchandise and in protecting it from spoilage and theft are important everywhere and may be especially difficult to achieve at branches. The *retail inventory method* described in Chapter 10 is especially effective for this purpose. It involves keeping a record at a head office of the retail value of merchandise shipped to the branch. Sales of the branch represent reductions of the retail value that should be on hand. Periodically a physical inventory of the goods at the branch is taken at retail prices. If this differs materially from the calculated retail value that should be on hand, investigations are made, and if the condition persists, personnel may be changed. This control is used by chain stores; it is applied at the zone office as a control over individual stores in large chains.

Review of reports is a fundamental device for management of any large enterprise because of the impossibility of high officials being able to observe everything directly. It is needed in management of branches because of the physical distance of the branch. Reports take the forms suitable to the business. For example, a branch flour mill will make reports showing the number of bushels of wheat ground and the number of barrels of flour and other products produced from them. A branch may periodically send in an aged list of accounts receivable balances, which is reviewed by a credit officer. It is important that reports be designed for the needs of the official who is to review them, that they be prepared as promptly as possible after the events they describe, and that they be discontinued when they no longer serve a useful purpose. Sometimes reports that no one wants get built into the office routine and are prepared long after they should be discontinued.

An *internal audit* is an examination of accounts by employees of the concern being audited. It is a popular device of large concerns with many branches. It enables the officials to know whether or not the reports from the branch reflect the accounting methods prescribed by the head office. It also allows them to discover new conditions that might not otherwise be called to their attention. According to the qualifications of the internal auditors and the policies of the company, the auditors may look into matters of operating efficiency as well as examining the financial records.

MANAGERIAL DECISION TO OPEN OR NOT TO OPEN A BRANCH

Possibilities of improving profit through the use of branches include:

1. Close contact with customers and better customer service
2. More economical use of field sales staff
3. Savings in delivery costs

Closer contact with customers and other elements of customer service such as more prompt delivery are not weighed in accounting terms. Their value is a matter of managerial judgment. Accounting can determine whether or not the field sales staff can be more economically used if branches are established. Accounts for travel expenses, for example, when salesmen are stationed at a home office may be compared with actual experience at a branch if one exists or with carefully calculated estimates of what would be required to do the job from a branch. Presumably travel expense and travel time would be reduced by having the sales force operate from bases scattered around the country rather than from a single location. Savings in delivery costs are often possible through use of branches that further process or assemble the company's product. Freight rates are generally lower on raw materials and semifabricated products than on finished products. A company that quotes delivered prices may therefore save money by shipping a semifinished product or raw material to a branch for completion. A shorter shipment of the finished product to the customer results.

The decision to open, to continue, or to close a branch must also take into consideration the fact that control by top officers may be weakened by the establishment of branches at distant points. If the use of branches results in greatly increased executive travel, the savings in other travel may be dissipated. Similarly, if branches must be staffed with less-qualified personnel, the company's reputation and profits may suffer. Many of the factors involved are intangible, but accounting will aid in spotting trouble by compiling the cost of operating each branch. This can be compared between branches, and, making allowances for different circumstances, inefficient branches and out-of-line expenses can be identified and corrected. Furthermore, statistics such as the operating expense per dollar of sales can be calculated for one branch or many and compared with past results or budgeted figures. Uneconomical performances will again be identified.

PARENT AND SUBSIDIARY COMPANIES

When one corporation owns more than 50 percent of the voting stock of another, it is called a parent corporation and the other is a subsidiary. This ownership permits the officers of parent corporations to manage the two (or more) corporations as one business. This arrangement is made for various reasons: to operate legally or advantageously in a foreign territory; to segregate different parts of a business with different risks into separate legal organizations (separate companies for mining and refining ore, for example); to divide stock ownership differently for different segments of a business; to obtain an assured supply of raw material or an existing distribution organization without investing the total amount required for complete ownership. The fact that the parent company owns part of the subsidiary and can manage it means that the stockholders of the parent company have an interest in the subsidiary. The parent company's balance sheet shows this interest in an investment account. However, the investment account does not disclose the total amount and kinds of assets used by the whole enterprise and the liabilities connected with them. In order to present a complete picture the balance sheets of the parent and subsidiary companies are combined by a process called *consolidation.*

The parent and the subsidiary companies may have transactions with each other, just as do a home office and a branch, but the subsidiaries, being separate corporations, keep complete ledgers. Because of the separate legal existence, the investment account of the parent is kept separate from any current account the companies may have. The effect of intercompany transactions may have to be eliminated when consolidated statements are prepared. Thus there are many parallels between branch and parent-subsidiary accounts and statements, but the latter situation has special features. The following paragraphs explore only the elementary problems of consolidated balance sheets.

NATURE OF CONSOLIDATION

When balance sheets are consolidated, duplications in the combined figures must be eliminated. Duplications arise primarily from two sources: (1) The investment account on the parent's books represents a portion of the subsidiary's net assets. If the investment account is left in when the assets of the two companies are added together, the resulting balance sheet would have a larger total of assets than actually exists in the two companies. (2) There may be transactions between the companies resulting in receivables and payables. When the accounts of the two are consolidated and the whole business is presented as one enterprise, these intercompany accounts cancel out—as they must, as the enterprise cannot owe itself. Intercompany accounts include ordinary current accounts receivable and accounts payable, noncurrent advances or loans, and promissory notes or bonds of one company owned by the other. The parent's investment account is offset by the proprietorship accounts of the subsidiary, or by a portion of them if there is less than 100 percent ownership. Any portion of the subsidiary proprietorship not owned by the parent company remains in the consolidated balance sheet as a *minority interest.* The investment account of the parent and the proprietorship accounts of the subsidiary are called *reciprocal accounts.*

ILLUSTRATION OF A CONSOLIDATED BALANCE SHEET—CASE 1

The Trendor Company had the following balance sheet on December 31, 1966:

TRENDOR COMPANY
Balance Sheet
December 31, 1966

Assets			Liabilities and Capital		
Current Assets:			Current Liabilities:		
Cash	$100,000		Notes Payable	$ 40,000	
Accounts Receivable	80,000		Accounts Payable	108,000	
Note Receivable—			Taxes Payable	22,000	$170,000
Formex	60,000		Capital:		
Merchandise	250,000	$490,000	Capital Stock	$400,000	
Investment in Formex			Retained Earnings	208,000	608,000
Company		100,000			
Fixed Assets:					
Land	$ 60,000				
Building	108,000				
Equipment	20,000	188,000			
		$778,000			$778,000

During the year the company had formed a subsidiary corporation (Formex Company) by investing $100,000 cash in exchange for the entire capital stock of the subsidiary. The subsidiary purchased merchandise and other assets and borrowed on a note from the parent to get started in business, but had not done any business at December 31, 1966. At that date its balance sheet was:

FORMEX COMPANY
Balance Sheet
December 31, 1966

Assets			Liabilities and Capital	
Current Assets:			Current Liabilities:	
Cash	$20,000		Notes Payable—Trendor	$ 60,000
Merchandise	20,000	$ 40,000		
Fixed Assets:			Capital:	
Land	$10,000		Capital Stock	100,000
Building	70,000			
Equipment	40,000	120,000		
		$160,000		$160,000

These balance sheets are consolidated in the following work sheet. Note that the figures from the balance sheets are listed in the first two columns, the debit balances first and then the credit balances, so they can be added across. Note that the next two columns are used for the adjustments and eliminations that are necessary in consolidating. The last two give the combined figures for the consolidated balance sheet.

The eliminations made in this case are explained as follows (no adjustments were required):

1. The note payable of Formex is offset against the equivalent note receivable on the Trendor books.
2. The investment of Trendor is offset against the Capital Stock account of Formex.

TRENDOR COMPANY AND SUBSIDIARY
Consolidating Work Sheet [Case 1]
December 31, 1966

	Trial Balances		Adjustments and Eliminations		Consolidated Balance Sheet	
	Tren-dor Co.	For-mex Co.	Debit	Credit	Debit	Credit
Debits						
Cash....................	100 000	20 000			120 000	
Accounts Receivable........	80 000				80 000	
Note receivable—Formex....	60 000			(1) 60 000	—	
Merchandise..............	250 000	20 000			270 000	
Investment in Formex Co......	100 000			(2) 100 000	—	
Land....................	60 000	10 000			70 000	
Buildings.................	108 000	70 000			178 000	
Equipment...............	20 000	40 000			60 000	
	778 000	160 000				
Credits						
Notes Payable............	40 000	60 000	(1) 60 000			40 000
Accounts Payable..........	108 000					108 000
Taxes Payable............	22 000					22 000
Capital stock:						
Trendor Co.............	400 000					400 000
Formex Co.............		100 000	(2) 100 000			—
Retained Earnings:						
Trendor Co.............	208 000					208 000
Formex Co.............		—				—
	778 000	160 000	160 000	160 000	778 000	778 000

The consolidated balance sheet follows:

TRENDOR COMPANY AND SUBSIDIARY
Consolidated Balance Sheet

December 31, 1966

Assets			Liabilities and Capital		
Current Assets:			Current Liabilities:		
Cash	$120,000		Notes Payable	$ 40,000	
Accounts Receivable	80,000		Accounts Payable	108,000	
Merchandise	270,000	$470,000	Taxes Payable	22,000	$170,000
Fixed Assets:			Capital:		
Land	$ 70,000		Capital Stock	$400,000	
Buildings	178,000		Retained Earnings	208,000	608,000
Equipment	60,000	308,000			
		$778,000			$778,000

ACQUISITION OF A GOING CONCERN

In the case discussed above, the subsidiary was owned 100 percent by the parent from the moment of organization. This relationship results in an Investment account exactly equal to the subsidiary's Capital Stock account. When an investment is made in a subsidiary that is a going concern, it is unlikely that the price paid will exactly equal the amount of the subsidiary proprietorship bought. It has already been noted that the price of a corporation's stock depends on its record and prospects as well as on the recorded amounts of assets. These recorded amounts may also be different from current price levels. The difference between the price paid and the amount of proprietorship eliminated in consolidating remains in the consolidated balance sheet. If it is a debit, it represents an investment in excess of the net assets bought, and is often called *goodwill*. The presumption is that the excess was paid for a superior reputation or for some other advantage not reflected on the subsidiary's books. If there is evidence that the excess represents value of a particular asset above the recorded amount, it may be shown under that title in the balance sheet. The computation of goodwill may be illustrated as follows:

Subsidiary's Capital:		
Capital Stock	$100,000	
Retained Earnings	60,000	
Total	$160,000	
Book value of 80% of Stock Purchased by Parent Company ($160,000 × .8)	$128,000	
Paid by Parent Company	150,000	
Goodwill	$ 22,000	

If less than book value is paid, the difference is shown as an addition to capital called "Excess of Subsidiary Assets Acquired over Parents' Investment" or something similar. This figure has sometimes been called "Negative Goodwill" and sometimes "Consolidation Surplus."[1]

The amount paid in acquiring a subsidiary that is a going concern is usually paid to existing stockholders of the acquired company, and the transaction does not change the separate balance sheet of that company.

INTERCOMPANY PROFIT IN INVENTORIES

If one company of a consolidated group has sold merchandise to another, a gross margin or profit will normally be included in the price. From the viewpoint of the whole group, nothing has been earned by this sale, since no outside resource was added by it. The gross margin or profit, in so far as it remains in the inventory, must therefore be eliminated from the balance sheet. This elimination is accomplished by crediting Inventory and debiting Retained Earnings of the parent company.[2] For example, a subsidiary sold $40,000 of merchandise that had a gross margin of 20 percent to its parent. One half of this merchandise remained in inventory at closing time. The amount to be eliminated is:

$$\$40,000 \times 20\% \times \tfrac{1}{2} = \$8,000 \times \tfrac{1}{2} = \$4,000$$

The eliminating entry is:

Retained Earnings (parent company)................$4,000		
Merchandise..................................		$4,000

CHANGES IN SUBSIDIARY'S RETAINED EARNINGS AFTER PARENT'S ACQUISITION

The normal procedure is to carry the Investment account on the parent's books at cost, as is done with other assets. Dividends declared by the subsidiary and received by the parent are credited to Dividend Income by the parent. Earnings retained by the subsidiary after the date of the parent's acquisition of its stock thus have no recognition in the parent's Investment account. When the consolidated balance sheet is prepared, the parent's share of earnings made since its purchase of stock must be taken into the consolidated balance sheet along with retained earnings of the parent from its own books. Any portion of retained earnings belonging to minority stockholders is shown with their portion of the subsidiary's capital stock as "minority interest."

The figures for the consolidated balance sheet may be conveniently obtained by the following procedure of adjustment and elimination:

1. Eliminate any intercompany balances (receivables and payables).
2. Eliminate any intercompany profit in inventories.

[1] Bulletin 51 of the American Institute of Certified Public Accountants Committee on Accounting Procedure states that if such excess of book values over the amount paid cannot be distributed to and deducted from a particular asset or assets, it may be taken into income over a period of years. It would thus be shown as a part of Retained Earnings. The committee does not consider Capital Surplus an acceptable presentation of this figure.

[2] Bulletin 51 of the A.I.C.P.A. (referred to in footnote 1) states that the amount can be apportioned between the parent's earnings and the minority interest.

3. Debit Investment account and credit the parent's Retained Earnings for its share of any increase in the subsidiary's retained earnings accumulated since acquisition.
4. Debit the subsidiary's Capital Stock and Retained Earnings accounts and credit Minority Interest for the percent owned by the other stockholders of the subsidiary.
5. Eliminate the remaining balances of the subsidiary's Capital Stock and Retained Earnings accounts against the parent's adjusted Investment account; any difference is goodwill.

ILLUSTRATION OF A CONSOLIDATED BALANCE SHEET — CASE 2

The consolidation of balance sheets where the subsidiary was acquired from prior stockholders and has accumulated additional retained earnings after the acquisition is shown in a work sheet on pages 708-709. In this case N. W. Worth Company bought 90 percent of the capital stock of B. C. Gladd Company on January 1, 1966, for $175,000. It had purchased 75 percent of the stock of Azure Manufacturing Company on June 30, 1963, for $60,000. The proprietorships of these subsidiaries at the dates of the parent's investments, together with the calculation of goodwill involved, were as follows:

	B. C. Gladd Co.	Azure Mfg. Co.
Capital Stock...................	$100,000	$50,000
Retained Earnings...............	80,000	22,000
	$180,000	$72,000
Investment of Parent Company..........	$175,000	$60,000
Book Value of parent's Interest:		
B. C. Gladd Co. (90%).............	162,000	
Azure Mfg. Co. (75%).............		$54,000
Goodwill.......................	$ 13,000	$ 6,000

The illustration (pages 708-9) shows the consolidating work sheet for N. W. Worth Company and its subsidiaries at December 31, 1966. At this time each of the subsidiaries had increased its retained earnings above the level existing at the time of the parent's stock purchase. Other facts needed to consolidate the statements are given below in numbered memoranda that refer to the adjustments and eliminations on the work sheet (numbers refer to the numbered entries on the work sheet). The balances on the three sets of books at December 31, 1966, may be seen in the first three columns of the work sheet. The adjustments and eliminations in the consolidating work sheet are as follows:

(1) This eliminates an intercompany account of $10,000, carried in the Accounts Receivable of Worth and the Accounts Payable of Gladd.

(2) Notes of Azure held by Worth in the amount of $4,000 and by Gladd in the amount of $4,000 are eliminated.

(3) Merchandise inventory of Worth includes $10,000 of purchases from Azure. This was priced with a gross margin of 20 percent, so $2,000 of it is eliminated.

(4) This adds to Worth's investment its share of the earnings of Gladd accumulated since the parent's interest was acquired but retained by the subsidiary. The amount is:

```
Retained Earnings at Acquisition....................$80,000
Retained Earnings December 31, 1966...............  95,000
Increase.........................................   15,000
Parent's Share of Increase (90%)...................  13,500
```

The adjustment is a debit to the Investment in Gladd and a credit to the Retained Earnings of Worth.

(5) This adjustment is made for earnings of Azure, as adjustment 4 was for Gladd:

```
Retained Earnings at Acquisition....................$22,000
Retained Earnings at December 31, 1966..............  36,000
Increase...........................................   14,000
Parent's Share of Increase (75%)...................  10,500
```

(6) The minority interest in Gladd is segregated by this entry. It is calculated as follows:

	Per Books	Percent of Minority Interest	Amount of Minority Interest
Capital Stock...........$100,000		10	$10,000
Retained Earnings....... 95,000		10	9,500
			$19,500

The segregation is made by an adjusting journal entry debiting the subsidiary's Capital Stock and Retained Earnings accounts and crediting Minority Interests on a new line of the work sheet.

(7) This segregates the minority interest in Azure. It is calculated as follows:

	Per Books	Percent of Minority Interest	Amount of Minority Interest
Capital Stock...........$ 50,000		25	$12,500
Retained Earnings....... 36,000		25	9,000
			$21,500

(8) The investment in Gladd is eliminated. Only the parent's share of Gladd's Capital Stock and Retained Earnings is left in the subsidiary proprietorship accounts after the minority interest is removed. The balances of those accounts and the adjusted amount of the Investment account are closed, and the difference, which is goodwill, is recorded. In this case the figures after prior adjustments are:

N. W. WORTH COMPANY AND SUBSIDIARIES
Consolidating Work Sheet [Case 2]
December 31, 1966

	Trial Balances December 31, 1966			Adjustments and Eliminations		Consolidated Balance Sheet	
	Worth	Gladd	Azure	Debit	Credit	Debit	Credit
Debits							
Cash	26,000	10,000	6,000			42,000	
Notes Receivable	18,000	4,000	—		(2) 8,000	14,000	
Accounts Receivable	40,000	18,000	20,000		(1) 10,000	68,000	
Allowance for Doubtful Accounts	(4,200)	(1,000)	(1,600)				6,800
Merchandise	51,000	42,000	30,000		(3) 2,000	121,000	
Prepaid Insurance	2,000	1,400	1,200			4,600	
Investment in Gladd	175,000	—	—	(4) 13,500	(8)188,500		
Investment in Azure	60,000	—	—	(5) 10,500	(9) 70,500		
Land	22,000	12,000	—			34,000	
Buildings	180,000	150,000	—			330,000	
Accumulated Depreciation—Buildings	(14,000)	(20,000)	—				34,000
Furniture and Fixtures	20,000	49,000	61,000			130,000	
Accumulated Depreciation—Furniture and Fixtures	(5,800)	(8,400)	(1,600)				15,800
Patents	30,000	—	—			30,000	
	600,000	257,000	115,000				
Credits							
Notes Payable	48,000	20,000	8,000	(2) 8,000			68,000
Accounts Payable	52,000	30,000	15,000	(1) 10,000			87,000
Taxes Payable	20,000	12,000	6,000				38,000

	Worth–Gladd–Azure			Eliminations		Consolidated	
	Worth	Gladd	Azure	Dr.	Cr.	Dr.	Cr.
Capital Stock:							
Worth	400,000						400,000
Gladd		100,000		(6) 10,000 (8) 90,000			
Azure			50,000	(7) 12,500 (9) 37,500			
Retained Earnings:							
Worth	80,000			(3) 2,000	(4) 13,500 (5) 10,500		102,000
Gladd		95,000		(6) 9,500 (8) 85,500			
Azure			36,000	(7) 9,000 (9) 27,000			
Minority Interests				(8) 13,000 (9) 6,000	(6) 19,500 (7) 21,500		41,000
Goodwill						19,000	
	600,000	257,000	115,000	344,000	344,000	792,600	792,600

Capital Stock..................................	$ 90,000
Retained Earnings..............................	85,500
	$175,500
Investment....................................	188,500
Excess, or Goodwill............................	$ 13,000

The goodwill is recorded on a new line of the work sheet.
(9) The investment in Azure is similarly eliminated. The figures are:

Capital Stock..................................	$37,500
Retained Earnings..............................	27,000
	$64,500
Investment....................................	70,500
Excess, or Goodwill............................	$ 6,000

This concludes the adjustments and eliminations. Note that two lines are needed on the work sheet for most of the proprietorship accounts. The consolidated balance sheet for this case has the following appearance:

N. W. WORTH CO. AND SUBSIDIARIES
Consolidated Balance Sheet
December 31, 1966

Assets				Liabilities and Capital			
Current Assets:				Current Liabilities:			
Cash..............	$ 42,000			Notes Payable.......	$ 68,000		
Notes Receivable.....	14,000			Accounts Payable.....	87,000		
Accounts Receivable,				Taxes Payable.......	38,000	$193,000	
Net.............	61,200			Minority Interests in Subsidiary Companies.....................		41,000	
Merchandise.........	121,000						
Prepaid Insurance....	4,600	$242,800		Capital:			
Fixed Assets:				Capital Stock........	$400,000		
Land..............	$ 34,000			Retained Earnings....	102,000	502,000	
Buildings.. $330,000							
Less: Depreciation.... 34,000	296,000						
Furniture & Fixtures. $130,000							
Less: Depreciation.... 15,800	114,200	444,200					
Patents.......................		30,000					
Goodwill from Consolidation.......		19,000					
		$736,000				$736,000	

OTHER POSSIBILITIES IN CONSOLIDATED STATEMENTS

Consolidated income statements and consolidated retained earnings statements are also widely used. The same basic principles outlined above for balance sheets are followed: intercompany transactions are eliminated and minority interests are segregated. These introduce additional features to the consolidating working papers that are beyond the scope of the present treatment.

SUMMARY

Branches differ in many ways and the accounting appropriate to them also varies. Four general types of accounting systems for branches are: memorandum records only, memorandum records plus cash and accounts receivable records, incomplete general ledger at the branch, and complete general ledger at the branch.

Use of a branch ledger involves reciprocal accounts between it and the home-office books. These are Home Office account on the branch books and Branch Office account on the home-office books. Interbranch accounts for shipments between branches are also required so that accounts of the several offices can be combined without double counting. When branch accounts are combined for over-all company statements, the reciprocal and other interbranch accounts are eliminated.

Internal control devices especially useful for branches are: imprest fund account for disbursements, restricted deposit account, retail inventory control, review of reports, and internal audit.

The managerial decision to open, continue, or close a branch involves consideration of possible profit improvement through close contact with customers and better customer service, more economical use of field sales staff, and savings in delivery costs. It must also consider the disadvantages of more difficult control of operations that are spread out in branches. Many of the data for the decision are provided by accounting that compiles the cost of each branch. Statistics such as operating expenses per dollar of sales may also be computed for the branches and compared with budgeted figures.

Consolidated balance sheets and other consolidated statements are prepared to show the financial condition or results of operations of parents and subsidiary corporations as a group. In preparing a consolidated balance sheet it is necessary to offset the investment account of the parent against the proprietorship accounts of the subsidiary. This usually involves an element of goodwill (investment in excess of the parent's interest per the subsidiary's books) and a minority interest in the subsidiary. Other adjustments or eliminations that must be made include elimination of intercompany receivables and payables and any profit on inventory resulting from intercompany sales.

QUESTIONS

25.1   What types of branch accounting systems may one expect to find?

25.2   Assuming that a general ledger is kept at a branch, what connection will it have with the home-office general ledger?

25.3   A branch buys merchandise in the local market and also receives shipments from its home office. Is any distinction between these sources of supply necessary in the accounts? Explain your answer.

25.4   Specify whether the entry to the *reciprocal* account in each of the following cases is a debit or a credit:

(1) Home office records its remittance of $11,000 to branch.
(2) Branch records its remittance of $18,000 to home office.
(3) Branch records its receipt of machinery from home office.
(4) Home office records the earnings of branch for the period.
(5) Home office records transfer of automobile from branch to home office.
(6) Branch records payment of president's hotel bill, which is to be borne by home office.
(7) Home office records shipment of merchandise to branch.

25.5   Assuming that the transactions described in the preceding question are present, what accounts have to be eliminated when branch and home-office accounts are combined for over-all company statements?

25.6   What special controls may be placed on branch cash transactions?

25.7   What control is effective for branch inventories?

25.8   How can the executives in a home office obtain an effective review of branch transactions, apart from reading branch reports?

25.9   What possibilities of improved profits does the use of branches open up?

25.10   Under what circumstances are consolidated statements needed?

25.11   What must be eliminated from the accounts of the separate corporations when consolidated statements are prepared?

25.12   What element, if any, may the investment account of the parent contribute to the consolidated balance sheet?

25.13   What account or caption do many consolidated balance sheets have that never appears in the balance sheet of a single corporation?

25.14   State what difference there is likely to be between the consolidated balance sheet of a group formed from pre-existing corporations and one formed by a parent company that organizes its own subsidiaries and finances them.

25.15   What effect do retained earnings of a subsidiary, accumulated since acquisition of an interest by the parent company, have on the proprietorship shown for the stockholders of the parent company in the consolidated balance sheet?

EXERCISES

25.1   Swimwear of California, Inc., opened a branch office in Hawaii on December 1, 1966. The following transactions affecting the branch were completed in December:

(1) Swimwear deposited a check for $10,000 to the credit of the branch in a Hawaii bank.
(2) Swimwear shipped merchandise costing $12,000 to the branch.
(3) The branch made cash sales of $10,000.
(4) The branch paid $5,000 of expenses.
(5) The branch recorded its closing inventory of $6,000 and closed its books; net income was reported to the home office.

Required:

Journalize the transactions on the books of the home office and on the books of the branch.

25.2   The Crown Publishing Co. maintains a home office in New York and a branch in San Francisco. The branch ledger contains accounts for revenues, expenses, and related assets and liabilities; however, payroll checks are made out in New York and all payroll tax liabilities are kept in the home-office ledger. Accounts for the fixed assets of the branch are also kept at the home office.

Required:

Give the journal entries to be made by the branch and by the home office for the following transactions:

(1) The branch office issued a $4,000 check on its bank account for branch office equipment, and notified the home office of the acquisition by journal voucher.

(2) Branch salaries of $1,000 were paid less employee payroll taxes of $200.

(3) Employer payroll taxes of $80 were recorded on the above salaries.

(4) Depreciation on branch fixed assets was $300.

25.3 The trial balances of Norsco, Inc., and its branch at December 31, 1966, were as follows:

	Home Office		Branch Office	
Cash	$ 10,000		$ 8,000	
Merchandise, 12/1/66.	15,000		14,000	
Branch Office	30,000		—	
Other Assets	53,000		6,000	
Capital Stock.		$ 50,000		—
Retained Earnings		24,000		—
Home Office		—		$30,000
Sales.		50,000		40,000
Shipments to Branch		23,000		—
Purchases	27,000		10,000	
Shipments from Home Office.	—		23,000	
Expenses.	12,000		9,000	
	$147,000	$147,000	$70,000	$70,000

Inventories as of December 31, 1966, were $20,000 at the home office and $12,000 at the branch.

Required:

Prepare a work sheet combining the home office and branch accounts.

25.4 The December 31, 1966, balance sheet accounts of P Co. and its wholly owned subsidiary, S Co., are presented below. P acquired the investment in S on January 1, 1966, for $20,000, when S was incorporated.

	P Co.		S Co.	
Merchandise, 1/1/66	$ 18,000		—	
Investment in S	20,000		—	
Other Assets	63,000		$47,000	
Capital Stock:				
P Co.		$ 50,000		
S Co.				$20,000
Retained Earnings:				
P Co.		30,000		
Sales		60,000		55,000
Purchases	24,000		18,000	
Expenses.	15,000		10,000	
	$140,000	$140,000	$75,000	$75,000

During the year P Co. sold S Co. merchandise for $14,000. The inventories at December 31, 1966, were as follows: P, $9,000; S, $4,000. These inventories included no intercompany profit.

Required:

Prepare a work sheet consolidating the parent company and subsidiary accounts.

25.5 Balance sheets of H Co. and S Co. at December 31, 1966, were as follows:

H Co.

Cash	$200,000	Capital Stock	$400,000
Other Assets	300,000	Retained Earnings	100,000
	$500,000		$500,000

S Co.

Cash	$ 40,000	Capital Stock	$100,000
Other Assets	85,000	Retained Earnings	25,000
	$125,000		$125,000

Required:

Prepare a consolidated balance sheet reflecting the financial condition of the parent and subsidiary immediately after each of the following alternatives:

(1) H buys all the capital stock of S from its shareholders for $125,000.
(2) H buys 80 percent of the capital stock of S from its shareholders for $100,000.
(3) H buys all the capital stock of S from its shareholders for $140,000.
(4) H buys 80 percent of the capital stock of S from its shareholders for $120,000.

25.6 Consolidated Industries, Ltd., acquired an 80 percent interest in State Enterprises, Inc., when State had retained earnings of $20,000. The balance sheet accounts are as follows:

	Consolidated		*State*	
Cash	$ 30,000		$140,000	
Advances to State	20,000		–	
Merchandise	40,000		30,000	
Investment in State	100,000		–	
Advances from Consolidated . .	–			$ 20,000
Capital Stock		$100,000		100,000
Retained Earnings		90,000		50,000
	$190,000	$190,000	$170,000	$170,000

The merchandise inventory of State includes an intercompany profit of $5,000.

Required:

Give the journal entries that would appear on a consolidating work sheet.

25.7 The following accounts were taken from the ledgers of the Carousel Company and its wholly owned subsidiary, the Carousette Company:

	Carousel	*Carousette*
Sales	$820,000	$300,000
Cost of Goods Sold	600,000	180,000
Operating Expenses	240,000	75,000
Dividends Income	25,000	–
Dividends	35,000	20,000

Sales by Carousel to Carousette totaled $120,000, which included a markup of 40 percent on Carousel's selling price. The inventory of Carousette at the beginning of the year included goods acquired from Carousel for $30,000; the inventory of Carousette at the end of the year included goods acquired from Carousel for $50,000.

Required:

Prepare a consolidated income statement for the year.

25.8 On December 31, 1963, H Co. purchased 80 percent of the capital stock of S Co., at which date the retained earnings of S was $200,000.

Condensed financial statements as of December 31, 1966, are as follows:

Balance Sheets as of *December 31, 1966*	*Consolidation*	*H Co.*	*S Co.*
Cash and Accounts Receivable	$ 194,800	$ 70,000	$216,000
Inventories	244,000	80,000	180,000
Fixed Assets (including Land)	1,180,000	850,000	230,000
Investment in S Co. (at cost)	—	560,000	—
Temporary Investments............	56,000	—	256,000
	$1,674,800	$1,560,000	$882,000
Accounts Payable	$ 116,000	$ 138,400	$ 56,000
Dividend Declared and Unpaid	24,800	21,600	16,000
Mortgage Bonds, 5%	290,000	400,000	90,000
Capital Stock	600,000	600,000	400,000
Retained Earnings	480,000	400,000	320,000
Minority Interest.................	164,000	—	—
	$1,674,800	$1,560,000	$882,000

Income Statements for *Year Ended December 31, 1966*	*Consolidation*	*H Co.*	*S Co.*
Sales.........................	$1,520,000	$1,200,000	$800,000
Less: Cost of Sales	$ 806,000	$ 720,000	$560,000
Selling & Admin. Exp. & Bond Interest	381,400	276,400	115,000
	$1,187,400	$ 996,400	$675,000
	$ 332,600	$ 203,600	$125,000
Investment Income	2,000	25,600	12,000
	$ 334,600	$ 229,200	$137,000
Income Tax	179,000	112,000	67,000
	$ 155,600		
Minority Interest.................	14,000		
Net Income for Year.............	$ 141,600	$ 117,200	$ 70,000
Dividends Paid	43,200	43,200	32,000
Transfer to Retained Earnings	$ 98,400	$ 74,000	$ 38,000

Additional information:

(1) Inventories of S Co. at both beginning and end of year included markup on purchases from H Co.

(2) S Co.'s temporary investments include $200,000 par value H Co. bonds which were set up in the account at their purchase price on January 1, 1966, of $200,000 (excluding accrued interest).

(3) S Co. has not paid dividends prior to the current fiscal year.

Required:

1. Reconcile the retained earnings of H Co. as of December 31, 1966, to the consolidated retained earnings as of that date. Submit details of calculations.

2. What are the amounts of intercompany liabilities, other than for bonds, for each company?
3. Account for the difference between the total cost of sales for H Co. and S Co. of $1,280,000 and consolidated cost of sales of $806,000.

(ICAC — adapted)

PROBLEMS

25.1 The following transactions were completed during July 1966 between Amtex Co. in New York and its branch in San Francisco:

(1) Home office deposits $10,000 cash to begin branch operations.
(2) Branch pays three months' rent, $1,200.
(3) Home office ships merchandise costing $15,000 to branch.
(4) Branch purchases merchandise on credit for $8,000.
(5) Branch pays expenses totaling $2,000 (charge Expense).
(6) Branch pays $5,000 on accounts payable.
(7) Home office sends to the branch equipment in the form of two office machines. They have been used in the home office and cost $6,000; accumulated depreciation of $2,000 is recorded for them. Since the branch keeps its own ledger record of fixed assets, the whole record of the machines is transferred to the branch.
(8) Branch sells merchandise on credit, $40,000.
(9) Branch buys additional office equipment on credit, $7,000.
(10) Branch collects $8,000 from accounts receivable.
(11) Branch pays expenses of $6,000.
(12) Branch pays a cash travel advance of $500 to the vice-president, who is visiting the branch. This advance is to be carried on the home-office books.
(13) Branch writes off $400 of prepaid rent.
(14) Branch records its closing inventory of $8,000.
(15) Branch closes its revenues to Profit and Loss.
(16) Branch closes its costs and expenses (including Purchases and Shipments from Home Office) to Profit and Loss.
(17) Branch closes its Profit and Loss and reports the net income to home office.
(18) Branch remits $15,000 to the home office.

Required:

Prepare entries in general journal form to record the transactions. Use two columns, the left for the home office entries and the right for the branch entries, with entries for the same transaction on the two sets of books appearing side by side.

25.2 January transactions of the San Francisco branch of the California Trading Company are given below. Journalize them, using two columns, the left for the home office entries and the right for the branch entries, with entries for the same transaction on the two sets of books appearing side by side. An Expenses control account is used in both ledgers.

(1) Home office deposits $9,000 cash to begin branch operations.
(2) Branch pays three months' rent, $900.
(3) Home office ships merchandise costing $15,000 to branch.
(4) Branch purchases merchandise on credit for $5,500; 2/10 n/30. (The gross method is used.)
(5) Branch pays expenses totaling $3,200.

(6) Branch pays $2,450 on accounts payable. Discount is allowed on the portion paid.

(7) Home office sends two office machines to the branch. They have been used two years in the home office, cost $3,000, and have accumulated depreciation of $600. The branch keeps its own general ledger record of fixed assets.

(8) Branch sells merchandise on credit, $26,000.

(9) Branch buys additional office equipment on credit for $4,800 with an estimated useful life of ten years.

(10) Branch collects $18,500 from customers on account.

(11) Home office pays the branch manager's salary, $1,000.

(12) Branch pays a cash travel advance of $500 to the vice-president, who is visiting the branch. This advance is to be carried on the home-office books.

(13) Branch records expenses incurred on credit, $2,500.

(14) Branch prepares necessary adjusting entries as of January 31. (Depreciation for a full month is provided by the straight line method on all equipment; scrap values are ignored.) The ending inventory is $9,400.

(15) Branch closes its books and reports the net income to home office.

(16) Branch remits $12,000 to the home office.

25.3   (1) Set up T accounts for the branch of problem 2 and enter the transactions. (Cross reference the entries by use of the transaction numbers.)

       (2) Prepare financial statements for the branch.

25.4   The balances on the home-office and branch ledgers of the Marfak Company for July 31, 1966, appear below. Merchandise inventory on July 31 was: home office, $34,000; branch office, $9,000.

	Home Office		Branch Office	
Cash	$ 33,000		$31,000	
Notes Receivable	8,000		—	
Accounts Receivable	20,000		8,000	
Branch Office	32,000		—	
Merchandise, July 1, 1966 . .	28,000		12,000	
Accounts Payable		$ 14,000		$10,000
Taxes Payable		9,000		2,000
Capital Stock		50,000		—
Retained Earnings		28,000		—
Home Office		—		32,000
Sales		70,000		50,000
Shipments to Branch		15,000		—
Purchases	40,000		16,000	
Shipments from Home Office .	—		15,000	
Expense	25,000		12,000	
	$186,000	$186,000	$94,000	$94,000

Required:

Prepare a work sheet combining the accounts. (Ignore income taxes.)

25.5   National Corporation acquired 80 percent of the capital stock of Roma Company on June 30, 1966, when the major stockholder of Roma decided to retire. The two companies had done business for some time. At the time of the acquisition, National's accounts receivable included an account with Roma for $30,000. The balances of the two companies after closing on June 30, 1966, were as follows:

	National Corporation		Roma Company	
Cash	$ 56,000		$ 42,000	
Accounts Receivable	74,000		56,000	
Merchandise	165,000		128,000	
Investment in Roma	120,000		–	
Land	12,000		12,000	
Buildings	91,000		62,000	
Notes Payable		$ 60,000		$ 65,000
Accounts Payable		151,000		85,000
Capital Stock		200,000		100,000
Retained Earnings		107,000		50,000
	$518,000	$518,000	$300,000	$300,000

Required:

Prepare a consolidated balance sheet as of June 30, 1966.

25.6 The following data concern Calway Company and its subsidiary, Bay Stores. Calway acquired 90 percent of the stock of Bay Stores in 1963, when Bay had retained earnings of $9,000. The postclosing balances on the books of each corporation at July 1, 1966, were:

	Calway Company		Bay Stores	
Cash	$ 30,000		$ 51,000	
Notes Receivable	25,000		12,000	
Accounts Receivable	50,000		30,000	
Merchandise	95,000		74,000	
Investment in Bay Stores .	103,000		–	
Land	20,000		6,000	
Building	68,000		54,000	
Notes Payable		$ 65,000		$ 25,000
Accounts Payable		120,000		63,000
Capital Stock		200,000		100,000
Retained Earnings		6,000		39,000
	$391,000	$391,000	$227,000	$227,000

The following additional information is available:

(1) Calway Company holds a promissory note of Bay Stores for $10,000. Interest on the note is paid through July 1, 1966.

(2) Bay Stores owes Calway Company $15,000 on open account at July 1, 1966.

(3) Bay Stores has merchandise purchased from Calway for $20,000. Calway realized a gross profit of 40 percent on the selling price of this merchandise.

Required:

1. Consolidating work sheet.
2. Consolidated balance sheet.

25.7 Top Holding Company acquired an 80 percent interest in Saylor, Inc., two years ago, when Saylor had retained earnings of $75,000. Data on the financial condition of the companies at December 31, 1966, and other data follow:

	Top Holding Company		Saylor, Inc.	
Cash	$ 52,000		$ 20,000	
Notes Receivable	50,000		–	
Interest Receivable	1,000		–	
Accounts Receivable	58,000		42,000	
Merchandise	97,000		84,000	
Investment in Saylor	155,000		–	
Land	32,000		15,000	
Buildings	185,000		157,000	
Notes Payable		$ 20,000		$ 50,000
Interest Payable		–		1,000
Accounts Payable		80,000		42,000
Capital Stock		300,000		100,000
Retained Earnings		230,000		125,000
	$630,000	$630,000	$318,000	$318,000

Other facts available are:

(1) Saylor owes Top Holding $50,000 on a 6 percent promissory note that has been outstanding four months.

(2) Saylor's merchandise inventory includes $25,000 of goods purchased from Top Holding. Top Holding made a gross profit of 40 percent on the retail price of the sale.

Required:

1. Consolidating work sheet.
2. Consolidated balance sheet.

Funds and Cash Flow

Analysis and Statements

NATURE AND PURPOSE OF FUNDS STATEMENTS

"Funds" may mean cash alone; it may mean "working capital" (current assets less current liabilities); or it may refer to "all financial resources" (spending power involved in all external transactions). The purpose is to summarize on one basis or another, by sources, the buying power flowing into the concern for a period and to describe what has been done with it. For example, a concern may have acquired $100,000 of new buying power by selling its goods or services to earn a net income of that amount; it may have sold more capital stock or have issued bonds, and so on. It may have used the buying power acquired to purchase new equipment, to pay off debt, to retire capital stock, to increase cash or working capital, or otherwise. Information about these financial transactions has become more widely used in recent years; investment advisors seek it, and recommendations that it be provided regularly in published reports have recently been made by authoritative bodies.[1] Investment analysts are interested in the statement because it throws some light on the question of whether or not dividends can be paid, and because it brings out clearly the attitudes of management on retention of funds and their use in the business. Such information is useful to management in giving a periodic summary of the financial transactions, as it may be difficult to understand the overall trend when transactions are observed only on a day-to-day basis. For example, a traditional question raised by managers in this connection is: "Our income statement shows a profit but our cash is smaller than ever. What happened to the funds?" A funds statement answers this question.

FORM AND CONTENT OF THE FUNDS STATEMENT

It would be possible to list funds transactions in great detail, including cash received from sales, cash paid for merchandise, cash paid for salaries, and other details. This is not done because broader categories of activity are considered significant for purposes of funds analysis. Accordingly, the transactions mentioned above are all included under the heading of "Funds Provided by Operations," and other major activities, such as "Funds Applied to Purchase

---

[1] American Institute of Certified Public Accountants, *Opinions of the Accounting Principles Board, No. 3*, New York, 1963; the New York Stock Exchange, *Regulations*.

of Equipment" and "Funds Applied to the Payment of Bonds," are similarly used. The only general rule involved is that each significant source and application of funds be disclosed; because operations — the activity that gives rise to net income — are almost always important, a figure for operations appears as a regular item in funds statements.

A funds statement takes the form given in the accompanying statement of application of funds. The statement also may be called statement of source and application of funds, funds statement, or statement of balance sheet changes; variations to suit individual taste are common.

EWALD COMPANY
Statement of Application of Funds
Year ended December 31, 1966

Funds were provided by:

Operating at a profit	$ 42,000	
Sale of capital stock	100,000	
Sale of vacant land	80,000	$222,000

Funds were applied to:

Payment of mortgage	$ 20,000	
Construction of Building	100,000	
Purchase of equipment	92,000	212,000
Increase in working capital, per schedule		$ 10,000

Schedule of Working-Capital Changes

	Balances Begin-ning	Ending	Changes In-creases	De-creases
Cash	$10,000	$16,000	$ 6,000	
Accounts Receivable	20,000	48,000	28,000	
Merchandise	30,000	35,000	5,000	
Prepaid Insurance	1,400	2,200	800	
Notes Payable	6,000	24,000		$18,000
Accounts Payable	8,000	20,000		12,000
Accrued Interest Payable	1,200	1,000	200	
			$40,000	$30,000
Net Increase				10,000
			$40,000	$40,000

PREPARATION OF THE FUNDS STATEMENT

The first step in preparing a funds statement is to decide on the definition of "funds" to be employed. If cash alone is to be the basis, only transactions actually occurring in cash will be reported. If "working capital" is the definition of funds used, all transactions with outside parties that reflect a receipt or an expenditure (increase or decrease) of working capital will be involved. This definition recognizes that the significance of most financial transactions is not altered importantly by the fact that receipt or payment of cash is deferred a little, so that sales charged to Accounts Receivable or purchases credited to Accounts Payable are reported as funds transactions, even though they may not have given rise to cash receipts or cash disbursements by the end of the period reported on. This is the most popular definition of "funds" and is reflected in the illustrations in this text. The third possibility is to define funds on an "all resources" basis. This provides for including transactions that may not have actually gone through working capital, but which are significant in the financing of the concern nevertheless. For example, a company may acquire a factory building by paying $50,000 in cash and issuing a 10-year mortgage to the seller for $100,000. A strict interpretation of the working capital definition of funds would report only $50,000 as applied to the purchase of the building, with no corresponding source of funds; on the other hand an all-resources approach would show funds provided by issuance of the mortgage in the amount of $100,000 and funds applied to the purchase of the building in the amount of $150,000. People who use the working capital definition of funds often also include unusual but significant financial transactions that do not actually go through the working capital accounts, and thus really support the all-resources concept. The authors recommend the latter practice as most likely to give an adequate accounting. If desired, one may give the same information while adhering technically to the working capital definition by showing the gross amounts together in the statement and extending only the net effect on working capital into the main column, as follows:

Recommended

	Amount
Funds were applied to:	
Purchase of factory building:	
Total purchase	$150,000
Less: Mortgage issued	100,000
Working capital applied	$50,000

It would be possible to prepare a funds statement by going through all the transactions (in the journals, for example) and classifying them for purposes of the statement. This is not only cumbersome; it is unnecessary. Since only significant changes are to be reported, and only the net effect of the many individual transactions in obtaining net income is desired, the figures may be obtained by analysis of the accounts outside the current section of the balance sheet (when working capital is the definition of "funds"). The many transactions involving receipt and payment of cash in connection with accounts receivable, accounts payable, and so on, and various transfers within the working capital group, do not affect total working capital. Other transactions that involve the noncurrent accounts on the balance sheet frequently result in a net increase or decrease in working capital; this, along with the effects on the other accounts, is one of the figures reported in the funds statement. Thus, an analysis of changes in the noncurrent accounts in the balance sheet for a period provides the data needed. In this process certain transactions that do not enter into the use of working capital are eliminated; for example, a loss of $50,000 incurred in the destruction of a building by an uninsured casualty and charged directly to Retained Earnings would not be a "funds" item reported in the statement.

Two methods are available for preparation of the funds statement: the T account method and the work sheet method. Both are illustrated in the following paragraphs. The т account method has the advantages of simplicity and time-saving where there are few complexities in the problem, and is easier for those who find it confusing to think in terms of reversing a transaction. The work sheet method permits a better over-all view of the process and preserves the record in better form for those cases in which future reference may be made to it (in case of audit by a public accountant who must render an opinion on the statement, for example).

PREPARATION OF FUNDS STATEMENT BY т ACCOUNT METHOD—CASE 1

A comparative balance sheet of Wells Construction Company, with the current and noncurrent sections separated is given here. The company has

WELLS CONSTRUCTION COMPANY
Comparative Balance Sheet
December 31, 1965 and 1966
Current Section

Assets	1965	1966	Liabilities and Balance	1965	1966
Cash	$18,000	$20,000	Notes Payable	$10,000	$12,000
Accounts Receivable	31,000	36,000	Accounts Payable	13,000	15,000
Building Materials	42,000	41,000	Taxes Payable	7,500	8,200
Prepaid Insurance	1,600	1,800	Balance of Working		
	$92,600	$98,800	Capital.	62,100	63,600
				$92,600	$98,800

Noncurrent Section

Assets	1965	1966	Liabilities and Capital	1965	1966
Balance of Working					
Capital.	$62,100	$63,600	Capital Stock	$50,000	$100,000
Land	—	5,000	Retained Earnings	12,100	19,600
Building.	—	14,000			
Equipment	—	37,000			
	$62,100	$119,600		$62,100	$119,600

operated out of the homes of its owners and had no fixed assets before 1966. In that year it issued additional capital stock and acquired land and a building to house its operations and some equipment (it previously rented the equipment required). No dividends were paid in 1966.

To process the data by the т account method one sets up a т account for Working Capital and one for each of the other balance sheet accounts in which there has been any change during the year (if there are offsetting changes in an account, an account should be set up for these changes). The net change is then entered in each of the т accounts on the side where it would be entered if it were to be recorded as an ordinary transaction in the usual course of business. An increase in working capital goes on the debit side; a decrease, on the credit side. A line is then drawn to indicate that the net-change figure is to be distinguished from other entries in the T accounts. The net change serves as a memorandum of the net effect of the transactions which are subsequently to be posted to the account. The accompanying T accounts for the Wells Construction Company illustrate the procedure.

Entries may then be made in the T accounts which reflect the various changes. Note that it is desirable to list the transactions related to operations in the T account for working capital separately from the other transactions, as the funds provided by operations are to be reported together in the funds statement. Note also that entries are made in the same way that they would be made in the regular course of business; purchase of a fixed asset is entered as a debit to the fixed asset account and a credit to the Working Capital account. One can see when all the necessary transactions have been accounted for by noting whether or not the net-change balance entered first in the T accounts is equal to the net total of the individual transactions entered below it.

WELLS CONSTRUCTION COMPANY
T Account Method of
Funds Statement Preparation—Case 1

Working Capital		
Net change 1,500		
Sources	**Applications**	
Operations		
(1) Income 7,500		
Other	(2) Land 5,000	
(5) Sale of	(3) Building 14,000	
Stock 50,000	(4) Equipment 37,000	
57,500	56,000	

Land	
Net change 5,000	
(2) Purchase 5,000	

Building	
Net change 14,000	
(3) Purchase 14,000	

Equipment	
Net change 37,000	
(4) Purchase 37,000	

Capital Stock	
	Net change 50,000
	(5) Sale 50,000

Retained Earnings	
	Net change 7,500
	(1) Income 7,500

When the entries are complete, the Working Capital account will show all the information required for the funds statement, with funds provided on the debit side and funds applied on the credit side. It will be helpful to enter brief explanations of the transactions as they are written in the T accounts, so one can better review any account for missing data. Information about the changes in each account other than Working Capital must come from an analysis of the corresponding account in the regular general ledger of the concern. In the present case we have the following information: No dividends were paid in 1966; the new fixed assets were acquired late in the year, so that no depreciation was recorded on them; there were no unusual transactions in the noncurrent accounts. This means that the change in Retained Earnings represents only the net income for the year. It is convenient, but not essential, to begin one's analysis with the Retained Earnings account. The entries made in the accompanying T accounts for case 1 are as follows:

1. Working Capital . . . . $ 7,500
      Retained Earnings. . . . . $ 7,500
      (to record net income for the period)
2. Land . . . . $ 5,000
      Working Capital . . . . $ 5,000
      (to record purchase of land)
3. Building $14,000
      Working Capital. $14,000
      (to record purchase of building)
4. Equipment $37,000
      Working Capital. $37,000
      (to record purchase of equipment)
5. Working Capital $50,000
      Capital Stock. $50,000
      (to record sale of capital stock)

A glance at the accounts after these entries and any needed footings have been made shows that all changes have been accounted for, including the change in Working Capital—if there has been no error. The difference between the entries on the two sides must of course be taken to obtain the net-change figure in any case where entries appear on both sides. The funds statement for this case is given herewith; note that, in accordance with common practice a schedule of working capital changes (changes in current assets and current liabilities) accompanies it to give information on the change in composition of working capital.

WELLS CONSTRUCTION COMPANY
Statement of Application of Funds
Year ended December 31, 1966

Funds were provided by:
  Operating at a profit. . . . . $ 7,500
  Sale of capital stock. 50,000 $57,500
Funds were applied to:
  Purchase of land. . . . . $ 5,000
  Purchase of building. 14,000
  Purchase of equipment. 37,000   56,000
Increase in working capital, per schedule. . . . . $ 1,500

Schedule of Working-Capital Changes

| | Balances | | Changes | |
	Beginning	Ending	Increases	Decreases
Cash....................	$18,000	$20,000	$2,000	
Accounts Receivable...........	31,000	36,000	5,000	
Building Materials.............	42,000	41,000		$1,000
Prepaid Insurance.............	1,600	1,800	200	
Notes Payable...............	10,000	12,000		2,000
Accounts Payable............	13,000	15,000		2,000
Taxes Payable...............	7,500	8,200		700
			$7,200	$5,700
Net Increase..........				1,500
			$7,200	$7,200

PREPARATION OF FUNDS STATEMENT BY T ACCOUNT METHOD — CASE 2

Two complications are added at this juncture: (1) noncurrent accounts with more than one change during the period and (2) changes within the noncurrent section that do not involve working capital. If the procedures followed in case 1 are observed here, no difficulty should arise: several transactions can be entered in each of the noncurrent accounts as they were in case 1 in the Working Capital account, and any transactions that do not affect working capital will be confined to the noncurrent accounts automatically. These additions are illustrated by the transactions of Wilhoit Corporation for 1966. Comparative balance sheets for this company, divided into current and noncurrent sections as in case 1, are given on page 727.

Data on the composition of changes in the accounts follow. The items of information are numbered to correspond with entries in the T accounts appearing on pages 728-729 (the significance of the provision for Deductions from Operations in the Working Capital account will become apparent as we proceed).

(1) The Retained Earnings account is analyzed as follows:

Balance, June 30, 1965..........		$36,500
Add: Net income		29,600
		$66,100
Deduct: Dividends	$20,000	
Loss on building abandoned	4,000	24,000
Balance, June 30, 1966..........		$42,100

Each of the transactions in the Retained Earnings accounts is entered in the T account scheme, but when the third one (loss on building abandoned) is reached, we note that it involves other noncurrent accounts. We therefore look up the entry involved, in order to handle the transaction all at once in our analysis. We find that the abandoned building cost $16,000 and had $12,000 of accumulated depreciation on it at the time of abandonment. We enter this

WILHOIT CORPORATION
Comparative Balance Sheets
Years Ended June 30, 1965 and 1966

Current Section

Assets	1965	1966
Cash	$ 60,000	$ 64,000
Accounts Receivable	92,000	88,000
Merchandise	114,000	128,000
Supplies	4,100	4,700
	$270,100	$284,700

Liabilities and Balance	1965	1966
Notes Payable	$ 98,000	$ 90,000
Accounts Payable	106,000	111,000
Accrued Interest Payable	2,000	2,000
Balance of Working Capital	64,100	81,700
	$270,100	$284,700

Noncurrent Section

Assets	1965		1966	
Balance of Working Capital		$ 64,100		$ 81,700
Land		12,000		6,000
Buildings	$264,000		$288,000	
Less: Accumulated Depreciation	30,000	234,000	23,000	265,000
Furniture & Fixtures	$ 36,000		28,000	
Less: Accumulated Depreciation	15,200	20,800	12,200	15,800
Warehouse Equipment	$ 24,000		24,000	
Less: Accumulated Depreciation	4,800	19,200	7,200	16,800
		$350,100		$385,300

Liabilities and Capital	1965	1966
Bonds Payable	$100,000	$100,000
Premium on Bonds Payable	3,600	3,200
Capital Stock	210,000	240,000
Retained Earnings	36,500	42,100
	$350,100	$385,300

WILHOIT CORPORATION

T Account Method of Funds Statement Preparation — Case 2

Working Capital

Net change	17,600		

Operations:		Deductions from operations:	
(1A) Net income 29,600		(2) Gain on land sold. . 4,600	
(5) Depreciation 10,400		(4) Gain on F. & F. . . . 1,000	
		(6) Amort. of Bond	
Other:		Premium 400	
(2) Sale of land 10,600			
(4) Sale of F. & F. 3,000		Applications:	
(7) Sale of Stock 30,000		(1B) Dividends. 20,000	
		(3) Const. of bldg. 40,000	
	83,600	66,000	

Buildings

Net change	24,000		
(3) Construction 40,000		(1C) Abandonment 16,000	

Furniture and Fixtures

		Net change	8,000
		(4) Sale 8,000	

Warehouse Equipment

—		—	

Bonds Payable

—		—	

Capital Stock

		Net change	30,000
		(7) Sale of Stock 30,000	

Land

		Net change	6,000
		(2) Sale 6,000	

Accumulated Depreciation — Buildings

Net change	7,000		
(1C) Abandonment 12,000		(5) Depreciation	5,000

Accumulated Depreciation — F. & F.

Net change	3,000		
(4) Sale 6,000		(5) Depreciation	3,000

Accumulated Depreciation — Warehouse Equipment

		Net change	2,400
		(5) Depreciation	2,400

Premium on Bonds Payable

Net change	400		
(6) Amortization	400		

Retained Earnings

		Net change	5,600
(1B) Dividends 20,000		(1A) Net Income 29,600	
(1C) Abandonment loss . . 4,000			

information as entry 1C. The entries recording the analysis of Retained Earnings are:

```
(1A) Working Capital (net income) . . . . . $29,600
          Retained Earnings. . . . . . . . . . .        $29,600
     (to record net income)
(1B) Retained Earnings . . . . . . . . . . . . . $20,000
          Working Capital (dividends) . . . . .        $20,000
     (to record dividends paid)
(1C) Accumulated Depreciation — Buildings $12,000
          Retained Earnings . . . . . . . . . . . . .     4,000
          Buildings . . . . . . . . . . . . . . . . . . .        $16,000
     (to record abandonment of building)
```

(2) Analysis of the Land account shows that a piece of land costing $6,000 was sold for $10,600. The gain of $4,600 went to net income. The funds provided by this sale were actually $10,600; no funds in addition to this amount are involved. The gain of $4,600 recorded in net income is not properly a part of "funds provided by operations." The transaction is entered as entry 2, and the gain appears under "deductions from operations," where it will act to reduce the original book figure for net income to eliminate this gain from funds provided by operations.

This entry is:

```
(2) Working Capital (land sale). . . . . . . . . . $ 10,600
       Land . . . . . . . . . . . . . . . . . . . . . . . . .          $6,000
       Working Capital (gain on land) . . . . . .                       4,600
    (to record sale of land; the debit records the
    funds provided, and the credit to Working
    Capital reduces the figure for net income that
    originally included the gain)
```

(3) The Buildings account is analyzed as follows:

```
Balance, June 30, 1965 . . . . . . . . . . . . $264,000
Add: Building constructed . . . . . . . . . . .   40,000
                                                $304,000
Deduct: Building abandoned  . . . . . . . .       16,000
Balance, June 30, 1966 . . . . . . . . . . . . $288,000
```

The transaction recording abandonment of a building was already entered in connection with the analysis of the Retained Earnings account as entry 1C. The remaining entry, which records the funds applied to the construction of a building, is entry 3 — a debit to Buildings and a credit to Working Capital.

(4) Analysis of the Furniture and Fixtures account discloses a sale, for $3,000, of furniture that cost $8,000. It had $6,000 of depreciation on it; the gain was carried to net income. Once again, the gain is not a source of funds independent of the $3,000 actual sale price and does not represent operations, so it is recorded as a deduction from the funds provided from operations, as preliminarily indicated by the book figure for net income. The entry is number 4, and is as follows:

```
(4) Working Capital (sale of F. and F.) . . . . . . . $3,000
    Accumulated Depreciation — F. and F. . . . . . .  6,000
       Furniture and Fixtures . . . . . . . . . . . . . .           $8,000
       Working Capital (gain on F. and F.) . . . . .                 1,000
    (to record sale of furniture and fixtures; the
    $1,000 gain is deducted from net income in the
    working capital account since it is not funds)
```

(5) The Accumulated Depreciation — Buildings account is analyzed as follows:

```
Balance, June 20, 1965 . . . . . . . . . . . . . . . . . . . . . . . . $30,000
Add: Depreciation for the year . . . . . . . . . . . . . . . . . . . .   5,000
                                                                      $35,000
Deduct: Accumulated depreciation on building abandoned . .  12,000
Balance, June 30, 1966 . . . . . . . . . . . . . . . . . . . . . . . . $23,000
```

The transaction involving the abandoned building was previously entered in connection with the Retained Earnings account (entry 1C). Only the depreciation for the year remains; since this situation exists for the Furniture and Fixtures and Warehouse Equipment accounts, it is convenient to make the entry for all three at once. Notice that the original recording of depreciation resulted in a deduction in the income statement but did not involve use of funds for this period. Accordingly, to find the amount of funds provided by operations, we must add back to the book figure for net income any depreciation charges. Depreciation for the year on Furniture and Fixtures was $3,000 and on Warehouse Equipment $2,400. The three depreciation figures total $10,400 and are recorded in our T account scheme by entry 5, which is:

(5) Working Capital (depreciation) $10,400
    Accumulated Depreciation—Buildings $5,000
    Accumulated Depreciation—Furniture and Fixtures.   3,000
    Accumulated Depreciation—Warehouse Equipment   2,400
    (to record depreciation)

Since there was no other transaction in the Accumulated Depreciation—Warehouse Equipment account, we give it no further attention.

(6) Investigation of the change in the account for Premium on Bonds Payable shows that it is the regular amortization for the year. This resulted in a reduction of bond interest paid to disclose the effective interest cost in the net income calculation. The amortization figure did not represent any source of funds, however, so its effect on the book figure is eliminated by entry 6. A similar entry would be required for amortization of a patent or other asset. The entry is:

(6) Premium on Bonds Payable $400
    Working Capital (amortization of bond premium) $400
    (to record amortization of bond premium)

(7) The change in Capital Stock is found to have resulted from the issue of additional shares for cash. Entry 7 records this as a debit to Working Capital and a credit to Capital Stock. Note that we might wish to record it as a source of funds even though the shares were issued directly for acquisition of a non-current asset, since the effect would be the same as receipt of the funds and their use to buy the asset.

A review of the T accounts at this point reveals that all changes are accounted for, including the change in net working capital. Data for the resulting funds statement can be seen in the T account for Working Capital: the statement is shown on page 732. Once again it is accompanied by a schedule of changes in current assets and current liabilities.

PREPARATION OF THE FUNDS STATEMENT—WORK SHEET METHOD

The work sheet method assembles the data in work sheet form rather than using T accounts. It may begin with comparative postclosing trial balances or with the net changes. It obtains the same results as the T account method but uses entries in an adjustment column to eliminate changes that do not involve funds. It arranges for an accumulation of information about funds provided from operations by establishing a special section for net income and its adjustments, much as the T account method does. Columns provide for accumulating the adjusted data and also give a convenient means of obtaining the figures for the schedule of changes in Working Capital accounts. The figures of Wilhoit Corporation are used again in the illustration of the work sheet method that follows. Since some students or instructors may wish to concentrate on one of the methods to the relative exclusion of the other, the explanations are repeated, but are treated from the different viewpoint imposed by the work sheet

WILHOIT CORPORATION

Statement of Application of Funds

Year ended June 30, 1966

Funds were provided by:
Profitable operations:

Net income per income statement		$29,600	
Add: Depreciation charges		10,400	
		$40,000	
Deduct: Gain on sale of land	$4,600		
Gain on sale of furniture	1,000		
Amortization of bond premium	400	6,000	$34,000
Sale of capital stock		30,000	
Sale of land		10,600	
Sale of furniture		3,000	$77,600

Funds were applied to:

Construction of building	$40,000	
Payment of dividends	20,000	60,000
Increase in working capital, per schedule		$17,600

Schedule of Changes in Working Capital

	Balances Beginning	Ending	Changes Increases	Decreases
Cash	$ 60,000	$ 64,000	$ 4,000	
Accounts Receivable	92,000	88,000		$ 4,000
Merchandise	114,000	128,000	14,000	
Supplies	4,100	4,700	600	
Notes Payable	98,000	90,000	8,000	
Accounts Payable	106,000	111,000		5,000
			$26,600	$ 9,000
Net Increase				17,600
			$26,600	$26,600

method. The entries made under the two methods do not correspond one to one in these illustrations.

PREPARATION OF THE STATEMENT—WILHOIT CORPORATION—WORK SHEET METHOD

Two problems emphasized in this case are:

1. Some changes in balance sheet accounts are a composite of individual changes. These must be separated in order that the various sources and applications of funds may be described.

2. Some changes outside the current section of the balance sheet do not involve the working capital. The commonest example is depreciation; this reduces the amount shown as net income and the book value of the assets but has no direct effect on working capital. Such changes must be eliminated for purposes of the statement of application of funds.

The procedure for meeting these problems in the work sheet method consists of three steps:

1. Analyze the noncurrent accounts to determine what changes make up the net change for the period.
2. Make adjustments on the work sheet to separate the different changes that affect each caption.
3. Make entries on the work sheet to reverse changes that do not involve funds.

These steps are illustrated by the work sheet for the funds statement of Wilhoit Corporation shown on pages 734-735. Data on the composition of changes and explanations of the adjustments follow.

(1) The Retained Earnings account is analyzed as follows:

Balance June 30, 1965.		$36,500
Add: Net income.		29,600
		$66,100
Deduct: Dividends.	$20,000	
Loss on building abandoned.	4,000	24,000
Balance June 30, 1966.		$42,100

Adjustment 1 records the analysis by debiting Retained Earnings for the net change of $5,600, debiting Dividends Paid for $20,000, debiting Loss on Abandonment of Building $4,000, and crediting Net Income $29,600. The dividends, loss on building, and net income are entered on new lines of the work sheet. Space should be left after the net income line for more entries, as more are likely. "Net Income" should be set out at once, because the adjustments of the other accounts often involve entries to it. Such items as the loss on abandonment of building can be dealt with later when the related account is taken up.

(2) The change in the Land account is due to the sale of a piece of vacant land for $10,600. The land cost $6,000; the gain of $4,600 went to Net Income. The funds provided by this sale total $10,600; the gain is therefore taken out of Net Income and combined with the cost of the land sold to show the whole proceeds as a distinct source of funds. The entry debits Net Income and credits Land with the $4,600. If desired, another entry could be made transferring the $10,600 that now remains on the line for Land to a separate line, but the line for the Land account will serve as well.

(3) The Buildings account is analyzed as follows for the period:

Balance June 30, 1965.		$264,000
Add: Building constructed.		40,000
		$304,000
Deduct: Building abandoned.		16,000
Balance June 30, 1966.		$288,000

The loss on abandonment of the building that appeared separately in Retained Earnings was $4,000. The difference between this and the credit to Buildings

WILHOIT CORPORATION
Funds-Statement Work Sheet
Year ended June 30, 1966

	Balances		Net Changes		Adjustments		Funds		Working Capital	
	6-30-65	6-30-66	Debit	Credit	Debit	Credit	Applied	Provided	Increase	Decrease
Debits										
Cash	60,000	64,000	4,000						4,000	
Accounts Receivable	92,000	88,000		4,000						4,000
Merchandise	114,000	128,000	14,000						14,000	
Supplies	4,100	4,700	600						600	
Land	12,000	6,000		6,000		(2) 4,600		10,600		
Buildings	264,000	288,000	24,000		(3) 16,000	(4) 40,000				
Furniture and Fixtures	36,000	28,000		8,000	(5) 8,000					
Warehouse Equipment	24,000	24,000								
	606,100	630,700								
Credits										
Accumulated Depreciation—Buildings	30,000	23,000	7,000		(6) 5,000	(3) 12,000				
Accumulated Depreciation—Furniture and Fixtures	15,200	12,200	3,000		(7) 3,000	(5) 6,000				
Accumulated Depreciation—Equipment	4,800	7,200		2,400	(8) 2,400					
Notes Payable	98,000	90,000	8,000						8,000	
Accounts Payable	106,000	111,000		5,000						5,000
Accrued Interest Payable	2,000	2,000								
Bonds Payable	100,000	100,000								
Premium on Bonds Payable	3,600	3,200	400			(9) 400				

Account					Analysis Dr	Analysis Cr				
Capital Stock	210,000	240,000		30,000					30,000	
Retained Earnings	36,500	42,100		5,600						
	606,100	630,700	61,000	61,000						
Dividends Paid			30,000		(1) 5,600					
Net Income			5,600		(1) 20,000	(1) 29,600	20,000			
Deduct:										
Gain on sale of land					(2) 4,600					
Gain on sale of furniture					(5) 1,000					
Amortization of bond premium					(9) 400					
Add:								34,000		
Depreciation of Building						(6) 5,000				
Depreciation of Furniture and Fixtures						(7) 3,000				
Depreciation of Equipment						(8) 2,400				
Loss on Abandonment of Building					(1) 4,000	(3) 4,000				
Proceeds of Sale of Furniture						(5) 3,000	40,000	3,000		9,000
Construction of Building					(4) 40,000		60,000	77,600	26,600	17,600
					110,000	110,000				26,600
Increase in Working Capital							17,600			
							77,600	77,600	26,600	26,600

is the accumulated depreciation of $12,000 that applied to this building. In order to separate the transaction representing the construction of the new building from the change due to the abandonment of another building, and because the abandonment involved no funds, the original entry recording the abandonment is simply reversed. This requires a debit of $16,000 to Buildings, a credit of $12,000 to Accumulated Depreciation—Buildings, and a credit to Loss on Abandonment of Building of $4,000.

(4) To make the transactions perfectly clear, the building constructed is set out on a separate line by crediting Buildings and debiting Building Constructed for $40,000. This adjustment could be omitted, because the figures on the line for Buildings add across to the $40,000, and this could simply be carried to the Funds column.

(5) An analysis of the Furniture and Fixtures account shows that there was only one transaction—a $3,000 sale of furniture that cost $8,000. This furniture had $6,000 of depreciation accumulated against it. The gain of $1,000 was carried into the Net Income figure. The $3,000 received for the furniture is a significant item in relation to this company's income, so it is separated from net income and shown on a separate line; at the same time, the reductions in Furniture and Fixtures and Accumulated Depreciation—Furniture and Fixtures are reversed, since they do not represent funds. The entry is fourfold: debit Net Income for the gain of $1,000; debit Furniture and Fixtures, $8,000; credit Accumulated Depreciation—Furniture and Fixtures, $6,000; and credit Proceeds of Sale of Furniture, $3,000.

(6) The Accumulated Depreciation—Buildings account is analyzed as follows:

Balance June 30, 1965	$30,000
Add: Depreciation for the year	5,000
	$35,000
Deduct: Accumulated depreciation on building abandoned	12,000
Balance June 30, 1966	$23,000

Adjustment was made for the $12,000 deducted when the building was abandoned in entry 3, which reversed the item because no funds are involved in this debit to Accumulated Depreciation. The addition of $5,000 to Accumulated Depreciation with the corresponding debit to expense does not involve funds either. This amount is also reversed; it is added back to Net Income (a credit) and deducted from Accumulated Depreciation (a debit).

(7) The analysis of Accumulated Depreciation—Furniture and Fixtures is:

Balance June 30, 1965	$15,200
Add: Depreciation for the year	3,000
	$18,200
Deduct: Accumulated depreciation on furniture sold	6,000
Balance June 30, 1966	$12,200

The entry for accumulated depreciation on furniture sold was disposed of by adjustment 5 on the work sheet. The depreciation for the year does not require funds, so it is added back to Net Income by adjustment 7.

(8) The only change in the account for Accumulated Depreciation—Warehouse Equipment is the addition of depreciation for the year. This is added back to Net Income by entry 8.

(9) The change in Premium on Bonds Payable account represents the writeoff for the year. This is a debit to Premium and a credit against the interest paid out to give an interest expense less than the cash payment. It requires no funds and is not part of working capital, so it is reversed to Net Income also. The entry 9 is a credit to Premium account and a debit against Net Income.

The work sheet is completed as shown. The statement for Wilhoit Corporation is the same as before and is given on page 732. The reader may wonder why the accounts for Accumulated Depreciation were shown separately, while no account for Allowance for Doubtful Accounts is shown (the Accounts Receivable figure is net). The reason is that the allowance for doubtful accounts is part of the working-capital figure and so does not have to be set out separately; whereas the accounts for Accumulated Depreciation must be adjusted for their nonfunds transactions. This adjustment could be made on the line for the regular asset account if that were shown net of accumulated depreciation, but it would be more confusing.

Note that the statement of application of funds customarily shows the net income per the income statement, with the additions and deductions necessary to remove nonfund items. In a condensed statement, a single figure for the funds provided by profitable operations is given.

POPULAR FORM OF "CASH FLOW"

It has recently become commonplace for securities analysts to calculate a figure they call "cash flow" by merely adding depreciation back to the net income figure. This provides a fair approximation of funds provided by operations in many cases, but it ignores other possible adjustments that may be needed to compute the figure properly, such as other amortizations or writeoffs and net gains or losses on capital assets sold. Furthermore, there is a tendency to substitute this "cash flow" figure for net income in discussing the prospects of a security. This may be extremely misleading. If a concern is to be successful, it must replace the assets it uses up in producing its merchandise or its services; the deduction of depreciation from revenue along with other expenses to arrive at net income recognizes this, but the "cash flow" computation does not. The student should be wary of this misuse of funds data and should remember that it is useful only as an indication of financial strength or weakness in the ability to pay debts or to continue to pay them when revenue declines, and for its description of the financial policies followed by management in reinvesting funds in productive assets, paying dividends, or retaining idle cash, for example.

SUMMARY

A statement of application of funds typically summarizes the flow of working capital through the concern for a period, although it may reflect cash transactions alone or all external sources of purchasing power. The statement may be constructed by a T account method or a work sheet method, but an analysis of the noncurrent balance sheet accounts is required in either case. An important figure in the statement is the one for funds provided from operations; this is different from net income, because some of the components of net income do not involve the use of funds in the current period. The most important of these components is depreciation. Care should be taken not to confuse funds provided from operations with net income, as the popular use of the term "cash flow" (net income plus depreciation) often does. The funds statement is useful as an indication of financial strength or weakness and as a summary of management policy regarding financial matters.

QUESTIONS

26.1   The manager of a concern manufacturing stock feed tells you that his income statement shows a profit of $40,000 for the year but that he does not have enough money in the bank to pay a dividend, and that after looking at his accounts receivable and inventory of merchandise he is convinced that funds will not be available in the near future to pay a dividend. He does not understand why this condition should exist. What kind of accounting statement does the manager need?

26.2   Suggest different definitions of "funds" that may be used in the preparation of a funds statement. Explain briefly how the statement is prepared for each definition. Under what circumstances might each approach be appropriate?

26.3   List four basic sources of working capital for an organization and four basic applications.

26.4   During the year C Co. paid off a $50,000 6 month 6 percent bank loan. How will this transaction be shown on a funds statement for the year?

26.5   How would each of the items listed below be reflected in a funds statement, if at all? Classify each as an application, a source, or a nonfund item:

(1) Construction of a building
(2) Issuance of bonds
(3) Payment of installment on a mortgage
(4) Recording of depreciation on a building
(5) Payment of a dividend
(6) Purchase of machinery
(7) Sale of land
(8) Operations at a profit
(9) Amortization of premium on bonds payable

26.6   What are the items generally added back to net income to get the total of funds provided by operations?

26.7   A funds statement could be prepared by going through all the transactions in the journals and classifying them for purposes of the statement. Why is this not done?

26.8   The S. A. Zeff Company acquired land and buildings during the year by the issuance of preferred stocks. Explain how this transaction might be disclosed (1) in a funds statement applying the all resources concept of funds and (2) in a funds statement applying the working-capital concept of funds.

26.9 Explain how the T accounts method can be used to prepare a funds statement. Why are the net changes entered in the accounts? What subdivision of the Working Capital account may be useful?

26.10 Give the entry used on the work sheet for a statement of application of funds in each of the following situations:

(1) Net income included in the retained earnings change is $14,000.
(2) Depreciation of $6,000 represents the only change in the Accumulated Depreciation—Small Tools account.
(3) Premium on bonds payable has decreased $800 for the year.
(4) The net change in the Buildings account is $60,000. This represents a new building constructed for $100,000 and the retirement of an old one that cost $40,000. The old one was fully depreciated and had no salvage value.
(5) Cash increased $800.

26.11 In a recent letter to the stockholders of Consolidated Steel Co., Inc., the president stated that earnings for the year were $1.15 a share, but the "cash flow" amounted to $4.20 a share.

(1) How was "cash flow" probably computed?
(2) Discuss briefly the limitations of such a computation as an approximation to the excess of receipts over disbursements from operations.
(3) Comment briefly on the uses and misuses of the "cash flow" amount cited in the president's letter.

26.12 Inflation reduces the relative effectiveness of depreciation as a source of funds, and results in misleading the public as to the availability of current profits for distribution. In *real* terms, the retention of earnings does not necessarily indicate a growing business, but rather one striving simply to maintain its productive capacity.

(1) What justification is there for calling depreciation a source of funds?
(2) How does inflation create the illusion referred to in the above statement?
(3) Explain the influence of inflation on the nature of any long term financing which a corporation may wish to undertake during such a period.

(*CPCU — adapted*)

EXERCISES

26.1 The balance sheets of Oceanic Marine, Inc., at December 31, 1965 and 1966, follow:

	1965	*1966*
Cash.	$ 40,000	$125,000
Marine Equipment	500,000	590,000
Buildings	50,000	50,000
Land	10,000	30,000
Accumulated Depreciation	(100,000)	(180,000)
	$500,000	$615,000
Debentures Payable	$200,000	$250,000
Common Stock, $10 par	250,000	270,000
Retained Earnings.	50,000	95,000
	$500,000	$615,000

Cash dividends of $75,000 were charged to Retained Earnings in 1966; net income accounted for the remaining change in Retained Earnings. Additional land was acquired during the year by the issuance of common stock.

Over

Required:

Prepare a funds statement. *(funds are defined as working capital)*

26.2 The comparative financial condition of the C. L. Nelson Co. at December 31, 1965 and 1966, is summarized below:

Assets	December 31 1965	December 31 1966	Increase (Decrease)
Working Capital	$179,000	$235,300	$56,300
Plant and Equipment	82,000	120,000	38,000
Accumulated Depreciation	(41,000)	(43,000)	(2,000)
	$220,000	$312,300	$92,300

Liabilities and Capital	December 31 1965	December 31 1966	Increase (Decrease)
Bonds Payable	$ 30,000	$ 60,000	$30,000
Bond Discount	—	(5,700)	(5,700)
Common Stock, $100 par	100,000	140,000	40,000
Premium on Common Stock	50,000	70,000	20,000
Retained Earnings	40,000	48,000	8,000
	$220,000	$312,300	$92,300

The statement of net income and retained earnings for 1966 shows:

Net Income		$24,200
Less:		
Loss on Retirement of Equipment	$3,000	
Premium on Retirement of Bonds	1,200	4,200
Net Income after Nonrecurring Charges		$20,000
Dividends		12,000
Increase in Retained Earnings		$ 8,000

During the year equipment that cost $12,000 and that had a book value of $4,000 was sold for $1,000. On June 30 all of the outstanding bonds were purchased at 104. A new 10-year issue was sold on July 1 at 90.

Required:

Prepare a funds statement.

26.3 A comparative balance sheet of the E. V. Celeski Co. shows:

Assets	December 31 1965	December 31 1966	Liabilities and Capital	December 31 1965	December 31 1966
Working Capital	$15,000	$ 20,000	Capital Stock	$10,000	$ 80,000
Land		10,000	Retained Earnings	5,000	20,000
Buildings		30,000			
Equipment		40,000			
	$15,000	$100,000		$15,000	$100,000

An analysis of the noncurrent accounts discloses:

(1) The net income for the year was $15,000.

(2) Additional capital stock was issued for $70,000.

(3) Prior to 1966 the company rented its plant and equipment. In late December of 1966 the company purchased land, buildings, and equipment for cash.

Required: Prepare a funds statement (funds are defined as working capital).

1. Open T accounts for Working Capital and for each of the other accounts listed above. Enter the net changes and underscore them to distinguish these amounts from subsequent entries.
2. Prepare entries in journal form to reflect the changes.
3. Put the caption "Sources" over the debits in Working Capital, and the caption "Applications" over the credits. Post the entries to the T accounts. Include a brief explanation of each posting.
4. Prepare a funds statement in good form.

26.4   The December 31, 1965 and 1966 balance sheets of the B. T. Sanders Company include the following data:

Assets	1965	1966	Liabilities and Capital	1965	1966
Working Capital . .	$ 58,000	$ 81,650	Bonds Payable . . .	$ 30,000	$ 50,000
Land.	15,000	19,000	Bond Premium . . .	1,200	4,750
Buildings.	100,000	108,000	Capital Stock	100,000	118,000
Acc. Depr. – Bldgs.	(40,000)	(31,000)	Retained Earnings .	19,800	28,800
Furn. & Fixt.	30,000	36,000			
Acc. Depr. – F. & F.	(12,000)	(12,100)			
	$151,000	$201,550		$151,000	$201,550

The statement of net income and retained earnings shows:

Net Income		$24,000
Less:		
Loss on Land and Building	$5,000	
Cash Dividends	2,000	
Stock Dividend.	8,000	15,000
Increase in Retained Earnings.		$ 9,000

Changes in land and buildings for the year were as follows:

	Land	Buildings Cost	Buildings Acc. Depr.
Balance, January 1	$15,000	$100,000	$40,000
Additions	10,000	30,000	6,000
	$25,000	$130,000	$46,000
Retirements	6,000	22,000	15,000
Balance, December 31	$19,000	$108,000	$31,000

The company moved its main office during the year. It sold its old building in January and bought a new building in July. Changes in furniture and fixtures for the year were as follows:

	Cost	Acc. Depr.
Balance January 1	$30,000	$12,000
Additions	12,000	5,500
	$42,000	$17,500
Retirements	6,000	5,400
Balance December 31	$36,000	$12,100

Furniture and fixtures retired during the year realized $1,000; gain on the retirement was included in net income.

Bonds outstanding on January 1, 1966, were retired at their book value at that date; a new issue of 10-year bonds was sold on July 1 at 110.

Required:

Prepare a funds statement by the T account method.

26.5 The information below is available for the preparation of a funds statement for the T. P. Herrick Company. Present in journal form the entries that would appear in T accounts used to develop the funds statement.

	December 31	
	1965	1966
Office Equipment	$ 18,000	$ 24,000
Acc. Depr. — Office Equip.	6,000	3,400
Delivery Equipment	11,000	16,500
Acc. Depr. — Delivery Equip.	7,500	5,300
Discount on Bonds Payable	6,000	—
Bonds Payable	100,000	—
Common Stock, par $100	500,000	670,000
Premium on Common Stock	100,000	44,500
Appropriation for Bond Retirement	60,000	—
Retained Earnings.	120,000	73,600

The bonds payable were converted into common stock on July 1, 1966, at which date the unamortized discount on bonds payable was $5,500. An analysis of retained earnings for the year ended December 31, 1966 follows:

Retained Earnings, January 1, 1966		$120,000
Gain on disposal of delivery equipment, cost $3,500, acc. depr. $3,000	$ 300	
Cancellation of appropriation for bond retirement	60,000	
Net income for 1966	24,000	84,300
		$204,300
Less:		
Cash dividends paid	$ 10,000	
Loss on retirement of office equipment, cost $5,000, acc. depr. $3,800	700	
Stock dividend, 1,000 shares at $120	120,000	130,700
Retained Earnings, December 31, 1966		$ 73,600

26.6 Balance sheet accounts of the J. T. Wheeler Company at December 31, 1965 and 1966, are as follows:

| | December 31 | | Increase |
	1965	1966	(Decrease)
Working Capital	$ 820,000	$ 824,120	$ 4,120
Investment in Subsidiary	—	84,000	84,000
Machinery.	190,000	186,600	(3,400)
Buildings.	507,500	566,500	59,000
Land.	52,500	52,500	—
Bond Discount	—	4,680	4,680
	$1,570,000	$1,718,400	$ 148,400
Bonds Payable, 4%	$ —	$ 125,000	$ 125,000
Bonds Payable, 6%	100,000	—	(100,000)
Acc. Depr. — Buildings	400,000	407,000	7,000
Acc. Depr. — Machinery	130,000	141,000	11,000
Premium on Bonds Payable	1,600	—	(1,600)
Capital Stock — no par	1,163,400	1,011,400	(152,000)
Paid in Capital	—	14,000	14,000
Retained Earnings	(225,000)	20,000	245,000
	$1,570,000	$1,718,400	$ 148,400

Retained earning transactions were:

December 31, 1966	Balance (deficit)	$(225,000)
March 31, 1966	Profit for first quarter 1966.	25,000
April 1, 1966	Transfer from stated capital	200,000
	Balance	—
December 31, 1966	Profit for last three quarters 1966	$ 80,000
	Dividend declared — payable January 20, 1967	(60,000)
	Balance	$ 20,000

Additional information:

(1) On April 1, 1966, the existing deficit was written off against capital surplus created by reducing the stated value of the no-par stock.
(2) On November 1, 1966, 8,000 shares of no-par stock were sold for $62,000. The board of directors voted to regard $6 per share as stated capital.
(3) Machinery was purchased for $4,600 and installed in December 1966. A check for this amount was sent to the vendor in January 1967.
(4) During the year, machinery which had a cost basis of $8,000 and on which there was accumulated depreciation of $5,000 was sold for $1,000. No other fixed assets were sold during the year.
(5) The 6 percent 20-year bonds were dated and issued on January 2, 1954. Interest was payable on June 30 and December 31. The bonds were sold originally at 104. They were retired at 101 and accrued interest on March 31, 1966.
(6) The 4 percent 40-year bonds were dated January 1, 1966, and were sold on March 31 at 97 and accrued interest. Interest is payable semiannually on June 30 and December 31. Expense of issuance was $1,020.
(7) The J. T. Wheeler Company acquired 80 percent control of a subsidiary company on January 2, 1966, for $100,000. The income statement of the company for 1966 shows a net loss of $20,000.
(8) Extraordinary repairs to buildings of $7,000 were charged to Accumulated Depreciation — Building.

Required:

Prepare a work sheet for funds statement.

(AICPA — adapted)

26.7 From the data below, determine the cash received from customers in 1966.

	1965	1966
Accounts Receivable, December 31	$ 54,500	$ 55,000
Sales Discounts	5,000	4,000
Sales	625,000	590,000
Freight Out	7,000	6,700

26.8 From the data below, determine the payments made to merchandise creditors of B Co. in 1966.

	1965	1966
Accounts Payable, December 31	$ 18,000	$ 12,000
Merchandise Inventory, December 31	31,000	27,000
Cost of Sales	205,000	247,000

PROBLEMS

26.1 The following postclosing trial balances are available for the Farber Company:

	December 31			
	1965		1966	
Cash	$ 5,000		$ 8,000	
Accounts Receivable	32,000		37,000	
Merchandise	57,000		62,000	
Supplies	4,000		5,000	
Land	—		20,000	
Buildings	—		80,000	
Equipment	70,000		70,000	
Acc. Depr. — Equip.		$ 14,000		$ 22,000
Notes Payable		18,000		20,000
Accounts Payable		42,000		51,000
Taxes Payable		8,000		6,000
Mortgage Payable		—		60,000
Capital Stock		80,000		110,000
Retained Earnings		6,000		13,000
	$168,000	$168,000	$282,000	$282,000

All changes in the noncurrent accounts represent a single transaction except in the case of Retained Earnings. This account contains an entry for the net income for the year and an entry for $10,000 of dividends paid during the year.

Required:

Prepare a statement of application of funds with a schedule of working-capital changes.

26.2 The B. S. Lee Company expanded its facilities in 1966, and management has asked that a statement of application of funds be prepared. The following post-closing trial balances are available:

	1965		December 31	1966	
Cash	$ 4,000			$ 8,000	
Accounts Receivable	28,000			32,000	
Merchandise..............	51,000			60,000	
Supplies.................	2,000			2,800	
Land	—			5,000	
Buildings	—			50,000	
Equipment	70,000			65,000	
Acc. Depr.—Equipment		$ 14,000			$ 15,000
Notes Payable		18,000			20,000
Accounts Payable...........		31,000			42,000
Taxes Payable		8,000			6,000
Mortgage Payable...........		—			30,000
Capital Stock		80,000			100,000
Retained Earnings		4,000			9,800
	$155,000	$155,000		$222,800	$222,800

Equipment costing $5,000 with a book value of $3,000 was sold for $4,000. The gain was included in income. Retained Earnings contains an entry for net income and an entry for $15,000 of dividends.

Required:

Prepare a statement of application of funds with a supporting schedule of working capital changes. Use the T account method.

26.3 Comparative statements of the Tandy Toys, Inc., financial position as of December 31 are as follows:

Assets	1966	1965
Cash	$ 40,000	$ 37,000
Marketable Securities	74,000	58,000
Accounts Receivable	160,000	148,000
Inventories......................	110,000	90,000
Prepaid Expenses	6,000	12,000
W Company Bonds (long term)	30,000	60,000
Equipment	500,000	460,000
Buildings	700,000	540,000
Land	80,000	80,000
	$1,700,000	$1,485,000

Liabilities and Proprietorship		
Current Payables	$ 142,000	$ 231,000
Bonds Payable	170,000	60,000
Accumulated Depreciation:		
Equipment	148,000	130,000
Building	100,000	80,000
Preferred Stock	100,000	—
Common Stock...................	900,000	900,000
Premium on Preferred Stock	2,000	—
Retained Earnings.................	138,000	84,000
	$1,700,000	$1,485,000

Additional information:

(1) Net income after taxes for 1966 was $74,000.

(2) Dividends paid in 1966 were $20,000.

(3) No buildings or equipment were retired or sold in 1966.

Required:

Prepare a statement of source and application of funds and a schedule analyzing the change in working capital.

(CPCU — adapted)

26.4   The president of Grand Co. cannot understand why cash has decreased significantly during 1966. Following are the condensed balance sheets at December 31, 1965 and 1966:

Assets	*1965*	*1966*
Cash	$ 90,000	$ 9,000
Accounts Receivable	252,000	280,000
Allowance for Doubtful Accounts	(5,600)	(9,000)
Inventories	285,600	328,000
Prepaid Expenses	2,000	1,600
	$624,000	$609,600
Fixed Assets	$100,000	$158,000
Accumulated Depreciation	(50,000)	(64,300)
Goodwill	20,000	—
Organization Expense	4,000	3,200
	$ 74,000	$ 96,900
	$698,000	$706,500

Liabilities and Proprietorship

Bank Loans	$ 44,000	$ —
Accounts Payable	176,000	202,000
Estimated Income Taxes Payable	40,000	41,840
	$260,000	$243,840
Capital Stock — 6% Preferred	$100,000	$100,000
— Common	200,000	200,000
Retained Earnings	138,000	202,660
Treasury Stock Preferred (at cost)	—	(40,000)
	$438,000	$462,660
	$698,000	$706,500

The following additional information relates to the year ended December 31, 1966:

(1) Net income shown on the income statement was $99,460.

(2) Dividends were paid as follows:

Preferred Shares	$6,000
Common Shares	8,000

(3) A machine originally costing $6,000, against which depreciation of $1,500 had been accumulated, was sold at a profit of $500. The profit realized on the disposal was included in arriving at the net income of $99,460 for the year.

Required:

1. Prepare a funds statement supported by a schedule of working capital.
2. Write a brief note to the president discussing the principal factors explaining the decrease in cash.

(ICAC — adapted)

26.5   D. W. Walker Company had the following balances at the beginning and end of its fiscal year ended June 30, 1966:

	June 30			
	1965		1966	
Cash	$ 40,000		$ 32,000	
Notes Receivable	64,000		60,000	
Accounts Receivable	96,000		102,000	
Merchandise.............	220,000		121,000	
Land	40,000		43,000	
Buildings	200,000		222,000	
Acc. Depr. — Bldgs.........		$ 50,000		$ 48,000
Furniture and Fixtures	80,000		90,000	
Acc. Depr. — F. & F.		22,000		25,000
Trademark	18,000		—	
Notes Payable		60,000		64,000
Accounts Payable..........		134,000		65,000
Bonds Payable		100,000		80,000
Bond Premium		4,000		2,800
Capital Stock		200,000		200,000
Retained Earnings..........		188,000		185,200
	$758,000	$758,000	$670,000	$670,000

Retained Earnings contains a $20,000 charge for dividends as well as the net income figure for the year. The company follows the all-inclusive concept of net income.

Land and buildings were sold during the year for $16,000. The building had a cost of $20,000 and accumulated depreciation of $10,000. A new building was purchased for cash; $8,000 of the price was charged to Land.

The trademark was sold for $25,000.

The change in Premium on Bonds Payable consists of $800 paid on bonds retired and $400 of regular amortization. There was no loss or gain on retirement of the bonds.

Other noncurrent account changes represent one or one type of transaction for the year.

Required:

1. Prepare a funds statement work sheet.
2. Prepare a statement of application of funds and schedule of working-capital changes.

26.6   General ledger trial balances of King Co. as of December 31, 1965 and 1966 appeared as follows:

		December 31		Increase or (Decrease)
Debits		1965	1966	
Cash..........................	$	87,321	$ 173,076	$ 85,755
Accounts Receivable............		95,415	118,524	23,109
Marketable Securities		47,400	53,400	6,000
Inventories		256,287	238,941	(17,346)
Prepaid Expenses		5,862	11,625	5,763
Investment in Subsidiary Companies .		624,000	633,000	9,000
Land.........................		37,548	37,548	–
Buildings.....................		252,582	507,738	255,156
Equipment		411,624	748,071	336,447
Automobiles		58,224	63,627	5,403
Goodwill......................		60,000	45,000	(15,000)
Unamortized Bond Discount and Expense.......................		–	40,950	40,950
		$1,936,263	$2,671,500	

Credits

		1965	1966	
Accounts Payable	$	246,582	$ 285,585	$ 39,003
Loan Payable		52,227	69,813	17,586
First Mortgage Bonds Payable......		300,000	600,000	300,000
Estimated Income Taxes Payable....		17,841	21,867	4,026
Reserve for Contingencies		87,000	105,000	18,000
Allowance for Doubtful Accounts ...		10,950	12,600	1,650
Accumulated Depreciation.........		325,962	411,024	85,062
Capital Stock		600,000	900,000	300,000
Surplus.......................		295,701	265,611	(30,090)
		$1,936,263	$2,671,500	

Your examination discloses the following additional information relating to the year ended December 31, 1966:

(1) Fixed assets were sold during the year at a gain of $5,274, which was included in the income statement. The following amounts were removed from the asset and accumulated depreciation accounts:

	Cost	Accumulated Depreciation
Equipment...........	$10,500	$2,376
Automobile	6,000	1,500

(2) During the year marketable securities were purchased and recorded in the accounts at a cost of $16,500.

(3) A wholly owned subsidiary suffered a loss of $27,000 during the year, provision for which was charged to surplus.

(4) Additional income taxes and interest thereon in respect of 1964, amounting to $4,725, were paid during 1966 and charged to Surplus.

(5) The first-mortgage bonds outstanding at December 31, 1965, were redeemed on July 1, 1966, at 103 and immediately replaced by a new issue of $600,000 5½ percent 20-year first-mortgage bonds, which were sold at 95. Premium on redemption was charged to Surplus.

(6) Expenses of issuing the new bonds amounted to $12,000 and were deferred.

(7) During the year 3,000 6 percent preferred shares were issued at 102½, the premium being credited to Surplus. The expenses of issue amounted to $1,665 and were charged to Surplus.

(8) Dividends of $30,000 were paid during the year.

(9) Legal fees amounting to $6,000 were paid in regard to current litigation and charged to Reserve for Contingencies.

(10) The amortization of goodwill was shown as an expense on the income statement.

Required:

Prepare a funds statement.

(ICAC – adapted)

26.7 Information relating to Royal Co. for the year ended December 31, 1966, follows:

(1) Net income for the year, $240,000.

(2) Fixed asset accounts at the year end were:

	1965	1966
Machinery and Equipment	$1,000,000	$1,160,000
Buildings	500,000	580,000
Land	40,000	50,000
Construction in Progress.	150,000	—
	$1,690,000	$1,790,000
Less: Accumulated Depreciation.	400,000	541,400
	$1,290,000	$1,248,600

(3) Construction in Progress at December 31, 1965, included the cost to date of $40,000 for an addition to the company's main building and $110,000 for equipment in the addition. On completion of the addition in June 1966, the construction costs were transferred to the appropriate accounts.

(4) During 1966, equipment was disposed of as follows:

Turret lathe, purchased in 1961 for $32,000, sold for $10,000
Punch press, purchased in 1964 for $24,000, sold for $20,000
Dynamo, purchased in 1958 for $6,000, abandoned as useless

The adjustments necessary to reflect the disposals have been made, with profits and losses being charged off to operations. Depreciation is always provided annually on a straight line basis at 10 percent on the closing balances in the fixed asset accounts.

(5) A credit of $8,000 appeared in the Buildings account. This represented a refund of an amount billed twice in error during March 1966.

(6) A debit of $7,000 appeared in the Accumulated Depreciation account during the year. This represented the cost of two electric motors. These motors replaced two similar motors purchased twelve years ago for approximately the same cost, which are now fully depreciated.

(7) Cost of buildings includes $14,000 architects' fees, which were paid by the issue of 2,000 no-par-value shares of Royal Co.

(8) The following other transactions also occurred during the year or at the year end:

(a) Allowance for Doubtful Accounts increased by $2,000.

(b) Patent rights purchased for $13,500.

(c) Amortization of patent rights of $2,100.

    (d) Mortgage bonds converted to preferred stock, $25,400.

    (e) Mortgage bonds redeemed, $38,600.

    (f) Franchise agreement acquired through issue of $11,000 mortgage bonds.

Required:

Prepare a funds statement for Royal Co. for the year ended December 31, 1966. Submit details of your calculations.

(ICAC — adapted)

Analysis of
Financial Statements

NATURE AND PURPOSE OF STATEMENT ANALYSIS

Statements are analyzed to bring out significant relationships. Isolated facts are often of little use, but when considered in relation to other facts their significance becomes clear. For example, the fact that a corporation earned $4,000,000 in a given year can scarcely be interpreted in isolation but can be interpreted in the light of the fact that the stockholder investment in the corporation is $400,000,000. The earning may seem large when viewed by itself, but it appears unsatisfactory when it is known to be only 1 percent on the stockholders' investment. Statements are analyzed for significant relationships by the management of the enterprise, by stockholders or other owners, by creditors who extend short-term credit, by bondholders and other long-term creditors, and by prospective investors. Anyone concerned with the financial condition and the operations of a company, including its employees, will use statement analysis. The reliability of the accounting data is so important that audits of the statements by independent accountants are used to assure the adequacy of the data, and the audit is a regular annual procedure with almost all large concerns.

COMPUTATION OF RATIOS

Most computations in statement analysis are ratios. A ratio is obtained by dividing one quantity by another. The divisor is the *base*. When we say the ratio of A to B, we mean the result obtained by dividing A by B. Thus the ratio of 200 to 400 is 0.5. Ratios may be expressed as natural fractions or proportions as well as by decimal fractions. The decimal fraction 0.5 is the same as the natural fraction 2/4 or 1/2 and the proportion 2:4 or 1:2 (read "1 to 2"). Ratios are frequently converted to percents or percentages by multiplying them by 100. Thus the ratio 0.5 is 50 percent. For statement analysis purposes percentages need be carried to only one decimal place.

SUMMARY ANALYSIS OF THE INCOME STATEMENT

There are two aspects of the summary analysis of financial statements:

1. Relationships within one year
2. Year-to-year comparisons

The relationships within a single year are shown in the income statement by expressing each item in the statement as a percent of net sales. This was done in Chapter 2; see the illustration on page 61. See also the illustration on page 753, which presents a comparative income statement analyzed in this way, together with year-to-year comparisons. The effectiveness of the firm's merchandising activity is indicated to a considerable degree by the ratio of gross margin on sales to sales revenue; this indicates whether or not a satisfactory price above the cost of goods sold was obtained. The ratios of various expenses to sales also indicate something of the firm's efficiency; the concern that can obtain satisfactory sales by spending only 5 percent of the sales revenue for advertising, for example, is doing better than one of similar character that must spend 10 percent for advertising. The ratios for a year may be compared with the performance of other firms in the same industry in that year, or with a budget, or with one's own experience over a period. Care must be taken not to place too much reliance on the results of a single year. The percentage analysis of the statement just described is sometimes called a "vertical" analysis because of the vertical arrangement of the figures.

Year-to-year comparisons appear in "comparative" statements. The illustration on page 753 presents the figures for each of two years' operations and is therefore a comparative income statement. The comparison may be left entirely to the reader, in which case only the regular figures of each of the two or more years are presented. The comparison may be facilitated by showing the amount of increase or decrease between years. Since only two years are represented in the illustration, only one column of amounts of increase or decrease appears. The comparison may be further facilitated by presenting the increase or decrease in percent, as the illustration also does. Note that the percent of increase or decrease is obtained by dividing the amount of change by the amount existing in the *earlier* year. This year-to-year comparison is sometimes called a "horizontal" analysis. Comparative statements may be made up for a period of years; in fact, it is considered a very helpful practice to present very condensed comparative statements, especially income statements and related statistics, for a long period. At least one prominent company publishes such a statement that covers several decades.

SUMMARY ANALYSIS OF THE BALANCE SHEET

Summary analysis of the balance sheet follows the same pattern as the summary analysis of the income statement. The analysis for a single balance sheet consists of expressing each of the figures as a percent of the total assets (or of total liabilities and capital). The distribution of assets has significance when compared with that of similar concerns. A concern doing the same business with a smaller proportion of its assets in the fixed category would presumably be in a better position. The distribution of financial interests is more significant, and especially the proportion of liabilities as compared with the proportion of proprietorship. Since liabilities must be paid regardless of the profitability of the business, a large proportion of them represents a less secure position than a small proportion does. A large proportion of short-term debt is also often disadvantageous as compared with less short-term and more long-term debt. The analysis of each of the years in the comparative balance sheet illustrated on page 754 shows the "vertical" analysis of the balance sheet.

COMPARATIVE INCOME STATEMENT WITH SUMMARY ANALYSIS

THE HOOPER COMPANY
Comparative Income Statement
Years ended December 31, 1966 and 1965

	1966		1965		Change	
	Amount	% of net sales	Amount	% of net sales	Increase (De-crease)	%
Sales......................	$800,000	102.2	$760,000	102.2	$40,000	5.3
Sales Returns, Discounts, etc.....	17,000	2.2	16,000	2.2	1,000	6.3
Net Sales................	$783,000	100.0	$744,000	100.0	$39,000	5.2
Cost of Goods Sold..........	470,000	60.0	444,000	59.7	26,000	5.9
Gross Margin on Sales........	$313,000	40.0	$300,000	40.3	$13,000	4.3
Selling Expense..............	$102,000	13.0	$101,000	13.6	$ 1,000	1.0
General Expense.............	58,000	7.4	57,000	7.6	1,000	1.8
Total Operating Expense......	$160,000	20.4	$158,000	21.2	$ 2,000	1.3
Net Operating Income........	$153,000	19.6	$142,000	19.1	$11,000	7.7
Other Income...............	9,000	1.1	8,000	1.1	1,000	12.5
	$162,000	20.7	$150,000	20.2	$12,000	8.0
Other Deductions............	12,000	1.5	14,000	1.9	(2,000)	14.3
Net Income before Income Tax..	$150,000	19.2	$136,000	18.3	$14,000	10.3
Income Taxes...............	72,500	9.3	65,220	8.8	7,280	11.2
Net Income.................	$ 77,500	9.9	$ 70,780	9.5	$ 6,720	9.5

The same illustration also shows the year-to-year analysis of the balance sheet. This is made in the same way as in the income statement. It helps in observing trends that may require action, particularly when a span of several years is covered. For example, if there is a tendency for current assets or total assets to decline, creditors and others will be uneasy. As to these ratios, the year-to-year analysis will be useful chiefly in cases in which income statements are not available, since the reasons for declining assets will probably appear in the income statement.

A tendency for short-term debt to increase while long-term debt and proprietorship were constant or were declining would also be unfavorable. In the case of the Hooper Company, shown in the illustration under discussion, an unsatisfactorily high proportion of current debt in 1965 was changed by issuing additional preferred stock in 1966 that permitted the current debt to be reduced.

The year-to-year analysis is referred to as a "horizontal" analysis in the balance sheet as well as in the income statement.

COMPARATIVE BALANCE SHEET WITH SUMMARY ANALYSIS

THE HOOPER COMPANY
Comparative Balance Sheet

December 31, 1966 and 1965

	1966		1965		Change	
	Amount	% of Total	Amount	% of Total	Increase (De-crease)	%
Assets						
Current Assets:						
Cash................	$ 118,000	9.2	$ 92,000	7.2	$ 26,000	28.3
Accounts Receivable....	224,000	17.4	212,000	16.5	12,000	5.7
Merchandise..........	264,000	20.5	260,000	20.2	4,000	1.5
Prepaid Expense.......	16,000	1.3	14,000	1.1	2,000	14.3
Total current assets...	$ 622,000	48.4	$ 578,000	45.0	$ 44,000	7.6
Fixed assets:						
Land................	$ 40,000	3.1	$ 40,000	3.1	$ —	—
Buildings.............	280,000	21.8	286,000	22.3	(6,000)	2.1
Equipment............	156,000	12.1	176,000	13.7	(20,000)	11.4
Total fixed assets.....	$ 476,000	37.0	$ 502,000	39.1	(26,000)	5.2
Patents..............	$ 187,000	14.6	$ 204,000	15.9	(17,000)	8.3
Total assets........	$1,285,000	100.0	$1,284,000	100.0	$ 1,000	0.1
Liabilities and Capital						
Current Liabilities:						
Notes Payable.........	$ 100,000	7.8	$ 110,000	8.6	(10,000)	9.1
Accounts Payable......	170,000	13.2	279,000	21.7	(109,000)	39.1
Taxes Payable.........	40,000	3.1	35,000	2.7	5,000	14.3
Total Current Liabilities	$ 310,000	24.1	$ 424,000	33.0	(114,000)	26.9
Long-term Liability:						
Bonds Payable........	$ 200,000	15.6	$ 200,000	15.6	—	—
Total Liabilities.......	$ 510,000	39.7	$ 624,000	48.6	(114,000)	18.3
Capital:						
Preferred Stock........	$ 250,000	19.5	$ 150,000	11.7	$ 100,000	66.7
Common Stock.........	300,000	23.3	300,000	23.4	—	—
Retained Earnings......	225,000	17.5	210,000	16.3	15,000	7.1
Total Capital........	$ 775,000	60.3	$ 660,000	51.4	$ 115,000	17.4
Total Liabilities and Capital..........	$1,285,000	100.0	$1,284,000	100.0	$ 1,000	0.1

OTHER SUMMARY ANALYSES

Any financial statement or schedule may be analyzed in the fashion described and illustrated above for the income statement and the balance sheet.

Others commonly analyzed include the statement of retained earnings, combined statements of income and retained earnings, and schedules of cost of goods sold.

OTHER RATIOS

Many useful calculations and comparisons may be made between figures on opposite sides of the balance sheet and between figures on the balance sheet and those in the income statement. Most ratios are of interest to more than one group of persons and most of them have significance for different decisions. A great variety of ratios is available and one should choose those that appear useful and significant in each case. The ratios discussed in the remainder of this chapter may be conveniently classified according to their primary significance as follows:

1. Solvency ratios (primarily concerned with the ability of the firm to meet its debts):

    (a) Working-capital or current ratio
    (b) Acid-test ratio
    (c) Ratio of long-term debt to capital
    (d) Ratio of fixed assets to long-term debt
    (e) Times interest earned

2. Efficiency ratios or earning-power ratios:

    (a) Inventory turnover
    (b) Turnover and analysis of receivables
    (c) Other turnovers
    (d) Book value per share of stock
    (e) Earnings per share of stock
    (f) Times dividends earned
    (g) Rate of return on total assets
    (h) Rate of return on proprietorship

These ratios will be illustrated with data from the statements of the Hooper Company given on pages 753 and 754, and with such supplementary information as is needed.

WORKING-CAPITAL OR CURRENT RATIO

This ratio is computed by the following formula:

$$\frac{\text{current assets}}{\text{current liabilities}} = \text{working-capital ratio}$$

In the case of the Hooper Company for 1966 it is:

$$\frac{\$622,000}{\$310,000} = 2.0, \text{ or } 2 \text{ to } 1$$

The working-capital ratio is usually expressed as a proportion; in this case, 2 to 1. Also called the current ratio, it has traditionally been used to measure the concern's ability to meet its short-term debts. It was perhaps more important fifty years ago than today, because financing on a short-term basis with bank loans represented a larger proportion of the business financing then than now. In the intervening decades many businesses have obtained capital by retaining earnings, and for this and other reasons the relative importance of short-term loans is less. However, the ratio is still important to anyone extending short-term credit. The ratio indicates the ability of the concern to absorb losses for a period (which usually reduce current assets) and still have enough current assets to meet the debts. The ratio really refers to the possibility of liquidation, as only in liquidation would the current assets be taken by a creditor and collected or sold to meet the debts. The proportion of 2 to 1 has been a popular rule of thumb or standard for this ratio. It means that current assets could shrink one half in liquidation and still meet the current debts. Concerns that have steady earnings, such as public utilities, do not have to be concerned about maintaining an excess of current assets over current liabilities, since a steady stream of revenue permits the bills to be met regularly regardless of the size of the working capital. Partial liquidation from a serious drop in revenues and full liquidation by action of creditors are both remote possibilities in these cases. Because the significance of the working-capital ratio rests in the possibility of liquidation, most analysts exclude from the current asset group any item that does not give rise to cash rather directly or which cannot be fairly readily sold. Such items consist most frequently of prepaid expenses.

ACID-TEST RATIO

This ratio is a more stringent measure of the same character as the working-capital ratio. It is computed as follows:

$$\frac{\text{cash} + \text{receivables} + \text{marketable securities}}{\text{current liabilities}} = \text{acid-test ratio}$$

For the Hooper Company, in 1966 it was:

$$\frac{\$118,000 + \$224,000}{\$310,000} = \frac{\$342,000}{\$310,000} = 1.1 \text{ to } 1$$

This ratio has the same significance as the current ratio but is a more severe "test" of the solvency of the concern.

RATIO OF LONG-TERM DEBT TO CAPITAL

This ratio compares the investment of the long-term creditors with that of the stockholders or proprietors. It is computed as

$$\frac{\text{long-term debt}}{\text{capital (proprietorship)}} = \text{ratio of long-term debt to capital}$$

For the Hooper Company, in 1966 it is:

$$\frac{\$200,000}{\$775,000} = 0.26 \text{ or } 26 \text{ percent}$$

In this case long-term debt is about one-fourth as much as the capital or proprietary investment. For most industries this would be a favorable condition. Presumably a reasonable return can be earned on the total amount invested in a permanent or semipermanent way by the long-term creditors and owners. A small proportion of debt means that a drop in this earning power probably would not reduce income so much that interest on the debt could not be paid. A similar statistic is available in the summary analysis of the balance sheet; this gives the proportions of the total financial interests represented by long-term debt and proprietorship.

FIXED-ASSET-TO-LONG-TERM-DEBT RATIO

Fixed-asset-to-long-term-debt ratio is calculated by this formula:

$$\frac{\text{fixed assets}}{\text{long-term debt}} = \text{ratio of fixed assets to long-term debt}$$

For the Hooper Company, in 1966 it was:

$$\frac{\$476,000}{\$200,000} = 2.4 \text{ or } 2.4 \text{ to } 1$$

Sometimes long-term debt is secured by the fixed assets by means of a mortgage. In any case the fixed assets represent a permanent and tangible portion of the investment that can be reached by creditors in case of bankruptcy of the concern. This ratio indicates the extent to which the fixed assets could shrink in liquidation and still meet the long-term obligations. There are some "ifs" in this connection; for example, short-term debt may increase as a concern gets into difficulty. In this event the long-term debt may not be as secure as its relation to fixed assets would indicate. One may also think of the fixed assets as the major source of earning power to meet the interest on the long-term debt, but data on the earning power can be better obtained from the income statement.

TIMES INTEREST EARNED

A good indication of the ability of the concern to meet its interest obligations and therefore to stay out of bankruptcy is the number of times its earnings cover its interest requirements. The formula is:

$$\frac{\text{net income before interest}}{\text{interest requirements}} = \text{times interest earned}$$

Note that interest is deductible for income tax purposes; if interest takes all the income available before interest and tax, there is no tax. Note also that the interest requirements are often computed only for long-term debt, in which case the ratio may be expressed as "times fixed charges earned." This plan is all right if short-term interest-bearing obligations are transitory or insignificant. Otherwise they should be included, since a short-term creditor can foreclose as well as a long-term creditor can. In the case of the Hooper Company, the 1966 interest on the notes payable was $3,000 and on the bonds was $8,000, a total of $11,000. When this figure is added back to the net income before income tax, we get $150,000 + $11,000 = $161,000, the income before interest and income tax. The times interest is earned in 1966 is then calculated as:

$$\frac{\$161,000}{\$\ 11,000} = 14.6 \text{ times}$$

In this year at least, income could have been much smaller without endangering the ability to pay interest. One must not assume, however, that business could fall off to one fourteenth of its 1966 level without endangering interest payments; the elements of income do not move uniformly. A decline in sales by one half might leave the company with a large loss and make interest payments impossible. Also note that interest can often be paid for some time out of assets even though current income is unsatisfactory.

INVENTORY TURNOVER

Efficiency is well indicated by the summary analysis of the income statement, but other ways of measuring it are available. A prominent one is the inventory turnover. This gives the number of times that the average investment in merchandise (or finished goods, work in process, and materials) is sold during a year. The formula is:

$$\frac{\text{cost of goods sold}}{\text{average inventory}} = \text{inventory turnover}$$

For the Hooper Company, in 1966 the average inventory was:

Beginning	$260,000
Ending	264,000
Together	$524,000
Average	$262,000

The inventory turnover was:

$$\frac{\$470,000}{\$262,000} = 1.8 \text{ times}$$

In most industries 1.8 times would be slow; in jewelry stores selling expensive gems it would be good. Management often computes turnovers on individual items of stock to check on the amount carried; if turnover is slow the amount carried is reduced. This ratio, like many others, is most useful when computed over a series of periods and when compared with the performance of other firms.

Many concerns close their books at the end of their seasonal cycle (a desirable practice). Inventories at this date are typically at their low point for the year. and a turnover computed from them alone is higher than actually exists for the year. A more accurate ratio is obtained by averaging the inventories existing at the end of each month during the year.

TURNOVER AND ANALYSIS OF ACCOUNTS RECEIVABLE

Accounts receivable turnover, or number of times the average accounts receivable balance is collected during the year, is calculated by this formula:

$$\frac{\text{net sales on account}}{\text{average accounts receivable}} = \text{accounts receivable turnover}$$

The Hooper Company sells on credit exclusively; its accounts receivable turnover in 1966 was:

$$\frac{\$783,000}{(\$212,000 + \$224,000) \div 2} = \frac{\$783,000}{\$218,000} = 3.6 \text{ times}$$

The comment made about inventory turnover applies here also; a more accurate figure is obtained by using the average of the accounts receivable balances of the twelve months.

Another way of looking at this measure of efficiency is to recognize that the average balance of accounts receivable can be expressed as the sales of so many months; in this case:

$$\frac{1}{3.6} \times 12 = 3.33 = 3\frac{1}{3} \text{ months}$$

This is a rather long collection period; one and one-half months' sales would be favorable in most cases.

A similar computation often used is the number of days' sales on the books at a particular date. The formula is:

$$\frac{\text{accounts receivable}}{\text{average net sales per day}} = \text{number of days' sales on the books}$$

For Hooper, at December 31, 1966, it was:

$$\frac{\$224,000}{\$783,000 \div 365} = \frac{\$224,000}{\$2,145.2} = 104.4 \text{ days' sales}$$

The aging of accounts receivable that is especially helpful in assessing collectibility was discussed in Chapter 9. This analysis may be made available to creditors also.

OTHER TURNOVERS

Turnovers of various assets or asset groups are sometimes computed, such as turnover of current assets and turnover of fixed assets. These are computed by dividing the amount of the asset or group of assets into sales. These turnovers are not of the same kind as an inventory turnover, because the other assets are not sold; the calculations are simply ways of comparing certain assets with sales. The same purpose would be served by reversing the computation and dividing the amount of the asset *by* sales instead of dividing it *into* sales. Such computations enable analysts to make comparisons between periods and between firms. A concern that can preserve a sales level with fixed assets equal to one fourth the sales (a fixed-asset "turnover" of 4) is more efficient in its use of the fixed assets than one that uses fixed assets equal to one half the sales, other things being equal. In making such computations, the average balance of the asset for the period should be used, as in the case of the inventory turnover. The term "turnover" is not very appropriate in these cases; a term such as "ratio of sales to fixed assets" should be substituted.

BOOK VALUE PER SHARE OF STOCK

The book value per share of stock is computed to determine the amount of investment represented by each share of stock. This figure is calculated chiefly as a base for comparison with earnings or dividends per share. It is obtained by dividing the number of shares outstanding for each class of stock into the proprietorship figure for it. The formula is:

$$\frac{\left(\begin{array}{c}\text{proprietorship applicable} \\ \text{to the class of stock}\end{array}\right)}{\left(\begin{array}{c}\text{number of shares of} \\ \text{the class outstanding}\end{array}\right)} = \left(\begin{array}{c}\text{book value per share} \\ \text{for the class}\end{array}\right)$$

Where only one class of stock exists, the total figure for capital or proprietorship is used. Where there are two or more classes of stock, the capital must be divided between them. The basis for this division is what each class would get in case of liquidation of the company. If there is preferred stock with a par value, it presumably would be paid at par value plus any cumulative dividends in arrears. Sometimes preferred stock gets a premium in case of liquidation, under terms of its contract. Including the cumulative dividends in arrears and any premium has the effect of assigning a part of the retained earnings to the preferred stock; aside from these possibilities, all the retained earnings and any other "surplus" go to the "residual equity" or common stock. If the preferred is no-par-value stock, a liquidation value is ordinarily stated in the contract and this is substituted for par value in the book-value computation. After the total book value of preferred stock is calculated, this figure is deducted from the total capital to get the total book value of common. Book value per share is obtained by dividing these figures by the number of shares of each class outstanding.

The Hooper Company has 2,500 shares of preferred stock of $100 par value, there are no dividends in arrears, and it is entitled to no premium in liquidation, so the book value of this stock is $100 per share, $250,000 total. The company had 15,000 shares of common stock outstanding on December 31, 1966, and the book value of this stock was:

$$\frac{\$300,000 + \$225,000}{15,000} = \frac{\$525,000}{15,000} = \$35.00 \text{ per share}$$

EARNINGS PER SHARE OF STOCK

Total net income may be divided by the number of shares outstanding. The formula for earnings per share of preferred is:

$$\frac{\text{net income}}{\text{number of preferred shares outstanding}} = \left(\begin{array}{c}\text{income per share of}\\ \text{preferred stock}\end{array}\right)$$

In the case of the Hooper Company the preferred stock pays $6 per share, and 2,500 shares have been outstanding in 1966. The net income of $77,500 represents earnings per preferred share of:

$$\frac{\$77,500}{2,500} = \$31.00$$

This gives a wide margin of safety over the $6 dividend.

The earnings per share of common are calculated as the net income less the preferred dividend requirement. The formula for earnings per share of common is:

$$\frac{\text{net income less preferred dividends}}{\text{number of common shares outstanding}} = \left(\begin{array}{c}\text{earnings per share of}\\ \text{common stock}\end{array}\right)$$

For Hooper, in 1966 (15,000 shares outstanding) the computation is:

Net income	$77,500
Preferred dividend requirement	15,000
Available to common	$62,500

$$\frac{\$62,500}{15,000} = \$4.17 \text{ per common share}$$

This figure is compared with the book value per share to determine how effectively the investment of the common stockholder has been used to produce income. It is also compared with the market value of the stock as a check on the value established by traders for the stock and to find what return one can get by investing in this issue. Of course, not all the net income is paid out in dividends, and investors are concerned about the dividends they can expect. For this information they refer to dividends recently paid plus any data, such as increasing earnings, indicating that a change might be made.

TIMES DIVIDENDS EARNED

When a stock pays dividends regularly a computation similar to the "times interest earned" may be made for dividends. For preferred stock the formula is:

$$\frac{\text{net income}}{\text{preferred dividend}} = \text{times preferred dividend earned}$$

For Hooper, in 1966 this is (dividends are $6 per share on 2,500 shares):

$$\frac{\$77,500}{\$15,000} = 5.2 \text{ times}$$

The formula for common dividends is:

$$\frac{\text{net income less preferred dividend}}{\text{common dividend}} = \left(\begin{array}{c}\text{times common}\\\text{dividend earned}\end{array}\right)$$

The Hooper Company in 1966 earned its common dividend of $3 per share 1.4 times:

$$\frac{\$77,500 - \$15,000}{\$45,000} = 1.4$$

RATE OF RETURN ON TOTAL ASSETS

The rate of return on total assets may be calculated in two ways. The first method is an "after tax" method and the second one is a "before tax" computation. The formulas are:

$$\frac{\text{net income} + \text{interest}}{\text{average total assets}} = \left(\begin{array}{c}\text{rate of return on}\\\text{total assets}\end{array}\right) \quad (1)$$

$$\frac{\text{net income} + \text{interest} + \text{income tax}}{\text{average total assets}} = \left(\begin{array}{c}\text{rate of return on}\\\text{total assets}\end{array}\right) \quad (2)$$

The rate is expressed as a percentage. The Hooper Company in 1966 earned these rates as calculated under the two methods:

$$\frac{77,500 + 11,000}{(1,284,000 + 1,285,000) \div 2} = \frac{88,500}{1,284,500} = 6.9\% \quad (1)$$

$$\frac{77,500 + 11,000 + 72,500}{(1,284,000 + 1,285,000) \div 2} = \frac{161,000}{1,284,500} = 12.5\% \quad (2)$$

The interest is added back to net income to get the earnings before any payment is made to those who furnished the assets, regardless of whether they are creditors or owners. This formula also puts the computation on the same basis for all companies, regardless of their capital structures, and makes the rate comparable from one year to another within one concern as the capital structure of the concern changes. The interest added back is usually the interest on long-term debt alone, but where interest on short-term debt is significant, as in the case of the Hooper Company, it should be included.

Method 1, which uses the income available after income taxes are deducted, has the advantage of showing the amount finally retained to compensate the people who furnished assets. Method 2, which uses income available before income tax is deducted, has the advantage of removing the effects of variations in tax rates. These occur between companies because of the use of a graduated tax and between years because of changes made in the law.

The rate of return on total assets is a fundamental indication of earning power and therefore one of the most important ratios.

RATE OF RETURN ON PROPRIETORSHIP

The rate of return on proprietorship, capital, or stockholders' equity is computed as follows:

$$\frac{\text{net income}}{\text{proprietorship}} = \text{rate of return on proprietorship}$$

This ratio is usually expressed as a percent. The Hooper Company had the following rate in 1966:

$$\frac{\$\ 77,500}{\$775,000} = 10\%$$

This ratio shows the profitability of the stockholders' investment and is a major guide to investors. It reflects the effect of any leverage due to debt in the capital structure of the corporation. Leverage exists when a lower rate than is earned on the whole investment is paid to some investors — bondholders and other creditors.[1] In the case of the Hooper Company, the after-tax earnings on total assets were 6.9 percent. Because only 3 percent was paid to the holders of the notes payable and only 4 percent to the bondholders, the stockholder investment had a return of 10 percent.

A similar computation may be made for the common stockholders alone; the 1966 return to them in the Hooper case is:

$$\frac{77,500 - 15,000}{300,000 + 225,000} = \frac{62,500}{525,000} = 11.9\%$$

The 15,000 is the preferred stock dividend requirement.

CAUTIONS FOR USING FINANCIAL STATEMENT RATIOS

Ratios must be used with care against erroneous or superficial interpretation. The following precautions are fundamental:

1. Look out for effects due to changes in accounting methods. A smaller inventory with the same cost of goods sold looks favorable, but if it is due to switching from fifo to lifo no improvement in inventory management may be indicated.

2. See that results are not due to nonrecurring transactions. If net income is up because a patent was sold at a large gain, there is no indication that the company's general earning power has improved.

3. Interpret particular cases with reference to general business conditions. A doubling of net income is impressive unless most firms have been able to triple net income.

4. Look out for the effects of price-level changes and related effects. A concern that had twice as much working capital in 1966 as in 1946 evidently had not increased the purchasing power and therefore the usefulness of its working capital at all; it had merely reflected the change in price levels. Also, a firm that bought its equipment in 1966 will have higher depreciation expense under conventional accounting methods than will a firm that bought its equipment in 1956.

[1] Leverage may also exist between preferred and common stockholders.

5. Be careful about drawing conclusions from the data of one year alone. Data of several years are more reliable and trends are significant.

SUMMARY

Financial statements are analyzed to bring out significant relationships. Relationships within individual statements of one year are revealed to an important degree by the summary analysis that expresses each item as a percentage of a suitable base ("vertical" analysis). This is net sales in the income statement and total assets in the balance sheet.

Another set of useful relationships is given in comparative statements, where the change from year to year may be computed and expressed as a ratio of the earlier year ("horizontal" analysis).

Other ratios may be calculated with the use of different figures in a single statement or figures from different kinds of statements. For example, average inventory from the balance sheet may be divided into cost of goods sold from the income statement to get inventory turnover.

Precautions in using financial-statement ratios involve watching for changes in accounting methods, nonrecurring transactions, relationship to general conditions, price-level changes, and need to avoid relying on only one year's data.

QUESTIONS

27.1 Financial statements present many important facts for the information of owners, managers, creditors, and investors. What is added by analysis of the statements?

27.2 What base is used in the summary analysis of a balance sheet for a single year?

27.3 What is the base for the summary analysis of the income statement for a single year?

27.4 Describe what is meant by a comparative financial statement. What kind of summary analysis is possible when comparative statements are given?

27.5 Classify the following ratios as useful primarily to measure solvency or efficiency:
(1) Inventory turnover
(2) Number of days' sales in accounts receivable
(3) Acid test
(4) Rate of return on total assets
(5) Current ratio
(6) Earnings per share of stock

27.6 "The significance of the working-capital ratio lies in a liquidation concept." Explain this statement.

27.7 What danger is indicated by a high ratio of long-term debt to capital or proprietorship? Explain.

27.8 "Interest on this issue was earned 16 times in the past year." Explain this statement.

27.9 "We were going to reduce our stocks because our inventory turnover was too slow, but we adopted a higher selling-price policy and our turnover dropped, so we have not reduced stocks." Criticize this position. What fact would you want to investigate before being certain your criticism was justified?

27.10 "We had a plant turnover of 3 times in the last year and 2½ times the year before last." What is the meaning of this statement? Is it true in the same sense that a statement about inventory turnover can be true?

27.11 Dalman Company has dividends of $80,000 in arrears on its cumulative preferred stock. Its Retained Earnings account has a balance of $200,000. The preferred stock consists of 10,000 shares of par value $100 each and is entitled to a premium of $4 per share in liquidation. Common stock consists of 20,000 no-par shares with a stated value of $40 per share. There are no other capital accounts. What is the book value per share of the preferred stock? What is the book value per share of the common stock?

27.12 Holman, Inc., had a net income of $400,000 in the past fiscal year. It has 15,000 shares of $6 preferred stock and 10,000 shares of common stock outstanding. The common dividend is $10.
(1) What were the earnings per share of preferred?
(2) What were the earnings per share of common?
(3) How many times was the preferred dividend earned?
(4) How many times was the common dividend earned?

27.13 (1) What ratio can you suggest as a fundamental measure of the efficiency of a company in producing net income? What advantages does it have? (2) What fundamental ratio can you suggest as a basis for the decision to buy or not to buy a particular stock? (Disregard the factor of market price).

27.14 What cautions should be observed in using financial-statement ratios?

EXERCISES

27.1 The financial statements of the Morningside Company at December 31 contain the following data:

	1966	1965
Cash. . . . . $	20,000	$ 20,000
Marketable Securities	10,000	30,000
Accounts Receivable.	150,000	60,000
Merchandise Inventories	240,000	70,000
Current Liabilities	200,000	100,000
Sales.	1,000,000	600,000
Cost of Goods Sold.	650,000	360,000

Required:

1. Calculate for both 1966 and 1965 (a) the amount of working capital, (b) the current ratio, (c) the acid-test ratio, (d) the average day's sales on the books at December 31 (assuming a 365-day year and all sales on a credit basis), and (e) the merchandise turnover (the merchandise inventory on January 1, 1965, was $50,000).
2. Evaluate each of the above.

27.2 Summarized financial data for the Kensington Manufacturing Company appear below.

Income data for years ended December 31, in thousands of dollars:

	1966	1965	1964
Net Sales	$5,460	$3,130	$2,410
Cost of Goods Sold	3,559	2,046	1,581
Gross Margin	$1,901	$1,084	$ 829
Operating Expenses	1,622	919	701
Net Income	$ 279	$ 165	$ 128

Balance sheet data at December 31, in thousands of dollars:

	1966	1965	1964
Total Assets....................	$3,032	$1,739	$1,150
Total Liabilities	958	704	560

Required:

1. Calculate for each year (a) the percent of net income to sales, (b) the ratio of sales to total assets, (c) the rate of return on total assets, (d) the ratio of total liabilities to total assets, (e) the rate of return on proprietorship, and (f) the percent of gross margin to sales.
2. Evaluate each of the above ratios.

27.3 The comparative financial statements of the Donner Company for December 31, 1966 and 1965, show, in thousands of dollars:

	Years Ended December 31	
	1966	1965
Net Operating Income[a]................	$1,400	$1,000
Bond Interest........................	200	200
Net Income Before Income Taxes.........	$1,200	$ 800
Income Taxes........................	624	416
Net Income	$ 576	$ 384

	As of December 31	
	1966	1965
Fixed Assets	$6,400	$8,000
4% Bonds Payable	5,000	5,000
6% Preferred Stock, no par[b]	1,000	1,000
Common Stock $20 par	5,000	4,000
Retained Earnings....................	1,516	2,000

[a] After depreciation of $1,600,000 in 1966 and $2,000,000 in 1965.
[b] Preferred as to assets on liquidation at $110 a share, 10,000 shares issued and outstanding.

Required:

1. Compute for 1966 and 1965 (a) times fixed charges earned, (b) ratio of bonded debt to fixed assets, (c) ratio of cash flow (net operating income plus income taxes) to fixed charges, (d) net income per share of common stock, and (e) book value per share of common stock. (Assume that the data above includes all the material elements for purposes of the computations.)
2. Evaluate the ratios.

27.4 The R. B. Dollar Corporation had a current ratio of 2.4 to 1 and a book value per share of $125. What is the separate effect of each of the following transactions on (a) the current ratio and (b) book value per share?
  (1) Declared a cash dividend due in one month.
  (2) Paid the cash dividend.
  (3) Declared and issued a dividend of one share of Southwest Pacific Lines (a wholly owned subsidiary) for each share of R. B. Dollar Corporation.
  (4) Received a stock dividend, not previously recorded, on stock in another company.
  (5) Wrote off a known uncollectible account against Allowance for Bad Debts.
  (6) Paid merchandise creditors on account.

(7) Bought merchandise on credit.
(8) Stockholders donated 10 percent of their shares to the corporation.
(9) The company purchased treasury shares, $100 par, at $120 per share.
(10) The company purchased treasury shares, $100 par, at $130 per share.

27.5 The credit manager of Burlington Floor Coverings has been asked to analyze the financial statements of two applicants for an exclusive distributorship in a proposed new marketing area. Burlington can accept only one company. It plans to invest in the distributor and to extend it a line of credit. Condensed balance sheets at December 31, 1966, are as follows:

	Company X	Company Y
Cash	$ 16,500	$ 31,000
Accounts Receivable	58,000	30,000
Inventories	85,500	30,500
Plant and Equipment	120,000	128,500
Accumulated Depreciation	(80,000)	(20,000)
	$200,000	$200,000
Current Liabilities	$ 80,000	$ 61,000
Long-Term Debt, 8%	50,000	5,000
Capital	70,000	134,000
	$200,000	$200,000

No significant changes in individual assets or liabilities took place during the year.

Condensed income statements for the year ended December 31, 1966, are as follows:

	Company X	Company Y
Sales	$358,000	$365,000
Cost of Goods Sold	257,760	248,200
Gross Margin on Sales	$100,240	$116,800
Operating Expenses	78,760	76,700
Net Operating Income	$ 21,480	$ 40,100
Interest Expense	4,000	400
Net Income before Income Taxes	$ 17,480	$ 39,700
Income Taxes	5,200	12,000
Net Income	$ 12,280	$ 27,700

All sales are on account; there are only minor seasonal variations in sales.

Required:

1. Compare the current debt-paying ability of the two companies. (*Suggestion*: Compute the current ratios, acid-test ratios, days' sales in receivables, and days' costs of goods sold in inventories.)
2. Compare the operating profitability of the two companies. What factors account for the difference? (*Suggestion*: Compute the gross margins on sales, operating expense ratios, net operating income ratios, rates of turnover of total assets, and percents of net operating income to total assets.)
3. Compare the long-term debt-paying ability of the two companies. (*Suggestion*: Compute the times interest earned, ratios of long-term debt to net plant, ratios of long-term debt to capital, and ratios of net income to capital.)
4. What is your recommendation?

27.6   The Provident Insurance Company has been approached by the Kelso Manufacturing Corporation for a direct placement loan for the purpose of expanding the operations. Kelso has at this time total assets of $20,000,000 and is requesting a 10-year 5 percent serial loan of $10,000,000. The analyst for Provident, who has reviewed the expansion plans of Kelso, reports that they appear sound and that the market for the product seems adequate to absorb the increased output at favorable prices. The analyst submits the following ratios from the statements of the Kelso Corporation for the years 1964, 1965, and 1966:

	1964	1965	1966
Current	2.1 to 1	1.7 to 1	1.4 to 1
Gross margin	31%	33%	34%
Inventory turnover	8	7	6
Selling expenses	16%	17%	19%
Stockholders' equity	40%	42%	32%

Required:

1. Indicate the formula for each of the above ratios.
2. Indicate for each ratio whether the trend exhibited is favorable or unfavorable. Explain.
3. Explain the significance of the changes in the stockholders' equity ratio and indicate the probable cause for the change between (a) 1964 and 1965, and (b) 1965 and 1966.

(CPCU — adapted)

27.7   Robert Jones, a wealthy friend, has informed you that he plans to invest in the common stock of either A Co. or B Co., two unrelated companies. He has asked you to assist him in deciding which company he should choose. He has provided the following condensed comparative financial statements for the past four years:

BALANCE SHEETS
As of December 31
(in thousands of dollars)

	A CO.				B CO.			
	1966	1965	1964	1963	1966	1965	1964	1963
Current Assets	$185	$165	$155	$140	$480	$450	$410	$381
Current Liabilities	160	135	130	110	272	251	170	180
	$ 25	$ 30	$ 25	$ 30	$208	$199	$240	$201
Fixed Assets less Depreciation	535	397	392	378	599	603	572	601
	$560	$427	$417	$408	$807	$802	$812	$802
Bonds Outstanding:								
6%, due 1985	$120	—	—	—				
5½%, due 1982					$400	$400	$400	$400
Common Stock:								
5% cumulative preferred — par value $1	200	$200	$200	$200	200	200	200	200
Common — par value $1	100	100	100	100	50	50	50	50
Retained Earnings	140	127	117	108	157	152	162	152
	$560	$427	$417	$408	$807	$802	$812	$802

INCOME STATEMENTS
FOR YEARS ENDED DECEMBER 31
(in thousands of dollars)

	A CO.				B CO.			
	1966	1965	1964	1963	1966	1965	1964	1963
Sales................	$600	$540	$528	$516	$330	$220	$320	$270
Cost of Sales (excluding Depreciation)	460	430	420	410	105	75	100	90
	$140	$110	$108	$106	$225	$145	$220	$180
Variable Expenses.......	$ 25	$ 20	$ 17	$ 16	$ 15	$ 12	$ 12	$ 10
Fixed Expenses.........	45	30	33	34	140	143	148	146
Income Tax............	35	30	29	28	30	–	30	12
	$105	$ 80	$ 79	$ 78	$185	$155	$190	$168
Net Income (Loss) for Year	$ 35	$ 30	$ 29	$ 28	$ 40	$(10)	$ 30	$ 12
Dividends Paid – Preferred	$ 10	$ 10	$ 10	$ 10	$ 20	–	$ 10	$ 10
Dividends Paid – Common .	12	10	10	10	15	–	10	–

The following additional information is also available:

(1) Although both companies manufacture and sell the same type of commodity, B Co.'s product is much more luxurious and commands a far greater price than A Co.'s product.
(2) A Co. carried out an extensive plant expansion in 1966; as a result, productive capacity has been increased by 50 percent. In 1965, production was 95 percent of capacity. To date, B Co. has not operated at greater than 65 percent of capacity.
(3) Current stock market quotations for common shares are: A Co., $2.60; B Co., $5.

Required:

List, with an outline explanation, the features of both companies that you would bring to Jones's attention in assisting him to decide which of the companies he should invest in. Include such calculations as are necessary to support your answer.

(ICAC – adapted)

27.8 Shortly after taking up your new appointment as controller of the Trans-Canada Tank Mfg. Co., Inc., you receive the following memorandum from Lyle Morgan, the owner of the company:

(1) Attached are the company's most recent financial statements.
(2) Although the profit picture for the year seems satisfactory, it is my impression that our financial position is not as healthy as is desirable.
(3) I have been asked to quote a selling price on a number of tank installations which could, if proceeded with, double present manufacturing volume. By working two shifts rather than one, as at present, we could handle the increased volume with existing plant facilities.
(4) I am unable to make further cash advances to the company.
(5) Would you prepare a memorandum commenting on the company's financial position and the desirability of quoting on the installations mentioned in paragraph 3?

Additional information:

(1) Prior to incorporation four years ago, the business was owned and operated by Morgan as a proprietorship, with sales of approximately $500,000 annually.

(2) The company manufactures petroleum tanks which are (a) sold for cash, (b) sold on terms of ninety days, (c) sold under conditional sales contracts, or (d) sold under lease-purchase agreements. Some tanks are also constructed for rental for periods ranging from one month to many years.

(3) Construction of tanks is normally undertaken only after a sales contract or rental contract for at least thirty-six months is signed.

(4) As security for bank borrowing, the company has assigned its accounts receivable, while Morgan has personally guaranteed the loans and agreed to postpone his claims against the company.

(5) The statements of source and application of funds for 1964 and 1965 show a marked similarity to the statement for 1966. The following are identical: (a) advances from shareholders, (b) reduction of mortgage on building, and (c) reduction of mortgage on rental storage tanks.

TRANS-CANADA TANK MFG. CO., INC.

BALANCE SHEET
As of December 31, 1966

Assets

Current Assets:			
Cash on Hand.			$ 2,000
Accounts and Finance Contracts Receivable:			
Trade Accounts	$272,000		
Finance Contracts (due within one year)	56,000		
	$328,000		
Less: Allowance for Doubtful Accounts	37,000		291,000
Inventories:			
Raw Materials	$120,000		
Work in Progress	465,000		
Finished Goods	77,000		662,000
Prepaid Expenses			17,000
			$ 972,000
Finance Contracts Receivable.	$284,000		
Less: Contracts (due within one year—above)	56,000		228,000

Fixed Assets:	Cost	Acc. Depr.	
Land.	$ 45,000		
Plant and Equipment	223,000	$ 82,000	
Automotive Equipment	26,000	17,000	
Office Equipment and Fixtures	30,000	14,000	
Storage Tanks and Fittings	1,730,000	860,000	
	$2,054,000	$973,000	1,081,000
			$2,281,000

Liabilities and Shareholders' Equity

Current Liabilities:

Due to Bank – Demand Loans		$ 430,000
Estimated Income Taxes Payable		213,000
Accounts Payable		134,000
Accrued Liabilities		29,000
		$ 806,000
Mortgage Payable (due June 30, 1971)		43,000
Due to Shareholder		373,000

Capital Stock and Retained Earnings:

Capital Stock:

Authorized, issued and fully paid 10,000 shares of no par value		$ 10,000	

Retained Earnings:

Balance as of January 1, 1966. . . . $771,000			
Add: Net Income for year ended December 31, 1966.	278,000	1,049,000	1,059,000
			$2,281,000

TRANS-CANADA TANK MFG. CO., INC.
STATEMENT OF PROFIT AND LOSS
Year Ended December 31, 1966

Sales:

Tanks and Fittings			$1,498,000

Cost of Sales:

Inventory of Finished Goods, January 1, 1966 . . . $	46,000		
Add:			
Transfer of tanks from fixed assets at undepreciated cost . . . . $	100,000		
Manufacturing costs for year (including plant depreciation of $12,000)	1,772,000	1,872,000	
		$1,918,000	
Deduct:			
Cost of tanks constructed for rental transferred to fixed assets . . . . . $	486,000		
Inventory of Finished Goods December 31, 1966	77,000	563,000	1,355,000
Gross Margin on Sales			$ 143,000

Other Income:

Tank Rental		$1,062,000	
Finance Contract Interest		20,000	1,082,000
Gross Operating Income.			$1,225,000
General, Admin., & Selling Expenses. . . . . $		400,000	
Interest Expense		20,000	
Depreciation:			
Admin. Bldg. & Equip. . . . . $	19,000		
Automotive Equipment.	3,000		
Rental Storage Tanks	241,000	263,000	683,000
Net Income before Income Taxes.			$ 542,000
Provision for Taxes on Income			264,000
Net Income for year.			$ 278,000

TRANS-CANADA TANK MFG. CO., INC.
STATEMENT OF SOURCE AND APPLICATION OF FUNDS
Year Ended December 31, 1966

Source of Funds:
Profits from Operations:

Net Income for Year	$278,000	
Add: Depreciation	275,000	$553,000
Mortgage on Building Extension		43,000
Advances from Shareholder		100,000
Proceeds from Sales of Fixed Assets and Transfers to Inventory		109,000
		$805,000

Application of Funds:

Retirement of Mortgage on Building	$ 10,000
Increase in Finance Contracts Receivable (due after one year)	75,000
Increase in Investment in Fixed Assets	561,000
Retirement of Mortgage on Rental Storage Tanks	104,000
Increase in Working Capital	55,000
	$805,000

TRANS-CANADA TANK MFG. CO., INC.
STATEMENT OF CHANGE IN WORKING CAPITAL
Year Ended December 31, 1966

Increase in Accounts and Finance Contracts Receivable		$25,000
Increase in Inventories — Raw Materials	$ 5,000	
Work in Progress	50,000	
Finished Goods	10,000	65,000
Increase in Prepaid Expenses		5,000
		$95,000
Deduct: Increase in Bank Overdraft	$10,000	
Increase in Bank Loans	50,000	
Increase in Income Taxes Payable	25,000	
	$85,000	
Less: Decrease in Accounts Payable	45,000	40,000
Increase in Working Capital		$55,000

Required:

Outline the points that you would cover in the memorandum to Morgan. Detailed schedules are not necessary.

(ICAC — adapted)

PROBLEMS

27.1 The following amounts are taken from the balance sheet of the Zone Company:

Cash	$19,000
Accounts Receivable	31,000
Merchandise	44,000
Accounts Payable	30,000

Notes Payable.	15,000
Bonds Payable	30,000
Capital Stock	50,000
Retained Earnings	36,000
Fixed Assets.	67,000

The company had 10,000 shares of capital stock outstanding.

Required:

Compute (1) working-capital ratio; (2) acid-test ratio; (3) long-term debt to capital ratio; (4) book value per share.

27.2 Following is the income statement for the Zone Co.:

Sales		$500,000
Cost of Goods Sold		300,000
Gross Margin on Sales		$200,000
Selling Expense.	$76,000	
General Expense.	54,000	130,000
Net Operating Income		$ 70,000
Interest Expense		3,000
Net Income before Income Taxes		$ 67,000
Income Tax		26,000
Net Income		$ 41,000

Required:

Compute (1) ratio of gross margin to sales; (2) times interest earned; (3) ratio of net operating income to sales; and (4) times dividend earned (dividend is $1.50 per share on 10,000 shares).

27.3 Using the figures in problems 1 and 2, compute the (1) inventory turnover; (2) accounts receivable turnover; (3) rate of return on total assets (use the "after tax" method); and (4) earnings per share of stock.

27.4 Referring to the figures in problems 1 and 2, compute the (1) number of days' sales in accounts receivable; (2) turnover of plant; (3) rate of return on proprietorship; (4) ratio of fixed assets to long-term debt.

27.5 The financial statements of Scott Company are as follows:

SCOTT COMPANY
COMPARATIVE BALANCE SHEET
December 31, 1966 and 1965

Assets	1966	1965
Current Assets:		
Cash.	$ 12,900	$ 11,400
Accounts Receivable.	90,000	84,300
Marketable Securities	34,500	24,000
Merchandise	190,000	105,000
Prepaid Expenses	1,500	1,200
	$328,900	$225,900
Fixed Assets:		
Land.	$ 65,000	$ 50,000
Buildings.	91,000	63,000
Equipment	36,000	33,000
	$192,000	$146,000
Total	$520,900	$371,900

Liabilities and Capital

Current Liabilities:

Notes Payable............................	$ 20,000	$ 30,000
Accounts Payable	85,000	60,000
Accrued Wages............................	10,000	10,000
Taxes Payable............................	8,000	5,000
	$123,000	$105,000
6% Bonds Payable ($100,000 par value)........	$100,800	$101,000
Capital:		
5% Preferred Stock ($100 par value)	$ 50,000	–
Premium on 5% Preferred Stock	3,000	–
Common Stock ($10 stated value)	155,000	$ 95,000
Retained Earnings	89,100	70,900
	$297,100	$165,900
Total Liabilities and Capital	$520,900	$371,900

SCOTT COMPANY
COMPARATIVE INCOME STATEMENT
Years Ended December 31, 1966 and 1965

	1966	*1965*
Sales	$170,000	$130,000
Cost of Goods Sold	95,000	70,000
Gross Margin on Sales	$ 75,000	$ 60,000
Selling Expense	$ 24,000	$ 21,500
General and Administrative Expense.............	11,200	12,300
Total Operating Expenses....................	$ 35,200	$ 33,800
Net Operating Income	$ 39,800	$ 26,200
Other Income.............................	3,000	4,100
	$ 42,800	$ 30,300
Other Deductions: Interest	5,800	5,800
Net Income before Income Taxes	$ 37,000	$ 24,500
Income Tax	11,260	5,390
Net Income	$ 25,740	$ 19,110

Compute the following:

1. Working-capital ratio, December 31, 1966.
2. Percent of change in current assets.
3. Ratio of net operating income to sales, 1966.
4. Ratio of long-term debt to capital, December 31, 1966.
5. Percent of change in retained earnings.
6. Times interest earned, 1966.
7. Turnover of fixed assets, 1966.
8. Percent of change in fixed assets.
9. Ratio of selling expense to sales, 1966.
10. Book value per share of preferred stock at December 31, 1966. This stock is entitled to par value plus a premium of $5 per share in liquidation. No dividends are in arrears.
11. Rate of return on total assets in 1966, using the "after tax" method.

27.6 Using the figures of problem 5, compute the following:

1. Acid-test ratio, December 31, 1966.
2. Percent of change in proprietorship.

3. Ratio of gross margin to sales, 1966.
4. Ratio of capital to total assets, December 31, 1966.
5. Percent of change in sales.
6. Book value per share of common stock on December 31, 1966 (preferred is entitled to par value plus $5 per share premium in liquidation; no preferred dividends are in arrears).
7. Turnover of inventory in 1966.
8. Percent of change in net income.
9. Ratio of long-term debt to total assets, December 31, 1966.
10. Times preferred dividend earned in 1966.
11. Rate of return on common stockholders' investment, 1966.
12. Percent of sales uncollected.

27.7 Following are condensed financial statements of the Northland Co. for the three years ended December 31, 1966, 1965 and 1964.

NORTHLAND CO.
COMPARATIVE BALANCE SHEET
As of December 31

	1966	1965	1964
Current Assets:			
Bank	$ 20,500	$ 7,600	$ 17,000
Receivables	38,000	30,000	20,000
Inventory	60,000	40,000	30,000
Prepaid Expenses	1,500	2,400	3,000
Total Current Assets	$120,000	$ 80,000	$ 70,000
Plant and Equipment	260,000	150,000	76,000
	$380,000	$230,000	$146,000
Current Liabilities:			
Accounts Payable and Accruals	$ 98,000	$ 78,000	$ 48,500
Income Taxes Payable	2,000	2,000	1,500
Total Current Liabilities	$100,000	$ 80,000	$ 50,000
Mortgage Bonds	50,000	50,000	–
Stated Capital, $100 par value	200,000	80,000	80,000
Retained Earnings	30,000	20,000	16,000
	$380,000	$230,000	$146,000

NORTHLAND CO.
COMPARATIVE INCOME STATEMENT
Years Ended December 31

	1966	1965	1964
Sales	$210,000	$120,000	$100,000
Cost of Sales	157,500	80,000	55,000
Gross Margin on Sales	$ 52,500	$ 40,000	$ 45,000
General and Selling Expenses	42,500	36,000	37,000
Net Income	$ 10,000	$ 4,000	$ 8,000

Additional information:
(1) The company's inventory as of December 31, 1963 was $20,000.
(2) Credit terms are net 60 days from date of invoice.

Required:

   1. From the above information calculate the following for each of the three
      years:
      (a) Working-capital (current) ratio
      (b) Acid-test (liquidity) ratio
      (c) Inventory turnover
      (d) Average age of outstanding accounts receivable
      (e) Gross profit margin percentage
      (f) Earnings per share
      (g) Ratio of fixed assets to shareholders' equity
   2. Comment on the significant features in the company's financial position and
      operating results which are apparent from the calculations in requirement (1)
      and from the financial statements.

                                                            (ICAC — adapted)

27.8   The following ratios and other data pertain to the financial statements of the
        Lansing Co. for the year ended December 31, 1966.

Working capital (current) ratio	1.75 to 1
Acid-test (liquidity) ratio	1.27 to 1
Working capital	$33,000
Fixed assets to shareholders' equity ratio	0.625 to 1
Inventory turnover (based on cost of closing inventory).	4 times
Gross profit percentage	40%
Earnings per share.	$0.50
Average age of outstanding accounts receivable (based on calendar year of 365 days)	73 days
Share capital outstanding	20,000 par value shares
Earnings for year as a percentage of share capital . . .	25%

The company had no prepaid expenses, deferred charges, intangible assets, or
long-term liabilities.

Required:

Reconstruct, in as much detail as is possible, the company's balance sheet and
income statement for the year ended December 31, 1966. Give details of your
calculations.

                                                            (ICAC — adapted)

Index

Account
  definition, 16
  expense, 38
  forms of, 16, 283, 514
  relationships, 37
  revenue, 38
Accounting
  cash vs. accrual basis, 79, 402
  entity, 7
  equation, 9
  fields of, 5
  matrix formulation of, 19, 20, 62
  nature of, 3
  specialization in, 5–6
  steps in the process of, 58
  users of, 7
Accounting control, nature of, 3
Accounts payable
  control account and subsidiary ledger, 183
  nature of, 8
Accounts receivable
  aging, 288
  bad debts, estimating, 287
  bad debts transactions, 281–282
  collectible amount, estimation of, 286
  collection, 292
  control account and subsidiary ledger, 150–151
  credit policy, 292
  customer's statement, 284–285
  direct posting, 284
  identifying customers whose credit is acceptable, 290–291
  internal control, 289
  machine posting, 286
  management problems in extending credit, 290
  nature of, 8
  possible deductions, 286
  records, 282
  sales discounts and, 279
  transactions, 279
Accruals
  defined, 79
  expense, 81
  revenue, 80
  summary table, 88
Acid-test ratio, 756

Acquisition costs, 174
Adjusting entries, definition, 79
Allowance for doubtful accounts
  bad debt recoveries, 282
  entries for, 109–110, 281
  use of, 109–110
Analysis of financial statements
  acid-test ratio, 756
  balance sheet, summary analysis of, 754, 756
  book value per share of stock, 760
  cautions for using financial statement ratios, 763
  computation of ratios, 751
  earnings per share of stock, 761
  fixed-asset-to-long-term-debt ratio, 757
  income statement, summary analysis of, 751, 753
  inventory turnover, 758
  nature and purpose, 751
  rate of return on proprietorship, 763
  rate of return on total assets, 762
  ratio of long-term debts to capital, 756
  summary analyses, 754
  times dividends earned, 761
  times interest earned, 757
  turnover and analysis of accounts receivable, 759
  turnovers, 759
  working capital on current ratio, 755
Analysis sheet
  departmental expense, 521
  payroll, 564
  sales, 161
Analysis of variance (see Standard costs)
Application of funds statement (see Statement of application of funds)
Appraisal capital, 492
Assets
  definition and examples, 8
  identity with financial interests, 9
Average cost method, 310, 312–313

Bad debts
  defined, 109
  entries for, 110–111, 281
  estimating, 287
  recoveries, 282

Balance sheet
  bond discount and premium, 377
  comparative, 727, 754
  consolidated, 701–708
  definition, 9
  equations, 9
  form of, 21–22
  illustrated, 9, 247, 259, 547, 704, 754
  managerial uses, 23–24
  popularized, 259
  summary analysis of, 752, 754
Bank reconciliation, 217–219
Bank statement, 215
Bill of lading, 154–155
Bonds
  definition, 367
  discount on, 375
  illustration, 369
  internal control, 379
  investments in, 376
  issuing, 374
  kinds of, 374
  management problems, 379–380
  nature of, 367
  premium on, 375
  purchased between interest dates, 377
  recording discount on bonds payable, 375
  recording premium on bonds payable, 375
Book value per share of stock, 760
Branch accounting
  branch-office account, 691
  combined statements, 697
  home-office account, 691
  illustration, 692–696
  interbranch accounts, 691–692
  internal control, 697–699
  managerial decisions on opening a branch, 700
  multiple branches, 697
  systems, 690
Break-even analysis, 622–625
Budgeting
  advantages, 643
  budgeted balance sheet, 651, 654
  budgeted income statement, 648–649
  cash receipts from customers, 647–648
  employee motivation and budget levels, 644
  journal entries for, 655–656
  operating expense, 646–647
  organization for, 644
  payments on merchandise purchases, 648
  purchases, 645–646
  sales, 645
  summary cash budget, 649–651
  work sheet, 652–653

Capital budgeting
  accounting for capital budgeting decisions, 679
  administration and control, 681
  cost of capital, 677
  definition, 667
  discounted cash flow method, 670
  economic life of equipment, 678
  payout period method, 668
  present value of annuity of $1 table, 673
  present value method, 675
  present value of $1 table, 671
  rate of return on average investment method, 669
  steps in, 667
Capital stock (see Corporations)
Cash
  bank reconciliation, 217–219
  bank statement, 215
  basic procedure, 205
  budget, 222, 647–648, 649–651
  check, described, 214
  check forms, 208, 214
  check register, 210
  daily report, 216
  deposit slip, 213
  disbursements journal, 208–209
  internal control, 219–221
  managerial decisions, 221
  nature of, 205
  over and short, 212
  petty, 211
  receipt form, 206
  receipts journal, 206–207
  voucher, petty cash, 211
Cash vs. accrual accounting, 79, 402
Cash disbursement system with vouchers, 189
Cash disbursements journal, 209, 210
Cash discounts
  purchase, 175
  purchase discounts lost, 176
  sales, 142–144
Cash receipts journal, 207
Chain discounts, 144–145
Check register, 210
Checks, illustrated, 208, 214
Classification
  assets, 246–248
  income statement (content of), 35–36, 248–251
  liabilities, 248
  proprietorship, 248
Closing
  defined, 45
  entries, 46–57, 252–254
  illustration, 46–57
  steps in, 241
Computers, 19, 63, 156
Consolidated balance sheet
  acquisition of a going concern, 704
  changes in subsidiary's retained earnings after parent's acquisition, 705
  illustrations: case 1, 701–704; case 2, 706–708
  intercompany profit in inventories, 705
  nature of consolidation, 701

Consolidated balance sheet (*Continued*)
  other possibilities, 709
  parent and subsidiary companies, 700–701
Contribution theory
  applications in special cost analysis, 626–628
  departments and, 523–524
  sales and, 162–163
Controllable vs. uncontrollable costs, 506, 631
Copyrights, 8, 344
Corporations
  appraisal capital, 492
  appropriations of retained earnings, 483
  capital stock, 459, 460, 461
  definition and nature, 457
  dividends, 484–490 (*see also* Dividends)
  entries for issue of capital stock, 462–464
  management problems in decision to use
      corporate form, 469–471
  managerial problems and dividends, 492–493
  organization of, 458
  paid-in surplus, 462
  par vs. no-par stock, 461
  preferred vs. common stock, 460
  proprietorship in, 458
  quasi reorganization, 490
  retained earnings, 482–484
  special corporate records, 468–469
  stock split-up, 490–492
  subscriptions to capital stock, 464–465
  treasury stock, 465–468
Cost analysis (*see* Standard costs; Special cost
    analysis)
Cost of goods sold, adjustment for, 88–89
Cost-or-market pricing, 316–319
Costs, matching with revenue, 76, 104
Credit
  definition, 17
  equality of credits and debits, 17
  memorandum, 156
Credit policy, 292–293
Current ratio, 755
Customer's order (purchase order), 177–178

Debit
  definition, 17
  equality of debits and credits, 17
  memorandum, 155
Deferrals
  expense, 85–88
  income, 81–84
  revenue, 81–84
  summary table, 88
Departmental accounting
  accounts, 512
  bases for distribution of indirect expenses,
    519
  departmental contribution, 523
  departmental expenses in ledger, 523
  departmental income statement, 520, 522
  direct and indirect expenses, 515
  forms of accounts, 512–513, 514

income statement with departmental gross
    margins, 515, 518
  internal control, 524
  journals, 513, 516–517
  objectives, 511
  sales revenue as a distribution base, 520
  selling and service departments, 519
  work sheet for departmental expense dis-
    tribution, 521
Depletion, 343, 346
Deposit slip, 213
Depreciation
  accumulated depreciation account, 109
  defined, 89
  double checking balance calculation, 341
  fallacies about, 339
  nature of, 338
  periodic method of calculation, 339
  service units calculation, 339
  straight line calculation, 341
  sum-of-years'-digits method, 342
Direct posting, accounts receivable, 284
Dividends
  entries for ordinary dividends, 486
  financing, 487
  liquidating, 489
  managerial problem and, 492–493
  nature of liability for, 487
  ordinary, 484
  significant dates, 486
  stock, 489
  of wasting asset companies, 488

Earnings per share of stock, 761
Employee's withholding exemption certificate,
    400
Equivalent units, 592–593
Errors, adjustments for, 89
Excise taxes, 141
Expense
  accounts, 38–39
  accrued, 81
  prepaid (deferred), 85
  recognition of, 77

Federal income tax (*see* Income tax, federal)
F.I.C.A. tax (*see* Payroll taxes)
Financial interests
  definition and examples, 8
  identity with assets, 9
Financial statement analysis (*see* Analysis of
    financial statements)
First-in, first-out, 308, 311
Fixed and intangible assets
  abandonment, 347
  accounting for acquisition, 337
  amortization of intangibles, 343
  balance sheet presentation, 346
  calculation of depreciation, 339–342 (*see
    also* Depreciation)
  copyrights, 344

Fixed and intangible assets (*Continued*)
  defined, 337
  depletion, nature and calculation, 343; revision, 346
  equipment record (illustrated), 340
  fallacies about depreciation, 339
  franchises, 344
  goodwill, 345
  internal control, 349
  leaseholds and leasehold improvements, 345
  management decisions, 350–352' (*see also* Managerial decisions)
  nature and recording of depreciation, 338
  organization costs, 345
  patents, 344
  plant ledger accounts, 338
  retirement, 347
  revision of depreciation or depletion, 346
  sale, 347
  trade-in, 348; tax rule, 348
  trademarks, 345
Fixed-asset-to-long-term-debt ratio, 757
Franchises, 344
Freight in, entry for, 173
Freight paid for customers, 145
Funds statement (*see* Statement of application of funds)

Goodwill, 345
Gross profits method, 319

Identified unit cost, 308
Income
  defined, unearned or accrued (*see* Revenue)
  disposition of, 59
Income statement
  combined with retained earnings statement, 252
  comparative, 753
  content of, 35–36, 248–251
  current operating vs. all-inclusive, 251
  defined, 16, 35
  departmental, 515–518
  with departmental gross-margin figures, 518
  illustrated, 16, 36, 249, 260, 518, 753
  single step, 260
  uses of, 60
Income tax, federal
  capital gains and losses, 405
  cash vs. accrual basis, 402
  corporation tax, 408
  deductions from adjusted gross income, 404
  deductions from gross income, 403
  deferred income taxes payable, 408–409
  estimated tax, 408
  exemptions, 405
  expenditures not deductible, 405
  in general, 402
  gross income, content of, 403
  individual, illustration of computation, 406–407
  internal control, 409–410
  management problems, 410–411
  personal, outline of computation of, 403
  rates, 405–406
  withholding table, 395
Income taxes, accrual of, 112–113
Individual earnings record, 400
Intangible assets (*see* Fixed and intangible assets)
Interest, calculation of, 367–368
Internal control
  branches, 697–698
  cash, 219–221
  definition, 157
  departmental, 524
  elements of, 157–159
  fixed and intangible assets, 349
  income tax, 409–410
  job order costs, 575, 577
  merchandise, 321–322
  notes and bonds, 379
  payroll, 400, 402
  process costs, 597
  purchases, 181, 184
  sales, 157, 159–160
  voucher system, 189–190
Inventory, 8, 104–108, 307–324 (*see also* Merchandise; Manufacturing accounts, inventories)
Inventory turnover, 758
Invoice register, 180, illustrated, 182

Job order costs
  diagram, 561
  factory overhead cost, 564–565
  factory overhead variance, 565–566
  finished goods, 566
  illustration, 566–575
  internal control, 575, 577
  job cost sheet, 561, 563
  job order method, 560
  labor, 563–564
  managerial decisions, 577–578
  materials, 561–562
  payroll analysis sheet, 564
  storeroom requisition, 565
  stores ledger account, 562
Journal
  definition, 39
  general journal illustrated, 40, 43, 50–51
  special journals illustrated, 147, 149, 180, 182, 188, 207, 209, 210, 516, 517
  usefulness of, 41
Journalizing, steps in, 41

Land, nature of, 8
Last-in, first-out, 309–310
Leaseholds and leasehold improvements, 345
Ledger
  definition, 18

Ledger (*Continued*)
  illustrated (partially), 46–49, 52–55
  managerial uses, 19

Machinery and equipment, nature of, 8
Managerial decisions
  branch, opening, 700
  corporate form, use of, 469–471
  cost accounting and, 577–578
  credit extension and policy, 292
  dividends, 492–493
  income taxes, problems with, 410–411
  inventory, 322–324
  major new investments in fixed assets, 350–353 (*see also* Capital budgeting)
  notes and bonds payable, problems surrounding, 380–381
  partnership, forming and operating, 441–444
  payout period for fixed assets, 350 (*see also* Capital budgeting)
  price-level problem and fixed assets, 352
  replacement of a fixed asset, 351
  sales, 160–161
  with simple manufacturing accounts, 549
  statements, problems regarding, 257–260
Manufacturing accounts
  accounts used, 541–542
  adjusting and closing entries, 545–546
  elements of production costs, 541
  in income statement, 542–543
  inventories, 546; pricing, 546–548
  job order costs (*see* Job order costs)
  manufacturing cycle, 540
  manufacturing work sheet, 543, 550–551
  nature of, 540
  pricing of inventories, 546–548
  process costs (*see* Process costs)
  production cost accounts, nature of, 540
  simple manufacturing accounts as managerial device, 549
  standard costs (*see* Standard costs)
  statement of cost of goods manufactured, 543
  work sheet, 550–551
Market price method, 315–316
Matrix formulation of accounting, 19, 20, 62
Merchandise
  accounts, 104
  estimated inventories, 319
  gross profit inventory method, 319–320
  in income statement, 106–107
  internal control, 321–322
  management problems, 322–324
  market price inventory method, 315–316
  nature of, 8
  operations research approach to inventory management, 323
  periodic inventory method, 105, 307; with Cost of Goods Sold account, 105–106; without Cost of Goods Sold account, 106
  perpetual inventory method, 104, 310–314;

  advantages, 313–314
  pricing periodic inventory, 308–310, 316–319
  retail inventory method, 320–321
  stores ledger accounts, illustrated, 311, 313
  summary of effects of different cost pricing methods, 315
Mortgages
  nature of, 8, 367
  paid on installment plan, 378–379
  payable, 8

Notes
  contingent liability on notes receivable discounted, 373
  discounting notes payable, 371
  discounting notes receivable, 372
  dishonored notes receivable, 373
  illustration, 367
  internal control, 379
  management problems, 380
  payable, 8, 370
  promissory note, definition, 366
  receivable, 370

Office furniture and equipment, nature of, 8
Organization costs, 345

Partnerships
  admission of additional partner, 434–438
  definition, 427
  division of net income, 430–433
  drawing accounts, 429
  formation by cash investment, 428
  legal characteristics, 427–428
  liquidation, 440–441
  management considerations in forming and operating, 441–444
  statement of capital accounts, 433–434
  withdrawal of a partner, 438–440
Patents, 8, 344
Payroll
  entries, 398
  individual earnings record, illustrated, 401
  internal control, 400, 402
  records, 396
  summary (sheet or book), illustrated, 399
  taxes (*see* Payroll taxes)
  timecard, illustrated, 397
  withholding, 394–395
Payroll taxes
  entries, 393–394
  nature and purposes, 392–393
  rates, 393
Petty cash, 211–212
  voucher, 211
Popularized balance sheet, 259
Posting, defined, 42
Prepaid (deferred) expense
  entries, 85–88
  nature of, 8, 85

Process costs
   definition, 588
   diagrams of, 588, 590
   equivalent units, 592–594
   general ledger accounts, 588–589
   illustration, 597–598
   internal control, 597
   journal entries, 596–597
   original records, 592
   under seasonal production, 591
   sequential, 589
   service departments, 591
   unit cost computations, 592
   unit cost statement, 594–596
Property taxes
   accounts for, 111
   accounts illustrated, 112–113
Proprietorship, nature of, 8
Purchases
   accounts in income statement, 176
   book, multicolumn, 182
   book, single column, 180
   cash discounts, 175
   discounts lost, 176
   internal control, 181, 184
   managerial decisions, 190–191
   order, 178
   receiving report, 179
   requisition, 177
   returns and allowances, 174
   transactions, 173

Quasi reorganization, 490

Rate of return on proprietorship, 763
Rate of return on total assets, 762
Ratio of long-term debt to capital, 756
Receiving report, 179
Requisition, 177
Responsibility accounting
   bases for effective use, 506
   case illustration, 510–511
   cost reports, 501–510
   nature of, 506
   organization chart, 507
Retail inventory method, 320–321
Retained earnings, 482–484
Returns and allowances
   purchases, 174
   sales, 145–146
Revenue
   accounts, 38
   accrued, 80
   matching with costs, 76
   recognition of, 77
Reversing entries, 255–258

Sales
   analysis sheet, 162–163
   bill of lading, 155
   cash discounts on, 142–144
      computers, 156
      distribution, 161
      freight on, 145
      internal control, 157, 159–160
      invoice, 151
      journal, 146–147
      managerial problems, 160
      multicolumn journal, 148, 149
      records, 146
      returns and allowances, 145
      shipping order, 154
      slip, 152
      taxes, 141–142
      trade discounts, 144
      transactions, 141
Sales invoice, 151
Sales slip, 152
Sales taxes, 141–142
Shipping order, 154
Sinking funds, 378
Social security taxes (*see* Payroll taxes)
Source and application of funds statement
      (*see* Statement of application of funds)
Special cost analysis
   applications of contribution theory, 626
   appraisal of sales effort, 628
   break-even analysis, 622
   break-even point, computation of, 626
   differential cost and price discrimination,
      628–630
   make or buy, 630
   opportunity costs and price level, 630–631
   planning, 626–627
   product selection, 627–628
Standard costs
   advantages, 606
   analysis of material and labor variances,
      612–615
   analysis of overhead variance, 615
   budget variance, 615
   capacity variance, 615–616
   diagrams, 605, 607
   efficiency variance, 616
   general ledger accounts, 606
   illustration, 609–612, 613
   limitations of historical costs, 605
   original records, 607–609
   standard cost card, 608
Statement of application of funds
   definition of funds, 721
   illustration of statement, 721
   nature and purpose, 720
   popular form of "cash flow," 737
   preparation, T account method, 723–731
   preparation, work sheet method, 731–737
Statements
   balance sheet, 9, 247, 259, 547, 704, 754
   consolidated balance sheet, 704, 754
   funds statement, 720–738
   income statement, 16, 36, 249, 260, 518, 753
   retained earnings statement, 485

Statements (*Continued*)
  statement of cost of goods manufactured, 543
  unit cost statement, 595
Stock
  in corporations (*see* Corporations, capital stock)
  in trade (*see* Merchandise)
Store equipment, nature of, 8
Stores ledgers, 311, 313
Subsidiary ledgers
  accounts payable, 181; illustrated, 183
  accounts receivable, 148; illustrated 150–151
Supplies, nature of, 8
Supplies used, adjustment for, 88–89
Surplus
  paid-in, 462
  retained earnings, 482–484

Taxes payable, nature of, 8
Timecard, 397
Times dividends earned, 761
Times interest earned, 757
Trade discounts, 144
Trademarks, 8, 345
Transactions
  analysis of, 10
  definition, 10

illustrated, 11–15
Trial balance
  defined, 42
  illustration, 45, 254
  postclosing, 254
Turnover and analysis of accounts receivable, 759 (*see also* Accounts receivable, aging)

Unemployment tax (*see* Payroll taxes)

Variance analysis (*see* Standard costs)
Voucher system
  advantages, 184, 190
  cash disbursement system with vouchers, 189, 210
  check register, 210
  internal control, 189
  records used, 185
  register, 187, 188
  variations in, 187
  voucher document, 185–186

Withheld taxes
  calculation, 394
  table, 395
Working capital ratio, 755
Work sheet, illustrated, 116–117, 244–245, 521, 550–551, 652–653, 698, 710–711, 734–735.